ARCANA CAELESTIA

EMANUEL SWEDENBORG

ARCANA
CAELESTIA

Principally a Revelation of the
inner or spiritual meaning of
Genesis and Exodus

VOLUME SEVEN
Paragraphs 4954–5727

GENESIS
Chapters 39–43

TRANSLATED FROM
THE ORIGINAL LATIN BY
JOHN ELLIOTT

LONDON
THE SWEDENBORG SOCIETY
1990

Published by The Swedenborg Society
Swedenborg House, 20-21 Bloomsbury Way, London WC1 2TH

© Swedenborg Society 1990

Designed by James Butler MSIAD
Typeset in Palatino by
Goodfellow & Egan Phototypesetting Ltd, Cambridge
Printed and bound in Great Britain at the
University Press, Cambridge

ISBN 0 85448 110 9 Hard covers
ISBN 0 85448 111 7 Paperback

TRANSLATOR'S NOTES

The section headed TREATMENT OF THE SCRIPTURES in my introduction in Volume One begins as follows:

The Latin version of every chapter of Genesis and Exodus when compared with the original Hebrew is found to be utterly literal, and in this new English edition of 'the Arcana' the effort has been made to preserve that literalism wherever English usage will allow. Where it will not do so the literal meaning is indicated at some point in a footnote.....

In the course of explaining the first two books of the Divine Word Swedenborg also quotes extensively from the rest, though from some far more than from others. In many places the sections quoted are explained in the same way as Genesis and Exodus and are for that reason just as much close word for word renderings of the original Hebrew or Greek.....

If therefore readers of this translation of *Arcana Caelestia* find the language used in Scriptural passages strange and unidiomatic they should bear in mind the translator's endeavour to reproduce Swedenborg's indications, for expository purposes, of how the original Hebrew or Greek is actually worded. Four examples – two that appear in earlier volumes and two in the present one – will suffice to illustrate this matter:

1 At Genesis 11:1 the New King James Version (or Revised Authorised Version) of the Bible reads, 'Now the whole earth had one language and one speech'. This represents in idiomatic English what the Hebrew says in its own idiomatic way; but in *Arcana Caelestia* the presentation of the inner or spiritual meaning demands a very literal rendering of the original Hebrew – 'And the whole earth was of one lip, and its words were one.' The expressions 'lip' and 'words' are indispensable here, as the reader of paragraphs 1284-1288 will realize.

2 The Hebrew verb meaning 'said' occurs four times in Genesis 22:7, as Swedenborg himself observes in 2802. English translations employ one or two synonyms at this point, such as 'spoke' or 'replied'; and so do Latin versions other than Swedenborg's. But for him the idiom of the original language must be expressed in his translation. Thus the English version is, 'And

Isaac *said* to his father – he *said* – My father. And he *said*, Here am, my son. And he *said*.....'

3 Genesis 42:23 begins in NKJ (or RAV) 'But they did not know that Joseph understood [them]'; and other English versions are very similar. The Hebrew word behind 'understood' normally means 'heard', and Swedenborg retains that meaning (to be exact he reproduces the Hebrew participle 'hearing'). A better English wording would result if in the sentence 'And they did not know that Joseph was hearing' the last word were changed to 'listening'; but Swedenborg's reference back to previous paragraphs where 'heard' is the subject (2542, 3869, 5017) precludes the use of that more idiomatic synonym.

4 In his rendering of Matthew 25:36 Swedenborg uses a word, also found in the Schmidius Latin version, that means 'clothe around' (*circuminduo*). Though the inclusion of 'around' in 'naked and you clothed Me around' leads to unusual English it represents an element in the original Greek which Swedenborg, it seems, wished to bring over to his readers.

Once more I wish to record my thanks to the Rev. Norman Ryder, Miss Madeline Waters, Dr John Chadwick, Mr Norman Pettersen, and especially my chief consultant, the Rev. Dennis Duckworth, for their different contributions to the work. In addition I would like to thank Mr David Glover for his help and advice in the purchase and use of an appropriate word-processor or personal computer, and Mrs Lisa Hyatt Cooper, who as 'American reader' has made countless helpful suggestions to the translator.

Finally, for all the knowledge and insights available to the world in *Arcana Caelestia*, May Jesus Christ be praised!

London 1990   JOHN ELLIOTT

Chapters and Paragraphs to Volumes of the Latin Edition

Volume				Paragraphs	
Volume	1	Genesis	1–15	Paragraphs	1–1885
	2		16–21		1886–2759
	3		22–30		2760–4055
	4		31–40		4056–5190
	5		41–50		5191–6626
	6	Exodus	1–15		6627–8386
	7		16–24		8387–9442
	8		25–40		9443–10837

Chapters and Paragraphs to Volumes of the English Edition

Volume				Paragraphs	
Volume	1	Genesis	1–9	Paragraphs	1–1113
	2		10–17		1114–2134
	3		18–22		2135–2893
	4		23–27		2894–3649
	5		28–31		3650–4228
	6		32–38		4229–4953
	7		39–43		4954–5727
	8		44–50		5728–6626
	9	Exodus	1–12		6627–8032
	10		13–21		8033–9111
	11		22–28		9112–9973
	12		29–40		9974–10837

39

4954　The preliminary section of the previous chapter contained an explanation of what the Lord said about judgement on the good and on the evil, in Matthew 25:31–33; see 4807–4810. In the present preliminary section what the Lord said next in that connection comes up for explanation, that is to say, the following words,

Then the King will say to those at His right hand, Come, O blessed of My Father, inherit the kingdom prepared for you from the foundation of the world; for I was hungry and you gave Me food, I was thirsty and you gave Me drink, I was a stranger and you took Me in, naked and you clothed Me around, I was sick and you visited Me, I was in prison and you came to Me.　Matt. 25:34–36.

4955　What these words hold within them in the internal sense will be evident from what is presented below. But first of all one needs to know that by these works listed one after another the essential ingredients of charity in their own ordered sequence are meant. This cannot be seen by anyone if he is unacquainted with the internal sense of the Word, that is, unless he knows what is really meant by giving food to the hungry, giving drink to the thirsty, taking in a stranger, clothing the naked, visiting the sick, and coming to those in prison. Anyone who restricts himself to the sense of the letter when thinking about these actions assumes that good works in the outward form these take are meant by them and that nothing deeper lies concealed within them, when in fact each action that is described contains some deeper reality, which is of a Divine nature because it has its origin in the Lord. But at the present day no understanding of any deeper reality exists because at the present day nothing is taught about charity. For after people separated charity from faith, teachings to do with charity perished, and in place of these, teachings to do with faith were accepted and invented, that is, teachings which provide no information at all about what is meant by charity or by the neighbour.

Teachings that existed among the Ancients specified all the genera and species of charity. They also taught who the neighbour was towards whom charity should be exercised, and how one person was the neighbour in a different degree and different respect from another, and consequently how charity was to be exercised in different ways according to the individual needs of the neighbour. The Ancients also made classifications of the neighbour and gave names to each of these. Some people they called the poor, the needy, the wretched, and the afflicted; some they called the blind, the lame, the maimed, as well as orphans and widows; and others they called the hungry, the thirsty strangers, the naked, the sick, the bound, and so on. From these classifications they knew what they ought to do for one person and what for another. But, as stated, such teachings have perished, and with them any understanding of the Word too. They have perished so completely that no one at the present day knows anything else than this, that when the poor, widows, and orphans are mentioned in the Word none but those who are literally called such are meant. The same applies whenever mention is made of the hungry, the thirsty, strangers, the naked, the sick, and those in prison. But the truth of the matter is that these names are used to describe charity – what it is like in its essence and what the exercise of charity ought to be like in a charitable life.

4956   Essentially charity towards the neighbour is an affection for goodness and truth and a recognition of oneself as being nothing but evil and falsity. Indeed the neighbour is one and the same as goodness and truth, and to have an affection for these is to have charity, while the opposite of the neighbour is evil and falsity, which a person who has charity turns away from. Anyone therefore who has charity towards the neighbour is moved by an affection for goodness and truth because they come from the Lord, and such a one turns away from evil and falsity because these come from himself. When he does this, humility is present in him as a consequence of his recognition of what he is in himself; and when such humility is present his state is one in which goodness and truth are received from the Lord. These essential ingredients of charity are the message in the internal sense of the following words used by the Lord,

I was hungry and you gave Me food, I was thirsty and you gave Me drink, I was a stranger and you took Me in, naked and you clothed Me around, I was sick and you visited Me, I was in prison and you came to Me.

Except from the internal sense no one can know that these words hold the essential ingredients of charity within them. The ancients who possessed teachings regarding charity knew these things, but at the present day matters such as these seem so far-fetched that everyone will be astonished by the assertion that those words hold the essential ingredients of charity within them. What is more, the angels present with a person do not perceive those words in any other way, for by 'the hungry' they perceive those led by affection to desire good, by 'the thirsty' those led by affection to desire truth, by 'a stranger' those wishing to receive instruction, by 'the naked' those acknowledging that no goodness or truth at all is present within them, by 'the sick' those acknowledging that within themselves there is nothing but evil, and by 'the bound' or 'those in prison' those acknowledging that within themselves there is nothing but falsity. All these if taken as a whole mean the aspects of charity described immediately above.

4957   From all this it may be seen that all the things the Lord spoke about held matters of Divine concern within them, though it seems to people whose interests are entirely worldly, and especially to those whose interests are bodily ones, that He spoke about the same kinds of things as anyone else might have spoken. Indeed those immersed in bodily interests will say of these and all other words spoken by the Lord that they are no more full of grace and therefore do not carry any more weight than the sermons and preaching of those in our own day and age who, because of their learning, are excellent speakers. But in fact their sermons and preaching are like the shell and husk when compared with the kernel inside them.

4958   The reason 'hungering' means being led by affection to desire good is that in the internal sense 'bread' means the good of love and charity, while food in general means good, 2165, 2177, 3478, 4211, 4217, 4735. The reason 'thirsting' means being led by affection to desire truth is that wine and also water mean the truth of faith – wine, 1071, 1798, water, 2702. 'A stranger' means one who wishes to receive instruction, see 1463, 4444; and one who is 'naked' means a person who acknowledges that no good or truth at all exists within him, one who is 'sick' a person who acknowledges that evil is present within him, and one who is 'bound' or 'in prison' a person who acknowledges that falsity is present, as is evident from many places in the Word where such names are used.

4959   The reason the Lord speaks of all these things being done to Himself is that He is present in those kinds of people, which is why He also says,

Truly I say to you, insofar as you did it to one of the least of these My brothers you did it to Me.   Matt. 25:40,45.

GENESIS 39

1 And Joseph was made to go down to Egypt, and Potiphar bought him – Pharaoh's bedchamber servant, the chief of the attendants, an Egyptian man – from the hand of the Ishmaelites who made him go down there.

2 And Jehovah was with Joseph, and he was a prosperous man; and he was in the house of his lord the Egyptian.

3 And his lord saw that Jehovah was with him, and everything that he did Jehovah made to prosper in his hand.

4 And Joseph found favour in his eyes, and ministered to him; and he put him in charge over his house, and whatever he had he gave into his hand.

5 And it happened from the time he put him in charge in his house and over all that he had, that Jehovah blessed the Egyptian's house for Joseph's sake; and the blessing of Jehovah was on all that he had in the house and in the field.

6 And he left all that he had in Joseph's hand, and did not concern himself with anything¹ except the bread that he ate. And Joseph was beautiful in form and beautiful in appearance.

7 And it happened after these events, that his lord's wife lifted up her eyes towards Joseph and said, Lie with me.

8 And he refused and said to his lord's wife, Behold, my lord does not concern himself with anything² in the house, and all that he has he has given into my hand.

9 He himself is no greater in this house than I am, and he has not held back anything from me except yourself, in that you are his wife. How then shall I do this great evil, and sin against God?

10 And it happened as she spoke to Joseph day after day, that he did not listen to her, to lie with her, to be with her.

11 And it happened on a certain day, that he went to the house to do his work, and none of the men³ of the house was there in the house.

12 And she took hold of him by his garment, saying, Lie with me. And he left his garment in her hand and fled, and went out of doors.

13 And it happened as she saw that he had left his garment in her hand and had fled out of doors,

14 That she cried out to the men of her house, and said to them – she said, See, he has brought us a Hebrew man to make sport of us. He came to me to lie with me, and I cried out with a loud voice.

15 And it happened as he was hearing [me], that I lifted up my voice and cried out, and he left his garment with me, and fled, and went out of doors.

16 And she kept his garment with her until his lord came to his house.

17 And she spoke to him in⁴ these words, saying, The Hebrew slave whom you have brought to us came to me, to make sport of me.

18 And it happened as I lifted up my voice and cried out, that he left his garment with me and fled out of doors.

19 And it happened – as his lord heard his wife's words which she spoke to him, saying, This is what⁵ your slave did to me – that his anger flared up.

---

¹ *lit.* did not know anything with him
² *lit.* does not know what is with me
³ *lit.* no man from the men
⁴ *lit.* according to
⁵ *lit.* According to these words

20 And Joseph's lord took him and committed him to the prison-house,
a place where the king's bound ones were bound; and he was there in
the prison-house.
21 And Jehovah was with Joseph, and showed mercy to him, and gave
him favour in the eyes of the governor¹ of the prison-house.
22 And the governor¹ of the prison-house gave into Joseph's hand all
the bound who were in the prison-house; and everything they did
there, he was the doer of it².
23 The governor of the prison-house oversaw nothing whatever that
was in his hand, in that Jehovah was with him; and whatever he did,
Jehovah made it prosper.

CONTENTS

4960   The internal sense deals here with the way in which the Lord
made His Internal Man Divine. 'Jacob' was the External Man, the
subject in preceding chapters, now 'Joseph' is the Internal Man, the
subject in the present chapter and those that follow it.

4961   And because the making Divine of His Internal Man was
carried out in conformity with Divine order, that order is described
here. Temptation too is described, such temptation being the means by
which a joining together is effected.

THE INTERNAL SENSE

4962   Verse 1 **And Joseph was made to go down to Egypt, and
Potiphar bought him – Pharaoh's bedchamber servant, the chief of the
attendants, an Egyptian man – from the hand of the Ishmaelites who
made him go down there.**
'And Joseph' means the celestial of the spiritual from the rational. 'Was
made to go down to Egypt' means to factual knowledge which the
Church possessed. 'And Potiphar bought him – Pharaoh's bedchamber
servant' means among facts of a more internal kind. 'The chief of the
attendants' means which facts come first and foremost in explanations.
'An Egyptian man' means natural truth. 'From the hand of the Ishmaelites' means from simple good. 'Who made him go down there' means a
descent from this simple good to that factual knowledge.

¹ *lit.* prince *or* chief
² *i.e. it was done under his instructions*

5

4963 'And Joseph' means the celestial of the spiritual from the rational. This is clear from the representation of 'Joseph' as the celestial-spiritual man that comes from the rational, dealt with in 4286. Here therefore, since the Lord is the subject, the Lord's Internal Man is represented by him. Everyone born a human being is external and internal. His external man is that which is seen with the eyes; it is that which enables him to live in association with other people and enables him to carry out what belongs properly to the natural world. But the internal man is one that is not seen with the eyes; it is what enables a person to live in association with spirits and angels and to carry through what belongs properly to the spiritual world. Everyone has an internal and an external, that is, the internal man and the external man exist, to the end that through man heaven may be joined to the world. For heaven flows by way of the internal man into the external and from that influx gains a perception of what exists in the world, while the external man in the world gains from the same influx a perception of what exists in heaven. It is to this end that the human being has been created the way he has.

2 The Lord's Human too had an External and an Internal because it pleased Him to be born like any other human being. The External, or His External Man, has been represented by 'Jacob' and after that by 'Israel', but His Internal Man is represented by 'Joseph'. The latter – the Internal Man – is what is called the celestial-spiritual man from the rational; or what amounts to the same, the Lord's Internal, which was the Human, was the celestial of the spiritual from the rational. This, and the glorification of it, are dealt with in the internal sense of the present chapter and those that follow it in which Joseph is the subject. What the celestial of the spiritual from the rational is has been explained already in 4286, 4585, 4592, 4594, namely that which comes above the celestial of the spiritual from the natural, represented by 'Israel'.

3 The Lord was indeed born like any other human being. But it is well known that everyone who is born depends for his make-up on both his father and his mother; also that he derives his inmost self from his father, but his more external aspects, or those which clothe his inmost self, from his mother. That is to say, both what he derives from his father and what he derives from his mother are defiled with hereditary evil. But in the Lord's case it was different. That which He derived from His mother possessed a hereditary nature essentially the same as that existing in any other human being; but what He derived from His Father, who was Jehovah, was Divine. Consequently the Lord's Internal Man was unlike the internal of any other human being, for His Inmost Self was Jehovah. Being intermediate this is therefore called the celestial of the spiritual from the rational. But in the Lord's Divine mercy more will be said about this later on.

4964 'Was made to go down to Egypt' means to factual knowledge which the Church possessed. This is clear from the meaning of 'Egypt' as knowledge, or factual knowledge in general, dealt with in 1164, 1165, 1186, 1462. But no explanation of the essential nature of that factual knowledge properly meant by 'Egypt' has been provided as yet. In the Ancient Church there was doctrinal knowledge and there was factual knowledge. Doctrinal knowledge had regard to love to God and charity towards the neighbour, whereas factual knowledge had to do with the correspondences of the natural world with the spiritual world, and with the representations of spiritual and heavenly realities within natural and earthly ones. Such was the factual knowledge of those in the Ancient Church.

Egypt was one of those parts of the world and one of those kingdoms where the Ancient Church also existed, 1238, 2385; but since in that land mainly factual knowledge was handed down from one generation to another, 'Egypt' means factual knowledge in general. This also explains why frequent reference is made to Egypt in the prophetical part of the Word, where that knowledge is meant specifically by 'Egypt'. What is more, the actual magic practised by the Egyptians had its origin in the same knowledge; for they were acquainted with the correspondences of the natural world with the spiritual, and at a later time, after the Church among them had come to an end, they misused these in magical practices. Now because such factual knowledge existed among them – that is to say, knowledge which taught correspondences, and also representatives and meaningful signs – and because this factual knowledge was the servant of the doctrinal teachings of the Church, especially in their understanding of things stated in their Word (for the Word of the Ancient Church was both prophetical and historical, like the Word that exists today, though this is a different Word, see 2686) 'he was made to go down to Egypt' consequently means made to go down to the factual knowledge which the Church possessed.

Because the Lord is represented by 'Joseph' and the words 'Joseph was made to go down to Egypt' are used here, the meaning is that when the Lord was to glorify His Internal Man, that is, make it Divine, He first of all assimilated the factual knowledge possessed by the Church. Then, starting from and using that knowledge He advanced towards things increasingly interior and at length even to those that were Divine. For it pleased Him to glorify or make Himself Divine in conformity with the same kind of order as that by which He regenerates the human being or makes him spiritual, 3138, 3212, 3296, 3490, 4402. That is to say, there is a gradual advance from external ideas, which are known facts and the truths of faith, towards internal ones, which are ideas of charity towards the neighbour and of love to Him. From this one may see what is meant by the following words in Hosea,

When Israel was a boy I loved him, and *out of Egypt I called My son.*   Hosea 11:1.

These words refer to the Lord, see Matt.2:15.

4965   'And Potiphar bought him – Pharaoh's bedchamber servant' means among facts of a more internal kind. This is clear from the meaning of 'Pharaoh's bedchamber servant' as facts of a more internal kind, dealt with in 4789. 'Buying' means that He availed Himself of them, 4397, 4487. Facts of a more internal kind are those that come closer to spiritual ideas, being facts that are applied to heavenly matters. For heavenly matters are what the internal man sees when the external man sees no more than the facts in the outward form these take.

4966 'The chief of the attendants' means which facts come first and foremost in explanations. This is clear from the meaning of 'the chief of the attendants' as the facts which come first and foremost in explanations, dealt with in 4790. Ones which come first and foremost in explanations are those which are pre-eminently suitable for explaining the Word, and so for coming to understand teachings drawn from the Word about love to God and charity towards the neighbour. It should be recognized that the factual knowledge of the people of old was entirely different from that existing at the present day. As stated above, the factual knowledge of the people of old had to do with the correspondences of things in the natural world with realities in the spiritual world. Knowledge which at the present day is called philosophical knowledge, such as Aristotelian systems and their like, did not exist among them. This is also evident from the books written by ancient authors, most of which consisted of descriptions of such things as were signs of, represented, and corresponded to more internal realities, as may be seen from the following evidence, and ignoring all else.

2 They envisaged Helicon on a mountain and took it to mean heaven, and Parnassus on a hill below that, and took it to mean factual knowledge. They spoke of a flying horse, called Pegasus by them, which broke open a fountain there with its hoof; they called branches of knowledge virgins; and so on. For with the help of correspondences and representatives they knew that 'a mountain' meant heaven, 'a hill' the heaven beneath this, which is heaven as it exists among men, 'a horse' the power of understanding, 'its wings with which it flew' spiritual things, 'its hoof' that which was natural, 'a fountain' intelligence, while three virgins called 'the Graces' meant affections for good, and virgins who were named 'the Heliconians' and 'the Parnassians' meant affections for truth. To the sun they likewise allotted horses, whose food they called ambrosia and whose drink they called nectar; for they knew that 'the sun' meant heavenly love, 'horses' powers of the understanding which sprang from that love, while 'food' meant celestial things and 'drink' spiritual ones.

3 The Ancients are also the originators of customs that are still followed when kings are crowned. The king has to sit on a silver throne, wear a purple robe, and be anointed with oil. He has to wear a crown on his head, while holding in his hands a sceptre, a sword, and keys. He has to ride in regal splendour on a white horse shod with horseshoes made of silver; and he has to be waited on at table by the chief nobles of the

kingdom. And many other customs are followed besides these. The Ancients knew that 'a king' represented Divine Truth that is rooted in Divine Good, and from this they knew what was meant by a silver throne, a purple robe, anointing oil, crown, sceptre, sword, keys, white horse, horseshoes made of silver, and what was meant by being waited on at table by the chief nobles. Who at the present day knows the meaning of any of these customs, or where the information exists to show him their meaning? People refer to them as symbols, but they know nothing at all about correspondence or representation. All this evidence shows what the factual knowledge possessed by the Ancients was like, and that this knowledge gave them a discernment of spiritual and heavenly realities, which at the present day are scarcely known to exist.

The factual knowledge that has replaced that of the Ancients, and which strictly speaking is called philosophical knowledge, tends to draw the mind away from knowing such things because such knowledge can also be employed to substantiate false ideas. Furthermore, even when used to substantiate true ones it introduces darkness into the mind, because for the most part mere terms are used to substantiate them, which few people can understand and which the few who do understand them argue about. From this it may be seen how far the human race has departed from the learning of the Ancients, which led to wisdom. Gentiles received their factual knowledge from the Ancient Church, whose external worship consisted in representatives and meaningful signs and whose internal worship consisted in the realities represented and meant by these. This was the kind of factual knowledge that is meant in the genuine sense by 'Egypt'.

4967   'An Egyptian man' means natural truth. This is clear from the meaning of 'a man' as truth, dealt with in 3134, and from the meaning of 'Egypt' as factual knowledge in general, dealt with immediately above in 4964, 4966. And since 'Egypt' means factual knowledge it also means the natural, for all the factual knowledge present with a person constitutes his natural since it resides in his natural man, and includes knowledge about spiritual and heavenly realities. The reason for this is that the natural is the position within which and from which he sees those realities. Those which he does not see from that position are unintelligible to him. But a regenerate person, who is called spiritual, sees them in one way, an unregenerate person, who is called merely natural, in another. In the case of a regenerate person factual knowledge has the light of heaven shed upon it, but not so in the case of an unregenerate one. The light shed on the unregenerate person's factual knowledge comes by way of spirits governed by falsity and evil, a light which, it is true, begins as the light of heaven but among such spirits is reduced to a dim light like that of evening or night. Indeed spirits of this kind, and consequently men like them, see in the way owls do – clearly at night but dimly during the daytime. That is, they see falsities clearly and truths dimly, and therefore worldly things clearly but heavenly ones dimly, if at all. From this one may recognize that genuine factual knowledge is natural truth; for all genuine factual knowledge that is of the kind meant in the good sense by 'Egypt' is natural truth.

4968 'From the hand of the Ishmaelites' means from simple good. This is clear from the representation of 'the Ishmaelites' as those in whom simple good is present, dealt with in 3263, 4747, and therefore here as natural truth which is received from simple good. Chapter 37:36 says that *'the Midianites* sold Joseph into Egypt to Potiphar, Pharaoh's bedchamber servant, the chief of the attendants'; but now it is said that 'Potiphar, Pharaoh's bedchamber servant, the chief of the attendants, bought him from the hand of *the Ishmaelites*, who made him go down there'. The matter is stated in these different ways for the sake of the internal sense. Previously – in Chapter 37 – the subject was the alienation of Divine truth, which is done not by those in whom simple good exists but by those in whom simple truth is present, whom 'the Midianites' represent, see 4788. But now the subject is the acquisition or the availing oneself of factual knowledge; also natural truth, which is acquired from simple good. This is why the expression 'from the Ishmaelites' is used, for these people represent those in whom simple good is present. From this it is evident that the matter is stated in the way it is for the sake of the internal sense. Nor is there any discrepancy in the historical narrative, for this states that the Midianites drew Joseph out of the pit and then handed him over to the Ishmaelites by whom he was led away into Egypt. Thus since the Midianites handed him over to the Ishmaelites who were going to Egypt, it was the Midianites who sold him to Egypt.

4969 'Who made him go down there' means a descent from this simple good to that factual knowledge. This is clear from the representation of 'the Ishmaelites who made him go down' as those in whom simple good is present, dealt with immediately above in 4968, and from the meaning of Egypt, to which 'there' refers here, as factual knowledge in general, dealt with just above in 4964, 4966. The expression 'going down' is used because the subject is factual knowledge which is exterior. For in the Word passing from interior things to exterior ones is described as 'going down', and passing from exterior to interior ones as 'going up', see 3084, 4539.

4970 Verses 2–6 **And Jehovah was with Joseph, and he was a prosperous man; and he was in the house of his lord the Egyptian. And his lord saw that Jehovah was with him, and everything that he did Jehovah made it to prosper in his hand. And Joseph found favour in his eyes, and ministered to him; and he put him in charge over his house, and whatever he had he gave into his hand. And it happened from the time he put him in charge in his house and over all that he had, that Jehovah blessed the Egyptian's house for Joseph's sake; and**

the blessing of Jehovah was on all that he had in the house and in the field. And he left all that he had in Joseph's hand, and did not concern himself with anything[1] except the bread that he ate. And Joseph was beautiful in form and beautiful in appearance.

'And Jehovah was with Joseph' means that the Divine existed within the celestial of the spiritual. 'And he was a prosperous man' means that all things had been provided. 'And he was in the house of his lord the Egyptian' means to enable it to be introduced into natural good. 'And his lord saw that Jehovah was with him' means a perception within natural good that the Divine existed within it. 'And everything that he did Jehovah made to prosper in his hand' means that all things were the conferments of Divine Providence. 'And Joseph found favour in his eyes' means that it had found acceptance. 'And ministered to him' means that factual knowledge was assigned to its own good. 'And he put him in charge over his house' means that this good applied itself to that factual knowledge. 'And whatever he had he gave into his hand' means that all that belonged to that good was seemingly subject to the power and control of its associated truth. 'And it happened from the time he put him in charge in his house and over all that he had' means a second state, after this good had applied itself to that truth and had made all that belonged to it seemingly subject to the power and control of that truth. 'That Jehovah blessed the Egyptian's house for Joseph's sake' means that at this point the Divine imparted the celestial-natural to that truth. 'And the blessing of Jehovah was' means increases. 'On all that he had in the house and in the field' means in life and in doctrine. 'And he left all that he had in Joseph's hand' means that it seemed as though all things were subject to its power and control. 'And did not concern himself with anything except the bread that he ate' means that the good from there was its own. 'And Joseph was beautiful in form' means the good of life springing from this. 'And beautiful in appearance' means the truth of faith springing from it.

4971   'And Jehovah was with Joseph' means that the Divine existed within the celestial of the spiritual. This is clear from the representation of 'Joseph' as the celestial of the spiritual from the rational, dealt with above in 4963; and because the Lord is the subject, at this point His Internal Man within His Human, 'Jehovah was with him' means that the Divine existed within it. The Divine existed within His Human because He had been conceived from Jehovah. The Divine does not exist within angels; it is merely present with them, because they are merely forms receiving the Divine coming forth from the Lord.

4972   'And he was a prosperous man' means that all things had been provided. This is clear from the meaning of the phrase 'being made to prosper', when used in reference to the Lord, as provision being made so that He might be enriched with all good.

---

[1] *lit.* did not know anything with him

4973 'And he was in the house of his lord the Egyptian' means to enable it to be introduced into natural good. This is clear from the meaning of 'lord' as good, dealt with below, and from the meaning of 'the Egyptian' as factual knowledge in general, and from this as that which is natural, dealt with in 4967. The reason 'being in the house' means being introduced is that 'house' is the mind in which good dwells, 3538, in this case the natural mind. Moreover 'house' is used in reference to good, 3652, 3720. The human being has both a natural mind and a rational mind. The natural mind exists within his external man, the rational within his internal. Known facts make up the truths that belong to the natural mind, and these are said to be there 'in their own house' when they are joined to good there; for good and truth together constitute a single house like husband and wife. But the forms of good and the truths which are the subject at present are of a more interior kind, for they are suited to the celestial of the spiritual from the rational, which is represented by 'Joseph'. Those suitable interior truths within the natural are applicable to useful purposes, while interior forms of good in the same are the useful purposes themselves.

2 The expression 'lord' is used many times in the Word, but unless a person is acquainted with the internal sense he assumes that 'lord' has no other meaning than what the word has when used in ordinary conversation. But 'lord' is used nowhere in the Word other than in reference to good, as is similarly the case with the name 'Jehovah'. When however reference is being made to truth, 'God' and also 'king' are used. This then is the reason why 'lord' means good, as may also be seen from the following places: In Moses,

Jehovah your God, He is God of gods, and *Lord of lords.* Deut. 10:17.

In David,

Confess Jehovah, confess the God of gods, confess *the Lord of lords.* Ps. 136:1–3.

In these places Jehovah or the Lord is called 'God of gods' by virtue of Divine Truth which goes forth from Him, and 'Lord of lords' by virtue of Divine Good which exists within Him.

3 Similarly in John,

The Lamb will overcome them, for He is *Lord of lords*, and King of kings. Rev. 17:14.

And in the same book,

The One sitting on the white horse has on His robe and on His thigh the name written, King of kings and *Lord of lords.* Rev. 19:16.

The Lord is called 'King of kings' by virtue of Divine Truth, and 'Lord of lords' by virtue of Divine Good, as is evident from the individual expressions used here. 'The name written' is His true nature, 144, 145, 1754, 1896, 2009, 2724, 3006. 'His robe' on which it is written is the truth of faith, 1073, 2576, 4545, 4763. 'His thigh' on which likewise that nature is written is the good of love, 3021, 4277, 4280, 4575. From this too it is evident that by virtue of Divine Truth the Lord is called 'King of kings' and by virtue of Divine Good 'Lord of lords'. For more about the Lord being called King by virtue of Divine Truth, see 2015, 2069, 3009, 3670, 4581.

From this it is also plain what 'the Lord's Christ' means in Luke,

Simeon received an answer from the Holy Spirit that he would not see death until he had seen *the Lord's Christ.* Luke 2:26.

'The Lord's Christ' is the Divine Truth that goes with Divine Good, for 'Christ' is one and the same as Messiah, and Messiah is the Anointed or King, 3008, 3009, 'the Lord' in this case being Jehovah. The name Jehovah is not used anywhere in the New Testament Word, but instead of Jehovah, the Lord and God are used, see 2921, as again in Luke,

Jesus said, How can they say that the Christ is David's son when David himself says in the Book of Psalms, *The Lord* said to *my Lord,* Sit at My right hand? Luke 20:41,42.

The same appears in David as follows,

Jehovah said to *my Lord,* Sit at My right hand. Ps.110:1.

It is obvious that Jehovah in David is called Lord in the gospel, 'Lord' in this case standing for the Divine Good of the Divine Human. Omnipotence is meant by 'sitting at the right hand', 3387, 4592, 4933(end).

While in the world the Lord was Divine Truth, but once He was glorified, that is, had made the Human within Him Divine, He became Divine Good, from which Divine Truth subsequently goes forth. This explains why after the Resurrection the disciples did not call Him Master, as they had before, but Lord, as is evident in John 21:7,12,15–17,20, and also in the other gospels. Divine Truth – which the Lord was while in the world and which subsequently goes forth from Him, that is, from Divine Good – is also called 'the Angel of the Covenant', in Malachi,

Suddenly there will come to His temple *the Lord* whom you are seeking, and *the Angel of the Covenant* in whom you delight. Mal.3:1.

Because 'Lord' is used to mean Divine Good and 'King' Divine Truth, therefore in places where the Lord is spoken of as having dominion and a kingdom 'dominion' has reference to Divine Good and 'a kingdom' to Divine Truth. For the same reason the Lord is called 'Lord of the nations' but 'King of the peoples', for 'nations' means those governed by good, 'peoples' those governed by truth, 1259, 1260, 1849, 3581.

Good is called 'lord' as against a servant, and 'father' as against a son, as in Malachi,

A son should honour his father, and *a servant his lord.* If I am a Father, where is My honour? And if I am *a Lord,* where is the fear of Me? Mal. 1:6.

And in David,

To be *a slave* JOSEPH was sold. The word of Jehovah tested him. *The king* sent and released him, *he who had dominion over nations* set him free and placed him as *lord of his house* and as *one with dominion* over all his possessions.
Ps. 115:17,19–22.

Here, as is evident from each individual expression, 'Joseph' is used to mean the Lord, 'lord' in this instance being the Divine Good of the Divine Human.

4974 'And his lord saw that Jehovah was with him' means a perception within natural good that the Divine existed within it. This is clear from the meaning of 'seeing' as understanding and discerning, dealt with in 2150, 3764, 4339, 4567, 4723, and from the meaning of 'lord' as good, dealt with immediately above in 4973, in this case natural good because it is 'the Egyptian' who is the lord. The existence inwardly of the Divine is meant by 'Jehovah was with him', as above in 4971.

4975 'And everything that he did Jehovah made to prosper in his hand' means that all things were the conferments of Divine Providence. This is clear from the meaning of 'being made to prosper' as being provided for, dealt with above in 4972. Consequently 'Jehovah made it prosper in his hand' is Divine Providence.

[4975a] 'And Joseph found favour in his eyes' means that it had found acceptance, that is to say, by natural good meant by 'his lord'. This is clear from the meaning of 'finding favour in someone's eyes' as finding acceptance. The expression 'in his eyes' is used because 'favour' has reference to the understanding, and this is meant by 'the eyes', 2701, 3820, 4526.

4976 'And ministered to him' means that factual knowledge was assigned to its own good. This is clear from the meaning of 'ministering' as serving by supplying what another has need of, in this case as being assigned to since the subject is natural good to which factual knowledge is to be assigned. 'Ministering' is also used to describe known facts, for in the Word a minister and a servant mean factual knowledge or natural truth because this is subservient to good as its lord. Factual knowledge stands in relation to delight present in the natural man – or what amounts to the same, natural truth stands in relation to its good – in exactly the same way as water does to bread, or drink to food. Water or drink enables bread or food to be dissolved, and once dissolved to be conveyed into the blood, from which it passes into all parts around the body and nourishes them. Without the water or drink the bread or food is not broken down into extremely small particles and carried around the body to fulfill its purpose.

2 The same applies to factual knowledge in relation to delight, or truth in relation to good. That being so, good longs for and desires truth, and does so because of the purpose such truth can fulfill by ministering to it and serving it. Food and drink also correspond to these. No one in the next life is nourished by any natural food or natural drink, only by

spiritual food and spiritual drink, spiritual food being good, and spiritual drink truth. This is why, when bread or food is mentioned in the Word, angels understand spiritual bread or food, which is the good of love and charity; and when water or drink is mentioned they understand spiritual water or drink, which is the truth of faith. From this one may see what the truth of faith without the good of charity is, and also what kind of nourishment the former without the latter is able to supply to the internal man; that is to say, it is like the nourishment supplied by water or drink alone without bread or food. It is well known that a person fed on water or drink alone wastes away and dies.

4977 'And he put him in charge over his house' means that this good applied itself to that factual knowledge. This is clear from the meaning of his 'lord', who put him in charge, as good, dealt with above in 4973, and from the meaning of 'putting him in charge over his house' as applying itself to it – to factual knowledge or natural truth. This meaning is evident from what follows, where it says that 'whatever he had he gave into his hand', meaning that all belonging to that good was seemingly subject to the other's power and control. For good is the lord and truth its minister, and when it says that the lord put the minister in charge, that is, that good put truth in charge, the meaning in the internal sense is not that the lordship ceased to rest with that good but that it applied itself to the truth. For in the internal sense one perceives what a thing really is, whereas the sense of the letter presents it in the form of an appearance. The lordship always rests with good, but good applies itself so that truth may be joined to it.

While a person is governed by truth, as happens before he has been regenerated, he knows scarcely anything at all about good. For truth flows in by an external route, or that of the senses, whereas good flows in by an internal route. Before he has been regenerated a person is aware of that which flows in by the external route, but not of that which comes by the internal one. Consequently unless in that state which comes first the lordship seemed to be given to truth, that is, unless good applied itself to it, that truth could never become attached to this good as its own. This is the same factor as has been presented many times before – that truth seemingly occupies the first place, that is, it is so to speak the lord, while a person is being regenerated, but that good plainly occupies the first place and is the lord once he has been regenerated, for which see 3539, 3548, 3556, 3563, 3570, 3576, 3603, 3701, 4925, 4926, 4928, 4930.

4978 'And whatever he had he gave into his hand' means that all that belonged to that good was seemingly subject to the power and control of its associated truth. This is clear from the meaning of 'whatever he had' as all that belonged to it, and from the meaning of 'hand' as power, dealt with in 878, 3091, 3387, 3563, 4931–4937. 'Giving into his hand' accordingly means placing under its power and control. Yet because this is only the appearance of what happens, the phrase 'seemingly subject to its power and control' is used. As regards its being what is apparently or seemingly the situation, see immediately above in 4977.

4979 'And it happened from the time he put him in charge in his house and over all that he had' means a second state, after this good had applied itself to that truth and had made all that belonged to it seemingly subject to the power and control of that truth. This is clear from the meaning of 'it happened' or 'so it was' – an expression used many times in the Word – as that which implies something new and therefore a second state (similarly in verses 7,10,11,13,15,18,19 below); from the meaning of 'from the time he put him in charge in his house' as after good had applied itself to that truth, dealt with above in 4977; and from the meaning of 'over all that he had' as all that belonged to such good was made seemingly subject to the power and control of that truth, also dealt with above, in 4978.

4980 'That Jehovah blessed the Egyptian's house for Joseph's sake' means that at this point the Divine imparted the celestial-natural to that truth. This is clear from the meaning of 'being blessed' as being enriched with celestial and spiritual good, so that an imparting by the Divine is meant by 'Jehovah blessed'; and from the meaning of 'the Egyptian's house' as the good dwelling in the natural mind, as above in 4973. From this it follows that the words 'Jehovah blessed the Egyptian's house' mean that at this point the Divine imparted the celestial-natural to it. The celestial-natural is good present in the natural which corresponds to the good belonging to the rational, that is, which corresponds to the celestial of the spiritual from the rational, meant by 'Joseph', 4963.

2   The term celestial, like spiritual, is used in reference both to the rational and to the natural, that is, both to the internal man, which is the rational man, and to the external, which is the natural man. For essentially, the spiritual is Divine Truth which goes forth from the Lord, while the celestial is Divine Good present within that Divine Truth. When Divine Truth containing Divine Good is received by the rational, or by the internal man, it is called the spiritual within the rational, but when it is received by the natural, or by the external man, it is called the spiritual within the natural. The same is so with Divine Good present within Divine Truth. When this good is received by the rational, or by the internal man, it is referred to as the celestial within the rational, but when it is received by the natural, or by the external man, it is referred to as the celestial within the natural. In man's case these two flow in both directly from the Lord and indirectly from Him through angels and spirits; but in the Lord's case while He was in the world they flowed in from Himself because the Divine existed within Him.

4981 'And the blessing of Jehovah was' means increases. This is clear from the meaning of 'the blessing of Jehovah'. In the genuine sense 'the blessing of Jehovah' means love to the Lord and charity

16

towards the neighbour, for those who are endowed with these are called 'the blessed of Jehovah' since they are in that case endowed with heaven and eternal salvation. Consequently 'the blessing of Jehovah' in the external sense, that is, in the sense which has to do with a person's state in the world, means resting content in God and on that account being content with one's position in society and with the amount of wealth one possesses, whether one is among the highly honoured and is wealthy or among the not so honoured and the poor. For the person who rests content in God regards positions and wealth as means to fulfill useful purposes; and when he thinks about these and at the same time about eternal life, he rates them as nothing and eternal life as that which is essential.

Because 'the blessing of Jehovah (or the Lord)' implies such increases in the genuine sense, blessing also implies countless other benefits and consequently means the various gifts which flow from it, such as enrichment with spiritual and celestial good, 981, 1731; fruitfulness resulting from the affection for truth, 2846; undergoing rearrangement into heavenly order, 3017; being endowed with the good of love and thereby being joined to the Lord, 3406, 3504, 3514, 3530, 3584; and joy, 4216. What is meant by 'blessing' therefore in any specific instance becomes clear from the context in which it appears. Here the meaning of 'the blessing of Jehovah' as increases in good and truth, that is, in life and doctrine, is evident from what follows it, for there it says that this blessing of Jehovah was 'in the house and in the field', and 'house' means good which is the good of life, while 'field' means truth which is the truth of doctrine. From this it is evident that increases in these are meant in this case by 'the blessing of Jehovah'.

4982   'On all that he had in the house and in the field' means in life and in doctrine. This is clear from the meaning of 'the house' as good, dealt with in 2048, 2233, 2234, 2559, 3128, 3652, 3720, and as 'the house' means good it also means life, since all good is the good of life; and from the meaning of 'the field' as the Church's truth, dealt with in 368, 3508, 3766, 4440, 4443, and as this means the Church's truth it also means doctrine, for all truth is the truth of doctrine. House and field are also referred to several times in other parts of the Word, and when in such places the celestial man is the subject, 'house' means celestial good and 'field' spiritual good. In this case celestial good is the good of love to the Lord, and spiritual good is the good of charity towards the neighbour. But when the spiritual man is the subject 'house' means the celestial as it exists with him, which is the good of charity towards the neighbour, while 'field' means the spiritual as it exists with him, which is the truth of faith. 'The house' and 'the field' have the same meanings in Matthew,

Let him who is on the roof of *the house* not go down to take anything out of *his house*; and let him who is in *the field* not turn back to get his clothing. Matt. 24:17,18.

See 3652.

4983 'And he left all that he had in Joseph's hand' means that it seemed as though all things were subject to its power and control. This is clear from what has been explained above in 4978 where practically the same words occur, and also from what has been stated in 4977.

4984 'And he did not concern himself with anything except the bread that he ate' means that the good from there was made its own. This is clear from the meaning of 'bread' as good, dealt with in 276, 680, 3478, 3735, 4211, 4217, 4735; and from the meaning of 'eating' as being made one's own, dealt with in 3168, 3513(end), 3596, 3832, 4745. 'He did not concern himself with anything except the bread' means that it took to itself nothing else than good. One might think that when good makes truth its own, it makes its own that kind of truth which is the truth of faith; but in fact it makes the good of truth its own. Truths that have no useful purpose do indeed come near it but they do not enter into it. All useful purposes led to by truths are instances of the good of truth. Truths which have no useful purpose are separated, some of which are then retained, others laid aside. The ones that are retained lead in some direct or else more remote way to good and actually have a useful purpose. Ones that are laid aside do not lead to good, nor do they become linked to it. Initially all useful purposes exist as the truths of doctrine, but they move on to become forms of good. They become such when a person acts in conformity with them, for it is what the person actually practises that imparts such a nature to those truths. Every action springs from the will, and the will is what causes that which existed initially as truth to become good. From this it is evident that, when in the will, truth is no longer the truth of faith but the good of faith, and that it is not the truth of faith but the good of faith that brings happiness. For the latter exerts an influence on the essential constituent of a person's life, that is to say, on the intentions in his will, bringing him interior delight or bliss, and in the next life happiness that is called heavenly joy.

4985 'And Joseph was beautiful in form' means the good of life springing from this, 'and beautiful in appearance' means the truth of faith springing from it. This is clear from the meaning of 'beautiful in form and beautiful in appearance', for 'the form' is the essence of a thing, whereas 'the appearance' is the outward manifestation derived from it. And since good is the actual essence and truth is the outward manifestation springing from it, 'beautiful in form' means the good of life and 'beautiful in appearance' the truth of faith. For the good of life is a person's essential being (*esse*) since it resides in his will, while the truth of faith is the manifestation of it since it inhabits his understanding. Indeed whatever inhabits the understanding is a manifestation of something that originates in the will. The essential being (*esse*) constituting a person's life resides in the intentions of his will, and the manifestation (*existere*) of his life resides in the thoughts of his understanding. A person's understanding is nothing else than an unfolding of his will, also the imparting of a form to it that enables its true nature to be seen in an outward appearance.

From this one may see where the beauty – the beauty of the interior man – comes from. That is, it comes from the good present in the will by way of the truth of faith. The truth of faith presents that beauty in an outward form, but the good in the will is the supplier of that beauty and the producer of the outward form. Here is the reason for the indescribable beauty of the angels of heaven, for each is so to speak love and charity embodied in a form. When therefore anyone sees them in their beauty his deepest feelings are stirred. For the good of love received from the Lord shines forth from them through the truth of faith, enters into him, and stirs those feelings within him. From this, as also in 3821, one may see what is meant in the internal sense by 'beautiful in form and beautiful in appearance.

4986   Verses 7-9 **And it happened after these events, that his lord's wife lifted up her eyes towards Joseph and said, Lie with me. And he refused and said to his lord's wife, Behold, my lord does not concern himself with anything[1] in the house, and all that he has he has given into my hand. He himself is no greater in this house than I am, and he has not held back anything from me except yourself, in that you are his wife. How then shall I do this great evil, and sin against God?**

'And it happened after these events' means a third state. 'That his lord's wife lifted up her eyes towards Joseph' means unspiritual natural truth wedded to natural good, and its perception. 'And said, Lie with me' means that it desired a joining together. 'And he refused' means an aversion. 'And he said to his lord's wife' means a perception regarding that truth. 'Behold, my lord does not concern himself with anything in the house' means that natural good did not have even the desire to make anything its own. 'And all that he has he has given into my hand' means that everything was subject to its power and control. 'He himself is no greater in this house than I am' means that that good is prior in respect of time but not of state. 'And he has not held back anything from me except yourself' means that becoming joined to the truth wedded to that good was forbidden. 'In that you are his wife' means because this truth must not be joined to any other good. 'How then shall I do this great evil, and sin against God?' means that, this being so, they exist set apart and not joined together.

4987   'And it happened after these events' means a third state. This is clear from the meaning of 'it happened' or 'so it was' as that which implies something new, as above in 4979, and therefore at this point a third state; and from the meaning of 'after these events' as after those things were completed. In the original language one line of thought is not separated from another by punctuation marks[2], as in other lan-

---

[1] *lit.* does not know what is with me
[2] *i.e. before the introduction of Masoretic pointing and punctuation*

guages, but the text seems to run so to speak from start to finish without any breaks in it. Ideas in the internal sense follow one another in a similar way without breaks, moving on from one state of a thing into another state of it. But when one state comes to an end and another major one takes its place, this is indicated by the expression 'so it was' or 'it happened', while a minor change of state is indicated by the word 'and'. This is the reason why these expressions occur so frequently. This third state described now is more internal than the previous one.

4988 'That his lord's wife lifted up her eyes towards Joseph' means unspiritual natural truth wedded to natural good, and its perception. This is clear from the meaning of 'wife' as truth wedded to good, dealt with in 1468, 2517, 3236, 4510, 4823, and in this case as unspiritual natural truth wedded to natural good since that kind of truth and this kind of good are described – the good to which that truth is joined being meant here by 'lord', 4973; and from the meaning of 'lifting up the eyes' as thought, attention, and also perception, dealt with in 2789, 2829, 3198, 3202, 4339.

2   'Wife' in this instance means natural truth, but not natural truth that is spiritual, while her husband, to whom 'lord' refers here, means natural good, but not natural good that is spiritual. But some explanation is needed to show what is meant by natural good and truth that are not spiritual and what is meant by natural good and truth that are spiritual. With the human being, good has two different origins – one being heredity and consequently that which is adventitious, the other being the doctrine of faith and charity or, in the case of gentiles, their religious belief. Good arising from the first origin is unspiritual natural good, whereas good arising from the second is spiritual natural good. Truth too comes from a like origin, for all good has its own truth wedded to it.

3   Natural good arising from the first origin, which is hereditary and consequently adventitious, bears many similarities to natural good arising from the second origin, which is the doctrine of faith and charity or some other set of religious beliefs. But those similarities are confined to outward appearances; inwardly the two are completely different. Natural good arising from the first origin may be compared to the good that is also present among living creatures of a gentle nature, whereas natural good arising from the second is peculiar to the human being who uses his reason when he acts, and who consequently knows how to administer what is good in different ways, in keeping with useful purposes that need to be served. These different ways in which good has to be administered are what the doctrine regarding what is right and fair teaches, and in a higher degree what the doctrine regarding faith and charity teaches; and in the case of people who are truly rational, reason also serves in many instances to corroborate what doctrine teaches.

4   Those whose performance of good arises from the first origin are moved

as if by blind instinct in their exercise of charity, whereas those whose performance of good arises from the second origin are moved by an inner sense of duty and so with their eyes so to speak fully open to what they are doing. In short, those whose performance of good arises from the first origin are not led by any conscientious regard for what is right and fair, still less by any such regard for spiritual truth and good; but those whose performance of good arises from the second origin are led by conscience. See what has been stated already on these matters in 3040, 3470, 3471, 3518, and what is said below in 4992. But what is involved in all this cannot possibly be explained intelligibly; for anyone who is not spiritual, that is, not regenerate, sees good from the point of view of the outward form it takes. He does this because he does not know what is meant by charity or by the neighbour; and the reason why he does not know this is that no doctrinal teachings regarding charity exist. Such matters can be seen very clearly in the light of heaven, and they can consequently be seen clearly by spiritual or regenerate persons because they dwell in the light of heaven.

4989 'And said, Lie with me' means that it desired a joining together. This is clear from the meaning of 'lying with me' as a joining together, that is to say, of spiritual natural good, meant here by 'Joseph', and unspiritual natural truth, meant by 'his lord's wife'; but this would be an unlawful joining together. Joinings together of good and truth, and of truth and good, are described in the Word by means of marriages, see 2727-2759, 3132, 3665, 4434, 4837, and therefore unlawful joinings together are described by means of liaisons with prostitutes. Here therefore the joining of unspiritual natural truth to spiritual natural good is described by his lord's wife's wanting to lie with him. No joining together of these exists internally, only externally, where they appear to be joined together but in fact have no more than a mere association with each other. This also is the reason why it says that she took hold of him by his garment and that he left his garment in her hand; for in the internal sense 'a garment' means what is external, by means of which the two only appear to be joined, that is, they have no more than a mere association with each other, as will be seen below at verses 12,13.

These meanings cannot be seen as long as the mind or thought concentrates solely on the historical details, for in that case there is no thought of anything else than Joseph, Potiphar's wife, and Joseph's flight after leaving behind his garment. But if the mind or thought were to concentrate on what is meant spiritually by 'Joseph', 'Potiphar's wife', and the 'garment', it would be seen that some spiritual but unlawful joining together was also meant here. When this is so, the mind or thought is able to concentrate on what is meant spiritually, provided the belief is present that the historical Word is Divine not by virtue of the mere historical narrative but by virtue of what is spiritual and Divine contained within it. If a person possessed such a belief he would know that its spiritual and Divine content was concerned with the goodness and truth present in the Church and in the Lord's kingdom, and in the highest sense with the Lord Himself. When a person enters the next life, which happens immediately after death, if he is one of those who are being raised up to heaven he will come to realize that he retains none of the historical details recorded in the Word. He knows nothing whatever about Joseph, nor anything about Abraham, Isaac, and Jacob, but only about the spiritual and Divine realities which he has learned from the Word and made part of his own life. These therefore are the kinds of matters inwardly present in the Word, which are called its internal sense.

4990   'And he refused' means an aversion. This is clear from the meaning of 'refusing' as being filled with aversion – with aversion for that joining together – for anyone whose refusal is so great that he even flees out of doors is filled with aversion.

4991   'And he said to his lord's wife' means a perception regarding that truth. This is clear from the meaning in the historical narratives of the Word of 'saying' as perceiving, often dealt with already, and from the meaning of 'his lord's wife' as unspiritual natural truth, wedded to natural good, dealt with above in 4988.

4992   'Behold, my lord does not concern himself with anything in the house' means that natural good did not have even the desire to make anything its own. This is clear from the meaning of 'his lord' as natural good, dealt with in 4973, and from the meaning of 'not concerning himself with anything in the house' as having no desire to make anything its own. This meaning of these words cannot be seen except from the train of thought in the internal sense, for now the subject is a third state, in which the celestial of the spiritual was present in the natural. In this state natural good and truth which are spiritual are separated from natural good and truth which are not spiritual. Consequently 'not concerning himself with anything in the house' means that no desire existed to make anything its own. But being arcana, these matters cannot be seen clearly without the help of examples.

2   Let the following serve to shed light on the matter. If mere lust leads a man to be joined to his wife, this is something natural which is unspiritual; but if conjugial love leads him to be joined to her this is something natural which is spiritual. And if after that – when he is her husband – it is mere lust that joins him to her, he considers himself to be a sinner who is no different from someone behaving in a sexually immoral way; which being so he has no further wish to make such lust his own. Or let another example be given. To do good to a friend, regardless of his character and simply because he is one's friend, is a natural action that is unspiritual; but to do good to a friend on account of the good residing with him, all the more so when one regards good itself as the friend to whom one is to do good, is a natural action that is

spiritual. When this attitude exists with a person, he realizes that he himself is a sinner if he does good to a friend who is evil; for in that case he does evil to others through that friend. When this is his state he turns away from making his own that unspiritual natural good which had existed with him previously. The same is so with everything else.

4993 'And all that he has he has given into my hand' means that everything was subject to its power and control. This is clear from what has been stated above in 4978, where similar words occur. But the difference is that there the subject is the second state which the celestial of the spiritual within the natural passed through, for at that point natural good applied itself to truth and made this its own, 4976, 4977. In that state good in actual fact had dominion, though truth appeared to do so, which was why the words used there meant that everything belonging to that good was seemingly subject to its power and control. Now however the subject is the third state which the celestial of the spiritual passed through when that good present within the natural was made spiritual. And because in this state spiritual natural good makes nothing its own, the words now used therefore mean that all was subject to the power and control of the celestial of the spiritual.

4994 'He himself is no greater in this house than I am' means that that good is prior in respect of time but not of state. This is clear from the meaning of 'his being no greater in this house than I am' as the fact that the lordship of the one has equal status with that of the other, and therefore both are prior. But from the train of thought in the internal sense it is evident that unspiritual natural good is prior in respect of time, and that spiritual natural good is prior in respect of state, as is also plain from what has been shown above in 4992. To be prior in respect of state means to be superior as regards essential nature.

4995 'And he has not held back anything from me except yourself' means that becoming joined to truth wedded to that good was forbidden. This is clear from the meaning of 'having held back from him' as that which has been forbidden, and from the meaning of the wife whom he held back, to whom 'yourself' refers here, as unspiritual natural truth, dealt with in 4988.

4996 'In that you are his wife' means because this truth must not be joined to any other good. This is clear from the meaning of 'wife' as truth wedded to its own good, dealt with in 1468, 2517, 3236, 4510, 4823, in this case unspiritual natural truth wedded to unspiritual natural good, as above in 4988.

4997 'How then shall I do this great evil, and sin against God?' means that, this being so, they exist set apart and not joined together. This is clear from the meaning of 'evil' and likewise of 'sin' as a state when things are set apart and not joined together. That is to say, it describes what happens if spiritual natural good is joined to unspiritual natural truth; being unlike and incompatible the two pull away from each other. The expressions 'doing evil' and 'sinning against God' are used because regarded in itself evil, and sin too, is nothing else than being parted from good. Also, evil exists essentially in disunion, as is evident from what good is. Essentially good is a joining together because all good stems from love to the Lord and love towards the neighbour. The good of love to the Lord joins a person to the Lord and consequently to all good that goes forth from the Lord; and the good of love towards the neighbour joins him to heaven and the communities there, so that by means of this love as well he is joined to the Lord. For properly speaking, heaven is the Lord since He is the All in all there.

2   But with evil the opposite applies. Evil stems from self-love and love of the world. Evil stemming from self-love sets a person apart not only from the Lord but also from heaven, for he loves no one but himself and others only insofar as he sees them as part of his self-interest, or as they identify themselves with him. Consequently he turns everyone's attention towards himself and entirely away from others, most of all away from the Lord. When a large number act like this within a single community it follows that all are set apart from one another; inwardly each sees another as his enemy. If anyone acts contrary to his self-interest he hates that person and takes delight in his destruction. The evil of the love of the world is not dissimilar, for this consists in a longing for other people's wealth and goods, and in a longing to gain possession of everything owned by others; and these longings too lead to all kinds of enmity and hatred, though in a lesser degree. For anyone to come to know what evil is, and so what sin is, let him merely try to see what self-love and love of the world are; and to come to know what good is, let him merely try to see what love to God and love towards the neighbour are. By trying to do this he will come to see what evil is, and as a consequence what falsity is; and from this he will come to see what good is, and as a consequence what truth is.

4998   Verses 10-15 **And it happened as she spoke to Joseph day after day, that he did not listen to her, to lie with her, to be with her. And it happened on a certain day, that he went to the house to do his work, and none of the men[1] of the house was there in the house. And she took hold of him by his garment, saying, Lie with me. And he left his garment in her hand and fled, and went out of doors. And it happened as she saw that he had left his garment in her hand and had fled out of doors, that she cried out to the men of her house, and said to them – she said, See, he has brought us a Hebrew man to make sport of us. He came to me to lie with me, and I cried out with a loud voice. And it happened as he was hearing [me], that I lifted up my voice and cried out, and he left his garment with me, and fled, and went out of doors.**

'And it happened' means a fourth state. 'As she spoke to Joseph day after day' means thought regarding that matter. 'That he did not listen to her, to lie with her' means that it was filled with aversion to such a

---

[1] *lit.* no man from the men

oining together. 'To be with her' means lest it should thereby be made
one with it. 'And it happened on a certain day' means a fifth state. 'That
he went to the house to do his work' means when engaged in the work
of being joined to spiritual good within the natural. 'And none of the
men of the house was there in the house' means without the help of any
other. 'And she laid hold of him by his garment' means that unspiritual
truth attached itself to the outermost existence of spiritual truth.
Saying, Lie with me' means to the end that a joining together might be
effected. 'And he left his garment in her hand' means that this
outermost truth was removed. 'And fled, and went out of doors' means
that this being so it did not have that truth with which to protect itself.
'And it happened as she saw' means a perception regarding this matter.
'That he had left his garment in her hand and had fled out of doors'
means regarding the separation of that outermost truth. 'That she cried
out to the men of the house' means falsities. 'And said to them – she
said' means an urgent demand. 'See, he has brought us a Hebrew man'
means something servile. 'To make sport of us' means that this rose up.
'He came to me to lie with me' means that that truth wanted to be
joined to it. 'And I cried out with a loud voice' means that it was filled
with aversion. 'And it happened as he was hearing [me]' means when it
was discerned. 'That I lifted up my voice and cried out' means that there
was a great aversion. 'And he left his garment with me' means evidence
that an approach had been made. 'And fled, and went out of doors'
means that it nevertheless separated itself.

4999   'And it happened' means a fourth state. This becomes clear
from what has been stated above in 4979, 4987.

5000   'As she spoke to Joseph day after day' means thought regarding that matter. This is clear from the meaning of 'speaking' as
thinking, dealt with in 2271, 2287, 2619, that is to say, thought regarding
Joseph, and so regarding the matter which 'Joseph' represents here.
'Day after day' or every day means intently. The reason why in the
internal sense 'speaking' means thinking is that thought is an inward
conversing, and when a person is thinking he is conversing with
himself. Things of an inward kind are expressed in the sense of the
letter by means of the outward ones that correspond to them.

5001   'That he did not listen to her, to lie with her' means that it was
filled with aversion to such a joining together. This is clear from the
meaning of 'not listening to' as not hearkening to or not obeying, dealt
with in 2542, 3869, in this case as being filled with aversion since he
refused to hearken to her, so much so that he left his garment in her
hand and fled; and from the meaning of 'lying with her' as being
unlawfully joined together, dealt with in 4989.

5002   'To be with her' means lest it should thereby be made one with
it. This is clear from the meaning of 'being with someone' as existing
joined more closely or united together. The reason 'being' means

existing united is that the actual being (*esse*) of a thing is good, and al good flows from love, love being essentially a spiritual togetherness o oneness. This explains why in the highest sense the Lord is calle 'Being' (*Esse*), or Jehovah; for all good flowing from love or spiritua togetherness is derived from Him. Because the love that is derived from Him and returned to Him through the acceptance of it, and also mutua love, make heaven one, heaven is therefore called a marriage, which gives it its 'being'. One would be able to say the same of the Church i love and charity existed there as its essential being. Therefore where nc togetherness or unity exists, the Church has no 'being', for unless something were present there to unite its members or make them one, the Church would disintegrate and cease to exist.

2 The same happens to civil society if everyone there is out only for himself and nobody, except for his own purposes, takes any interest in anyone else. Without laws to unite its members, and without any fears for loss of gain, position, reputation, or life, society would fall completely to pieces. Therefore the 'being' of such a society in which everyone is out for himself consists in its members being joined or united together, but at a purely external level. Internally that society does not have any 'being'. Consequently in the next life people like this are confined to hell, where in a similar way they are kept in check by external restraints, especially by fears. But as often as those restraints are eased, one individual hastens to destroy another, there being nothing he wants to do more than to destroy another completely. It is different in heaven, where love to the Lord and mutual love deriving from that love join its members together at an internal level. When external restraints are removed there, angels become even more closely joined to one another. And being thereby drawn nearer to the Divine Being (*Esse*) coming to them from the Lord, they are filled deeper still with affection, and from this with a sense of freedom, and as a consequence with feelings of blessedness, happiness, and joy.

5003 'And it happened on a certain day' means a fifth state. This is clear from the meaning of 'it happened' or 'so it was' as that which implies something new, as above in 4979, 4987, 4999, and so a new state, in this case a fifth one.

5004 'That he went to the house to do his work' means when engaged in the work of being joined to spiritual good within the natural. This becomes clear from the fact that it is this joining together that 'Joseph' serves to describe in this chapter, and therefore when it says 'he went to the house to do his work' the work involved in that joining together is meant.

5005 'And none of the men of the house was there in the house' means without the help of any other. This becomes clear from the fact that this statement means that Joseph was alone; and because in the internal sense 'Joseph' is descriptive of the Lord, of how He glorified

His Internal Human or made this Divine, these words are used to mean that He made it so without the help of any other. This truth that the Lord made His Human Divine by His own power, and so without the help of any other, may be recognized from the consideration that because He was conceived from Jehovah, the Divine was within Him, and thus that the Divine was His own. Therefore when He was in the world and made the Human within Him Divine, He did so with the aid of the Divine, which was His own, that is, He did it by Himself. This is described in Isaiah as follows,

Who is this who is coming from Edom, with spattered clothes from Bozra, He that is glorious in His apparel, *marching in the vast numbers of His strength? I have trodden* the winepress *alone*, and from *the peoples no man was with Me*. I looked about but there was *none helping*, and I wondered, but there was *not one to uphold*; therefore *My own arm brought salvation to Me*.   Isa.63:1,3,5.

And elsewhere in the same prophet,

He saw that there was no man, and as it were wondered that there was no intercessor; therefore *His own arm brought salvation to Him*, and His righteousness lifted Him up. Consequently He put on righteousness as a breastplate, and a helmet of salvation upon His head.   Isa.59:16,17.

For more about the Lord making the Human within Him Divine by His own power, see 1616, 1749, 1755, 1812, 1813, 1921, 1928, 1999, 2025, 2026, 2083, 2500, 2523, 2776, 3043, 3141, 3382, 3637, 4286.

5006   'And she took hold of him by his garment' means that unspiritual truth attached itself to the outermost existence of spiritual truth. This is clear from the representation of Potiphar's wife, to whom these words refer, as unspiritual natural truth, dealt with in 4988; from the meaning of 'taking hold of' in this case as attaching itself; and from the meaning of 'garment' as truth, dealt with in 1073, 2576, 4545, 4763, in this case the outermost existence of spiritual truth, which in this state is Joseph's – 'Joseph' here representing spiritual natural good, 4988, 4992. For it was to the truth belonging to this good that unspiritual natural truth wished to become joined, as is evident from the train of thought in the internal sense.

But as to what a wish on the part of unspiritual natural truth to become joined to spiritual natural truth may be and what is implied by it, this is a mystery at the present day, chiefly because few people have any concern or wish to know what spiritual truth is and what unspiritual truth is. Indeed that lack of concern is so great that people are hardly willing to listen when the word spiritual is used, for at the mere mention of this a kind of darkness instantly descends upon them, and along with this a melancholy feeling, which gives rise to a distaste for the word and so a rejection of it. The truth of this has also been demonstrated to me. While I was once pondering on these matters, some spirits from the Christian world were present, who were then taken back into the state that had been theirs in the world. The mere thought of spiritual good and truth not only gave them a melancholy feeling; it also seized them with such loathing on account of their aversion to it that they said they felt as they had done in the world when they wanted to vomit. But I was allowed to tell them that this happened because their affections were centred solely on earthly bodily, and worldly interests; and when a person is concerned solely with these, the things of heaven nauseate him. I also told those spirits that when they had gone to church where the Word was preached they had not gone out of any wish to know the things of heaven, but out of some other desire present in them since early childhood. This experience showed me what the Christian world is like at the present day.

3 The overall reason why this is the situation is that the Christian Church at the present day preaches faith alone, not charity, and so doctrine, not life. And when the Church fails to preach life, no one acquires any affection for good; and when there is no affection for good, neither is there any for truth. Consequently most people find it contrary to their life's delight to listen to anything about the things of heaven beyond what they have known since they were young children.

4 But the fact of the matter is that a person exists in the world to the end that he may be introduced through the services he renders there into the things of heaven. But his life in the world lasts barely a moment so to speak, compared with his life after death; for the latter goes on for ever. Yet there are few who believe that they will be alive after death, which explains why heavenly things are of little importance to them. And this I can positively declare, that a person is in the next life as soon as he has died, carrying on to the full the life he was leading in the world; the nature of his life remains the same as it was in the world. I can positively declare this to be so because I know it to be so. I have talked to almost all those I knew during their earthly lives after these were over. I have therefore been allowed to know through actual experience the nature of the lot that awaits everyone – that each person's lot is determined by the life he has led. But the kind of people mentioned above do not believe any of this. As to what a wish on the part of unspiritual natural truth to become joined to spiritual natural truth may be, and what is implied by it, meant by 'she took hold of Joseph by his garment', this will be discussed in what follows immediately below.

5007 'Saying, Lie with me' means to the end that a joining together might be effected. This is clear from the meaning of 'lying' as a joining together, dealt with above in 4989, 5001, in this case to the end that a joining together might be effected, that is, with the consequent object that one might be joined to the other.

5008 'And he left his garment in her hand' means that this outermost truth was removed. This is clear from the meaning of 'leaving in her hand' as leaving to its power and control, for 'the hand' means power or power and control, 878, 3091, 3387, 3563, 4931-4937, a removal being meant here since it is said that 'she took hold of his garment'; and rom the meaning of 'a garment' as outermost truth, dealt with above in ,oo6. No one can begin to understand what is meant by a wish on the part of unspiritual natural truth to join itself to spiritual natural truth, or by the latter being filled with aversion to such a joining together and therefore leaving the outermost truth behind, that is, allowing this to be removed, except with the help of examples to shed light on the matter. But first, see what unspiritual natural truth is, and what spiritual natural truth is, in 4988, 4992; also the fact that the two are associated with each other so far as outermost things are concerned but that they are in no way joined to each other [4989].

But, as has been said, examples will help to shed light on this matter. Take this one first. Within the Church there exists the unspiritual natural truth which says that good should be done to the poor, widows and orphans, and that doing good to these is the charity which is commanded in the Word. But unspiritual truth, or rather, people guided by unspiritual truth, understand the poor, widows and orphans to be those who are literally called such, whereas spiritual natural truth, or rather, people guided by this kind of truth – while giving their firm assent to this unspiritual natural truth – place such an understanding of the expression 'poor, widows and orphans' in the last or outermost position. For in their hearts they say that not all people calling themselves the poor are in fact such, and also that some of those who are poor lead very wicked lives, fearing neither God nor men, and ready to plunge into every unmentionable deed but for the fear that holds them back. They also say in their hearts that in the Word the expression 'the poor' is used to mean those who are such spiritually, that is to say, those who know and in their hearts confess that nothing good or true at all that originates in themselves resides with them and that everything that is there has been freely given them. The expressions 'widows' and 'orphans' are considered by them in a similar way, the difference being that each involves some different state. From this example it may be seen that to people guided by spiritual natural truth doing good to the poor, widows and orphans who are literally called such is an outermost truth, and that this outermost truth is like a garment covering the things within. One may also see that this outermost truth fits in with the truth as understood by those guided by unspiritual natural truth; and that even so the two are not joined together but have merely an association with each other.

Take the example of doing good to the neighbour. Those guided by spiritual natural truth consider every individual person to be their neighbour, yet each one to be such in a different manner and degree. In their hearts they say that those governed by good are pre-eminently the neighbour to whom good should be done. They also say that those governed by evil are likewise the neighbour, but that good is done to these if they suffer the punishments prescribed by laws, because those punishments serve to correct them, as well as to prevent evil being done to the good by them and the bad examples they set. Those within the

Church who are guided by unspiritual natural truth likewise call every individual person the neighbour; but they do not take into consideration the degree or manner in which each one is a neighbour. Therefore if motivated by natural goodness they do good indiscriminately, to everyone who moves them to pity, most of all to the evil rather than the good because the evil in their malice know how to arouse feelings of pity. From this example too one may see that this outermost truth brings together those guided by unspiritual natural truth and those guided by spiritual natural truth, and yet the two are still not joined together but have merely an association with each other since one has a different idea and different perception from the other of the neighbour and of charity towards him.

4 Take a further example. Those guided by spiritual natural truth say in general that the poor and the wretched are to inherit the kingdom of heaven. But for them this is an outermost truth since they gather up within this the belief that 'the poor' and 'the wretched' are those who are spiritually such, and that these are the ones meant in the Word, to whom the heavenly kingdom will belong. But those within the Church who are guided by unspiritual natural truth say that no others can inherit the kingdom of heaven but those who in the world have been reduced to poverty, live in wretched circumstances, and suffer greater affliction than everyone else. They also call riches, important positions, and worldly joys just so many distractions or means that divert a person from heaven. This example also shows what an outermost truth is and the nature of the harmony between the two kinds of natural truth; it shows that they are not joined together, but have merely an association with each other.

5 Take this example too. Those guided by spiritual natural truth consider it an outermost truth that those objects which in the Word are called holy really were holy, such as the ark and mercy seat, the lampstand, the incense, the loaves, and so on, as well as the altar; also the temple; and Aaron's vestments too, which are called vestments of holiness – in particular the ephod together with the breastplate where the urim and thummim were. Yet the idea they have so far as this outermost truth is concerned is that those objects were not in themselves holy, nor had they had any holiness instilled into them, but that they were holy in a representative sense, that is to say, they represented the spiritual and celestial realites of the Lord's kingdom, and in the highest sense the Lord Himself. People guided by unspiritual natural truth however also call those objects holy, but holy in themselves because holiness has been instilled into them. From this one may see that the two kinds of truth meet but do not become joined to each other; for as the spiritual man's conception of that outermost truth is different from that of the merely natural man, a different form is taken by each.

6 Take yet another example. To the spiritual man it is an outermost truth that all Divine truths can be substantiated from the literal sense of the Word, and also by means of the rational or intellectual concepts known

o the enlightened. That same outermost or general truth is also
accepted by the natural man, but he has the simple belief that
everything is true which can be substantiated from the Word, above all
that which he himself has substantiated from it. The spiritual man and
the natural man meet each other therefore in their common acceptance
of the idea that every Divine truth can be substantiated; yet one sees
this general truth in a different way from the other. The merely natural
man believes that whatever he himself has substantiated for himself, or
else has heard others substantiate, is a Divine truth. He does not realize
that falsity can be substantiated just as easily as truth, and that, once
substantiated, falsity has all the appearance of truth; indeed it appears
to be more true than the truth itself, because the illusions of the senses
enter in and present it in the light of the world separated from the light
of heaven.

This too shows what outermost spiritual truth seems like to the natural
man – like a garment. It also shows that when this garment is removed
nothing at all is left to draw the two together, as a consequence of which
the spiritual man no longer has anything with which to protect himself
from the natural man, which considerations are meant by Joseph's
leaving his garment behind, fleeing, and going out of doors. For the
merely natural man does not acknowledge interior truths, and therefore
when exterior ones are taken away or removed a severance instantly
takes place. What is more, all the ideas introduced by the spiritual man
to substantiate outermost truth are called falsities by the natural man
since he has no ability to see whether the idea substantiated by the
spiritual man is really true. It is not possible to see by natural light what
belongs to spiritual light, for to do so is contrary to order. But seeing by
spiritual light what belongs to natural light is in keeping with order.

5009   'And fled, and went out of doors' means that this being so it
did not have that truth with which to protect itself. This is clear from
the meaning of 'fleeing and going out of doors' after he had left his
garment behind, as a separation that had taken place, or the fact that the
two no longer had anything in common. Consequently, since 'a
garment' means outermost truth, the meaning is that it had no truth
with which to protect itself, regarding which see what has been shown
immediately above, towards the end of 5008.

5010   'And it happened as she saw' means a perception regarding
this matter. This is clear from the meaning of 'seeing' as perception,
dealt with in 2150, 3764, 4567, 4723. The matter that was perceived is the
separation which came about through the non-acknowledgement of
outermost truth any longer, meant by 'he left his garment in her hand
and fled out of doors', as is evident from what has been stated above in
5008, 5009.

5011   'That she cried out to the men of the house' means falsities.
This is clear from the meaning of 'a cry' as falsity, dealt with in 2240,

and consequently 'crying out' is used in reference to falsity. In the genuine sense 'the men of the house' are truths in the service of good, but in the contrary sense they are falsities in the service of evil. The fact that they are falsities which Potiphar's wife tells the men of the house now, and her husband later on, is evident from what she actually tells them. For the natural truth that is meant here by 'Potiphar's wife' is incapable of telling anything but falsities, which are the opposite of the truth, once outermost spiritual truth, the most external aspect of which can seemingly effect a joining together, has been torn away, see above towards the end of 5008.

5012 'And said to them – she said' means an urgent demand. This is clear from the meaning of 'saying' here as an urgent demand, for in the internal sense 'saying' means perception, 2862, 3395, 3509, and also communication, 3060, 4131. Here therefore, because the expression 'she cried' is used, followed by 'said – she said', a communication delivered with intense feeling, that is, an urgent demand to listen, is meant.

5013 'See, he has brought us a Hebrew man' means something servile. This is clear from the meaning of 'a Hebrew man', an expression that is used to refer to servitude, dealt with in 1703. The meaning is also plain from what follows below, for there Joseph is called 'a Hebrew slave' and also simply 'a slave' – *'The Hebrew slave* whom you have brought to us came to me' verse 17, and 'this is what *your slave* did to me' verse 19. The principal reason why 'a Hebrew man' here means something servile is that those governed by unspiritual natural truth and good, represented here by 'Potiphar and his wife', do not regard spiritual truth and good, represented here by 'Joseph', as anything other than their slave. So far as both the life and the doctrine of these people are concerned, order is upside down, for with them the natural is lord and the spiritual is slave, whereas, when true order exists, the spiritual is lord and the natural is slave. For the spiritual is prior, more internal and higher, also closer to the Divine, while the natural is posterior, more external and lower, and further removed from the Divine. For this reason both with the individual person and within the Church the spiritual is compared to heaven and also actually called heaven, and the natural is compared to the earth and also actually called the earth. This also explains why, when spiritual people – that is, those with whom the spiritual is lord – are seen in the next life in the light of heaven, they have their heads pointing upwards towards the Lord and their feet downwards towards hell. But when natural people – that is, those with whom the natural is lord – are seen in the light of heaven, they have their feet pointing upwards and their heads downwards; and this is so, even though they are seen differently in their own light, which is a feeble light produced by the evil desires and consequent false notions they are steeped in, 1528, 3340, 4214, 4418, 4531, 4532.

2   The way natural people look upon spiritual things as so to speak a body

of slaves was also represented by the way the Egyptians regarded the Hebrews as nothing else than their slaves; for the Egyptians represented those who are preoccupied with natural knowledge, and so are natural people, whereas the Hebrews represented those who belong to the Church and so are spiritual when considered in relation to the Egyptians. Furthermore the Egyptians thought the Hebrews were of so low or slave-like a degree that it was an abomination to them to eat with Hebrews, Gen.43:32; also the sacrifices which Hebrews offered were an abomination to them, Exod.8:26.

5014   'To make sport of us' means that this rose up. This is clear from the train of thought in the internal sense, and also from the meaning of 'making sport of', when this is stated with intense feeling, as rising up.

5015   'He came to me to lie with me' means that that truth – spiritual natural truth – wanted to be joined to it. This is clear from the meaning of 'coming' in this case as wanting, for anyone who comes intent on something is wanting it; and from the meaning of 'lying with' as joining together, dealt with above in 4989, 5001, 5007.

5016   'And I cried out with a loud voice' means that it was filled with aversion. This is clear from the meaning of 'a cry' as speaking falsely, dealt with in 5011, and therefore 'crying out' here implies the same. That is to say, false speaking is implied in her crying out to the men of the house for help, meaning that the unspiritual natural truth felt repelled by the spiritual; it is also implied by her assertion that she cried out with a loud voice, meaning that it was filled with aversion to the spiritual.

5017   'And it happened as he was hearing [me]' means when it was discerned. This is clear from the meaning of 'hearing' as obeying and also discerning. As regards obeying being meant, see 2542, 3869; but the fact that discerning is meant as well is evident from the actual function performed by the ear and consequently from the nature of hearing. The function of the ear is to receive what is spoken by another and to convey this to the general seat of sensation, so that this may discern from what has been conveyed to it the other person's thought. This is the reason why 'hearing' means discerning. The nature of hearing therefore is to carry one person's utterances expressing his thought to another's thought, and from there into his will, and from there into actions. This is the reason why 'hearing' means obeying. Such are the two functions proper to hearing, and in spoken languages they are distinguished from each other by the expressions 'to hear someone', meaning to discern what he says, and 'to listen to someone' or hearken to him, meaning to obey him. The reason hearing has these two functions is that the human being is unable to communicate the contents of his thought and also of his will in any other way; nor can he do other than use reasons to persuade and lead others to do and obey what he wills. From this one may see the circle through which desires and ideas are communicated – from will into thought and thus into speech, then from speech by way of his ear into another's thought and will. From this one may also see why spirits and angels who correspond to the ear or sense of hearing in the Grand Man are not only 'discernments' but also 'obediences'. As regards their being 'obediences', see 4652-4660; and being these they are also 'discernments', for the one entails the other.

5018 'That I lifted up my voice and cried out' means that there was a great aversion. This is clear from the meaning of 'crying out with a loud voice' as aversion, dealt with above in 5016; here therefore 'lifting up the voice and crying out' means a great aversion.

5019 'And he left his garment with me' means evidence that an approach had been made. This is clear from the meaning of 'leaving one's garment' as removing outermost truth, dealt with in 5008, but in this case as evidence, for the garment in her hand which she showed – that is, outermost truth by which it gave proof that it wished to be joined – would be evidence that an approach had been made. This meaning, it is true, seems rather far-fetched; nevertheless it is what her words hold within them, see below in 5028.

5020 'And fled, and went out of doors' means that it nevertheless separated itself. This is clear from the meaning of 'fleeing, and going out of doors' as separating itself, as above in 5009. These then are the falsities told by Potiphar's wife to the men of the house regarding Joseph, meaning in the internal sense the falsities which unspiritual natural truth tells regarding spiritual natural truth or which the unspiritual natural man tells regarding the spiritual natural man, see 4988, 4992, 5008.

5021 Verses 16-18 **And she kept his garment with her until his lord came to his house. And she spoke to him in[1] these words, saying, The Hebrew slave whom you have brought to us came to me, to make sport of me. And it happened as I lifted up my voice and cried out, that he left his garment with me and fled out of doors.**
And she kept his garment with her' means that it retained outermost truth. 'Until his lord came to his house' means so that it might communicate with natural good. 'And she spoke to him in these words' means speaking falsely. 'Saying, The Hebrew slave whom you have brought to us came to me' means that servile thing. 'To make sport of me' means that it rose up. 'And it happened as I lifted up my voice and cried out' means when it discerned the great aversion. 'That he left his garment with me' means proof. 'And fled out of doors' means that at that point it separated itself.

5022 'And she kept his garment with her' means that it retained outermost truth. This is clear from the meaning of 'keeping with oneself' as retaining, and from the meaning of 'a garment' as outermost

---

[1] lit. according to

ruth, dealt with above, in 5006, 5008; for once that truth is removed the spiritual man no longer has anything with which he may protect himself against people who are merely natural, 5008(end), 5009, and so he suffers harm. For any utterance made in this case by the spiritual man is declared by those who are merely natural to be something they do not perceive and also something that is not true. At the mere mention of anything internal or spiritual they either ridicule it or else call it something arcane, as a result of which any link they may have with the spiritual man is severed. And once that link has been severed the spiritual man undergoes trying experiences at the hands of those who are merely natural. This is also represented by the fact that after the wife used the garment to prove to her husband the accusation she was making, Joseph was thrown into the prison-house.

5023   'Until his lord came to his house' means so that it might communicate with natural good. This is clear from the meaning of 'lord' as unspiritual natural good, dealt with in 4973, 4988. 'House' in the internal sense is the natural mind, for the natural mind, like the rational mind also, resembles a house. 'The husband' in it is good, 'the wife' truth; 'the daughters and sons' are affections for good and truth, as well as being forms of good and truth which are begotten from that aforesaid good and truth as their parents, while 'the women servants and the men servants' are the desires and the known facts that minister to and support them. Here therefore 'until his lord came to his house' means when natural good comes to its own dwelling-place, where also there is the truth that is joined to it, though in this case it is falsity which convinces the good that it is truth. For unspiritual natural good is easily convinced that falsity is truth and that truth is falsity. The expression 'his lord' is used because the unspiritual natural looks on the spiritual as something servile, 5013.

The fact that a person's natural mind, like his rational mind, is called 'a house' is evident from the following places: In Luke,

When the unclean spirit has gone out of a person he passes through dry places seeking rest; and if he does not find any he says, *I will return to my house* out of which I came. And if when he comes he finds it swept and decorated, he goes away and brings seven other spirits more evil than himself, and they enter in and dwell there.   Luke 11:24-26.

'House' here stands for the natural mind, which is called a house that is 'empty and swept'[1] when there are no forms of good and truth in it meant by 'husband and wife', no affections for good and truth meant by 'daughters and sons', nor anything such as supports these meant by 'women servants and men servants'. The person himself is 'the house' because the rational mind together with the natural mind constitutes a human being. Without the inhabitants just mentioned – that is, without the forms of good and truth, and without the affections for these, and the service rendered by those affections – a person is not a human being but a beast.

[1] empty and swept *belongs to* Matthew 12:44.

3 The human mind is again meant by 'a house' in the same gospel,

Every kingdom divided against itself is laid waste, and *house falls upon house*. Luke 11:17.

And in Mark,

If a kingdom is divided against itself, this kingdom cannot stand. Also, if *a house* is divided against itself, *this house* cannot stand. No one can *go into the house* and plunder the vessels of a strong man unless he first binds the strong man, and then he may plunder his *house*. Mark 3:24,25,27.

'Kingdom' means truth, 1672, 2547, 4691, and 'house' good, 2233, 2234, 3720, 4982, 'house' meaning good on account of its greater importance.

4 In Luke,

If the householder had known at what hour the thief was coming he would certainly have been awake and *would not have permitted his house to be broken into*. Luke 12:39.

In the same gospel,

From now on there will be *in one house* five divided, three against two, and two against three. Father will be divided against son and son against father, mother against daughter and daughter against mother. Luke 12:52,53.

This refers to the spiritual conflicts which members of the Church enter into once the internal or spiritual contents of the Word have been opened up to them. 'House' stands for the actual person or his mind, while the 'father', 'mother', 'son', and 'daughter' in it are forms of good and truth together with affections for these, or in the contrary sense evils and falsities together with affections for these, which are the source of conflict and the things to be grappled with in such conflict.

5 The Lord commanded His disciples, in Luke,

Whatever house you enter, first say, *Peace be to this house*! And if indeed a son of peace is there, your peace shall rest on it; but if not, it shall return to you. *But remain in the same house*; eat and drink what they have there. *Do not pass on from house to house*. Luke 10:5-7.

This represented the requirement for them to remain with genuine good, that is, with the good of love to the Lord and of charity towards the neighbour, and not to pass on to any other kind. For more about the actual person or his mind being meant by 'a house', see also 3538, 4973.

5024 'And she spoke to him in these words' means speaking falsely. This is clear from what follows, for the things she told her husband were false.

5025 'Saying, The Hebrew slave whom you have brought to us came to me' means that servile thing. This is clear from what has been stated above in 5013. Here 'that servile thing' is used to mean spiritual truth and good, which at this particular point is represented by 'Joseph'. This truth and good is seen by the unspiritual natural man as something servile. For example, the desire on the part of spiritual truth and good is that a person's delight should lie not at all in eminent positions or any kind of superiority over others but in the services rendered by him to his country and to communities corporately and individually, thus that a person's delight should lie in the purpose that positions of importance are meant to serve. The merely natural man is entirely ignorant of what this delight is and denies the existence of it. Although he too can in a hypocritical manner say much the same thing, he nevertheless makes 'a lord' out of the delight received from important positions existing for his own benefit and 'a slave' out of such positions existing for the benefit of communities corporately and individually. For in every single thing he does he regards himself first and communities only after himself, promoting their welfare only insofar as they promote his.

Take another example. If one says that the purpose and end in view determine whether something is spiritual or unspiritual – spiritual when the purpose and end have the common good, the Church, and God's kingdom in view, but unspiritual when the purpose and end have, preponderating over these, oneself and one's own family and friends in view – the natural man is indeed able to affirm this with his lips but not in his heart. He can do so with his lips because of the instruction received by his understanding, but he cannot do so in his heart because his understanding has been ruined by evil desires. Consequently he makes 'a lord' out of the purpose and end that has himself in view, and 'a slave' out of the purpose and end that has the common good, the Church, and God's kingdom in view. Indeed he says in his heart, How can anyone possibly be any different from this?

In short, everything that the natural man regards as being separated from himself is considered utterly worthless by him and is cast aside; and everything that he regards as being linked to himself is considered by him to be valuable and acceptable. The natural man neither knows nor wishes to know about any spiritual way of thinking in which a person sees himself linked to everyone who is governed by good, whether or not he is actually acquainted with him, and separated from everyone who is governed by evil, whether or not he is actually acquainted with him. For when this is a person's way of thinking he is linked to those in heaven and cut off from those in hell. But since the natural man does not experience any delight in that spiritual attitude, for the reason that he does not entertain any spiritual influence, he therefore looks upon it as something utterly base and servile, thus something worthless compared with the delight he experiences, coming to him through his physical senses and through the desires of his selfish and worldly love. But this delight is a dead one because it originates in hell, whereas the delight brought by a spiritual influence is living, since this delight, which comes by way of heaven, begins in the Lord.

5026   'To make sport of me' means that it rose up. This is clear from the meaning of 'making sport of' as rising up, as above in 5014.

5027 'And it happened as I lifted up my voice and cried out' means when it discerned the great aversion. This is clear from the meaning of 'lifting up the voice and crying out' as a great aversion, also as above, in 5018.

5028 'That he left his garment with me' means proof. This is clear from the meaning of 'leaving his garment with her' as evidence that an approach had been made, dealt with in 5019. 'A garment' in the internal sense means truth, and 'leaving a garment' means removing outermost truth, 5008. The reason why evidence or proof that an approach had been made is meant here is that when outermost truth is left behind or removed it supplies to the natural man evidence against the spiritual man. For it seems as though the spiritual man is joined to the natural man by means of outermost truth, but it is not in fact so joined, see 5008 – the reason being that when the spiritual man explains that truth the lack of any similarity between the two becomes apparent. But let the examples introduced previously in 5008 serve to illustrate this.

2 The spiritual man says, just as the natural man does, that good should be done to the poor, widows, and orphans; but the spiritual man thinks that good should not be done to the poor, widows, or orphans who are evil, or who call themselves poor when in fact they are rich; for then they would mislead simply by the words they use. From this the spiritual man is led to deduce that the poor, widows, and orphans mentioned in the Word mean those who are spiritually so. But the natural man thinks that good should be done to the poor, widows, and orphans who are literally called such, and that none other than these are meant in the Word; nor is he interested in whether they are evil or good people. What the poor, widows, and orphans may be on a spiritual level he neither knows nor wishes to know. From this one may see that this outermost truth – that good should be done to the poor, widows, and orphans – appears to be the same with both the spiritual man and the natural man; but when it is explained no such similarity exists. But when the lack of any similarity comes out, the two are consequently parted from each other, and then outermost truth serves the natural man as evidence or proof that an approach has been made. Therefore it speaks falsely against the spiritual man who no longer has anything with which to protect himself. Accordingly this example too serves to show why and in what way 'a garment' means evidence or proof.

3 Take another example. The spiritual man says, just as the natural man does, that good should be done to the neighbour. He also says that everyone is his neighbour, yet he thinks that one person is his neighbour in a different respect and degree from another, and that to do good to an evil person because he calls himself his neighbour is to do evil to the neighbour. The natural man joins the spiritual man in subscribing to that outermost truth – the truth that good should be done to the neighbour, and also the truth that everyone is the neighbour. But he supposes that the neighbour is anyone who is

favourably disposed towards him; and he has no interest in whether that person is good or evil. This example too shows that the two appear to be joined together so far as outermost truth is concerned, but that there is no real joining together, also that as soon as that truth is explained they become parted from each other. Once they are parted outermost truth serves the natural man as evidence against the spiritual man that the latter has been making sport of it so to speak. The same can be seen in all the other examples [in 5008].

5029   'And fled out of doors' means that at that point it separated itself. This is clear from the meaning of 'fleeing out of doors' as separating itself, as above in 5020, as a consequence of which it has no truth with which to protect itself, as in 5009.

5030   Verses 19,20 **And it happened – as his lord heard his wife's words which she spoke to him, saying, This is what[1] your slave did to me – that his anger flared up. And Joseph's lord took him and committed him to the prison-house, a place where the king's bound ones were bound; and he was there in the prison-house.**
'And it happened' means a new state. 'As his lord heard his wife's words which she spoke to him' means the communication of falsity which looked like the truth. 'Saying, This is what your slave did to me' means corroboration. 'That his anger flared up' means an aversion to spiritual truth. 'And Joseph's lord took him' means temptation coming from the natural. 'And committed him to the prison-house' means involving false-speaking against good. 'A place where the king's bound ones were bound' means the state of those governed by falsities. 'And he was there in the prison-house' means the duration of that temptation.

5031   'And it happened' means a new state. This is clear from the meaning of 'it happened' or 'so it was' as that which implies something new or a new state, dealt with in 4979, 4987, 4999, in this case the state of spiritual natural good, represented by 'Joseph', after the outermost covering of truth has been removed from it, and so after it has ceased to be joined any longer to unspiritual natural truth and good.

5032   'As his lord heard his wife's words which she spoke to him' means the communication of falsity which looked like the truth. This is clear from the meaning of 'hearing the words' as communication, for 'hearing' means discerning, 5017, and so being communicated; from the meaning of 'wife' as unspiritual natural truth, dealt with already, though in this case falsity is meant. Actual false-speaking is meant by the things she told him, as above in 5024, and the one to which the falsity is communicated is unspiritual natural good, meant here by 'his lord', as above in 5023. The idea that to that good this falsity looked like the truth is clear from what follows below.

[1] *lit.* According to these words

2 Dealt with here is the fact that unspiritual natural good is easily convinced, so easily that to it falsity looks altogether like truth. For what unspiritual natural good is and what it is like – that is, who those people are with whom that good resides, and what they are like – see above in 4988, 4992, 5008, 5013, 5028. In these places it is shown that they are those who by heredity and consequently adventitiously are disposed to be meek and upright, and so who do what is good from some natural inclination and not from any religious motive. Doing good from some natural inclination is entirely different from doing it from a religious motive. In the world a person cannot distinguish one from the other because he is not immediately aware of inward things; but in the next life he can clearly tell the difference because in that world inward things are laid bare. There thoughts, intentions, and ends in view reveal themselves, being laid bare as if in broad daylight.

3 This being so I have been allowed to know what those people are like with whom unspiritual good resides and what those like with whom spiritual good resides. Those with whom unspiritual natural good resides allow themselves to be persuaded by no matter whom, easily so by the evil, for evil spirits and genii are in their element or their life's delight when they can get into another's desires; and once they have entered them they allure that person into every kind of evil. For at such times they convince him that what is false is true. This they can easily do to those with whom unspiritual natural good resides. They cannot do the same to those with whom spiritual good resides because these know from within themselves what evil and falsity are. The reason for this is that when those with whom spiritual good resides lived in the world they welcomed whatever doctrine prescribed, and disciplined their internal man in the same, thereby enabling heaven to act upon their internal man. But when those with whom unspiritual natural good resides lived in the world they did not welcome anything prescribed by doctrine or discipline their internal man in the same. Consequently they have nothing laid down in them into which heaven can operate, but whatever enters them from heaven passes straight through; and when this enters the natural man it is not welcomed there because evil ones, that is, the devil's crew, instantly remove it by smothering it, or repelling it, or perverting it.

4 Therefore those whose good is wholly natural suffer severely in the next life. Sometimes they complain profusely about being among those in hell even though, they believe, they have done good, just as has everyone else. But they have been told that in their doing of good they were no different from harmless living creatures that are not endowed with reason. They had shown no concern, they are told, for anything good and true that is known to the Church; and since, as a consequence of this, nothing existed in their internal man to receive what was good and true, they now have nothing enabling angels to protect them. Furthermore, under a cloak of goodness, they had performed very many evil deeds.

5033   'Saying, This is what your slave did to me' means corroboration. This becomes clear from his firm belief that his wife had spoken the truth, and that as a result her accusation, so far as he was concerned, was corroborated. The wife who convinced him means unspiritual natural truth, though at this point falsity is meant; for unspiritual natural good easily allows itself to be convinced by falsity, see immediately above in 5032. It is well known that falsities can be corroborated to look exactly like truths. This is evident from all heresies and from every aspect of any heresy. Though they are falsities, corroborations of them nevertheless cause people who adhere to a heresy to see them as truths. The same point is evident in people who are not religious. These people in their thinking set themselves firmly against things of the Church, so firmly that they see as the truth the idea that the Church exists merely to keep the common people down. They also see as the truth the idea that natural forces are the be-all and end-all and that the Divine is so remote as to be virtually nothing at all, as well as the idea that in death the human being is no different from any animal. People with whom unspiritual natural good resides allow themselves, more easily than others, to be persuaded and convinced of these and similar ideas, for they have no mirror so to speak within themselves, only one outside themselves which makes illusions look like realities.

5034   'That his anger flared up' means an aversion to spiritual truth. This is clear from the meaning of 'anger' as a departure from the good of charity, dealt with in 357, and so an aversion, in this case an aversion to spiritual truth since that truth is the subject here. The reason 'anger' means an aversion is that as long as a person is angry with another he feels averse to him; for anger arises or is aroused in someone when the love linking him to some other person, or to some particular object, is offended by that person or object. When the link is broken, that person flares up or becomes angry, as though something in his life that gives him delight, and thus something of his own life, has been lost. This sorrow turns into grief, and the grief into anger.

5035   'And Joseph's lord took him' means temptation coming from the natural. This is clear from what follows immediately after this, for the narrative goes on to refer to the committal of Joseph to the prison-house, describing in the internal sense the temptation of spiritual good within the natural. This being the implication of the words 'Joseph's lord took him', it is also their spiritual meaning. There are two kinds of temptations – those which involve truths and those which involve forms of good. Temptations involving truths are the work of spirits, but those involving forms of good are the work of genii. Spirits in the next life are distinguished from genii by the fact that spirits act upon the understanding part of the mind, and so upon matters of faith, whereas genii act upon the will part and so upon matters of love. That is to say, such spirits allow themselves to be seen, and also reveal

themselves by making utterances, but genii make themselves inconspi-
cuous and do not reveal themselves except by their entry into a person's
passions and desires. They also exist separated in the next life, for the
evil or hellish spirits appear in front and to either side beneath the
lower earth, whereas the evil or hellish genii are beneath and to the
rear, deep down at the back underneath the lower earth. Temptations
involving truths are the work, as stated, of evil spirits, but temptations
involving forms of good are the work of evil genii. From here onwards
the subject is temptations – those which are the work of evil spirits, and
so ones that involve false-speaking against good. These temptations are
milder than those which are the work of evil genii; they also arise
before the latter kind do.

5036 'And committed him to the prison-house' means involving
false-speaking against good. This is clear from the meaning of 'being
committed to the prison-house' and 'being kept bound there' as being
subjected to temptations involving false-speaking against good, dealt
with below. But first of all something must be said about temptations.
At the present day scarcely anyone in the Christian world knows where
temptations originate. Those who undergo them do not believe them to
be anything more than the feelings of anguish which creep in because
of the evils residing inwardly with a person, which first make him
uneasy, then fill him with anxiety, and finally torment him. But he is
totally unaware of the fact that they are the work of the evil spirits
present with him. The reason he is unaware that this is so is that he
does not believe he is in the company of spirits while he is living in the
world; indeed he has scarcely any belief that any spirit at all is present
with him, when in fact a person, so far as his interiors are concerned,
exists in constant association with spirits and angels.

2 As for temptations themselves, they are going on while a person is in
the actual process of being regenerated, for no one can be regenerated
unless he also undergoes temptations; and the evil spirits around him
are the means through which those temptations are brought about. In
temptation the person is brought into a state in which the evil that
possesses him, that is, possesses his own essential self, is dominant.
Once he enters this state evil and hellish spirits surround him, and
when they realize that inwardly he is protected by angels those evil
spirits reactivate the false ideas he has previously contemplated and the
evil deeds he has committed. But the angels defend him from within.
This conflict is what the person experiences as temptation, yet the
experience is so vague that he is aware of it as scarcely anything more
than a feeling of anxiety. For a person, especially one who has no belief
at all in influx, dwells in a state of complete obscurity and discerns
scarcely the smallest fraction of the things over which evil spirits and
angels are engaged in conflict. Yet a battle is taking place at such a time
over that person and his eternal salvation, with both sides using what is
within him; for both draw on what resides with the person and engage

in conflict over it. The truth of this I have been led most certainly to know. I have heard such conflict going on, I have perceived the influx taking place, and I have seen the spirits and the angels, to whom I spoke at the time and subsequently about what was happening.

As stated, temptations arise primarily when a person is becoming spiritual, for at that time he is gaining a spiritual understanding of the truths of doctrine. The person himself is often unaware that this is happening; even so, the angels present with him see spiritual concerns within his natural ones since his interiors at this time are open towards heaven. (This also explains why, after living in the world, a person who has been regenerated is among angels, where he both sees and perceives the spiritual concerns which had previously appeared to him as natural ones.) When therefore a person is such as this, it is possible for the angels to defend him in temptation when he is assailed by evil spirits; for the angels then have a place that has been established in him into which they can operate; that is, they can flow into the spiritual level established in him, and through this into that which is natural.

Once therefore outermost truth has been removed, with the result that the person does not possess anything to protect himself from those who are natural, dealt with in 5006, 5008, 5009, 5022, 5028, he enters into temptations in which evil spirits, all of whom are wholly natural, make accusations against him, especially that of false-speaking against good. They say, for example, that he has thought and said that good should be done to the neighbour and has also given proof of this in his actions, yet by the neighbour he now means only those with whom good and truth are present, not those with whom evil and falsity are present and who are incapable of receiving correction. Consequently, because he is no longer willing to do good to the evil, apart from punishing them so as to correct them and to protect his neighbour from what is evil, they accuse him of having thought and spoken what was false and of not thinking as he speaks.

Take another example. Because a person, once he has become spiritual, no longer believes it to be a holy and godly act to give to monasteries or even churches where great wealth exists, and because prior to his becoming spiritual he had thought it a holy and godly thing to do, those spirits accuse him of falsity. They reactivate all the thoughts he had cherished previously about such holy and godly giving, as well as all his actual deeds resulting from that way of thinking. Those spirits make similar accusations in countless other instances which these examples serve merely to illustrate somewhat. In particular those spirits enter the affections which the person possessed previously and reactivate these, reactivating also the falsities and evils which he had thought and committed, and in this way they fill him with anxiety and quite often with doubt extending to the point of despair.

Such then is the origin of spiritual kinds of anxiety and of those feelings called the pangs of conscience. What makes these appear to exist essentially within himself is influx and communication. Anyone who knows and believes this may be compared to a person who sees himself in a mirror but knows that it is not he himself who appears in the mirror or on the other side of it, only his image, whereas anyone who does not know and believe this may be compared to a person who sees himself in the mirror and supposes that he himself, not his image, appears there.

5037 The reason why 'being committed to the prison-house' and 'being kept bound there' mean being subjected to temptations involving false-speaking against good is that the expression 'the prison-house' is used for the entire place just beneath and round about the soles of the feet where those undergoing vastation are kept. Those undergoing vastation there are people who, in spite of their false assumptions and of their evil life arising from falsity, have nevertheless had good intentions. Such people cannot be received into heaven until they have divested themselves of their false assumptions and also of a living delight in them which sprang from these assumptions. People in that place are subjected to temptations, for the false assumptions and the living delights springing from these cannot be ousted except by means of temptations. The place where those people are, or rather the state which they are passing through, is meant in general by 'the prison-house' and those actual places by 'pits'. Regarding vastations in the next life, see 698, 699, 1106-1113, 2699, 2701, 2704. Those undergoing vastations are called 'the bound'; not that they are literally bound in any way but that they lack freedom so far as their previous thoughts and resulting affections are concerned.

2 Such is the condition of those meant in the Word by 'the bound' and by 'those who are in prison', as is evident from other places in the Word: In Isaiah,

> I will give You to be a covenant of the people, a light of the nations, to open the blind eyes, *to bring the bound out of prison, out of the dungeon-house* those who sit in darkness. Isa.42:6,7.

This refers to the Lord and His Coming. Here 'opening the blind eyes and bringing the bound out of prison, and out of the dungeon-house those who sit in darkness' stands for those who have no knowledge of goodness and truth but who nevertheless have the desire to know and be taught about these. But in this instance a different word is used in the original language to describe a prison.

3 In the same prophet,

> All the young men are hidden *in prison-houses*; they have become a prey, and none delivers *and none says, Bring out.* Isa.42:22.

'The young men' in the internal sense are the truths of faith, which are said 'to be hidden in prison-houses and to become a prey' when they are not acknowledged any longer. In the same prophet,

> It will be on that day, that Jehovah will visit the host of the height on high, and the kings of the ground on the ground, and *the bound will be gathered together*

over the pit, and they will be shut *in*[1] *the dungeon*; after a multitude of days they will be visited.   Isa.24:21,22.

'The bound over the pit' stands for those undergoing experiences of vastation, that is, temptation.
In the same prophet,

What will you do on the day of visitation and vastation? It will come from afar. To whom will you flee for help? [Anyone] who has not bowed himself down will fall *beneath the bound* and beneath the slain.   Isa.10:3,4.

'Beneath the bound' stands for the hell which lies below the places of vastation. 'The slain' stands for those who through the false assumptions adopted by them have destroyed the truths of faith to a smaller extent than those pierced [by the sword] have done, dealt with in 4503.
In Zechariah,

He will speak peace to the nations, and His dominion will be from sea to sea, and from the river even to the ends of the earth. Also as for You, through the blood of Your covenant *I will let out the bound ones from the pit* in which there is no water. Return to the stronghold, *O bound ones of hope.*   Zech.9:10-12.

'Letting out the bound ones from the pit' stands for those who are undergoing vastation and temptation; for the places where such undergo vastation are called 'pits', see 4728, 4744. In David,

Jehovah hears the needy and *does not despise His bound ones.*   Ps.69:33.

In the same author,

Let *the groaning of him who is bound come* before You.   Ps.79:11.

In the same author,

Jehovah looked from the heavens towards the earth to hear *the groaning of him who was bound*, to open to the sons of death.   Ps.102:19,20.

'Those who are bound' stands for those who are undergoing vastation and temptations. In Isaiah,

In a time of good pleasure I have answered You, and in a day of salvation I have helped[2] You; I have also guarded You, and I have given You for a covenant of the people to restore the land, to apportion the inheritances that have been laid waste, *to say to those that are bound, Go out*; and to those who are in darkness, Reveal yourselves. They will feed[3] along the roads, and on all slopes will their pasture[4] be. And *they will neither hunger nor thirst.*   Isa.49:8–10.

In the same prophet,

The Spirit of the Lord Jehovih is upon Me, Jehovah has anointed Me; to bring good tidings to *the poor* He has sent Me, and to bind up the broken in heart; to preach liberty to *captives*, and *to those who are bound, to him who is blind*; to proclaim the year of Jehovah's good pleasure.   Isa.61:1,2.

---

[1] *lit.* over
[2] *The Latin means* heard, *but the Hebrew means* helped.
[3] *lit.* pasture
[4] *The Latin means* good pasture, *but the Hebrew means* their pasture, *which Sw. has in other places where he quotes this verse.*

In David,

Jehovah who executes judgement for the oppressed, who gives *bread to the hungry;* Jehovah who *sets the bound free;* Jehovah who opens the *blind* [eyes]; Jehovah who lifts up the bowed down; Jehovah who loves the righteous; Jehovah who guards *strangers,* upholds *the orphan* and *the widow.* Ps.146:7-9.

'The bound' stands for those who are undergoing vastation and temptations because of falsities.

From all these places it is also evident who are meant in Matthew by those who are bound or 'in prison' and likewise who are meant by 'the hungry, the thirsty, and strangers',

Then the King will say to those at His right hand, *I was hungry* and you gave Me food, *I was thirsty* and you gave Me drink, I was *a stranger* and you took Me in, naked and you clothed Me around, I was sick and you visited Me, *I was in prison* and you came to Me. Matt.25:34-36.

Regarding these verses, see the preliminary section of the present chapter, 4954-4958.

5038 'A place where the king's bound ones were bound' means the state of those governed by falsities. This is clear from the meaning of 'a place' as a state, dealt with in 2625, 2837, 3356, 3387, 4321, 4882; and from the meaning of 'the king's bound ones' as those who are governed by falsities and who, being governed by falsities, undergo vastation, and those who, while being regenerated in the world, undergo temptation. For temptation involves the laying waste of falsity and at the same time the consolidation of truth. The expression 'the king's bound ones' is used because 'a king' in the internal sense means truth, 1672, 1728, 2015, 2069, 3009, 3670, 4575, 4581, 4789, 4966, and therefore 'his bound ones' means those governed by falsity. The places where the king's bound ones were kept were also called 'pits', which was why Joseph said, in verse 15 of the next chapter,

By theft I have been taken out of the land of the Hebrews, and here also I have not done anything for which they should have put me *in the pit.*

As regards 'a pit' meaning a place of vastation, see 4728, 4744.

5039 'And he was there in the prison-house' means the duration of that temptation. This is clear from the meaning of 'the prison-house' as vastation and also temptation, dealt with just above in 5036, 5037, and from the meaning of 'being in that house' as staying there, and so the duration.

5040 Verses 21-23 **And Jehovah was with Joseph, and showed mercy to him, and gave him favour in the eyes of the governor[1] of the prison-house. And the governor[1] of the prison-house gave into Joseph's hand all the bound who were in the prison-house; and everything they did there, he was the doer of it[2]. The governor of the**

---

[1] *lit.* prince *or* chief
[2] *i.e. it was done under his instructions*

prison-house oversaw nothing whatever that was in his hand, in that Jehovah was with him; and whatever he did, Jehovah made it prosper.
'And Jehovah was with Joseph' means that the Divine was inwardly present. 'And showed mercy to him' means Divine love within every individual thing. 'And gave him favour in the eyes of the governor of the prison-house' means consequent support in temptations. 'And the governor of the prison-house gave' means the truth governing in a state of temptations. 'Into Joseph's hand all the bound who were in the prison-house' means from Him over all falsities. 'And everything they did there, he was the doer of it' means absolute power and control. 'The governor of the prison-house oversaw nothing whatever that was in his hand' means that He Himself governed truth. 'In that Jehovah was with him' means from the Divine that was within Him. 'And whatever he did, Jehovah made it prosper' means that the Divine Providence began in Himself.

5041   'And Jehovah was with Joseph' means that the Divine was inwardly present, that is, present within the Lord, who is represented in the highest sense by 'Joseph'. At this point the Divine presence in temptations is meant, temptations being the subject here. For the Divine itself is Jehovah, whose existence or presence within the Lord is meant by 'Jehovah was with Joseph'. Because the sense of the letter is dealing with Joseph the expression 'with Joseph' is used, but in the internal sense, where the Lord is the subject, 'within the Lord' is meant. Anybody within the Church can recognize this from the consideration that the Lord was conceived from Jehovah and for that reason calls Him His Father on so many occasions. A person's essential being (*esse*) and consequently the inmost centre of life in him is received from his father, its coverings or outward clothing from his mother. Therefore the Lord's Essential Being (*Esse*) and consequently the inmost centre of life in Him was the Divine because it was Jehovah Himself, while its coverings or outward clothing constituted the human which He took upon Himself from His mother by being born from her. The nature of this human was such that it could undergo temptation, for it was defiled by hereditary evil received from His mother. But because the inmost centre of Him was the Divine, He was able by means of the power that was His own to cast out that hereditary evil received from His mother. This casting out took place in succeeding stages by means of temptations, until He underwent the final temptation, that on the Cross, at which point He fully glorified His Human, that is, made it Divine. From this one may see what is meant when it is said that the Divine was inwardly present.

5042   'And showed mercy to him' means Divine love within every individual thing. This is clear from the meaning of 'mercy' in the highest sense as Divine Love, dealt with in 1735, 3063, 3073, 3120, 3875. The Divine Being (*Esse*) itself is that Love which is meant in the highest sense and is completely beyond human comprehension. Acting by means of truth, that Love brings all things into being and keeps them in being, both those which are animate and those which are inanimate. This Divine Love that emanated from that Essential Being (*Esse*) was flowing through the inmost centre of life within the Lord into every individual thing He did from the human which He had taken to Himself from His mother; it directed His attention towards particular ends, leading on to the final one, which was that the human race might be saved. And because the Lord could see, from the Divine itself present within Him, the essential nature of His human – that owing to its heredity it was steeped in evil – the words 'Jehovah showed mercy to him' are used, meaning in the highest sense the presence of Divine Love within every single thing. Divine mercy (*misericordia*) is nothing else than Divine Love directed towards those trapped in misery (*miseriae*), 1049, 3063, 3875, that is, towards those undergoing temptations. For people who undergo temptations dwell in misery, and these primarily are meant in the Word by 'the wretched' (*miseri*).

5043   'And gave him favour in the eyes of the governor of the prison-house' means consequent support in temptations. This is clear from the meaning of 'giving favour' as support, for 'giving favour' in temptations is bringing comfort and supporting with hope; from the meaning of 'the governor (or the prince)' as primary truth, dealt with in the next paragraph; and from the meaning of 'the prison-house' as the laying waste of falsity, and therefore temptation, dealt with above in 5038, 5039.

5044   'And the governor of the prison-house gave' means the truth governing in a state of temptations. This is clear from the meaning of 'the governor (or the prince)' as the primary and so governing truth, dealt with below; and from the meaning of 'the prison-house' as the laying waste of falsity, and therefore temptation, dealt with above in 5038, 5039, 5043. What the truth governing in a state of temptations is must first be discussed. With all who are undergoing temptations truth from the Lord is flowing in, and this truth rules and governs their thoughts, uplifting them every time they are given to doubt and also to feelings of despair. This truth is what that governing truth is, and it is the kind of truth which they have learned from the Word and from doctrine and which they themselves have confirmed. Other kinds of truth may also be called on at such times, but these do not govern those persons interiorly. Sometimes the truth governing them does not make itself clearly visible in their understanding but lies obscured, yet continues to govern. For the Lord's Divine flows into that governing truth and in so doing keeps the interior parts of the mind within its domain, so that when it comes out into the light the person undergoing temptation receives comfort from it and is uplifted by it.

2   Not the actual truth but an affection for it is what the Lord uses to govern those undergoing temptations; for the Divine does not flow into anything except that which is regarded with affection. Truth that has

been implanted and become rooted in a person interiorly has been implanted and become rooted there through affection. Absolutely nothing grows there without affection. Truth that has been implanted and become rooted through affection sticks in the mind, and it is recollected through an affection for it. Furthermore when that truth is recollected it also manifests the affection attached to it, an affection which in that person is a reciprocal one. This being what goes on in a person who undergoes temptations, no one is therefore allowed to experience any spiritual temptation until he reaches adult years and so has acquired some truth by means of which he may be governed. Without that truth he goes under, in which case his latter state is worse than his former one. From all this one may see what is implied by the truth governing in a state of temptations, meant by 'the governor of the prison-house'.

The reason 'a prince (or a governor)' means a primary truth is that 'a king' in the internal sense means the truth itself, 1672, 1728, 2015, 2069, 3009, 3670, 4575, 4581, 4789, 4966, and consequently because 'princes' are the king's chief subjects the primary features of that truth are meant by them. For this meaning of 'princes', see 1482, 2089; yet because those two paragraphs have not shown that meaning from other places in the Word, let some be introduced here: In Isaiah,

To us a boy is born, to us a son is given, *on whose shoulder will be the government*[1] – *the prince of peace*, increasing *government*[2] and peace [to which] there will be no end.   Isa.9:6,7.

This refers to the Lord. 'The government upon his shoulder' means all Divine Truth in the heavens originating in Him, for the heavens are distinguished into separate principalities in keeping with the varieties of truth derived from good, which also explains why angels are called principalities. 'Peace' means the state of bliss in the heavens which inmostly affects what is good and true, 3780. This is why the Lord is called 'the prince of peace' and why it speaks of Him 'increasing government and peace to which there will be no end'.

In the same prophet,

The princes of Zoan are foolish, the wise counsellors of Pharaoh. How do you say to Pharaoh, I am a son of the wise, *a son of the kings of old? The princes of Zoan* have become fools, *the princes of Noph* deluded, and they have led Egypt astray, the corner-stone of the tribes.   Isa.19:11,13.

This refers to Egypt, by which the Church's factual knowledge is meant, 4749, and so natural truth, which is the last and lowest degree of order. For the same reason Egypt is here called 'the corner-stone of the tribes', for by 'the tribes' are meant all aspects of truth in their entirety, 3858, 3862, 3926, 3939, 4060. Here however 'Egypt' is factual knowledge that perverts the truths known to the Church, and so is truths in the lowest degree of order that have been falsified, meant by 'the princes of Zoan

---

[1] *lit.* principality *or* princely rule
[2] *lit.* multiplying the principality *or* princely rule

and the princes of Noph'. The reason Egypt calls itself 'a son of the kings of old' is that the factual knowledge which existed in that land had its origin in the truths known to the Ancient Church. Actual truths are meant by 'kings', as shown above, and the truths known to the Ancient Church by 'the kings of old'.

5 In the same prophet,

Asshur does not think what is right and his heart does not consider what is right, for his heart is to destroy, and to cut off nations not a few, for he says, *Are not my princes kings?* Isa.10:7,8.

'Asshur' stands for reasoning about Divine truths which gives rise to falsities, and so stands for perverted reason, 1186. Truths falsified in this way, that is, falsities, which are the product of reasoning and look altogether like truths, are meant when Asshur says 'Are not my princes kings?' As long as a person's mind is fixed on the historical sense of the letter he cannot see or consequently believe that 'Asshur' means reasoning, and that 'princes who are kings' means major falsities which are regarded as supreme truths. Still less can he believe this if he refuses to entertain the idea that there is something holier and more universal within the Divine Word than that which is seen in the literal sense. Yet in the internal sense 'Asshur' is used to mean in the Word nothing else than reason and reasoning, and 'kings' to mean actual truths, 'princes' the primary features of truth. Also, those in heaven have no knowledge as to what or who 'Asshur' may be, besides which angels put away from themselves the idea of a king or a prince; and when they detect this idea residing with man they transfer it to the Lord and then perceive that which goes forth from the Lord and which is the Lord's in heaven, namely His Divine Truth going forth from His Divine Good.

6 In the same prophet,

Asshur will fall by the sword, not of man (*vir*), and a sword, not of man (*homo*), will devour him. Also his rock will pass away by reason of terror, and *his princes* will be dismayed by the ensign. Isa.31:8,9.

This too refers to Egypt, by which the Church's factual knowledge once it has been perverted is meant. Reasoning based on known facts regarding Divine truths which leads to perversion and falsification is meant by 'Asshur', those perverted and falsified truths being 'his princes'. 'The sword by which Asshur will fall' is falsity engaged in conflict with truth and bringing about the devastation of it, 2799, 4499. In the same prophet,

The strength of Pharaoh will become shame for you, and trust in the shadow of Egypt ignominy, when *his princes* will be *in Zoan*. Isa.30:3,4.

'Princes in Zoan' stands for truths that have been falsified, and so stands for falsities, as above.

7 In the same prophet,

The spoon-bill and the duck will possess it, and the owl and the raven will dwell in it; and he will stretch over it the line of emptiness, and the plumb-line of a waste place. Let them call its nobles who are not there a kingdom, and *all its princes will be nothing.* Isa.34:11,12.

'The spoon-bill', 'the duck', 'the owl', 'the raven' stand for varieties of falsity which arise when Divine truths in the Word are rendered valueless. The desolation and laying waste of truth is meant by 'the line of emptiness and the plumb-line of a waste', while the falsities, which are primary truths so far as the people described here are concerned, are meant by 'its princes'. In the same prophet,

I will render *the princes of holiness* profane, and I will give Jacob to utter destruction and Israel to reproaches. Isa.43:28.

'Rendering the princes of holiness profane' refers to holy truths. The annihilation of the truth known to the Church – the internal Church and the external – is meant by 'giving Jacob to utter destruction and Israel to reproaches', 'Jacob' being the external Church and 'Israel' the internal, see 4286.

In Jeremiah,

There will enter through the gates of this city *kings* and *princes* seated on the throne of David, riding in chariots and on horses, *they* and their *princes.* Jer.17:25.

Anyone who understands the Word at this point according to its historical sense cannot know that anything deeper and holier lies hidden within these words than the idea that kings and princes will enter through the gates of the city in chariots and on horses, from which he gathers that the duration of the kingdom is meant. But one who is aware of what is meant by 'city' in the internal sense, and what is meant by 'kings', 'princes', 'the throne of David', and 'riding in chariots and on horses' sees deeper and holier matters in this description. For 'the city', which is Jerusalem, means the Lord's spiritual kingdom, 2117, 3654; 'kings' Divine Truths, as shown above; 'princes' the primary features of truth; 'the throne of David' the Lord's heaven, 1888; and 'riding in chariots and on horses' the existence in the Church of a spiritual understanding, 2760, 2761, 3217.

In the same prophet,

O sword against the Chaldeans and against the inhabitants of Babel, and against *its princes* and against its wise men! O sword against the liars! O sword against its horses and against its chariots! Jer.50:35–37.

'Sword' stands for truth engaged in conflict with falsity, and for falsity in conflict with truth and laying it waste, 2799, 4799. 'The Chaldeans' stands for those who profane truths, and 'the inhabitants of Babel' for those who profane good, 1182, 1283, 1295, 1304, 1307, 1308, 1321, 1322, 1326, 1327(end). 'Princes' stands for falsities, which to such people are primary truths. 'Horses' stands for the Church's possession of understanding, and 'chariots' for its doctrinal teaching, the laying waste of these being meant by 'a sword against its horses and against its chariots'.

10 In the same prophet,

> How in His anger the Lord covers the daughter of Zion with a cloud! The Lord has swallowed up – He has not spared – all the dwelling-places of Jacob. He has destroyed in His wrath the strongholds of the daughter of Judah; He has cast them down to the ground; He has profaned the kingdom *and her princes*. The gates have sunk into the ground; He has broken in pieces her bars; her *king* and *princes* are among the nations.   Lam.2:1,2,9.

'The daughter of Zion and Judah' stands for the celestial Church, in this case for that Church when it has been destroyed. 'The kingdom' stands for the truths of doctrine there, 2547, 4691, 'king' for truth itself, and 'princes' for the primary features of this truth.

11 In the same prophet,

> Our skins have been blackened like an oven because of the storms of famine; they have ravished women in Zion, virgins in the cities of Judah. *Princes have been hung up by their hands.*   Lam.5:10-12.

'Princes hung up by their hands' stands for the fact that truths have been made profane, for being hung up represented the damnation brought about by profanation. And because being hung up represented that profanation the command was also given that when the people went whoring after Baalpeor and worshipped their gods, *the princes were to be hung up* before the sun, Num.25:1-4, since 'to go whoring after Baalpeor and to worship their gods' was to make worship profane. In Ezekiel,

> The king will mourn, and the prince will be wrapped in stupidity, and the hands of the people of the land will be all atremble; I will deal with them in their way.   Ezek.7:27.

Here likewise 'the king' stands for truth in general, and 'the prince' for the primary features of it.

12 In the same prophet,

> The prince who is in the midst of them will be carried on the shoulder under darkness and will go forth; they will dig through the wall to lead out through it; he will cover his face, so that with the eye he does not see the earth.   Ezek.12:12.

Here it is quite evident that 'the prince' does not mean a prince but truth known to the Church. When the words 'will be carried on the shoulder under darkness' are used in reference to it, the meaning is that total power is used to bear away among falsities, 'darkness' meaning falsities. 'Covering the face' means that truth is completely out of sight; 'so that with the eye he does not see the earth' means that nothing of the Church is visible, 'earth' or 'land' meaning the Church, see 662, 1066, 1067, 1262, 1413, 1607, 1733, 1850, 2117, 2118(end), 2928, 3355, 4447, 4535. In Hosea,

> The children of Israel will sit many days with *no king* and *no prince*, and no sacrifice, and no pillar, and no ephod, and no teraphim.   Hosea 3:4.

13 And in David,

> All glorious is *the king's daughter* within, in her clothing with gold interweav-

52

ings; in embroidered robes she will be led to *the king*. Instead of your fathers will be your sons; *you will set them as princes in the whole earth.*   Ps.45:13,14,16.

'The king's daughter' means the Lord's spiritual kingdom. It is called His spiritual kingdom by virtue of the Lord's Divine truth, which in this instance is described by means of 'clothing consisting of gold interweavings and of embroidered robes'. 'Sons' are the truths of that kingdom which are derived from the Lord's Divine, which are going to be 'the princes', that is, the primary features of it.

'The prince' who is described – he and his possession in the New Jerusalem and in the new land – in Ezekiel 44:3; 45:7,8,17; 46;8,10,12,16,18; 48:21, means, in general, truth that is derived from the Lord's Divine. For 'the New Jerusalem' in these places, 'the New Temple', and 'the new land' are used to mean the Lord's kingdom in heaven and on earth, which kingdom is described here in Ezekiel by means of representatives such as figure elsewhere in the Word.

5045   'Into Joseph's hand all the bound who were in the prison-house' means received from Him over all falsities, that is to say, the truth governing in a state of temptations was received from Him. This is clear from the meaning of 'giving into Joseph's hand' as placing under its power and control ('the hand' means power and control, 5008, thus that which is received from Him – for anything done by the use of His power is something done by Him – while 'Joseph' means the Lord in the internal sense, as has often been shown above); and from the meaning of 'the bound in the prison-house' as falsities, dealt with above in 5037, 5038. Thus 'the governor of the prison-house gave into Joseph's hand all the bound who were in the prison-house' means the truth governing in the state of temptations that was received from Him and had power over all falsities, that is, He Himself was the source of the truth by means of which He governed falsities in the state of temptations. Here and in what follows at the end of this present chapter the subject in the internal sense is the Lord and the government executed by Him in a state of temptations. That is, it describes how He overcame, by His own power, the hells which were steeped in evils and falsities, and which were constantly pouring out evils and falsities onto the human race. For details about the Lord overcoming them and bringing them into subjection to Himself by His own power, thereby also glorifying the Human within Him or making it Divine, see 1616, 1749, 1755, 1813, 1904, 1914, 1921, 1935, 2025, 2026, 2083, 2159, 2574, 2786, 2795, 3036, 3382, 4075, 4286, 5005. This is clear from many places in the Word, including the following in John,

I lay down My life[1], so that I may receive it again. No one takes it from Me, but I lay it down of Myself; I have power to lay it down and I have power to receive it again.   John 10:17,18.

---

[1] *lit.* soul

The passion of the Cross was the last temptation, by which He fully glorified the Human within Him, that is, made it Divine, as is also evident from many places in the Word, such as John 13:31,32; 17:1,5; Luke 24:26.

5046 'And everything they did there, he was the doer of it' means absolute power and control. This may be seen without explanation, for these words imply that all things were of His doing, thus that He had absolute power and control to carry them out or leave them undone.

5047 'The governor of the prison-house oversaw nothing whatever that was in his hand' means that He Himself governed truth. This is clear from the meaning of 'the governor of the prison-house' as truth governing in a state of temptations, dealt with above in 5044, and from the meaning of 'overseeing nothing whatever that was in his hand' as His acting of Himself, and so with absolute power and control, as above in 5045, 5046.

5048 'In that Jehovah was with him' means from the Divine that was within Him. This is clear from what appears above in 5041.

5049 'And whatever he did, Jehovah made it prosper' means that the Divine Providence began in Himself. This is clear from the meaning of 'causing to prosper' as providence, dealt with in 4972, 4975. The Divine nature of this providence is meant by 'Jehovah', and its beginning in Himself by 'whatever he did'. The reason why in the highest sense 'causing to prosper' means providence is that all prosperity witnessed in the outermost things forming the natural dimension owes its origin to the Lord's Divine Providence. The truth of this, and also that everything which people call fortune owes its origin to the same, will in the Lord's Divine mercy be demonstrated elsewhere from experiences in the spiritual world.

CORRESPONDENCE WITH
THE GRAND MAN – *continued*
IN THIS SECTION THE CORRESPONDENCE OF
THE LOINS AND THE ORGANS OF
GENERATION WITH IT

5050   Who exactly in the Grand Man or heaven belong to the province of the hands, the arms, and the feet has been shown from experience at the end of the previous chapter, in 4931-4953. Now this present section must state which particular communities in heaven or the Grand Man are the ones to which the loins, also the parts associated with the loins called the generative organs, correspond. In general it should be recognized that the loins and associated organs correspond to genuine conjugial love and consequently to those communities where angels live who possess that love. The inhabitants of those communities are the most heavenly ones and in their lives they enjoy greater peace and delight than any others do.

5051   In a peaceful dream I once saw some trees planted in a wooden receptacle, one of which was tall, another shorter, and two were small. The shorter tree gave me very great delight, and all the while a very lovely feeling of peacefulness, beyond my ability to describe, was filling my mind. When I woke up from my sleep I talked to those among whom my dream had originated. They were angelic spirits, see 1977, 1979, who told me what was meant by that sight – conjugial love. The tall tree meant a husband, the shorter his wife, and the two small ones their children. Those angelic spirits went on to say that the very lovely feeling of peacefulness which filled my mind served to indicate the loveliness of the peace enjoyed by those in the next life who have led lives of genuine conjugial love. They added that people like these are the ones who belong to the province of the thighs immediately above the knees, and that those whose state is yet more lovely belong to the province of the loins. I was also shown that this province communicates through the feet with the soles and heels. The existence of this communication is also evident from the large nerve in the thigh which sends out its branches not only through the loins to the generative parts, which are the organs of conjugial love, but also through the feet to the soles and heels. Those angelic spirits also disclosed to me at this time the meaning in the Word of the acetabulum and the nerve in the thigh which was put out of joint when Jacob wrestled with the angel, Gen.32:25,31,32, dealt with in 4280, 4281, 4314-4317.
After this I saw a large dog, like the one which very ancient authors call Cerberus. It had horrible, gaping jaws. I was told that a dog such as this means the guard which is set to prevent a person crossing over from heavenly conjugial love to a love of adultery, which is a hellish love. For heavenly conjugial love consists in one living, content in the Lord,

together with one's partner whom one loves very tenderly, and with one's children. In the world this brings a person a deeper pleasure, and in the next life heavenly joy. But if people cross over from that love to its opposite, and this opposite love seems to them to hold heavenly delight within it, though in fact it is a hellish delight, a dog resembling Cerberus presents itself as if on guard to prevent any communication of opposite delights.

5052   The heaven through which the Lord imparts conjugial love is the inmost one, whose inhabitants enjoy greater peace than all others. Peace in the heavens may be compared to spring in the world which makes everything delightful; for in origin peace is something utterly heavenly. The angels inhabiting that inmost heaven are the wisest of all, and because of their innocence they are seen by others as young children. They themselves also love young children far more than even their forebears and mothers do. They are present with infants in the womb, and through them the Lord takes care of the nourishment and proper development of infants in the womb. Thus angels from that heaven are placed in charge of those who are pregnant.

5053   There are heavenly and celestial communities to which the organs and parts dedicated to generation correspond – every single one in both sexes. Those communities are distinct and separate from others, even as that province in a man or woman is rightly distinct and separate from all the rest. The reason those communities are heavenly and celestial ones is that conjugial love is the fundamental love of all loves, 686, 2733, 2737, 2738. It also serves an incomparable purpose and as a consequence affords a delight that surpasses all other delights, for marriages are the seed-beds of the entire human race, also the seed-beds of the Lord's heavenly kingdom since heaven consists of members of the human race.

5054 . People who have had a very tender love of young children, such as mothers with that love, are in the province of the womb and organs round about it; that is, they are in the province of the cervix and ovaries. The life of those in that province is absolutely sweet and delightful, and their heavenly joy is greater than that of all others.

5055   But I have not been allowed to know the identity and essential nature of the communities that belong to specific organs of generation because those communities are far too internal for anyone in a lower sphere to discern. Those communities also correlate with hidden functions served by these organs, hidden and also unknown to science for the providential reason that things such as these, which in essence are utterly heavenly, must not suffer any damage from filthy thoughts. They must not be damaged by thoughts that accompany wantonness, whoredom, or adultery and that are aroused in most people by the mere mention of those organs. This being so, let me describe some things witnessed by me which took place further away.

5056   A certain spirit from another planet was once present with me.
(Spirits from other planets will in the Lord's Divine mercy be spoken
about elsewhere.) He asked me earnestly to intercede on his behalf to
enable him to enter heaven. He said he was not aware of having done
what was evil, only of having reprimanded inhabitants of that planet;
for on his planet there are people who reprimand and chastise others
when they do not lead correct lives. (Reference will be made to these
people too when the inhabitants of other planets are dealt with.) That
spirit added that after he reprimanded people he instructed them; and
as he said this his voice seemed to crack. He also had the ability to
arouse feelings of pity. The only answer I could give him however was
that I was unable to help him in any way. Entrance into heaven, I told
him, rested with the Lord alone; but if he was worthy he could
entertain the hope of gaining it. At that point however he was sent back
to be among upright spirits who belonged to his own planet; but those
spirits said that he could not remain in their company because he was
not like them. Nevertheless because his intense desire made him
demand that he should be let into heaven, he was sent to a community
of upright spirits belonging to our own planet. But these too told him
that he could not remain with them. In addition to this his colour seen
in the light of heaven was black, though he himself said it was not black
but a ruddy brown.
I was told that this is what people of this sort are like initially, before
they are received among those who constitute the province of the
seminal vesicles, for in these vesicles sperm (*semen*)[1] is gathered
together along with the suitable fluid with which the sperm is com-
bined. That combination places the sperm in the right condition, so that
once it has been sent forth it is released from the fluid at the cervix and
thus serves to bring about conception. This kind of substance also holds
within it the endeavour and so to speak desire to fulfill the same
purpose and so to cast aside the fluid that clothes it. Something similar
to this was seen to happen to that spirit. He returned to me, but now he
was dressed in humble clothing. He said he had a burning desire to
enter heaven and recognized that now he was in a fit state to remain
there. I was led to say to him that this was perhaps a sign that he would
be received there shortly. At this point angels told him to cast aside his
clothing, which in his desire to do so he cast aside so quickly that
hardly anything could have been done more quickly. This represented
the nature of the desires of those in the province to which the seminal
vesicles correspond.

5057   I once saw a mortar, standing by which there was a man who
had an instrument made of iron. In his delusion the man thought he
was pounding human beings in the mortar, tormenting them dread-
fully. He took great delight in what he was doing, and that delight was

---

[1] *In Latin* semen *is the sperm or seed within the seminal fluid, not – as in
English – both the sperm and the fluid.*

communicated to me to enable me to know the nature of it and how strong it was in people of his kind. It was a hellish delight, and angels told me that it was the kind that reigned among the descendants of Jacob. These never felt more delighted than when they could treat gentile nations in a cruel fashion, exposing those they had slain to be devoured by wild animals and by birds, cutting up with saws and axes those who were still alive, and making them pass through the brickkiln, 2 Sam.12:31, also striking little children and hurling them to the ground. No one has ever been commanded to behave in these ways, nor has anyone ever been permitted to do so other than the kind of people in whom the nerve in the thigh has been put out of joint, 5051. Such spirits live beneath the right heel, where the adulterers who are also cruel dwell.

2   In view of this it is astonishing that anyone should ever believe that that nation was chosen or elected in preference to any other one. Believing that they were so elected many people go on to convince themselves of the idea that one's life is of no consequence at all but that election and consequent acceptance into heaven is attributable to mercy alone, irrespective of the life one has led. Yet anyone of sound reason can see that to think in that way is to think contrary to the Divine. The Divine is mercy itself, and therefore if the attainment of heaven were attributable to mercy alone irrespective of the life one leads, all would be accepted, no matter how many these might be. To thrust anyone down into hell to suffer torment there, when it was possible for him to be received into heaven, would not be mercy but the opposite of mercy, and to elect one in preference to another would not be righteousness but the opposite of righteousness.

3   Consequently those who have believed and convinced themselves of the idea that some have been elected and the rest have not been elected, also of the idea that admittance into heaven is attributable solely to mercy regardless of the life they have led, have been for the most part the kind of people who have led evil lives. These are told, as I have also heard and seen on several occasions, that the Lord never refuses anyone entrance into heaven, and that if they like they can find this out from experience. They are therefore raised up into some community of heaven whose inhabitants have led their lives under the influence of an affection for good, that is, they have led charitable lives. But when those raised up arrive there they begin, being evil, to suffer pain and inner torment because their life is contrary to that of heaven. And when heavenly light shines on them they look in that light like devils that are almost wholly devoid of human appearance. Some have sunken faces; some are all teeth, looking like crates; and some, who are different again, look like monsters. Thus they are horrified at themselves and hurl themselves headfirst into hell; and the deeper they can go, the better it is for them.

5058   There was another spirit who in the world had been one of the quite distinguished. I had been acquainted with him then, though not with what he was like inwardly. In the next life however, after his state of life underwent a number of changes, he was shown to be deceitful. Having been some while among deceitful ones in the next life and having suffered severely there, he wished to be parted from them. I heard him saying at this time that he wished to enter heaven, for he too had believed that acceptance there was attributable to mercy alone. But he was told that if he entered heaven he would not be able to remain there and that he would suffer torment like those in the world experiencing death-throes. But in spite of being told this he persisted with his desire. He was allowed into a community where some of the simple good dwelt, in front overhead. But once he entered that community he began, in keeping with the life he had led, to act cunningly and deceitfully. Soon after this the simple good there started to complain that he was taking away their perception of what was good and true and consequently their delight, and that he was destroying their state as he did so. At that point some light from a more internal heaven was let in. In that light he looked like a devil, with the upper part of his nose horribly disfigured from some dreadful wound; and he also began to suffer torment within himself. Having experienced that torment he thrust himself away from there into hell. From this it is evident that what leads to heaven is not election and acceptance attributable to mercy, but a person's life. Yet every aspect of a life consisting of goodness and every aspect of a faith composed of truth is, so far as those in the world who are recipients of mercy are concerned, attributable to mercy. To them being accepted into heaven is an act of mercy, and these are the ones who are called the elect, 3755(end), 3900.

5059 When those who have lived in ways that are the opposite of conjugial love – that is, in adulterous ways – have drawn near me, they have introduced pain into my loins, the severity of which has depended on the nature of the adulterous life led by them. That influx also demonstrated that the loins corresponded to conjugial love. Furthermore their hell is situated beneath the area behind the loins, under the buttocks, where they live in filth and excrement. These are also the things that give them delight, for such filth and excrement correspond to the pleasure they gain in the spiritual world from such things. But in the Lord's Divine mercy more will be said about these spirits when the hells are described as a whole and individually.

5060 Who exactly correspond to the testicles has in a similar way been made clear to me from those whose love is the opposite of conjugial love and who strike pain into the testicles. For when communities are at work they act into those parts and members of the body to which they correspond – heavenly communities acting into them by an influx that is gentle, sweet, and delightful, hellish communities who love the opposite of what is heavenly by an influx that is vicious and causes pain. Yet their influx is not perceptible to any except those whose interiors have been opened and who as a consequence are able to perceive their communication with the spiritual world. Those whose love is the opposite of conjugial love and who strike pain into the testicles are spirits who use love, friendship, and kind deeds to behave treacherously. When such spirits came near me they wished to talk to me in secret, being very much afraid that someone else might be present with us. For this is what those spirits were like during their lifetime, and being such then, they are no different in the next life. For everyone's life follows on with him.

2   From the region round Gehenna there once rose up something so to speak air-like and barely visible. It was a band of spirits who were like those just described. But after that, although there were quite a number of them, they looked to me like a single spirit, who was impeded by bandages which however he seemed to himself to remove. This was a sign meaning their desire to remove obstructions, for in the world of spirits representative images like this one serve to reveal people's thoughts and intentions, and as soon as those images are seen their meaning is recognized instantly. After this, one who looked like a small snowy-white spirit seemed to come out of that band of spirits and to make his way towards me. This was a representation of their thought and intention, which was a wish to assume a state of innocence so that no one could suspect them of being what they were in fact like. When he reached me he stooped down towards my loins, where he seemed to wind himself all round them. This represented their wish to present themselves as spirits filled with chaste conjugial love. After this he seemed to twist like a coil around my feet, which represented their wish to worm their way in by means of such things as are naturally delightful. At length the small spirit became practically invisible, which represented their wish to lie completely out of sight.

3   Angels told me that worming their way in like this is characteristic of those who deal treacherously in respect of conjugial love. That is to say, being intent on committing adultery with other men's wives they would worm their way in, when they were in the world, by talking about conjugial love in a chaste and wholesome manner, by fondling the children and praising the husband in every possible way. They did all this so as to be considered friendly, chaste, and above suspicion, when in fact they were deceitful adulterers. Such being their true nature therefore, this was revealed, for once the incidents described above had taken place, the small snowy-white spirit became visible again. But now he had a dusky and very black appearance, and also a misshapen one. He was cast out into his own hell, which too was deep down below the middle of the loins, where the inhabitants live among utterly disgusting excrement, and also among the robbers, described in 4327, who correlate with general and involuntary sensory activity. I have spoken subsequently to spirits of this kind, who have been amazed that anyone should have any conscientious objection to committing adultery, that is to say, that his conscience should forbid him to lie with

another man's wife even if allowed to do so. Indeed when I have talked to them about conscience they have refused to believe that anyone possesses a conscience. I have been told that spirits like these come mainly from the Christian world, and only rarely do any come from other parts.

5061 To end with let the following noteworthy incident be added. There were some spirits who lay shut up for a long time in a hell unlike any other, from which they could not break out. I wondered several times who exactly they might be. One evening they were let out, at which point a quite tumultuous grumbling sound was heard to be coming from them, which lasted for a long time. Having been given the opportunity to do so, I could hear them making jeering remarks about me, and I perceived that their desire and endeavour was to come up and destroy me. I asked the angels the reason for this. They replied that those spirits had hated me during their lifetime even though I had not done them any harm at all. I also learned that when spirits of this kind merely perceive the sphere of one whom they have hated they long for his destruction. But they were taken back to their own particular hell. From this it became clear that those who have hated one another in the world meet in the next life and set out to inflict many injuries on one another, as other examples of such hatred witnessed by me on a number of other occasions have also led me to know. For hatred is the opposite of love and charity, and is a turning away and so to speak spiritual antipathy. Consequently the moment such spirits in the next life perceive the sphere of one they have hated they go into a seeming frenzy. From this one may see what is implied by what the Lord has said in Matthew 5:22-26.

5062 Correspondence with the Grand Man is continued at the end of the next chapter.

40

5063   The opening section of the previous chapter contained an explanation of what the Lord said about the judgement on the good and on the evil, in Matthew 25:34–36. There now follows what He said after that,

Then the righteous will answer Him, saying, Lord, when did we see You hungry and feed You, or thirsty and give You drink? When did we see You a stranger and take You in, or naked and clothe You? When did we see You sick, or in prison, and come to You? But the King answering will say to them, Truly I say to you, Insofar as you did it to one of the least of these My brothers you did it to Me. Then He will also say to those on the left, Depart from Me, O cursed ones, into eternal fire prepared for the devil and his angels; for I was hungry and you gave Me no food, I was thirsty and you gave Me no drink, I was a stranger and you did not take Me in, naked and you did not clothe Me, sick and in prison and you did not visit Me. Then they also will answer Him, saying, Lord, when did we see You hungry or thirsty or a stranger or naked or sick or in prison and did not minister to You? Then He will answer them, saying, Truly I say to you, Insofar as you did not do it to one of the least of these you did not do it to Me. And these will go away into eternal punishment, but the righteous into eternal life.   Matt.25:37–46.

5064   The preliminary section of the previous chapter, 4954–4959, contained an explanation of what is meant in the internal sense by giving food to the hungry, giving drink to the thirsty, taking in a stranger, clothing the naked, visiting one sick or in prison. That section shows that what charity is essentially is implied and described by all these actions. By one who is hungry, thirsty, or a stranger is meant an affection for what is good and true; and by one who is naked, sick, or in prison is meant a recognition of what one's own selfhood is like, see 4956, 4958.

5065   The same particular actions occur three times in the verses quoted above, but since, as has been stated, an explanation of such actions has appeared already, there is no need to deal with them individually, that is, to explain what each word means in the internal sense. All that needs to be stated here is the meaning of the reply given both by those on the right and by those on the left – that they had not seen Him hungry, thirsty, a stranger, naked, sick, or in prison. Then the meaning of 'the King' needs to be given, also the meanings of 'the righteous' and 'eternal life', and the meanings of 'him who is cursed' and 'eternal fire'.

5066   The reply of those on the right was,

Lord, when did we see You hungry and feed You, or thirsty and give You drink? When did we see You a stranger and take You in, or naked and clothe You? When did we see You sick, or in prison, and come to You?

This reply means that if they had seen the Lord Himself, all of them would have performed these acts of kindness to Him. Yet it would not have been love towards Him that would have led them to do so, only fear because He was about to come and judge the whole world. Nor would they have acted for His sake but their own, and so not because of anything present more internally in them, in their hearts, but for quite external reasons, and in outward conduct alone. They may be likened to a person who, when he sees his king whose favour he wishes to secure so that he may become great or rich, therefore conducts himself in a submissive manner before the king. Or they may be likened to those who engage in external holy worship in which so to speak they see the Lord and are submissive before Him. They do this because they believe that by engaging in such worship they will receive eternal life, even though they have no charity and do not do good to anyone except for selfish reasons, thus solely for their own benefit. Those on the right are like people who outwardly show great respect to their king yet scoff at what he commands because in their hearts they despise him. These and other examples like them are what are meant by the reply given by those on the right. And because the outward actions of the evil as well are similar, the reply given by those on the left was practically the same.

5067   Since therefore the Lord is not concerned about external things, only about those that are internal, and a person bears witness to internal ones not through worship alone but through charity and acts that express it, the Lord replied,

Truly I say to you, Insofar as you did it to one of the least of these My brothers you did it to Me.

The word 'brothers' is used to describe those in whom the good of charity and life is present; for since good itself is present in them, the Lord resides with them. These are the ones who are meant, strictly speaking, by the neighbour. Yet the Lord does not present Himself even within these, for compared with Him they are worthless. But a person presents himself before the Lord by worshipping Him with his inner being.

5068   The reason the Lord calls Himself 'the King' in the following words – 'When the Son of Man comes in His glory, He will sit on the throne of [His] glory.....Then the King will say to them' – is that the Lord's kingly rule is Divine Truth, on which judgement is based and in accordance with which it is executed. But the basis and execution of judgement in the case of the good is different from what it is with the evil. Because the good have accepted Divine Truth, the basis on which they are judged is good, and so mercy; but because the evil have not accepted Divine Truth, the basis of their judgement is truth, but not mercy, for the reason that they have cast mercy aside and as a consequence are constantly casting it aside in the next life. The acceptance of Divine Truth implies not only possessing faith but also expressing that faith in action, that is, making what doctrine teaches a matter of life. These are the reasons why the Lord calls Himself 'the King'. The Lord's kingly rule consists in Divine Truth, see 1728, 2015(end), 3009, 3670, 4581, 4966.

5069   The expression 'the righteous', used of those on the right in the following statements – '*The righteous* will answer Him, saying, etc.' and '*the righteous* will go into eternal life' – means that the Lord's righteousness dwells with them. All in whom the good of charity is present are called 'the righteous'; not that of themselves they are righteous but that they are made such by the Lord, whose right-eousness they take to themselves. Those who believe that of themselves they are righteous, or that they have been made righteous to such an extent that no evil at all is present in them any longer, are not among the righteous but among the unrighteous. For they attribute good to themselves and also make that good meritorious; and people like them cannot possibly possess true humility with which to worship the Lord. Therefore in the Word those people are called 'righteous and holy' who know and acknowledge that all good comes from the Lord and all evil from themselves, that is, they possess it from hell.

5070   The eternal life which is imparted to the righteous is life flowing from good. Good has life within it because it comes from the Lord, who is life itself. Included within the life which comes from the Lord there is wisdom and intelligence; for wisdom consists in receiving good from the Lord and then making it the object of one's will, while intelligence consists in receiving truth from the Lord and then believ-ing it. And those who receive such wisdom and intelligence have life. Also, because happiness is linked to that kind of life, eternal happiness too is meant by that life. The opposite is the case with those governed by evil. They do, it is true, seem – especially to themselves – to possess life; but it is the kind of life which in the Word is called death, and is in actual fact spiritual death; for they do not have any wise apprehension of what is good or any intelligent understanding of what is true. This may be seen by anyone who considers the matter carefully, for since it is good and the truth rooted in such good that hold life within them, no life can exist in evil or in the falsity springing from it, because these are by nature the reverse of good and truth and destructive of life. Consequently the people under consideration here have no other life than the kind which the insane have.

5071   The reason why the expression 'cursed' is used of those on the left and why their punishment is called 'eternal fire' in the following statements – 'Then He will also say to those on the left, Depart from Me,

O *cursed* ones, into *eternal fire* prepared for the devil and his angels' and 'these will go away into eternal *punishment*' – is that they have turned away from good and truth and have turned towards evil and falsity 'Cursing' in the internal sense of the Word means a turning away, 245, 379, 1423, 3530, 3584. The eternal fire into which they were to depart is not material fire, nor is it a tormented conscience, but a craving for evil. For cravings like this in a person are spiritual fires which consume him during the life of the body and torment him in the next life. Because of these fires burning within them, the inhabitants of hell use dreadful methods to torture one another.

2   Eternal fire is clearly not material fire; and the reason it is not a tormented conscience is that none who are governed by evil have any conscience; and those who have had no conscience during their lifetime cannot have any in the next life. But the reason eternal fire is a craving is that the entire fire of life in a person is fuelled by his loves, a heavenly fire by the love of what is good and true, a hellish fire by the love of what is evil and false. Or what amounts to the same, a heavenly fire is fuelled by love to the Lord and love towards the neighbour, and a hellish fire by self-love and love of the world. Anyone can see, if he stops to think, that all the fire or heat burning within a person is fuelled by his loves. This also explains why love is called spiritual heat and why in the Word fire and heat have no other meaning, 934(end), 1297, 1527, 1528, 1861, 2446, 4906. The fire of life in the evil is also such that when they feel very strong cravings, a kind of fire is also burning in them, which inflames them with an intense and furious desire to torment others. But the fire of life in the good is such that when a higher level of affection exists with them, a kind of fire is alight in them too. But this fire inflames them with a loving and zealous desire to do good to others.

GENESIS 40

1 And so it was after these words[1], that they sinned – the cupbearer of the king of Egypt, and the baker – against their lord the king of Egypt.

2 And Pharaoh was incensed with his two courtier-ministers, with the chief of the cupbearers and with the chief of the bakers.

3 And he put them in the custody of the house of the chief of the attendants, at the prison-house, the place where Joseph was bound.

4 And the chief of the attendants set Joseph over them and he ministered to them; and they were in custody for days[2].

5 And they both dreamed a dream, each his dream in one night, each according to the interpretation of his dream, the cupbearer and the baker to the king of Egypt, who were bound in the prison-house.

6 And Joseph came to them in the morning, and he saw them, and behold, they were troubled.

7 And he asked Pharaoh's courtier-ministers who were with him in the custody of his lord's house, saying, Why are your faces sad[3] today?

8 And they said to him, We have dreamed a dream and there is no interpreter for it. And Joseph said to them, Do not interpretations belong to God? Tell it to me, I beg you.

9 And the chief of the cupbearers told his dream to Joseph, and said to him, In my dream, and behold, a vine before me.

10 And on the vine three shoots, and it was as though budding; its blossom came up, and its clusters ripened into grapes.

11 And Pharaoh's cup was in my hand, and I took the grapes and pressed them into Pharaoh's cup, and put the cup onto Pharaoh's palm.

12 And Joseph said to him, This is the interpretation of it: The three shoots are three days.

13 In yet three days Pharaoh will lift up your head and will restore you to your position, and you will put Pharaoh's cup into his hand, according to the former manner when you were his cupbearer.

14 But remember me when it is well with you, and show, I beg you, mercy to me, and make mention of me to Pharaoh, and bring me out of this house.

15 For I have indeed been taken by theft out of the land of the Hebrews, and here also I have not done anything for which they should put me in the pit.

16 And the chief of the bakers saw that he had interpreted what was good, and he said to Joseph, I also was in my dream, and behold, three baskets with holes in them were on my head.

17 And in the highest basket there was some of every kind of food for Pharaoh, the work of the baker, and the birds were eating them out of the basket, from upon my head.

---

[1] *i.e.* things, *see* 5075
[2] *i.e.* for a considerable length of time
[3] *lit.* evil

18 And Joseph answered and said, This is the interpretation of it: The three baskets are three days.

19 In yet three days Pharaoh will lift up your head from upon you, and will hang you on wood; and the birds will eat your flesh from upon you.

20 And it happened on the third day, Pharaoh's birthday, that he made a feast for all his servants, and he lifted up the head of the chief of the cupbearers, and the head of the chief of the bakers, in the midst of his servants.

21 And he restored the chief of the cupbearers to his supervision over [Pharaoh's] drink, and he put the cup onto Pharaoh's palm.

22 And the chief of the bakers he hanged, as Joseph had interpreted to them.

23 And the chief of the cupbearers did not remember Joseph, and forgot him.

CONTENTS

5072 The internal sense of this chapter continues to deal with the state of temptations, by means of which bodily things could be brought into a state of agreement. Rightly called bodily ones, those things are the powers of the senses, of which there are two kinds, some sensory powers being subordinate to the understanding part of the mind, others to the will part. Those subordinate to the understanding part are represented by the cupbearer of the king of Egypt, and those subordinate to the will part by the baker. The eventual retention of the former but casting away of the latter is represented by the fact that the cupbearer returned to the position he had held previously, whereas the baker was hanged. Everything else will become evident from the train of thought.

THE INTERNAL SENSE

5073   Verses 1–4 **And so it was after these words[1], that they sinned –
the cupbearer of the king of Egypt, and the baker – against their lord
the king of Egypt. And Pharaoh was incensed with his two courtier-
ministers, with the chief of the cupbearers and with the chief of the
bakers. And he put them into the custody of the house of the chief of
the attendants, at the prison-house, the place where Joseph was bound.
And the chief of the attendants set Joseph over them and he ministered
to them; and they were in custody for days[2].**

'And so it was' means a new state and the things that followed. 'After
these words' means after the things prior to this. 'That they sinned'
means that order had become turned around. 'The cupbearer of the
king of Egypt' means among the things of the body which are subject to
the understanding part of the mind. 'And the baker' means among the
things in the body which are subject to the will part. 'Against their lord
the king of Egypt' means that these were contrary to the new state in the
natural man. 'And Pharaoh was incensed' means that the new natural
man turned away. 'With his two courtier-ministers' means from both
kinds of sensory powers in the body. 'With the chief of the cupbearers
and with the chief of the bakers' means in general from the sensory
powers subordinate to the understanding part and to the will part. 'And
he put them into the custody' means a casting aside. 'Of the house of
the chief of the attendants' means the things that are first and foremost
in explanations. 'At the prison-house' means among falsities. 'The place
where Joseph was bound' means the state of the celestial of the natural
now in relation to these things. 'And the chief of the attendants set
Joseph over them' means that under the influence of the things first and
foremost in explanations the celestial of the natural taught those bodily
senses. 'And he ministered to them' means that it instructed them.
'And they were in custody for days' means that they lay in a state when
they were cast aside for a long time.

5074   'And so it was' means a new state and the things that follow.
This is clear from the fact that in the Word 'so it was' or 'it happened'
implies a new state, see 4979, 4999. Furthermore in the original
language this expression serves to mark off series of prior events from
subsequent ones, 4987. This is why 'and so it was' means the things
that follow.

5075   'After these words' means after the things prior to this. This is
clear from the meaning of 'words' in the original language, in which the
same expression also means things. This therefore is why 'after these
words' here means after these things, and so after those that happened

---

[1] *i.e.* things, *see* 5075
[2] *i.e.* for a considerable length of time

prior to this. The reason 'words' in the original language also means things is that in the internal sense 'words' means the truths of doctrine, on account of which all Divine Truth in general is called the Word; and in the highest sense the Lord Himself, the source of all Divine Truth, is the Word, 1288. A further reason is that no thing which comes into being anywhere in the world has any existence, that is, any reality, unless it has been created by Divine Good acting through Divine Truth. It explains why in Hebrew the same expression is used for things as for words. The truth that no thing anywhere in the world has any existence, that is, any reality, unless it has been created by Divine Good acting through Divine Truth, that is, through the Word, is evident in John,

In the beginning was *the Word*, and *the Word was with God*, and *the Word* was God. All things were made through Him, and without Him nothing was made that was made. John 1:1,3.

2 The interior meanings that words possess have their origin for the most part in the interior man, which dwells with spirits and angels. For as to his spirit, that is, as to his true self which lives after the death of his body, everyone lives in communion with angels and spirits, though the external man is not conscious of this. Living in communion with them he is also among those who use a universal language and so use that which is the origin of verbal expressions. It is for this reason that words have many spiritual meanings attached to them which to outward appearance seem to be out of keeping with them; but inwardly they are in keeping, as with the meaning of 'words' here as things. The same is true of very many other expressions, as when for instance a person's understanding is called his inner sight and is said to possess light, or as when his apprehension of and obedience to something is called hearing and listening, or as when his detection of something is called smelling, and so on.

5076 'That they sinned' means that order had become turned around. This is clear from the meaning of 'sinning' as acting contrary to Divine order, anything whatever contrary to that order being sin. Essentially, Divine order is Divine Truth grounded in Divine Good; and this order exists with everyone whose truth is grounded in good, that is, whose faith is grounded in charity, truth being the essence of faith and good the essence of charity. But everyone acts contrary to that order whose truth is not grounded in good, consequently whose truth or else falsity is grounded in evil. Nothing else than this is meant by sin. Here 'they sinned' – the cupbearer and the baker – means that the order in which the external senses existed in relation to interior things had become turned around, so that the former were not in accord or did not agree with the latter.

5077 'The cupbearer of the king of Egypt' means among the things of the body which are subject to the understanding part of the mind.

This is clear from the meaning of 'the cupbearer' as the external or bodily senses that are subordinate or subject to the understanding part of the internal man, dealt with in what follows below; and from the meaning of 'the king of Egypt' as the natural man, dealt with below in 5079. Since the cupbearer and the baker are the subject of the narrative that follows and these mean the external senses belonging to the body, something must first be said about these. It is well known that the external or bodily senses are five in number – sight, hearing, smell, taste, and touch – and also that these constitute the entire life of the body. For without those senses the body has no life at all, for which reason also when deprived of them it dies and becomes a corpse. The actual bodily part of the human being therefore is nothing else than a receiver of sensory impressions and consequently of the life resulting from these. The part played by the senses is the principal one and that by the body the instrumental. The instrumental without its principal which it is fitted to serve cannot even be called the body that a person carries around while living in the world; but the instrumental together with its principal, when they act as one, can be called such. The two together therefore constitute the body.

A person's external senses are directly related to his internal ones, for they have been given to a person and placed within his body to serve his internal man while he is in the world and to exist subject to the sensory powers of that internal man. Consequently when a person's external senses begin to rule his internal ones he is done for. When this happens his internal sensory powers are regarded as no more than servants whose function is to reinforce whatever the external senses imperiously demand. When this is the state in which the external senses operate, order in their case has become turned around, a situation dealt with immediately above in 5076.

A person's external senses are, as stated, directly related to his internal ones, in general to the understanding and to the will. Consequently some external senses are subject or subordinate to the understanding part of the human mind, others are subject to the will part. One sensory power specifically subject to the understanding is sight; another subject to the understanding, and after that to the will also, is hearing. Smell, and more especially taste, are subject to both simultaneously, while the power subject to the will is touch. Much evidence could be introduced to show that the external senses are subject to the understanding and the will, and also to show how they are subject; but it would take up too much space to carry the explanation so far. Something of what is involved may be recognized from what has been shown at the ends of preceding chapters about the correspondence of those senses.

In addition it should be recognized that all truths that are called the truths of faith belong to the understanding part, and that all forms of good which are those of love and charity go with the will part. Consequently it is the function of the understanding to believe, acknowledge, know, and see truth – and good also. But the function of the will is to feel an affection for that truth and to love it; and whatever a person feels an affection for and loves is good. But how the understanding influences the will when truth passes into good, and how the will influences the understanding when it puts that good into effect, are matters for still deeper examination. In the Lord's Divine mercy those matters will be discussed at various points further on.

5 The reason 'the cupbearer' means the senses subject or subordinate to the understanding part of the internal man is that everything which serves as drink, or which is consumed as such, for example, wine, milk, or water, is related to truth, which feeds the understanding and so belongs to the understanding. Also, because the external or bodily senses play a ministering role, 'a cupbearer' therefore means those senses or what is perceived by them. For in general 'drinking' has reference to truths which feed the understanding, see 3069, 3071, 3168, 3772, 4017, 4018; the specific meaning of 'wine' is truth deriving from good, or faith from charity, 1071, 1798, while 'water' means truth, 680, 2702, 3058, 3424, 4976. From all this one may now see what 'the cupbearer' means.

5078 'And the baker' means among the things in the body which are subject to the will part. This is clear from the meaning of 'the baker' as the external or bodily senses which are subordinate or subject to the will part of the internal man. The reason 'the baker' has this meaning is that everything which serves as food or is consumed as such, for example, bread, solid foods in general, and anything made by a baker, has reference to good and so to the will; for all good feeds the will, just as every truth feeds the understanding, as stated immediately above in 5077. By 'bread' is meant what is celestial, or goodness, see 1798, 2165, 2177, 3478, 3735, 3813, 4211, 4217, 4735, 4976.

2 The reason why here and in the rest of this chapter external sensory powers of both kinds are dealt with in the internal sense is that the previous chapter dealt with how the Lord glorified or made Divine the interior aspects of His Natural, and therefore the present chapter deals with how the Lord glorified or made Divine the exterior aspects of that Natural. The exterior aspects of the natural are rightly called bodily ones, being both kinds of sensory powers of perception together with their recipient members and organs; for these recipients together with those powers make up that which is referred to as the body, see above in 5077. The Lord made Divine all that constituted His body, both its sensory powers and their recipient members and organs, which also explains why He rose from the grave with His body, and after the Resurrection told His disciples,

See My hands and My feet, that it is I Myself; handle Me, and see; for a spirit does not have flesh and bones as you see Me have. Luke 24:39.

3 Most people at the present day who belong to the Church believe that everyone is going to rise again on the last day and to do so at that time with his body. This supposition is so universal that scarcely anyone,

because of what he is taught, believes anything different. But that supposition has gained strength because the natural man imagines that the body alone is the possessor of life. Consequently if he were not allowed to believe that this body is going to receive life once again he would refuse to believe in any resurrection at all. But the truth of the matter is that a person rises again immediately after death, at which point he seems to himself to be in his body just the same as when he was in the world, having a face and members, arms, hands, feet, breast, belly, and loins like the ones he had before. Indeed when he sees himself and touches himself he says he is exactly as he was in the world. However, that which he sees and touches is not his external which he carried round in the world but the internal which constituted the real person. That internal is what had life within it, but it had the external surrounding it, or outside every individual part of it, enabling it to exist in the world where it could act in the right way and carry out its functions.

The actual earthly body is of no further use to him. He is in another world where he possesses other functions and other strengths and powers for which the kind of body he has there is suited. He sees that body with his own eyes – not the eyes he had in the world but those he now has in that other world. They are the eyes of his internal man, the ones he had used previously to see with through the eyes of his body and behold worldly and earthly objects. He also touches and feels that body – not with the hands or sense of touch he had been given in the world but with the hands and sense of touch which he is given in that other world and which had lain behind his sense of touch in the world. Furthermore each of the senses in that other world is keener and more perfect because it belongs to the internal man released from the external. The internal dwells in a greater state of perfection, because it is this that supplies sensory awareness to the external, though when it acts into the external, as it does in tne world, that power is blunted and reduced. What is more, the sensory perception of the internal is·a perception of what is internal, that of the external a perception of what is external. This being so, people can see one another after death, and they exist grouped together in communities on the basis of what they are inwardly like. In order to become quite sure of this I have been allowed to touch actual spirits and to talk to them many times on this subject, see 322, 1630, 4622.

People after death – who are then called spirits or, if they have led good lives, angels – are utterly amazed at what the member of the Church believes about himself. For he believes that he will not see eternal life until the last day when the world is destroyed, and that at that time he will be reclothed with the dust that has been cast away; when yet one who belongs to the Church knows that he rises again after death. For who does not say, when someone dies, that his soul or spirit is in heaven, or in hell? Who does not say about his young children who have died that they are in heaven? Who does not comfort a person who is [incurably] sick or one who is condemned to death by saying that shortly he will enter the next life? And one who is in the throes of death and has been prepared for it does not believe anything different. Indeed such a conviction about a person's rising again after he has died is what leads many to claim that they have the power to release others from places of condemnation and to admit them into heaven, and to say masses for their souls. Is anyone unacquainted with what the Lord said to the robber, 'Today you will be with Me in paradise', Luke 23:43, or with what the Lord said about the rich man and Lazarus, that the former was carried off into hell, whereas the latter was taken by the angels into heaven, Luke 16:22,23? Or is anyone unacquainted with what the Lord taught about the resurrection when He said that God is not the God of the dead but of the living, Luke 20:38?

6 A person acquainted with all this thinks in these ways and speaks in these ways when his spirit guides his thought and speech. But when his thought and speech are guided by what doctrine teaches that person says something entirely different, namely that he will not rise again until the last day. But in fact each person's last day is at hand when he dies, and this is his time of judgement too, as many also declare. As to what is meant by 'being encompassed by my skin' and 'out of my flesh seeing God' in Job 19:25,26, see 3540(end). These things were said so that people may know that no one rises again in the body that encompassed him in the world except the Lord alone. He did so because, while in the world, He glorified His body, that is, He made it Divine.

5079 'Against their lord the king of Egypt' means that these – the external or bodily senses, meant by 'the cupbearer and the baker' – were contrary to the new state in the natural man. This is clear from the meaning of 'the king of Egypt' as factual knowledge in general, dealt with in 1164, 1165, 1186, 1462, 4749, 4964, 4966; for, the king being the head of the nation, 'the king of Egypt' is similar in meaning to 'Egypt', the same as in other places where the king of any nation is referred to or named, 4789. Since factual knowledge in general is meant by 'the king of Egypt', so also is the natural man meant by him; for all factual knowledge is truth as it exists in the natural man, 4967, while the actual good there is meant by 'the lord', 4973. The reason a new state in the natural man is meant is that the previous chapter dealt with the interior aspects of the natural, which were made new, or – in the highest sense, in which the Lord is the subject – were glorified, whereas the present chapter deals with the exterior aspects of the natural which are to be brought into accord or agreement with those interior ones. These interior aspects of the natural which have been made new – or, what amounts to the same, a new state in the natural man – are what are meant by 'the lord the king of Egypt', while the exterior aspects which have not been brought into a state of order and are consequently contrary to it are meant by 'the cupbearer and the baker'.

There are interior aspects of the natural and there are exterior ones. The interior aspects of the natural are known facts and the affections for them, but the exterior aspects are both kinds of sensory perception spoken of above in 5077. When a person dies he leaves behind those exterior aspects of the natural; but the interior aspects of the natural he takes with him into the next life where they serve as the foundation on which spiritual and celestial things can be based; for when a person dies he loses nothing apart from his flesh and bones. He keeps his memory in which everything he has done, spoken, or thought is recorded, and he keeps every natural affection and desire, and so every interior aspect of the natural. He does not need its exterior aspects, for he does not see anything that is in the world, or hear anything that is in the world, or smell, taste, or touch anything that is in the world, only what is in the next life. Things in the next life, it is true, seem for the most part to be like those in the world, but they are not, for they hold what is living within them, such as things proper to the natural world do not hold within them. For every single thing in the next life owes the beginning and the continuance of its existence to the Sun there, which is the Lord, as a consequence of which it has that which is living within it. But every single thing in the natural world owes the beginning and the continuance of its existence to the sun there, which is material fire, as a consequence of which it does not have that which is living within it. What gives it the appearance of having life within it is that its origin lies solely in the spiritual world, that is, in the Lord through the spiritual world.

5080   'And Pharaoh was incensed' means that the new natural man turned away. This is clear from the representation of 'Pharaoh' or the king of Egypt as the new natural man or a new state in the natural man, dealt with immediately above in 5079, and from the meaning of 'being incensed' or being angry as turning away, dealt with in 5034; so that the meaning here is that the interior natural which had been made new turned away from the exterior natural, or the bodily senses, because the latter were not in agreement with it.

5081   'With his two courtier-ministers' means from both kinds of sensory powers in the body; that is to say, from these [the new natural man] turned away. This is clear from the meaning of 'courtier-ministers', who in this case are the cupbearer and the baker, as both kinds of sensory powers, dealt with above in 5077, 5078. In relation to the interior man, meant by 'lord the king', the bodily senses – sight, hearing, smell, taste, and touch – are also ministers, courtiers so to speak. For they serve to provide the interior man with evidence gathered from experience in the visible world and in human society, thereby enabling it to become intelligent and wise. For the human being is born with not even any knowledge, let alone with any intelligence or wisdom. He is born with no more than the capacity to receive and be endowed with these. Such reception and endowment is effected through two different channels, an internal channel and an external one. By the internal channel that which is from the Divine flows in, by the external that which is from the world. The two meet within a person, in which case, so far as the person allows himself to receive light from the Divine, he enters into wisdom. The things that flow in by the external channel come through the bodily senses; yet they do not flow in of their own accord but are called forth by the internal man to serve as a base laid down for celestial and spiritual things flowing in from the Lord by the internal channel. From this it may be seen that the bodily senses are like courtier-ministers. In general everything exterior, in relation to what is interior, is a minister; the entire natural man in relation to the spiritual man is nothing else.

2 The word used in the original language means minister, courtier, bed-chamber servant, and eunuch. In the internal sense the good and truth of the natural man are meant, as is the case here. But specifically the good of the natural man is meant, as in Isaiah,

> Do not let the son of the foreigner who clings to Jehovah say, Jehovah surely separates me from being with His people. Do not let *the eunuch* say, Behold, I am dry wood. For thus said Jehovah to *the eunuchs* who keep My sabbaths and choose that in which I delight, and are holding fast to My covenant, I will give those in My house and within My walls a place and a name better than sons and daughters; I will give them an eternal name which will not be cut off. Isa.56:3–5.

In this case 'the eunuch' stands for the good of the natural man, and 'the son of the foreigner' for the truth of the natural man; for the Lord's Church is both external and internal. Those who belong to the external Church are natural; those who belong to the internal Church are spiritual. Those who are natural and yet are governed by good are 'the eunuchs', while those governed by truth are 'the sons of the foreigner'. Also, since the truly spiritual or internal ones are to be found solely within the Church, 'the sons of the foreigner' in addition means therefore those who are outside the Church – the gentiles – who are nevertheless governed by the truth as taught by their religion, 2049, 2593, 2599, 2600, 2602, 2603, 2861, 2863, 3263, while 'the eunuchs' means those governed by good.

5082 'With the chief of the cupbearers and with the chief of the bakers' means in general from the sensory powers subordinate to the understanding part and to the will part. This is clear from the meaning of 'the cupbearer' as the senses subordinate and subject to the understanding, dealt with above in 5077; from the meaning of 'the baker' as the senses subordinate and subject to the will, also dealt with above, in 5078; and from the meaning of 'the chief (or prince)' as that which is first and foremost, dealt with in 1482, 2089, 5044, in this case in general or commonly so throughout; for that which is first and foremost is also common throughout since it reigns throughout the rest of the whole. In relation to particular details, things that are first and foremost exist as what is general and overall, making everything one and removing any signs of incongruity.

5083   'And he put them into the custody' means a casting aside. This is clear from the meaning of 'putting into custody' as a casting aside, for anyone put into custody is cast aside.

5084   'Of the house of the chief of the attendants' means the things that are first and foremost in explanations. This is clear from the meaning of 'the chief of the attendants' as the things which are first and foremost in explanations, dealt with in 4790, 4966. The meaning here therefore is that both kinds of sensory impressions were cast aside by the things which are first and foremost in explanations, that is to say, by those which belong to the Word in the internal sense. Sensory impressions are said to be cast aside when the things that are first and foremost in explanations place no reliance on them; for they are indeed sensory impressions, and impressions received by the mind directly through the senses are illusions. The senses are the source of all the illusions that reign in a person, and they are the reason why few have any belief in the truths of faith and why the natural man is opposed to the spiritual man, that is, the external man to the internal. Consequently if the natural or external man starts to have dominion over the spiritual or internal man, no belief at all in matters of faith exists any longer, for illusions cast a shadow over them and evil desires smother them.

Few know what the illusions of the senses are and few believe that these cast a shadow over rational insights and most of all over spiritual matters of faith – a shadow so dark that it blots them out. This happens especially when at the same time what a person delights in is the result of desires bred by a selfish and worldly love. But let examples be used to shed some light on this matter, first some examples of illusions of the senses which are purely natural ones, that is, illusions about things within the natural creation, then some examples of such illusions in spiritual things.

i It is an illusion of the senses – a purely natural one, or an illusion about the natural creation – to believe that the sun is borne round this globe once a day, and that the sky too and all the stars are borne round at the same time. People may be told that it is impossible and therefore inconceivable that so vast an ocean of fire as the sun, and not only the sun but also the countless stars, should revolve once a day without undergoing any changes of position in relation to one another. They may be told in addition that one can see from the planetary system that our own globe performs a daily movement and an annual one, by rotations on its axis and by revolutions. This can be recognized from the fact that the planets are globes like ours, some of which have moons around them and all of which, as observation shows, perform daily and annual movements like ours. But for all that they are told, the illusion of the senses prevails with very many people – that things really are as the eye sees them.

3 ii It is an illusion of the senses – a purely natural one, or an illusion about the natural creation – that the atmosphere is a single entity, except that it becomes gradually and increasingly rarified until a vacuum exists where the atmosphere comes to an end. A person's external senses tell him nothing else than this when their evidence alone is relied on.

iii It is an illusion of the senses, a purely natural one, that the power which seeds have to grow into trees and flowers and to reproduce themselves was conferred on them when creation first began, and that that initial conferment is what causes everything to come into being and remain in being. People may be told that nothing can remain in being unless it is constantly being brought into being, in keeping with the law that continuance in being involves a constant coming into being, and with another law that anything that has no connection with something prior to itself ceases to have any existence. But though they are told all this, their bodily senses and their thought that is reliant on their senses, cannot take it in. Nor can they see that every single thing is kept in being, even as it was brought into being, through an influx from the spiritual world, that is, from the Divine coming through the spiritual world.

4 iv This gives rise to another illusion of the senses, a purely natural one, that single entities exist called monads and atoms. For the natural man believes that anything comprehended by his external senses is a single entity or else nothing at all.

v It is an illusion of the senses, a purely natural one, that everything is part of and begins in the natural creation, though there are indeed purer and more inward aspects of the natural creation that are beyond the range of human understanding. But if anyone says that a spiritual or celestial dimension exists within or above the natural creation, this idea is rejected; for the belief is that unless a thing is natural it has no existence.

vi It is an illusion of the senses that only the body possesses life and that when it dies that life perishes. The senses have no conception at all of an internal man present within each part of the external man, nor any conception that this internal man resides in the inward dimension of the natural creation, in the spiritual world. Nor consequently, since they have no conception of it, do the senses believe that a person will live after death, apart from being clothed with the body once again, 5078, 5079.

5 vii This gives rise to the further illusion of the senses that no human being can have a life after death any more than animals do, for the reason that the life of an animal is much the same as that of a human being, the only difference being that man is a more perfect kind of living creature. The senses – that is, the person who relies on his senses

to think with and form conclusions – have no conception of the human being as one who is superior to animals or who possesses a life superior to theirs because of his ability to think not only about the causes of things but also about what is Divine. The human being also has the ability to be joined through faith and love to the Divine, as well as to receive an influx from Him and to make what flows in his own. Thus because of his response to such influx from the Divine it is possible for the human being to receive it, which is not at all the case with animals.

viii This gives rise to yet another illusion, which is that what is actually living in the human being – what is called the soul – is merely something air-like or flame-like which is dispersed when the person dies. Added to this is the illusion that the soul is situated either in the heart, or in the brain, or in some other part of him, from where it controls the body as if this were a machine. One who relies on his senses has no conception of an internal man present in every part of his external man, no conception that the eye sees not of its own accord, and that the ear hears not of its own accord, but under the direction of the internal man.

ix It is an illusion of the senses that no other source of light is possible than the sun or else material fire, and that no other source of heat than these is possible. The senses have no conception of the existence of a light that holds intelligence within it, or of a heat that holds heavenly love within it, or that all angels are bathed in that light and heat.

x It is an illusion of the senses when a person believes that he lives independently, that is, that an underived life is present within him; for this is what the situation seems to be to the senses. The senses have no conception at all that the Divine alone is one whose life is underived, thus that there is but one actual life, and that anything in the world that has life is merely a form receiving it, see 1954, 2706, 2886–2889, 2893, 3001, 3318, 3337, 3338, 3484, 3742, 3743, 4151, 4249, 4318–4320, 4417, 4523, 4524, 4882.

xi The person who relies on his senses can be misled into a belief that adulterous relationships are allowable; for his senses lead him to think that marriages exist merely for the sake of order which the upbringing of children necessitates, and that provided this order is not destroyed it makes no difference who fathers the children. He can also be misled into thinking that the married state is no different from having sex with someone, except that it is allowable. That being so, he also believes that it would not be contrary to order for him to marry several wives if the Christian world, basing its ideas on the Sacred Scriptures, did not forbid it. If told that a correspondence exists between the heavenly marriage and marriages on earth, and that no one can have anything of marriage within him unless spiritual good and truth are present there, also that a genuinely conjugial relationship cannot possibly exist between one man and several wives, and consequently that marriages are intrinsically holy, the person who relies on his senses rejects all this as worthless.

8   xii It is an illusion of the senses that the Lord's kingdom, or heaven, is like an earthly kingdom, that joy and happiness there consist in one person holding a higher position than another and as a consequence possessing more glory than another. For the senses have no conception at all of what is implied by the idea that the least is the greatest and the last is the first. If such people are told that joy in heaven or among angels consists in serving the welfare of others without any thought of merit or reward, it strikes them as a sorrowful existence.

xiii It is an illusion of the senses that good works earn merit and that to do good to someone even for a selfish reason is a good work.

xiv It is also an illusion of the senses that a person is saved by faith alone, and that faith may exist with someone who has no charity, as well as that faith, not life, is what remains after death.

One could go on with very many other illusions of the senses; for when a person is governed by his senses the rational degree within him, which is enlightened by the Divine, does not see anything. It dwells in thickest darkness, in which case every conclusion based on sensory evidence is thought to be a rational one.

5085   'At the prison-house' means among falsities. This is clear from the meaning of 'the prison-house' as the vastation of falsity, and consequently as falsity itself, dealt with in 4958, 5037, 5038.

5086   'The place where Joseph was bound' means the state of the celestial of the natural now in relation to these things. This is clear from the meaning of 'the place' as a state, dealt with in 2625, 2837, 3356, 3387, 4321, 4882; from the representation of 'Joseph' as the celestial of the spiritual from the rational, dealt with in 4286, 4585, 4592, 4594, 4963, at this point the celestial of the natural because it was now in the natural, from which temptations arise, 5035, 5039; and from the meaning of 'bound' as a state of temptations, dealt with in 5037. The subject in the previous chapter was the state of temptations undergone by the celestial of the spiritual within the natural, involving those things which belonged to the interior natural, whereas in this chapter it is the state of temptations involving things that belong to the exterior natural.

5087   'And the chief of the attendants set Joseph over them' means that under the influence of the things first and foremost in explanations the celestial of the natural taught those bodily senses. This is clear from the meaning of 'the chief of the attendants' as the things that are first and foremost in explanations, dealt with in 4790, 4966, 5084; from the representation of 'Joseph' as the celestial of the natural, dealt with immediately above in 5086; and from the meaning of 'being set over' here as teaching, for one who is 'set over' things that are cast aside so that they may be examined and corrected performs the function of a teacher.

5088   'And he ministered to them' means that it instructed them. This is clear from the meaning of 'ministering to' as instructing. Here 'ministering to' clearly does not mean ministering as a servant, for the very reason that Joseph was set over those men. 'Ministering to' here means supplying what was suitable to them. And because the subject here is a new sensory or external part in the natural, 'being set over' means teaching and 'ministering to' means instructing. 'To be set over' is used in reference to good which is the essence of life, 'to minister to' in reference to truth which is the essence of doctrine, 4976.

5089   'And they were in custody for days' means that they lay in a state when they were cast aside for a long time. This is clear from the meaning of 'days' as states, dealt with in 23, 487, 488, 493, 893, 2788, 3462, 3785, 4850; so that 'for days' here means lying in a particular state for a long time – in a state when they were cast aside, meant by 'custody', 5083. A more lengthy explanation of the details contained in the internal sense here is not possible because they are not the kind of matters about which any idea can be gained with the help of things in the world, such as details about the celestial-of-the-spiritual man, about this man's state within the natural when the interior natural is being made new, and after that when it has been made new and the exterior natural has been cast aside. But some idea of these matters and others like them can be gained from things in heaven, which is the kind of idea that does not pass into any notion gained from things in the world, except in the case of people who, in their thinking, can be led away from sensory impressions.

Unless a person's thought can be raised above sensory impressions so that these are beheld as existing so to speak beneath him, he cannot possibly discern any interior aspect of the Word, let alone things of heaven such as are totally removed from those of the world, since the senses take hold of them and stifle them. This explains why people who rely on their senses and have focused their attention on known facts rarely understand anything about the things of heaven; for they have immersed their thoughts in the kinds of things that belong to the world, that is, in terms and in definitions formed from these, and so in what the senses perceive, from which they can no longer be raised up and so preserved in a way of looking at things that is higher than the senses. Nor can their thought range freely any longer over the whole field of matters recorded in the memory, selecting those which agree and casting aside those which are contrary, and using those which are in any way appropriate. For their thought is locked up and immersed in terms, as has been stated, and consequently in sensory impressions, so that it cannot look round about. This is the reason why the learned possess less belief than the simple, and also indeed why they possess less discernment in heavenly matters. For the simple can view something from a position that is above mere terms and above known facts, and so above sensory evidence. This the learned cannot do; their viewpoint is based on terms and known facts because their mind is immersed in these. Thus they are bound so to speak in a dungeon or prison.

5090 Verses 5–8 **And they both dreamed a dream, each his dream in one night, each according to the interpretation of his dream, the cupbearer and the baker to the king of Egypt, who were bound in the prison-house. And Joseph came to them in the morning, and he saw them, and behold, they were troubled. And he asked Pharaoh's courtier-ministers who were with him in the custody of his lord's house, saying, Why are your faces sad[1] today? And they said to him, We have dreamed a dream and there is no interpreter for it. And Joseph said to them, Do not interpretations belong to God? Tell it to me, I beg you.**

'And they both dreamed a dream' means foresight regarding them. 'Each his dream in one night' means regarding what the outcome would be, which to them lay in obscurity. 'Each according to the interpretation of his dream' means which they held within them. 'The cupbearer and the baker' means regarding both kinds of sensory powers. 'To the king of Egypt' means which were subordinate to the interior natural. 'Who were bound in the prison-house' means which were among falsities. 'And Joseph came to them in the morning' means that which was revealed and made clear to the celestial of the natural[2]. 'And he saw them' means perception. 'And behold, they were troubled' means that they were passing through a sad state. 'And he asked Pharaoh's courtier-ministers' means those sensory powers. 'Who were with him in the custody of his lord's house' means which had been cast aside. 'Saying, Why are your faces sad today?' means, What affection gives rise to this sadness? 'And they said to him' means perception regarding these matters. 'We have dreamed a dream' means a fore-telling. 'And there is no interpreter for it' means that no one knows what they hold within them. 'And Joseph said to them' means the celestial of the natural. 'Do not interpretations belong to God?' means that the Divine is within them. 'Tell it to me, I beg you' means that it might be known.

5091 'And they both dreamed a dream' means foresight regarding them. This is clear from the meaning of 'a dream' as foresight, dealt with in 3698, 'they both' being both kinds of sensory powers meant by 'the cupbearer and the baker', whose dreams have reference to themselves, as is evident from what follows. The reason 'a dream', in the highest sense, means foresight is that dreams which come directly from the Lord by way of heaven foretell things to come. Such was the nature of Joseph's dreams, the cupbearer's dream and the baker's dream, Pharaoh's dream, Nebuchadnezzar's dream, and prophetical dreams in general. The things to come that are foretold in dreams have no other origin than the Lord's Divine foresight. From this one may also realize that every single thing is foreseen by Him.

---

[1] *lit.* evil

[2] the celestial of the spiritual *is possibly intended here; see* 5097.

5092   'Each his dream in one night' means regarding what the outcome would be, which to them lay in obscurity. This is clear from the meaning of 'a dream' as foresight and consequent foretelling – and because a foretelling is meant, so also is the outcome, it being the outcome that is foretold; and from the meaning of 'night' as obscurity. In the spiritual sense 'night' means a state of shade brought about through falsity that is the product of evil, 1712, 2353, and so also obscurity, that is to say, mental obscurity. The obscurity belonging to night in the world is natural obscurity, but the obscurity belonging to night in the next life is spiritual obscurity. Natural obscurity comes about because the sun of the world is absent and the light received from it is lost, whereas spiritual obscurity comes about because heaven's sun, which is the Lord, is absent and the light, that is, intelligence received from it, is lost. This latter loss does not arise because the sun of heaven sets as the sun of the world does, but because a person or a spirit is living amid falsity that is the product of evil. He himself moves away from that sun and brings obscurity to himself.

An idea simply of night and of the obscurity that comes with it is sufficient to enable one to see how the spiritual sense and the natural sense of something are related to each other. Furthermore there are three kinds of spiritual obscurity – the first being that which is due to falsity that is a product of evil; the second being that which is due to ignorance of the truth; and the third being the obscurity in which exterior things dwell, compared with interior ones, and so the obscurity in which ideas formed by the senses and present in the external man dwell, compared with the rational concepts present in the internal man. All three kinds of obscurity arise however because the light of heaven, or intelligence and wisdom flowing from the Lord, is not received. This light shines unceasingly, but falsity that is a product of evil either rejects, smothers, or else perverts it; ignorance of truth receives only a little; while ideas formed by the senses that are present in the external man reduce it to a dim light by making it a general or ordinary one.

5093   'Each according to the interpretation of his dream' means which – that is, the outcome – they held within them. This is clear from the meaning of 'the interpretation of a dream' as an explanation and therefore a knowledge of the outcome, thus the outcome which they held within them. For 'a dream' means the outcome, see immediately above in 5092.

5094   'The cupbearer and the baker' means regarding both kinds of sensory powers. This is clear from the meaning of 'the cupbearer' as the sensory powers subordinate to the understanding part of the mind, dealt with in 5077, and from the meaning of 'the baker' as the sensory powers subordinate to the will part, dealt with in 5078, which, as stated above in 5083, 5089, were cast aside by the interior natural. But it should be realized that the actual powers of the senses were not cast aside –

that is to say, sight, hearing, smell, taste, and touch, for the life of the body is dependent on these – but the insights or thoughts, as well as the affections and desires, that are dependent on them. Objects belonging to the world enter a person's external or natural memory by way of his senses on the one hand and by way of his rational thought on the other. These objects then divide themselves off from one another in that memory; those entering through rational thought place themselves in a more internal position, whereas those entering through the senses do so in a more external one, as a consequence of which the natural comes to have two parts – the interior part and the exterior – as has also been stated above.

2   The interior natural is what 'Pharaoh king of Egypt' represents, while the exterior natural is what 'the cupbearer and the baker' represents. The nature of the difference between the two becomes clear from the different ways they look at things, that is, from their thoughts and their conclusions based on those thoughts. The person who uses the interior natural to think with and to form conclusions is rational, and is so insofar as he has absorbed what comes to him through rational thought; but the person who uses the exterior natural to think with and form conclusions is governed by his senses, and is so insofar as he has absorbed what comes to him from sensory evidence. Such a person is called one governed by his senses, whereas the other is called one who is rational-natural. When a person dies he has the entire natural with him; and its form remains the same as that which it took in the world. He is also rational-minded to the extent he has absorbed ideas from rational thought, but sensory-minded to the extent he has absorbed ideas from his senses. The difference between the two is that, to the extent it has absorbed ideas from rational thought and made them its own, the natural looks down on the senses belonging to the exterior natural and controls them by disparaging and casting aside illusions formed by the senses. But to the extent that it has absorbed ideas formed by the bodily senses and made them its own the natural looks down on rational thought by disparaging this and casting it aside.

3   An example of the difference between the two may be seen in the ability of the rational-natural man to comprehend that no one's life is self-existent but that it comes to him through an influx of life from the Lord by way of heaven, and the inability of one governed by the senses to comprehend the same. For the latter says his senses tell him and he can plainly see that his life is self-existent and that it is pointless to contradict the evidence of the senses. Let another example be given. The rational-natural man comprehends the existence of a heaven and a hell; but one governed by his senses denies the existence of these because he has no conception of another world purer than the one he sees with his eyes. The rational-natural man comprehends the existence of spirits and angels who are not visible to him; but one governed by the senses cannot comprehend the same, for he imagines that what he cannot see or touch has no existence.

Here is another example. The rational-natural man comprehends that it is the mark of an intelligent being to have ends in view, and with foresight to be directing means towards some final end. When he looks at the natural creation from the point of view of the order of everything, he sees the natural creation as a complex system of means and realizes that an intelligent Supreme Being has given them direction, though to what final end he cannot see unless he becomes spiritual. But a person governed by his senses does not comprehend how anything distinct and separate from the natural creation can exist or how some Being superior to the natural order can do so. He has no notion of what exercising intelligence, exercising wisdom, having ends in view, or giving direction to means may be unless all these activities are being spoken of as natural ones; and when they are spoken of as such, his idea of them is like that of one who is designing a machine. These few examples show what is meant by the interior natural and the exterior natural, and by the powers of the senses being cast aside – not sight, hearing, smell, taste, and touch in the body, but the conclusions reached by these about interior matters.

5095   'To the king of Egypt' means which were subordinate to the interior natural. This is clear from the representation of Pharaoh or 'the king of Egypt' in this chapter as a new state of the natural man, dealt with in 5079, 5080, consequently as the interior natural since this had been made new. As to what the interior natural is, and the exterior natural, see immediately above in 5094. The nature of the internal sense of the Word in the historical sections and in the prophetical parts must be stated briefly. When the historical sense mentions a number of persons – as when Joseph, Pharaoh, the chief of the attendants, the cupbearer, and the baker are mentioned here – various things are indeed meant by them in the internal sense, yet only as all these exist in one person. The reason for this is that names mean different spiritual things, as they do here: 'Joseph' represents the Lord as regards the celestial-spiritual from the rational and also within the natural, 'Pharaoh' represents Him as regards the new state of the natural man, that is, as regards the interior natural, 'the cupbearer and the baker' as regards the things that belong to the external natural. Such is the nature of the internal sense. The same is so in other places, for example when Abraham, Isaac, and Jacob are mentioned; in the sense of the letter they are three different persons, but in the highest sense all three represent the Lord – 'Abraham' the Divine itself, 'Isaac' His Divine Intellectual[1], and 'Jacob' His Divine Natural. The same may be seen in the Prophets where sometimes the text consists of mere names, either of persons or of kingdoms or of cities; yet all of them together present and describe a single entity in the internal sense. Anyone unaware of this may be easily misled by the sense of the letter into visualizing a variety of things, with the result that the idea of a single entity disappears.

[1] *previously the expression* Divine Rational *has been used to describe* Isaac's *representation; cp* 5998.

5096 'Who were bound in the prison-house' means which were among falsities. This is clear from the meaning of 'being bound in the prison-house' as being among falsities, dealt with in 4958, 5037, 5038, 5085. Those who are engrossed in falsities, more so those steeped in evils, are called 'the bound' and 'in prison', not because they are held in any physical bonds but because they are not in freedom; for people who are not in freedom are inwardly in bonds. Indeed once they subscribe to falsity they no longer have any freedom to choose or receive what is true; and those who subscribe heavily to it do not have any freedom even to see it, let alone acknowledge it and believe it, because they are quite convinced that what is false is true and what is true is false. That conviction is so powerful in them that it removes all freedom to think anything different, and is so strong that it holds their actual thought in bonds, in prison so to speak. This has been made clear to me from considerable experience among those in the next life who have become quite convinced of falsity by harbouring ideas that serve to prove to it. They are the kind of people who do not entertain any truths at all but turn or drive these away, doing so with a degree of ruthlessness which matches the intensity of their conviction. This is primarily so when such falsity is the product of evil, that is, when evil causes them to be convinced of it. These are the ones who are meant in the Lord's parable in Matthew,

Other seeds fell on the hard path, and the birds came and devoured them. Matt.13:4.

'Seeds' means Divine truths, 'hard rock' conviction, and 'birds' false assumptions.

2 People like these are not even aware that they are in bonds or in prison, for they are full of affection for their falsity, loving it because of the evil which produces it. This leads them to think that they are in freedom, since everything they have an affection for or love seems to make them feel free. But those who have not really subscribed to falsity, that is, who have not become convinced of it, entertain truths easily. They see them, choose them, and are full of affection for them, after which they look down on falsities so to speak, and then see how those convinced of falsity have come to be in bonds. Having such freedom they are able in their contemplation and thought to roam so to speak through the whole of heaven in search of countless truths. But nobody can have this freedom except one who is governed by good; for it is by virtue of good that he is in heaven and by virtue of good that truths are seen there.

5097 'And Joseph came to them in the morning' means that which was revealed and made clear to the celestial of the spiritual. This is clear from the representation of 'Joseph' as the celestial of the spiritual, dealt with in 4286, 4592, 4963, and from the meaning of 'the morning' as a state of enlightenment, dealt with in 3458, so that what was revealed and made clear is meant. The reason 'the morning' has these meanings is that all the periods of a day, like all the seasons of a year, mean the various states that arise owing to variations of the light of heaven. Variations of the light of heaven are not like the daily and annual variations of light in the world; they are variations of intelligence and love. For the light of heaven is nothing else than Divine Intelligence flowing from the Lord, which also shines before the eyes as light, while the warmth accompanying that light is the Lord's Divine Love, which is also felt as a radiated warmth. It is that light which provides a person with understanding, and that warmth which provides him with both vital heat and a will desiring what is good. In heaven morning is a state of enlightenment, of enlightenment in matters involving goodness and truth; and this state arises when there is an acknowledgement, more so when there is a perception that good is indeed good and truth is indeed truth. Perception is a revelation that takes place internally, and therefore 'the morning' means something that has been revealed. And because that which has previously been obscure is now made clear, 'the morning' as a consequence also means that which has been made clear.

In addition to this, 'morning' in the highest sense means the Lord Himself, for the reason that the Lord is the sun from which all light in heaven flows; He is always a rising sun and so is always a morning one. He is rising always on everyone who receives truth that is the truth of faith and good that is the good of love; but He is setting on everyone who does not receive these. Not that the sun there ever sets, for as has been stated, it is always a rising one, but that anyone who does not receive that truth or good causes it so to speak to set on himself. This may be compared in some measure to the changes which the sun of the world undergoes so far as the inhabitants on earth are concerned. Here too the sun does not really set since it remains all the time in its own fixed position, from where it is constantly shedding light. Yet it does seem to set because the earth spins daily on its axis, and as it goes round it takes its inhabitants out of sight of the sun, see the first example given in 5084. Thus the sun does not actually go down but anyone inhabiting the earth is removed from its light. This comparison is used to illustrate a particular point; but the phenomenon referred to is in itself instructive because every detail of the natural creation is representative of the Lord's kingdom. The instruction held within that phenomenon is that a loss of the light of heaven, that is, of intelligence and wisdom, does not come about because the Lord, the Sun of intelligence and wisdom, sets on anyone. It comes about because the inhabitant of His kingdom takes himself away, that is, he allows hell to be his leader and so take him away.

5098   'And he saw them' means perception. This is clear from the meaning of 'seeing' as understanding and perceiving, dealt with in 2150, 3764, 4567, 4723.

5099   'And behold, they were troubled' means that they were passing through a sad state. This is clear without explanation.

5100 'And he asked Pharaoh's courtier-ministers' means those sensory powers. This is clear from the meaning of 'Pharaoh's courtier-ministers' as both kinds of sensory powers, namely those subordinate to the understanding part and those subordinate to the will part, dealt with above in 5081.

5101 'Who were with him in the custody of his lord's [house]' means which had been cast aside. This is clear from the meaning of 'being put into custody', and so being in custody, as a state when one has been cast aside, also dealt with above, in 5083.

5102 'Saying, Why are your faces sad today?' means, What affection gives rise to this sadness? This is clear from the meaning of 'faces' as the things that are within, dealt with in 358, 1999, 2434, 3527, 4066, 4796, 4797, and so as the affections, for a person's interiors from which his thoughts spring – which are also things that are within – are his affections; and being aspects of his love, these affections are essentially his life. It is well known that the affections reveal themselves in the faces of those who are in a state of innocence; and when those affections reveal themselves, so too does a general impression of their thoughts, for people's thoughts are the forms their affections take. Regarded in itself therefore the face is nothing else than an image representing the things that are within.

2   No face is looked at by the angels in any other way, for angels do not see the material but the spiritual form that a person's face takes; that is, they see the form presented by his affections and the thoughts springing from those affections. These are the essential components of the human face, as anyone may recognize from the fact that when bereft of thought and affections the face is completely dead, and that the face is enlivened by them and owes its pleasing looks to them. The sadness expressing some affection, or an affection which gives rise to sadness, is meant by Joseph's words, Why are your faces sad today?

5103 'And they said to him' means perception regarding these matters. This is clear from the meaning of 'saying' in the historical narratives of the Word as perception, often dealt with already.

5104 'We have dreamed a dream' means a foretelling. This is clear from the meaning of 'a dream' as foresight and a consequent foretelling, dealt with above in 5091.

5105 'And there is no interpreter for it' means that no one knows what they hold within them. This is clear from the meaning of 'the interpretation' as the explanation of what something holds within it, dealt with above in 5093, and so of what those dreams held within them.

5106 'And Joseph said to them' means the celestial of the natural. This is clear from the representation of 'Joseph' as the celestial of the natural, dealt with above in 5086.

5107 'Do not interpretations belong to God?' means that the Divine is within them. This is clear from the meaning of 'the interpretation', when used in reference to dreams, as that which these hold within them, as just above in 5105 – that which is Divine being meant by 'God'.

5108 'Tell it to me, I beg you' means that it might be known. This is clear from the meaning of 'tell me, I beg you' as an expression implying a plea that it might be made known – as is also evident from what follows.

5109 Verses 9–13 **And the chief of the cupbearers told his dream to Joseph, and said to him, In my dream, and behold, a vine before me. And on the vine three shoots, and it was as though budding; its blossom came up, and its clusters ripened into grapes. And Pharaoh's cup was in my hand, and I took the grapes and pressed them into Pharaoh's cup, and put the cup onto Pharaoh's palm. And Joseph said to him, This is the interpretation of it: The three shoots are three days. In yet three days Pharaoh will lift up your head and will restore you to your position, and you will put Pharaoh's cup into his hand, according to the former manner when you were his cupbearer.**

'And the chief of the cupbearers told his dream to Joseph' means that the celestial of the spiritual discerned what the outcome would be for the sensory impressions subject to the understanding part of the mind, which until then had been cast aside. 'And said to him' means revelation resulting from perception. 'In my dream' means a foretelling. 'And behold, a vine before me' means the understanding part. 'And on the vine three shoots' means derivatives from this even to the final one. 'And it was as though budding' means an influx that allows rebirth to be effected. 'Its blossom came up' means the state next to regeneration. 'And its clusters ripened into grapes' means spiritual truth when joined to celestial good. 'And Pharaoh's cup was in my hand' means an influx of the interior natural into the exterior natural, and the beginning of reception. 'And I took the grapes and pressed them into Pharaoh's cup' means a reciprocal influx into good deeds that have a spiritual origin. 'And put the cup onto Pharaoh's palm' means that the interior natural made these its own. 'And Joseph said to him, This is the interpretation of it' means revelation resulting from perception received from the celestial within the natural as to what it held within it. 'The three shoots are three days' means continuous derivatives even to the final one. 'In yet three days' means that at that point a new state is arrived at. 'Pharaoh will lift up your head' means that which has been provided and therefore decided. 'And will restore you to your position' means that the impressions received through the senses subject to the under-standing part were restored to order, to occupy the lowest position. 'And you will put Pharaoh's cup into his hand' means in order that they might consequently serve the interior natural. 'According to the former manner' means in keeping with the law of order. 'When you were his cupbearer' means as is the normal position for sensory impressions of this kind.

5110 'And the chief of the cupbearers told his dream to Joseph' means that the celestial of the spiritual discerned what the outcome would be for the sensory impressions subject to the understanding part of the mind, which until then were cast aside. This is clear from the representation of 'Joseph' as the celestial of the spiritual, dealt with in 4286, 4585, 4592, 4594, 4963; from the meaning of 'a dream' as foresight and consequently the outcome, dealt with above in 5091, 5092, 5104, and so as foresight or discernment of the outcome; and from the meaning of 'the chief of the cupbearers' as the powers of the senses in general that are subject to the understanding part, dealt with in 5077, 5082, a casting aside being meant by being in custody, 5083, 5101. All this shows that the internal sense of the words used here is as has been stated, in addition to which it is clear from what follows below that 'Joseph', representing the celestial of the spiritual, discerned what the outcome would be.

2 When the expression 'the celestial of the spiritual' is used, the Lord is meant by it. But it may also be used to refer to an abstract quality in Him, for He is the Celestial itself and the Spiritual itself, that is, He is Good itself and Truth itself. No one, it is true, can have any conception of an abstract quality separate from an actual person because what is natural enters into every individual idea present in his thought. But even so, if one holds in mind the idea that everything within the Lord is Divine and that the Divine transcends one's entire thought, altogether transcending even what angels can comprehend; and if as a consequence one removes from one's mind everything comprehensible, one is left with the idea of pure Being (*Esse*) and the Manifestation (*Existere*) of that Being. That is to say, one then has an idea of the Celestial itself and the Spiritual itself, which are Good itself and Truth itself.

3 However, the human being is such that he cannot form in his mind any idea at all of abstract realities unless he associates with them some natural imagery that has come to him from the world through his senses; for without any such imagery his thought becomes lost so to speak in an abyss and is dissipated. Therefore to prevent the idea of the Divine becoming lost in the case of a person immersed in bodily and worldly interests, and to prevent the defilement of this idea, and at the same time of everything celestial or spiritual from the Divine, by foul thoughts in the case of anyone with whom it remained, Jehovah has been pleased to make Himself known as He exists essentially and as He manifests Himself in heaven, namely as a Divine Man. For the whole of heaven combines together and presents itself in the human form, as may be seen from what has been shown at the ends of chapters dealing with the correspondence of all parts of the human being with the Grand Man, which is heaven. This Divine, that is, Jehovah's manifestation of Himself in heaven, is the Lord from eternity. It is also the appearance

assumed by the Lord when He glorified, that is, made Divine, the Human within Him, as is also quite evident from the form in which He appeared before Peter, James, and John at His transfiguration, Matt. 17:1,2, and in which He appeared on a number of occasions to prophets. All this being so, anyone can think of the Divine itself as Man, and at the same time of the Lord in whom the entire Divine and perfect Trinity dwell; for within the Lord the Divine itself is the Father, the Divine that manifests itself in heaven is the Son, and the Divine proceeding from these is the Holy Spirit – from which it is clear that these three are one, as He Himself teaches.

5111   'And said to him' means revelation resulting from perception. This is clear from the meaning of 'saying' in the historical narratives of the Word as perception, dealt with in 1791, 1815, 1819, 1822, 1898, 1919, 2080, 2619, 2862, 3395, 3509, and so as revelation too, since revelation is internal perception and is the result of that perception.

5112   'In my dream' means a foretelling. This is clear from the meaning of 'a dream' as foresight, and from this a foretelling, dealt with above in 5091, 5092, 5104.

5113   'And behold, a vine before me' means the understanding part. This is clear from the meaning of 'a vine' as the understanding part of the mind as it exists in the spiritual Church, dealt with below. Because 'the cupbearer' means the sensory powers that are subject to the understanding part, and because the subject here is the flow of the understanding into the sensory powers subordinate to it, there appeared in the dream therefore a vine with shoots, blossom, clusters, and grapes, which are used to describe its flow into those powers and the rebirth of them. With regard to the understanding part as it exists in the spiritual Church, it should be recognized that when that Church is the subject in the Word, its understanding is in many instances dealt with too, for the reason that it is the understanding part which is regenerated and made the Church in the case of one belonging to that Church.

There are in general two Churches – the celestial and the spiritual. The celestial Church exists with the person in whom the will part of the mind can be regenerated or made the Church, whereas the spiritual Church exists with one in whom, as stated, solely the understanding part can be regenerated. The Most Ancient Church before the Flood was a celestial one because there existed with those who belonged to it some degree of wholeness in the will part, whereas the Ancient Church after the Flood was a spiritual one because among those who belonged to it no degree of wholeness existed in the will part, only in the understanding part. This explains why, when the spiritual Church is dealt with in the Word, its understanding is dealt with in many instances too. Regarding these Churches, see 640, 641, 765, 863, 875, 895, 927, 928, 1023, 1043, 1044, 1555, 2124, 2256, 2669, 4328, 4493. As regards its being the understanding part that is regenerated in the case of those who belong to the spiritual Church, this may also be recognized from the fact that the member of that Church does not have any good from which he may perceive truth, as those who belonged to the celestial Church had. Rather, he must first learn the truth of faith and absorb it into his understanding, and so come to recognize with the aid of truth what good is. Once truth enables him to recognize what good is, he can think about it, then desire it, and at length put it into practice, in which case he now has a new will formed by the Lord in the understanding part of his mind. The Lord then uses this to raise the spiritual man up to heaven, though evil still remains in the will that is properly his own, which at this point is miraculously set aside. This is accomplished by a higher power which withholds him from evil and maintains him in good.

3 In the case of the member of the celestial Church however the will part was regenerated. From earliest childhood he was absorbing the good of charity, and once he could see with perception what that good was, he was led on to perceive what love to the Lord was. Consequently all the truths of faith were seen by him in his understanding as if in a mirror. His understanding and will formed one complete mind; for those truths enabled him to perceive in his understanding that which existed as a desire in his will. This is what the wholeness of that first human being consisted in, by whom the celestial Church is meant.

4 As regards 'the vine' meaning the understanding part in the case of the spiritual Church, this is clear from many other places in the Word, as in Jeremiah,

What have you to do with the way to Egypt, to drink the waters of Shihor? Or what have you to do with the way to Assyria, to drink the waters of the River? Yet I have *planted you as a wholly choice vine*, a seed of truth. How therefore have you *turned* from Me *into the degenerate branches of a strange vine*? Jer.2:18,21.

This refers to Israel, which means the spiritual Church, 3654, 4286. 'Egypt' and 'the waters of Shihor' stand for factual knowledge which leads to perversion, 1164, 1165, 1186, 1462; 'Assyria' and 'the waters of the River' stand for reasoning based on this, that is, on factual knowledge, against the good of life and the truth of faith, 119, 1186. 'A choice vine' stands for the member of the spiritual Church, who is called 'a vine' because of his understanding, while 'the degenerate branches of a strange vine' stands for someone belonging to the perverted Church.

5 In Ezekiel,

A riddle and a parable about the house of Israel. A great eagle took some of the seed of the land and planted it in a seed field. It sprouted and became *a spreading vine*, low in height, so that *its branches* turned towards him and its roots were under him. So it became *a vine* which brought forth *branches* and sent out *shoots* towards the eagle. *This vine* directed its roots and sent *its branches* towards him in a good field by many waters. It was planted to produce a branch, that it might be *a magnificent vine*. Ezek.17:2,3,5–8.

'An eagle' stands for rational thought, 3901, 'the seed of the land' for truth known to the Church, 1025, 1447, 1610, 1940, 2848, 3038, 3310, 3373. Its becoming 'a spreading vine' and 'a magnificent vine' stands for becoming a spiritual Church, which is called 'a vine' because wine is obtained from it – 'wine' meaning spiritual good or the good of charity, the source of the truth of faith implanted in the understanding part. In the same prophet,

Your mother was like *a vine* in your likeness, planted beside the waters, fruitful, and made full of branches by reason of many waters. Consequently it had strong rods as sceptres for those who had dominion, and its stature rose up among entangled boughs, so that it was seen in its height amid the multitude of its branches.   Ezek.19:10,11.

This too refers to Israel, by whom the spiritual Church is meant, which Church is compared to 'a vine' for a similar reason to that mentioned immediately above. It is a description of its derivatives even to the final ones in the natural man, that is to say, even to factual knowledge based on sensory impressions, meant by 'entangled boughs', 2831. In Hosea,

I will be as the dew of *Israel*. His branches will go out, and his beauty will be like the olive's, and his odour like that of Lebanon. Those dwelling in its shadow will turn back, they will quicken the grain and will blossom as *the vine*; the memory of it will be as *the wine of Lebanon*. O Ephraim, what have I to do any more with idols?   Hosea 14:5–8.

'Israel' stands for the spiritual Church, the blossoming of which is compared to 'the vine', and the memory of it to 'the wine of Lebanon', because of the good of faith when that good has been implanted in the understanding part. 'Ephraim' means the understanding part as it exists in the spiritual Church, 3969. In Zechariah,

The remnant of the people will be the seed of peace; *the vine will give its fruit*, and the land will give its increase, and the heavens will give their dew. Zech.8:11,12.

'The remnant of the people' stands for truths stored away by the Lord within the interior man, 468, 530, 560, 561, 660, 798, 1050, 1738, 1906, 2284. 'The seed of peace' stands for good there, 'the vine' for the understanding part. In Malachi,

I will rebuke the devourer for you, so that he does not ruin for you the fruit of the land, *nor will the vine in the field fail you*.   Mal.3:11,12.

'The vine' stands for the understanding part. The expression 'a vine that does not fail' is used when the understanding part is not left bereft of the truths and goods of faith; on the other hand 'an empty vine' is used when falsities exist there together with derivative evils, as in Hosea,

Israel is an empty vine, it bears fruit like itself.   Hosea 10:1.

10 In Moses,

> He will bind his ass's colt *to the vine,* and the foal of his she-ass *to a choice vine* after he has washed his clothing *in wine,* and his garment in *the blood of grapes* Gen.49:11.

This is the prophecy of Jacob, who by then was Israel, regarding his twelve sons, in this case regarding 'Judah', who represents the Lord 3881. 'The vine' here stands for the understanding part as it exists in the spiritual Church, and 'a choice vine' for the understanding part as it exists in the celestial Church.

11 In David,

> O Jehovah, You caused *a vine* to journey *out of Egypt.* You cast out the nations, and You planted *it.* You cleared the way in front of *it* and caused *its* roots to be rooted, so that it might fill the land. The mountains were covered with the shadow of *it,* and the cedars of God with its branches. You sent out *its shoots* even to the sea, and its *little branches* to the Euphrates. The boar out of the forest tramples on *it,* and the wild animal of the fields feeds on *it.* Ps.80:8–11,13.

'A vine out of Egypt' stands in the highest sense for the Lord, the glorification of His Human being described by it and its shoots. In the internal sense 'a vine' here means the spiritual Church and the member of that Church – what he is like when the understanding and will parts of him have been made new or regenerated by the Lord. 'The boar in the forest' means falsity, and 'the wild animal of the fields' evil, which destroy the Church and faith in the Lord.

12 In John,

> The angel sent his sickle into the earth and *harvested the vine of the earth,* and cast it into the great winepress of the wrath of God. The winepress was trodden outside the city, and the blood went out of the winepress up to the horses' bridles. Rev.14:19,20.

'Harvesting the vine of the earth' stands for destroying the understanding part in the Church. And since 'the vine' means that understanding part it is also said that 'the blood went out of the winepress up to the horses' bridles'; for the powers of understanding are meant by 'horses', 2761, 2762, 3217. In Isaiah,

> It will happen on that day, that every place in which *there have been a thousand vines,* worth a thousand [shekels] of silver, will be briers and brambles. Isa.7:23.

In the same prophet,

> The inhabitants of the land will be scorched and hardly any men (*homo*) left. The new wine will mourn, and *the vine will languish.* Isa.24:6,7.

In the same prophet,

> They beat themselves on their breasts for the fields of *unmixed wine,* for *the fruitful vine;* for over the land of My people the thorn, the prickle is coming up. Isa.32:12–14.

In these places the subject is the spiritual Church when laid waste as regards the good and truth of faith, and so as regards the understanding part, since, as stated above, the truth and the good of faith exist in the understanding part of the mind of the member of that Church. Anyone may see that in these places 'the vine' is not used to mean the vine, nor 'the land' to mean the land, but some feature of the Church.

In the genuine sense 'the vine' means good present in the understanding part, and 'the fig' good present in the natural part; or what amounts to the same, 'the vine' means good present in the interior man, and 'the fig' good present in the exterior man. This being so, when the vine is mentioned in the Word, so also on many occasions is the fig, as in the following places: In Jeremiah,

I will completely devour them. There will be *no grapes on the vine or figs on the fig tree*; and its leaf has come down.   Jer.8:13.

In the same prophet,

I will bring upon you a nation from afar, O house of Israel, which will devour *your vine* and *your fig tree*.   Jer.5:17.

In Hosea,

I will lay waste *her vine* and *her fig tree*.   Hosea 2:12.

In Joel,

A nation has come up over the land. It has turned *My vine* into a waste, and *My fig tree* into froth. It has stripped *it* completely bare and cast *it* aside; *its branches* have been made white. *The vine* has withered and *the fig tree* languishes. Joel 1:6,7,12.

In the same prophet,

Fear not, you beasts of My fields, for the dwelling-places of the wilderness have been made green; for the tree will bear its fruit, and *the fig tree* and *the vine* will give their full yield.   Joel 2:22,23.

In David,

He smote *their vines* and *their fig trees*, and broke to pieces the trees of their borders.   Ps.105:33.

In Habakkuk,

The fig tree will not blossom; neither will there be any yield *on the vines*. Hab.3:17.

In Micah,

Out of Zion will go forth teaching, and the Word of Jehovah from Jerusalem. They will sit every one *under his vine* and *under his fig tree*, unafraid. Micah 4:2,4.

In Zechariah,

On that day you will shout, each to his companion, *under his vine* and *under his fig tree*.   Zech.3:10.

In the first Book of Kings,

In Solomon's time there was peace from all the border-crossings round about, and Judah and Israel dwelt with confidence, *every one under his vine* and *under his fig tree*.   1 Kings 4:24,25.

'The fig tree' means the good of the natural or exterior man, see 217.

14 'The vine' may also mean an understanding part that has been made new or regenerated by means of good obtained from truth and of truth obtained from good. This is clear from the Lord's words addressed to the disciples after He instituted the Holy Supper, in Matthew,

> I tell you that I shall not drink from now on *of this fruit of the vine* until that day when I drink it new with you in My Father's kingdom.   Matt.26:29.

The good obtained from truth and the truth obtained from good, by means of which the understanding is made new, that is, by which a person is made spiritual, is meant by 'the fruit of the vine', while making such one's own is meant by 'drinking'. For 'drinking' means making one's own, and is used in reference to truth, see 3168. The fact that this is fully accomplished only in the next life is meant by 'until that day when I drink it new with you in My Father's kingdom'; for 'the fruit of the vine', it is quite plain, is not used to mean new wine or matured wine but something of a heavenly nature belonging to the Lord's kingdom.

15 Because the understanding part of the spiritual man's mind is made new and regenerated by means of truth which comes solely from the Lord, the Lord therefore compares Himself to 'the vine'. He then compares those who are secure in the truth which comes from Him and consequently is His to 'the branches', and the good produced by them to 'the fruit', in John,

> I am the true vine, and My Father is the vinedresser. Every branch in Me that does not bear fruit He takes away, but every one that does bear fruit He prunes, that it may bear more fruit. Abide in Me, and I in you. As the branch cannot bear fruit by itself unless it abides in the vine, neither can you unless you abide in Me. I am the vine, you are the branches. He who abides in Me, and I in him, he it is that bears much fruit; for apart from Me you cannot do anything. This is My commandment, that you love one another as I have loved you.   John 15:1–5,12.

16 Because in the highest sense 'the vine' means the Lord as regards Divine Truth, and from this it means, in the internal sense, a member of the spiritual Church, 'a vineyard' therefore means the spiritual Church itself, 1069, 3220.

17 Since 'the Nazirite' represented the celestial man – who is regenerated by means of the good of love and not, like the spiritual man, by means of the truth of faith, so that, as may be seen stated above, it is not in the understanding part but in the will part of the celestial man's mind that the regeneration takes place – the Nazirite was therefore forbidden *to eat anything that came from the vine* and so was forbidden *to drink wine*, Num.6:3,4; Judg.13:14. From this also it is evident that 'the vine', as has been shown, means the understanding part, which belongs to the spiritual man. For details about 'the Nazirite' representing the celestial man, see 3301. From this one may also see that nobody can possibly know why the Nazirite was forbidden anything that came from the vine, and many other things besides, unless he knows what 'the vine' means in the proper sense, and also unless he knows of the existence of

a celestial Church and of a spiritual Church, and that the member of the celestial Church is regenerated in a different way from a member of the spiritual Church. The former is regenerated by means of seed implanted in the will part, the latter by seed implanted in the understanding part. These are the kinds of arcana stored away in the internal sense of the Word.

5114   'And on the vine three shoots' means derivatives from this even to the final one. This is clear from the meaning of 'the vine' as the understanding part, dealt with immediately above in 5113; from the meaning of 'three' as complete and continuous even to the end, dealt with in 2788, 4495; and from the meaning of 'shoots' as derivatives; for since 'the vine' means the understanding part, 'shoots' means nothing else than derivatives from this. Because 'three' means that which is continuous even to the end, that is, which goes from first to last, 'three shoots' means derivative degrees extending from the understanding part to the final level, which is that of the senses. The first in the sequence is the actual understanding part, and the last is the senses. In general the understanding part is the sight which the internal man possesses and which sees by the light of heaven radiating from the Lord; and everything it sees is spiritual or celestial. But the senses, in general, belong to the external man; and here the sensory power of sight is meant because this corresponds to and is subordinate to the understanding part. The sensory power of sight sees by the light of the world radiating from the sun; and everything it sees is worldly, bodily, or earthly.

In the human being there exist derivatives from the understanding part that dwells in the light of heaven; and they extend to the senses which dwell in the light of the world. Unless these derivatives existed the senses could not possess any life of a human quality. A person does not owe the life which his senses possess to what he sees by the light of the world, for the light of the world holds no life within it; he owes it to what he sees by the light of heaven, for this light does hold life within it. When the light of heaven falls on the perceptions a person has gained by the light of the world, it brings life to them and enables him to see objects in an intelligent manner, and thus as a human being. In this way a person possessing factual knowledge born from things which he has seen and heard in the world, and therefore from those which have entered in through the senses, comes to possess intelligence and wisdom, on which in turn he bases his public, private, and spiritual life.

As regards derivatives specifically, the nature of their existence in a person is such that no brief explanation of them is possible. They exist as degrees, like steps, from the understanding part down to the senses. But no one can have any conception of those degrees unless he knows how they are related to one another, that is to say, that they are quite distinct and separate from one another, so distinct that interior degrees can come into being and remain in being without exterior ones, but no exterior degrees without interior ones. For example, a person's spirit can remain in being without a material body, as it also actually does when death separates it from the body. For a person's spirit exists in an interior degree, his body in an exterior one. Similarly with a person's spirit after death. If he is one of the blessed his spirit exists in a final and outermost degree when in the first heaven; in a more interior degree when in the second; and in the inmost one when in the third. When it exists in the inmost it exists at the same time in the other degrees, though these are inactive with him, almost as the human body is inactive during sleep, but with this difference that interiorly angels are at such times fully awake. Therefore as many distinct and separate degrees exist in the human being as there are heavens, apart from the final one, which is the body and the bodily senses.

4 From all this regarding a person's spirit one may gain some idea of the way derivatives are related to one another from the first to the final one, that is, from the understanding part to the senses. A person's life, which he receives from the Lord's Divine, passes through these degrees from the inmost to the final one. At every degree there exists a derivative of that life which becomes increasingly general, until in the final degree it is the most general. Derivatives in the lower degrees are merely combinations – or to put it more appropriately, structured forms – of the individual and particular constituents of the higher degrees ranged consecutively, with the addition of the kinds of things drawn from purer nature, and after that from grosser nature, that can serve as containing vessels. Once these vessels are done away with, the individual and particular constituents of the higher degrees, which had received form in those vessels, move back to the degree immediately above. And because in the case of the human being there is a link with the Divine, and his inmost being is such that it can accept the Divine – and not only accept but also make Him its own, by acknowledging and having an affection for the Divine, thus by a reciprocal response to Him – and because he thereby has the Divine implanted within him, he can never die. Indeed what is eternal and infinite exists with him, not only through their flowing into him but also through his reception of them.

5 From this one may see how uninformed and senseless in their thinking regarding the human being those people are who compare him to animals and imagine that he will not be alive after death any more than they are. Such people do not take into consideration the fact that with animals there is no acceptance of the Divine or any acknowledgement or affection leading to a reciprocal response to the Divine by making Him their own, or any consequent joining to Him. Nor do those people take into consideration the fact that, as the animal state is like this, the recipient forms of life which these possess are inevitably dissipated; for with animals that which flows into them passes through their organic forms into the world, where it comes to an end and melts away, never to make any return there.

5115   'And it was as though budding' means an influx that allows rebirth to be effected. This is clear from the meaning of 'budding' – that is, bringing forth leaves, and also blossom later on – as the first stage of rebirth. The reason an influx is meant is that when a person is being born again spiritual life flows into him, even as a tree, when it starts to bud, is receiving its life through heat from the sun. The birth of a human being is compared in various places in the Word to members of the vegetable kingdom, especially trees. The reason for this comparison is that the entire vegetable kingdom, like the animal kingdom also, represents the kind of things that exist with the human being, and consequently the kind of things that exist in the Lord's kingdom. For the human being is heaven in its least form, as may be seen from what has been shown at the ends of chapters regarding correspondence of the human being with the Grand Man, which is heaven. This also explains why the ancients referred to man as the microcosm; and if more had been known about the heavenly state they would have called him a miniature heaven too. For the whole natural system is a theatre representative of the Lord's kingdom, see 2758, 3483, 4939.

But in particular it is a person who is being born anew, that is, being regenerated by the Lord, who is called heaven; for during that time Divine good and truth from the Lord, and consequently heaven, are implanted in him. Indeed, like a tree, a person who is being born again begins from a seed, which is why in the Word 'seed' means truth obtained from good. Also, like a tree, he brings forth leaves, then blossom, and finally fruit; for he brings forth the kind of things that belong to intelligence, which again in the Word are meant by 'leaves', then the kind of things that belong to wisdom, which are meant by 'blossoms', and finally the kind of things that are matters of life, namely forms of the good of love and charity expressed in action, which in the Word are meant by 'fruits'. Such is the representative likeness that exists between a fruitful tree and a person who is being regenerated, a likeness so great that one may learn from a tree about regeneration, provided that something is known first of all about spiritual good and truth. From this one may see that 'the vine' in the cupbearer's dream serves to describe fully in a representative fashion the process by which a person is born again so far as the sensory power subject to the understanding part is concerned. That process is described first by the three shoots, then by the buds that were formed, after that by the blossom, followed by the ripening of the clusters into grapes, and finally by his pressing them into Pharaoh's cup and his giving this to him.

Furthermore the dreams which come from the Lord by way of heaven are never anything else than scenes based on representatives. Anyone therefore who does not know what this or that in the natural world represents, more so one who is totally unaware of anything at all being representative there, inevitably supposes that those representatives are merely comparisons such as anybody may use in ordinary conversation. They are indeed comparisons; but they are the kind which are also correspondences and which therefore present themselves as visible objects in the world of spirits while the angels positioned more internally in heaven are talking about spiritual or celestial things belonging to the Lord's kingdom. Regarding dreams, see 1122, 1975, 1977, 1979–1981.

5116 'Its blossom came up' means the state next to regeneration. This is clear from the meaning of 'the blossom' which appears on the tree before the fruit as the state before regeneration. The budding and fruiting of a tree represents, as stated immediately above in 5115, the person's rebirth. Becoming covered with leaves represents the first state, with blossom the second, that is, the one immediately before regeneration, and fruiting the third, which is the actual state of one who has been regenerated. Consequently 'leaves' means the things that belong to intelligence, which are the truths of faith, 885, for these come first in a person's rebirth or regeneration. By 'blossoms' however are meant the things that belong to wisdom, which are the goods of faith, since these come immediately before rebirth or regeneration, while 'fruits' means the things that are matters of life, which are the works of charity, in that these come after rebirth and constitute the actual state of one who is regenerate.

2 These features of the vegetable kingdom owe their existence to the influx of the spiritual world into it; but people who attribute everything to natural forces and nothing to the Divine are in no way able to believe this. Those however who attribute everything to the Divine and nothing to natural forces have the ability to see that every single thing owes its existence to that influx. Not only that, each individual thing also has a corrrespondence, and because it has a correspondence it is a representative. In the end such people have the ability to see that the whole natural system is a theatre representative of the Lord's kingdom, thus that the Divine exists within each individual thing, so much so that the whole natural system is a representation of that which is eternal and infinite – eternal because the reproduction of species continues without end, infinite because the multiplication of seeds is unlimited. Such endeavours to reproduce and multiply could not possibly come to exist in each individual thing in the vegetable kingdom if the Divine were not flowing into it unceasingly. This influx is what provides the impulse to reproduce and to multiply; the impulse brings the power to make this a reality, and that power leads to the actual realization of it.

3 People who attribute everything to natural forces say that such impulses to reproduce and to multiply were introduced into fruits and seeds when things were first created, and because of the power which they have received from those impulses fruits and seeds ever since then are carried spontaneously into such activities. But those people do not take into consideration the fact that continuance in being is constant coming into being, or what is much the same, that reproduction is creation

taking place constantly. Nor do they take into consideration the fact that an effect is the continuation of its cause, and that when a cause ceases to exist so does the effect, and consequently that without constant influx from its cause every effect perishes in an instant. Neither do they take into consideration the fact that anything that is not linked to the first being of all, consequently to the Divine, instantly ceases to have any existence; for to have any being, what is posterior must have what is prior existing unceasingly within it.

If those attributing everything to natural forces and little, scarcely anything, to the Divine were to take these facts into consideration they would also be able to acknowledge that every single thing in the natural system represents something akin to it in the spiritual world, and therefore something akin to it in the Lord's kingdom, where the closest representation of the Lord's Divine exists. This is why reference has been made to an influx coming from the spiritual world; but by this is meant an influx from the Lord's Divine coming by way of the spiritual world. The reason adherents to naturalism do not take such facts into consideration is that they are not willing to acknowledge them, since they are immersed in earthly and bodily interests and as a consequence in the life belonging to self-love and love of the world. As a result, so far as things belonging to the spiritual world, that is, to heaven are concerned, the complete reverse of true order exists with them; and to view such matters from within a state in which order is turned around is not possible, since higher things are then seen as lower ones, and lower things as higher ones. This also accounts for the fact that, when persons like these are seen in the next life in the light of heaven, they are seen with their heads pointing downwards and their feet upwards.

Who among these, when he sees blossom on a tree or on anything else that grows, thinks of it as an expression of gladness so to speak that fruit and seeds are now being brought forth? All that such persons see is that blossom comes first and remains until rudimentary forms of the fruit and seeds are formed within it, whereby sap is conveyed into them. If they knew anything about human rebirth or regeneration, or rather if they wanted to know, they would also see in that blossom, because of the similarity there, a representative of a person's state before regeneration. They would see that because of the good which his intelligence and wisdom desires he is in a similar way blooming, that is, he possesses an inner gladness and beauty, because now he is endeavouring to implant these – that is to say, forms of good desired by intelligence and wisdom – in his life; that is, he is endeavouring to bear fruit. Such persons cannot know about the nature of this state because knowledge of what that inner gladness and inner beauty so represented are does not exist at all with people who feel no gladness other than that which accompanies love of the world and no delight other than that connected with self-love. Worldly or selfish feelings of gladness or delight cause inner ones to be seen as the opposite of gladness and delight, so much so that those persons loathe them. In loathing them they also brush them aside as something worthless or as something that has no actual existence. As a consequence they refuse to accept them, and at the same time they refuse to accept that what is spiritual or celestial is really anything at all. This is how the absurd thinking of the present day which is believed to be wisdom comes about.

5117 'And its clusters ripened into grapes' means spiritual truth when joined to celestial good. This is clear from the meaning of 'ripening' as the advancement of rebirth or regeneration even to the point where truth is joined to good, and so the two are joined together; and from the meaning of 'clusters' as the truth of spiritual good, and 'grapes' as the good of celestial truth; in this instance both of these as they exist within the sensory awareness represented by 'the cupbearer' is meant. The joining together of them within that sensory awareness may be likened to the ripening of clusters into grapes, for in rebirth or regeneration every truth aims to become joined to good. At first truth is unreceptive of life and is not therefore fruitful. This stage is represented in the fruits of trees while they are ripening. In unripe fruit, called 'clusters' here, that state when truth is still predominant is represented, whereas in ripe fruit, called 'grapes' here, the state when good has predominance is represented. This predominance of good is also represented in the flavour and the sweetness that one finds in ripe grapes. But regarding the joining together of truth and good within the sensory awareness subject to the understanding part, nothing more can be said as these are arcana too deep for anyone to understand. First of all one needs to have a thorough knowledge of the state of the celestial-spiritual and of sensory awareness, and also of the state of the natural in which that joining together of truth and good takes place.

2 'Grapes' means the good of the spiritual man, and so means charity. This may be seen from many places in the Word, as in Isaiah,

> My beloved had *a vineyard* on a very fertile hill[1]. He looked for it *to yield grapes*, but it yielded *wild grapes*. Isa.5:1,2,4.

'A vineyard' stands for the spiritual Church; 'he looked for it to yield grapes' for the good deeds of charity; 'but it yielded wild grapes' for the bad deeds of hatred and revenge.

3 In the same prophet,

> Thus said Jehovah, As *the new wine* is found *in the cluster*, and one says, Do not destroy it, for there is a blessing in it. Isa.65:8.

'The new wine in the cluster' stands for truth obtained from good within the natural.

4 In Jeremiah,

> I will surely gather them, says Jehovah; there will be *no grapes on the vine*, and no figs on the fig tree. Jer.8:13.

---

[1] *lit.* on a horn of a son of oil

'No grapes on the vine' stands for the non-existence of any interior or rational good, 'no figs on the fig tree' for the non-existence of any exterior or natural good; for 'the vine' means the understanding part, as shown just above in 5113. When truth and good exist joined together there, 'the vine' means the rational, for the rational exists as a result of that joining together. As regards 'the fig' meaning the good of the natural or exterior man, see 217.

In Hosea,

Like *grapes in the wilderness* I found Israel, like the firstfruit on the fig tree, in its beginning, I saw your fathers.   Hosea 9:10.

'Grapes in the wilderness' stands for rational good not yet made spiritual; 'the firstfruit on the fig tree' in a similar way for natural good. 'Israel' stands for the ancient spiritual Church when it first began, 'fathers' here and elsewhere being not the sons of Jacob but those people among whom the Ancient Church was first established.

In Micah,

There was no *cluster* to eat; my soul desired the firstfruit. The holy man has perished from the earth, and there is none upright among men.   Micah 7:1,2.

'Cluster to eat' stands for the good of charity in its first beginnings, 'the firstfruit' for the truth of faith at the same stage also.

In Amos,

Behold, the days are coming, so that the ploughman catches up with the reaper, and *the treader of grapes* with him who sows seed. The mountains will drip new wine, and all the hills will flow down with it. And I will bring again the captivity of My people, in order that they may build the devastated cities, and may settle down and *plant vineyards,* and *may drink their wine,* and *make gardens* and eat their fruit.   Amos 9:13,14.

This refers to the establishment of the spiritual Church, which is described in this manner. The joining of spiritual good to its truth is foretold by the statement that the ploughman will catch up with the reaper, and the joining of spiritual truth to its good by the statement that the treader of grapes will catch up with the one who sows seed. The good deeds of love and charity resulting from that joining together are meant by the statement that the mountains will drip new wine and the hills will flow down with it. 'Bringing again the captivity of the people' stands for deliverance from falsities, 'building the devastated cities' for the correction of falsified teachings regarding the truth, 'settling down and planting vineyards' for a development of what constitutes the spiritual Church, 'drinking their wine' for making the truths of that Church one's own, which truths teach about charity, and 'making gardens and eating their fruit' for making one's own the forms of good derived from these. Anyone can see that building cities, planting vineyards, drinking wine, making gardens and eating their fruit are descriptions of merely natural activities, which but for the spiritual sense would hold nothing Divine within them.

8 In Moses,

> He washes his clothing *in wine,* and his garment in *the blood of grapes.*
> Gen.49:11.

This refers to the Lord. 'Wine' stands for spiritual good originating in Divine love, 'the blood of grapes' for celestial good originating in the same.

9 In the same author,

> Butter from the herd, and milk from the flock, with the fat of lambs and of rams, the breed[1] of Bashan, and of goats, with kidney-fat of wheat; and of *the blood of the grape* you drink unmixed wine.   Deut.32:14.

This refers to the Ancient Church whose good deeds of love and charity are described in this manner. Each particular product referred to means some specific kind of good. 'The blood of the grape' means spiritual-celestial good, the expression used for the Divine in heaven, coming forth from the Lord. Wine is also called 'the blood' of grapes because wine and blood mean holy truth coming forth from the Lord, though 'wine' is used in reference to the spiritual Church and 'blood' to the celestial Church. For the same reason wine has also been prescribed in the Holy Supper.

10 In the same author,

> From the vine of Sodom comes their vine, and from the fields of Gomorrah; *its grapes are grapes of poison, they have clusters of bitterness.*   Deut.32:32.

This refers to the Jewish Church. 'From the vine of Sodom comes their vine, and from the fields of Gomorrah' stands for the fact that the understanding part is occupied by falsities that are the product of hellish love. 'Its grapes are grapes of poison, they have clusters of bitterness' stands for the fact that the will part is in the same predicament; for as 'the grape' in the good sense means charity, it is therefore used in reference to the will part, though to the will present within the understanding part. The same is true in the contrary sense, for all truth belongs essentially to the understanding, and all good essentially to the will.

11 In John,

> The angel said, Put in your sharp sickle and *gather the clusters of the earth,* for *its grapes have ripened.*   Rev.14:18

'Gathering the clusters of the earth' stands for destroying all existence of charity.

12 In Matthew,

> By their fruits you will know them. *Do people gather grapes from thorns,* and figs from thistles?   Matt.7:16.

And in Luke,

---

[1] *lit.* the sons

Every tree is known by its own fruit; for people do not collect figs from thorns, nor do they gather grapes from a bramble-bush.   Luke 6:44.

The subject here being charity towards the neighbour, it is said that they will be recognized 'by their fruits', which are the good deeds of charity. Internal good deeds of charity are meant by 'grapes', external ones by 'figs'.

The law was laid down in the Jewish Church,

When you enter your companion's vineyard you shall eat *grapes* at your pleasure until you have had enough[1]; but you shall not put them into your vessel. Deut.23:24.

This law implies that when anyone is among others whose teachings and religion are different from his own, he is free to learn about and welcome their charitable deeds, but he is not free to adopt the same charitable practices and link them into his own truths. 'A vineyard', meaning the Church, describes a place where teaching or religion exists; 'grapes' means the good deeds of charity, 'vessel' the truth that the Church possesses.

5118   'And Pharaoh's cup was in my hand' means an influx of the interior natural into the exterior natural, and the beginning of reception. This is clear from the representation of 'Pharaoh' as the interior natural, dealt with above in 5080, 5095; from the representation of 'the cupbearer' as the exterior natural, dealt with in 5077, 5082 – 'my hand' being the cupbearer's; from the meaning of 'cup' as that which contains, and also at the same time that which is contained in it, dealt with below in 5120. From these meanings and from the train of thought in the internal sense 'Pharaoh's cup was in my hand' means the influx of the interior natural into the exterior natural, and the beginning of reception there. What the interior natural and the exterior natural are has been stated already – the interior natural is that which communicates with the rational and into which the rational enters, while the exterior natural is that which communicates with the senses, that is, through the senses with the world, and so that which the world flows into.

As regards influx, this begins with the Lord and extends continuously through the rational into the interior natural and then through this into the exterior natural; but what flows through undergoes change and is converted according to the way it is received. With those who are not regenerate all good is converted there into evil, and all truth into falsity; but with those who are regenerate all good and truth presents itself there as in a mirror. For the natural is nothing else than a face so to speak that is representative of spiritual characteristics of the internal man; and the face becomes representative when exteriors correspond to interiors. From this one may gain some idea of what is meant by an

---

[1] *lit.* eat grapes in accordance with your soul, to your satisfaction

influx of the interior natural into the exterior natural, and the beginning of reception there.

5119 'And I took the grapes and pressed them into Pharaoh's cup' means a reciprocal influx into good deeds that have a spiritual origin. This is clear from the meaning of 'grapes' as the good deeds of charity, dealt with just above in 5117, and so as good deeds that have a spiritual origin, since every good deed of genuine charity originates there; and from the meaning of 'pressing into Pharaoh's cup' as a reciprocal influx. The expression 'reciprocal influx' does not mean that the exterior natural flows into the interior natural, for that is not possible. Exterior things cannot by any means flow into interior ones, or what amounts to the same, lower or posterior things into higher or prior ones. The reciprocal influx takes place when the rational calls forth things present in the interior natural, and also, by means of the interior natural, those present in the exterior natural. Not that it calls forth what actually exists there but what is deduced or so to speak extracted from what is there. This is what the reciprocal influx is.

2 It does seem as though things in the world pass by way of the senses into what is present within; but that is an illusion of the senses. The reality is that what exists within flows into what is outward, and that this influx is what enables discernment to take place. I have discussed these matters with spirits on several occasions and have been shown through actual experiences that the interior man sees and discerns within the exterior man what is taking place outside the exterior man, and that the life of the senses has no other origin; that is, neither the ability to perceive with the senses nor actual sensory perception has any other origin. But the nature and power of this illusion are such that it cannot by any means be banished from the natural man, nor even from the rational, unless the rational man can be made to stand aside from sensory impressions. All this has been mentioned to show what reciprocal influx is.

5120 'And put the cup onto Pharaoh's palm' means that the interior natural made these its own. This is clear from the meaning of 'putting the cup' to drink (and so the wine in the cup) as making one's own, for 'drinking' means making truth one's own, see 3168; and from the representation of 'Pharaoh' as the interior natural, dealt with in 5080, 5095, 5118. As is evident from what has gone before, the subject here is the regeneration of the sensory power meant by 'the cupbearer' which is subject to the understanding part of the interior man; consequently the subject is also the influx of truth and good and their reception in the exterior natural. But since these matters are quite beyond the understanding of those who do not have any distinct idea about the rational and about the natural, or any about influx, all further explanation is therefore abandoned.

2 But there is more to be said about 'a cup' mentioned very many times in

the Word – about how in the genuine sense it has the same meaning as wine, namely spiritual truth or the truth of faith which is derived from the good of charity, and about how in the contrary sense it means falsity which produces evil, and also falsity which is a product of evil. The reason 'a cup' has the same meaning as 'wine' is that the cup is the container and the wine the content and therefore the two constitute a single entity, with the result that one is used to mean the other. This meaning of 'a cup' in the Word is evident from the following places:
In David,

O Jehovah, You will spread a table before me in the presence of enemies and will make my head fat with oil; *my cup will overflow.* Ps.23:5.

'Spreading a table' and 'making the head fat with oil' stand for being endowed with the good of charity and love. 'My cup will overflow' stands for the fact that the natural will thereby be filled with spiritual truth and good. In the same author,

What shall I render to Jehovah? *I will take the cup of salvation* and call on the name of Jehovah. Ps.116:12,13.

'Taking the cup of salvation' stands for making the goods of faith one's own.
In Mark,

Whoever *gives you drink from a cup of water* in My name, because you are Christ's, truly I say to you, he will not lose his reward. Mark 9:41.

'Giving drink from a cup of water in My name' stands for imparting the truths of faith from a small measure of charity.
In Matthew,

Then *taking a cup*, and giving thanks, He gave it to them, saying, Drink from this, all of you; for this is My blood – that of the New Testament. Matt.26:27,28; Mark 14:23,24; Luke 22:20.

The word 'cup' is used, not wine, because 'wine' has reference to the spiritual Church but 'blood' to the celestial Church. Both wine and blood however mean holy truth going forth from the Lord, though in the spiritual Church the holiness of faith springing from charity towards the neighbour is meant, whereas in the celestial Church the holiness of charity springing from love to the Lord is meant. The spiritual Church differs from the celestial in that the spiritual is moved by charity towards the neighbour, whereas the celestial is moved by love to the Lord. Furthermore the Holy Supper was established to represent and be a sign of the Lord's love towards the whole human race and man's reciprocal love towards Him.
Because 'a cup' meant that which served to contain and 'wine' that which was contained, 'the cup' consequently meaning the external aspect of man and 'wine' the internal aspect of him, the Lord therefore said,

Woe to you Scribes and Pharisees, hypocrites! For you cleanse *the exterior of the cup* and of the plate but the interiors are full of pillage and lack of restraint. Blind Pharisee! cleanse first *the interior of the cup* and of the plate and the exterior will be made clean also.   Matt.23:25,26; Luke 11:39.

Here also 'cup' is used to mean in the internal sense the truth of faith. Cultivating the truth of faith without the good of faith is 'cleansing the exterior of the cup', the more so when the interiors are full of hypocrisy, deceit, hatred, revenge, and cruelty; for in this case the truth of faith exists solely in the external man and not at all in the internal, whereas cultivating and embracing the good of faith causes truths to be joined to good in the interior man. Furthermore when the truth of faith is cultivated without the good of faith, false ideas are accepted as truths; this is meant by 'cleansing first the interior of the cup, and the exterior will be made clean also'.

7   It is similar with matters recorded in Mark,

There are many other things which the Pharisees and Jews have received carefully, *the washing¹ of cups* and of pots, and of bronze vessels, and of beds. Forsaking the commandment of God you keep to human tradition, *the washing¹ of pots* and *of cups*; and many other similar things you do. You reject the commandment of God, so that you may keep to your tradition.   Mark 7:4,8,9.

8   As regards 'a cup' meaning in the contrary sense falsity which produces evil and also falsity produced by evil, this is clear from the following places: In Jeremiah,

Thus said Jehovah, the God of Israel, to me, *Take this cup of the wine of anger* from My hand, and make all the nations to which I send you *drink* it, in order that they may drink and stagger, and go mad because of the sword which I am going to send among them. So I took *the cup* from Jehovah's hand, and made all the nations drink to whom Jehovah sent me.   Jer.25:15–17,28.

'The cup of the wine of anger' stands for falsity that produces evil. The reason falsity producing evil is meant is that as wine can make people drunk and make them of unsound mind, so too can falsity. Spiritual drunkenness is nothing other than unsoundness of mind caused by reasonings regarding matters of belief when a person does not believe anything which he does not apprehend – which unsoundness of mind leads to falsities and to evils that are the product of falsities, 1072. Hence the statement 'in order that they may drink and stagger, and go mad because of the sword which I am going to send'. 'Sword' means falsity at war against truth, 2799, 4499.

9   In the Book of Lamentations,

Rejoice and be glad, O daughter of Edom, dweller in the land of Uz; *to you also the cup will pass*, you will be made drunk and uncovered.   Lam.4:21.

'Being made drunk by the cup' stands for being made unsound in mind by falsities. 'Being uncovered', or shamelessly laid bare, stands for resulting evil, 213, 214.

10   In Ezekiel,

---

¹ *lit.* baptisms *or* dippings

You have walked in the way of your sister, *therefore I will give her cup into your hand*. Thus said the Lord Jehovih, *You will drink your sister's cup*, which is deep and wide; you will be laughed at and mocked, as an ample recipient. You will be filled with drunkenness and sorrow, with *the cup* of devastation and desolation. You will drink *the cup of your sister* Samaria, and crush it and crumple the pieces. Ezek.23:31–34.

This refers to Jerusalem, by which the spiritual aspect of the celestial Church is meant. 'The cup' in this case stands for falsity that is a product of evil; and because such falsity lays waste or destroys the Church, the expression 'the cup of devastation and desolation' is used. In Isaiah,

Stir, stir, surge up, O Jerusalem, you who have drunk from the hand of Jehovah *the cup of His anger*; you have drunk the dregs of *the cup of consternation*. Isa.51:17.

In Habakkuk,

Drink, you also – that your foreskin may be revealed. *The cup of Jehovah's right hand* will come round to you, so that disgusting vomit may be upon your glory. Hab.2:16.

In David,

A cup is in the hand of Jehovah; and He has mixed the wine, filled it with the mixed, and poured out from it. But they will suck out the dregs of it; all the wicked of the earth will drink from it.   Ps.75:8.

In these places 'a cup' also stands for the insanity caused by falsities and resulting evils. It is called 'the cup of Jehovah's anger' and also 'of His right hand' for the reason that the Jewish nation believed, as the common people believe, that evils, and the punishments of evils and falsities, had no other origin than Jehovah, though in fact they originate in man and in the hellish crew who are present with him. From the appearance, and from a belief based on it, such statements occur many times; but the internal sense teaches how one ought to understand them and what to believe. On these matters, see 245, 592, 696, 1093, 1683, 1874, 1875, 2335, 2447, 3605, 3607, 3614.

2 Since 'a cup', like 'wine', in the contrary sense means falsities that produce evils, and also falsities produced by evils, 'cup' as a consequence also means temptation, for temptation arises when falsity conflicts with truth and therefore evil with good. The word cup is used instead of and in reference to such temptation in Luke,

Jesus prayed, saying, If You are willing, let this *cup* pass from Me; nevertheless not My will, but Yours, be done.   Luke 22:42; Matt.26:39; Mark 14:36.

'Cup' here stands for temptation. Similarly in John,

Jesus said to Peter, Put your sword into its sheath; *the cup* which the Father has given Me, shall I not drink it?   John 18:11.

And also in Mark,

Jesus said to James and John, You do not know what you are asking. *Are you able to drink the cup that I drink*, and to be baptized with the baptism with which I am baptized? They said, We are able. But Jesus said to them, *The cup indeed that I drink you will drink*; and with the baptism with which I am baptized you will be baptized.   Mark 10:38,39; Matt.20:22,23.

From this it is evident that 'cup' means temptation, for temptation comes about when evils use falsities to enter into conflict with goods and truths. 'Baptism' means regeneration which, being effected by means of spiritual conflicts, consequently means temptation also.

13 In the completely contrary sense 'cup' means falsity that is a product of evil among those who are profaners, that is, with whom inwardly the exact opposites of charity are present but who put on an outward show of holiness. The word is used in this sense in Jeremiah,

Babel was *a golden cup* in Jehovah's hand, making the whole earth drunken. All nations have drunk of *her wine*, therefore the nations are mad.
Jer.51:7.

'Babel' stands for people with whom there is holiness outwardly but unholiness inwardly, 1182, 1326. The falsity which they veil with holiness is meant by 'a golden cup'. 'Making the whole earth drunken' stands for the fact that they lead those who belong to the Church, meant by 'the earth', into erroneous and insane ways. The profanities which they conceal beneath outward holiness involve nothing else than this – their intention to become the greatest and the wealthiest of all, to be worshipped as gods, the possessors of heaven and earth, and so to have dominion over people's souls as well as their bodies. And the means used by them is their outward display of respect for Divine and holy things. Consequently they look, so far as their external man is concerned, like angels; but so far as their internal man is concerned they are devils.

14 A similar description of Babel exists in John,

The woman was clothed in purple and scarlet, and covered[1] with gold and precious stones and pearls, *holding in her hand a golden cup*, full of abominations and the uncleanness of her whoredom.   Rev.17:4.

In the same book,

It has fallen, Babylon the great has fallen and become a dwelling-place of demons; for she has given all nations drink *from the wine of the fury* of her whoredom; and the kings of the earth have committed whoredom with her. I heard a voice from heaven, saying, Render to her as she has rendered to you; in *the cup* which she mixed, mix double for her.   Rev.18:2–4,6.

In the same book,

The great city was divided into three parts, and the cities of the nations fell. The remembrance of Babylon the great was established before God, *to give her the cup of the fury of the anger of God.*   Rev.16:19.

In the same book,

The third angel said with a loud voice, If anyone worships the beast and his image, *he will drink from the wine of God's anger, poured unmixed as it is in the cup of His anger*; and he will be tormented with fire and brimstone.   Rev.14:9,10.

---

[1] *lit.* gilded

5121   'And Joseph said to him, This is the interpretation of it' means revelation resulting from the perception received by the celestial within the natural as to what it held within it. This is clear from the meaning of 'saying' in the historical narratives of the Word as perception, dealt with in 1791, 1815, 1819, 1822, 1898, 1919, 2080, 2619, 2862, 3509, 3395, in this case as revelation resulting from perception, since the subject is a dream and its interpretation, and all revelation is either the result of talking to angels through whom the Lord speaks or else the result of perception, dealt with below; from the representation of 'Joseph' as the celestial within the natural, dealt with above in 5086, 5087, 5106; and from the meaning of 'the interpretation' as what it held within it, also dealt with above, in 5093, 5105, 5107. From this it is evident that 'Joseph said to him, This is the interpretation of it' means revelation resulting from the perception received by the celestial within the natural as to what it held within it.

With regard to revelations resulting either from perception or from talking to angels through whom the Lord speaks, it should be recognized that people who are governed by good and from this by truth, especially those who are governed by good flowing from love to the Lord, receive revelation as a result of perception. But those who are not governed by good or from this by truth can indeed receive revelations, but not those that are the result of perception, only those which come to them through a voice which they hear speaking within themselves and so through angels from the Lord. This kind of revelation is external, whereas the other kind is internal. Revelation resulting from perception is the kind that angels, especially celestial ones, receive. It was also the kind received by members of the Most Ancient Church, and by some members of the Ancient Church too; but scarcely anyone receives such at the present day. Very many people however, including those who have not been governed by good, have received revelations from conversations [with angels] which did not involve any perception, the same as with those receiving revelations through visions or through dreams.

Most of the revelations received by the prophets in the Jewish Church were of this kind – they heard a voice, saw a vision, or dreamed a dream. But because they had no perception these were merely verbal or visual revelations which did not involve any perception about what was really meant by them. For genuine perception comes from the Lord through heaven; it fills the understanding with spiritual ideas and leads it, as may be perceived, to think along the lines of, and inwardly to recognize, the true nature of a thing. The source of that power of recognition is not known, but the understanding imagines that it begins within itself and springs from the interconnected ideas it has present within itself. But in fact that power is a dictate coming from the Lord by way of heaven into the interior parts of one's thought regarding the things that are above and beyond the natural and the senses, that is, the kinds of things that belong to the spiritual world or heaven. From all this one may see what revelation resulting from perception is. But the revelation resulting from perception which the Lord, who is represented here by 'Joseph', had – which revelation is the subject here in the internal sense – sprang from the Divine within Himself, and so originated in Himself.

5122 'The three shoots are three days' means continuous derivatives even to the final one. This is clear from the meaning of 'three' as a single period and the continuity of it from start to finish, dealt with in 2788, 4495; from the meaning of 'shoots' as derivatives, dealt with in 5114; and from the meaning of 'days' as states, dealt with in 23, 487, 488, 493, 893, 2788, 3462, 3785, 4850. From all this it follows that 'the three shoots are three days' means the state in which the sensory power represented by 'the cupbearer' undergoes rebirth, from the first to the final degrees of it, its consecutive derivatives being meant by 'shoots'.

2   The states of rebirth which each sensory power and every aspect of the natural, as well as every aspect of the rational, pass through have from beginning to end their own progressive stages. When they attain any end they also begin at that point something else that is new; that is to say, they pass on from the end they had been striving to attain in a prior state to the realization of some further end, and so on after that. Eventually order is turned around, so that what has been last becomes first. This is what happens when a person is being regenerated, both in the case of his rational and in that of his natural. While his regeneration is taking place the phases that make up the first state are the stages of a movement from the truths of faith towards forms of the good of charity, when the truths of faith seemingly play the leading role while forms of the good of charity play a secondary one; for the truths of faith have the good of charity as their end in view. Phases like these continue until the person's regeneration is completed. Once this is completed charity then moves from the final place to the first in the line, and so becomes the point from which new states begin. These states develop in two directions – in an increasingly inward direction and also in a more outward one. Inwardly they move closer to love to the Lord, while outwardly they move closer first to the truths of faith, then to natural truths, and after that to truths as these are perceived by the senses. Then these three degrees of truths are brought into agreement one after another with forms of the good of charity and love present within the rational and so are brought into heavenly order.

3   These are the matters that are meant by progressive stages of development and by continuous derivatives even to the final one. Such stages and derivatives are unending in the case of a person who is being regenerated. They begin when he is a young child and continue through to the final phase of his life in the world; indeed they continue for ever after that, though his regeneration can never reach the point when he can by any means be called perfect. For there are countless, indeed a limitless number of things to be regenerated, both within his

rational and within his natural. Everything there has limitless shoots, that is, stages of development and derivatives that progress in both inward and outward directions. A person has no immediate awareness at all of this, but the Lord is aware of every particular detail and is making provision for it moment by moment. If He were to stop doing this for a single instant every stage of development would be thrown into confusion. For one stage looks to the next in an unending sequence and produces chains of sequences which never cease. From this it is evident that Divine Foresight and Providence exist in every particular detail, and that if they did not, or did so in a merely overall way, the human race would perish.

5123 'In yet three days' means that at that point a new state is arrived at. This is clear from the meaning of 'three' as that which is continuous even to the end, and so also that which is complete, dealt with in 2788, 4495; and from the meaning of 'days' as states, dealt with above in 5122. From this it is evident that 'three days' means a complete state; consequently 'in three days', that is, after three days, means a new state, 4901, for once a state is completed a new one begins.

5124 'Pharaoh will lift up your head' means that which has been provided and therefore decided. This is clear from the meaning of 'lifting up the head' as reaching a decision, and in the highest sense as providing; for a decision taken by the Divine and the carrying of that decision into effect is Providence. 'Lifting up the head' was an expression commonly used by the Ancients when it was decided that those who were bound, that is, those in prison, should either be allowed to live or else be condemned to death. When they were allowed to live the expression 'lifting up the head' was used, as also in the second Book of Kings,

Evil-merodach king of Babel, in the year he became king, *lifted up the head of Jehoiachin* king of Judah *from the prison-house*; and he spoke to him that which was good, and set his throne above the throne of the kings who were with him in Babel.   2 Kings 25:27,28.

Similarly in Jeremiah,

Evil-merodach king of Babel, in the [first] year of his reign, *lifted up the head of Jehoiachin* king of Judah and brought him *from the prison-house*. Jer.52:31.

But when someone was condemned to death the expression 'lifting up the head from upon him' was used, as in verse 19 further on which refers to the baker,

In yet three days Pharaoh *will lift up your head from upon you.*

This phrase expressing the decision that someone should live or be put to death originated with the Ancients, among whom representatives existed; it originated in their representation of those who were bound in prison or the pit. Because those in prison represented people undergoing vastation beneath the lower earth, 4728, 4744, 5038, 'lifting up the head' therefore meant their release from this condition. For when they are released they are raised or brought up from that vastation to heavenly communities, see 2699, 2701, 2704. Being brought or raised up implies advances made towards interior things, for the expression raised up or high is used to refer to things that are interior, 2148, 4210. And because advances made towards interior things are meant, an advance towards heaven is meant, since heaven exists within interior things. Such is the meaning of 'lifting up the head'. But 'lifting up the head from upon someone' meant his condemnation to death, for in this case those who were above the ones in the pit or undergoing vastation were raised up to heaven, while those in the pit were sent down into the nether regions. These things meant by this phrase expressing the decision whether one should live or be put to death are the reason for its usage in the Word. From this it is evident that 'lifting up the head' means that which has been decided; and as this is meant, that which has been provided is meant in the highest sense, since the Divine makes provision for that on which He has made a decision.

5125 'And will restore you to your position' means that the impressions received through the senses subject to the understanding part were restored to order, to occupy the lowest position. This is clear from the representation of 'the cupbearer', regarding whom these words are said, as the powers of the senses subject to the understanding part, dealt with in 5077, 5082, and therefore the impressions received through the senses in the external natural (for it is not the actual powers of the senses that are restored to order but the impressions which have come through the senses into the person's false notions); and from the meaning of 'restoring to a position' as restoring to order. And because sensory impressions, that is, images which have come in from the world by way of the external sensory organs, occupy the lowest position, where they minister to or serve more interior things, those impressions too are meant. In the case of regenerate persons sensory impressions do occupy the lowest position, but in the case of those who are not regenerate they occupy the first, see 5077, 5081, 5084, 5089, 5094.

2 A person can easily tell, if he pays the matter any attention, whether sensory impressions occupy the first or else the last and lowest position in him. If he says yes to everything his senses urge or desire and plays down all that his understanding tells him, then sensory impressions occupy the first position. When this is the case that person is carried along by natural desires and is ruled completely by his senses. The condition of a person like this is little different from that of animals, which are not endowed with reason; for animals are carried along by nothing else than their senses. Indeed that person's condition is worse than theirs if he misuses his power of understanding or reason to lend support to evils and falsities which the senses urge and tend towards. But if he does not say yes to these, but from within himself recognizes that they can mislead him into false beliefs and incite desires for evil in

him, and he strives to discipline them – thereby bringing them into a position of subservience, that is, making them subject to the understanding part and the will part which belong to the interior man – sensory impressions are in that case restored to order, to occupy the last and lowest position. When sensory impressions occupy that position, happiness and bliss radiate from the interior man into the delights of the senses and make these delights a thousand times better than they were before. Having no understanding of this, one who is ruled by his senses has no belief in it either; and feeling no other delight than that of the senses, and so imagining that no higher kind of delight exists, he regards the happiness and bliss that can be inwardly present in the delights of the senses as worthless. For what a person has no knowledge of is not thought by him to have any real existence.

5126   'And you will put Pharaoh's cup into his hand' means in order that they might consequently serve the interior natural. This is clear from the meaning of 'putting the cup to drink' as making one's own, dealt with above in 5120, besides the obvious meaning of serving; and from the representation of 'Pharaoh' as the interior natural, dealt with in 5080, 5095, 5118. For there is an interior natural and there is an exterior natural, the exterior natural being made up of impressions which enter in directly from the world by way of the senses into the natural mind, that is to say, they enter the memory belonging to that mind and therefore enter the place where mental images are formed, see 5118.

So that people can know what the exterior natural and what the interior natural are like, which make up the exterior man, and from this can know what the rational is which makes up the interior man, a brief reference to them must be made here. From infancy to childhood a person relies solely on his senses, for during those years he is receiving, through his bodily senses, nothing but earthly, bodily, and worldly impressions, which during those years are also the raw material from which he forms his ideas and thoughts. Communication with the interior man has not yet been opened up, except insofar as he is able to take in and hold on to those impressions. The innocence which exists in him at this time is solely external, not internal, because true innocence resides within wisdom. But the Lord uses this – his external innocence – to bring order into what enters through the senses. If innocence did not come to him from the Lord in that first period no foundation would ever be laid down on which the intellectual or rational degree of the mind proper to a human being could be established.

From childhood to early youth communication is opened up with the interior natural, by the person's learning about what is decent, public-spirited, and honourable, both through what parents and teachers tell him and through his own efforts to find out about such matters. During early youth to later youth however communication is opened up between the natural and the rational, by his learning about what is true and what is good so far as his public life and private life are concerned, and above all about what is good and what is true so far as his spiritual life is concerned, all of which he learns about through listening to and reading the Word. Indeed insofar as he uses truths to immerse himself in good deeds, that is, insofar as he puts the truths he learns into practice, the rational is opened up; but insofar as he does not use truths to immerse himself in good deeds, or does not put truths into practice, the rational is not opened up. Nevertheless the things he has come to know remain within the natural; that is to say, they remain in his memory, left on the doorstep so to speak outside the house.

4　But insofar – during these years and the next period of life – as he impairs the things he knows, refuses to accept them, and acts contrary to them, that is, insofar as he believes falsities and practises evils instead, the rational is closed, as is the interior natural also. But in spite of that, the Lord's Divine Providence enables communication to remain open enough to give him the ability to understand the good or truth he knows about. But he does not make these his own unless he truly repents and for a long while after that wrestles with falsities and evils. With people however who allow themselves to be regenerated the opposite takes place; for gradually, that is, in consecutive stages, their rational is opened up, the interior natural then becoming ranged in order beneath it, and the exterior natural beneath that. This occurs especially in the period from late youth to adulthood; it also continues in progressive stages to the final period of those regenerating people's lives, and after that in heaven for ever. From all this one may know what constitutes a person's interior natural and what his exterior natural.

5127　'According to the former manner' means in keeping with the law of order. This is clear from the meaning of 'the former manner' as the law of order. The law of order demands that exterior things should be subject to interior ones, or what amounts to the same, lower things should be subject to higher ones, serving them like domestic servants. Indeed exterior or lower things are nothing else than such servants, whereas interior or higher things in relation to them are their lords. The reason 'after the former manner' has this meaning is that as the cupbearer, being a servant, had previously served Pharaoh as his lord, in keeping with the law of subordination, so too was it in keeping with the law of order that the sensory power represented by 'the cupbearer' should serve the interior natural represented by 'Pharaoh'.

2　The fact that the law of order requires lower or exterior things to serve higher or interior ones is totally unknown to a person governed by his senses. For anyone who relies solely on his senses has no knowledge of what is interior, nor thus of what is exterior in relation to this. He knows about his thought and speech, and about his will and action, and from this presumes that thought and will are interior, speech and action exterior. But he is not aware of the fact that thought based solely on

sensory experience, and action based solely on natural impulses, belong
to the external man, so that his thought and will are activities of his
exterior man alone. He is particularly unaware of this when his
thoughts are false thoughts and his desires evil desires. And since in
the case of anyone like him communication with his interiors is closed
he therefore has no idea of what interior thought is or what interior will
is. If he is told that interior thought is based on truth and that interior
will is based on doing what is good, he does not begin to understand it.
He understands still less if he is told that the interior man is distinct
and separate from the exterior – so distinct that the interior man can,
from a higher position so to speak, see what is going on in the exterior
man – and that the interior man has the ability and power to discipline
the exterior, and the ability not to will or think what the exterior man
sees as a result of his having false notions and longs for as a result of his
having evil desires.

As long as his external man is in control and reigning he sees none of
this. But when not in this state, when for example he suffers any pain or
grief owing to misfortune or sickness, he can see and grasp it because
the external man ceases at that time to be in control. For a person's
ability or power to understand is always preserved by the Lord, but it is
largely obscured in the case of those steeped in falsities and evils, and is
always more apparent as falsities and evils become dormant. The Lord's
Divine is constantly coming to a person and bringing him light, but
when falsities and evils are present, that is, things contrary to truths
and forms of good, the light of the Divine is then either cast aside,
smothered, or perverted. Just enough is received, through chinks so to
speak, to allow him to think and to speak by the use of ideas received
through the senses, and also to think and to speak about spiritual
matters with the help of expressions registered in the natural or bodily
memory.

5128   'When you were his cupbearer' means as is the normal
position for sensory impressions of this kind. This is clear from the
meaning of 'cupbearer' as the powers of the senses, that is, those of
them that are subject to the understanding part of the mind, dealt with
in 5077, 5082 – the normal position being meant by the expression
'when you were'. The need for sensory impressions to be subject and
subordinate to rational ideas has been referred to already in what has
gone before; but since the subjection and subordination of them is the
subject here in the internal sense, something more must be said about
the nature of this.

The person with whom the senses have been made subject is called a
rational person, but a person with whom they have not is called one
ruled by his senses. But whether a person is rational or whether he is
one ruled by his senses is scarcely discernible by others; only the
individual himself can know, if he examines himself inwardly, that is, if
he examines what he wills and what he thinks. Others cannot know

from a person's speech whether he is one ruled by his senses or whether he is a rational person, nor can they know it from his actions, because the life of his thought held within his speech and the life of his will held within his actions cannot be perceived by any of the physical senses. These hear merely the sound he utters, or they see the movement made by his body together with the affection that impels him to make it. One cannot tell whether this affection is artificial or genuine. In the next life however those who are governed by good perceive clearly both what is held within a person's speech and what is held within his actions, and so perceive the nature of the life within them and where that life has its origin. Yet even in the world several indications exist which enable one to deduce to some extent whether the senses are subject to the rational, or the rational to the senses; or what amounts to the same, whether a person is rational or ruled solely by his senses. Those indications are as follows: If one notices that a person who makes false assumptions is not ready to become more enlightened but casts truths altogether aside, dispenses with reason, and obstinately defends falsities, this is an indication that he is ruled by his senses and is not a rational person. His rational is closed, so that it does not let in the light of heaven.

3 Ruled even more by their senses are those who are quite convinced by what is false, for such a conviction closes the rational altogether. It is one thing to make false assumptions, another to be convinced by what is false. Those convinced by what is false do have some light shining within their natural, but this is like the light in winter. When it shines among them in the next life that light is as bright as snow; but as soon as the light of heaven falls on it, it becomes a dull light, the degree and nature of their conviction making it dark as night. The same is also evident in these people while they are living in the world, for during that time they are unable to see the faintest glimmer of truth. Indeed because of the dullness and benightedness due to the falsity of which they are convinced, they see no value at all in truths and laugh at them. To the simple those people sometimes give the impression that they are rational, for by means of that snowy-white wintry light they are able to employ clever reasonings to substantiate falsities and make them look like truths. This kind of conviction exists in many of the learned, more than in every other kind of person, for they have used syllogistic and philosophical reasonings, and finally much factual knowledge to become firmly convinced by falsities. Among the ancients such people were called serpents belonging to the tree of knowledge, 195–197, but today they may be called those who are ruled inwardly by their senses and are devoid of true rationality.

4 The main indication that shows whether someone is ruled wholly by his senses or whether he is a rational person exists in the life he leads. By this one does not mean the kind of life that is evident in his words and deeds but the kind that is held inwardly in these. For the source of the life within his words is his thought, and the source of the life within

his deeds is his will, both having their origin in his intentions or end in view. The nature therefore of the intentions or end in view present within his words and deeds determines the nature of the life they hold within them, for without the life within them words are mere sounds, while deeds are mere motions. This kind of life is also what is meant when one speaks of life continuing after death. If a person is rational his words flow from right thinking and his deeds from right willing; that is, his words are a product of faith and his deeds a product of charity. But if a person is not rational he can, it is true, make a pretence of acting as one who is rational, and likewise of speaking as one who is such; but no life at all is coming from his rational. For a life of evil closes entirely the path to or communication with the rational, which causes him to be a merely natural person or one ruled by his senses.

There are two things which not only close that path of communication but also rob a person of the ability ever to become rational – deceit and profanation. Deceit is like a subtle poison which affects the inward parts, while profanation is that which mixes up falsities with truths and evils with forms of good. The two completely destroy the rational. Present with everyone there are forms of good and truth which have been stored away by the Lord since earliest childhood. In the Word these forms of good and truth are called remnants, regarding which see 468, 530, 560, 561, 661, 1050, 1738, 1906, 2284; and it is these remnants that deceit poisons and that profanation mixes up with falsities and evils. For what profanation is, see 593, 1008, 1010, 1059, 1327, 1328, 2051, 2426, 3398, 3402, 3489, 3898, 4289, 4601. All these indications show to some extent who a rational person is and who one ruled by his senses is.

When the senses have become subject to the rational, the sensory powers that serve to form a person's first mental images receive light which comes through heaven from the Lord; they are at the same time brought into a state of order that enables them to receive that light and agree with the rational. Once they exist in this condition sensory impressions are no longer a barrier that prevents truths from being either acknowledged or seen, for those that are not in keeping with truths are instantly set aside, while those which are in keeping are accepted. Those that are in keeping are now so to speak at the centre and those that are not are on the fringes. Those at the centre are so to speak raised up towards heaven, while those on the fringes are hanging downwards. Those at the centre receive light from the rational, and when they are manifested visually in the next life they look like small glittering stars which radiate light, gradually decreasing, out to the fringes. This is the kind of form that natural or sensory images are being brought into when the rational has dominion and the senses exist subject to it. This is what happens to a person while he is being regenerated, bringing him as a consequence into a state in which truths can be seen and acknowledged by him in abundance. But when the rational is subject to the senses the opposite happens, for in this case falsities are in the middle or at the centre and truths are on the fringes. The falsities at the centre dwell in a certain kind of light, which however is an inferior and deceptive one, like that emitted by a coal fire. Into this there is flowing light on every side from hell. This inferior light is that which is called darkness, for as soon as any light from heaven flows into it, it is converted into darkness.

5129 Verses 14,15 **But remember me when it is well with you, and show, I beg you, mercy to me, and make mention of me to Pharaoh, and bring me out of this house. For I have indeed been taken away by theft out of the land of the Hebrews, and here also I have not done anything for which they should put me in the pit.**
'But remember me' means the reception of faith. 'When it is well with you' means when a correspondence exists. 'And show, I beg you, mercy to me' means the reception of charity. 'And make mention of me to Pharaoh' means communication with the interior natural. 'And bring me out of this house' means a release from evils. 'For I have indeed been taken away by theft' means that evil caused celestial things to become alienated. 'Out of the land of the Hebrews' means from the Church. 'And here also I have not done anything' means innocence. 'For which they should put me in the pit' means a casting away among falsities.

5130 'But remember me' means the reception of faith. This is clear from the representation of 'Joseph', who says this about himself, as the Lord as regards the celestial within the natural, dealt with in 5086, 5087, 5106; and from the meaning of 'remember me' as the reception of faith, for remembering and being mindful of the Lord do not flow from anything other than faith. Consequently 'remember me' implies a desire to receive faith. As regards faith, anyone who receives and possesses faith is constantly mindful of the Lord. This is so even when he is thinking or talking about something other than Him, or else when he is carrying out his public, private, or family duties, though he is not directly conscious of his mindfulness of the Lord while he is carrying them out. Indeed that mindfulness of the Lord present in those who possess faith governs their whole being, but that which governs their whole being is not noticed by them except when they turn their thought specifically to that matter.

2 This may be illustrated by many aspects of human character. One who is governed by some love, whatever this may be, is thinking constantly about things connected with that love. This is so even when other matters occupy his mind, conversation, or action. This is quite evident in the next life from the spiritual spheres which surround everyone individually. From those spheres alone one can detect what the faith is and what the love is that are present in all who are there, even though they may be thinking or talking about something completely different, 1048, 1053, 1316, 1504–1520, 2489, 4464. For that which governs a

person's whole being produces the sphere surrounding him and reveals to others what his life is. From this one may see what is meant by the statement that one ought to be thinking constantly about the Lord, salvation, and life after death. All who possess faith that is grounded in charity do so, as a consequence of which they do not entertain evil thoughts regarding their neighbour, and that which is just and fair is present in every aspect of their thought, speech, and action; for that which governs the person's whole being enters every particular aspect of it, both leading it and controlling it. Indeed the Lord holds the mind to those concerns that are charitable and are therefore matters of faith, and in so doing He fits every single thing in the mind into its proper place. The sphere of faith grounded in charity is the sphere which reigns in heaven, for the Lord flows in with love, and by means of love with charity, and as a consequence with truths which are the truths of faith. This explains why those in heaven are said to be in the Lord.

The subject in what follows next is the rebirth of the sensory power subject to the understanding part represented by 'the cupbearer'; and as the rebirth of this is the subject, so also is the reception of faith. Indeed sensory awareness, like the rational, is born again by means of faith, but by faith into which charity is flowing. Unless charity flows into faith and imparts life to it, faith cannot possibly exist throughout a person's whole being, for it is what a person loves that reigns in him, not what he merely knows and retains in his memory.

5131   'When it is well with you' means when a correspondence exists. This is clear from the meaning – when the subject is the rebirth or regeneration of the exterior natural or sensory power – of 'being well with you' as a correspondence that exists, for until that power corresponds things are not well with it. What correspondence is may be seen at the ends of chapters. There is a correspondence of sensory impressions with natural ideas, a correspondence of natural ideas with spiritual realities, a correspondence of spiritual realities with celestial entities, and finally a correspondence of celestial entities with the Lord's Divine. Thus a sequence of correspondences exists extending from the Divine down to the last and lowest degree of the natural.

Since it is difficult for anyone to have any conception of the nature of correspondences if he has not previously given any thought to them, a brief statement must therefore be made about them. It is well known from philosophy that the end is prior to the cause, and the cause prior to the effect. To enable end, cause, and effect to follow one another and act as one, the effect must correspond to the cause, and the cause must correspond to the end. Nevertheless the end does not manifest itself as the cause, nor does the cause manifest itself as the effect. Rather, to enable the cause to exist the end must act on the level where the cause belongs, calling on assistant means to help it – the end – to bring the cause into existence; and to enable the effect to exist the cause likewise must act on the level where the effect belongs, by calling on assistant means to help it – the cause – to bring the effect into existence. These assistant means are ones that correspond; and because they correspond, the end can exist within the cause and bring the cause into operation, and the cause can exist within the effect and bring the effect into operation. Consequently the end uses the cause to bring the effect into operation. But it is different when no correspondence exists. In this case the end does not have a cause in which it may exist, let alone any effect in which it may do so. Instead the end undergoes change and variation within the cause, and finally within the effect, according to the form which the assistant means create.

3 All things without exception within the human being, indeed all things without exception in the natural creation, follow one another as end, cause, and effect. When these correspond to one another in this way they act as one, for in this case the end is the all in all of the cause, and through the cause is the all in all of the effect. Take for example heavenly love, when this is the end, the will is the cause, and action is the effect. If the three exist in correspondence with one another – that love flowing into the will, and the will into action – they then act as one, so much so through their correspondence with one another that the action is seen as the love. Or take for another example faith grounded in charity. When this is the end, thought is the cause, and conversation is the effect. If the three exist in correspondence with one another – if faith grounded in charity is flowing into a person's thought, and this into his conversation – they then act as one, so much so that through their correspondence with one another his conversation is seen as if it were the end. But to enable the cause to exist, which is will or thought, the end, which is love or faith, must call on assistant means within the rational mind which must correspond. For without the corresponding assistant means the end, which is love and faith, has nothing to receive it, even though it flows in from the Lord through heaven. From this it is evident that both the interior and the exterior aspects of the human being, that is, his rational concepts, natural ideas, and sensory impressions, must be brought into a state of correspondence so that the Divine can flow in and be received by a person, consequently so that he may be born again, prior to which all is not well with him. From all this one may see that 'when it is well with you' here means [when] a correspondence exists.

5132 'And show, I beg you, mercy to me' means the reception of charity. This is clear from the meaning of 'mercy' as love, dealt with in 3063, 3073, 3120, 5042, in this case love towards the neighbour, which is charity, since the reception of faith is spoken of above in 5130; for on the level of the senses, when these are born again, faith and charity must make one. The reason 'mercy' means charity is that all who have charity have mercy, that is, all who love their neighbour are merciful towards him. This also explains why the Word describes the practice of charity as acts of mercy, as in Matthew,

I was hungry and you gave Me food, I was thirsty and you gave Me drink, I was a stranger and you took Me in, naked and you clothed Me, I was sick and you visited Me, I was in prison and you came to me. Matt.25:35,36.

And in other places the practice of charity is described as acts of mercy done to the poor, the afflicted, widows, and orphans.

Charity consists essentially in desiring the welfare of one's neighbour, in having an affection for what is good, and in acknowledging that since what is good is one's neighbour, those who are governed by good are consequently one's neighbour, but varyingly so, depending on the amount of good that governs the individual person. Therefore since charity consists in having an affection for what is good, it also consists in feelings of mercy for those in distress. The good of charity holds such feelings within it because it comes down from the Lord's love towards the whole human race, a love which is 'mercy' because the whole human race is in distress. Mercy sometimes seems to exist among the evil who have no charity. But this is a case of pain because of their own suffering; for it consists in a concern for friends whom they identify with themselves, and when those friends suffer, they suffer too. This kind of mercy is not the mercy that belongs to charity but that which goes with friendship based on self-interest, which regarded in itself is the opposite of mercy. That kind of person despises and hates everyone else apart from himself, and so everyone else apart from the friends whom he identifies with himself.

5133   'And make mention of me to Pharaoh' means communication with the interior natural. This is clear from the meaning of 'making mention to someone' as communicating, and from the representation of 'Pharaoh' as the interior natural, dealt with 5080, 5095. By communication with the interior natural one means a joining together with it that has been effected through correspondence. The interior natural is that which receives ideas of truth and good from the rational and stores these away for the use they may serve, and is consequently that which communicates directly with the rational. The exterior natural however is that which receives images, and from these the ideas of things coming from the world by way of the senses.

Unless these latter ideas receive light from ideas present in the interior natural they give rise to illusions, which are called the illusions of the senses. When subject to such illusions a person believes nothing apart from that which is in agreement with them or to which they lend support, as is the situation if no correspondence exists. Nor does any correspondence exist if that person is not endowed with charity, for charity is the means which brings about union because the good of charity contains life from the Lord. That life arranges truths into order, thereby giving charity an outward form, that is, an image in which it can present itself. This form is manifested visually in the next life and is the angelic form itself. All the angels consequently are forms of charity, the beauty of this charity being received from the truths of faith, and the life within the beauty being received from the good of charity.

5134 'And bring me out of this house' means a release from evils. This is clear from the meaning of 'bringing out' as a release, and from the meaning of 'house' as good, dealt with in 710, 1708, 2048, 2233, 3128, 3652, 3720, 4982, and therefore, in the contrary sense, as evil. From this it is evident that 'bring me out of this house' means a release from evils, a meaning that also follows the preceding train of thought, which is this: When faith is received within the exterior natural, which is the subject here, 5130, a correspondence is effected, 5131, and when charity is received, 5132, and a communication is thereby effected with the interior natural, 5133, the exterior natural is at that point released from the evils which had caused the celestial represented by 'Joseph', 5086, 5087, 5106, to become alienated – that alienation being meant by the words which follow next, stating that he was taken away by theft. Furthermore, when the natural is regenerated by means of charity and faith it is released from evils; for when it is regenerated the evils are set apart and cast away from the centre, where they were previously, to the fringes, which the light of truth from good does not reach. In man's case evils are set apart in this manner; yet they still remain, for they cannot be completely destroyed. But with the Lord, who made the natural within Himself Divine, evils and falsities were cast out and completely destroyed. For the Divine cannot have anything at all in common with evils and falsities, or be encompassed by them, as is the case with man; for the Divine is the Essential Being (*Esse*) of good and truth, and that Being exists an infinite distance away from everything evil and false.

5135 'For I have indeed been taken away by theft' means that evil caused celestial things to become alienated. This is clear from the representation of 'Joseph', who says this about himself, as the celestial within the natural, dealt with in 5086, 5087, 5106, and consequently the celestial things there; and from the meaning of 'being taken away by theft' as undergoing alienation caused by evil. For 'to commit theft' means to alienate, while 'theft' itself means the evil which causes alienation, as well as meaning evil which lays claim to the things existing there in the natural. 'Theft' means an alienation caused by evil that happens in the place which such evil takes possession of; for it expels everything good and true and fills up that place with evils and falsities. 'Theft' also means its laying claim to what belongs to others; for it takes to itself everything good and true in that place and makes such its own as well as attaching it to evils and falsities. But to enable anyone to know what is meant by 'theft' in the spiritual sense, a statement must be made about what happens to evils and falsities when they enter in and take possession of a place, and also when they lay claim to everything good and true there.

2 From infancy to childhood, and sometimes on into early youth, a

person is absorbing forms of goodness and truth received from parents and teachers, for during those years he learns about those forms of goodness and truth and believes them with simplicity – his state of innocence enabling this to happen. It inserts those forms of goodness and truth into his memory; yet it lodges them only on the edge of it since the innocence of infancy and childhood is not an internal innocence which has an influence on the rational, only an external one which has an influence solely on the exterior natural, 2306, 3183, 3494, 4563, 4797. When however the person grows older, when he starts to think for himself and not, as previously, simply in the way his parents or teachers do, he brings back to mind and so to speak chews over what he has learned and believed before, and then he either endorses it, has doubts about it, or refuses to accept it. If he endorses it, this is an indication that he is governed by good, but if he refuses to accept it, that is an indication that he is governed by evil. If however he has doubts about what he has learned and believed before, it is an indication that he will move subsequently either into an affirmative attitude of mind or else into a negative one.

The truths that a person learns and believes in his earliest years when he is a young child but which later on he either endorses, has doubts about, or refuses to accept, are in particular these: There is God, and He is one; He created everything; He rewards those who do what is good and punishes those who do things that are bad; there is life after death, when the bad go to hell and the good go to heaven, and so there is a hell and a heaven; the life after death lasts for ever; also, people ought to pray every day and to do so in a humble way; they ought to keep the sabbath day holy, honour their parents, and not commit adultery, kill, or steal; and many other truths like these. Such truths are learned and absorbed by a person from earliest childhood; but if, when he starts to think for himself and to lead his own life, he endorses them, adding to them further truths of a more interior kind, and leads a life in conformity with them, all is well with him. But if he starts to disobey them, refusing at length to accept them, then even though outwardly he leads a life in conformity with them, because the law and society expect him to do so, he is governed by evil.

This evil is what is meant by 'theft', to the extent that thief-like it usurps the position held previously by good. With many people it is thief-like to the extent that it takes away the forms of goodness and truth previously there and uses them to lend support to evils and falsities. So far as is possible with these people the Lord removes the forms of goodness and truth absorbed in early childhood from where these are to a more internal position, where – within the interior natural – He stores them away for future use. These forms of goodness and truth that are stored away within the interior natural are meant in the Word by 'the remnant', dealt with in 468, 530, 560, 561, 660, 661, 1050, 1738, 1906, 2284. But if evil steals the forms of goodness and truth there and uses them to lend support to evils and falsities, especially if it does so by the use of deceit, it destroys those remnants; for in this case it mingles evil with good, and falsity with truth, to such an extent that one cannot be separated from the other; and then a person is done for.

5 The fact that 'theft' means the kinds of things mentioned above may be seen from the mere use of that word to refer to what constitutes a person's spiritual life. For the only riches in that life are cognitions of good and truth, and the only possessions and inheritances are the different forms of happiness in life which are gained from forms of good and from truths deriving from these. The stealing of such things, as stated above, is what 'theft' relates to in the spiritual sense, and therefore by the thefts mentioned in the Word nothing else is meant in the internal sense, as in Zechariah,

> I lifted up my eyes and saw, and behold, a flying scroll. Then he said to me, This curse is going out over the face of the whole land, for *everyone committing theft* from now on, according to it, will be innocent, and everyone swearing falsely, according to it, will be innocent. I have cast it forth, that *it may enter the house of the thief*, and the house of him swearing falsely by My name, and may pass the night in his house and consume it, both its timbers and its stones. Zech.5:1–4.

Evil which takes away remnants of good is meant by 'one committing theft' and by 'the house of the thief', and falsity which takes away remnants of truth by 'one swearing falsely' and by 'the house of him swearing falsely'. 'The face of the whole land' stands for the whole Church, which is why the statement is made that the curse will consume the house, both its timbers and its stones – 'house' meaning the natural mind or a person so far as that mind is concerned, 3128, 3538, 4973, 5023, 'timbers' the forms of good present there, 2784, 2812, 3720, 4943, and 'stones' the truths, 643, 1298, 3720.

6 Profanation and a consequent removal of goodness and truth are meant in the spiritual sense by the action of Achan, who took some of 'the devoted things' – a mantle of Shinar, two hundred shekels of silver, and a wedge of gold – and hid them in the earth in the middle of his tent, on account of which he was stoned and everything was burned, as described in Joshua,

> Jehovah said to Joshua, Israel has sinned; they have transgressed My covenant which I commanded them, and have taken some of that which was devoted; *they have committed theft*, have lied, and have put it among their own vessels. Josh.7:11,12,25.

'The devoted things' meant falsities and evils, which were not on any account to be mixed with anything holy. 'A mantle of Shinar, two hundred shekels of silver, and a wedge of gold' in the spiritual sense are specific types of falsity. 'Hiding them in the earth in the middle of the tent' meant a mingling with things that are holy – for 'a tent' means that which is holy, see 414, 1102, 1566, 2145, 2152, 3312, 4128, 4391, 4599. Such was the meaning of the declaration that they had committed theft, lied, and put [what was devoted] among their own vessels; for 'vessels' means holy truths, 3068, 3079, 3316, 3318.

In Jeremiah,

I will bring the disaster[1] of Esau upon him, the time I will visit him. If grape-gatherers come to you, will they not leave grape-gleanings? *if thieves in the night*, will they not destroy a sufficiency? I will strip Esau bare, I will uncover his secret places, and he will not be able to be concealed. His seed has been laid waste, and his brothers, and his neighbours; and he is no more.   Jer.49:8–10.

'Esau' stands for the evil of self-love to which falsities have been allied, 3322. The destruction by this evil of the remnants of good and truth is meant by the statements that 'thieves in the night will destroy a sufficiency' and that 'his seed has been laid waste, also his brothers and his neighbours, and he is no more'. 'Seed' stands for truths which are those of faith grounded in charity, 1025, 1447, 1610, 1940, 2848, 3038, 3310, 3373; 'brothers' for forms of good which are those of charity, 367, 2360, 2508, 2524, 3160, 3303, 3459, 3815, 4121, 4191; 'neighbours' for the adjoining and related forms of truth and good which belong to it.
A similar reference to Esau occurs in Obadiah,

If *thieves come to you*, if *those who overturn in the night* – how you will have been cut off! – *will they not steal that which is enough for themselves?* If grape-gatherers come to you, will they not leave some clusters?   Obad.verse 5.

'Grape-gatherers' stands for falsities which are not a product of evil. These falsities do not destroy the forms of goodness and truth – that is, the remnants – stored away by the Lord in a person's interior natural. But falsities that are the product of evils do destroy them, for they steal forms of truth and good and also use them, through misapplication of them, to lend support to evils and falsities.
In Joel,

A great and mighty people, like heroes they will run, like men of war they will scale the wall; and they will pass on, every one on his way. They will run about the city, they will run on the wall, they will climb into the houses, *they will go in through the windows like a thief.*   Joel 2:7,9.

'A great and mighty people' stands for falsities fighting against truths, 1259, 1260; and because they fight in a mighty way, by destroying truths, they are spoken of as 'heroes' and 'like men of war'. 'The city' through which they are said to run about stands for matters of doctrine regarding truth, 402, 2268, 2449, 2712, 2943, 3216; 'the houses which they will climb into' stands for the forms of good which they destroy, 710, 1708, 2048, 2233, 3128, 3652, 3720, 4982; 'the windows which they will go through' stands for intellectual concepts and for reasonings derived from these, 655, 658, 3391. This being so, those falsities are compared to a thief because they usurp the position held previously by truths and forms of good.

---

[1] *Reading* Exitium(disaster) – *which Sw. has in his rough draft, and also in another place where he quotes this verse – for* Exitum (departure)

10 In David,

Since you hate discipline and cast away My words behind you, *if you see a thief you run with him*, and your part is with adulterers. You open your mouth towards evil, and with your tongue you frame deceit. Ps.50:17–19.

This refers to someone wicked, 'running with a thief' standing for his use of falsity to alienate truth from himself.

11 In Revelation,

They did not repent of their murders, or of their enchantments, or of their whoredoms, *or of their thefts*. Rev.9:21.

'Murders' stands for evils which destroy forms of good, 'enchantments' for falsities from these which destroy truths, 'whoredoms' for falsified truths, 'thefts' for forms of good that have consequently been alienated.

12 In John,

Truly, truly, I say to you, he who does not enter by the door into the sheepfold but climbs in by another way, that man is *a thief* and *a robber*. But he who enters by the door is the shepherd of the sheep. I am the door; if anyone enters through Me he will be saved, and will go in, and will go out, and will find pasture. *The thief does not come except to steal* and to kill and to destroy. John 10:1,2,8–10.

'A thief' in this instance also stands for the evil of merit-seeking, for anyone who takes away from the Lord that which is His and claims it as his own is called 'a thief'. This evil closes the path so as to prevent the flow of good and truth from the Lord, for which reason it is referred to as 'killing and destroying'. Much the same is meant in the Ten Commandments, at Deut.5:19, by *You shall not steal*, 4174. From all this one may see what is meant in the spiritual sense by the laws laid down in the Jewish Church regarding thefts, such as those at Exod.21:16; 22:1–4; Deut.24:7; for all laws in that Church had their origin in the spiritual world, and they therefore correspond to the laws of order which exist in heaven.

5136 'Out of the land of the Hebrews' means from the Church; that is to say, evil caused celestial things to be alienated from it. This is clear from the meaning of 'the land of the Hebrews' as the Church, 'the land of the Hebrews' being in this case the land of Canaan, for this was the place from which Joseph was taken away. The reason why in the Word 'the land of Canaan' means the Church is that the Church had existed there since most ancient times, first the Most Ancient Church, which came before the Flood; then the Ancient Church, which came after the Flood; after that the second Ancient Church, which is called the Hebrew Church; and at length the Jewish Church. So that the Jewish Church might be established there Abram was commanded to move from Syria to that land, where he received the promise that the land would be given as an inheritance to his descendants. This explains why in the Word 'land' or 'earth' means the Church, and 'the whole land' – an expression found in various places – the universal Church, and why 'a new heaven and a new earth' means a new Church, internal and external.

The reason the Church existed there continuously since most ancient times was that the member of the Most Ancient Church, who was celestial, was the kind of person who saw within every single object in the world and on earth something representative of the Lord's kingdom. Worldly and earthly objects were the means that enabled him to think about heavenly realities. This was where all the representatives and meaningful signs known subsequently in the Ancient Church had their origin, for these had been gathered together by the people meant by 'Enoch', and preserved for the use of others descended from them, 519, 521, 2896. This was how it came about that each specific place, and also each specific mountain or river in the land of Canaan, where the most ancient people lived, came to be representative, as did all the surrounding kingdoms. Now because the Word could not be written unless representatives and meaningful signs were used, including those connected with places, those consecutive dispensations of the Church were to that end kept in existence in the land of Canaan. But after the Lord's Coming the Church was transferred elsewhere because representatives were now done away with. From all this it is evident that the land of Canaan, called the land of the Hebrews here, means the Church.

But see what has been presented already on these matters – in the following places:

The Most Ancient Church, the one before the Flood, existed in the land of Canaan, 567, 3686, 4447, 4454.
Part of the Ancient Church, the Church after the Flood, existed there, 3686, 4447.
The second Ancient Church, called the Hebrew Church, also existed there, 4516, 4517.
Abram was therefore commanded to go there, and the land was given to his descendants, 3686, 4447.
Consequently the land of Canaan represented the Lord's kingdom, 1607, 3038, 3481, 3705, 4240, 4447.
This explains why in the Word 'the land' means the Church, 566, 662, 1066, 1067, 1262, 1413, 1607, 1733, 1850, 2117, 2118(end), 3355, 4447, 4535.

5137   'And here also I have not done anything' means innocence. This becomes clear without explanation, for 'not doing anything evil' is a declaration of innocence.

5138   'For which they should put me in the pit' means a casting away among falsities. This is clear from the meaning of 'the pit' as falsity, dealt with in 4728, 4744, 5038. In what appears above evil was the subject, that is to say, the fact that evil caused celestial things to become alienated, 5134, 5135; but now falsity is the subject, for when the one is mentioned in the Word, so also is the other. That is to say, when evil is mentioned, so also is falsity, for the reason that when good is mentioned there, so also is truth, in order that a marriage may exist in every individual part of the Word. The heavenly marriage is a marriage of good and truth, but the hellish marriage is one of evil and falsity. For where evil exists, so also does falsity, falsity linking itself to evil like a wife to her husband; and where good exists, so also does truth, truth joining itself to good like a wife to her husband. Consequently one can see from a person's life the essential nature of his faith, for good, or else evil, is the inner essence of his life, and truth, or else falsity, is the inner essence of his faith. As regards a marriage existing in every individual part of the Word, see 683, 793, 801, 2173, 2516, 2712, 4138(end).

5139   Verses 16–19 **And the chief of the bakers saw that he had interpreted what was good, and he said to Joseph, I also was in my dream, and behold, three baskets with holes in them were on my head. And in the highest basket there was some of every kind of food for Pharaoh, the work of the baker, and the birds were eating them out of the basket, from upon my head. And Joseph answered and said, This is the interpretation of it: The three baskets are three days. In yet three days Pharaoh will lift up your head from upon you, and will hang you on wood; and the birds will eat your flesh from upon you.**

'And the chief of the bakers saw' means the discernment of the sensory power subject to the will part of the mind. 'That he had interpreted what was good' means what was going to take place. 'And he said to Joseph' means the perception of the celestial within the natural. 'I also was in my dream' means a foretelling. 'And behold, three baskets' means consecutive degrees forming the will. 'With holes in them were on my head' means without a termination anywhere at all in the middle. 'And in the highest basket' means the inmost degree of the will. 'There was some of every kind of food for Pharaoh' means full of celestial good for nourishing the natural. 'The work of the baker' means according to every useful purpose served by that power of the senses. 'And the birds of the air were eating them out of the basket, from upon my head' means that falsity originating in evil would consume it. 'And Joseph answered and said' means revelation resulting from the perception received by the celestial within the natural. 'This is the interpretation of it' means what it held within it. 'The three baskets' means the consecutive degrees of the will. 'Are three days' means even to the final one. 'In yet three days' means that within the final one. 'Pharaoh will lift up your head from upon you' means a decision based on foresight. 'And will hang you on wood' means a casting aside and condemnation. 'And the birds will eat your flesh from upon you' means that falsity originating in evil will consume every one of those sensory impressions.

5140   'And the chief of the bakers saw' means the discernment of the sensory power subject to the will part of the mind. This is clear from the meaning of 'seeing' as understanding and discerning, dealt with in 2150, 2807, 3764, 4723, and from the meaning of 'the chief of the bakers' as in general the sensory power subject to the will part, and so its sensory perceptions, dealt with in 5078, 5082.

5141   'That he had interpreted what was good' means what was going to take place. This is clear from the meaning of 'interpreting' as what it held within itself, or what lay within it, dealt with above in 5093, 5105, 5107, 5121, and thus also what was going to take place. The discernment that what was good was going to take place was a sensory discernment which, compared with other kinds of discernment, is an obscure one. To be exact, there is the power of discernment exercised by the senses or the exterior natural; the power of discernment exercised by the interior natural; and the power of discernment exercised by the rational. When a person is led by affection to think on a more interior level and to divorce his mind from what his senses and his body tell him, his discernment is of the rational kind. For in his case lower ideas, that is, those conceived by his external man, become dormant, and that person is virtually in his spirit. But when, for reasons that arise in the world, his thought exists on a more exterior level his power of discernment is that exercised by the interior natural. The rational is, it is true, exerting an influence, but not with any living affection. When however a person is engrossed in mere pleasures and the delights engendered by a love of the world, and also by self-love, his power of discernment is that exercised by the senses. His life in this case is focused on external interests or the body, and he has no room for anything internal apart from what will prevent him from breaking out into shameful and unseemly kinds of behaviour. But the more external his discernment is, the more obscure it is; for in relation to interior things exterior ones are general. Countless details that are interior manifest themselves in that which is exterior as one simple whole.

5142   'And he said to Joseph' means the perception of the celestial within the natural. This is clear from the meaning of 'saying', in the historical narratives of the Word, as perception, often dealt with already; and from the representation of 'Joseph' as the celestial within the natural, dealt with in 5086, 5087, 5106.

5143   'I also was in my dream' means a foretelling. This is clear from the meaning of 'a dream' as a foretelling regarding the outcome, dealt with in 5092, 5104, 5112.

5144   'And behold, three baskets' means consecutive degrees forming the will. This is clear from the meaning of 'three' as complete and continuous even to the end, dealt with in 2788, 4495, 5114, 5122, thus things that are consecutive; and from the meaning of 'baskets' as degrees forming the will. The reason 'baskets' means degrees forming the will is that they are vessels which serve to contain food, and 'food' means celestial and spiritual kinds of good, which are contained in the will. For all good belongs to the will, and all truth to the understanding. As soon as anything goes forth from the will it is perceived as good. Up to this point the subject has been the sensory power subject to the understanding, which has been represented by 'the cupbearer'; but now the subject is the sensory power subject to the will, which is represented by 'the baker', see 5077, 5078, 5082.

2. The consecutive or continuous degrees of the understanding were represented by the vine, its three shoots, blossom, clusters, and grapes; and then truth which belongs properly to the understanding was represented by 'the cup', 5120. But the consecutive degrees forming the will are represented by the three baskets on the baker's head, in the highest of which 'there was some of every kind of food for Pharaoh, the work of the baker'. By consecutive degrees of the will are meant degrees in consecutive order, beginning with the one inmostly present with a person and ending with the outermost degree where sensory awareness resides. Those degrees are like a flight of steps from the inmost parts to the outermost, 5114. Good from the Lord flows into the inmost degree, then through the rational degree into the interior natural, and from there into the exterior natural, or the sensory level. That good passes down a flight of steps so to speak, the nature of it being determined at each distinct and separate level by the way it is received. But more will be said later on about the nature of this influx and those consecutive degrees it passes through.

3. Elsewhere in the Word 'baskets' again means degrees of the will, in that forms of good are contained in these, as in Jeremiah,

Jehovah showed me, when behold, there were *two baskets of figs*, set before the temple of Jehovah; *in one basket* extremely good figs, like first-ripe figs, *but in the other basket* extremely bad figs, which could not be eaten because of their badness. Jer.24:1–3.

In this case a different word is used in the original language for 'a basket'[1], which is used to describe the natural degree of the will. The figs in the first basket are forms of good in the natural, but those in the second are forms of evil there.

4. In Moses,

When you have come into the land which Jehovah your God will give you, you shall take some of the first of all the fruit of the land, which you shall bring from your land, and *you shall put it in a basket*, and you shall go to the place which Jehovah has chosen. Then the priest shall take *the basket* from your hand, and place it before the altar of Jehovah your God. Deut.26:1–4.

Here yet another word for 'a basket' is used[1], which means a new will within the understanding part of the mind. 'The first of the fruit of the land' are the forms of good produced from that new will.

5. In the same author,

To consecrate Aaron and his sons, Moses was to take unleavened bread, unleavened cakes mixed with oil, and unleavened wafers anointed with oil; he was to make them of fine wheat flour. And *he was to put them in one basket*, and to bring them near *in the basket*. Aaron, then his sons, were to eat the flesh of the ram, and the bread *in the basket*, at the door of the tent of meeting. Exod.29:2,3,32.

[1] *Sw. reflects these differences by the use of three different Latin words for* basket.

In this case the same word is used for 'a basket' as here [in the baker's dream]. It means the will part of the mind, which has within it forms of good that are meant by bread, cakes, oil, wafers, flour, and wheat. The expression 'the will part of the mind' describes that which serves as a container; for good from the Lord flows into those interior forms within man, as the proper vessels to contain it. If those forms have been set to receive it they are 'baskets' containing such good.

In the same author, when a Nazirite was being inaugurated,

He shall take *a basket of unleavened* [loaves] of fine flour, cakes mingled with oil, and unleavened wafers anointed with oil, together with their minchah and their drink-offerings. He shall also offer a ram as a sacrifice of peace-offerings to Jehovah, in addition to *the basket of unleavened* things. And the priest shall take the cooked shoulder of the ram, and one unleavened cake *from the basket*, and one wafer from the unleavened, and he shall place them on the hand of the Nazirite, and [the priest] shall wave them as a wave-offering before Jehovah. Num.6:15,17,19,20.

Here also 'a basket' stands for the will part of the mind serving as a container. Cakes, wafers, oil, minchah, cooked shoulder of the ram serve to represent forms of celestial good; for a Nazirite represented the celestial man, 3301.

In those times things like these which were used in worship were carried in baskets; even the kid which Gideon brought to the angel under the oak tree was carried in one, Judg.6:19. The reason for this was that 'baskets' represented things serving as containers, while the things in those baskets represented the actual contents.

5145 'With holes in them were on my head' means without a termination anywhere at all in the middle. This is clear from the meaning of 'with holes in' as that which is open from top to bottom, thus that which is not closed and therefore has no termination anywhere at all in the middle; and from the meaning of 'the head' as interior degrees, in particular those that constitute the will. For the head is the primary location where all substances and forms exist, and is therefore the place to which all sensations travel and register themselves, and the place from which all actions spring and are derived. The powers of the mind too – the power of understanding and that of the will – are plainly located there, which is why interior degrees are meant by 'the head'. 'The baskets' [in the baker's dream] represented those powers within 'the head'.

The subject at present is the sensory impressions subject to the will part of the mind, 'baskets on the head with holes in them' meaning that interior degrees existed without a termination anywhere at all in the middle. Therefore those sensory impressions, as follows from this, were cast aside and condemned. But some explanation must be given of what is meant by 'without a termination anywhere at all in the middle'. Interiorly the human being is divided into separate degrees, and each degree has its own termination that serves to separate it from the degree beneath it. This is so with every degree from the inmost one to the outermost. The interior rational constitutes the first degree, the degree in which celestial angels are, that is, where the inmost or third heaven is. The exterior rational makes up the second degree, the one in which spiritual angels are, that is, where the middle or second heaven is. The interior natural makes up the third degree, the one in which good spirits are, that is, where the last and lowest or first heaven is. And the exterior natural, the level of the senses, makes up the fourth degree, in which man is.

3 These degrees also exist within man, each degree completely distinct and separate. Consequently, if he leads a good life, he is interiorly a miniature heaven; that is, his interiors correspond to the three heavens. Also, if he has led a life of charity and love he can be taken after death all the way up to the third heaven. But if he is to be someone like this, each degree within him must be furnished with its own specific termination that makes it separate from the next one. When those degrees do have those terminations, making them distinct and separate from one another, each degree has a floor on which good flowing in from the Lord can rest and where it is received. Without such terminations acting as floors that good is not received but passes straight through, as if through a sieve or through 'a basket with holes in it', down to the sensory level. There, because it has not received any direction on the way, this good is turned into something foul, though it is seen as good by the recipients of it at that lowest level. That is to say, the good is turned into the kind of delight that belongs to a selfish and worldly love, and consequently into the kind of delight that belongs to hatred, revenge, cruelty, adultery, and avarice, or into sheer self-gratification and personal extravagance. This is what happens if the degrees of a person's will exist without a termination anywhere at all in the middle, that is, if 'they have holes in them'.

4 One can also actually know whether these terminations and therefore floors exist; people's abilities to perceive what is good and true point to the existence of them, as do their consciences. In the case of those who, like celestial angels, have the ability to perceive what is good and true, terminations exist in every degree, from the first to the last. Unless each degree has its own termination, no perceptive abilities such as these can exist. Regarding these abilities, see 125, 202, 495, 503, 511, 536, 597, 607, 784, 865, 895, 1121, 1383, 1384, 1387, 1919, 2144, 2145, 2171, 2515, 2831. In the case of those who, like spiritual angels, have conscience, terminations likewise exist, but only in the second degree or else in the third down to the last. For them the first degree is closed. One must say in the second degree or else in the third because conscience is twofold – interior and exterior. Interior conscience is one that concerns itself with what is spiritually good and true, exterior conscience one that concerns itself with what is just and fair. Conscience itself is an interior floor which provides inflowing Divine Good with a termination; but those who have no conscience do not have any interior floor to receive that influx. In their case good passes straight through to the exterior natural,

or the natural level of the senses, where it is turned, as has been stated, into foul delights. These people sometimes feel pain like that of conscience, but this is not conscience. The pain is caused by the loss of what they delight in, such as the loss of position, gain, reputation, life, pleasures, or the friendship of others who are like themselves. They suffer pain because the terminations which they possess consist in those kinds of delights. From all this one may see what is meant in the spiritual sense by 'baskets with holes in them'.

Particularly so in the next life one can discern whether or not the degrees of a person's will have been furnished with terminations. In the case of one who has been furnished with them, a zeal exists for what is spiritually good and true or for what is just and fair. For such persons had done what was good for the sake of what was good or for the sake of what was true, and had practised what was just for the sake of what was just or for the sake of what was fair, not for the sake of gain, position, and the like. All whose interior degrees of the will have been furnished with terminations are raised up to heaven, for the inflowing Divine is able to lead them there. But all whose interior degrees of the will have not been furnished with terminations make their way to hell, for what is Divine passes straight through and is turned into that which is hell-like, as when the heat of the sun falls on foul excrement and a disgusting stench is given off by it. Consequently all who have had conscience are saved, but those who have had none are incapable of being saved.

Degrees of the will are said to have holes in them, or to have no terminations, when there is no affection for goodness and truth, or for justice and equity, and when these virtues are considered to be of little or no value at all compared with anything else, or are esteemed solely for the sake of acquiring gain or position. The affections are what supply terminations and serve to close off, which is also why they are called bonds or restraints – affections for what is good and true being internal bonds, and affections for what is evil and false external ones, 3835. Unless the affections for what is evil and false acted as bonds or restraints the person would be insane, 4217; for insanity is nothing else than the removal of such restraints, so that no terminations are present in such persons. Even so, though these people do not possess any internal restraints and are therefore inwardly insane, so far as their thoughts and affections are concerned, an eruption of these is held back by external restraints, which consist in affections for gain, position, or reputation for their own sake, and consequently in a fear of the law or of loss of life. This was represented in the Jewish Church by the law that in the house of one who had died every open vessel which had no covering [or] cord [to fasten it] was unclean, Num.19:15.

Much the same is also meant by 'works full of holes' in Isaiah,

Those that make silk thread, and those that weave *works full of holes*, will blush.

And its foundations will be broken to pieces – all those making pools of the soul[1] their wages. Isa.19:9,10.

And by 'holes' in Ezekiel,

The Spirit brought the prophet to the door of the court, where he looked, and behold, *a hole in the wall.* And He said to him, Son of man, *bore a hole through the wall. He therefore bore a hole through the wall,* and behold, a door. Then He said to him, Go in and see the abominations that they do here. When he went in and saw, behold, every likeness of creeping thing and of beast, an abomination; and all the idols of the house of Israel, portrayed on the wall round about, etc. Ezek.8:7–10.

5146 'And in the highest basket' means the inmost degree of the will. This is clear from the meaning of 'a basket' as a degree of the will, dealt with above in 5144; and from the meaning of 'the highest' as the inmost part, dealt with in 2148, 3084, 4599. The reason 'the highest' means the inmost part is that while a person is an inhabitant of space, interior things are seen by him as higher and exterior ones as lower. But when spatial ideas are laid aside, as happens in heaven and also in a person's interior thought, the idea of height and depth is also laid aside; for height and depth belong to spatial ideas. Indeed in the inner heaven not even the idea of interior things and exterior ones exists because even that idea has a spatial element attached to it. Rather, the idea in that heaven is of a state of greater or lesser perfection; for interior things exist within a greater state of perfection than exterior ones because interior things are nearer to the Divine and exterior ones more remote from Him. This is the reason why that which is highest means that which is inmost.

2   Nevertheless no one can have a mental grasp of the relationship of what is interior to what is exterior unless he knows about degrees, regarding which see 3691, 4154, 5114, 5145. Man has no other notion of what is interior and consequently more perfect than the ever increasing purity of something the more one breaks it down. But greater purity and greater grossness can exist simultaneously in one and the same degree, owing not only to the expanding and condensing of it but also to the limitation of it and to the introduction of similar or else dissimilar elements into it. With an idea such as that regarding his interiors man cannot possibly do other than think that exterior things are attached in a continuous manner to interior ones, and so act entirely as one with them. But if a proper idea regarding degrees is formed one may grasp how interior and exterior things are distinct and separate from one another, so distinct that interior things can come into being and remain in being without exterior ones, whereas exterior things can never do so without interior ones. One may also grasp the nature of the correspondence of interior things within exterior ones, as well as the way in which the exterior things can represent interior ones. This explains why, other than hypothetically, the learned are unable to examine the

---

[1] *What Sw. understands by this literal rendering of the Hebrew is not clear.*

question regarding the interaction of the soul and the body. Indeed it also explains why many of them believe that life belongs intrinsically to the body, and thus that when their body dies their interiors will die too since these are closely attached to the body. But in actual fact only the exterior degree dies; the interior degree survives and goes on living.

5147 'There was some of every kind of food for Pharaoh' means full of celestial good for nourishing the natural. This is clear from the meaning of 'food' as celestial good, dealt with below; and from the representation of 'Pharaoh' as the interior natural, dealt with in 5080, 5095, and also the natural in general, since the interior natural and the exterior natural make one when they correspond. And because food exists to provide nourishment, 'every kind of food for Pharaoh' means full of celestial good for nourishing the natural. It is said that this food was in the highest basket, meaning that the inmost degree of the will was full of celestial good. For good from the Lord flows in by way of the inmost degree in a person; and from there it passes degree by degree, so to speak down a flight of steps, to what is more exterior. For in relation to other degrees the inmost one exists in the most perfect state, and can therefore receive good from the Lord directly, in a way the lower ones cannot. If these were to receive good from the Lord directly, they would either obscure it or pervert it, since they are less perfect in comparison with the inmost degree.

As regards the influx of celestial good from the Lord and the reception of it, it should be recognized that the will part of the human mind is the receiver of good and the understanding part is the receiver of truth. The understanding part cannot possibly receive truth so as to make this its own unless at the same time the will part receives good; and vice versa. For one flows as a result into the other and disposes that other to be receptive. All that constitutes the understanding may be compared to forms which are constantly varying, and all that constitutes the will may be compared to the harmonies resulting from those variations. Consequently truths may be compared to variations, and forms of good may be compared to the delights which those variations bring. And this being pre-eminently the case with truths and forms of good it is evident that one cannot exist without the other, as well as that one cannot be brought forth except by means of the other.

The reason 'food' means celestial good is that angels' food consists in nothing else than forms of the good of love and charity, and that these serve to enliven angels and to rejuvenate them. Especially when they are expressed in action or practice do those forms of good cause angels to feel rejuvenated, for they are the desires they have; for it is a well known fact that when a person's desires are expressed in action he feels rejuvenated and enlivened. Those desires also nourish a person's spirit when material food supplies nourishment to his body, as may be recognized from the fact that when no delight is taken in food it is not very nutritious, but when delight is taken in it, it is nutritious. The delight taken in food is what opens the meatus or channels which serve to convey it into the blood, whereas the opposite closes them. Among angels those delights are forms of the good of love and charity, and from this one may deduce that these are spiritual kinds of food which correspond to earthly ones. Also, just as forms of good are meant by different kinds of food, so truths are meant by 'drink'.

4 In the Word 'food' is mentioned in many places, yet someone unacquainted with the internal sense will inevitably suppose that in those places ordinary food is meant. In fact spiritual food is meant, as in Jeremiah,

All the people groan *as they search for bread*. They have given their desirable things *for food to restore the soul*. Lam.1:11.

In Isaiah,

Everyone who *thirsts*, come to the waters, and he who has no money, come, buy, and *eat*! Come, buy *wine* and *milk* without money and without price. Isa.55:1.

In Joel,

The day of Jehovah is near, and as destruction from the thunderbolt-hurler will it come. *Is not the food cut off before our eyes*, gladness and joy from the house of our God? *The grains* have rotted under their clods, *the storehouses* have been laid waste, *the granaries* have been destroyed, because *the grain* has failed. Joel 1:15–17.

In David,

Our storehouses are full, yielding *food and still more food*; our flocks are thousands, and ten thousands in our streets. There is no outcry in our streets. Blessed are the people for whom it is thus. Ps.144:13–15.

In the same author,

They all look to You, *that You may give them their food in due season*. You give to them – they gather it up; You open Your hand – they are *satisfied with good*. Ps.104:27,28.

5 In these places celestial and spiritual food is meant in the internal sense when material food is referred to in the sense of the letter. From this one may see how the interior features of the Word and its exterior features correspond to one another, that is, how what belongs inwardly to its spirit and what belongs to its letter do so; so that while man understands those things according to the sense of the letter, the angels present with him understand the same things according to the spiritual sense. The Word has been written in such a way that it may serve not only the human race but heaven also, and for this reason all expressions are used to mean heavenly realities, and every matter described there is representative of these realities. This is so with the Word even to the tiniest jot.

6 Furthermore the Lord Himself explicitly teaches that good is meant in the spiritual sense by 'food': In John,

Do not *labour for the food* which perishes, but *for the food* which endures to eternal life, which the Son of Man will give you. John 6:27.

In the same gospel,

My flesh is truly *food*, and My blood is truly drink.   John 6:55.

'Flesh' means Divine Good, 3813, and 'blood' Divine Truth, 4735. And in the same gospel,

Jesus said to the disciples, *I have food to eat* of which you do not know. The disciples said to one another, Has anyone brought Him [anything] to eat? Jesus said to them, *My food is* to do the will of Him who sent Me, and to finish His work.   John 4:32–34.

'Doing the will of the Father and finishing His work' means Divine Good when expressed in actions or practice, which in the genuine sense is 'food', as stated above.

5148   'The work of the baker' means according to every useful purpose served by that power of the senses. This is clear from the meaning of 'the work' as according to every useful purpose, dealt with below; and from the meaning of 'the baker' as the sensory power subject to the will part, dealt with in 5078, 5082. The reason 'the work' means a useful purpose is that this expression is used in reference to the will part, that is, to the sensory part subject to the will part. Whatever is effected by means of this and may be called 'the work' must be a useful purpose. No work of charity is anything else, for the works of charity are works performed by the will, and these are the realization of useful purposes.

5149   'And the birds were eating them out of the basket, from upon my head' means that falsity originating in evil would consume it. This is clear from the meaning of 'the birds' as intellectual concepts and also thoughts, and consequently the things which flow from them – in the genuine sense truths of every kind, and in the contrary sense falsities – dealt with in 40, 745, 776, 778, 866, 988, 3219; from the meaning of 'eating' as consuming (in the original language the verb to eat also denotes to consume); and from the meaning of 'the basket' as the will part of the mind, dealt with in 5144, 5146, in this case evil coming from the will part since the basket has holes in it, 5145. From this it follows that 'the birds were eating them out of the basket, from upon his head' means that falsity originating in evil would consume it.
Falsity has two different origins, doctrine and evil. Falsity originating in doctrine does not consume any form of good, for a person can have such falsity in his mind and yet desire what is good, which is why people taught any kind of doctrine, including gentiles, can be saved. But falsity originating in evil is falsity which does consume good. Evil itself is opposed to good; yet it does not by itself consume any good but relies on falsity to do so. For falsity attacks the truths which are the defenders of good, those truths being so to speak the ramparts behind which good resides. Falsity is used to attack those ramparts, and once this has been done, good is given over to destruction.

3   Anyone unacquainted with the fact that 'birds' means intellectual concepts will inevitably suppose that when mentioned in the Word the expression 'birds' is either used to mean birds literally or else is used, as in everyday speech, in a figurative sense. Except from the internal sense no one can know that 'birds' means things belonging to the understanding, such as thoughts, ideas, reasonings, basic assumptions, and consequently truths or falsities, as in Luke,

> The kingdom of God is like a grain of mustard seed, which someone took and sowed in his garden, and it grew and became a big tree *so that the birds of the air dwelt in its branches.*   Luke 13:19.

'The birds of the air' here stands for truths.

4   In Ezekiel,

> It will turn into a noble cedar, and *under it will dwell every bird of every sort[1]*; in the shade of its branches they will dwell.   Ezek.17:23.

'Bird of every sort' stands for truths of every kind. In the same prophet,

> Asshur was a cedar in Lebanon. In its branches *all the birds of the air* made their nests, and under its branches every beast of the field brought forth, and in its shadow dwelt all great nations.   Ezek.31:3,6.

'The birds of the air' stands in a similar way for truths.

5   In the same prophet,

> Upon its ruin will dwell *every bird of the air*, and on its branches will be every wild animal of the field.   Ezek.31:13.

'Bird of the air' stands for falsities. In Daniel,

> Nebuchadnezzar saw in a dream. Behold, a tree in the midst of the earth; under it the beasts of the field had shade, and *in its branches dwelt the birds of the air.* Dan.4:10,12,14,21.

Here also 'the birds of the air' stands for falsities.

6   In Jeremiah,

> I looked, and behold, there was no man; and *every bird of the air* had flown away. Jer.4:25.

'No man' stands for no good, 4287, 'the birds of the air which had flown away' for the fact that truths had been dispersed. In the same prophet,

> *From bird of the air* even to beast they have flown away, they have gone away. Jer.9:10.

Here the meaning is the same. In Matthew,

> A sower went out to sow; and some fell on the pathway, and *the birds came and devoured it.*   Matt.13:3,4.

Here 'the birds of the air' stands for reasonings, and also for falsities. The same meaning may be seen in many other places.

---

[1]   *lit.* of every wing

5150   'And Joseph answered and said' means revelation resulting from perception received by the celestial within the natural. This is clear from the meaning of 'answering and saying' as revelation resulting from perception, dealt with above in 5121; and from the representation of 'Joseph' as the celestial within the natural, dealt with in 5086, 5087, 5106. The reason 'Joseph' here means the celestial within the natural is that the natural is the subject. With regard to the celestial and the spiritual, the celestial itself and the spiritual itself which flow into heaven from the Lord's Divine reside principally in the interior rational, for the forms there are more perfect ones and apt receivers. Even so, the celestial and the spiritual also flow from the Lord's Divine into the exterior rational, and into the natural too, doing so both indirectly and directly. They flow indirectly by way of the interior rational, and directly from the Lord's Divine itself. What flows in directly is that which brings order, and what flows in indirectly is that to which order is brought. This is what happens in the exterior rational, as also in the natural. From this one may recognize what the celestial within the natural is.

The celestial has its origin in Divine Good and the spiritual in Divine Truth – both having their origin in the Lord. When they exist in the rational they are called the celestial and spiritual within the rational, and when they exist in the natural they are called the celestial and spiritual within the natural. The rational and natural are used to mean the person himself insofar as he has been formed to receive the celestial and spiritual; but the rational is used to mean his internal and the natural his external. By reason of what flows into him, and depending on his reception of it, a person is called a celestial man or else a spiritual man – a celestial man if the Lord's Divine Good is received in the will part of his mind, a spiritual man if it is received in the understanding part.

5151   'This is the interpretation of it' means what it held within it. This is clear from the meaning of 'the interpretation' as what something holds within it, that is, what lies within, dealt with above in 5093, 5105, 5107.

5152   'The three baskets' means the consecutive degrees of the will. This is clear from the meaning of 'the three baskets' as consecutive degrees of the will, dealt with above in 5144.

5153   'Are three days' means even to the final one. This is clear from the meaning of 'three' as a single period and the continuation of it from beginning to end, and so even to the final phase, dealt with in 2788, 4495, 5122.

5154   'In yet three days' means that within the final one. This is clear from what has been stated just above in 5152 about the meaning of 'three'.

5155 'Pharaoh will lift up your head from upon you' means a decision based on foresight. This is clear from the meaning of 'lifting up the head' as that which has been provided and therefore has been decided, or a decision based on providence, dealt with above in 5124; but here a decision based on foresight is meant because the prediction follows that he would be hanged on wood, by which a casting aside and condemnation are meant. The reason why a decision based on foresight, not on providence, is meant is that providence is used with reference to good but foresight with reference to evil. For all good flows in from the Lord and is therefore what is provided by Him; but all evil flows from hell, that is, from the human proprium which makes one with hell, and is therefore what is foreseen by Him. In its dealings with evil, providence is nothing else than the directing and steering of evil towards a milder evil, and so far as possible towards good; but evil itself is foreseen. Since therefore the subject at this point is the sensory power subject to the will part and the casting aside of this on account of evil, it is foresight that is meant.

5156 'And will hang you on wood' means a casting aside and condemnation. This is clear from the meaning of 'being hanged on wood' as a casting aside and condemnation; for hanging someone on wood was a curse, and a curse is being cast aside from the Divine and consequently is condemnation. The fact that hanging someone on wood was a curse is clear in Moses,

If a man has committed a crime punishable by death and he has been slain, *so that you hang him on wood*, his dead body shall not remain all night on the wood, but you must bury him the same day, for *the one hanged is the curse of God*. For you shall not defile the land which Jehovah your God is giving you for an inheritance. Deut.21:22,23.

'It shall not remain all night on the wood' meant casting aside for ever. For in the evening a new day began; therefore if those who had been hanged were not cast away before the evening, the failure to cast evil aside and consequently the failure to rid the land of that evil were represented. The land was defiled; hence the addition of the words 'You shall not defile the land which Jehovah your God is giving you for an inheritance'. They were left hanging until evening, but no later, see Josh.8:29; 10:26. Among the Jewish nation two chief forms of punishment existed, stoning and hanging. The existence of stoning was due to falsity, that of hanging on wood to evil, for the reason that 'stone' means truth, 643, 1298, 3720, and in the contrary sense falsity, while 'wood' means good, 2784, 2812, 3720, and in the contrary sense evil. This is why frequent reference is made in the prophetical part of the Word to 'committing adultery with stone and wood', meaning the perversion of truth, which is falsity, and the adulteration of good, which is evil.

5157   'And the birds will eat your flesh from upon you' means that falsity originating in evil will consume every one of those sensory impressions. This is clear from the meaning of 'eating' as consuming, dealt with above in 5149; from the meaning of 'the birds' as falsity, also dealt with above in 5149; from the meaning of 'flesh' as good, dealt with in 3812, 3813, and therefore in the contrary sense as evil (for most things in the Word also have a contrary sense, which is discerned from their meaning in the genuine sense); and from the meaning of 'from upon you' as from the sensory impressions subject to the will part, since those impressions are represented by 'the baker', 5078, 5082. The fact that these were evil and had therefore to be cast aside is clear from what has gone before.

The significance of all this – that the sensory impressions subject to the understanding part, which are represented by 'the cupbearer', were retained, whereas those subject to the will part, which are represented by 'the baker', were cast aside – is an arcanum that is completely unintelligible unless it has light shed on it. Let the following serve to shed some such light. By sensory impressions are meant those known facts and those delights which have been introduced through the five external or bodily senses into a person's memory and into his longings, and which together constitute the exterior natural, by virtue of which a person is called one governed by the senses. The facts are subject to the understanding part of his mind, whereas the delights are subject to the will part. Also, the facts link up with the truths which belong to the understanding, while the delights link up with the forms of good which belong to the will. The former are represented by 'the cupbearer' and were retained, but the latter are represented by 'the baker' and were cast aside.

The reason those known facts were retained is that in time they were able to accord with ideas in the understanding; but the reason the delights were cast aside is that they were by no means able to accord with what was in the will. For the will within the Lord, who is the subject in the highest internal sense, was from conception Divine and was the Divine Good itself; but the will received through His birth from His mother was evil and therefore had to be cast aside, and a new will had to be acquired in place of it. This new will was to be acquired from the Divine Will through the [Divine] Understanding, that is, from Divine Good through Divine Truth, and so was acquired by His own power. This is the arcanum which is described here in the internal sense.

5158   Verses 20–23 **And it happened on the third day, Pharaoh's birthday, that he made a feast for all his servants, and he lifted up the head of the chief of the cupbearers, and the head of the chief of the bakers, in the midst of his servants. And he restored the chief of the cupbearers to his supervision over [Pharaoh's] drink, and he put the cup onto Pharaoh's palm. And the chief of the bakers he hanged, as**

Joseph had interpreted to them. And the chief of the cupbearers did not remember Joseph, and forgot him.

'And it happened on the third day' means in the final phase. 'Pharaoh's birthday' means when the natural was to be regenerated. 'That he made a feast for all his servants' means the introduction and joining to the exterior natural. 'And he lifted up the head' means according to what was of providence and what was of foresight. 'Of the chief of the cupbearers, and the head of the chief of the bakers' means the sensory powers subject to both parts, the understanding part and the will part. 'In the midst of his servants' means which were among the things present in the exterior natural. 'And he restored the chief of the cupbearers to his supervision over [Pharaoh's] drink' means that the sensory impressions belonging to the understanding part were accepted and made subordinate. 'And he put the cup onto Pharaoh's palm' means and subservient to the interior natural. 'And the chief of the bakers he hanged' means that the sensory impressions belonging to the will part were cast aside. 'As Joseph had interpreted to them' means as foretold by the celestial within the natural. 'And the chief of the cupbearers did not remember Joseph' means that a complete joining to the celestial of the natural did not as yet exist. 'And forgot him' means removal.

5159 'And it happened on the third day' means in the final phase. This is clear from the meaning of 'the third day' as the final phase of a state; for 'day' means state, 23, 487, 488, 493, 893, 2788, 3462, 3785, 4850, and 'third' that which is complete, and so comes last, 1825, 2788, 4495. By the final phase of a state is meant the point when the previous state comes to an end and the new one begins. In the case of the person who is being regenerated a new state begins when order is turned around. The change takes place when interior things are given dominion over exterior ones, and exterior things begin to serve interior ones – which involves both ideas in the understanding and desires in the will. People who are being regenerated are conscious of this change as an inner urge not to allow sensory delights and bodily or earthly pleasures to take control, and draw ideas present in the understanding over to their own side to support them. When this change takes place the previous state has reached its final phase and the new one is entering its first. This is what is meant by 'on the third day'.

2　In everyone, whether or not he is being regenerated, changes of state take place, and order is turned around. Yet such changes are different in the case of those who are being regenerated than in the case of those who are not being regenerated. With those who are not being regenerated those changes of state or order are due to physical causes or are attributable to causes associated with life in the community. Physical causes are those impulses which arise at one stage in life and subside at another, in addition to the giving of deliberate thought to physical health and a long life in the world. The causes connected with life in the community are the external, visible curbs a person has to place on his real desire, so that he may earn a reputation for being a wise person and a lover of what is righteous and good, when in fact the acquisition of position and material gain is his real reason for pursuing such. But in the case of people who are being regenerated, such changes of state or order are attributable to spiritual causes which spring from goodness and righteousness themselves; and when a person starts to have an affection for these he is at the end of the previous state and at the beginning of the new one.

But as few are capable of seeing the truth of all this, let an example serve to shed light on the matter. Anyone who does not allow himself to be regenerated loves things of the body for their own sake, not for any other reason; and he loves the world too for its own sake. His love does not reach any higher because at heart he refuses to accept anything higher or more interior. On the other hand one who is being regenerated also loves things of the body, and worldly things likewise. Yet he loves them for higher or more interior reasons. He loves things of the body because he wishes to have a healthy mind inside a healthy body. Also, he loves his own mind and its healthiness for an even more interior reason, namely that he may have a wise discernment of what is good and an intelligent understanding of what is true. He also loves worldly things as much as others do, yet for the reason that the world, worldly wealth, possessions, and positions of importance may serve him as the means to put what is good and true or what is just and fair into effect.

This example enables one to see what each one – the regenerate and the unregenerate – is really like, and to see that outwardly the two are apparently alike but that inwardly they are totally different. From this one may also recognize the identity and the essential nature of the causes which bring about the changes of state and turnings around of order that take place with people who are not being regenerated and those that take place with people who are being regenerated. One may also see that in the case of regenerate persons interior things have dominion over exterior ones, whereas in the case of unregenerate persons exterior ones have dominion over interior. The reasons or the ends that a person has in view are what have dominion, for those ends subordinate everything else in a person and make it subject to themselves. The person's whole life is conditioned entirely by his end in view, for that end is what he loves all the time.

5160   'On Pharaoh's birthday' means when the natural was to be regenerated. This is clear from the meaning of 'being born' as being regenerated, dealt with below; and from the representation of 'Pharaoh' as the interior natural, dealt with in 5080, 5095, in this case the natural in general because among regenerate persons the agreement of the interior natural with the exterior natural causes the two to act as one.

The reason 'being born' means being regenerated is that in the internal sense spiritual matters are meant, and spiritual birth is regeneration, which is also called rebirth. When therefore birth is spoken of in the Word no other birth is understood in heaven than a birth effected through water and the spirit, that is, through faith and charity. For being born again or regenerated makes a person truly human and entirely different from animals, because in this case he becomes a son and heir of the Lord's kingdom. As regards the births which are mentioned in the Word meaning spiritual births, see 1145, 1255, 3860, 3868, 4070, 4668.

5161 'That he made a feast for all his servants' means the introduction and joining to the exterior natural. This is clear from the meaning of 'a feast' as the introduction to a joining together, dealt with in 3832, and also as a joining together through love and a making one's own, 3596; and from the meaning of 'servants' as the things which belong to the exterior natural. For when a person is being regenerated lower things are made subordinate and subject to higher ones, that is, exterior things are made so to interior ones. When this happens the exterior things become servants, and the interior become masters. This is the meaning 'servants' has in the Word, see 2541, 3019, 3020. But the kinds of people who become 'servants' are those who are loved by the Lord, for it is mutual love which joins them together and leads them to see their service to Him not as bondage but as whole-hearted allegiance, since good enters from within to produce that kind of delight there. In former times feasts were held for various reasons; and they meant an introduction into mutual love and so meant a joining together. Feasts were also held on birthdays; these represented the new birth or regeneration, which is a joining, through love, of a person's interiors to his exteriors, consequently a joining together in him of heaven and the world. For what is worldly or natural in a person is joined to what is spiritual and celestial.

5162 'And he lifted up the head' means [according to] what was of providence and what was of foresight. This is clear from the meaning of 'lifting up the head' as a decision attributable to providence and also to foresight, dealt with above in 5124, 5155. Providence is at work in the case of that power of sensory perception which is subject to the understanding part and is retained as something good, this being represented by 'the cupbearer'; but foresight is at work in the case of that sensory perception which is subject to the will part and is cast aside as something evil, this being represented by 'the baker'. That which is good is of providence while that which is evil is of foresight because everything good originates in the Lord but everything evil in hell or in the human proprium. As regards the human proprium being nothing but evil, see 210, 215, 694, 874–876, 987, 1023, 1044, 1047, 1581, 3812(end), 4328.

5163   'Of the chief of the cupbearers, and the head of the chief of the bakers' means regarding the sensory powers subject to both parts, the understanding part and the will part. This is clear from the representation of 'the cupbearer' as the sensory power subject to the understanding part, dealt with in 5077, 5082; and from the representation of 'the baker' as the sensory power subject to the will part, dealt with in 5078, 5082.

5164   'In the midst of his servants' means which were among the things present in the exterior natural. This is clear from the meaning of 'in the midst' as among those things; and from the meaning of 'servants' as the things within the exterior natural, dealt with just above in 5161. In the Word all things that occupy a lower position and are therefore subordinate and subject to higher ones are called 'servants'. This is so in the case of things present in the exterior natural – that is, the sensory impressions there – when considered in relation to the interior natural. The things present in this interior natural, when considered in relation to the rational, are also referred to as 'servants'. Consequently every single thing present in a person, inmost ones no less than outermost, are called such when considered in relation to the Divine, since the Divine is the highest of all.

The servants here in whose midst Pharaoh the king passed judgement on the cupbearer and the baker were chief courtiers and nobles. The reason why these, like other subjects belonging to any other rank of society, are called servants when considered in relation to the king is that, as is the case in any kingdom even today, kingship represents the Lord as regards Divine Truth, 2015, 2069, 3009, 3670, 4581, 4966, 5068. Considered in relation to Him all are equally servants, no matter what rank of society they belong to. Indeed in the Lord's kingdom, that is, in heaven, those who are the greatest there, that is, who are the inmost ones, are pre-eminently servants because their obedience is the greatest of all, and their humility is greater than that of any others. These are the ones who are meant by the least who will be the greatest, and the last who will be the first,

The first will be last, and *the last will be first.*
Matt.19:30; 20:16; Mark 10:31; Luke 13:30.
He who presents himself as *least* among you will be *great.*   Luke 9:48.

They are also meant by the great who are ministers, and by the first who are servants,

Whoever would be great among you must be your *minister*; and anyone who would be *first* among you must be *the servant* of all.   Mark 10:44; Matt.20:26,27.

They are called 'servants' in relation to the Divine Truth which originates in the Lord and 'ministers' in relation to the Divine Good which originates in Him. The reason 'the last who are the first' are servants, and more so than any others, is that they know, acknowledge, and perceive that the whole of their life, and therefore the whole of the power which they possess, originates in the Lord, and none at all in themselves; and those who do not perceive this because their acknowledgement of it is not so great are 'servants' too, though more because that acknowledgement is one that is on their lips rather than in their hearts. Those however whose attitude is completely the reverse also call themselves servants in relation to the Divine; yet their real wish is to be masters. For they are annoyed and angry if the Divine does not show them favour or so to speak does not obey them, and at length they set themselves against the Divine, when they take away all power from Him and attribute everything to themselves. Very many like these exist within the Church; they do not accept the Lord, though they do say that they acknowledge a supreme being.

5165 'And he restored the chief of the cupbearers to his supervision over [Pharaoh's] drink' means that the sensory impressions belonging to the understanding part were accepted and made subordinate. This is clear from the representation of 'the chief of the cupbearers' as in general the sensory impressions subject to the understanding part, dealt with above; and from the meaning of 'restoring to his supervision over [Pharaoh's] drink' as restoring to order beneath the understanding part. 'Restoring to a position' means restoring to order so as to occupy the lowest position, see 5125; but here a restoration to supervision over the drink is spoken of because that supervision and the kinds of drink that were the objects of it, such as wine, new wine, strong drink, and water, have reference to things of the understanding, as also do giving to drink and actual drinking, 3069, 3168, 3772, 4017. From this it is evident that 'restoring the chief of the cupbearers to his supervision over [Pharaoh's] drink' means a restoration to order of the sensory impressions belonging to the understanding, and thus the acceptance and subordination of them.

2 Those sensory impressions are accepted and made subordinate when they minister to and serve interior things as the means both to the realization of these in actions and to the acquisition of insights into them. For within the sensory impressions present in his exterior natural a person can see interior things, in much the same way as he sees people's affections within their faces and even more interior affections within their eyes. Without an interior face or mirror such as this no one is able, while living in the body, to engage in any thought at all about things that are above the senses; for what he sees within the sensory impressions may be likened to someone's recognition of other people's affections and thoughts within their faces, without the payment of any attention by him to their actual faces. Or it may be likened to someone listening to another speaking; he pays no attention to the words the speaker uses, only to the meaning of what is uttered by him. The actual words that are used are a mirror in which the inner meaning can be seen. The same is so with the exterior natural; if this did not serve interior things as a mirror in which they see themselves as if in a

looking-glass, a person could not engage in any thought at all. This being so, the mirror is formed first – in earliest childhood onwards. But these are matters about which people have no knowledge because what is going on inside a person is not evident unless one stops to reflect on what takes place inwardly.

The nature of the exterior natural is plainly evident in the next life, for the faces of spirits and of angels are shaped by and in conformity with it. In the light of heaven interior things, especially intentions and ends in view, shine through those faces. If love to the Lord and charity towards the neighbour have formed the interiors, then these cause a brightness to shine in the face, and the face itself is a visual form of love and charity. But if self-love and love of the world, and therefore all kinds of hatred, revenge, cruelty, and the like, have formed the interiors, these cause a devilish appearance to be manifested in the face, and the face itself is a visual form of hatred, revenge, and cruelty. From this one may see what the exterior natural is and the use it serves, also what it is like when made subject to interior things, and what it is like when these are made subject to itself.

5166   'And he put the cup onto Pharaoh's palm' means and subservient to the interior natural. This is clear from what has been stated above in 5126, where similar words occur.

5167   'And the chief of the bakers he hanged' means that the sensory impressions belonging to the will part were cast aside. This too is clear from what has been explained above, in 5156, where again similar words occur.

5168   'As Joseph had interpreted to them' means as foretold by the celestial within the natural. This is clear from the meaning of 'interpreting' as stating what the dream holds within itself or what lies within it, and also what was going to take place, dealt with in 5093, 5105, 5107, 5141, and so means a foretelling; and from the representation of 'Joseph' as the celestial within the natural, dealt with in 5086, 5087, 5106. As to what the words used here hold within them – namely the teaching that sensory impressions belonging to the understanding part were retained, whereas those belonging to the will part were cast aside – see above in 5157.

This chapter deals in the internal sense with the subordination of the exterior natural, which has to be made subordinate so that it may serve the interior natural as a mirror for it, see 5165. Indeed unless it is made subordinate, interior forms of truth and good, and consequently interior thoughts possessing what is spiritual and celestial within them, do not have any place where they can be represented, for these manifest themselves so to speak in their own face or so to speak in a mirror. Therefore when no such subordination exists a person cannot possess any interior thought, or indeed any faith, since no ability exists, neither a weak nor a strong one, to grasp such matters, and therefore no discernment exists of them either. Only one thing can make the natural subordinate and bring it into a state of correspondence, and this is good that has innocence within it, a good which in the Word is called charity. Sensory impressions and factual knowledge are merely the means into which that good may flow, to present itself in a visual form and make itself available for every useful purpose it can serve. But even if it consisted of actual truths of faith, factual knowledge that has no good within it would be nothing else than scales amid filth, which fall off.

3 But as regards the way in which good, relying on factual knowledge and the truths of faith as its means, causes exterior things to be restored to order and to be brought into correspondence with interior ones, this at the present day is less able to be understood than it was in former times. There are many reasons why this is so, the main one being that within the Church at the present day no charity exists any longer. For the final period of the Church has arrived and consequently no affection for knowing such things exists. This being so, a kind of aversion is instantly encountered when anything is mentioned which lies inside of or above sensory evidence, and consequently when anything from among such things as constitute angelic wisdom are expressed. Yet because such matters are contained in the internal sense – for what the internal sense contains is wholly suited to angels' wisdom – and because the internal sense of the Word is now being explained, those matters must be stated, however remote they may seem to be from sensory evidence.

5169 'And the chief of the cupbearers did not remember Joseph' means that a complete joining to the celestial of the natural did not as yet exist. This is clear from the meaning of 'remembering Joseph' as the reception of faith, dealt with above in 5130 – and consequently as a joining together too (faith is the means by which the joining together is effected, and therefore 'not remembering' here means that a complete joining together did not as yet exist); from the representation of 'the chief of the cupbearers' as the sensory perception belonging to the understanding part, and from the representation of 'Joseph' as the celestial of the natural, both of which representations are dealt with above.

5170 'And forgot him' means removal. This is clear from the meaning of 'forgetting' – when 'not remembering' means the non-existence of any joining together – as removal; for insofar as no joining together exists, removal takes place. Anything that becomes forgotten is also removed; and the same is so with sensory impressions subject to the understanding part. Though they are retained they are not joined to the celestial of the natural, because they are not as yet wholly free from illusions. But as they come to be freed from these, so the joining together takes place. But these matters are dealt with in the next chapter, where the cupbearer remembers Joseph.

CORRESPONDENCE WITH
THE GRAND MAN–*continued*
IN THIS SECTION THE CORRESPONDENCE OF
THE INTERNAL ORGANS WITH IT

5171   The particular provinces to which angelic communities belong
can be ascertained in the next life from the positions they occupy in
relation to the human body, as well as from the way they act and flow
in. For angelic communities flow into and act upon that organ or
member in which they are located. But their flowing in and action can
be perceived only by those who are in the next life. It cannot be
perceived by man unless his interiors have been opened all the way
through to that life, and not even then if the Lord does not impart to
him the ability to reflect on the sensations he feels and to do so with
perception.

5172   There are certain upright spirits who do not have to cogitate
and who can therefore express quickly whatever ideas occur to them
without having to think about them. They enjoy an interior kind of
perception, which does not reveal itself in thought and reflection, as is
the case with other spirits. For during the course of their lives they had
taught themselves about the goodness of things but not so much about
the truth of them. I have been shown that such spirits belong to the
province of the *Thymus Gland*; for the thymus is a gland that is
primarily of service to young children, at whose time of life that gland is
soft. With the spirits who belong to that province a child-like softness is
preserved into which a perception of what is good can flow; and from
that perception a general impression of what is true is created. Those
spirits can be in the midst of utter turmoils and yet they themselves are
not in any turmoil, as may also be the case with that gland.

5173   In the next life very many ways of harrying people are
employed, and also very many methods that involve introducing them
into a kind of spiralling. Harryings are represented in the body by the
purifications of the blood, also the serum or lymph as well as the chyle,
which too are accomplished by various refining processes, while
introductions into spiralling are represented by the subsequent assign-
ment of those refined fluids to particular services. It is very common in
the next life for spirits to be brought, after they have been harried, into
a state of tranquillity and delight, and then to be brought to those
communities which they are to be introduced into and become attached
to.
The idea that the refining processes and purifications of the blood,
serum, and chyle, and also of the food in the stomach, correspond to
such processes in the spiritual world is bound to seem strange to those
who presume that natural things hold no more than what is natural

within them, and even stranger to those who are quite convinced that this is so and accordingly deny that anything spiritual, active or reactive, does or can lie within natural things. Yet the reality is that every single thing in the natural world and its three kingdoms possesses something acting into it from the spiritual world. If this were not so, nothing whatever in the natural world could accomplish any cause and effect, and therefore nothing would be brought forth. That which natural things hold within them from the spiritual world is described as a force implanted since creation began; but in fact it is an endeavour, and when that endeavour ceases, action or motion ceases. All this demonstrates that the whole visible world is a theatre representative of the spiritual world.

3   The case is the same with the movement of the muscles and consequent action. Unless the movement of them held within it an endeavour originating in the person's thought and will, it would instantly cease; for laws well known to the learned world state that when the endeavour ceases so does the movement, and also that the person's entire direction of mind is present within the endeavour, as well as that nothing real other than the endeavour expresses itself within the movement. The force or endeavour within the action or movement is, it is plain, something spiritual within something natural; for thought and will are spiritual activities, whereas action and movement are natural ones. People whose thought does not extend beyond the natural world have no grasp of this at all; yet they are not able to deny it. Nevertheless what exists in the will, and from there in the thought, is the producer of the action, though it is not similar in form to the action which it produces. For the action merely represents what the mind wills and thinks.

5174   It is well known that food in the stomach is subjected to many processes which harry it so that its essential nourishment – which goes on to perform some useful purpose, that is, which passes into the chyle and then into the blood – may be extracted from it, after which it undergoes further processing in the intestines. Harryings of this kind are represented by the initial harryings that spirits undergo – every one of which is determined by the lives they led in the world – so that evils may be separated and the forms of good which have some useful purpose to perform may be gathered together. So far as souls or spirits are concerned therefore, it may be said that a little while after their departure or release from the body they come first so to speak into the region of the stomach where they are harried and purified. After those with whom evils have gained predominance have been harried to no avail they are conveyed through the stomach into the intestines, right on to the end of them – to the colon and the rectum. From there they are excreted into the latrine, which is hell. But those with whom forms of good have gained predominance are converted, after several experiences involving harrying and purification, into chyle and pass on into the blood, some by a longer route, others by a shorter one. Some are subjected to harsh harrying experiences, others to mild ones, and some to scarcely any whatever. Those subjected to scarcely any are represented in the food-juices that are absorbed instantly through the veins into the bloodstream, even into the brain, and so on.

5175 When a person dies and enters the next life, his life may be likened to food which is received in a gentle manner by the lips and is then passed down through the mouth, throat, and oesophagus into the stomach, the whole process being conditioned by his character which has been formed during his lifetime by the things he did. To begin with, the treatment that most spirits receive is mild, for they are kept in the company of angels and good spirits. This is represented by what happens to food, when at first it is touched gently by the lips and then tasted by the tongue to see what it is like. Food that is soft, containing that which is sweet, oily, and spirituous is received instantly through the veins and carried away into the bloodstream, whereas food that is hard, containing that which is bitter, disagreeable, and of little nutritive value, is harder to break down, being sent down through the oesophagus into the stomach where it is refined by various methods and violent actions. Food that is even harder, even less agreeable, and of even less value is forced down into the intestines and at length into the rectum where the first hell is situated, and is then finally expelled and becomes excrement. Analogous to all this is a person's life after death. At first he is confined to matters of an external nature; and because in matters of an external nature he has led a decent and respectable life, he is among angels and upright spirits. But once he ceases to be confined to them, what he had been like inwardly – what he had been like so far as his thoughts and affections were concerned, and at length so far as his ends in view were concerned – is revealed; and those ends determine the life that awaits him.

5176 As long as spirits remain in that state in which they are like food in the stomach they are not within the Grand Man but are at the stage of being introduced into it. But once, representatively speaking, they are within the blood they are within the Grand Man.

5177 Those who have worried much about the future, and more so those who have as a consequence become grasping and avaricious, appear in the region where the stomach is situated. Many have appeared to me there. The sphere of their life may be likened to a nauseating smell emitted from the stomach and also to an ache caused by indigestion. People like these remain in that region for a long time, for worries about the future, when these are compounded by the way such people act, seriously impair and slow down the inflow of spiritual life. This is because these people assign to themselves that which is the business of Divine Providence, and those who do this put a stop to that inflow and so cut themselves off from the life of goodness and truth.

5178 Since worrying about the future produces feelings of anxiety in a person, and since such spirits appear in the region of the stomach, feelings of anxiety therefore have a greater effect on the stomach than on all other internal organs. I have also been allowed to recognize how those anxious feelings have increased or diminished as those spirits have become present or been removed. I have noticed that some anxious feelings exist more internally, others more externally, some higher up, others lower down, depending on the differences in origin, derivation, and direction taken by such kinds of worry. Here also lies the reason why, when such feelings of anxiety take hold of the mind, the area around the stomach is tense and sometimes pain is felt there, and also why feelings of anxiety seem to surge up from there. The same also explains why, when a person ceases to worry about the future or when everything is turning out right for him so that he no longer fears any misfortune, the area around the stomach is free and relaxed, and he has the feeling of delight.

5179 On one occasion I experienced an anxious feeling in the pit of my stomach, which told me that spirits of that kind were present. I spoke to them, telling them that it would be better if they went away, because their sphere which created the feeling of anxiety was not compatible with the spheres of the spirits who were residing with me. At that time I talked to them about spheres, to the effect that many spiritual spheres surround a person but that people neither know nor wish to know about the existence of them, for the reason that they deny the existence of everything that is called spiritual, some denying the existence of everything that cannot be actually seen or touched. So I went on to say that certain spheres from the spiritual world surround a person, spheres that are in keeping with the life he leads, and that by means of these he exists in the company of spirits whose affection is similar to his own. Those spheres, I added, were also what gave rise to very many things, the existence of which is denied by the person who attributes everything to natural forces or else is ascribed by him to some rather more hidden natural cause such as chance. For experience leads some people to feel quite convinced that some hidden force is at work which they call chance, though they do not know the origin of that force. The fact that its origin exists in a spiritual sphere and that it is the last and lowest degree of Providence will in the Lord's Divine mercy be described elsewhere, when I shall draw on experience to bear witness to it.

5180 There are genii and spirits who subject the head to a kind of sucking or drawing out, which they do in such a way that pain is felt at the point where that drawing or sucking out takes place. I have experienced a definite sensation of suction, altogether as if a membrane was being sucked out. I doubt whether anyone else could put up with the pain of it; but because I have become accustomed to the experience I have at length come to bear it without noticing the pain. The chief place subjected to suction was the top of my head, and from there it spread towards the region of my left ear and also towards that of my left eye, the spread towards the eye being caused by spirits and that towards the ear by genii. These genii and spirits belong to the province of the *Cisterna Chyli* and its *ducts,* to which point chyle is drawn from everywhere around, even though other chyle is being sent forth at the same time from there. Besides those genii and spirits there were also others acting inside my head in almost the same manner, though not with so great a power of suction. I was told that these are the ones to whom the fine chyle corresponds – the fine chyle which is conveyed towards the brain and there mingled with new animal spirit[1] so as to be sent down to the heart. At first I had seen those acting on the outside in front, a little to the left; but subsequently I saw them in a higher position there, which made me realize that their region extended from the level of the septum of the nose upwards to the level of the left ear. Those who constitute this province are of two kinds, for some are quite constrained while others are impudent. The constrained are ones who have sought to know other people's thoughts to the end that they might gain those people's interest and become attached to them; for a person who knows another's thoughts knows his secret and inner feelings, and these link the two together. The end in view is company and friendship. These constrained spirits desire to know simply about the good things, finding out more about these and placing a good interpretation on all else. But the impudent ones have a longing to know – and strive in various ways to fish out – other people's thoughts, their end in view being to take advantage of those people or harm them. Now because that kind of longing and striving is present in them they fix another person's mind steadfastly on the matter which they themselves wish to know about, showing him affection and approval as they do so. By acting in this way they get out of him even his secret thoughts. They behave in the same way in the next life within the communities there, yet in a more expert manner. There too they do not allow another to stray from whatever idea he has in mind; indeed they foster it and thereby get it out of him. As a consequence these impudent spirits then have a hold so to speak on others and subject them to their own will; for they know what those others' evils are. These spirits however, being some of those who are wanderers, suffer frequent punishment.

5181   From the spirallings also one can gain some idea about which particular province in the Grand Man, and correspondingly in the body, spirits and angels belong to. The spirallings of those who belong to the province of the *Lymphatic System* are thin and quick in action, like water flowing smoothly, so that scarcely any spiralling movement can be detected. Those who belong to the lymphatic system are eventually brought into places which, they have said, are the counter-

[1] *See* 4227:3.

part to the *Mesentery*. I have been told that here there are labyrinths so to speak, from which, like chyle in the body, they are then borne away to various places in the Grand Man to serve some useful purpose there.

5182   There are spirallings into which spirits who are recent arrivals in the next life have to be introduced, for the purpose of enabling them to live in the company of other spirits and of enabling them both to speak and to think in unison with these. In the next life all must exist in accord and harmony with one another if they are to be a unified whole, even as all the individual parts of the human being, which are varied throughout the body, are nevertheless in harmony with one another and so make a unified whole. The same applies to the Grand Man, in which one person's thought and speech must accord with the thought and speech of all the others if they are to achieve the same end. It is absolutely essential that the thought and speech of each member in a community should accord with the rest, otherwise discord is detected, which sounds in the minds of the others like a harsh grating noise. Furthermore everything discordant is destructive of unity; it is an imperfection that must be cast out. This imperfection resulting from discord is represented by impurity residing with and present within the blood, from which it must be expelled. The expulsion of this impurity is effected by harrying processes, which are nothing else than various kinds of temptations, and after this by means of introductions into spirallings. The purpose of a first introduction into spirallings is to enable spirits to become adjusted to one another; the purpose of a second is that their thought may accord with their speech; the purpose of a third is that they may all agree with one another in thought and affection; and the purpose of a fourth is that they may agree in truth and good.

5183   I have beeen allowed to watch the spirallings of those who belong to the province of the *Liver*, and to do so for a whole hour. These spirals were gentle ones, flowing round in varying ways in keeping with the operation of that organ; and they gave me a great feeling of delight. The operation of the spirits is diverse, but in general they proceed in a circular manner. The diversity of their operation is also represented in the functions performed by the liver, in that these too are diverse. For the liver draws in blood and separates it. It introduces the best blood into the veins, sends that of medium quality into a hepatic duct, and leaves that of poorest quality for the gall bladder. This is so in adult persons, but in embryos the liver receives blood from the mother's womb and purifies it. It passes the purer blood to the veins so that it may flow into the heart by a shorter route, and act as protectors in front of the heart.

5184   Those who belong to the *Pancreas* act in a more incisive way – employing so to speak a sawing action which also sounds like such an action. The actual sound they make is audible to spirits, but not to man unless while in the body he is in the spirit. Their region lies between that of the spleen and that of the liver, more to the left. Those in the province of the *Spleen* are almost directly overhead; but when they operate they come down into that organ.

5185 There are spirits who correlate with the *Pancreatic Duct*, the *Hepatic Duct*, and the *Cystic Duct*, and who consequently correlate with the bile present in them, which is excreted by the intestines. These groups of spirits are distinct and separate, yet they work together as demanded by the state of those in whom they operate. They are present in particular at chastisements and punishments, which they would like to be in charge of. The worst of them are so stubborn that they have no wish at all to desist unless they are frightened off by fears and threats; for they are afraid of being punished themselves, and so will promise to do anything. They are spirits who during their lifetime stuck rigidly to their own opinions, not so much because they led an evil life as because they were naturally perverse. When in their own natural state they have no real thought at all (a person has no real thought at all when he has vague thoughts about many things simultaneously but has no distinct idea about any one thing in particular). Their delights consist in the work of chastisement and doing good by carrying it out; but they do not refrain from foul deeds.

5186 Those who constitute the province of the *Gall Bladder* are at the back. They are spirits who during their lifetime despised uprightness and to a certain extent godliness, and also spirits who sneered at these virtues.

5187 A certain spirit once came to me, asking whether I knew a place where he could stay. I thought he was an upright spirit, and when I told him that he could perhaps stay where I was, harrier spirits who belonged to this province came along and harried him piteously. This grieved me, and I sought in vain to stop them. At this point I became aware of the fact that I was in the province of the gall bladder. The harrying spirits were some of those who despised uprightness and godliness. I was allowed to witness one kind of harrying there, which consisted in compelling a spirit to speak faster than he could think. This they accomplished by severing his own speech from his thought and then compelling him to speak what they were speaking, a painful experience. By means of this form of harrying the slow are introduced into thinking and speaking more quickly.

5188 There are certain people in the world who, when they act, employ tricks and lies to accomplish evil deeds. I have been shown what those people are like and the ways in which they act – how, when persuading others, they use as their agents those who will do no one any harm, and also how they induce other persons to speak in a certain way while they themselves remain silent on the matter. In short they employ evil means to attain whatever end they have in view, means that involve the use of deceit, lies, and trickery. Such spirits have their counterpart in malignant growths, called *Spurious Tubercles*, which usually develop in the lungs or other membranes. When these are deep-rooted their malignancy becomes widespread, so that at length they wreck the entire membrane.

2 Spirits of this kind undergo severe punishment. Theirs is different from the punishments suffered by other spirits; it involves their being whirled around. They are whirled around from left to right, like an object which is flat at first but swells out as it spins round. Then this tubercle-like swelling seems to be pressed in and made hollow, at which point the speed is increased. Amazingly, this swelling out of them is shaped like and is an imitation of tubercular lumps or apostemes. I noticed that while they were spinning round those spirits tried to draw others, for the most part blameless ones, into their orbit and so path of destruction. Thus they did not care at all whom they dragged into that path of destruction, so long as it seemed to them that those dragged in were being destroyed.

3 I also noticed that those spirits had very keen sight. They took only an instant to scan everything thoroughly so to speak and so seize upon whatever would serve them as means favouring their own ends. Thus they are more sharp-witted than all others. They may also be called deadly ulcers, wherever these occur within the cavity of the chest, whether in the pleura, or in the pericardium, or in the mediastinum, or in the lungs. I was shown that following punishment spirits of this kind are cast away into a deep place at the rear, where they lie face and belly downwards. There only a little human life is left to them, and the sharp-sightedness which they possessed when they lived like wild animals has been taken away from them. Their hell is situated in a deep place beneath the right foot, a little towards the front.

5189 Some spirits once came in front of me, though not before I had detected a sphere emanating from those who were evil. That sphere led me to suppose that those who were approaching were evil spirits, but in fact they were the enemies of such spirits. I gathered they were their enemies from the antagonistic and hostile feeling they showed towards them. As they came they positioned themselves overhead and addressed me, saying that they were men (*homo*). I replied that they were not men endowed with bodies like those which people in the world possess, who are accustomed to call themselves men because of the form their bodies take, but that they were nevertheless men because a person's spirit is in a true sense the man. I detected no objection to this, for they supported what I had said and went on to say that they were men who were all different from one another. Because it seemed impossible to me that a community of people who were all different from one another could exist in the next life, I therefore discussed the matter with them. I said that if a common cause were to make them a unified whole they could form a community, since they would all accordingly have the same end in view. They then said that they were by nature such that each individual spoke differently from all the rest and yet all thought alike. This they also demonstrated by examples, from which it could be seen that the perception of all was the same but that their utterances were diverse.

After this they spoke into my left ear, saying that they were good spirits and that this was their normal manner of speaking. I was told that these spirits arrive on the scene in large numbers, and that it is not known where they come from. I perceived that the sphere of the evil spirits was extremely hostile towards them, for evil spirits are subjected by them to harrying. Their community, which is a wandering one, was represented by a man and a woman in a room, dressed in a garment that was turned into a robe of bright blue. I perceived that they correlated with the *Isthmus* in the brain, which lies between the cerebrum and the cerebellum and through which fibres pass to spread out in various directions, acting in different ways wherever they go in external parts. In addition I perceived that they correlated with the *Ganglia* in the body into which nerves pass and from where they are distributed into numerous fibres, some of which go one way, others another, and in the outermost parts act in differing ways; yet they all have the same starting-point. Thus in the outermost parts they are seen to be different from one another; but so far as the end in view is concerned they are all alike. It is also a well known fact that a single force acting within the extremities can be made to vary in all kinds of ways, depending on the form those extremities take. Ends in view are also represented by the starting-points of fibres, like such starting-points in the brain, in which the fibres originate. The thoughts arising out of those ends are represented by the fibres leading from those starting-points, and the consequent actions by the nerves that are made up of the fibres.

5190   Correspondence with the Grand Man is continued at the end of the next chapter.

41 [1]

1 And it happened at the end of two years of days*, that Pharaoh was dreaming, and behold, he was standing next to the river.

2 And behold, out of the river seven cows were coming up, beautiful in appearance and fat-fleshed; and they fed in the sedge.

3 And behold, seven other cows were coming up after them out of the river, bad in appearance and thin-fleshed, and stood by the [other] cows on the bank of the river.

4 And the cows bad in appearance and thin-fleshed devoured the seven cows beautiful in appearance and fat. And Pharaoh awoke.

5 And he fell asleep and dreamed a second time, and behold, seven heads of grain were coming up on one stalk, fat and good.

6 And behold, seven heads, thin and scorched by an east wind, were sprouting after them.

7 And the thin heads swallowed up the seven fat and full heads. And Pharaoh awoke, and behold, it was a dream.

8 And it happened early in the morning, that his spirit was troubled, and he sent and called all the magi of Egypt, and all its wise men; and Pharaoh told them his dream, and there was no one to interpret them for Pharaoh.

9 And the chief of the cupbearers spoke to Pharaoh, saying, I remember my sins today.

10 Pharaoh was incensed with his servants, and put me into custody in the house of the chief of the attendants, me and the chief of the bakers.

11 And we dreamed a dream in one night, I and he; we dreamed each according to the interpretation of his own dream.

12 And a Hebrew boy was there with us, a servant to the chief of the attendants; and we told him, and he interpreted our dreams for us, to each according to his dream he gave the interpretation.

13 And it happened, that as he interpreted to us, so it came about. He restored me to my position, and he hanged him.

---

[1] *Volume Five of the Latin, which begins here, does not have any preliminary sections to chapters.*

[2] *i.e.* two full years

14 And Pharaoh sent and called Joseph, and they hurried him out of the pit; and he clipped [his hair and beard], and changed his clothes, and came to Pharaoh.

15 And Pharaoh said to Joseph, I have dreamed a dream, and there is no one who can interpret it; and I have heard about you – it is said that when you hear a dream you can interpret it.

16 And Joseph answered Pharaoh, saying, It is not mine; God will give an answer of peace, O Pharaoh.

17 And Pharaoh spoke to Joseph, In my dream, behold, I was standing on the bank of the river.

18 And behold, out of the river seven cows were coming up, fat-fleshed and beautiful in form; and they fed in the sedge.

19 And behold, seven other cows were coming up after them, weak and extremely bad in form and lean-fleshed; I have not seen any like them in all the land of Egypt for badness.

20 And the lean and bad cows devoured the first seven fat cows.

21 And they devoured them completely[1], and no one would have known that they had devoured them completely[2]; and their appearance was malign, as it had been in the beginning. And I awoke.

22 And I saw in my dream, and behold, seven heads of grain were coming up on one stalk, full and good.

23 And behold, seven heads, dried up, thin, and scorched by an east wind, were sprouting after them.

24 And the thin heads swallowed up the seven good heads. And I told it to the magi, and there was no one to point out the meaning to me.

25 And Joseph said to Pharaoh, Pharaoh's dream, it is one; what God is doing He has pointed out to Pharaoh.

26 The seven good cows are seven years, and the seven good heads of grain are seven years; the dream, it is one.

27 And the seven thin and bad cows coming up after them are seven years; and the seven empty heads of grain, scorched by an east wind, will be seven years of famine.

28 This is the word which I have spoken to Pharaoh; what God is doing He has caused Pharaoh to see.

29 Behold, seven years are coming, [in which there will be] a great abundance of corn in all the land of Egypt.

30 And seven years of famine will arise after them, and all the abundance of corn in the land of Egypt will be thrust into oblivion, and the famine will consume the land.

31 And the abundance of corn in the land will not be known because of the famine from then on, for it will be extremely severe.

32 And as for the dream being presented[3] to Pharaoh twice, this is because the thing is established by God, and God is hastening to do it.

---

[1] *lit.* they came to their viscera
[2] *lit.* it was not known that they had come to their viscera
[3] *lit.* repeated

33 And now let Pharaoh see[1] a man with intelligence and wisdom, and set him over the land of Egypt.

34 Let Pharaoh do this, and let him place governors in charge over the land, and let him take up the fifth part of the land of Egypt in the seven years of abundance of corn.

35 And let them gather all the food of these good years that are coming, and let them store up grain under the hand of Pharaoh – food in the cities; and let them guard it.

36 And let the food be for a reserve for the land, for the seven years of famine which there will be in the land of Egypt, and the land will not be cut off in the famine.

37 And the thing was good in Pharaoh's eyes and in the eyes of all his servants.

38 And Pharaoh said to his servants, Shall we find a man like this, in whom is the spirit of God?

39 And Pharaoh said to Joseph, After God has caused you to know all this, no one has wisdom and intelligence like you.

40 You shall be over my house, and all my people shall kiss on your mouth; only in the throne will I be great, more than you.

41 And Pharaoh said to Joseph, See, I have set you over all the land of Egypt.

42 And Pharaoh took off his ring from upon his hand and put it onto Joseph's hand, and clothed him in robes of fine linen, and placed a chain of gold onto his neck.

43 And he made him ride in the second chariot that he had; and they cried out before him, Abrek! and he set him over all the land of Egypt.

44 And Pharaoh said to Joseph, I am Pharaoh, and without you no man shall lift up his hand or his foot in all the land of Egypt.

45 And Pharaoh called Joseph's name Zaphenath Paneah, and gave him Asenath, the daughter of Potiphera the priest of On, for a wife; and Joseph went out over the land of Egypt.

46 And Joseph was a son of thirty years when he stood before Pharaoh king of Egypt; and Joseph came out from before Pharaoh, and went through all the land of Egypt.

47 And in the seven years of abundance of corn the land yielded bunches.

48 And he gathered all the food of the seven years which were in the land of Egypt, and laid up[2] the food in the cities; the food of the field of a city which was round about it he laid up[2] in the midst of it.

49 And Joseph stored up grain like the sand of the sea, very much, until he left off numbering, because it was beyond number.

50 And to Joseph were born two sons before the year of famine came, whom Asenath, the daughter of Potiphera the priest of On, bore to him.

---

[1] *i.e.* select *or* look out. *See* 5286.
[2] *lit.* gave

51 And Joseph called the name of the firstborn Manasseh – for God has made me forget all my labour and all my father's house.

52 And the name of the second he called Ephraim – for God has made me fruitful in the land of my affliction.

53 And the seven years of abundance of corn ended, which was in the land of Egypt.

54 And the seven years of famine began to come, even as Joseph had said; and the famine was in all lands, and in all the land of Egypt there was bread.

55 And all the land of Egypt suffered famine, and the people cried out to Pharaoh for bread. And Pharaoh said to all Egypt, Go to Joseph; do what he tells you.

56 And the famine was over all the face of the earth; and Joseph opened all the places in which [there was grain] and sold to Egypt. And the famine was becoming great in the land of Egypt.

57 And all the earth came to Egypt to buy [grain], to Joseph; for the famine became great in all the earth.

CONTENTS

5191 In this chapter the subject in the internal sense is the second state of the celestial of the spiritual, which is 'Joseph'; that is to say, the subject is the raising up of this above the things belonging to the natural or external man, and so above all the factual knowledge there, which is 'Egypt'.

5192 'Pharaoh' is the natural in general which has now become inactive, leaving everything to the celestial of the spiritual, which is 'Joseph'. The seven years of the abundance of corn in the land of Egypt are the factual knowledge to which good from the celestial of the spiritual can be attached, while the seven years of famine are subsequent states when no good is present within factual knowledge except that coming from the Divine celestial of the spiritual, which is received from the Lord's Divine Human. A detailed explanation of this is given in what follows below.

THE INTERNAL SENSE

5193 Verses 1-4 **And it happened at the end of two years of days[1], that Pharaoh was dreaming, and behold, he was standing next to the river. And behold, out of the river seven cows were coming up, beautiful in appearance and fat-fleshed; and they fed in the sedge. And behold, seven other cows were coming up after them out of the river, bad in appearance and thin-fleshed, and stood by the [other] cows on the bank of the river. And the cows bad in appearance and thin-fleshed devoured the seven cows beautiful in appearance and fat. And Pharaoh awoke.**

'And it happened at the end of two years of days' means after the state when the joining together took place. 'That Pharaoh was dreaming' means provision made for the natural. 'And behold, he was standing next to the river' means from boundary to boundary. 'And behold, out of the river' means in the boundary. 'Seven cows were coming up' means the truths belonging to the natural. 'Beautiful in appearance' means which are expressions of faith. 'And fat-fleshed' means which are embodiments of charity. 'And they fed in the sedge' means instruction. 'And behold, seven other cows were coming up after them out of the river' means falsities belonging to the natural which are also at the boundary. 'Bad in appearance' means which are not expressions of faith. 'And thin-fleshed' means which are not embodiments of charity. 'And stood by the [other] cows on the bank of the river' means at the boundaries where truths were present. 'And the cows bad in appearance and thin-fleshed devoured.....' means that falsities which were not expressions of faith and were not embodiments of charity would banish..... 'The seven cows beautiful in appearance and fat' means the truths in the natural which are expressions of faith and embodiments of charity. 'And Pharaoh awoke' means a state of enlightenment.

5194 'And it happened at the end of two years of days' means after the state when the joining together took place, that is to say, when the powers of the senses belonging to the exterior natural and those belonging to the interior natural were joined together, both of which powers are dealt with in the previous chapter. This is clear from the meaning of 'two years of days', that is, a period of two years, as a state involving a joining together; for 'two' means a joining together, 1686, 3519, while 'years' means states, as does 'days'. For the meaning of 'years' as states, see 487, 488, 493, 893, and for that of 'days', 23, 487, 488, 493, 2788, 3462, 3785, 4850. The reason 'two' means a joining together is that every single thing in the spiritual world, and consequently in the natural world, has two forces associated with it – goodness and truth. Good is an active inflowing force, truth a passive, recipient one. Also, because everything has these two forces associated with it, and because

---

[1] *i.e.* two full years

nothing can ever be brought forth unless the two are made one by becoming so to speak married to each other, a joining together is therefore meant by them.

2   This type of marriage exists in every single thing within the natural order and its three kingdoms; without it nothing whatever can come into existence. For anything to come into existence within the natural order there needs to be heat and light, heat in the natural world corresponding to the good of love in the spiritual world, and light corresponding to the truth of faith. These two – heat and light – must act as one if anything is to be brought forth. If they do not act as one, as is the case in winter-time, nothing at all is brought forth. The same holds true on a spiritual level, as is quite evident with the human being, who has two mental powers – will and understanding. The will has been formed so that it may receive spiritual heat, that is, the good of love and charity, while the understanding has been formed so that it may receive spiritual light, that is, the truth of faith. Unless these two residing with a person make one nothing is brought forth, for the good of love devoid of the truth of faith cannot give definition and particular character to anything, while the truth of faith devoid of the good of love cannot bring anything into effect. So that the heavenly marriage may exist in a person therefore, or rather so that a person may be in the heavenly marriage, those two entities must make one in him. This explains why the ancients likened every single thing in the world, and every single thing within the human being, to a marriage, 54, 55, 568, 718, 747, 917, 1432, 2173, 2516, 2731, 2739, 2758, 3132, 4434, 4835, 5138. From all this one may see why it is that 'two' means a joining together.

5195   'That Pharaoh was dreaming' means provision[1] made for the natural. This is clear from the representation of 'Pharaoh' as the natural, dealt with in 5079, 5080, 5095, 5160, and from the meaning of 'dreaming' as a foretelling of things to come, and so in the highest sense as Foresight, dealt with in 3698, 4682, 5091, 5092, 5104. Now since Foresight or the foreseen is meant, Providence or provision is meant too, because Foresight and Providence cannot exist one without the other. For Providence has in view the state that is to last for ever; but unless it foresees what this state is, it cannot make any provision towards it. A provision for present needs without at the same time any foresight of future ones, and so no simultaneous provision for future needs within present ones, would imply a lack of any end in view, or of any order, or of consequently any wisdom and intelligence, and so it would not be something having a Divine origin. But when reference is made to what is good the term Providence is used, whereas Foresight is used in reference to what is not good, 5155. One cannot use the term Foresight when speaking of what is good because good resides within the Divine, comes forth from the Divine Himself, and exists in accord

---

[1] *Reading* provisum (what is provided) *for* praevisum (what is foreseen) *cp* 5193, 5211

with the Divine. Rather, this term is used when one refers to what is not good or to what is evil since this comes forth from outside the Divine, from others opposed to the Divine. Thus because Providence is used when reference is made to what is good, the term is also used to refer to the joining of the natural to the celestial of the spiritual. This is the reason why 'dreaming' at this point means provision that had been made.

5196   'And behold, he was standing next to the river' means from boundary to boundary. This is clear from the meaning of 'the river' – which in this case is the River of Egypt, or the Nile – as a boundary. The reason 'the river' means a boundary is that the major rivers, the Euphrates, the Jordan, and the Nile, and besides these the sea, were the final boundaries of the land of Canaan. Because the land of Canaan itself represented the Lord's kingdom, and all locations in that land therefore represented various features of that kingdom, the rivers accordingly represented its final limits or boundaries, see 1866, 4116, 4240. The Nile or River of Egypt represented sensory impressions subject to the understanding part of the mind and so represented factual knowledge gained from those impressions; for that factual knowledge is the final limit of spiritual things that belong to the Lord's kingdom. The reason why from boundary to boundary is meant is that, referring to Pharaoh, it says 'he was standing next to the river'; and 'Pharaoh' represents the natural in general, 5160. Viewing something from within through to its final outward limit is represented by 'standing next to the river', as happens in the spiritual world. And because in the present context such a view extends from boundary to boundary, that is what is therefore meant in the internal sense.

5197   'And behold, out of the river' means in the boundary. This is clear from the meaning of 'the river' as the boundary, dealt with immediately above in 5196. The reason 'out of the river' means in the boundary is that that was where the cows appeared.

5198   'Seven cows were coming up' means the truths belonging to the natural. This is clear from the meaning of 'cows' as the truths belonging to the natural, dealt with below. The reason there were seven is that 'seven' means that which is holy, 395, 433, 716, and therefore this number contributes to any matter under consideration the idea of holiness, dealt with in 881. The matter under consideration here is likewise of a holy nature since it concerns a further rebirth of the natural through the joining of this to the celestial of the spiritual. As regards 'cows' or 'young cows' meaning the truths belonging to the natural, this becomes clear from the fact that 'bulls' and 'young bulls' mean forms of good belonging to the natural, 2180, 2566, 2781, 2830. For in the Word, when a male means good, its female means truth, and conversely when the male means truth its female means good, so that 'a cow' means some truth belonging to the natural, because 'a bull' means some form of good belonging to it.

2   All beasts without exception that are mentioned in the Word mean affections, evil and useless beasts meaning evil affections, gentle and useful ones meaning good affections, see 45, 46, 142, 143, 246, 714, 715, 719, 776, 1823, 2179, 2180, 3218, 3519. The reason why they have such a meaning lies in the representations that occur in the world of spirits, for whenever a discussion about affections is taking place in heaven, beasts corresponding to affections of the kind under discussion are represented in the world of spirits, as I have also been allowed quite often to see. On several occasions I have wondered about the origin of that phenomenon, but have been led to perceive that the lives led by beasts are nothing else than affections; for they respond instinctively, devoid of reason, to their innate affections and are led by these to fulfill their specific functions. No other physical forms are suited to these affections devoid of reason than the kinds in which they are seen on earth. This explains why, when the discussion in heaven is about affections alone, the ultimate forms that those affections take in the world of spirits are the same in appearance as the physical forms of such beasts; for those affections cannot be clothed with any other forms than ones such as correspond to them. I have also seen beasts, the like of which do not appear anywhere at all in the natural world. They were the forms taken by affections that are not known and by affections that are mingled together.

3   Here then is the reason why in the Word affections are meant by 'beasts', though which particular affections are meant cannot be seen from anywhere else than the internal sense. 'Bulls' means the good belonging to the natural, as may be seen in the paragraphs listed above; and as for the meaning of 'cows' as the truths belonging to the natural, this becomes clear from other places where they are referred to, such as Isaiah 11:7; Hosea 4:16; Amos 4:1, as well as from the reference in Num.19:2-10 to the water of separation by which they were to be made clean and which was prepared from *the red cow* burned to ashes outside the camp, with which cedar wood was mixed, hyssop, and twice-dyed scarlet. When the meaning of this procedure is disclosed with the help of the internal sense, it shows that 'the red cow', meaning unclean truth within the natural, is made clean by 'burning', and also by the kinds of things meant by 'cedar wood, hyssop, and twice-dyed scarlet'. The water prepared by that process represented the means of purification.

5199   'Beautiful in appearance' means which are expressions of faith. This is clear from the meaning of 'beauty' and 'appearance'. Spiritual 'beauty' is essentially an affection for interior truth, while spiritual 'appearance' is essentially faith, so that 'beautiful in appearance' means an affection for the truth of faith, see 553, 3080, 3821, 4985. The reason spiritual beauty is an affection for interior truth is that truth is the outward form taken by good. The good which they receive in heaven from the Divine provides angels with the life they possess; but the outward form taken by that life is provided by the truths springing from that good. The truth of faith however does not provide the beauty but the affection itself present within the truths of faith springing from good. Beauty that is provided solely by the truth of faith is like the beauty of a face seen in a painting or a sculpture, but the beauty provided by an affection for truth springing from good is like the beauty of a real face full of life imparted to it by heavenly love; for as is the love – that is, as is the affection – which shines out of the form provided by the face, so is the beauty seen there. This being so, the outward appearance of the angels is indescribably beautiful. Their faces are radiant with the good of love passing through the truth of faith, which good and truth not only present themselves visually but can also be felt from the spheres that emanate from them.

The reason why this is the source of beauty is that heaven in its entirety is the Grand Man and has a correspondence with every single part of the human being. Everyone therefore who has the good of love and for that reason the truth of faith present in him has the form which heaven possesses present within him; and as a consequence of this there is also imparted to him the beauty which heaven possesses, heaven being a place where the Divine going forth from the Lord is the All in all. This also explains why those in hell, being the opposite of what is good and true, are horribly ugly, and in the light of heaven do not look like human beings but like monsters. The reason why spiritual appearance (*aspectus*) is faith is that in the internal sense 'looking at (*aspicere*) and seeing' means understanding, and in a sense more internal than this having faith is meant, see 897, 2150, 2325, 2807, 3863, 3869, 4403-4421.

5200 'And fat-fleshed' means which are embodiments of charity. This is clear from the meaning of 'fat' or 'fatness' as that which is celestial and which is used here to refer to good which flows from love and charity, dealt with in 353; and from the meaning of 'flesh' as the will part of the mind when made living by good received from the Lord, 148, 149, 780, 999, 3812, 3813, and thus also good which flows from love and charity. From this it follows that 'fat-fleshed' means matters of charity, while 'beautiful in appearance' means matters of faith. Thus the truths belonging to the natural, meant by 'the cows', are described here – what they are so far as form is concerned and what they are essentially. In form they are matters of faith, in essence they are matters of charity. The truth of this cannot be seen from the sense of the letter.

5201 'And they fed in the sedge' means instruction. This is clear from the meaning of 'feeding' as receiving instruction, dealt with below, and from the meaning of 'the sedge', or longer grass that grows near rivers, as facts known to the natural man. Since such factual knowledge is meant by 'grass' or 'plant', as is plain from the Word, 'feeding in the sedge' therefore means receiving instruction in factual knowledge, and through this knowledge instruction regarding things that are true and good. For factual knowledge serves as a means. Indeed it is like a mirror in which an image of interior things reveals itself; and this image is like another mirror in which forms of the truth and the good of faith, and therefore things which belong to heaven and are called spiritual, reveal and represent themselves. But being an interior one, this image is seen by none but those who have faith that is rooted in charity. This is what is meant in the genuine sense by 'feeding in the sedge'.

2   The meaning of 'feeding' as receiving instruction is evident from those places in the Word where one reads the expression, such as in Isaiah,

> Then He will give rain for your seed with which you sow the land, and bread of the produce of the land; and there will be fatness and wealthiness. On that day, *they will feed* your cattle *in a broad grassland.*   Isa.30:23.

'Cattle' stands for those in whom goodness and truth are present, 'feeding in a broad grassland' for receiving abundant instruction.

3   In the same prophet,

> I have given You as a covenant of the people – to restore the land; to share out the devastated inheritances; to say to the bound, Go out; to those who are in darkness, Reveal yourselves. *They will feed along the ways*, and on all slopes will their *pasture* be.   Isa.49:8,9.

This refers to the Lord's Coming. 'Feeding along the ways' stands for receiving instruction in truths, 'the ways' being truths, 627, 2333. 'Pasture' stands for the actual instruction. In Jeremiah,

> Woe to *the shepherds* destroying and scattering the flock of *My pasture*! Therefore said Jehovah God of Israel against *the shepherds feeding My people*.....   Jer.23:1,2.

'The shepherds' stands for those who give instruction, and 'the flock' for those who receive it, 343, 3795, so that 'feeding' means giving instruction.

4   It has become customary to refer to those who teach as 'pastors' or 'shepherds' and to those who learn as 'the flock'. For this reason the use of the expression 'feeding' has become commonly accepted when talking about preaching or about instruction given in doctrine or the Word. But when the expression is used in this way it is only a comparison and not, as when it occurs in the Word, one that holds any spiritual meaning within it. The reason 'feeding', when used in the Word, has a spiritual meaning is that when instruction and doctrine based on the Word are being talked about in heaven, that discussion is represented in a visual way in the world of spirits, where spiritual realities make their appearance within natural images. That representation consists of grasslands that are lush with grass, plants, and flowers, and where also there are flocks; and every variation of this scene occurs, as determined by the nature of the discussion that is taking place in heaven regarding instruction and doctrine.

5   In the same prophet,

> I will bring back Israel to his habitation so that *he may feed* on Carmel and

Bashan; and on mount Ephraim and in Gilead his soul will be satisfied.
Jer.50:19.

'Feeding on Carmel and Bashan' stands for receiving instruction in
forms of the good of faith and charity. In the same prophet,

There has gone out from the daughter of Zion all her majesty; her princes have
become like deer, they have not found *pasture*.   Lam.1:6.

In Ezekiel

I will feed them in a good pasture, and their *fold* will be on the mountains of the
loftiness of Israel; and they will lie down in *a good fold,* and *on fat pasture they
will feed* upon the mountains of Israel.   Ezek.34:14.

In Hosea,

Now Jehovah *will feed* them like a sheep in a broad place.   Hosea 4:16.

'Feeding in a broad place' stands for giving instruction in truths, for 'a
broad place' means truth, see 1613, 3433, 3434, 4482. In Micah,

You, Bethlehem Ephrath, from you will come forth for Me one who will be Ruler
in Israel. He will stand and *feed* [His flock] in the strength of Jehovah.
Micah 5:2,4.

In the same prophet,

Guide[1] your people with your staff, the flock of your inheritance which is dwelling
alone. *Let them feed* in Bashan and Gilead as in the days of old.   Micah 7:14.

In Zephaniah,

The remnant of Israel *will feed* and rest, with none making them afraid.
Zeph.3:13.

In David,

Jehovah is *my Shepherd*; He will make me lie down in *green pastures[2]*; He will
lead me away to still waters.   Ps.23:1,2.

In the same author,

He made us and not we ourselves, His people and *the flock of His pasture*;
therefore we are His, His people and the flock of His *pasture[3]*.   Ps.100:3.

In the Book of Revelation,

The Lamb who is in the midst of the throne *will feed them* and will guide them to
living springs of water.   Rev.7:17.

In John,

I am the door. If anyone enters through Me he will be saved, and will go in and
out, and *find pasture*.   John 10:9.

---

[1] *or* Feed *or* Pasture
[2] *lit.* pastures of the plant
[3] *The first and second halves of this sentence are in fact alternative ways of
understanding the original Hebrew.*

In the same gospel,

Jesus said to Peter, *Feed* My lambs; a second time, *Feed* My sheep; and a third time, *Feed* My sheep.   John 21:15-17.

5202   'And behold, seven other cows were coming up after them out of the river' means falsities belonging to the natural which are also at the boundary. This is clear from the meaning of 'cows' as the truths belonging to the natural, dealt with just above in 5198, so that in the contrary sense 'cows' means falsities (for most things in the Word have a contrary meaning that can be recognized from the genuine one, and therefore since truths of a natural kind are meant by 'cows' in the genuine sense, falsities of the same kind, thus falsities within the natural, are meant in the contrary sense); and from the meaning of 'the river' as the boundary, also dealt with above, in 5196, 5197. The presence of those falsities at the boundary is also evident from the use of the words 'came up out of the river', for coming or going up is used in reference to an advance made from what is exterior towards things that are interior, 3084, 4539, 4969.

2   The implications of this, since it forms the subject in what follows, must be stated here. The previous chapter dealt with the exterior natural, with the fact that some impressions were the kind that belonged to the understanding while others were the kind that belonged to the will. The former were accepted, but the latter were cast aside. Impressions such as belonged to the understanding were represented by 'the cupbearer', and those such as belonged to the will by 'the baker'. Also, because the kind belonging to the understanding were accepted, they were also made subordinate to the internal natural. These were the matters that were dealt with in the previous chapter, in which the first stage in the rebirth of the natural is described.

3   In the present chapter however the subject is the influx of the celestial of the spiritual into the impressions in the natural which were retained, that is to say, the impressions belonging to the understanding part there, which are meant now by 'the cows beautiful in appearance and fat-fleshed'. But as the natural cannot undergo any rebirth solely so far as ideas belonging to the understanding are concerned, desires belonging to the will must also be involved; for every individual part of the natural, to be anything at all, must include some element belonging to the understanding and at the same time another element belonging to the will. But because the will element that was present previously has been cast aside a new one must therefore enter in to replace it. This new element is received from the celestial of the spiritual which, together with its influx into the natural, is the subject in the present chapter. What the natural is like in this state is described in the internal sense – a state in which the truths there have been banished by falsities, so that the natural has been left exposed to the celestial of the spiritual. These are the considerations that are meant by the devouring of the good cows by the bad cows and the swallowing up of the full heads of grain

by the empty ones, and after this by Joseph's making provision for all the land of Egypt. But in the Lord's Divine mercy more regarding these matters will be stated in what follows.

They are, what is more, the kind of considerations that scarcely fall within the area of light within the human understanding, for they are the arcana of regeneration which in themselves are countless but about which a person knows barely anything at all. The person with whom good is present is undergoing rebirth every moment, from earliest childhood to the final stage of his life in the world, and after that for ever. This is happening to him not only interiorly but also exteriorly; and this rebirth involves processes that are amazing. They are processes which for the most part constitute angelic wisdom, and that wisdom, as is well known, is indescribable, embracing such things as ear has not heard, nor eye seen, and such as have never entered man's thought[1]. The internal sense deals with such matters and so is suited to angelic wisdom; and when this sense passes into the sense of the letter it becomes suited to human wisdom, and in an unseen way it stirs the affections of those who, motivated by good, have the desire to know truths received from the Word.

5203 'Bad in appearance' means which are not expressions of faith. This is clear from the meaning of 'beautiful in appearance' as things which are matters of faith, dealt with just above in 5199, and therefore 'bad in appearance' here means things which are not matters of faith.

5204 'And thin-fleshed' means which are not embodiments of charity. This is clear fom the meaning of 'fat-fleshed' as things which are matters of charity, also dealt with above, in 5200, and therefore 'thin-fleshed' here means things which are not matters of charity, for the two are contraries.

5205 'And stood by the [other] cows on the bank of the river' means at the boundaries where the truths were present. This is clear from the meaning of 'standing by, on the bank of the river' as at the boundaries, 'the river' meaning a boundary, see 5196, 5197; and from the meaning of 'the cows' as the truths belonging to the natural, dealt with above in 5198. The implications of this – of falsities standing at the boundaries where truths were – will be evident from what appears further on, in particular at the point where the meaning in the internal sense of the seven years of famine in the land of Egypt comes up for explanation, those seven years being foretold and meant by the seven cows that were bad in appearance and thin-fleshed, and also by the seven heads of grain that were thin and scorched by an east wind.

5206 'And the cows bad in appearance and thin-fleshed devoured.....' means that falsities which were not expressions of faith and were not embodiments of charity would banish..... This is clear

---

[1] *This well-known saying occurs in 1 Cor.2:9.*

from the meaning of 'devouring' as consuming, dealt with in 5149, 5157, here as banishing because truths present in the natural, before they have received life through the celestial of the spiritual and so have been regenerated, have been so to speak banished by falsities; from the meaning of 'cows bad in appearance' as things which are not expressions of faith, dealt with just above in 5203; and from the meaning of 'thin-fleshed' as things which are not embodiments of charity, also dealt with above, in 5204.

5207 'The seven cows beautiful in appearance and fat' means the truths of the natural which are expressions of faith and embodiments of charity. This is clear from the meaning of 'cows' as the truths belonging to the natural, dealt with above in 5198; from the meaning of 'beautiful in appearance' as expressions of faith, dealt with in 5199; and from the meaning of 'fat' as embodiments of charity, dealt with in 5200. As regards this particular matter – that truths were banished from the natural by falsities at the boundaries – it should be recognized that this is what happens initially whenever regeneration takes place. For the truths which are implanted initially in a person are in themselves truths, yet they are not truths residing with that person until good has been linked to them. Once it has been so linked good causes those truths to be truths indeed, for good is the inward essence, while truths are the outward form of that essence. Initially therefore falsities stand close to truths; that is, where at the boundaries truths are present, so also are falsities.

2 But as good is joined to the truths, the falsities are put to flight. This is what actually happens in the next life. There the sphere of falsity attaches itself to the truths, depending on how much good passes into the truths. When little good enters in, the sphere of falsity is nearby; when more good enters in, the sphere of falsity moves further away; and when good is wholly linked to the truths the sphere of falsity is completely dispersed. When the sphere of falsity is close by, which is the case initially, as has been stated, the truths are so to speak banished. Actually they are for the time being concealed in a more interior place where they are filled with good and from where they are brought back in consecutive stages. These are the considerations that are meant by seven cows and seven heads of grain, and further on by seven years of abundance of corn and by seven years of famine. But anyone who does not know anything about regeneration or anything about a person's internal state fails to understand any of this.

5208 'And Pharaoh awoke' means a state of enlightenment. This is clear from the meaning of 'awakening' as receiving enlightenment, dealt with in 3715; and from the representation of 'Pharaoh' as the natural, dealt with previously, from which it is evident that 'Pharaoh awoke' means a state of enlightenment within the natural. The word enlightenment is used here to mean a general enlightenment coming from the celestial of the spiritual, and so from what is within. In that which is lower the enlightenment that comes or flows from what is within is a general one, but it becomes gradually less general, and at length becomes particular as truths from good are implanted there. For every truth from good is a shining light and a source of enlightenment. This now explains the statement made just above in 5206, that truths in the natural were banished. These truths are banished so that the natural may then be enlightened generally from what is within, after which truths in their own proper order are restored there within that general light, causing the enlightenment of the natural to be made a particular one.

A state of agreement between a person's spiritual and his natural, or between his internal and his external, is effected in this manner. For truths are acquired first, but then they are so to speak banished. They are not in fact banished but are hidden, at which point what is lower has a general light shed upon it from what is higher, or what is without receives that light from what is within; and in that light the truths are restored to their own proper order. As a consequence of this all the truths there become images of the general whole to which they belong, and they then exist in a state of agreement. In every single thing that comes into being not only in the spiritual world but also in the natural world, what is general comes first; then less general aspects are gradually inserted, and at length particular details. Unless this kind of insertion or filling in takes place, nothing holds together at all; for whatever is not part of a general whole and does not depend for its existence on that general whole ceases to be anything, see 917, 3057, 4269, 4325(end), 4329(middle), 4345, 4383.

5209   Verses 5-7 **And he fell asleep and dreamed a second time, and behold, seven heads of grain were coming up on one stalk, fat and good. And behold, seven heads, thin and scorched by an east wind, were sprouting after them. And the thin heads swallowed up the seven fat and full heads. And Pharaoh awoke, and behold, it was a dream.**

'And he fell asleep' means a state of obscurity. 'And dreamed a second time' means the provision that had been made. 'And behold, seven heads of grain were coming up on one stalk' means facts known to the natural, which facts existed linked together. 'Fat and good' means into which facts matters of faith and charity could be instilled. 'And behold, seven heads, thin' means facts that are useless. 'And scorched by an east wind' means full of evil desires. 'Were sprouting after them' means appearing next to them. 'And the thin heads swallowed up the seven fat and full heads' means that the facts which were useless banished the facts that were good. 'And Pharaoh awoke' means a general state of enlightenment. 'And behold, it was a dream' means in that obscurity.

5210   'And he fell asleep' means a state of obscurity. This is clear from the meaning of 'sleeping' as a state of obscurity. 'Sleep' has no other meaning than this in the spiritual sense, even as 'wakefulness' means nothing else than a state of brightness; for spiritual sleep is a time when truths remain in obscurity, spiritual wakefulness when truths exist in brightness. And to the extent that truths are in the one state or else the other, spirits are awake or asleep. From this it is evident that 'falling asleep' is a state of obscurity.

5211 'And he dreamed a second time' means the provision that had been made. This is clear from the meaning of 'dreaming' as provision that has been made, dealt with in 5195.

5212 'And behold, seven heads of grain were coming up on one stalk' means facts known to the natural, which facts existed linked together. This is clear from the meaning of 'heads' or 'tips' as facts known to the natural, dealt with below, and from the meaning of 'on one stalk' as existing linked together, for all present on one stalk are linked together by their common origin. The reason facts are meant by 'heads' or 'tips' is that 'grain' means the good of the natural, 3580; for facts are the containers of natural good, just as heads are of grain. In general all truths are vessels for containing good; and so too are facts since these are truths of the lowest order. Truths of the lowest order, that is, the truths belonging to the exterior natural, are called known facts because they reside in a person's natural or external memory. They are also called such because for the most part they are dependent on the light of the world and can for that reason be presented and represented to others by the use of words, that is, by the use of ideas put into words that draw on things such as belong to the world and the light of the world. The contents of the interior memory however are not called facts but truths since these are dependent on the light of heaven. Without the aid of that light they are unintelligible, and without the use of words, that is, of ideas put into words that draw on things such as belong to heaven and the light of heaven they are inexpressible. The facts meant here by 'heads' or 'tips' are ones that are known to the Church, regarding which see 4749, 4844, 4964, 4965.

2 The reason there were two dreams, one about seven cows, the other about seven heads of grain, was that in the internal sense both parts of the natural are dealt with, the interior natural and the exterior natural, the rebirth of the two being the subject in what follows. By 'the seven cows' are meant things in the interior natural which have been called the truths belonging to the natural, 5198; by 'the seven heads of grain' are meant the truths in the exterior natural, which are called facts.

3 Interior facts and exterior ones are meant by 'the tips of the river Euphrates even to the river of Egypt' in Isaiah,

So it will be on that day, that Jehovah will smite *from the tip of the river even to the river of Egypt*, and you will be gathered one to another, O children of Israel. So it will be on that day, that a great trumpet will be blown, and they will come – those who are perishing in the land of Asshur, and those who are outcasts in the land of Egypt – and they will bow themselves down to Jehovah on the holy mountain, in Jerusalem. Isa.27:12,13.

'Those perishing in the land of Asshur' stands for interior truths, and 'the outcasts in the land of Egypt' for exterior truths, which are facts. Comparison with the blade, the tip or the ear, and the full grain also implies the rebirth of a person by means of factual knowledge, the truths of faith, and the good deeds of charity, in Mark,

Jesus said, The kingdom of God is like when someone casts seed onto the land. Then he sleeps and rises, by night and by day, but the seed sprouts and grows, he himself knowing not how; for the earth bears fruit of its own accord, first *the blade*, then *the ear*, after that *the full grain in the ear*. Once the fruit has been brought forth, he will immediately put in the sickle, because the harvest is established.   Mark 4:26–29.

'The kingdom of God', which is compared to the blade, the ear, and the full grain, is heaven existing with a person through regeneration; for one who has been regenerated has the kingdom of God within him and he becomes an image of the kingdom of God, that is, of heaven. 'The blade' is factual knowledge, which comes first; 'the ear' is knowledge of what is true that develops out of that; and 'the full grain' is the good that develops out of this. In addition the laws laid down regarding *gleanings*, Lev.19:9; 23:22; regarding the freedom *to pluck the ears* on a companion's standing grain, Deut.23:25; and also regarding the non-eating of bread or of *dried ears* or of *green ones* before they had brought a gift to God, Lev.23:14, represented such things as are meant by 'ears'.

5213   'Fat and good' means into which facts matters of faith and charity could be instilled. This is clear from the meaning of 'fat' when used in reference to known facts meant by 'heads of grain' (in that facts are able to receive the good of faith and can therefore have matters of faith instilled into them; for facts are vessels, and when 'fatness' is used in reference to them, the ability to receive such things as are matters of faith springing from charity is meant); and from the meaning of 'good' when used in reference to known facts meant by 'heads of grain' (in that facts are able to receive the good of charity and can therefore have matters of charity instilled into them). 'Fat' has regard to matters of faith and 'good' to matters of charity because these are their usual connotations throughout the Word. For whenever these two adjectives are applied to the same thing, one is connected with matters of faith, the other with matters of charity; and this is so on account of the marriage of truth and good present in every individual part of the Word, 683, 793, 801, 2173, 2516, 2712, 4137(end), 5138. The fact that 'fat' means matters of faith and 'good' matters of charity is also evident from the previous parallel description regarding the cows, 5199, 5200.

The facts which are able to have matters of faith and charity instilled into them are very many. They include all facts known to the Church which are meant in the good sense by 'Egypt', dealt with in 4749, 4844, 4964, 4965, consequently all facts which are truths about correspondences, representatives, meaningful signs, influx, order, intelligence and wisdom, affections. Indeed they include all truths, both visible and invisible ones, that are descriptive of the interior and the exterior aspects of the natural world, because such truths correspond to spiritual truths.

5214 'And behold, seven heads, thin' means facts that are useless. This is clear from the meaning of 'heads' as facts, dealt with above in 5212, and from the meaning of 'thin' as ones that are useless. For thin is the opposite of full, and the expression full is used to refer to what has a use, or what amounts to the same, what is good; for everything good has a use to serve. Consequently 'thin' describes that which is useless. Useless facts are those which have no other end in view than personal glory and pleasure. Such ends are useless because they do not benefit one's neighbour.

5215 'And scorched by an east wind' means full of evil desires. This is clear from the meaning of 'being scorched by an east wind' as being consumed by the fire of evil desires. For 'an east wind' and 'the east' in the genuine sense mean love to the Lord and love towards the neighbour, 101, 1250, 3249, 3708, 3762, and therefore in the contrary sense self-love and love of the world, and so cravings and evil desires since these spring from those loves. The word 'fire' is used to refer to such desires for the reason dealt with in 5071, and therefore 'being scorched' is used also.

2   There are two sources of heat, as there are also two sources of light, the one source of heat being the sun of this world, the other souce of heat being the sun of heaven, which is the Lord. It is a well known fact that the sun of this world pours out heat into its own world and onto everything there, but it is a less well known fact that the sun of heaven pours out heat into the whole of heaven. Yet this too may become an equally well known fact if one reflects merely on the heat which exists intrinsically in the human being but which has nothing in common with the heat of the world, that is, if one reflects on what is called vital heat. From this one could know that this heat is of a different nature from the world's heat. That is to say, the former is a living heat but the latter is not at all a living one; also the former, being a living one, fires a person interiorly, namely his will and understanding, imparting to him desires and loves, and affections too. This also explains why desires, loves and affections are spiritual forms of heat, and are also called such. The fact that they are forms of heat is quite evident, for heat is radiated from all parts of the bodies of live persons, even where it is intensely cold. More than that, when desires and affections, that is, when loves, increase, the body grows correspondingly warmer. This kind of heat is what is meant in the Word by 'heat', 'fire', and 'flame'; in the genuine sense celestial and spiritual love is meant, in the contrary sense bodily and earthly love. From this it becomes clear that here 'being scorched by an east wind' means being consumed by the fire of evil desires, and that when used in reference to known facts meant by 'heads' that are 'thin', facts full of evil desires are meant.

'The east wind' means the blasts of evil desires and of derivative false notions, as is clear from places in the Word where that wind is mentioned, for example, in David,

He caused *an east wind* to blow[1] in the heavens, and by His power He brought forth the south wind; and He caused flesh to rain onto them like the dust, winged birds like the sand of the sea. Ps.78:26,27.

'The flesh' which that wind brought meant cravings, and 'winged birds' resulting false notions, as is evident in Num.11:31-35, where it is said that the name of the place where the people were struck down for eating flesh was called 'the graves of *craving*, for there they buried the people who *had the craving'*.

In Ezekiel,

Behold, the vine that was planted, will it thrive? When *the east wind* strikes it, *will it not wither completely? It will wither* on the small spaces where it began to grow. Ezek.17:10.

And in the same prophet,

The vine has been plucked up in anger, it has been cast down onto the ground, and *the east wind has dried* its fruit. They have been plucked out and *have withered*, each rod of its strength; *fire* has consumed each one. For *fire* has gone out from a rod of its branches and has consumed its fruit, so that there is no rod of strength in it, a sceptre for dominion. Ezek.19:12,14.

Here 'the east wind' stands for the blasts of evil desires. In Isaiah,

He gave thought to *His rough wind*, on the day of the east wind. Isa.27:8.

In Hosea,

An east wind will come, Jehovah's wind rising up from the desert, and his spring *will become dry,* and his fountain *dried up*. It will strip his treasury of every precious vessel. Hosea 13:15.

Here also 'an east wind' stands for blasts of evil desires. Similarly in Jeremiah,

Like *an east wind* I will scatter them before the enemy. Jer.18:17.

In David,

By means of *an east wind* You will shatter the ships of Tarshish. Ps.48:7.

In Isaiah,

You have forsaken Your people, the house of Jacob, because they have been filled from *the east wind*, and they are diviners like the Philistines. Isa.2:6.

In Hosea,

Ephraim feeds the wind, and pursues *the east wind*. All the day long he multiplies lies and devastation. Hosea 12:1.

'The wind' here stands for false notions, and 'the east wind' for evil desires. Something similar is also meant in the internal sense by 'an

---

[1] *lit.* set out

east wind' by means of which 'locusts were brought forth' and by means of which 'the locusts were cast into the sea'[1], Exod.10:13,19, and also by means of which 'the waters of the sea Suph' were divided, Exod.14:21.

5216 'Were sprouting after them' means appearing next to them. This is clear from the meaning of 'sprouting' here as appearing, and from the meaning of 'after them' as next to or at the boundary, which is the same meaning as that in the reference to the bad or thin cows coming up 'after them', that is, after the beautiful and fat ones, 5202. The reason 'after them' means next to them is that 'after' describes a subsequent point of time; and in the spiritual world, consequently in the spiritual sense, no notion of time exists, but instead of this the kind of state that corresponds to it.

5217 'And the thin heads swallowed up the seven fat and full heads' means that the facts which were useless banished the facts that were good. This is clear from the meaning of 'the thin heads' as facts that are useless, dealt with above in 5214; from the meaning of 'fat and full heads' as facts into which matters of faith and charity could be instilled, dealt with in 5213, which are consequently facts that are good; and from the meaning of 'swallowing up' as banishing, which is similar to 'devouring', as said of the cows above in 5206. Regarding the banishment of good facts by useless ones, or the banishment of truths by falsities, see 5207.

2   The same applies in the spiritual world. Where falsities are present no truths can remain; and conversely, where truths are present no falsities can remain. The one group banishes the other, since they are complete opposites, for the reason that falsities originate in hell and truths in heaven. Sometimes it does seem as though falsities and truths are present together in the same subject; but the falsities in this case are not complete opposites of the truths there, but ones that are attached to those truths through the ways they are used. A subject in which truths and falsities that are complete opposites exist together is called lukewarm, while a subject in which falsities and truths have become mixed together is called profane.

5218 'And Pharaoh awoke' means a general state of enlightenment. This is clear from the explanation above in 5208, where the same words occur.

5219 'And behold, it was a dream' means in that obscurity. This is clear from the meaning of 'a dream' as a state that was obscure, dealt with in 1838, 2514, 2528, 5210. The word obscure is used because truths have been banished; indeed where there are no truths obscurity exists. The light of heaven flows solely into truths, that light being Divine Truth received from the Lord, the source of truths residing with angels

[1] *According to* Exodus 10:19 *a* west *wind cast the locusts into the sea.*

and spirits, and with men too. They are subsidiary lights; but they derive their light from Divine Truth through the good present within those truths. For unless truths are rooted in good, that is, unless truths have good present within them, they cannot acquire any light from the Divine. They acquire it through good, for good is like a fire or flame, and truths are like lights radiating from it. In the next life there are also some truths that shine which are devoid of good; but the light shining from them is a wintry light which turns into thick darkness on the arrival of the light of heaven.

From all this one may now see what is meant here by obscurity, namely a natural state when facts that are good are banished by those that are useless. Such obscurity is one that can receive a general enlightenment, 5208, 5218. But obscurity caused by falsities can by no means receive any enlightenment, for falsities are so many masses of darkness which blot out the light of heaven and in so doing bring obscurity which cannot be lightened until those falsities have been removed.

5220 Verse 8 **And it happened early in the morning, that his spirit was troubled, and he sent and called all the magi of Egypt, and all its wise men; and Pharaoh told them his dream, and there was no one to interpret them for Pharaoh.**

'And it happened early in the morning' means in that new state. 'That his spirit was troubled' means a turmoil. 'And he sent and called all the magi of Egypt, and its wise men' means in consulting factual knowledge, interior as well as exterior. 'And Pharaoh told them the dream' means regarding things to come. 'And there was no one to interpret them for Pharaoh' means that no knowledge existed of what was going to happen.

5221 'And it happened early in the morning' means in that new state. This is clear from the meaning of 'it happened', or so it was, as that which implies something new, dealt with in 4979, 4987; and from the meaning of 'early' or 'the morning' as a state of enlightenment, dealt with in 3458, 3723, this state being the new one that is meant, about which see just above in 5218. The subject here is that state and the nature of it, namely one of turmoil owing to the obscurity that exists regarding the things that are taking place. But scarcely anyone can know anything about what that state is like unless he has come into a spiritual sphere and at the same time takes note of what is going on inside himself.

Unless he does so he cannot begin to know what is meant by receiving a general enlightenment or by receiving a particular enlightenment. He cannot even know what is meant by receiving enlightenment, let alone the idea that within a state of general enlightenment[1] turmoil exists

---

[1] *The first Latin edition reads* within a general state of enlightenment, *but Swedenborg's rough draft reads* within a state of general enlightenment.

initially and that there is no respite until truths rooted in good are restored in their proper order. Angels have a clear perception of all this, and so do good spirits, because they live in a spiritual sphere. To know about such matters and to think them over is a source of delight to them. But to someone in a natural sphere, more so to someone in a sphere of sensory-mindedness, and more so still to one who is completely sensory-minded and concerned only with ideas gained from bodily and earthly things, such matters are of no interest.

5222 'That his spirit was troubled' means a turmoil. This is clear from the meaning of 'being troubled in spirit' as being placed in a turmoil. 'Spirit' is used here, as it is several times elsewhere in the Word, to mean a person's interior affection and thought, which also constitute his spirit. The ancients called these his spirit, but specifically they used spirit to mean the interior man who would go on living after the body died. At the present day however, when people read about the spirit where it has that meaning, they understand by it solely the faculty of thought, without anything else subject to it apart from the body in which it resides.

2   The reason for this different understanding is that people no longer believe that the interior man is a person's true self. Rather, they believe that the interior man, which ordinary people call the soul or spirit, is merely the faculty of thought without anything else compatible with and subject to it. Consequently they believe that because that faculty has nothing subject to it in which to reside, it will be dissipated after death in the way something air-like or flame-like is dissipated. This is the kind of meaning spirit possesses at the present day, as when the expression 'troubled in spirit', 'saddened in spirit', 'joyful in spirit', or 'exultant in spirit' is used. But in reality it is the actual interior man that is called the spirit and that is troubled, saddened, joyful, or exultant. And this interior man – existing within an entirely human form, though this is unseen by the eyes of the body – is where the faculty of thought resides.

5223   'And he sent and called all the magi of Egypt, and its wise men' means in consulting factual knowledge, interior as well as exterior. This is clear from the meaning of 'the magi' in the good sense as interior factual knowledge, dealt with below, and from the meaning of 'wise men' as exterior factual knowledge, also dealt with below. The reason 'the magi and wise men of Egypt' means factual knowledge is that Egypt had been one of the kingdoms where the representative Ancient Church existed, 1238, 2385. But in Egypt the facts known to that Church were the particular objects of care and attention, being knowledge about correspondences, representatives, and meaningful signs. For that knowledge was used to explain what had been written in the books of the Church, and to explain the things that were done in their sacred worship, 4749, 4964, 4966. This was how it came about that 'Egypt' meant factual knowledge in general, 1164, 1165, 1186, 1462, as did

'Pharaoh' its king too. The leading people among them who were well-versed in and imparted that knowledge were called magi and wise men. The magi were those well-versed in mystical knowledge, the wise men those well-versed in non-mystical, so that the facts known to the magi were interior ones, while those known to the wise men were exterior. This explains why such factual knowledge is meant in the Word by those two kinds of men. But after they began to misuse the Church's interior factual knowledge and to turn it into magic, 'Egypt', and likewise 'the magi of Egypt and its wise men', began to mean factual knowledge that led to perversions.

The magi in those times had a knowledge of the kinds of things that belong to the spiritual world, and in their teaching about these they employed the correspondences and the representatives known to the Church. For this reason many of those magi also communicated with spirits and learned the arts of illusion which they used to perform miracles that involved magic. But those who were called the wise men had no interest in anything like this. Instead they provided the answers to hard questions and taught about the causes lying behind natural things. It was primarily in arts such as these that the wisdom of those times consisted, and the ability to practise them was called wisdom. This becomes clear from what is recorded about Solomon in the first Book of Kings,

Solomon's wisdom surpassed *the wisdom* of all the sons of the east, and all *the wisdom of the Egyptians*, so much so that he was *wiser* than all people – than Ethan the Ezrahite, and Heman, and Chalcol, and Darda, the sons of Mahol. He spoke three thousand *proverbs*, and his songs were one thousand and five. In addition he spoke about trees, from the cedars which are in Lebanon even to the hyssop which comes out of the wall. He also spoke about beasts, and about birds, and about creeping things, and about fish. Therefore they came from all peoples to hear *the wisdom* of Solomon, from all kings of the earth who had heard about *his wisdom*. 1 Kings 4:30–34.

Also there is what is recorded about the queen of Sheba in the same book,

She came to test him with *hard questions*; and Solomon gave her an explanation for every matter she mentioned[1]. There was not a matter[2] hidden from the king for which he could not give her an explanation.
1 Kings 10:1 and following verses.

From this one may see what was described in those times as wisdom and who exactly those people were who were called wise men, not only in Egypt but also elsewhere – in Syria, Arabia, and Babel. But in the internal sense 'the wisdom of Egypt' means nothing else than knowledge about natural things, while 'that of the magi' means knowledge about spiritual realities, so that exterior factual knowledge is meant by 'the wise men', and interior factual knowledge by 'the magi', 'Egypt' meaning knowledge in general, 1164, 1165, 1186, 1462, 4749, 4964, 4966.

[1] *lit.* all her words
[2] *lit.* word

Egypt and its wise men had no other meaning in Isaiah,

The princes of Zoan are foolish, the counsel of *the wise counsellors of Pharaoh* has become brutish. How does one say to Pharaoh, *I am a son of the wise*, a son of the kings of old? Where are your *wise* men now? Isa.19:11,12.

4   The fact that the term 'magi' was applied to those who had a knowledge of spiritual realities, and who also for that reason received revelations, is clear from *the magi* who came from the east to Jerusalem, asking where the King of the Jews was to be born and saying that they had seen His star in the east and had come to worship Him, Matt.2:1,2. The same is also clear from Daniel, who is called *the chief of the magi* in Dan.4:9. And in another place,

The queen said to King Belshazzar, There is a man in your kingdom in whom is the spirit of the holy gods. And in the days of your father, light and intelligence and wisdom, like the wisdom of the gods, were found in him. Therefore King Nebuchadnezzar your father set him up as *chief of the magi*, diviners, Chaldeans, and determiners. Dan.5:11.

And in yet another place,

Among them all none was found like Daniel, Hananiah, Mishael, and Azariah; for when they were to stand before the king, every matter of wisdom [and] understanding which the king asked of them *exceeded* ten times [that of] *all the magi*, the diviners who were in his kingdom. Dan.1:19,20.

5   It is well known that in the contrary sense 'magi'[1] is used to mean those who pervert spiritual realities and thereby practise magic, like those mentioned in Exod.7:9-12; 8:7,19; 9:11. For magic is nothing else than a perversion, being the perverted use of those kinds of things that constitute true order in the spiritual world, a perverted use that gives rise to magic. But at the present day such magic is called natural, for the reason that no recognition exists any longer of anything above or beyond the natural order. People refuse to accept the existence of anything spiritual unless one means by this an interior dimension of what is natural.

5224   'And Pharaoh told them the dream' means regarding things to come. This is clear from the meaning of 'the dream' as foresight, foretelling, and outcome, dealt with in 5091, 5092, 5104, and so things to come. What this implies in the internal sense is clear from the whole train of thought. The present verse deals with a new state in the natural when this dwells in obscurity because truths have been banished from it; at this particular point it deals with the turmoil involved in consulting factual knowledge regarding things to come. For when that kind of obscurity exists, thought about what the outcome is to be instantly arises. Because this is what generally happens in every state such as this when a person is being regenerated, that state is therefore described here in the internal sense.

---

[1] *The same Latin noun* magus *describes* a wise man *or* philosopher *in a good sense, but* a magician *in a bad sense.*

But such states are not known about at the present day, because for one thing few are being regenerated and because for another those who are being regenerated do not stop to reflect on these matters. No one is interested at the present day in what goes on in a person interiorly, because external interests have a complete hold; that is, when external interests are the ends in view in people's lives, internal interests are of no importance at all to them. Regarding the obscurity referred to here they would say, Of what concern is that to me when there is nothing to be gained from it, and no honour in knowing it? Why give any thought to the state of the soul or state of the internal man, and why ask whether this is in obscurity when truths are banished or in clearness when truths are restored there? What advantage is there in knowing this? I doubt whether any internal man exists or whether any state of the soul exists apart from that of the body. Indeed I even doubt the existence of a soul that lives after death. Has anyone every returned from the dead to show us? These are the kind of things that the member of the Church says to himself at the present day and the kind of thoughts he has when he hears or reads anything about the state of the internal man. From this one may see how it comes about that the things which go on inside a person are in obscurity and wholly unknown about at the present day. Such obscurity of understanding never existed among the ancients. Their wisdom consisted in fostering more internal things and so in perfecting both powers of the mind, which are the understanding and the will, and so consisted, because they did this, in seeing to the needs of the soul. The fact that these were the kinds of things the ancients were concerned about is plain from their writings which are extant at the present day, and in addition to this from everyone's desire to hear Solomon,

Therefore they came from all peoples to hear the wisdom of Solomon, from all the kings of the earth who had heard about his wisdom.   1 Kings 4:34.

This was the reason why the queen of Sheba came to him; and because of the blessing she received from Solomon's wisdom she said,

Blessed are your men, blessed are these your servants, who stand continually before you and hear your wisdom.   1 Kings 10:8.

Would anyone today say that he is blessed on that account?

5225   'And there was no one to interpret them for Pharaoh' means that no knowledge existed of what was going to happen. This is clear from the meaning of 'interpreting' as knowing what was going to happen, dealt with in 5141, and therefore 'no one to interpret' means no knowledge of it since 'no one' in the internal sense means the absence and so non-existence of some reality. For the idea of a person is converted in the internal sense into that of some reality. For example, the idea of a man, husband, woman, wife, son, daughter, boy, or virgin is converted into the idea of some truth or form of good. Or, as above in 5223, the idea of a magus and a wise man is converted into that of factual knowledge, interior and exterior. The reason for this is that in the spiritual world, that is, in heaven, angels' attention is fixed not on persons but on spiritual realities. For persons narrow an idea down and focus it on some finite thing, whereas spiritual realities do not involve any such narrowing down or focusing but spread to what is Infinite, and so to the Lord. This explains too why in heaven no one ever perceives a person mentioned in the Word; instead they perceive the reality represented by that person. Nor for the same reason does anyone in heaven perceive a people or nation, only its essential nature. Indeed in heaven they have no knowledge at all of any historical detail in the Word about any person, nation, or people; consequently they have no knowledge of who Abraham, Isaac, Jacob, or the people of Israel are, nor of who the Jewish people are. Instead they perceive what is represented by Abraham, Isaac, Jacob, the people of Israel, the Jewish people, and so on with everything else. This explains why angelic language has no limitations and is also a universal one compared with other languages.

5226 Verses 9–13 **And the chief of the cupbearers spoke to Pharaoh, saying, I remember my sins today. Pharaoh was incensed with his servants, and put me into custody in the house of the chief of the attendants, me and the chief of the bakers. And we dreamed a dream in one night, I and he; we dreamed each according to the interpretation of his own dream. And a Hebrew boy was there with us, a servant to the chief of the attendants; and we told him, and he interpreted our dreams for us; to each according to his dream he gave the interpretation. And it happened, that as he interpreted to us, so it came about. He restored me to my position, and he hanged him.**

'And the chief of the cupbearers spoke to Pharaoh' means thought formed by the sensory power subject to the understanding part of the mind. 'Saying' means the perception resulting from this. 'I remember my sins today' means regarding a state of separation. 'Pharaoh was incensed with his servants' means when the natural turned away. 'And put me into custody in the house of the chief of the attendants' means a casting aside from what exists first and foremost in explanations. 'Me and the chief of the bakers' means both kinds of sensory power. 'And we dreamed a dream in one night' means that which was foreseen in obscurity. 'I and he' means regarding both kinds of sensory power. 'We dreamed each according to the interpretation of his own dream' means what was to be the outcome of both. 'And a Hebrew boy was there with us' means that owing to temptation the guiltlessness of the Church had been cast away there. 'A servant of the chief of the attendants' means in which there was truth that served that which came first and foremost in explanations. 'And we told him' means resulting perception. 'And he interpreted our dreams for us' means what the things foreseen in obscurity held within them. 'To each according to his dream he gave the interpretation' means from [a knowledge of] the truth. 'And it happened, that as he interpreted to us, so it came about' means that so was the outcome. 'He restored me to my position' means that the sensory power belonging to the understanding part of the mind was accepted. 'And he hanged him' means that the sensory power belonging to the will part was cast aside.

5227   'And the chief of the cupbearers spoke to Pharaoh' means thought formed by the sensory power subject to the understanding part of the mind. This is clear from the meaning of 'speaking' as thinking, dealt with in 2271, 2287, 2619; and from the representation of 'the chief of the cupbearers' as the sensory power subject to the understanding part, dealt with in 5077, 5082. As to what thought formed by a power of the senses may be, see 5141.

5228   'Saying' means the perception resulting from this. This is clear from the meaning of 'saying' as perceiving, dealt with in 1791, 1815, 1819, 1822, 1898, 1919, 2080, 2619, 2862, 3395, 3509. No intelligible explanation of what is meant by perception resulting from thought can be given because no one at all at the present day knows what spiritual perception is; and what he knows nothing about makes no sense to a person, no matter how well it is described to him. For perception is nothing else than the speech or the thought of the angels who are present with a person. When that speech or thought passes into him it becomes the perception of whether something is true or untrue. This however happens to none but those in whom the good of love and charity is present, good being the channel through which it reaches him. With these people that perception is what engenders their thoughts; for the power of perception which they possess is the general source of their thought. In reality there is no such thing as perception resulting from thought; it is only an appearance. But nothing more can be said about this arcanum because, as has been stated, no one at all at the present day knows what perception is.

5229   'I remember my sins today' means regarding a state of separation. This is clear from the meaning of 'sins' as the faults that belong to an inversion of true order, dealt with in 5076, and from the meaning of 'remembering' as a joining together, dealt with in 5169, so that 'remembering one's sins' means becoming attached to those faults that belong to an inversion of order, and as a consequence becoming separated from the natural represented by 'Pharaoh'. For that which is attached to the faults present in inverted order is separated from what constitutes true order. The reason 'remembering' means a joining together is that in the next life the remembrance of a person links one up with him. For as soon as any spirit calls another spirit to mind, the latter becomes present with him, so fully that the two can converse with each other. This explains why angels and spirits are able to meet, see, and talk in person to everyone they have been acquainted with or heard about, if the Lord lets them call such persons to mind, 1114.

5230 'Pharaoh was incensed with his servants' means when the natural turned away. This is clear from the explanation given above, in 5080, 5081, where similar words occur.

5231 'And put me into custody in the house of the chief of the attendants' means a casting aside from what exists first and foremost in explanations. This too is clear from the explanation given above, in 5083, 5084, where similar words occur.

5232 'Me and the chief of the bakers' means both kinds of sensory power. This is clear from the representation of the chief of the cupbearers, to whom 'me' refers here, as the sensory power subject in general to the understanding part of the mind, dealt with in 5077, 5082, and from the representation of 'the chief of the bakers' as the sensory power in general subject to the will part, dealt with in 5078, 5082, so that 'me and the chief of the bakers' means both kinds of sensory power. The expression 'both kinds of sensory power' is used because in the human being there are two mental powers – the will and the understanding – which make up his life, and these have a connection with every single thing within him. The reason there are in the human being two mental powers which constitute his life is that there are two elements which compose life in heaven, namely goodness and truth. Goodness is connected with the will, truth with the understanding. From this one may see that there are two elements which compose the spiritual man and as a consequence constitute blessedness in the next life; these are charity and faith. For charity is essentially goodness, and faith essentially truth, so that charity is connected with the will and faith with the understanding. Every single thing in the natural world too has a connection with these two, goodness and truth; it comes into being from these and is kept in being by them.

2 The fact that every single thing in the natural world has a connection with those two elements is perfectly plain from the existence of heat and light. Heat has a connection with good and light a connection with truth, and therefore spiritual heat is the good of love, while spiritual light is the truth of faith. Since every single thing in the entire natural creation has a connection with these two – with goodness and truth – and since good is represented in heat, and faith in light, anyone can judge for himself what a person is like if he possesses faith alone without any charity, or what amounts to the same, if he possesses an understanding of truth alone without any desire for good. Does he not resemble the situation in winter, when light shines and yet every single thing is dormant for lack of heat? That is what the state is like of the person who possesses faith alone and no good of love. His state is one of cold and darkness, of cold because he is averse to goodness, of darkness because he is on that account averse to truth. For anyone averse to goodness is also averse to truth, no matter how much it may seem to him that he is not; for the one aversion leads to the other. This is what that person's state comes to be like after death.

5233   'And we dreamed a dream in one night' means that which was foreseen in obscurity. This is clear from the meaning of 'a dream' as that which is foreseen, dealt with in 3698, 5091, and from the meaning of 'night' as a state of shade, dealt with in 1712, and so obscurity.

5234   'I and he' means regarding both kinds of sensory power. This is clear from the representation of the cupbearer, to whom 'I' refers here, as one kind of sensory power, and from the representation of the baker, to whom 'he' refers, as the other kind of sensory power, dealt with just above in 5232.

5235   'We dreamed each according to the interpretation of his own dream' means what was to be the outcome of both. This is clear from the meaning of 'interpretation' as what it held within it and what was to take place, dealt with in 5093, 5105, 5107, 5141, and so what the outcome was to be – [evident] from what was foreseen, meant by 'a dream', 5233.

5236   'And a Hebrew boy was there with us' means that owing to temptation the guiltlessness of the Church had been cast away there. This is clear from the meaning of 'a boy' as guiltlessness, dealt with below; and from the meaning of 'Hebrew' as a person belonging to the Church, dealt with in 5136, thus some attribute of the Church. His having been cast away there owing to temptation is meant by the words 'was there', that is to say, in custody; for 'custody', in which Joseph had been placed, means a state of temptation, 5036, 5037, 5039, 5044, 5045, that state being the subject in Chapters 39 and 40.
The reason 'a boy' [or older 'child']¹ means guiltlessness is that in the internal sense a young child means innocence. References are made in the Word to suckling, young child, and older child, by whom three degrees of innnocence are meant, the first degree being meant by 'suckling', the second degree by 'young child', and the third by 'older child'. But because an older child is one who is beginning to lose his innocence, he therefore means the kind of innocence that is called guiltlessness. Because three degrees of innocence are meant by 'suckling', 'young child', and 'child', three degrees of love and charity are also meant by them, for the reason that celestial and spiritual love, which is love to the Lord and charity towards the neighbour, can have no existence except within innocence. It should be recognized however that the innocence of sucklings, young children, and older ones is purely external and that no internal innocence exists with anyone until he has been born anew, that is, has so to speak become a suckling, young child, and older child once again. These are the states meant in the Word by these three, for the internal sense of the Word has only that which is spiritual as its meaning, and therefore has purely spiritual birth – called rebirth and also regeneration – as its meaning.

¹ *The Latin word* puer *used for* a boy *may also be used to mean simply* a child, *male or female, as in several places in the remainder of this paragraph.*

3   The fact that the innocence called guiltlessness is meant by 'a child' is clear in Luke,

Jesus said, Whoever does not receive the kingdom of God like *a child* will not enter it.   Luke 18:17.

'Receiving the kingdom of God like *a child*' means receiving charity and faith because of one's innocence. In Mark,

Jesus took *a child*, set him in the midst of them and took him up in His arms. He said to them, Whoever takes up one of such *children* in My name is taking up Me.   Mark 9:36,37; Luke 9:47,48.

'A child' here is a representation of innocence; anyone who takes this up is taking up the Lord because He is the Source from which every trace of innocence is derived. Anyone may see that 'taking up a child in the Lord's name' does not mean taking up a child, so that something heavenly is represented by such an action.

4   In Matthew,

When *the children* in the temple cried out, Hosanna to the son of David, [the chief priests and scribes] were indignant. Therefore Jesus said to them, Have you not read that out of the mouth of *young children* and *sucklings* You have perfected praise?   Matt.21:15,16; Ps.8:2.

The children's cry 'Hosanna to the son of David' was voiced so as to represent the truth that innocence alone acknowledges and accepts the Lord, that is, that those who have innocence within them do so. The words 'out of the mouth of young children and sucklings You have perfected praise' mean that there is no other path than innocence along which praise can go to the Lord. Along this path alone can any communication be established, any influx take place, or consequently any approach be made. This is why the Lord says, in the same gospel,

Unless you are converted and become as *children* you will not enter the kingdom of heaven.   Matt.18:3.

5   In the following places too 'a boy' [or 'a child'] means innocence: In Zechariah,

The streets of the city will be full of *boys* and *girls* playing in the streets. Zech.8:5.

This refers to a new Jerusalem, or the Lord's kingdom. In David,

Praise Jehovah, young men and also virgins, old men and *children*.   Ps.148:12.

In the same author,

Jehovah redeems[1] your life from the pit. He satisfies your mouth with what is good, so that *your youth* is renewed like the eagle's[2].   Ps.103:4,5.

In Joel,

---

[1] *The Latin means* renews, *but the Hebrew means* redeems, *which Sw. has in another place where he quotes this verse.*
[2] *lit.* so that you are renewed like the eagle with *your childhood*

Over My people they have cast lots, for they have given *a boy* for a harlot and have sold *a girl* for wine which they have drunk.   Joel 3:3.

In Jeremiah,

I will scatter throughout you man and woman, and I will scatter throughout you old man and *boy*, and I will scatter throughout you young man and virgin. Jer.51:22.

In Isaiah,

To us a boy is born, to us a son is given, upon whose shoulder is the government; and He will call His name, Wonderful, Counsellor, God, Hero, Father of Eternity, Prince of Peace.   Isa.9:6.

5237   'A servant of the chief of the attendants' means in which there was truth that served that which came first and foremost in explanations. This is clear from the use of 'a servant' to refer to truth, dealt with in 2567, 3409; and from the meaning of 'the chief of the attendants' as things which come first and foremost in explanations, dealt with in 4790, 4966, 5084. And since truth is of service to explanations – to explanations of the Word – 'a servant of the chief of the attendants' here means truth that is of service.

5238   'And we told him' means resulting perception. This is clear from the meaning of 'telling' as perception, dealt with in 3209.

5239   'And he interpreted our dreams for us' means what the things foreseen in obscurity held within them. This is clear from the meaning of 'interpreting' as what was held within, dealt with in 5093, 5105, 5107; and from the meaning of 'dreams' as the things foreseen in obscurity, dealt with above in 5233.

5240   'To each according to his dream he gave the interpretation' means from [a knowledge of] the truth; 'and it happened, that as he interpreted to us so it came about' means that so was the outcome. As regards the meaning 'so was the outcome', this may be seen from the fact that the words used here mean the outcome of the matter, which from [a knowledge of] the truth was exactly as he had foretold.

5241   'He restored me to my position' means that the sensory power belonging to the understanding part of the mind was accepted. This is clear from the meaning of the cupbearer, meant by 'me' here, as the sensory power belonging to the understanding part, dealt with above; and from the meaning of 'restoring to one's position' as restoring to order and making subordinate, dealt with in 5125, 5165, and so also as accepting.

5242   'And he hanged him' means that the sensory power belonging to the will part was cast aside. This is clear from the meaning of the baker, meant here by 'him', as the sensory power belonging to the will part, dealt with above; and from the meaning of 'hanging' as casting aside, dealt with in 5156, 5167. There is no need to explain these meanings any further because they have been explained already. They are details such as have been restated for the sake of the sequence of thought.

5243 Verse 14 **And Pharaoh sent and called Joseph, and they hurried him out of the pit; and he clipped [his hair and beard], and changed his clothes, and came to Pharaoh.**
'And Pharaoh sent' means the inclination of the new natural. 'And called Joseph' means to accept the celestial of the spiritual. 'And they hurried him out of the pit' means a hasty casting aside of such things as, belonging to a state of temptation, were a hindrance, and a consequent change that was made. 'And he clipped [his hair and beard]' means a casting aside and the change made so far as the coverings of the exterior natural were concerned. 'And changed his clothes' means the change made so far as the coverings of the interior natural were concerned, by the putting on of what was rightly suited to this. 'And came to Pharaoh' means a communication in this guise with the new natural.

5244 'And Pharaoh sent' means the inclination of the new natural. This is clear from the representation of 'Pharaoh' as the new natural man, dealt with in 5079, 5080. An inclination to accept the celestial of the spiritual is the meaning of the words 'sent and called Joseph'. Such an inclination is evident from what follows, in verses 40–43, where it is stated that Pharaoh set him over his house and over all the land of Egypt and said that all his people would kiss him on the mouth. The implications of this are that when the state is complete, that is, when everything has been made ready in the natural to accept an influx from what is interior or higher and to link itself to what flows into it, the natural too possesses that inclination, which is an affection disposed to accept [the celestial of the spiritual]. The one accordingly becomes compatible with the other when a person is being renewed by the Lord.

5245 'And called Joseph' means to accept the celestial of the spiritual. This is clear from the representation of 'Joseph' as the celestial of the spiritual, dealt with in 4286, 4585, 4592, 4594, 4963 – an inclination to accept it being meant by the word 'called', see immediately above in 5244.

5246 'And they hurried him out of the pit' means a hasty casting aside of such things as, belonging to a state of temptation, were a hindrance, and a consequent change that was made. This is clear from the meaning of 'the pit' as a state in which vastation and also temptation take place, dealt with in 4728, 4744, 5038; and from the meaning of 'hurrying him out of it' as a hasty casting aside of such things as belong to this – to a state of temptation. For as 'the pit' describes a state of temptation, 'hurrying someone out of it' describes the removal of such things as belong to that state, consequently the casting aside of them, as is evident from what follows next – he cast aside what belonged to the pit, that is, he clipped [his hair and beard] and changed his clothes.

In comparison with the state that follows it, a state in which temptation takes place is like conditions in a pit or prison – squalid and unclean. For when a person undergoes temptation unclean spirits are near him and round about him. They activate the evils and falsities residing with him; and they also confine him to these, increasing them to the point where he reaches despair. So it is that the person dwells at such times amid uncleanness and squalor; and when a visual presentation of that state is made in the next life (for there they can present visually the nature of any spiritual state) it is seen as a cloud issuing from filthy places. And one also smells the stench emanating from the same source. A sphere such as this is what surrounds someone undergoing temptation and also someone undergoing vastation, that is, one who is in the pit on the lower earth, dealt with in 4728.

But when the state involving temptation comes to an end the cloud is dispersed and the air is made clear. The reason this happens is that temptations are the means by which the evils and falsities residing with a person are exposed and removed, the cloud presenting itself while they are being exposed, the clear air when they are-being removed. The change that takes place in that state is also meant by Joseph clipping [his hair and beard] and changing his clothes.

One may also compare the state in which temptation takes place to a person's condition when he falls among robbers. When he gets away his hair is dishevelled, his face is rough, and his clothes are torn. If he yields in temptation he remains in that state; but if he overcomes in temptation his condition is happy and peaceful once he has attended to his face, combed his hair, and changed his clothes. What is more, there are hellish spirits and genii who, behaving at such times like robbers, surround and attack him, and so subject him to temptations. From all this it is now evident that 'they hurried him out of the pit' means a hasty casting aside of such things as, belonging to a state of temptation, were a hindrance, and a consequent change that was made.

5247   'And he clipped [his hair and beard]' means a casting aside and the change made so far as the coverings of the exterior natural were concerned. This is clear from the meaning of 'clipping' – that is, clipping the head and beard – as casting aside the coverings of the exterior natural. For 'hair' which was clipped means the exterior natural, see 3301. Also, both hair on the head and that composing the beard correspond in the Grand Man to the exterior natural. This explains why in the light of heaven sensory-minded people – that is, those who have had no belief in anything apart from that which is natural, and have had no desire to understand how anything more internal or purer can exist apart from that which they can perceive with their senses – have a hairy appearance in the next life. They look so hairy that their faces are scarcely anything else than hairy beards. I have seen faces covered with hair like these on many occasions. But rationally-minded people, that is, spiritually-minded ones, with whom the natural has played a correctly subordinate role, are seen with tidy hair. Indeed from the state of people's hair in the next life one can tell what the natural with them is like. The reason spirits appear with hair on their heads is that in the next life spirits look exactly like people on earth. This too is why the Word sometimes includes a description of the hair of the angels people have seen.

2 From all this one may now see what is meant by 'clipping', as in Ezekiel,

> The priests the Levites, the sons of Zadok, shall put off *their garments* in which they have been ministering and lay them in the holy chambers, and *they shall put on other garments,* and they shall not sanctify the people in *their own garments.* And *they shall not shave their head* and *shall not let their hair grow long; they shall surely clip their heads.*   Ezek.44:15,19,20.

This refers to a new Temple and a new priesthood, that is, to a new Church. 'Putting on other garments' means holy truths; 'not shaving their head, and not letting their hair grow long, but surely clipping their heads' means not casting aside the natural but taking measures to make it conformable, and so to make it subordinate. Anyone who believes that the Word is indeed holy can see that these and all the other details mentioned by the prophet which describe a new land, a new city, and a new Temple and priesthood must not be taken literally. The statement, for example, that the priests the Levites, the sons of Zadok, will minister there, at which time they will put off their ministerial garments and put on new ones, and will also clip their heads, is not meant literally; rather, each and all the details given by the prophet have as their meaning such things as are aspects of a new Church.

3 The following rules were laid down for the high priest, the sons of Aaron, and the Levites, in Moses,

> The priest who is chief among his brothers, on whose head the anointing oil has been poured and who has been consecrated[1] *to wear the garments, shall not shave his head* or *rend his garments.*   Lev.21:10.
> The sons of Aaron *shall not introduce any baldness on their head or shave the corner of their beard.* They shall be holy to their God, and they shall not profane the name of their God.   Lev.21:5,6.
> You shall purify the Levites like this: Sprinkle over them the water of expiation, *and they shall pass a razor over their flesh* and wash *their garments,* and they shall be pure.   Num.8:7.

These rules would never have been given unless they had held holy ideas within them. Can there be anything holy or anything of the Church in the actual rule forbidding the high priest to shave his head or rend his garments, or in the actual rule forbidding the sons of Levi to introduce any baldness on their head or shave the corner of their beard, or in that commanding the Levites to shave their flesh with a razor

---

[1] *lit.* whose hand has been filled

when they underwent purification? Rather, the possession of an external or natural man made subordinate to the internal or spiritual man, both of which have thereby been made subordinate to the Divine, is the holy idea within those rules; and it is also what angels perceive when man reads about them in the Word.

The same goes for what is said about a Nazirite who was holy to Jehovah. If someone next to him happened to die suddenly and so defile his consecrated head, the Nazirite was required *to clip his head* on the day of his cleansing; on the seventh day *he had to clip it*. On the day that the days of his Naziriteship were completed *he had to clip his consecrated head* at the door of the Tent of Meeting and to take *the hair from his head* and put it on the fire which was under the sacrifice of peace offerings, Num.6:8,9,13,18. For the meaning of a Nazirite and what aspect of holiness he represented, see 3301. No one can possibly understand why anything holy existed within the Nazirite's hair unless he knows from correspondence what is meant by 'the hair' and from this what aspect of holiness a Nazirite's hair corresponded to. Nor can anyone likewise understand how the source of Samson's strength lay in his hair, which he told Delilah about in the following description,

No razor has come upon my head, for I have been a Nazirite of God from my mother's womb. *If I am shaved,* my strength will depart from me, and I shall become weak and be like anyone else. And Delilah called a man *who shaved off the seven locks of his hair*; and his strength departed from him. After that, *when the hair on his head began to grow, even as it had been shaved off,* his strength returned to him.   Judg.16:17,19,22.

Without any knowledge of correspondence who can see that the Lord's Divine Natural was represented by 'a Nazirite', or that 'Naziriteship' had no other meaning than this, or that Samson's strength was due to that representation?

Anyone who does not know, and more so one who does not believe that the Word has an internal sense, and that the sense of the letter serves to represent the real things contained in the internal sense, will recognize scarcely anything holy at all in these matters, when in fact the greatest holiness lies within them. Anyone who does not know, and more so one who does not believe that the Word has an internal sense that is intrinsically holy cannot know what the following texts enfold within them: In Jeremiah,

Truth has perished and has been cut off from their mouth. *Cut off the hair of your Naziriteship* and throw it away.   Jer.7:28,29.

In Isaiah,

On that day the Lord *will shave by means of a razor hired* at the crossing-places of the River – by means of the king of Asshur – *the head* and *the hair of the feet*; and it will consume *the beard* also.   Isa.7:20.

In Micah,

Make yourself bald, and *shave your head* for the children of your delight; *extend your baldness* like an eagle, for they have departed from you.   Micah 1:16.

Nor will anyone know the aspect of holiness contained in the reference to Elijah's being *a man covered with hair*, who wore a skin girdle around his loins, 2 Kings 1:8. Nor will he know why the children who called Elisha *baldhead* were torn apart by the bears out of the forest, 2 Kings 2:23,24.

6 Both Elijah and Elisha represented the Lord as to the Word, and so represented the Word itself, specifically the prophetical part, see Preface to Genesis 18, and 2762. Being covered with hair and having a skin girdle meant the literal sense, 'a man covered with hair' meaning that sense so far as truths were concerned, 'wearing a skin girdle around his loins' so far as forms of good were concerned. For the literal sense is the natural sense of the Word since it employs ideas formed from things that exist in the world, whereas the internal sense is the spiritual sense because it employs ideas formed from things existing in heaven. These two senses are related to each other in the way that the internal and the external are related in the human being. But because the internal can have no existence without the external, the external being the last and lowest degree of order within which the internal is held in being, the calling of Elisha 'baldhead' therefore meant the shameful accusation made against the Word that it lacked so to speak an external and so lacked a sense suited to man's capacity to understand it.

7 From all this one may see that every particular detail in the Word is holy. However, this holiness within the Word is discerned by no one unless he is acquainted with the internal sense; yet an inkling of it flows from heaven into someone who believes that the Word is holy. The internal sense known to the angels is the channel through which that influx comes; and even if the person has no understanding of that sense it nevertheless stimulates an affection in him, because the affection felt by the angels who know that sense is communicated to him. From this it is also evident that the Word was given to man so that he might have a means of communication with heaven and so that by flowing into him Divine Truth in heaven might stimulate affection in him.

5248 'And changed his clothes' means the change made so far as coverings of the interior natural were concerned, by the putting on of what was rightly suited to this. This is clear from the meaning of 'changing' as removing and casting aside, and from the meaning of 'clothes' as the coverings of the interior natural, dealt with below. The putting on of what was rightly suited, meant by 'new clothes', follows on from this. Frequent reference is made in the Word to clothes, by which are meant lower or outward things which, being such, serve to cover higher or inward ones. 'Clothes' consequently means the external part of man and therefore what is natural, since this covers the internal and the spiritual part of him. In particular 'clothes' means truths that are matters of faith since these cover forms of good that are embodiments of charity. This meaning of 'clothes' has its origin in the clothes that spirits and angels are seen to be wearing. Spirits are seen dressed in clothes that have no brightness, whereas angels are seen dressed in clothes full of brightness and so to speak made of brightness. For the actual brightness that surrounds them looks like a robe, much like the Lord's garments when He was transfigured, which were 'as the light', Matt.17:2, and 'glistening white', Luke 9:29. From the clothes they wear one can also tell what kinds of spirits and angels they are so far as truths of faith are concerned since these are represented by their clothes, though only truths of faith such as exist within the natural. The truths of faith such as exist within the rational are revealed in the face and in the beauty it possesses. The brightness of their garments has its origin in the good of love and charity, for that good shines through and is the producer of the brightness. From all this one may see what is represented in the spiritual world by clothes and as a consequence what is meant in the spiritual sense by 'clothes'.

But the clothes which Joseph changed – that is, cast aside – were those of the pit or prison-clothing, which mean the delusions and false ideas that are stirred up by evil genii and spirits in a state involving temptations. Consequently the expression 'he changed his clothes' means a casting aside and a change made in the coverings of the interior natural. And the clothes which he put on were ones such as were properly suitable, so that the putting on of what was rightly suited is meant. See what has been stated and shown already regarding clothes,

Celestial things are unclothed, but not so spiritual and natural ones, 297.
'Clothes' are truths, which are of a lower nature when they are compared with what they cover, 1073, 2576.
'Changing one's garments' was representative of the need to put on holy truths, and therefore 'changes of garments' had the same meaning, 4545.
'Rending one's clothes' was representative of mourning on account of the loss of truth, 4763.
What is meant by someone entering who was not wearing a wedding garment, 2132.

5249   'And came to Pharaoh' means a communication with the new natural. This is clear from the meaning of 'coming' in this instance as a communication through influx; and from the representation of 'Pharaoh' as the new natural, dealt with in 5079, 5080, 5244. What the words in this verse hold within them is evident from the explanations of them that have been given; for those words describe how Joseph was set free from the pit and came to Pharaoh. In the internal sense 'Joseph' represents the Lord so far as the celestial of the spiritual is concerned, while 'Pharaoh' represents the natural or external man. 'The pit' in which Joseph was confined represents a state of temptation endured by the Lord which involved the celestial of the spiritual, while his being called from the pit by Pharaoh means a state of release from temptations, and also a state of influx and communication after that with the new natural. From all this it is evident that the internal sense contains a description at this point of how the Lord made His Natural new and at length Divine.

2 These are the matters that celestial angels contemplate when such historical details are read by man. To contemplate such matters is also their greatest delight, for they live in the Lord's Divine sphere and so they are as it were in the Lord. They know the deepest joy when they are thinking about the Lord and about the salvation of the human race, which took place because the Lord made the Human within Himself Divine. Also, to enable angels to go on experiencing that most heavenly joy and at the same time wisdom, a full description of that Divine process has therefore been given in the internal sense of the Word. This sense includes at the same time the process by which man is regenerated, for man's regeneration is an image of the Lord's glorification, 3138, 3212, 3296, 3490, 4402. Many will perhaps be wondering what angels talk about to one another and consequently what people after death who become angels talk about. Let those who so wonder know that angels talk about the kinds of matters that are contained in the internal sense of the Word, that is to say, about the Lord's glorification, His kingdom, the Church, the regeneration of man by means of the good of love and the truth of faith. But when they do so they use profound ideas which for the most part are beyond description.

5250 Verses 15,16 **And Pharaoh said to Joseph, I have dreamed a dream, and there is no one who can interpret it; and I have heard about you – it is said that when you hear a dream you can interpret it. And Joseph answered Pharaoh, saying, It is not mine; God will give an answer of peace, O Pharaoh.**

'And Pharaoh said to Joseph' means a perception expressed by the natural but belonging to the celestial of the spiritual. 'I have dreamed a dream' means a foretelling. 'And there is no one who can interpret it' means ignorance about what it held within it. 'And I have heard about you' means the ability of the celestial of the spiritual. 'It is said that when you hear a dream you can interpret it' means to discern what it is that things foreseen hold within them. 'And Joseph answered Pharaoh' means awareness. 'Saying, it is not mine' means that it does not have a purely human origin. 'God will give an answer of peace, O Pharaoh' means that the Divine Human was the origin of it, through its being joined to it.

5251 'And Pharaoh said to Joseph' means a perception expressed by the natural but belonging to the celestial of the spiritual. This is clear from the meaning of 'saying' in the historical narratives of the Word as perceiving, often dealt with already; from the representation of 'Pharaoh' as the natural, dealt with in 5079, 5080, 5095, 5160; and from the representation of 'Joseph' as the celestial of the spiritual, dealt with in 4286, 4592, 4594, 4963, 5086, 5087, 5106, 5249. The reason why a perception expressed by the natural but belonging to the celestial of the spiritual is meant is that the Lord is represented by both 'Joseph' and 'Pharaoh'. 'Joseph' represents His celestial of the spiritual and 'Pharaoh' His natural, and therefore 'Pharaoh said to Joseph' means a perception which the Lord had, which originated in the celestial of the spiritual and was present in the natural. But nothing intelligible can be stated regarding the identity and essential nature of that perception unless some idea has been formed first of what spiritual perception and the celestial of the spiritual are, as well as some idea about the essential nature of the natural being distinct and separate from that of the spiritual. Some reference has indeed been made previously to these matters; but one needs to be reminded of them.

5252   'I have dreamed a dream' means a foretelling. This is clear from the meaning of 'a dream' as foresight and consequently a foretelling, dealt with in 3698, 5091, 5092, 5104, 5233. The fact that at this point 'a dream' means a foretelling is also evident from what follows, for in the dream the seven years of abundance of corn and the seven years of famine were foretold.

5253   'And there is no one who can interpret it' means ignorance about what it held within it. This is clear from the meaning of 'interpreting' as what something held within it, dealt with in 5093, 5105, 5107, 5141 – ignorance about what it held within it therefore being meant by 'no one who can interpret it'. In the internal sense 'no one' does not mean no one or nobody, but simply absence or non-existence. Here therefore that which is 'not' is meant, thus something that is unknown to people or of which they are ignorant. The explanation for this is that one does not see in the internal sense any particular person, or indeed anything that has to do specifically with any person, see 5225; and by the expression 'no one' or 'nobody' no more than some general aspect of a person is implied.

There are in general three elements which depart from the literal sense of the Word when it becomes the internal sense; these are the temporal, the spatial, and the personal. The reason for this is that neither time nor space exists in the spiritual world. These two elements belong properly to the natural order, which also accounts for its being said that those who die depart from the realm of time, leaving temporal concerns behind them. And the reason why in the spiritual world they do not see anything that has to do specifically with some person is that any focusing, when they speak, on some particular person narrows down and limits the idea they have in mind; such a focusing prevents any broadening or removal of limits to their idea. Their use, when they speak, of broadened and unlimited ideas renders their language universal, a language that includes and enables them to express countless and also wondrous ideas. This is what the language used by angels is like, especially that used by celestial angels, which, compared with that employed by others, knows no limitations. This being so, the whole of their speech reaches into what is infinite and into what is eternal, consequently into the Divine of the Lord.

5254 'And I have heard about you' means the ability of the celestial of the spiritual; and 'it is said that when you hear a dream you can interpret it' means to discern what it is that things foreseen hold within them. This is clear from the meaning of 'hearing about you' as discerning and coming to know that its nature is such and therefore that it possessed that kind of ability; from the representation of 'Joseph', to whom these words are addressed, as the celestial of the spiritual, dealt with in 4286, 4592, 4594, 4963, 5086, 5087, 5106; from the meaning of 'hearing' as discerning, dealt with in 5017; from the meaning of 'a dream' as that which is foreseen, dealt with just above in 5252; and from the meaning of 'interpreting' as what it held within it, also dealt with above, in 5253. From all these meanings it is evident that 'I have heard about you – it is said that when you hear a dream you can interpret it' means the ability which the celestial of the spiritual possesses to discern what it is that things foreseen hold within them.

5255 'And Joseph answered Pharaoh' means awareness. This is clear from the meaning of 'giving an answer to something', when any question is posed regarding it, as imparting knowledge and thereby showing an awareness of the nature of the matter.

5256 'Saying, It is not mine' means that it does not have a purely human origin. This becomes clear from the meaning of 'it is not mine' or not belonging to himself – when these words refer to the Lord, who is represented by 'Joseph' – as that it does not have a purely human origin but a Divine one; for the Divine foresees and consequently knows what something holds within it. When He was in the world the Lord possessed foresight and providence; the two were indeed present in the human, but they had their origin in the Divine. After that time however, once He was glorified, they had their origin in the Divine alone, for the Human, having been glorified, is Divine. Regarded in itself the human is nothing else than a form that receives life from the Divine; but the Lord's glorified Human, or His Divine Human, is not a form that receives life from the Divine but is the actual inner Being (*Esse*) of that life and so the source from which it comes forth. This is the kind of idea about the Lord that angels have. But as for members of the Christian Church at the present day who enter the next life, almost all think of the Lord as they do of any other human being. Not only do they have an idea of Him separate from the Divine, though they do attribute Divinity to Him; they also have an idea of Him separate from Jehovah. In addition they have an idea of Him separate from the holy one that goes forth from Him. They talk, it is true, about one God, yet they think of three and in practice divide the Divine into three. For they distinguish the Divine into separate persons, calling each one God and attributing a distinct property to each. Consequently Christians are said in the next life to worship three Gods, for their thoughts are of three however much they may talk about one.

But those who are gentile converts to Christianity worship the Lord alone in the next life. They do so because they believed that it could have been none else than the supreme Deity who revealed Himself on earth as man and that this supreme Deity is a Divine Man. They also believed that if they did not have that idea of the supreme Deity they could not have any idea at all and so could not have any thought about God, nor consequently have any knowledge of Him, let alone love for Him.

5257 'God will give you an answer of peace, O Pharaoh' means that the Divine Human was the origin of it, through its being joined to it. This becomes clear from what has been stated immediately above in 5256, and from the meaning of 'peace of which God will give an answer' as the Lord's Divine Human as the origin of it. 'God', as is clear without explanation, means the Divine; while 'peace' in the highest sense means the Lord, see 3780, 4681. The reason it is the origin through its being joined to it – to the celestial of the spiritual, and through this to the natural – is that this joining together is the subject here.

5258 Verses 17–24 **And Pharaoh spoke to Joseph, In my dream, behold, I was standing on the bank of the river. And behold, out of the river seven cows were coming up, fat-fleshed and beautiful in form; and they fed in the sedge. And behold, seven other cows were coming up after them, weak and extremely bad in form and lean-fleshed; I have not seen any like them in all the land of Egypt for badness. And the lean and bad cows devoured the first seven fat cows. And they devoured them completely[1], and no one would have known that they had devoured them completely[2]; and their appearance was malign, as it had been in the beginning. And I awoke. And I saw in my dream, and behold, seven heads of grain were coming up on one stalk, full and good. And behold, seven heads, dried up, thin, and scorched by an east wind, were sprouting after them. And the thin heads swallowed up the seven good heads. And I told it to the magi, and there was no one to point out the meaning to me.**

'And Pharaoh spoke to Joseph' means thought expressed by the natural but belonging to the celestial of the spiritual. 'In my dream' means what has been foreseen in a state of obscurity. 'Behold, I was standing on the bank of the river' means from boundary to boundary. 'And behold, out of the river' means at the boundary. 'Seven cows were coming up' means the truths belonging to the natural. 'Fat-fleshed' means which were embodiments of charity. 'And beautiful in form' means which were expressions of faith resulting from these. 'And they fed in the sedge' means instruction. 'And behold, seven other cows were coming

---

[1] *lit.* they came to their viscera
[2] *lit.* it was not known that they had come to their viscera

up after them' means falsities present in the natural close by them. 'Weak and extremely bad in form' means empty and lacking in faith. 'And lean-fleshed' means lacking in charity too. 'I have not seen anything like them in all the land of Egypt for badness' means which were such that they could not by any means be joined to forms of truth and good. 'And the lean and bad cows devoured.....' means that falsities which were not expressions of faith and not embodiments of charity would banish..... 'The first seven fat cows' means truths which were expressions of faith derived from charity. 'And they devoured them completely' means an interior banishing. 'And no one would have known that they had devoured them completely' means that the truths of good were no longer discernible. 'And their appearance was malign, as it had been at the beginning' means that no communication or joining together existed. 'And I awoke' means a state of enlightenment. 'And I saw in my dream' means still more foreseen in obscurity. 'And behold, seven heads of grain were coming up on one stalk' means facts known to the natural, which facts existed linked together. 'Full and good' means into which facts matters of faith and charity could be instilled. 'And behold, seven heads, dried up, thin, and scorched by an east wind' means facts that are useless and full of evil desires. 'Were sprouting after them' means appearing close by them. 'And the thin heads swallowed up the seven good heads' means that the facts which were useless banished the facts which were useful. 'And I told it to the magi' means a consultation with facts of an interior kind. 'And there was no one to point out the meaning to me' means that nothing at all was discerned from these.

5259 'And Pharaoh spoke to Joseph' means thought expressed by the natural but belonging to the celestial of the spiritual. This is clear from what has been stated above in 5251, where the same words occur, except that there it says that Pharaoh *said* to Joseph, here that he *spoke* to him; for 'said' means perception, whereas 'spoke' means thought, 2271, 2287, 2619. The reason 'Pharaoh spoke to Joseph' means thought which is expressed by the natural but belongs to the celestial of the spiritual, and not the other way round, is that when thought is going on in what is exterior, the source of such thought does not lie there but in what is interior. Or what amounts to the same, when thought is going on in what is lower, nothing else than what is higher is the source of it. Even so, while the thought belonging to what is interior or higher is going on in what is exterior or lower, it does seem as though the exterior or lower is itself the source of the thought going on in it. But that is an illusion. It is like a person who sees some object in a mirror but does not know that the mirror is there. He supposes that the object exists where it appears to do so, but in reality it does not exist there.

2   Now because the celestial of the spiritual is interior or higher, and the natural is exterior or lower, 'Pharaoh spoke to Joseph' therefore means in the internal sense thought expressed by the natural but belonging to

the celestial of the spiritual. In short, nothing in a lower position possesses anything self-derived whatsoever. Any ability it possesses comes from what is higher, which being so it plainly follows that the Highest one of all, that is, the Divine, is the source of everything. Consequently the source of a person's thought proceeding from his understanding and of his activity proceeding from his will is the Highest one or the Divine. If however a person thinks false ideas and acts in evil ways, this is due to the form he has stamped on his own character; but if he thinks right ideas and acts in ways that are good, it is due to the form he has received from the Lord. For it is well known that one and the same power and force produces differing movements which are determined by the ways in which the intermediate and outermost parts are structured, so that in the human being life from the Divine produces differing thoughts and actions, determined by the forms existing there.

5260   The details that follow in this passage are practically the same as those explained already in this chapter, in 5195–5217, and therefore one can pass over them without any further explanation.

5261   Verses 25–27 **And Joseph said to Pharaoh, Pharaoh's dream, it is one; what God is doing He has pointed out to Pharaoh. The seven good cows are seven years, and the seven good heads of grain are seven years; the dream, it is one. And the seven thin and bad cows coming up after them are seven years; and the seven empty heads of grain, scorched by an east wind, will be seven years of famine.**
'And Joseph said to Pharaoh' means a perception which the natural received from the celestial of the spiritual. 'Pharaoh's dream, it is one' means that a similar situation existed in both parts, which was foreseen. 'What God is doing He has pointed out to Pharaoh' means that the natural was allowed to discern what was provided. 'The seven good cows are seven years' means a state when truth within the interior natural is multiplied. 'And the seven good heads of grain are seven years' means a state when truth within the exterior natural is multiplied. 'The dream, it is one' means that both will be such through a joining together. 'And the seven thin and bad cows coming up after them are seven years' means a state when falsity attacking the interior natural is multiplied. 'And the seven empty heads of grain, scorched by an east wind' means a state when falsity attacking the exterior natural is multiplied. 'Will be seven years of famine' means a consequent absence and seeming deprivation of truth.

5262   'And Joseph said to Pharaoh' means a perception which the natural received from the celestial of the spiritual. This is clear from the meaning of 'saying' in the historical narratives of the Word as perceiving, from the representation of 'Joseph' as the celestial of the spiritual, and from the representation of 'Pharaoh' as the natural, which specific meaning and representations have often been dealt with already.

5263 'Pharaoh's dream, it is one' means that a similar situation existed in both parts, which was foreseen. This is clear from the meaning of 'dream' as that which was foreseen, dealt with in 3698, 5091, 5092, 5104, 5233; from the representation of 'Pharaoh' as the natural, dealt with in 5079, 5080, 5095, 5160; and from the meaning of 'it is one' here as a similar situation existing in both parts – in the interior natural and in the exterior natural. For the natural has two parts, see 5118, 5126. What Pharaoh dreamed about involving the cows was a foresight regarding the interior natural, and what he dreamed about involving the heads of grain was a foresight regarding the exterior natural; and since both parts of the natural must act as a single unit through their existing joined together, a similar situation in both parts is meant.

5264 'What God is doing He has pointed out to Pharaoh' means that the natural was allowed to discern what was provided. This is clear from the meaning of 'what God is doing' as what was provided, dealt with below; from the meaning of 'pointing out' as communicating and allowing one to discern, dealt with in 3608, 4856; and from the representation of 'Pharaoh' as the natural, dealt with above in 5263. From this it is evident that 'what God is doing He has pointed out to Pharaoh' means that the natural was allowed to discern what was provided.

2   The reason why 'what God is doing' means what has been provided is that everything done by God, that is, by the Lord, constitutes His Providence. Every act of Providence is Divine, for it holds what is eternal and infinite within it. It holds what is eternal because its view is not limited by any beginning or end, and it holds what is infinite because its view comprehends simultaneously the entire whole within any specific part, and every specific part within the entire whole. All this is called 'Providence'; and because every single one of the Lord's acts holds what is eternal and infinite within it, no other expression than Providence exists to describe it. This truth that every single one of the Lord's acts holds what is infinite and eternal within it will in the Lord's Divine mercy be illustrated elsewhere with the help of examples.

5265 'The seven good cows are seven years' means a state when truth within the interior natural is multiplied. This is clear from the meaning of 'the cows' in the good sense as the truths belonging to the interior natural, dealt with in 5198; and from the meaning of 'years' as states, dealt with in 482, 487, 488, 493, 893. There were seven because 'seven' means that which is holy and therefore adds the idea of holiness to the matter under discussion, dealt with in 395, 433, 716, 881, as well as implying a whole period from start to finish, 728. This explains why in the dream seven cows and seven heads of grain were seen, and after that why there were seven years of abundance of corn and seven years of famine. It also explains why the seventh day was made holy, why in the representative Church the seventh year was a sabbatical year, and why after seven times seven years there was a Jubilee.

'Seven' means things that are holy because of the meanings that numbers have in the world of spirits. Each number there holds some spiritual reality within it. Visual indications of numbers have appeared to me frequently, simple and compound ones, and also on one occasion a long sequence of them, when I have wondered what meanings they possessed. I have been told that they have their origin in conversations held by angels, and that it is customary from time to time to use numbers to express spiritual realities too. These numbers are not seen in heaven but in the world of spirits, where the visual presentation of such things takes place. The most ancients, who were celestial people and who talked to angels, knew all about this, which was why they used numbers to express an evaluation of the Church. The numbers used by them conveyed a general overall idea of matters for which words served to provide a detailed description. The meaning contained within every number did not however continue to be known among the descendants of these people; only the meanings of the simple numbers survived, that is to say, the meanings of two, three, six, seven, eight, twelve, and from these the meanings of twenty-four, seventy-two, and seventy-seven. In particular their descendants knew that 'seven' meant that which was most holy – that is to say, that in the highest sense 'seven' meant the Divine Himself, and in the representative sense the celestial element of love – and that the state of the celestial man was therefore meant by 'the seventh day', 84-87.

It is quite evident from the numbers used plentifully in the Word that numbers mean spiritual realities, such as the following ones in John,

Let him who has intelligence reckon the number of the beast, for it is the number of a man, that is, its number is six hundred and sixty-six. Rev.13:18.

And elsewhere in the same book,

The angel measured the wall of the holy Jerusalem, a hundred and forty-four cubits, which is the measure of a man, that is, of an angel. Rev.21:17.

The number one hundred and forty-four is twelve squared and twice seventy-two.

5266   'And the seven heads of grain are seven years' means a state when truth within the exterior natural is multiplied. This is clear from the meaning of 'heads of grain' in the good sense as factual knowledge, dealt with in 5212, and therefore as the truths known to the exterior natural, for such truths are called facts; and from the meaning of 'years' as states, dealt with immediately above in 5265, where the meaning of 'seven' may also be seen.

5267   'The dream, it is one' means that both will be such through a joining together. This is clear from what has been stated above in 5263.

5268   'And the seven thin and bad cows coming up after them are seven years' means a state when falsity attacking the interior natural is multiplied. This is clear from the meaning of 'cows' in the genuine sense as truths within the interior natural, dealt with in 5198, 5265, but in the contrary sense as falsities there, dealt with in 5202, so that the former are called 'good cows', but the latter 'thin and bad'; from the meaning of 'coming up' as an advance made towards things that are interior, dealt with in 5202; and from the meaning of 'years' as states, dealt with just above in 5265. Even as 'seven' means that which is holy, so in the contrary sense it means that which is unholy. For most things in the Word have a contrary meaning as well, the reason for this being that when the selfsame things as come into being in heaven pass downwards in the direction of hell, they are converted into things of an opposite nature and become in actual fact their opposites. Consequently things that are holy, meant by 'seven', are made in that place into those that are unholy.

2   Let references to the number seven found solely in the Book of Revelation serve to prove that 'seven' is used to mean both holy things and unholy ones. The following are places where holy things are meant,

John to *the seven Churches*: Grace and peace from Him who is and who was and who is to come, and from *the seven spirits* who are before His throne.   Rev.1:4.
These things says He who has *the seven spirits* and *the seven stars*.   Rev.3:1.
From the throne there were coming *seven lamps* of fire burning before the throne, which are *the seven spirits* of God.   Rev.4:5.
I saw on the right hand of Him sitting on the throne a book written within and on the back, sealed with *seven seals*.   Rev.5:1.
I looked, and behold, in the midst of the throne, a Lamb standing as though it had been slain, having *seven horns* and *seven eyes*, which are *the seven spirits of God* sent out into all the earth.   Rev.5:6.
To *the seven angels* were given *seven trumpets*.   Rev.8:2.
In the days of the voice of *the seventh angel* the mystery of God was to be fulfilled.   Rev.10:7.
Out of the temple came *the seven angels* having *the seven plagues*, clothed in linen, white and splendid, and girded around their breasts with golden girdles. Then one of the four living creatures gave to *the seven angels seven golden bowls*.   Rev.15:6,7.

3   The fact that 'seven' in the contrary sense means things that are unholy is evident from the following places, also in the Book of Revelation,

Behold, a great fiery-red *dragon* having *seven heads* and ten horns, and on his heads *seven jewels*.   Rev.12:3.
I saw a beast coming up out of the sea, which had *seven heads* and ten horns, and on its horns ten jewels, but on its heads a blasphemous name.   Rev.13:1.
I saw a woman sitting on a scarlet beast, full of blasphemous names; and it had *seven heads* and ten horns. Here is the understanding of this – if anyone has the wisdom: The *seven heads* are *seven mountains* on which the woman is seated; and they are *seven kings*. The beast which was, and is not, he is the eighth king, and is *of the seven*, and is going away into perdition.   Rev.17:3,7,9–11.

5269   'And the seven empty heads of grain, scorched by an east wind' means a state when falsity attacking the exterior natural is multiplied. This is clear from the meaning of 'heads' as facts that are truths known to the exterior natural, dealt with above in 5266, and so in the contrary sense as falsities there, 5202–5204. For the meaning of 'empty' and 'scorched by an east wind' see above.

5270   'Will be seven years of famine' means a consequent absence and seeming deprivation of truth. This is clear from the meaning of 'famine' as an absence of cognitions, dealt with in 1460, 3364, and so a deprivation of truth. For falsities banished truths to such an extent that the latter did not seem to exist any longer, which is the meaning of the descriptions in verses 4,7,20,21,24 – 'the lean and bad cows devoured the seven fat cows; they devoured them completely and no one would have known that they had devoured them', and also 'the thin heads swallowed up the seven good heads', 5206, 5207, 5217. The implication of all this – the idea that at first truth will be multiplied in both parts of the natural, but that subsequently there will be an absence of truth so great that it scarcely seems to exist – is an arcanum which can be known to none except him who is allowed to know the nature of human reformation and regeneration. Such being the subject in the internal sense of what follows after this, a brief statement about it needs to be made in advance here.

When a person is being reformed he begins by learning truths from the Word, or from what he is taught, and then storing those truths away in his memory. The person who is unable to be reformed imagines that once he has learned truths and stored them away in his memory there is nothing more to be done. But he is much mistaken. The truths he has taken in need to be introduced and joined to good; but they cannot be so introduced and joined to good as long as the evils of self-love and love of the world remain in the natural man. These two loves served initially in the introduction of such truths, but the latter cannot possibly become joined to them. Therefore so that a joining to good may be effected the truths that have been introduced and held there by those loves must first be banished, though they are not actually banished but are withdrawn to a more interior position, with the result that they do not seem to exist, which is why the expression 'a seeming deprivation of truth' is used. Once this has happened the natural receives light from within and the evils of self-love and love of the world give way; and to the extent that they do give way the truths are restored and joined to good. In the Word a state when a person is seemingly deprived of truths is called desolation. It is also compared to the evening in which a person dwells before he moves on into morning, which was why in the representative Church the day began in the evening, 883.

5271   Verses 28–32 **This is the word which I have spoken to Pharaoh; what God is doing He has caused Pharaoh to see. Behold, seven years are coming, [in which there will be] a great abundance of corn in all the land of Egypt. And seven years of famine will arise after them, and all the abundance of corn in the land of Egypt will be thrust into oblivion, and the famine will consume the land. And the abundance of corn in the land will not be known because of the famine from then on, for it**

will be extremely severe. And as for the dream being presented[1] to Pharaoh twice, this is because the thing is established by God, and God is hastening to do it.

'This is the word which I have spoken to Pharaoh' means what the natural was led to think by the celestial of the spiritual. 'What God is doing' means regarding what was provided. 'He has caused Pharaoh to see' means discernment by the natural. 'Behold, seven years are coming' means a state of providence. 'A great abundance of corn in all the land of Egypt' means the multiplication of truth in both parts of the natural. 'And seven years of famine will arise after them' means subsequent states when there will be an absence of truth. 'And all the abundance of corn in the land of Egypt will be thrust into oblivion' means the removal of truth and the seeming deprivation of it in both parts of the natural. 'And the famine will consume the land' means even to the point of despair. 'And the abundance of corn in the land will not be known' means that no discernment at all regarding the truth present previously will exist there. 'Because of the famine from then on, for it will be extremely severe' means on account of such an absence [of truth]. 'And as for the dream being presented to Pharaoh twice' means because what was foreseen had regard to both parts of the natural. 'This is because the thing is established by God' means that it is Divine. 'And God is hastening to do it' means a total fulfillment.

5272 'This is the word which I have spoken to Pharaoh' means what the natural was led to think by the celestial of the spiritual. This is clear from the meaning of 'the word' as the real thing, dealt with below; from the meaning of 'speaking' as thinking, dealt with in 2271, 2287, 2619, 5259; from the representation of 'Joseph', who is the speaker here, as the celestial of the spiritual, and from the representation of 'Pharaoh' as the natural, both of whom are dealt with above. From all this it is evident that 'this is the word which I have spoken to Pharaoh' means the real thing, or what the natural was led to think by the celestial of the spiritual; see also 5262. Regarding the term 'the word', this is used in the original language to express the idea of the real thing. This also explains why Divine revelation is called the Word, and why too in the highest sense the Lord Himself is called such. And when 'the Word' is used to refer to the Lord, as also when it is used to refer to revelation received from Him, Divine Truth – the source of every real thing that comes into being – is meant in the proximate sense.

2   This idea that all real things have been brought and are being brought into being by means of Divine Truth going forth from the Lord, thus by means of the Word, is an arcanum which has yet to be disclosed. People's belief and understanding of this is that all things have been created because God has spoken and issued His command, as a king does in his kingdom. But that is not what is meant by saying that all things have been made and created by the Word. Rather, the meaning

[1] *lit.* repeated

is that Divine Truth which goes forth from Divine Good, that is, which goes forth from the Lord, is the originator of all things that have been brought and are being brought into being. Divine Truth going forth from Divine Good is the ultimate reality and the essential being within all creation; and this Divine Truth is what makes and creates all things. But scarcely anyone has any other idea of Divine Truth than this – a word or utterance issuing from a speaker's mouth and transmitted into the air. This idea about Divine Truth leads to the notion that 'the Word' means simply a command, so that all things that have been made exist solely because a command has been delivered, not because of some reality that has come forth from the Lord's Divine. But as has been stated, the Divine Truth going forth from the Lord is the ultimate reality and essential being from which all things derive their existence. Every form of what is good and true owes its existence to this. But in the Lord's Divine mercy more will be said later on regarding this arcanum.

5273   'What God is doing' means regarding what was provided. This is clear from the meaning of 'what God is doing' as what is provided, dealt with above in 5264.

5274   'He has caused Pharaoh to see' means discernment by the natural. This is clear from the meaning of 'seeing' as understanding and discerning, dealt with in 2150, 2325, 2807, 3764, 4567, 4723; and from the representation of 'Pharaoh' as the natural, dealt with previously.

5275   'Behold, seven years are coming' means a state of providence. This is clear from the meaning of 'years' as states, dealt with in 487, 488, 493, 893; and from the meaning of 'coming' as an act of providence. For 'coming' and being done, when used in reference to the Divine, or to that which God does, means what happens providentially and is therefore an act of providence; for providence is meant by that done by God, see above in 5264, 5273. Regarding the seven years of abundance of corn and the seven years of famine that are the subject in what follows, where 'years' means states, 'the years of abundance of corn' are states when truth is multiplied in the natural, and 'the years of famine' are states when there is an absence and deprivation of truth in the natural. In general the seven years of abundance of corn and the seven years of famine in the land of Egypt describe in the internal sense the state when a person is reformed and regenerated, and in the highest sense the state when the Lord's Human was glorified. To represent these things was why such events took place in the land of Egypt. The reason that land was the one where they took place is that in the internal sense 'the land of Egypt' and 'Pharaoh' mean the natural, the glorification of which within the Lord is the subject here.

2   It should be recognized that the events which took place at that time and have been recorded in the Word were representative in the highest sense of the Lord Himself and of the glorification of His Human, and in the representative sense of His kingdom, and consequently of the

Church at a corporate level and also of the Church at an individual level. They were accordingly representative of a person's regeneration, for regeneration is the means by which a person becomes a Church at the individual level. The representation of such things by the events happening at that time was primarily for the sake of the Word – so that this could be written and thus be a Word that would contain the kinds of matters that would represent Divine, celestial, and spiritual realities in a continuous line of thought, and so would be of service not only to the member of the Church but also to the angels in heaven. From those representative descriptions angels perceive Divine realities and are thereby filled with holy feelings which are communicated to the person who reads the Word with affection; for he too receives a feeling of holiness. This is the reason why such events took place in the land of Egypt.

5276 'A great abundance of corn in all the land of Egypt' means the multiplication of truth in both parts of the natural. This is clear from the meaning of 'an abundance of corn' as a multiplication of truth, dealt with below; and from the meaning of 'the land of Egypt' as both parts of the natural. For knowledge is meant by 'Egypt', see 1164, 1165, 1186, 1462, 4749, 4964, 4966; and since knowledge is meant by that land, so also is the natural meant by it, for the reason that as the expression 'factual knowledge' is used to describe what is stored in the natural, 'the land of Egypt' therefore means the natural mind in which factual knowledge is stored. This being so, 'all the land of Egypt' means both parts of the natural – the interior natural and the exterior natural, regarding which, see 5118, 5126. The reason 'an abundance of corn' means a multiplication of truth is that the expression describes the opposite of 'famine', by which an absence of truth is meant. The word used in the original language to express an abundance of corn – an antonym to 'famine' – means in the internal sense a vast wealth and sufficiency of religious knowledge; for 'famine' means an absence of it. Religious knowledge consists in nothing else than the truths present in a person's natural man which have not yet been made his own by him. The multiplication of such truths is what is meant here. Religious knowledge does not come to be truths residing with a person until that knowledge finds acceptance in his understanding, which happens when he firmly embraces it; and what are then truths residing with him are not made his own until he lives in conformity with them. For nothing is made a person's own other than that which is made part of his life; thus because those truths form his life, his true self is invested in them.

5277 'And seven years of famine will arise after them' means subsequent states when there will be an absence of truth. This is clear from the meaning of 'years' as states, dealt with in 482, 487, 488, 493, 893; from the meaning of 'famine' as an absence of religious knowledge or cognitions, dealt with in 1460, 3364; and from the meaning of 'after them' as subsequent ones.

5278   'And all the abundance of corn in the land of Egypt will be thrust into oblivion' means the removal of truth and the seeming deprivation of it in both parts of the natural. This is clear from the meaning of forgetting or 'being thrust into oblivion' as a removal and the seeming deprivation that results from this; from the meaning of 'the abundance of corn' as the multiplication of truth, that is, truth that has been multiplied, dealt with just above in 5276; and from the meaning of 'the land of Egypt' as the natural mind or a person's natural, both parts of it in this case, as just above in 5276.

The reason forgetting or 'being thrust into oblivion' means a removal and seeming deprivation is that something akin to this happens to the memory and to thought that relies on it. The actual matters that a person is thinking about are immediately beneath his attention, while related matters spread out in order around them, extending to unrelated ones furthest away, which at that time are in oblivion. Matters of a contrary nature are separated from these, hanging downwards and revealing themselves underneath, where they serve to counterbalance what is above them. This ordered arrangement is effected by means of good flowing in. Such is the way in which the whole of a person's thought is ordered. The truth of this can be seen from people's thoughts in the next life. There in the light of heaven it is quite normal for people's thoughts to be presented sometimes in a visual manner, at which times the form in which those thoughts are arranged is demonstrated. From this it may be seen that 'forgetting' in the internal sense means nothing else than a removal and seeming deprivation.

5279   'And the famine will consume the land' means even to the point of despair. This is clear from the meaning of 'famine' as an absence of religious knowledge or cognitions and a consequent deprivation of truth, dealt with above in 5277, 5278; and from the meaning of 'the land', in this case the land of Egypt, as the natural mind, also dealt with above, in 5276, 5278. The reason even to the point of despair is meant is that the words 'the famine will consume the land' are used. Since 'the land' means the natural mind, and 'famine' the deprivation of truth, nothing else than despair is meant, for at that time, in a spiritual manner, a consuming takes place. The description here is of a state of desolation owing to a deprivation of truth, the final stage of that state being despair. The reason despair is the final stage of that state is that despair is the means by which the delight that belongs to self-love and love of the world is removed, and the delight connected with the love of what is good and true is instilled in place of it. The despair experienced by those who are to be regenerated has to do with the attainment of spiritual life and with being deprived of truth and good. For when such people are deprived of truth and good they are in despair about the attainment of spiritual life; consequently they have feelings of delight and bliss when they come out of their despair.

5280 'And the abundance of corn in the land will not be known' means that no discernment at all regarding the truth present previously will exist there. This is clear from the meaning of 'being known' as being discerned; from the meaning of 'the abundance of corn' as truth that has been multiplied, dealt with above in 5276, 5278; and from the meaning of 'the land', in this case the land of Egypt, as the natural mind, also dealt with above, in 5276, 5278, 5279. From these meanings it is evident that 'the abundance of corn in the land will not be known' means that no discernment at all regarding the truth present previously will exist in the natural.

2 This verse deals with the final state of desolation, when despair, which comes immediately before regeneration, is experienced; and this being the matter dealt with in this verse, something must be said about the nature of it. Everyone has to be reformed, and to be born anew or regenerated, so that he may enter heaven,

No one, unless he is born again, can see the kingdom of God. John 3:3,5,6.

The human being is born into sin which has increased as it has come down in a long line of descent from ancestors, grandparents, and parents; it has become hereditary and so has been handed down to offspring. At birth a person is born into so many inherited evils which have gradually increased, as described, that he is nothing but sin; therefore unless he undergoes regeneration he remains wholly immersed in sin. But to be regenerated, he must first undergo reformation, which is effected by means of the truths of faith; for he must learn from the Word, and from teaching drawn from it, what good is. Items of knowledge regarding what is good that have been acquired from the Word – that is, from teaching drawn from there – are called the truths of faith; for all truths of faith well up out of good and flow in the direction of good, good being the end they have in view.

3 This state comes first and is called the state of reformation. Most people within the Church are introduced into it during the period from young childhood through to adolescence, though few are regenerated because most people within the Church learn the truths of faith – or religious knowledge about what is good – for the sake of reputation and position and for the sake of material gain. Since therefore the truths of faith have been introduced through his love of these things, a person cannot be born anew or be regenerated until that love has been removed. To enable such love to be removed that person is launched into a state of temptation, which takes place in the following way: His love of reputation, position, and material gain is activated by the hellish crew, for that crew's desire is to live immersed in the love of those things. But at the same time angels activate affections for what is true and good which were implanted in the state of innocence during early childhood

and then stored away interiorly and preserved there for this particular purpose. As a result conflict between evil spirits and angels takes place, and this conflict taking place within a person is experienced by him as temptation. And because the action at this time involves truths and forms of good, the actual truths which were instilled initially are so to speak banished by the falsities infused by the evil spirits – so banished that they are not seen – dealt with above in 5268–5270. And as the person allows himself at this time to be regenerated, the Lord introduces through an internal route the light of truth radiated from good in the natural, in which light the truths are restored there in their proper order.

This is what happens to a person who is being regenerated, but few at the present day are permitted to enter that regenerative state. So far as they allow it to happen, all people, it is true, start to be reformed through the instruction they receive in the truths and forms of good that belong to spiritual life; but as soon as they reach adolescent years they allow the world to distract them. So they turn away into those parts where hellish spirits are, who gradually alienate these people from heaven; the spirits alienate them so completely that they scarcely believe any longer in the existence of heaven. Consequently those people cannot be launched into any spiritual temptation; for if they were they would go under instantly, in which case their latter state would be worse than their former one, Matt.12:45. From all this one may see the nature of what the internal sense contains here, namely the state of reformation and the state of regeneration. This particular verse however describes the final state in temptation, which is a state of despair – this state being dealt with immediately above in 5279.

5281   'Because of the famine from then on, for it will be extremely severe' means on account of such absence [of truth]. This is clear from the meaning of 'the famine' as an absence of religious knowledge or cognitions regarding what is good, and therefore an absence of truth, dealt with above in 5277, 5278, and despair finally on account of that absence [of truth], 5279; and from the meaning of 'extremely severe' as that which is vast. The final state of desolation, which is one of despair, and the increasing severity of it, dealt with above in 5279, is continued here.

5282   'And as for the dream being presented to Pharaoh twice' means because what was foreseen had regard to both parts of the natural. This is clear from the meaning of 'the dream' as foresight, dealt with in 3698, 5091, 5092, 5104; from the representation of 'Pharaoh' as the natural, dealt with in 5079, 5080, 5095, 5160; and from the meaning of 'presented twice' as that which has regard to both parts of the natural, that is to say, the interior part and the exterior part – for the natural has two parts, the interior and the exterior, see 5118, 5126. That which had regard to the interior natural was foreseen in the first dream, the one about the cows, 5198, 5202; that which had regard to the exterior natural was foreseen in the second dream, the one about the heads of grain, 5212. Therefore 'presented twice' has regard to both parts.

5283 'This is because the thing is established by God' means that it is Divine. This becomes clear without explanation, for when the expression 'the thing [or the word]' is used in connection with God, Divine Truth is meant. When this is said 'to be established by God' the meaning is a total fulfillment.

5284 'And God is hastening to do it' means a total fulfillment. This is clear from the meaning of 'doing', when used in reference to God, as providence, dealt with in 5264, and therefore also the fulfillment, for what is of Divine Providence is certainly fulfilled; and from the meaning of 'hastening to do' as a total fulfillment. 'Hastening' or hastiness does not in the internal sense describe swiftness but certainty, also completeness, and so it means a total fulfillment. For hastiness has a temporal connotation, but in the spiritual world there is no time. Instead of time there is state, so that hastiness, which has temporal associations, is connected in that world with the kind of state that corresponds to hastiness. The nature of that corresponding state is one in which many forces are at work simultaneously, and these are such as accomplish certain and complete fulfillment.

5285 Verses 33–36 **And now let Pharaoh see[1] a man with intelligence and wisdom, and set him over the land of Egypt. Let Pharaoh do this, and let him place governors in charge over the land, and let him take up the fifth part of the land of Egypt in the seven years of abundance of corn. And let them gather all the food of these good years that are coming, and let them store up grain under the hand of Pharaoh – food in the cities; and let them guard it. And let the food be for a reserve for the land, for the seven years of famine which there will be in the land of Egypt, and the land will not be cut off in the famine.**

'And now let Pharaoh see' means provision to be made by the natural. 'A man with intelligence and wisdom' means with regard to inflowing truth and good. 'And set him over the land of Egypt' means which will set in order all that is in the natural mind. 'Let Pharaoh do this' means a further provision. 'And let him place governors in charge over the land' means the ordering of general wholes within the natural. 'And let him take up the fifth part of the land of Egypt' means which are to be preserved and then stored away. 'In the seven years of abundance of corn' means which are instilled during the times when truths along with forms of good have been multiplied. 'And let them gather all the food' means all things that have a useful purpose. 'Of these good years that are coming' means which are to be taken in during those times. 'And let them store up grain' means at the same time every good of truth. 'Under the hand of Pharaoh' means for when there is need and the consequent power of disposal in the natural. 'Food in the cities'

---

[1] *i.e.* select *or* look out

means such things present in the interior parts of the natural mind. 'And let them guard it' means to be stored away there. 'And let the food be for a reserve for the land' means that it should be kept there for every useful purpose served by the natural. 'For the seven years of famine' means as need arises when there is an absence [of truth]. 'Which there will be in the land of Egypt' means which will exist in the natural. 'And the land will not be cut off in the famine' means lest the person perishes.

5286 'And now let Pharaoh see' means provision to be made by the natural. This is clear from the meaning of 'seeing' as making provision; for 'seeing' here implies an action, one that Pharaoh is to take. But when 'seeing' does not imply the taking of an action, it means understanding and discerning, as shown in 2150, 2325, 2807, 3764, 3863, 4403–4421, 4567, 4723, 5114. The situation so far as provision made by the natural is concerned is this: A person's natural – that is, his natural mind which is beneath his rational mind – cannot by itself see to any provision whatever that has to be made. It seems to do so by itself, but any provision it does make is seen to by what is interior. This sees within the exterior what provision needs to be made, almost as a person sees himself in a mirror in which his image seems to exist. This particular matter is presented in the internal sense by Joseph speaking in the way he does to Pharaoh – 'Joseph' representing the celestial of the spiritual, which is what is interior, and 'Pharaoh' the natural, which is what is exterior – and by its seeming to Pharaoh that Joseph was the very man with intelligence and wisdom, about whom Joseph was speaking.

5287 'A man with intelligence and wisdom' means with regard to inflowing truth and good. This is clear from the meaning of 'a man with intelligence' as truth, and of 'a man with wisdom' as accompanying good. It should be recognized that 'a man with intelligence and wisdom' is not used in the internal sense to mean any actual man such as this but to mean, without reference to any actual person, that which makes someone intelligent and wise – to mean truth and good therefore. In the next life, especially in the heavens, all thought and consequently all language consists of images that do not involve any actual persons, so that thought and language there are universal and, compared with other forms of them, are free of limitations. For insofar as thought and language limit themselves to specific persons, especially to their personal characteristics, and insofar as they limit themselves to names and also to words, that thought and language become less universal; for these then limit themselves to something specific and do not stray from it. Insofar however as they do not focus on such things but on realities quite apart from them, they no longer limit themselves to something specific but spread out beyond themselves, with the result that a superior and therefore more universal picture is obtained.

2   One may see the truth of this quite clearly in the way a person thinks. Insofar as his thought fixes its attention on the actual words a speaker uses, its attention is not fixed on their meaning. Also, insofar as his attention is fixed on particular ideas imprinted in his memory and remains concentrated on these, he has no perception of the essential nature of things. More than this, insofar as self-regard is present in everything he thinks he cramps his thought and denies himself an overall picture of anything. This explains why, insofar as anyone loves himself more than others, he is lacking in wisdom. From all this one may now see why in the internal sense matters which have no reference to actual persons are meant by those descriptions which in the sense of the letter do limit themselves to such persons. See also 5225.

Various places in the Word draw a distinction between wisdom, intelligence, and knowledge. Wisdom is used to mean that which springs from good, intelligence to mean that which springs from truth, and knowledge to mean both of these as they exist in a person's natural, as in Moses,

> I have filled Bezalel with the spirit of God, so far as *wisdom*, and *intelligence*, and *knowledge*, and all workmanship are concerned.   Exod.31:2,3; 35:30,31.

And in the same author,

> Choose[1] *wise*, and *intelligent*, and *knowledgeable men*, according to your tribes, and I will make them your heads.   Deut.1:13.

5288   'And set him over the land of Egypt' means which will set in order all that is in the natural mind. This is clear from the meaning of 'setting over something' as appointing one who will set in order, thus as setting in order; and from the meaning of 'the land of Egypt' as the natural mind, as above in 5276, 5278, 5279. The pronoun 'him' used here refers to a man with intelligence and wisdom, by whom truth and good are meant. From this it is evident that the words used here mean that truth and good will set in order all that exists in the natural. It is indeed good and truth which set every single thing in order in the natural mind, for when good and truth flow in, they do so from within and in that way place every single thing in its proper position.

2   The person who does not know about the nature of the human power of thought, or who does not know about the human ability to look at things, see what they are, analyse them, form conclusions regarding them, and finally transmit them to the will and through the will into action, will see nothing wondrous in any of this. Such a person imagines that all this happens naturally; he is totally unaware of the fact that every single thought flows in from the Lord by way of heaven, and that but for that inflow from the Lord a person cannot have any thought at all, and also that as that inflow is diminished, so is his thought. Nor therefore does that person know that good flowing in from the Lord by

---

[1] *lit.* Give yourselves

way of heaven sets all things in order, shaping them into an image of heaven, so far as the person allows this to happen. Nor consequently does he know that such inflowing thought possesses the heavenly form. The heavenly form is the form in which the communities of heaven exist set in their proper order, a form that accords with the one which good and truth going forth from the Lord produce.

5289 'Let Pharaoh do this' means a further provision. This is clear from the explanation given above in 5286.

5290 'And let him place governors in charge over the land' means the ordering of general wholes within the natural. This is clear from the meaning of 'placing in charge' as setting in order; from the meaning of 'governors' as general wholes, dealt with below; and from the meaning of 'the land' – in this case the land of Egypt – as the natural mind, as just above in 5288. The reason 'governors' means general wholes is that particular aspects are contained within and subordinated to those wholes, see 917, 4269, 4325(end), 4329, 4345, 4383, 5208, whereas 'princes' means things that come first and foremost, 1482, 2089, 5044.

5291 'And let him take up a fifth part of the land [of Egypt]' means which are to be preserved and then stored away. This is clear from the meaning of 'taking up a fifth part' as that which implies something similar to taking tenths. In the Word 'taking tenths' means preserving remnants, and preserving remnants is a gathering together and then storing away of forms of truth and good. For remnants are the forms of good and truth that the Lord has stored away in the interior man, see 468, 530, 560, 561, 661, 1050, 1906, 2284, 5135, and 'tenths' is used in the Word to mean remnants, 576, 1738, 2280, and so also is 'ten', 1906, 2284. And the number five, which is half of ten, is likewise used to mean the same. Half or twice any number when used in the Word holds the same meaning as the number itself. Twenty for example holds the same meaning as ten, four the same as two, six the same as three, twenty-four the same as twelve, and so on. A multiplication of a number also holds the same meaning. A hundred or a thousand for example holds the same as ten; seventy-two and also a hundred and forty-four hold the same as twelve. Therefore what it is that composite numbers hold within them may be seen from the simple numbers of which they are the products. What the more simple numbers hold within them may be seen in a similar way from their integers. Five for example may be seen from ten, two and a half from five, and so on. In general it should be recognized that multiples hold the same meaning as their factors, yet more completely, while quotients hold the same meaning as their dividends, yet less completely.

As regards the number five specifically, this has a dual meaning. First, it means that which is little and consequently something; second, it means remnants. It receives its meaning of that which is little from its relationship with other numbers meaning that which is much, namely a thousand and a hundred, and therefore ten also. For 'a thousand' and 'a hundred' mean that which is much, see 2575, 2636, and so therefore does 'ten', 3107, 4638, as a consequence of which 'five' means that which is little, and also something, 649, 4638. But 'five' means remnants when it has a connection with ten, 'ten' in this case meaning remnants, as stated above. For all numbers used in the Word have spiritual realities as their meaning, see 575, 647, 648, 755, 813, 1963, 1988, 2075, 2252, 3252, 4264, 4495, 4670, 5265.

3 Anyone who does not know that the Word has an internal sense which is not visible in the letter will be utterly astonished by the idea that spiritual realities too are meant by the numbers used in the Word. The specific reason for his astonishment is his inability to use numbers to give shape to any spiritual idea, when yet the spiritual ideas known to angels present themselves as numbers, see 5265. The identity of those ideas or spiritual realities to which numbers correspond can, it is true, be known; but the origin of such correspondence remains hidden, such as the origin of the correspondence of 'twelve' to all aspects of faith, the correspondence of 'seven' to things that are holy, as well as that of 'ten' and also 'five' to forms of good and truth stored up by the Lord within the interior man, and so on. Even so, it is enough if people know simply that such a correspondence does exist and that by virtue of that correspondence each number used in the Word denotes something present in the spiritual world, consequently that what is Divine has been inspired into them and so lies concealed within them.

4 Examples of this are seen in the following places where 'five' is mentioned, such as the Lord's parable in Matt.25:14 and following verses about the man who, before going away to a foreign country, placed his resources in the hands of his servants. To the first he gave *five talents*, to the second *two*, and to the third *one*. The servant who received *five talents* traded with them and earned *five talents* more. In a similar way the one who received *two* earned *two more*; but the servant who received *one* hid his master's money[1] in the earth. The person whose thought does not extend beyond the literal sense knows no other than this, that the numbers five, two, and one have been adopted merely to make up the story told in the parable and that they entail nothing more, when in fact those actual numbers hold some arcanum within them. The servant who received the five talents means those people who have accepted forms of good and truth from the Lord and so have received remnants. The one who received the two talents means those who at a more advanced stage in life have linked charity to faith, while the servant who received the one means someone who receives faith alone devoid of charity. Regarding this servant it is said that he hid his master's money[1] in the earth – the reason for this description being that the money[1] he is said to have received means in the internal sense truth which is the truth of faith, 1551, 2954; but faith that is

---

[1] or silver

devoid of charity cannot earn any interest, that is, it cannot be fruitful. These are the kinds of matters that numbers hold within them.

Much the same is contained in other parables, such as the parable in Luke 19:12 and following verses regarding someone who journeyed to a far country to receive a kingdom. He gave his servants *ten minas* and told them to trade with these until he came back. When he returned the first said, 'Sir, your mina has earned *ten minas*'. He said to him, 'Well done, good servant; because you have been faithful over a very little, be over *ten cities*'. The second said, 'Sir, your mina has made *five minas*', and to him too he said, 'You also, be over *five cities*'. The third had kept his mina stored away in a handkerchief. But the master said, 'Take the mina from him and give it to him who has *ten minas*'. Here in a similar way 'ten' and 'five' mean remnants, 'ten' rather more, 'five' somewhat less. The one who kept his mina stored away in a handkerchief describes those who acquire the truths of faith but do not join them to the good deeds of charity, so that these truths do not gain interest or become fruitful at all.

The same meaning exists in other places where the Lord uses these numbers, such as the place where He refers to what one of those invited to a supper said,

I have bought five yoke of oxen, and I am going away to test them.   Luke 14:19.

Also in the place where He refers to what the rich man said to Abraham,

I have *five brothers*; send [Lazarus] to speak to them, lest they come into this place of torment.   Luke 16:28.

And in the place where He talks about *ten* virgins, *five* of whom were wise and *five* were foolish, Matt.25:1–13. The following words spoken by the Lord in a similar way contain such numbers,

Do you think that I have come to give peace on earth? No, I tell you, but division; for from now on there will be in one house *five* divided; *three* against *two*, and *two* against *three*.   Luke 12:51,52.

And the following details given in the historical narrative also contain such numbers – the Lord fed *five thousand* people with *five* loaves and *two* fishes; He commanded them to sit down in groups of *a hundred* and groups of *fifty*; and after they had eaten they collected *twelve* baskets of broken pieces, Matt.14:15–21; Mark 6:38 and following verses; Luke 9:12–17; John 6:5–13.

It is hardly credible that the numbers included in such details, since these belong to a historical narrative, have a spiritual meaning. That is, five thousand, the number of people, has a spiritual meaning; so does five, the number of loaves, as well as two, the number of fishes. A hundred, and likewise fifty, the numbers of people sitting down together, each have a spiritual meaning; and so lastly does twelve, the number of baskets containing broken pieces. Though it may seem incredible, every detail holds some arcanum. Every single thing occurred providentially, to the end that Divine realities might be represented by them.

8 In the following places too 'five' means things of a similar nature in the spiritual world, and it corresponds to such in both senses, the genuine sense and the contrary one: In Isaiah,

Gleanings will be left in it, as in the shaking of an olive tree[1], *two or three* berries on the top of the [highest] branch, *four or five* on the branches of a fruitful tree. Isa.17:6,7.

In the same prophet,

On that day there will be *five* cities in the land of Egypt which speak in the lips of Canaan and swear to Jehovah Zebaoth. Isa.19:18.

In the same prophet,

One thousand at the rebuke of *one*, at the rebuke of *five* you are fleeing, until you remain like a flagstaff on top of a mountain, like a signal upon a hill. Isa.30:17.

In John,

The *fifth* angel sounded, at which point I saw a star that had fallen from heaven to the earth. To him was given the key of the pit of the abyss. It was given the locusts which were coming out from there, that they should not kill the people who did not have the seal of God on their foreheads, but that they should torment them *five months*. Rev.9:1,3,5,10.

In the same book,

Here is intelligence, if anyone has wisdom: The *seven* heads are *seven* mountains, on which the woman sits; and there are *seven* kings. *Five* have fallen; and *one* is, the other has not yet come. And when he comes he must remain a short time. Rev.17:9,10.

9 The number five holds a similar representative meaning in the following places,

The valuation for a man or for a woman was determined by their ages – between one month and *five years*, and *between five years and twenty years.* Lev.27:1–9.
If a field was redeemed, *one-fifth* was to be added. Lev.27:19.
If tithes were redeemed, again *one-fifth* was to be added. Lev.27:31.
The firstborn who were in excess [of the Levites] were to be redeemed for *five shekels* [each]. Num.3:46–end.
The firstborn of an unclean beast was to be redeemed with *the addition of one-fifth.* Lev.27:27.
In the case of any wrongs that were done *one-fifth* was to be added as a penalty. Lev.22:14; 27:13,15; Num.5:6–8.
Anyone who stole an ox or one of the flock, and who slaughtered it or sold it, had to restore *five oxen* for an ox, and *four of the flock* for one of the flock. Exod.22:1.

10 The fact that the number five contains some heavenly arcanum, as does ten also, is evident from the cherubs referred to in the first Book of Kings,

In the sanctuary Solomon made two cherubs of olive wood, each *ten cubits* high. The wing of one cherub was *five cubits*, and the wing of the other cherub *five*

---

[1] *The Latin means* fig tree, *but the Hebrew means* olive tree, *which Sw. has in other places where he quotes this verse.*

cubits; ten cubits from the tips of the wings of one to the tips of the wings of the other. Thus a cherub was *ten cubits*; both cherubs were the same size and same shape.   1 Kings 6:23-25.

The same fact is evident from the lavers around the temple, and also from the lampstands, described in the same book,

Five bases for the lavers were placed on the right side of the house[1], and *five* on the left side of the house[1]. Also, *five* lampstands were placed on the right, and *five* on the left in front of the sanctuary.   1 Kings 7:39,49.
The bronze sea was *ten cubits* from one brim to the other, and *five cubits* high, and *thirty cubits* in circumference.   1 Kings 7:23.

All this was prescribed so that holy things might be meant spiritually not only by the numbers ten and five but also by thirty, for although geometrically this number giving the circumference is not right for the stated diameter, it nevertheless implies spiritually what is meant by the rim of a vessel.

All numbers mentioned in the Word mean things existing in the spiritual world, as is clearly evident from the numbers used in Ezekiel, where a new land, a new city, a new temple, and a detailed measuring of these by the angel are described; see Chapters 40-43,45-49. Numbers are used in these chapters to describe practically every sacred object, and therefore anyone unacquainted with what those numbers hold within them can know scarcely anything about the arcana present there. The number ten and the number five occur there in Ezek.40:7,11,48; 41:2,9,11,12; 42:4; 45:11,14, in addition to the multiplications of such numbers, namely twenty-five, fifty, five hundred, and five thousand. As regards the new land, the new city, and the new temple mentioned in those chapters, these mean the Lord's kingdom in heaven, and therefore His Church on earth, as is clear from every detail mentioned there.

All the references above to 'five' have been gathered together for the reason that here and in what follows the subject is the land of Egypt, where, in the seven years of abundance, a fifth part of the corn was to be gathered and preserved for use in the succeeding years of famine. This demonstrates that 'the fifth part' means the forms of good and truth which a person has received from the Lord, who has stored them away and preserved them in that person for future use when there is a famine, that is, when there is an absence and deprivation of goodness and truth. For unless the Lord stored away in a person such forms of good and truth, there would be nothing to raise him up in a state of temptation and vastation and consequently to make it possible for him to be regenerated, so that he would be left without any means of salvation in the next life.

5292   'In the seven years of abundance of corn' means which are instilled during the times when truths along with forms of good have

---

[1] *lit.* beside the shoulder of the house towards the right/left

been multiplied. This is clear from the meaning of 'years' as states, and from these as periods of time, dealt with below; and from the meaning of 'abundance of corn' as the multiplication of truth, or truth that has been multiplied, dealt with above in 5276, 5278, 5280. Here therefore truths which, along with forms of good, have been multiplied are meant because truths are nothing unless they are accompanied by forms of good; nor are any truths stored away within the interior man – dealt with immediately above in 5291 – other than those which have been joined to forms of good. The reason 'years' means not only states but also periods of time is that in the internal sense 'years' means entire states, that is, periods in their entirety from the start to the finish of a state. No expression other than periods of time exists to describe such states; nor have the inhabitants of [space and] time any other way of understanding them than as periods of time. For 'days' and 'years' mean both states and periods of time, see 23, 487, 488, 493, 893, 2906.

5293   'And let them gather all the food' means all things that have a useful purpose. This is clear from the meaning of 'gathering' as drawing together and preserving; and from the meaning of 'food' as things which have a useful purpose. In the internal sense 'food' means, strictly speaking, those things which nourish a person's soul, that is, which nourish him when his bodily life is ended. For when this is ended his soul or spirit is living, and he no longer needs material food as he did in the world; but he does need spiritual food, which consists in everything that has a useful purpose and everything leading to this. That which leads to what has a useful purpose is knowing what goodness and truth are; and that which has such a purpose is the desire to realize these in actions. These are the things with which angels are nourished and which are therefore called spiritual and celestial foods. A person's mind – the place within him where his will and understanding, that is, his intentions or ends in view, reside – is nourished by no other kind of food, even while he lives in the body. Material food does not extend as far as that; it extends only to his bodily parts, which are sustained by that material food to the end that the mind may be sustained by food for the mind while the body is sustained by food for the body, that is, to the end that there may be a healthy mind in a healthy body.

2   The reason 'food' in the spiritual sense means everything that has a useful purpose is that a person's entire knowledge, his entire understanding and wisdom, and so his entire will must have a useful purpose as its end in view. Consequently as is the nature of the purpose he has in view, so is the nature of his life. The truth that 'food' in the spiritual sense means everything with a useful purpose is evident from the following words spoken by the Lord,

Jesus said to the disciples, I have *food to eat* of which you do not know. The disciples said to one another, Has anyone brought Him anything to eat? Jesus said to them, *My food is to do the will of Him who sent Me, and to accomplish His work.* John 4:32–34.

And elsewhere,

Do not labour for *the food which perishes,* but for *the food* which endures to eternal life, which the Son of Man will give you. On Him the Father – God – has set His seal.   John 6:27.

5294   'Of these good years that are coming' means which are to be taken in during those times. This is clear from the meaning of 'years' as states and also periods of time, dealt with just above in 5292. 'The good years that are coming' therefore means the times when truths along with forms of good are multiplied, meant by 'the seven years of abundance of corn'.

5295   'And let them store up grain' means at the same time every good of truth. This is clear from the meaning of 'storing up' as collecting at the same time and preserving; and from the meaning of 'grain' as natural good, dealt with in 3580, in this case the good of truth present in the natural. For the good of truth is truth present in will and action. The reason 'grain' means good is that in the spiritual sense 'the field' is the Church, and therefore everything connected with the field – such as seed, sower, harvest, standing crop, grain, and also the head or tip of the grain, besides specifically wheat, barley, and much else – describes something to do with the Church. And everything to do with the Church has a connection with goodness and truth.

5296   'Under the hand of Pharaoh' means for when there is need and the consequent power of disposal in the natural. This is clear from the meaning of 'the hand' as power, dealt with in 878, 3387, 4931–4937, and therefore 'under the hand of' means at the disposal of when any need arises, since that which is within anyone's power is at his disposal; and from the representation of 'Pharaoh' as the natural, dealt with already.

5297   'Food in the cities' means such things present in the interior parts of the natural mind. This is clear from the meaning of 'food' as all things that have a useful purpose, dealt with just above in 5293; and from the meaning of 'cities' as the interior parts of the natural mind. In the universal sense 'cities' means matters of doctrine known to the Church, see 402, 2268, 2449, 2451, 2712, 2943, 3216, 4492, 4493, but in a particular sense it means the interior parts of a person where matters of doctrine exist, or rather where truths joined to good exist. For the forms of truth and good existing with a person form a city so to speak, see 3584, which is why a person who has the Church within him is called 'the city of God'. The meaning that 'a city' has is similar to the meaning that 'a house' has. In a universal sense 'a house' means good; in a particular sense however it means a person, 3128, and in a specific sense it means his mind so far as goodness and truth are joined together there, 3538, 4973, 5023. Also a house with its rooms, surrounding buildings, and courtyards is a city in miniature.

The interior parts of the natural mind are meant by 'cities' in Isaiah,

On that day there will be *five cities in the land of Egypt* which speak in the lips of Canaan and swear to Jehovah Zebaoth.   Isa.19:18.

Both forms of good and of truth present in the interior parts are meant by 'cities' in the Lord's parable in Luke,

He said to the one who used his mina to earn ten minas, Well done, good servant; because you have been faithful over a little, *be over ten cities.* And he said to the second who earned five minas, You also, *be over five cities.*
Luke 19:12 and following verses.

The recommendation here therefore that they should store up food in cities and should guard it means that truths joined to good were to be stored away in the interior parts of the natural mind. When these truths and forms of good have been stored away there they are called remnants. These remnants are where a person's actual spiritual life resides, and they are what a person is nourished by spiritually whenever need and desire, that is, whenever spiritual famine, arises.

5298   'And let them guard it' means to be stored away there. This is clear from the meaning of 'guarding' as storing away, that is to say, storing away in the interior parts of the natural mind, which are meant by 'cities', dealt with immediately above in 5297.

5299   'Let the food be for a reserve for the land' means that it should be kept there for every useful purpose served in the natural. This is clear from the meaning of 'food' as forms of good and truth, dealt with above in 5293; from the meaning of 'for a reserve' as what is stored away for every useful purpose, because it is so stored for use in the years of famine that follow; and from the meaning of 'the land', in this case the land of Egypt, as the natural mind, also dealt with above in 5276, 5278, 5279, 5288.

5300   'For the seven years of famine' means as need arises when there is an absence [of truth]. This is clear from the meaning of 'famine' as an absence of truth, dealt with above in 5277, 5278. The fact that the time when truth is absent is a time of need is self-evident; for in the internal sense 'years' are states, as has frequently been shown above, and therefore 'for those [seven] years' means for those states when need arises.

5301   'Which there will be in the land of Egypt' means which will exist in the natural. This is clear from the meaning of 'the land of Egypt' as the natural mind, dealt with in 5276, 5278, 5279, 5288. The expression 'the natural' is used here and in other places, and by it the natural mind is meant. For the human being has two minds, the rational mind and the natural mind. The rational mind belongs to the internal man, whereas the natural mind belongs to the external man; and it is the natural mind or external man that is meant when simply 'the natural' is used. The mind is a person's true self, as will be seen in what is spoken about next.

5302   'And the land will not be cut off in the famine' means lest the person perishes – through an absence of truth. This is clear from the meaning of 'being cut off' as perishing, and from the meaning of 'the land', in this case the land of Egypt, as the natural mind, dealt with immediately above in 5301; and because it is the natural mind, it is the person's true self, since a human being is a human being by virtue of his mind, it being the actual mind itself that constitutes a person, and the kind of mind he has that determines what kind of a person he is. By the mind is meant a person's understanding and will, consequently his essential life. People who are stupid imagine that a human being is a human being by virtue of his outward appearance, that is to say, because he possesses a human face. Others who are a little less stupid say that the human being is a human being because he has the ability to speak, while others again who are less stupid still say that the human being is a human being because he has the ability to think. But a human being is not a human being for any of these reasons but because he has the capacity to think what is true and to will what is good; and when he thinks what is true and wills what is good he has the capacity to behold what is Divine and, perceiving what it is, to accept it.

This is what distinguishes a human being from animals. Not merely his human appearance, or his ability to speak, or his ability to think make him a human being; for if he thinks what is false and wills what is evil, that makes him not only like but worse than an animal. For he then uses those abilities to destroy what is human within himself and to make a wild animal of himself. This is particularly evident from people of this kind in the next life, for when they are seen in the light of heaven, and also when angels see them, they look at that moment like monsters, and some of them like wild animals. The deceitful look like snakes, and others like something different again. But when they are taken away from the light of heaven and are returned to their own inferior light which they have in hell, they look to one another like human beings. But the implications of all this – of the fact that a person will perish in times when truth is absent if he has no forms of good and truth stored away by the Lord in the interior parts of his mind, meant by 'food kept as a reserve for the land, for the seven years of famine, so that the land is not cut off in the famine' – will be stated in the sections that follow next in the present chapter.

5303   Verses 37-40 **And the thing was good in Pharaoh's eyes and in the eyes of all his servants. And Pharaoh said to his servants, Shall we find a man like this, in whom is the spirit of God? And Pharaoh said to Joseph, After God has caused you to know all this, no one has intelligence and wisdom like you. You shall be over my house, and all my people shall kiss you on the mouth; only in the throne will I be great, more than you.**

'And the thing was good in Pharaoh's eyes' means that the natural was well-pleased. 'And in the eyes of all his servants' means that everything in the natural was well-pleased. 'And Pharaoh said to his servants' means the perception of the natural and of everything in it. 'Shall we find a man like this, in whom is the spirit of God?' means regarding an influx of truth containing good received from within, and so containing the celestial of the spiritual. 'And Pharaoh said to Joseph' means a perception present in the natural but received from the celestial of the spiritual. 'After God has caused you to know all this' means for the reason that Foresight and Providence belong to that celestial of the spiritual. 'No one has intelligence and wisdom like you' means that this alone is the source of truth and good. 'You shall be over my house' means that the natural mind shall be made subordinate and submissive to it. 'And all my people shall kiss you on the mouth' means that everything there shall obey it. 'Only in the throne will I be great, more than you' means that the natural will be seen as sovereign, because the celestial of the spiritual acts through the natural.

5304 'And the thing was good in Pharaoh's eyes' means that the natural was well-pleased. This is clear from the meaning of 'the thing being good' as to be pleasing (the expression 'in the eyes of' being part of everyday language; for 'the eye' means interior sight, and so means understanding, perception, observation, and many other powers which that sight possesses, 2701, 2789, 2829, 3198, 3202, 3820, 4083, 4086, 4339, 4403–4421, 4523–4534, which explains why 'the thing was good in Pharaoh's eyes' means a well-pleased feeling); and from the representation of 'Pharaoh' as the natural, often dealt with already.

5305 'And in the eyes of all his servants' means that everything in the natural was well-pleased. This is clear from the meaning of 'the thing being good in the eyes of' as a well-pleased feeling, dealt with immediately above in 5304; and from the meaning of 'servants' as what was in the natural, especially in the exterior natural. The word 'servant' occurs in places throughout the Word. In the internal sense it means that which is of service to another; and in general it means everything that is lower when considered in relation to what is above it. For order requires what is lower to serve what is higher; and insofar as it actually does so it is called 'a servant'. In the present context however things within the natural are being called 'servants', the natural in general being represented by 'Pharaoh'. The general or common whole has to be served by its individual parts, in the same way as the common good is served in any kingdom by its individual subjects. As regards 'Pharaoh' representing the natural in general, see 5160.

5306 'And Pharaoh said to his servants' means the perception by the natural and of everything in it. This is clear from the meaning of 'saying' in the historical narratives of the Word as perceiving, dealt with in 1791, 1815, 1819, 1822, 1898, 1919, 2080, 2061, 2238, 2619, 2862, 3395, 3509; from the representation of 'Pharaoh' as the natural, dealt with in 5079, 5080, 5095, 5160; and from the meaning of 'his servants' as everything in the natural, dealt with immediately above in 5305.

5307   'Shall we find a man like this, in whom is the spirit of God?' means regarding an influx of truth containing good received from within, and so containing the celestial of the spiritual. This is clear from the meaning of 'a man' as truth, dealt with in 3134, 3309, 3459, and from the meaning of 'the spirit of God' as good received from within, thus from the Divine. The spirit of God is that which goes forth from the Divine, and so from absolute good; for the Divine is absolute Good. That which goes forth from this is truth containing good, and it is this truth that is meant in the Word by 'the spirit of God'. Actually the spirit does not go forth, only truth containing good, which is holy truth. The spirit is the instrument by means of which it is brought forth. This truth containing good is the celestial of the spiritual, represented by 'Joseph'. Within the Church it is well known that in a spiritual sense 'Joseph' is the Lord, which also explains why the Lord is called the heavenly Joseph. But no one knows which aspect of the Lord is represented by 'Joseph'. For the Lord is represented by Abraham, also by Isaac, and by Jacob too. He is represented as well by Moses and Elijah, by Aaron, and also by David, in addition to many others in the Word. But each one nevertheless represents Him in a different way from any other. The aspect that Abraham represents is the Divine itself, 'Isaac' the Divine Rational, 'Jacob' the Divine Natural, 'Moses' the Law or historical part of the Word, 'Elijah' the prophetical part, 'Aaron' His priesthood, and 'David' His kingship. But what aspect is represented by 'Joseph' may be seen in 3969, 4286, 4585, 4592, 4594, 4669, 4723, 4727, 4963, 5249 – that aspect which 'Joseph' represents being the celestial of the spiritual deriving from the rational. No other description than this can be used, for the celestial is good received from the Divine, the spiritual is truth received from that good, making it the truth of good received from His Divine Human. This was what the Lord was when He lived in the world. But once He had glorified Himself, He rose up above it; even His Human was made absolute Divine Good, or Jehovah.

Nothing more specific can be stated regarding this arcanum than the following: Joseph came to Egypt, where first of all he served in the house of Potiphar, the chief of the attendants, then was held in custody, and after that was made the governor over Egypt, so that the way might be represented in which the Lord by progressive stages made the Human within Himself Divine, and so that all this might be written about in a Word that would contain matters of a Divine nature in its internal sense. This sense was intended to serve angels primarily, whose wisdom – which is beyond understanding or description when compared with human wisdom – is concerned with such Divine matters. It was intended at the same time to serve men who prefer historical to any other descriptions, in which, as men turn such descriptions over in their minds, angels can perceive – through an influx from the Lord – the matters of a Divine nature.

5308 'And Pharaoh said to Joseph' means a perception present in the natural but received from the celestial of the spiritual. This is clear from the meaning of 'saying' in the historical narratives of the Word as perception, dealt with just above in 5306; from the representation of 'Pharaoh' as the natural, and from the representation of 'Joseph' as the celestial of the spiritual, both of which have often been dealt with already.

5309 'After God has caused you to know all this' means for the reason that Foresight and Providence belong to that celestial of the spiritual. This is clear from the meaning of 'coming to know', when used in reference to God, as foresight and providence. For one cannot speak of God coming to know since He has an underived knowledge of all things, whereas man's capacity to know something is derived from Him. Therefore when used in reference to God, 'coming to know' means foresight and providence. Foresight is knowing from eternity to eternity, while providence is the performance of what is foreseen. The reason why foresight and providence belong to the celestial of the spiritual is that the Lord, who is the celestial of the spiritual represented by 'Joseph', is the subject at this point in the internal sense.

5310 'No one has intelligence and wisdom like you' means that this alone is the source of truth and good. This is clear from the meaning of 'one who has intelligence' as truth, and from the meaning of 'one who has wisdom' as good, both dealt with above in 5287. The reason why this alone, and no other, is meant by 'no one' is that no one, or nobody, in the internal sense describes an absence and so separation from all else, see 5225, 5253.

5311 'You shall be over my house' means that the natural mind shall be made subordinate and submissive to it. This is clear from the meaning of 'house' as the mind, dealt with in 3538, 4973, 5023, in this case the natural mind since the expression 'my house' is used by Pharaoh, who represents the natural. The need for it to be made subordinate and submissive [to the celestial of the spiritual] is meant by 'shall be over' it. The person who is set over someone's house is in practice the master there, and all who are in it are made subordinate and submissive to him, though the actual master, so far as appearances go, retains that name and status.

5312 'And all my people shall kiss you on the mouth' means that everything there shall obey it. This is clear from the meaning of 'kissing on the mouth' as accepting and carrying out what is commanded, and so being obedient; and from the meaning of 'all my people' as everything in the natural. 'People' means truths, see 1259, 1260, 3581, 4619, and so cognitions of good and truth, also factual knowledge, present in the natural, since these are truths as they exist within the natural, 5276.

5313   'Only in the throne will I be great, more than you' means that the natural will be seen as sovereign, because the celestial of the spiritual acts through the natural. This is clear from the meaning of 'being great, more than another' as being greater, in this case so far as what is seen or appears to be so; and from the meaning of 'the throne' at this point as the natural. The natural is meant by 'the throne' when the celestial of the spiritual is meant by the one who is seated on it; for the natural is like a throne for the spiritual or in this case the celestial of the spiritual. Generally what is lower is like a throne for what is higher; for the higher exists and acts within the lower, indeed acts through the lower. What is done by it seems to be the work of the lower because, as stated, it acts through the lower. This is the meaning of what Pharaoh said to Joseph – Only in the throne will I be great, more than you.

'Throne' is used frequently in the Word when reference is made to Divine Truth and judgement based on this. In these places 'throne' means in the internal sense that which is the essence of Divine kingship, and 'the one seated on it' is the Lord Himself acting as King or Judge. But the exact meaning of 'the throne', as with the meaning of quite a number of other things, is determined by the context. When the Lord's essential Divine Being and His Divine Human are meant by 'the one seated on the throne', Divine Truth going forth from Him is meant by 'the throne'. When however Divine Truth going forth from the Lord is meant by 'the one seated on the throne', the whole of heaven, which Divine Truth suffuses, is meant by 'the throne'. And when the Lord present with Divine Truth in the higher heavens is meant by 'the one seated on the throne', Divine Truth as this exists in the lowest heaven, and also as it exists in the Church, is meant by 'the throne'. Thus the context decides whatever specific meaning 'the throne' may have. The reason 'the throne' means that which belongs to Divine Truth is that in the Word 'king' means truth, and so too does 'kingdom'. For the meaning of 'king', see 1672, 1728, 2015, 2069, 3009, 3670, 4581, 4966, 5044, 5068; and for that of 'kingdom', 1672, 2547, 4691.

The specific meaning that 'throne' has at any point in the Word is evident from the train of thought in which it occurs, as in Matthew,

I say to you, You shall not swear at all, neither by *heaven*, for it is *God's throne*, nor by the earth, for it is *His footstool*, nor by Jerusalem, for it is the city of the great King.   Matt.5:34,35.

And elsewhere in the same gospel,

He who swears by *heaven* swears by *God's throne* and by Him who sits on it.   Matt.23:22.

Here it is explicitly stated that heaven is 'God's throne'. 'The earth', which is called 'a footstool', means that which is beneath heaven, and so means the Church – the Church being meant by 'the earth', see 566, 662, 1066, 1067, 1262, 1413, 1607, 1733, 1850, 2117, 2118, 2928, 3355, 4447, 4535. A similar usage is seen in Isaiah,

Thus said Jehovah, *The heavens are My throne* and the earth My footstool. Isa.66:1.

And in David,

Jehovah has established *His throne* in *the heavens.* Ps.103:19.

In Matthew,

When the Son of Man comes in His glory, and all the holy angels with Him, then He will sit *on the throne of His glory.* Matt.25:31.

This refers to a last judgement, 'the one seated on the throne' being called 'the King', in verses 34,40. In the internal sense here 'the throne of glory' is the Divine Truth that flows from Divine Good in heaven, 'the one seated on the throne' being the Lord, who – inasmuch as He is a judge by virtue of Divine Truth – is called 'the King'.

4   In Luke,

He will be great and will be called Son of the Most High; and the Lord will give Him *the throne of David* His father. Luke 1:32.

These words were spoken by the angel to Mary. It is clear to anyone that here 'the throne of David' is not the kingdom which David possessed; for it is not a kingdom on earth but one in heaven. Nor therefore is David meant by 'David' but the Lord's Divine kingship, while 'the throne' means Divine Truth that goes forth and constitutes His kingdom. In John,

I was in the spirit, and behold, *a throne set in heaven,* and *one seated upon the throne.* And the one seated was in appearance like a jasper stone and a sardis. There was a rainbow *around the throne,* in appearance like an emerald. *Around the throne were twenty-four thrones,* and *on the thrones* I saw twenty-four elders sitting. From *the throne* were coming forth lightnings and thunders and voices, and likewise seven lamps of fire burning *before the throne,* which are the seven spirits of God. In addition, *before the throne* there was a sea of glass, like crystal. Then *in the midst of the throne,* and *around the throne,* were four living creatures, full of eyes in front and behind. Whenever the four living creatures gave glory and honour and thanks to *the one seated on the throne,* who lives for ever and ever, the twenty-four elders would fall down before *the one seated on the throne* and would worship the one who lives for ever and ever, and would cast their crowns before *the throne.* Rev.4:2–end.

5   This description of the throne of the Lord's glory is used to depict Divine Truth which goes forth from Him. Representatives are used, but if someone has no knowledge of what is meant by these he will hardly be able to know anything at all about what the details of this prophecy hold within them and will suppose that all such details are devoid of any deeper Divine content. The person who knows no better cannot do other than conceive of the heavenly kingdom as one that is similar to a kingdom in the world. But in fact 'a throne set in heaven' means Divine Truth there, and so heaven as regards Divine Truth. 'One seated upon a throne' is used to mean the Lord; and the reason why in appearance He looked like 'a jasper stone and a sardis' is that those stones, like all precious stones in the Word, mean Divine Truth, 114, 3858, 3862, while

stones in general mean the truths of faith, 643, 1298, 3720, 3769, 3771, 3773, 3789, 3798.

'A rainbow around the throne' means truths made translucent by good, for in the next life colours are products of the light of heaven, and the light of heaven is Divine Truth. Regarding rainbows in the next life, see 1042, 1043, 1053, 1623–1625; and regarding colours there, 1053, 1624, 3993, 4530, 4922, 4677, 4741, 4742. By 'the thrones of the twenty-four elders around the throne' are meant all aspects of truth in their entirety, like the things meant by 'twelve'; for 'twelve' means all aspects of truth in their entirety, see 577, 2089, 2129, 2130, 3272, 3858, 3913. 'The lightnings, thunders, and voices which were coming forth from the throne' means the feelings of terror which Divine Truth produces in those who are not governed by good. 'The seven lamps of fire burning' are affections for truth which is rooted in good, which likewise usher in harmful consequences for those who are not governed by good and which are therefore called 'the seven spirits of God', who, as is evident from what comes later on[1], did usher in harmful consequences.

'The sea of glass before the throne' is every truth within the natural, thus the cognitions and the factual knowledge present there; for these are meant by 'the sea', see 28, 2850. 'The four living creatures which were in the midst of the throne and around the throne, and which were full of eyes in front and behind' are ideas in the understanding which are received from the Divine in heaven. 'Four' means the joining of those ideas to desires present in the will; for truths belong to the understanding part and forms of good to the will part of the human mind. This explains why it is said that 'they were full of eyes in front and behind', for 'the eyes' means ideas in the understanding and therefore in a higher sense matters of belief, 2701, 3820, 4403–4421, 4523–4534. 'Four' means a joining together, as likewise does 'two', 1686, 3519, 5194. The holiness of Divine Truth going forth from the Lord is described in what follows at this point [in the Book of Revelation].

Because 'the twenty-four thrones' and 'the twenty-four elders' mean all aspects of truth, or all aspects of faith, in their entirety, and 'twelve' has a similar meaning, as has just been stated, one may consequently see what 'the twelve thrones on which the twelve apostles were seated' is used to mean in the internal sense, namely all aspects of truth, the grounds upon which, and the standard by which judgement takes place. Their thrones are referred to in Matthew as follows,

Jesus said to the disciples, Truly I say to you, that you who have followed Me, in the regeneration, when the Son of Man sits on *the throne of His glory*, will also sit on *twelve thrones*, judging the twelve tribes of Israel.   Matt.19:28.

And in Luke,

---

[1] *i.e. in Chapter 8 of the Book of Revelation*

I bestow on you, just as My Father bestowed on Me, a kingdom, that you may eat and drink at My table in My kingdom, and *sit on thrones* judging the twelve tribes of Israel.   Luke 22:29,30.

'The twelve apostles' means all aspects of truth, see 2129, 2553, 3354, 3488, 3858, as do 'the twelve sons of Jacob' and therefore 'the twelve tribes of Israel', 3858, 3921, 3926, 3939, 4060, 4603. The apostles have no power to judge anyone at all, 2129, 2553.

9   Similarly in John,

I saw *thrones*, and they sat on them, and judgement was given to them. Rev.20:4.

Here also 'thrones' means all aspects of truth, which are the grounds upon which, and the standard by which judgement takes place. Much the same is also meant by 'the angels' with whom the Lord will come to the judgement, in Matt.25:31. When 'angels' are mentioned in the Word some attribute of the Lord is meant, see 1705, 1925, 2320, 2821, 3039, 4085, in this case truths received from the Divine, which truths are called 'judgements' in the Word, 2235.

10   There are very many more places in which Jehovah or the Lord has a throne attributed to Him because thrones embody within themselves that which is representative of the kingdom. When in a higher heaven they are talking about Divine Truth and judgement, a throne is seen in the lowest heaven. This is the reason why a throne is, as has been stated, representative and therefore why a throne is mentioned so many times in the prophetical part of the Word. It is also the reason why in most ancient times a throne became the sign to distinguish the king and why as such a sign it now denotes the office of a monarch. Further examples of the attribution of a throne to the Lord occur in the following places: In Moses,

Moses built an altar, and called its name Jehovah Nissi. Moreover he said, Because the hand is upon *the throne of Jah*, Jehovah will have war against Amalek from generation to generation.   Exod.17:15,16.

No one can know what is meant by 'the hand upon the throne of Jah' or by 'Jehovah having war against Amalek from generation to generation' except from the internal sense, and so unless he knows what is meant by 'the throne' and by 'Amalek'. In the Word 'Amalek' means falsities which assail truths, 1679, and 'the throne' the Divine Truth that is assailed.

11   In David,

O Jehovah, You have maintained *my judgement* and my cause; *You sat upon the throne, a Judge of righteousness.* Jehovah will remain there for ever; He has prepared *His throne for judgement.*   Ps.9:4,7.

In the same author,

Your throne, O God, will be for ever and ever (*in saeculum et aeternum*); a sceptre of uprightness is the sceptre of Your kingdom.   Ps.45:6.

In the same author,

Cloud and thick darkness are round Him, righteousness and judgement are *the foundation of His throne.*   Ps.97:2.

In Jeremiah,

At that time they will call Jerusalem *the throne of Jehovah,* and all the nations will be gathered to it.   Jer.3:17.

'Jerusalem' stands for the Lord's spiritual kingdom. This kingdom is again meant by the new Jerusalem in Ezekiel, and also by 'the holy Jerusalem coming down from heaven' in the Book of Revelation. The Lord's spiritual kingdom exists where that which is pre-eminent is Divine Truth holding Divine Good within it, whereas the Lord's celestial kingdom exists where that which is pre-eminent is Divine Good from which Divine Truth flows. From this one may see why Jerusalem is called 'the throne of Jehovah'. And in David,

In Jerusalem they sit – *the thrones for judgement.*   Ps.122:5.

But Zion is called 'the throne of Jehovah's glory' in Jeremiah,

Have you utterly rejected Judah, has your soul loathed Zion? Do not spurn [us], for Your name's sake; do not dishonour *the throne of Your glory.*   Jer.14:19,21.

'Zion' is used to mean the Lord's celestial kingdom.

3 The way in which the Lord when executing judgement is represented in heaven, where visual scenes like those described in various places in the Prophets come before people's eyes, may be seen in Daniel,

I saw, until *thrones were placed,* and the Ancient of Days was seated. His clothing was white as snow, and the hair of His head like pure wool. *His throne* was a flame of fire, its wheels burning fire. A river of fire issued and came forth before Him, a thousand thousands served Him, and ten thousand times ten thousand stood before Him. The judgement sat down, and the books were opened. Dan.7:9,10.

Sights like this occur constantly in heaven; all are representatives. They have their origin in what angels are discussing in the higher heavens, which discussion comes down from there and manifests itself in visual scenes. The angelic spirits to whom the Lord imparts perception know what is meant by such scenes. They know what is meant by 'the Ancient of Days', 'clothing white as snow', 'hair of the head like pure wool', 'a throne like a flame of fire', 'wheels that are a burning fire', and 'a river of fire going forth from Him'. 'A flame of fire' and 'a river of fire' in this case represent the Good of Divine Love, 934, 4906, 5071, 5215.

4 It is similar with what is said in Ezekiel,

Above the expanse that was above the heads of the cherubim, in appearance like a sapphire stone, there was *the likeness of a throne,* and above *the likeness of a throne* there was a likeness as the appearance of a man upon it.   Ezek.1:26; 10:1.

Likewise with what is said in the first Book of Kings,

I saw – the prophet Micah said – *Jehovah sitting on His throne,* and the entire host of heaven standing beside Him, on His right hand and on His left. 1 Kings 22:19.

Anyone who does not know what these particular descriptions represent, or what their consequent spiritual meanings are, cannot help supposing that the Lord has a throne in the way kings on earth do, and that things actually do exist as they are described by the prophets. But no such phenomena occur in the [higher] heavens; rather they are sights presented to those in the lowest heaven, within which – as within images – they see Divine arcana.

15 The Lord's kingship, by which one means the Divine Truth that goes forth from Him, was also represented by the throne that Solomon built, described in the first Book of Kings as follows,

Solomon made *a large throne of ivory*, and overlaid it with pure gold. There were six steps *to the throne*, and a rounded top to *the throne* at the back of it; there were armrests[1] on either side at the place of the seat, and two lions standing beside the armrests[1], and twelve lions standing there, above the six steps on either side.   1 Kings 10:18–20.

It was a throne of glory that was represented by all this. 'Lions' are Divine Truths engaged in conflict and overcoming, 'twelve lions' being all those Truths in their entirety.

16 Since almost everything in the Word has a contrary meaning, 'a throne' has such too. Its contrary meaning is a kingdom of falsity, as in John,

To the angel of the Church which is in Pergamum, I know your works, and where you dwell, where *Satan's throne* is.   Rev.2:12,13.

In the same book,

The dragon gave the beast coming up out of the sea his power, and *his throne*, and great authority.   Rev.13:2.

In the same book,

The fifth angel poured out his bowl onto *the throne of the beast*, and his kingdom became darkened.   Rev.16:10.

In Isaiah,

You said in your heart, I will go up into the heavens, above the stars of God I will raise *my throne*.   Isa.14:13.

This refers to Babel.

5314   Verses 41–44 **And Pharaoh said the Joseph, See, I have set you over all the land of Egypt. And Pharaoh took off his ring from upon his hand and put it onto Joseph's hand, and clothed him in robes of fine linen, and placed a chain of gold onto his neck. And he made him ride in the second chariot that he had; and they cried out before him, Abrek! and he set him over all the land of Egypt. And Pharaoh said to Joseph, I am Pharaoh, and without you no man shall lift up his hand or his foot in all the land of Egypt.**

'And Pharaoh said to Joseph' means a further perception present in the natural but received from the celestial of the spiritual. 'See, I have set

---

[1] *lit.* hands

you over all the land of Egypt' means dominion over both parts of the natural. 'And Pharaoh took off his ring from upon his hand' means a confirmation regarding the power which belonged at first to the natural. 'And put it onto Joseph's hand' means that it yielded all that power to the celestial of the spiritual. 'And clothed him in robes of fine linen' means an outward sign denoting the celestial of the spiritual, 'robes of fine linen' being truths going forth from the Divine. 'And placed a chain of gold onto his neck' means an outward sign denoting the joining of interior things to exterior ones, good being that which effects that joining together. 'And he made him ride in the second chariot' means an outward sign that the celestial of the spiritual was the source of all the teaching about goodness and truth. 'That he had' means which is imparted through the natural. 'And they cried out before him, Abrek!' means acknowledgement coming through faith, and homage. 'And he set him over all the land of Egypt' means that its authority was as described. 'And Pharaoh said to Joseph' means further perception still. 'I am Pharaoh' means that this made the natural what it was. 'And without you shall no man lift up his hand' means that all power in the spiritual was received from the celestial of the spiritual. 'Or his foot' means all power in the natural. 'In all the land of Egypt' means in both parts of the natural.

5315   'And Pharaoh said to Joseph' means a [further] perception present in the natural but received from the celestial of the spiritual. This is clear from the meaning of 'saying' in the historical narratives of the Word as perceiving, often dealt with already; and from the representation of 'Pharaoh' as the natural, and the representation of 'Joseph' as the celestial of the spiritual, both of which have also been dealt with already. The reason a perception present in the natural but received from the celestial of the spiritual is meant is that the natural receives all the perception it has from what is above it, which in this case is the celestial of the spiritual.

5316   'See, I have set you over all the land of Egypt' means dominion over both parts of the natural. This is clear from the meaning of 'setting someone over' as dominion, and from the meaning of 'all the land of Egypt' as both parts of the natural, dealt with above in 5276. Described at greater length here is the dominion which Pharaoh transferred to Joseph over the land of Egypt. That is to say, Pharaoh divested himself of his own authority and placed the whole of Egypt under Joseph. These events happened by Divine Providence so that Joseph might come to represent the celestial of the spiritual which was the Lord's when He was in the world – the celestial of the spiritual being that by means of which the Lord exercised control over His natural and also His sensory awareness, so that step by step He could make both of these Divine. The end in view with what happened to Joseph was this: When that part of the Word in which Joseph was the subject came to be written it was to contain Divine matters, thus such matters as are most sacred in heaven and suited to the angels in heaven. For the angels there abide in the Lord because they live within the sphere of Divine Truth that goes forth from the Lord. Therefore the Divine matters in the internal sense of the Word which have to do with the Lord and the glorification of His Human stir so much affection in them that they feel all the blessedness that belongs to their wisdom and intelligence.

5317 'And Pharaoh took off his ring from upon his hand' means a confirmation regarding the power which belonged at first to the natural. This is clear from the representation of 'Pharaoh' as the natural, dealt with already; from the meaning of 'ring' as a confirmation, dealt with below; and from the meaning of 'hand' as power, dealt with in 878, 3091, 3387, 4931–4937, 5296. From this it is evident that 'he took off the ring from upon his hand' means that the natural renounced the power which at first belonged to itself, and that 'he put it onto Joseph's hand', as stated next, means that it passed all that power over to the celestial of the spiritual. The fact that 'the ring upon the hand' means a confirmation regarding power is not easy to show from parallel places in the Word, because no references are made to rings worn on the hand, apart from the following in Luke, where the father of the son who had squandered everything said to his servants,

Bring out the best robe and put it on him, and put *a ring upon his hand* and shoes on his feet. Luke 15:22.

Here also, as before, 'a ring' means a confirmation regarding power in the house, such as a son possesses. The same meaning is evident even from the customs which have come down to us from ancient times, such as the customs followed at betrothals and weddings, also at inaugurations, when rings are placed upon the hand. By these rings too a confirmation regarding power is meant. In addition to this, signets, which were likewise worn on the hand, Jer.22:24, mean consent and confirmation, see 4874.

5318 'And put it onto Joseph's hand' means that it yielded all that power to the celestial of the spiritual. This is clear from the meaning of 'putting a ring onto another's hand' as a confirmation that one yields to another the power belonging to oneself, 5317; and from the representation of 'Joseph' as the celestial of the spiritual, often dealt with already.

5319 'And clothed him in robes of fine linen' means an outward sign denoting the celestial of the spiritual, 'robes of fine linen' being truths going forth from the Divine. This is clear from the meaning of 'robes' as truths, dealt with in 1073, 2576, 4545, 4763, 5248. The reason 'robes of fine linen' means truths going forth from the Divine is that a robe made of fine linen was absolutely white and at the same time shining, and truth going forth from the Divine is represented by robes which have that kind of brightness and splendour. And the reason for this is that heaven derives its brightness and splendour from the light that flows from the Lord; and the light that flows from the Lord is

Divine Truth itself, 1053, 1521–1533, 1619–1632, 2776, 3195, 3222, 3339, 3485, 3636, 3643, 3862, 4415, 4419, 4526, 5219. This explains why, when the Lord was transfigured before Peter, James, and John, *His clothing appeared as the light*, Matt.17:2; *glistening, intensely white like snow, as no fuller on earth could bleach them*, Mark 9:3; and *dazzling*, Luke 9:29. It was Divine Truth itself going forth from the Lord's Divine Human that was represented in this manner. But they are exterior truths that are represented in heaven by the brightness of robes, whereas interior truths are represented by the brightness and splendour of the face. This is why 'being clothed in robes of fine linen' at this point means an outward sign denoting truth going forth from the celestial of the spiritual, for this was what the Lord's Divine consisted in at this time.

There are other places too in the Word where truth going forth from the Divine is meant by 'fine linen' and 'robes of fine linen', as in Ezekiel,

I clothed you with embroidered cloth, and shod you with badger, and *swathed you in fine linen*, and covered you in silk. Thus were you adorned with gold and silver, and your robes were *fine linen*, and silk, and embroidered cloth. Ezek.16:10,13.

This refers to Jerusalem, which is used in these verses to mean the Ancient Church. The truths of this Church are described by robes made of embroidered cloth, fine linen, and silk, and by being adorned with gold and silver. 'Embroidered cloth' means truths existing as facts, 'fine linen' natural truths, and 'silk' spiritual truths.

In the same prophet,

Fine linen with embroidered work from Egypt was your sail, that it might be to you *an ensign*; violet and purple from the islands of Elishah was your covering. Ezek.27:7.

This refers to Tyre, which too is used to mean the Ancient Church, but so far as cognitions of good and truth are concerned. 'Fine linen with embroidered work from Egypt, which was its sail' means truth obtained from factual knowledge, which was the outward sign of that Church.

In John,

The merchants of the earth will weep and mourn over Babylon, since no one buys their wares any more, wares of gold, and silver, and precious stones, and pearls, and *fine linen*, and purple, and silk, and scarlet, and all thyine wood, and every vessel of ivory, and every vessel made of most precious wood, and bronze, and iron, and marble.   Rev.18:11,12.

All the specific commodities mentioned here mean the kinds of things that have to do with the Church and so truth and goodness. Here however they are used in the contrary sense because they are spoken of in reference to Babylon. Anyone may see that such commodities would never have been listed in the Word which has come down from heaven unless each one held something heavenly within it. What other reason can there be for a list of worldly wares when Babylon, meaning an unholy Church, is the subject? Similarly in the same book,

Woe, woe, the great city, *you that were clothed in fine linen*, and purple, and scarlet, covered[1] with gold, and precious stones, and pearls. Rev.18:16.

5   The fact that each commodity means something Divine and heavenly is quite evident in the same book where it states what fine linen is, namely the righteous acts of the saints,

The time of the marriage of the Lamb has come, and His wife has made herself ready. At that time she was given *fine linen, clean and shining, to wear; for the fine linen is the righteous acts of the saints.* Rev.19:7,8.

'Fine linen' is 'the righteous acts of the saints' for the reason that all those with whom truth received from the Divine exists are clothed with the Lord's righteousness. For their robes which are bright and shining are products of the light which flows from the Lord. Therefore in heaven truth itself is represented by 'brightness', 3301, 3993, 4007; and people who are being raised to heaven from a state of vastation are seen to be clothed with brightness because they are at this point casting off the robe of their own righteousness and putting on that of the Lord's righteousness.

6   So that truth from the Divine might be represented in the Jewish Church, they were commanded to use cotton or fine linen in Aaron's vestments, and also in the curtains around the Ark, referred to in Moses as follows,

You shall make in chequered pattern for Aaron *a tunic of cotton*, and you shall make *a turban of cotton.* Exod.28:39.
They made *tunics of cotton*, the work of a weaver, for Aaron and his sons. Exod.39:27.
You shall make the Dwelling-place, ten curtains – *fine-twined cotton*, violet and purple and twice-dyed scarlet. Exod.26:1; 36:8.
You shall make the court of the Dwelling-place. The hangings for the court shall be of *fine-twined cotton.* Exod.27:9,18; 38:9.
The screen for the gate of the court, the work of an embroiderer, violet and purple, and twice-dyed scarlet, and *fine-twined cotton.* Exod.38:18.

Cotton is fine linen, which they were commanded to use because each object in the Ark and around the Ark, also every detail of Aaron's vestments, were representative of spiritual and celestial realities. From this one may see that a person has only a meagre understanding of the Word if he does not know what such things represent, and scarcely any understanding at all if he thinks that the Word possesses no holiness other than that which presents itself in the letter.

7   When angels with whom truth from the Divine is present are seen by anyone they are clothed so to speak in fine linen, that is, in shining brightness, as is evident in John where 'a white horse' is referred to,

The One seated on *a white horse* was clothed in a garment dyed with blood, and His name is called the Word. His armies in heaven were following Him *on white horses; they were clothed in fine linen, white and clean.* Rev.19:11,13,14.

---

[1] *lit.* gilded

These words show quite plainly that 'fine linen' is an outward sign denoting truth from the Divine, for 'the One seated on a white horse' is the Lord as to the Word; indeed those words state quite explicitly that He is the Word. The Word is truth itself received from the Divine, and 'a white horse' is the internal sense of the Word, see 2760–2762. Consequently truths received from the Divine are meant by 'white horses', for such truths constitute the whole of the internal sense of the Word. This was why His armies were seen 'on white horses' and why 'they were clothed in fine linen, white and clean'.

5320   'And placed a chain of gold onto his neck' means an outward sign denoting the joining of interior things to exterior ones, good being that which effects that joining together. This is clear from the meaning of 'the neck' as a flowing in, also the communication of higher things with lower ones, or what amounts to the same, interior things with exterior ones, dealt with in 3542; and therefore 'a chain', because it goes around the neck, is a sign denoting the joining together of those things. 'A chain of gold' means a joining together by means of good; that is, good is the means which effects it, because 'gold' means good, 113, 1551, 1552. A sign denoting the joining of interior truth to exterior truth is meant by 'a chain onto the neck' in Ezekiel,

I adorned you with ornaments and put bracelets onto your hands and *a chain onto your neck*.   Ezek.16:11.

5321   'And he made him ride in the second chariot' means an outward sign that the celestial of the spiritual was the source of all the teaching about goodness and truth. This is clear from the meaning of 'the chariot' as teaching which has reference to goodness and truth, dealt with below, so that 'making him ride in the chariot' is a sign denoting that the celestial of the spiritual was the source of that teaching. This particular matter is connected with what Pharaoh has stated previously, in verse 40,

You shall be over my house, and all my people shall kiss you on the mouth; only in the throne will I be great, more than you.

The reason why teaching that has reference to goodness and truth is meant by 'Joseph' is that 'Joseph' represents the Lord's Divine Spiritual, 3971, 4669, and so Divine Truth going forth from the Lord's Divine Human, 4723, 4727, the celestial of the spiritual being an extension of that Divine Truth. The reason why all the teaching about goodness and truth is derived from the celestial of the spiritual is that in a real sense the Lord is that teaching since every detail of it comes forth from Him and every detail of it has reference to Him. For all that teaching has reference to the good of love and the truth of faith; and since the Lord is the source of these, He is not merely present within them but in a real sense is both of them. From this it is clear that teaching which has reference to goodness and truth has reference to the Lord alone, and that such goes forth from His Divine Human.

2 No doctrine at all can possibly go forth from the Divine itself except through the Divine Human, that is, through the Word, which in the highest sense is Divine Truth coming from the Lord's Divine Human. That which goes forth directly from the Divine itself cannot be understood even by angels in the inmost heaven. The reason for this is that it is infinite and so surpasses all understanding, even that of angels. But that which goes forth from the Lord's Divine Human is capable of being understood, for such truth refers to God as Divine Man, of whom some idea can be formed from His Human. No matter what kind of idea has been formed about that Human, it is an acceptable one if only the good of innocence has been inspired into it and the good of charity is present within it. This is the meaning of the Lord's words in John,

Nobody has ever seen God; the only begotten Son who is in the bosom of the Father, He has made Him known. John 1:18.

In the same gospel,

You have never heard the Father's voice nor seen His shape. John 5:37.

And in Matthew,

No one knows the Father except the Son, and he to whom the Son wishes to reveal Him. Matt.11:27.

3 Chariots are mentioned in very many places in the Word, yet scarcely anyone knows that matters of doctrine concerning goodness and truth, and also factual knowledge attached to those matters of doctrine, are meant by 'chariots'. The reason for such lack of knowledge is that nothing spiritual, only what is natural and historical, enters their thinking when 'a chariot' is mentioned, or similarly when the horses in front of a chariot are mentioned. But in the Word the powers of the understanding are meant by 'horses', 2760–2762, 3217, and therefore 'a chariot' means matters of doctrine and associated factual knowledge.

4 It has become clear to me from the chariots which I have seen so many times in the next life that 'chariots' means the matters of doctrine and also the factual knowledge which the Church possesses. There is also a place over on the right, around the lower earth, where chariots and horses, together with rows of stables, appear. In that place people who in the world were considered learned, and who thought that life was the end in view of learning, stroll and converse with one another. The origin of such chariots and horses seen by them lies with the angels in higher heavens; when these angels' conversation turns to intellectual concepts, and to matters of doctrine and to known facts, those chariots and horses are seen by the spirits around the lower earth.

5 The fact that such things are meant by 'chariots and horses' is perfectly plain from the occasion when Elijah was seen riding into heaven in a chariot of fire with horses of fire, and from what both he and Elisha were called – 'the chariot of Israel and its horsemen'. The two of them are spoken of in the second Book of Kings as follows,

Behold, *a chariot of fire* and *horses of fire* came between them, and Elijah went up in a whirlwind into heaven; Elisha saw this and cried out, My father, my father, *the chariot of Israel* and *its horsemen.*   2 Kings 2:11,12.

And in a reference to Elisha in the same book,

When Elisha was sick with the illness from which he died, Joash the king of Israel came down to him and wept before his face and said, My father, my father, *the chariot of Israel* and *its horsemen.*   2 Kings 13:14.

The reason they were called this is that both of them – Elijah and Elisha – represented the Lord as to the Word, see Preface to Genesis 18, and 2762, 5247(end). The Word itself is primarily doctrinal teaching about what is good and true, for the Word is the source of all doctrinal teaching. It was for the same reason that Elisha's servant, whose eyes had been opened by Jehovah, saw around Elisha,

A mountain full of horses and chariots of fire.   2 Kings 6:17.

The fact that 'chariot' means matters of doctrine and 'horse' intellectual concepts is also clear from other places in the Word, as in Ezekiel,

You will be filled at My table with *horse* and *chariot*, with mighty man and every man of war. Thus will I bring My glory to the nations.   Ezek.39:20,21; Rev.19:18.

This refers to the Lord's Coming. Anyone can see that here 'horse and chariot' does not mean horse and chariot, for people are not going to be filled with these at the Lord's table but with such things as are meant spiritually by 'horse and chariot', which are intellectual concepts and matters of doctrine regarding what is good and true.

Much the same is meant by 'horses' and 'chariots' in the following places: In David,

The chariots of God are myriad on myriad[1], thousands of peacemakers; the Lord is within them, Sinai is within the sanctuary.   Ps.68:17.

In the same author,

Jehovah covers Himself with light as with a garment; He stretches out the heavens like a curtain, laying the beams for His upper chambers[2] on the waters; *He makes the clouds His chariots*; He walks on the wings of the wind.   Ps.104:2,3.

In Isaiah,

The prophecy of the wilderness of the sea. Thus said the Lord to me, Set a watchman; let him announce what he sees. *He therefore saw a chariot, a pair of horsemen, a chariot of asses, a chariot of camels*, and he listened diligently, with great care. For a lion cried out on the watchtower, O Lord, I am standing continually during the daytime, and at my post I have been set every night. Now behold, *a chariot of men, a pair of horsemen.* And he said, Fallen, fallen has Babylon.   Isa.21:1,6–9.

In the same prophet,

At that time they will bring all your brothers in all nations as an offering to

---

[1] *lit.* two myriads
[2] *lit.* His couches

Jehovah, *on horses*, and *in chariots*, and *in covered waggons*, and *on mules*, and *on couriers*, to My holy mountain, Jerusalem. Isa.66:20.

In the same prophet,

Behold, Jehovah will come with fire, and *His chariots* will be like a whirl-wind. Isa.66:15.

In Habakkuk,

Has Jehovah been displeased with the rivers? Has Your anger turned against the rivers, has Your wrath turned against the sea, *that You ride on Your horses, Your chariots being salvation*? Hab.3:8.

In Zechariah,

I lifted up my eyes and saw, and behold, *four chariots* coming out from between two mountains; but the mountains were mountains of bronze. *The horses coupled to the first chariot* were reddish, *the horses coupled to the second chariot* were black, *the horses coupled to the third chariot* were white, and *the horses coupled to the fourth chariot* were mottled. Zech.6:1–3.

And in Jeremiah,

There will enter through the gates of this city kings and princes seated on the throne of David, *riding in chariots and on horses*, they and their princes, the men of Judah and the inhabitants of Jerusalem. And this city will be inhabited for ever. Jer.17:25; 22:4.

'The city that will be inhabited for ever' is not Jerusalem but the Lord's Church meant by 'Jerusalem', 402, 2117, 3654. The kings who will enter through the gates of that city are not kings but truths known to the Church, 1672, 1728, 2015, 2069, 3009, 3670, 4575, 4581, 4966, 5044, 5068. Thus 'princes' are not princes but the first and foremost aspects of truth, 1482, 2089, 5044. Those 'seated on the throne of David' are Divine Truths which go forth from the Lord, 5313; and those 'riding in chariots and on horses' are consequently intellectual concepts and matters of doctrine. Chariots are also mentioned many times in historical descriptions in the Word; and since historical events are representative of, and the words used to describe them mean, the kinds of things that exist in the Lord's kingdom and in the Church, 'chariots' have a similar meaning there also.

10 Since most things in the Word also have a contrary meaning, so too does 'chariots'. In that contrary sense matters of doctrine maintaining what is evil and false, also factual knowledge used to lend support to these, are meant by 'chariots', as in the following places: In Isaiah,

Woe to those who go down into Egypt for help and *rely on horses* and *trust in chariots* because they are many, and *on horsemen* because they are extremely strong, but do not look to the Holy One of Israel. Isa.31:1.

In the same prophet,

By the hand of your[1] servants you have spoken ill of the Lord and have said, *By the multitude of my chariots* I have gone up [to] the height of the mountains, the

---

[1] *The Latin means* my, *but the Hebrew means* your.

sides of Lebanon, where I will cut down the tallness of its cedars, the choice of its fir trees.   Isa.37:24.

This is a prophecy delivered in response to the haughty words spoken by the Rabshakeh, a leader serving the king of Assyria. In Jeremiah,

Behold, waters rising out of the north which will become a deluging stream, and they will deluge the land and all that fills it, the city and those who dwell in it. And every inhabitant of the land will wail at *the sound of the beat* of the hoofs *of the horses* his mighty ones, *at the noise of his chariot, the rumble of its wheels.*   Jer.47:2,3.

In Ezekiel,

By reason of the abundance of his horses their dust will cover you; *by reason of the noise of horseman, and wheels, and chariots,* your walls will be shaken, when he comes into your gates, like the entry into a city that has been breached. *By means of the hoofs of his horses* he will trample all your streets.   Ezek.26:10,11.

In Haggai,

I will overthrow the throne of kingdoms, and I will destroy the strength of the kingdoms of the nations. I will also overthrow *the chariots* and *those riding in them; the horses* and *their riders* will come down.   Hagg.2:22.

In Zechariah,

I will cut off *the chariot* from Ephraim, and *the horse* from Jerusalem, I will cut off the battle bow. On the other hand He will speak peace to the nations. Zech.9:10.

In Jeremiah,

Egypt comes up like the river, like the rivers his waters are tossed about. For he said, I will go up, I will cover the earth, I will destroy the city and those who dwell in it. *Go up, O horses*; rage, *O chariots.*   Jer.46:8,9.

2   The horses and chariots with which the Egyptians pursued the children of Israel and with which Pharaoh entered the Sea Suph, when the wheels of the chariots were made to come off, and much else regarding the horses and chariots which forms the major part of the description – Exod.14:6,7,9,17,23,25,26 and 15:4,19 – mean intellectual concepts, matters of doctrine, and known facts which maintain what is false. They also mean therefore reasonings which pervert and destroy the truths known to the Church. The destruction and death of such reasonings is described there.

5322   'That he had' means which – that is to say, doctrinal teaching about what is good and true – is imparted through the natural. This is clear from the train of thought in the internal sense, and also from the things explained above in 5313.

5323   'And they cried out before him, Abrek!' means acknowledgement coming through faith, and homage. This is clear from the meaning of 'crying out' as acknowledgement coming through faith, dealt with below, and from the meaning of 'Abrek!' as homage, because Abrek in the original language means 'bend your knees', and the bending of knees is homage. For every inward impulse of a person's will, thus of his love and affection, and consequently of his life, has corresponding outward actions and gestures. Those actions and gestures flow from the actual correspondence of exterior things with interior ones. Holy fear that leads to humility, and from this to homage, has corresponding actions or gestures, which are bending the knees, falling forward on the knees, and also prostration of the body flat on the ground. If in that state homage is a product of genuine humility, and if humility is the product of genuine holy fear, there is an absence of spirits, which leads to a falling downwards of the joints at the border or intermediate area where the spiritual is joined to the natural, and so where the knees are. For the parts below the knee correspond to natural things, while the parts above the knee correspond to spiritual ones. These are the reasons why bending the knees is a sign representative of homage. Among celestial people this action comes quite spontaneously, but in the case of spiritual people it is a deliberate act of their will.

2   In former times people bent their knees before kings when they rode by in a chariot. They bent them because kings represented the Lord's Divine Truth, while 'a chariot' meant His Word. This customary act of homage came into being when people knew what was represented by it, at which time kings did not think that such homage was paid to themselves but to their kingly authority, which was distinct from yet invested in their own persons. That authority invested in them was the law, and because this law had its origin in Divine Truth, it was the law invested in the person of the king, inasmuch as he was the guardian of the law, to which homage had to be paid. Thus a king did not attribute any royal authority to himself other than guardianship of the law. Insofar as he relinquished that guardianship he relinquished his royal authority; for he knew that homage arising from any other source than the law, that is, any other homage than that paid to the law itself, was idolatry. By royal authority is meant Divine Truth – see 1672, 1728, 2015, 2069, 3009, 3670, 4581, 4966, 5044, 5068 – and therefore that authority is the law, which essentially is truth reigning in that kingdom, in accordance with which its inhabitants conduct their lives. From all this it may be seen that 'Abrek!' or 'bend your knees' means homage.

3   Since 'a cry' is in a similar way an action which corresponds to a living confession or an acknowledgement that is a product of faith, crying out was also the custom followed by the ancients when an outward sign of such confession or acknowledgement needed to be made. The expression 'crying out' is therefore used in various places in the Word when confession and acknowledgement that are the product of faith are referred to, as in the description involving John the Baptist in John,

He bore witness to Jesus and *he cried out*, saying, This was He of whom I spoke, He who, though coming after me, was before me, for He was before me. I am *the voice of one crying* in the wilderness, Make straight the way of the Lord. John 1:15,23.

In the same gospel,

They took branches of palm trees, and went to meet Jesus, and *cried*, Hosanna! Blessed is He who comes in the name of the Lord, the King of Israel! John 12:13.

In Luke,

Jesus said to the Pharisees that if [the disciples] kept silent, the stones would *cry out*. Luke 19:40.

Because 'crying out' meant an acknowledgement that was the product of faith and consequently acceptance rising out of the acknowledgement, one therefore reads several times of the Lord's crying out, as in John 7:28,37; 12:44,45. Also in Isaiah,

Jehovah will go forth as a Mighty Man, as a Man of Wars He will arouse zeal; He will *shout aloud*, and also will *cry out*. Isa.42:13.

In the contrary sense 'crying out' means lack of acknowledgement and so aversion, see 5016, 5018, 5027. This usage has reference to falsity, 2240.

5324   'And he set him over all the land of Egypt' means that its authority was as described. This is clear from the meaning of 'setting him over all the land of Egypt' as dominion over both parts of the natural, dealt with above in 5316, though here its dominion was such as has been described in what has gone immediately before this, thus that its authority was as described.

5325   'And Pharaoh said to Joseph' means further perception still. This is clear from the meaning of 'saying', from the representation of 'Pharaoh', and from the representation of 'Joseph' as perception present in the natural but received from the celestial of the spiritual, dealt with in 5315, here a further perception because the expression is used once again.

5326   'I am Pharaoh' means that this made the natural what it was. This is clear from the representation of 'Pharaoh' as the natural, dealt with in 5079, 5080, 5095, 5160. The fact that 'I am Pharaoh' means that this made the natural what it was is evident from all that immediately follows. For the declaration 'without you shall no man lift up his hand or his foot in all the land of Egypt' means that the celestial of the spiritual was the origin of all the power in both parts of the natural. Also, because things present in the natural are meant by the words that follow, the expression 'I am Pharaoh' therefore comes first, the term natural being used to mean the natural which has the celestial of the spiritual as its origin. The implications of this are as follows: With someone who is being created anew, that is, being regenerated, the natural is entirely different from what it is with someone who is not being regenerated. In the case of someone who is not being regenerated, his natural is everything; it is the source of his thought, and it is the source of his desires. His rational is not the source of it, and his spiritual still less so, because these are closed and for the most part dead.

2 But in the case of someone who is being regenerated everything is made spiritual. The spiritual not only determines the thoughts and desires of the natural but also constitutes the natural in exactly the same way as a cause constitutes its effect; for nothing else acts within any effect except its cause. Thus the natural becomes like the spiritual, for the contents of the natural – such as any knowledge or cognition which springs from something in the natural world – do not act by themselves; they serve merely to support the spiritual so that it can act within and through the natural, and so act on the level of the natural. The same is so within an effect. An effect holds more things within itself than its cause does; yet the only purpose such things serve is to enable the cause to achieve the actual effect within the effect and to present itself in actual fact on the level of effect. From these few comments one may see what the natural is like in the case of a person who has been created anew, that is, regenerated – that regeneration, which made the natural what it was, being meant by 'I am Pharaoh'.

5327 'And without you shall no man lift up his hand' means that all power in the spiritual was received from the celestial of the spiritual. This is clear from the meaning of 'hand' as power, dealt with in 878, 3387, 4931–4937, 5296. Consequently 'no man lifting up his hand without you' means that they had no power at all except from this, thus that all power rested with this, that is to say, with the celestial of the spiritual. As regards power *in the spiritual* being meant by 'hand', this will be seen in the next paragraph.

5328 'Or his foot' means all power in the natural. This is clear from the meaning of 'foot' as the natural, dealt with in 2162, 3147, 3761, 3986, 4280, 4938–4952. Here power within the natural is meant because 'lifting up the foot', like 'lifting up the hand', means power, though 'lifting up the hand' means power in the spiritual, whereas 'lifting up the foot' means power in the natural; for the parts within the body that are above the feet correspond to spiritual things. This is especially evident from the Grand Man or the three heavens.

2 Whenever the whole of heaven is displayed visually as one human being, the inmost or third heaven presents itself as the head, the middle or second heaven presents itself as the body, and the lowest or first as the feet. The reason the inmost or third heaven presents itself as the head is that it is celestial; the reason the middle or second heaven presents itself as the body is that it is spiritual; and the reason the lowest or first presents itself as the feet is that it is natural. By 'the neck' therefore, since this is an intermediate part, is meant the inflow and communication of celestial things with spiritual ones; and by 'the knees', since these are likewise intermediate, is meant the inflow and

communication of spiritual things with natural ones. From this it is evident that 'lifting up the hand' means power within the spiritual, while 'lifting up the foot' means power within the natural, and therefore that the power meant by 'the hand' has regard to the spiritual, namely to truth grounded in good, 3091, 3563, 4932. By the spiritual is meant that within the natural which belongs to the light of heaven, and by the natural that within the natural which belongs to the light of the world; for everything belonging to the light of heaven is called spiritual, and everything belonging to the light of the world is called natural.

5329   'In all the land of Egypt' means in both parts of the natural. This is clear from the meaning of 'all the land of Egypt' as both parts of the natural, dealt with above in 5276. Matters like those that are being presented now are what angels perceive when man reads,

Pharaoh took off his ring from upon his hand and put it onto Joseph's hand, and clothed him in robes of fine linen, and placed a chain of gold onto his neck. And he made him ride in the second chariot that he had; and they cried out before him, Abrek! and he set him over all the land of Egypt.

For angels cannot have any perception at all of actual historical details since these are the kind of things that belong to the world and not to heaven; things that belong to the world are not seen by them. Yet because everything in the world has a correspondence with something in heaven angels therefore have a perception of heavenly things when man's perception is of worldly ones. If this were not so no angel from heaven could ever be present with man; but so that an angel can be present with him the Word has been provided, in which angels perceive a Divine holiness that they can communicate to the person with whom they are present.

5330   Verse 45 **And Pharaoh called Joseph's name Zaphenath Paneah, and gave him Asenath, the daughter of Potiphera the priest of On, for a wife; and Joseph went out over the land of Egypt.**
'And Pharaoh called Joseph's name Zaphenath Paneah' means the essential nature of the celestial of the spiritual at this point. 'And gave him Asenath, the daughter of Potiphera the priest of On, for a wife' means the essential nature of the marriage of truth to good, and of good to truth. 'And Joseph went out over the land of Egypt' means when both parts of the natural were His.

5331   'And Pharaoh called Joseph's name Zaphenath Paneah' means the essential nature of the celestial of the spiritual at this point. This is clear from the meaning of 'name' and 'calling the name' as the essential nature, dealt with in 144, 145, 1754, 1896, 2009, 2628, 2724, 3006, 3237, 3421. In the original language Zaphenath Paneah means the revealer of things that are hidden and the discloser of things to come. In the heavenly sense these names mean the Divine within him, for the revelation of things that are hidden and the disclosure of things to come belong to God alone. This essential characteristic is what is embodied in the name Joseph was given; and that characteristic is the essential nature of the celestial of the spiritual. For the celestial of the spiritual is the good of truth that has the Divine within it; that is, it is what flows directly from the Divine. This – the celestial of the spiritual that had the Divine within it – was the Lord's alone when He was in the world. It was the Human in which the Divine itself could be present and which could be cast aside when the Lord made the entire Human within Himself Divine.

5332 'And gave him Asenath, the daughter of Potiphera the priest of On, for a wife' means the essential nature of the marriage of truth to good, and of good to truth. This is clear from the meaning of 'giving for a wife' as a marriage. The reason the marriage of good to truth, and of truth to good, is meant is that nothing else is understood in a spiritual sense by 'marriages', and therefore nothing else is understood by 'marriages' in the Word. 'The daughter of the priest of On' means the truth of good, since 'a daughter' is the affection for truth and 'a priest' is good; but 'Joseph' is the good of truth that has the Divine within it, which is the same as the celestial of the spiritual. From this it is evident that the marriage of truth to good, and of good to truth, is meant. What is actually meant is the essential nature of this marriage; but this cannot receive any further explanation because the essential nature of what was the Lord's when He was in the world is beyond all understanding, beyond even that of angels. Just a vague idea of it can be formed from the kinds of things that exist in heaven – from the Grand Man and from the celestial of the spiritual existing there as a result of the influx of the Lord's Divine. But that idea is like the darkest shade compared with the light itself; for it is a very general idea indeed, thus scarcely anything compared with the reality it describes.

5333 'And Joseph went out over the land of Egypt' means when both parts of the natural were His. This is clear from the meaning of 'going out' here as flowing into, and from the meaning of 'the land of Egypt' as the natural mind, often dealt with already, and so both parts of the natural. Since 'going out' means flowing into, and 'the land of Egypt' means both parts of the natural, these words and the ones that come just before mean the essential nature of the celestial of the spiritual, and the essential nature of the marriage of good to truth, and of truth to good, when the celestial of the spiritual flowed in and made both parts of the natural its own. For what is meant by making the natural its own, see just above in 5326.

5334 Verses 46–49 **And Joseph was a son of thirty years when he stood before Pharaoh king of Egypt; and Joseph came out from before Pharaoh, and went through all the land of Egypt. And in the seven years of abundance of corn the land yielded bunches. And he gathered all the food of the seven years which were in the land of Egypt, and**

laid up¹ the food in the cities; the food of the field of a city which was
round about it he laid up¹ in the midst of it. And Joseph stored up
grain like the sand of the sea, very much, until he left off numbering,
because it was beyond number.

'And Joseph was a son of thirty years' means a state when the quantity
of remnants was complete. 'When he stood before Pharaoh king of
Egypt' means the presence of the celestial of the spiritual in the natural.
'And Joseph came out from before Pharaoh' means when the natural in
general belonged to it. 'And went through all the land of Egypt' means
when it made each thing there subordinate and submissive. 'And in the
seven years of abundance of corn the land yielded bunches' means
initial states when series of truths were multiplied. 'And he gathered all
the food of the seven years' means the preservation of truth linked to
good, multiplied in the initial phases. 'Which were in the land of Egypt'
means within the natural. 'And laid up food in the cities' means that it
stored them in the interior parts. 'The food of the field of a city' means
that these were proper to and suitable for those interior parts. 'Which
was round about it he laid up in the midst of it' means what existed first
in the exterior natural was stored away by it in the interior parts of the
interior natural. 'And Joseph stored up grain like the sand of the sea,
very much' means a multiplication of truth derived from good. 'Until he
left off numbering, because it was beyond number' means such as
holds the celestial from the Divine within it.

5335   'And Joseph was a son of thirty years' means a state when the
quantity of remnants was complete. This is clear from the meaning of
'thirty' as a completed number of remnants, dealt with below, and from
the meaning of 'years' as states, dealt with in 482, 487, 488, 493, 893. In
the Word the number thirty can mean some existence of conflict, or else
it can mean a completed number of remnants. The reason why that
number has this twofold meaning is that it is arrived at by multiplying
five and six, or else by multiplying three and ten. When it is the product
of five times six it means some existence of conflict, 2276, because 'five'
means some, 649, 4638, 5291, and 'six' conflict, 720, 737, 900, 1709. But
when thirty is the product of three times ten it means a completed
number of remnants, because 'three' means that which is complete,
2788, 4495, and 'ten' means remnants, 576, 1906, 2284. A composite
number implies much the same as the simple ones of which it is the
product, 5291. Remnants are the truths joined to good which have been
stored away by the Lord in a person's interior parts, see 468, 530, 560,
561, 576, 660, 1050, 1738, 1906, 2284, 5135.

A completed number of remnants is likewise meant by 'thirty' – as it is
also by 'sixty', and by 'a hundred' too – in Mark,

The seed which fell into good ground yielded fruit growing up and increasing.
One bore *thirty*-fold, and another *sixty*, and another *a hundred*.   Mark 4:8,20.

¹ *lit.* gave

Each of these numbers, being a multiple of ten, means a completed number of remnants. Also, because no one can be regenerated – that is, permitted to enter into spiritual temptations, by means of which regeneration is effected – until he has received a completed number of remnants, it was therefore laid down that no Levite should carry out any work in the tent of meeting until he was fully thirty years old. Their work or function is also called 'military service', being referred to in Moses as follows,

Take a census of the sons of Kohath from the midst of the sons of Levi – from *sons thirty years of age* and over, up to sons fifty years of age, *everyone coming to perform military service*, to do the work in the tent of meeting. Num.4:2,3.

Much the same is said regarding the sons of Gershon, and much the same regarding the sons of Merari, in verses 22,23,29,30, and then in verses 35,39,43 of that same chapter in Moses. And something similar is implied where it says that David began to reign when he was *a son thirty years of age*, 2 Sam.5:4.

3   From all this one may now see why the Lord did not make Himself known until He was *thirty years of age*, Luke 3:23. At that age a completed number of remnants existed with Him, though these remnants which the Lord possessed were ones that He Himself had acquired for Himself. They were also Divine ones and the means by which He united His Human Essence to His Divine Essence and made that Human Essence Divine, 1906. In Him therefore lies the reason why 'thirty years' means a state when the quantity of remnants is complete and why the priests the Levites began to perform their specific functions when they were thirty years old. And because he was to represent the Lord's kingship, David did not begin to reign until he was that same age. For every representative is derived from the Lord, and therefore every representative has reference to Him.

5336   'When he stood before Pharaoh king of Egypt' means the presence of the celestial of the spiritual in the natural. This is clear from the meaning of 'standing before someone' as the presence, and from the representation of 'Pharaoh king of Egypt' as a new state in the natural or a new natural man, dealt with in 5079, 5080, and so the natural which now had the celestial of the spiritual within it and which the celestial of the spiritual now made its own – which is also the meaning of the words that immediately follow, 'And Joseph came out from before Pharaoh'.

5337   'And Joseph came out from before Pharaoh' means when the natural in general belonged to it. This is clear from the meaning of 'coming out' as belonging to it, dealt with below; from the representation of 'Joseph' as the celestial of the spiritual, and of 'Pharaoh' as the natural, both dealt with above. As regards the meaning of 'coming out' as belonging to it, or being its own, this is evident from what is said before and after this. It is also evident from the spiritual sense of the expression, for in that sense 'coming out' or going forth is making oneself present before another in a form suited to this other. Thus one is still the same person; only the form in which one appears is different. The expression 'coming out' is used in this sense in reference to the Lord, in John,

Jesus said regarding Himself, *From God I came out* and now come.   John 8:42.
The Father loves you because you have loved Me and have believed *that I came out from God. I came out from the Father* and have come into the world; again I am leaving the world and going to the Father. The disciples said, We believe *that You came out from God.*   John 16:27,28,30.
They have received and know in truth *that I came out from You*[1].   John 17:8.

To show what is meant by 'coming out' or going forth let some examples be used. Truth is said to come out or go forth from good when truth is the form that good possesses, that is, when truth is good existing in a form intelligible to the understanding. The understanding too may be said to come out or go forth from the will when the understanding is the form that the will possesses, that is, when the will exists in a form discernible to a person's inner sight. Thought which is the activity of the understanding may in a similar way be said to come out or go forth when it is transformed into speech, and so may the will when this is transformed into action. Thought takes on a different form when it is transferred into speech; yet it is still thought which comes out or goes forth within such speech, for the words and sounds which are chosen are no more than adjuncts to thought which serve to present it in such a way that it can be discerned. The will in a similar way takes on a different form when it is transferred into action; yet it is still the will which is present in that different form. The gestures and movements which it adopts are no more than adjuncts to the will which serve to reveal this in a suitable way that enables it to be known. The external man may likewise be said to come out or go forth from the internal man, and to do so as that which manifests the substance, for the external man is nothing else than the form given to the internal man [or the substance], enabling it to function in a proper way in the world in which it exists. From all these examples one may see what is meant in the spiritual sense by 'coming out' or going forth, namely that when used in reference to the Lord, 'coming out' or going forth means the Divine existing within a human form, thus in a form suited to believers' perception. For these two [the Divine and the human form] exist as one.

5338   'And went through all the land of Egypt' means when it made each thing there, in the natural, subordinate and submissive. This is clear from the meaning of 'all the land of Egypt' as both parts of the natural, dealt with in 5276, 5278, 5280, 5288, 5301. The fact that 'going through that land' means making each thing in the natural subordinate and submissive follows from what has gone before.

[1] *The Latin means* God *but the Greek means* You, *which Sw. has in another place where he quotes this verse.*

5339 'And in the seven years of abundance of corn the land yielded bunches' means initial states when series of truths were multiplied. This is clear from the meaning of 'seven years' as initial states (for seven years in which there was an abundance of corn came first, followed by seven years in which there was famine – 'years' meaning states, see 482, 487, 488, 493, 893); from the meaning of 'an abundance of corn' as a multiplication of truth, dealt with in 5276, 5280, 5292 ('the land yielded' meaning that this multiplication took place in the natural – 'the land' here being the natural, as immediately above in 5338); and from the meaning of 'bunches' as series.

The role which the series meant by 'bunches' play is this: With a person who is undergoing reformation general truths are introduced first, then the particular aspects of those general truths, and after that the specific details of these particular aspects. Particular aspects are ranged in order beneath general truths, and specific details beneath particular aspects, 2384, 3057, 4269, 4325(end), 4329(middle), 4345, 4383, 5208.

2   These arrays or ordered arrangements of truths are meant in the Word by bundles, which at this point are called handfuls or 'bunches'. They are nothing else than truths which have been multiplied and are then arrayed in or arranged into series. With people who are regenerate these series follow the same ordered patterns as those in which the communities in heaven exist; but in the case of those who are not regenerate and are incapable of becoming such they follow the patterns in which the communities in hell exist. Consequently a person who is governed by evil, and by falsity rooted in evil, is a miniature hell, whereas one who is governed by good, and by truth rooted in good, is a miniature heaven. But more, in the Lord's Divine mercy, will be stated elsewhere about these series.

5340 'And he gathered all the food of the seven years' means the preservation of truth linked to good, multiplied in the initial phases. This is clear from the meaning of 'gathering' here as preserving (for it says that he gathered it and laid it up in the cities, in the midst of them, which means that he stored it in the interior parts and thereby preserved it; for it was put to use in the years of famine); from the meaning of 'the food' as everything by which the internal man is nourished, namely good and truth, as may be recognized from the correspondence of earthly food which nourishes the external man with spiritual food which nourishes the internal man. Here therefore truth linked to good is meant, because this is what is preserved and stored away in a person's interior parts. 'Seven years' means the initial phases, when truths become multiplied, 5339. From all this it is evident that 'he gathered all the food of the seven years' means the preservation of truth linked to good, multiplied in the initial phases.

2   The expression 'the preservation of truth linked to good' is used, but because few are aware of what truth linked to good is, let alone of how and when truth becomes linked to good, let something therefore be said

about this. Truth comes to be joined to good when a person finds joy in doing good to his neighbour for truth and goodness' own sake, and not for any selfish or worldly reason. When that affection moves a person the truths he hears or reads or thinks about become joined to good; and this can usually be seen in an affection for truth which has that end in view.

5341 'Which were in the land of Egypt' means within the natural. This is clear from the meaning of 'the land of Egypt' as the natural mind, 5276, 5278, 5280, 5288, 5301, and so the natural itself.

5342 'And laid up food in the cities' means that it stored them – truths linked to good – in the interior parts. This is clear from the meaning here of 'laying up' as storing; from the meaning of 'food' as truth linked to good, dealt with just above in 5340; and from the meaning of 'the cities' as the interior parts of the natural mind, dealt with above in 5297. The idea that truths linked to good are stored in the interior parts of the natural mind, and are preserved there for use subsequently in life, in particular for use in temptations when a person is being regenerated, is an arcanum known to few at the present day. Therefore the nature of this arcanum must be stated. The seven years of abundance of corn mean the truths multiplied initially, and the storage of grain in the cities, in the midst of them, means that those truths linked to good were stored away in a person's interior parts. The seven years of famine and the sustainment provided by the bunches that had been gathered means the state of regeneration effected by means of the truths that had been linked to good and stored away in the interior parts.

The arcanum is this: During the time from earliest infancy through to early childhood a person is led by the Lord into heaven; indeed he is placed among celestial angels who serve to keep him in a state of innocence. This state which infants pass through until early childhood is a well-known one. At the beginning of childhood a gradual shedding of that state of innocence takes place; but even so, the person is kept in a state of charity through the charitable affection which he and his companions feel for one another. During this state, which with many people lasts through to adolescence, he is among spiritual angels. Because he begins at this time to think from what is within himself and to act in accordance with this, he cannot be kept any longer in charity, as he was previously; for now he calls on hereditary evils and allows them to lead him. Once this state has arrived the forms of the good of charity and innocence adopted by him previously are banished, to the extent that forms of evil are present in his thinking and are reinforced by his actions. Actually those forms of good are not banished but are withdrawn by the Lord to interior parts where they are stored away.

But because he does not as yet know any truths, those forms of the good of innocence and charity which he has adopted during those two states do not possess any qualities as yet; for truths give good its qualities, while good gives truths their essence. From this time of life onwards therefore he is being equipped with truths by means of the teaching he receives, and especially by means of his own thoughts about and consequent verification of those truths. Insofar as he is moved at this time by an affection for good, the Lord joins truths to good in him, 5340, and stores them away for [future] use. This is the state that is meant by the seven years of abundance of corn. These truths linked to good are the ones which in a proper sense are called remnants. In the measure therefore that a person allows himself to be regenerated, the remnants serve a useful purpose; for the Lord draws in the same measure on that store of remnants and returns them to the natural. As a result a correspondence of exterior things with interior ones, or natural things with spiritual ones, is brought about; and this happens in the state that is meant by 'the seven years of famine'. This is the arcanum.

4   At the present day the member of the Church thinks that no matter what anyone's life is like he can nevertheless by an act of mercy be accepted into heaven and enjoy eternal blessedness there; for the member of the Church imagines that it is simply a matter of being let in. But he is much mistaken, because no one can be let into heaven and find acceptance there unless he has acquired spiritual life, and no one can acquire spiritual life unless he is being regenerated, and no one can undergo regeneration except by means of goodness of life coupled to truth taught by doctrine. This is the way spiritual life is acquired by him. The fact that no one can enter heaven unless he has acquired spiritual life through regeneration is stated plainly by the Lord in John,

Truly, truly I say to you, Unless anyone is born again he cannot see the kingdom of God.   John 3:3.

And just after this,

Truly, truly I say to you, Unless a person has been born from water and the spirit he cannot enter the kingdom of God.   John 3:5.

'Water' is the truth taught by doctrine, 2702, 3058, 3424, 4976, and 'the spirit' is goodness of life. No one enters the kingdom simply through being baptized; rather, baptism is the sign denoting regeneration which the member of the Church should call to mind.

5343   'The food of the field of a city' means that these – the truths linked to good in the interior parts – were proper to and suitable for those interior parts. This is clear from the meaning of 'the food' as truths linked to good, dealt with in 5340, 5342. Truths proper to the interior parts and suitable for them are meant by 'the food of the field of a city' for the reason that the field belonged to the city and formed the area encircling it. In the internal sense the parts which form an encircling area mean what is suitable and proper. This is also why the statement 'which was round about it he laid up in the midst of it' comes next. The reason the parts forming an encircling area mean what is proper to and suitable for is that all truths joined to good exist arranged into series, and the nature of these series is such that truth joined to good is positioned in the middle or inmost part of each one; then truths that are proper to and suitable for that middle or inmost part are positioned around the same, continuing to the outermost part where the series disappears.

The actual series too are positioned in relation to one another in a similar kind of way. But such positionings vary in keeping with the changes of state that take place. It is quite normal in the next life for such arrangements of truths joined to good to present themselves in a visual manner; for in the light of heaven, which holds intelligence and wisdom within it, visual images can be used to present such things. The same cannot be done in the light of the world, nor can it be done in the light of heaven if a person's interior parts have not been opened, though he still has the ability to recognize them through rational insights and so see them by the use of reason in the light of heaven. These ordered arrangements of truths owe their origin to the ordered arrangements of the angelic communities in heaven; for in whatever way the angelic communities are arranged, so also with regenerate persons are the series of truths joined to good arranged, because these series of truths correspond to those angelic communities.

5344 'Which was round about it he laid up in the midst of it' means that what existed first in the exterior natural was stored away by it in the interior parts of the interior natural. This is clear from the meaning of 'round about' as things on the outside and so in the exterior natural; and from the meaning of 'the midst' as things on the inside, dealt with in 1074, 2940, 2973, and so in the interior natural. The reason 'in the midst of it (the city)' means in the interior parts of the interior natural is that 'a city' means the interior parts, 5297, 5342. The interior parts of the interior natural are those parts in it which are called spiritual ones, and the spiritual parts in it are those parts which belong to the light of heaven and are therefore able to shed light on the parts there which belong to the light of the world, which strictly speaking are called natural ones. It is in the spiritual parts of the interior natural that the truths linked to good have been stored away.

Those spiritual parts there are what correspond to the angelic communities in the second heaven, and a person is in communication with this heaven through his remnants. This heaven is the one that is opened when a person is being regenerated, and it is the one that is shut when a person does not allow himself to be regenerated. For remnants – that is, truths and forms of good stored away in interior parts – are nothing else than correspondences with the communities belonging to that heaven.

5345 'And Joseph stored up grain like the sand of the sea, very much' means a multiplication of truth derived from good. This is clear from the meaning here of 'storing up' as multiplying; from the meaning of 'grain' as truth present in will and action, dealt with in 5295, the multiplication of which, when likened to 'the sand of the sea', means that it is derived from good, in this case from the good of the celestial of the spiritual through the influx of this. For truth in the interior parts is multiplied from no other source than good. A multiplication of truth that does not spring from good is not a multiplication of truth, because it is not truth, no matter how much it looks in outward appearance like truth. It is like a lifeless statue; and because such truth is dead it comes nowhere near being truth. For if a person's truth is to be truth it must receive life from good, that is, through good from the Lord; and when it does receive life in that manner, that truth can be said in a spiritual sense to be multiplied. The fact that good is the only source which enables truth to be multiplied may be seen from the consideration that nothing can be multiplied except from something marriage-like. Truth cannot enter into marriage with anything else than good. If it does do so with anything else, that is not marriage but adultery. That which is a multiplication resulting from marriage is legitimate, and thus is truth; but that which is the result of adultery is not legitimate. It is spurious and thus is not truth.

5346 'Until he left off numbering, because it was beyond number' means such as holds the celestial from the Divine within it. This becomes clear from the fact that truth holding the celestial from the Divine within it is unbounded and beyond number. This kind of truth has existed with no one except the Lord, when He was in the world – the Lord being represented here by 'Joseph' and the glorification of His Natural being the subject here in the highest sense.

5347 Verses 50–52 **And to Joseph were born two sons before the year of the famine came, whom Asenath, the daughter of Potiphera the priest of On, bore to him. And Joseph called the name of the firstborn Manasseh – for God has made me forget all my labour and all my father's house. And the name of the second he called Ephraim – for God has made me fruitful in the land of my affliction.**
'And to Joseph were born two sons' means the good and truth born from this. 'Before the year of famine came' means which were born through the natural. 'Whom Asenath, the daughter of Potiphera the priest of On, bore to him' means which were born from the marriage. 'And Joseph called the name of the firstborn Manasseh' means a new area of will within the natural, and the essential nature of it. 'For God has made me forget all my labour' means a removal after temptations have finished. 'And all my father's house' means the removal of hereditary evils. 'And the name of the second he called Ephraim' means a new area of understanding within the natural, and the essential nature of it. 'For God has made me fruitful' means leading to a multiplication of truth from good. 'In the land of my affliction' means where the temptations were undergone.

5348   'And to Joseph were born two sons' means the good and truth born from this, that is to say, from the influx of the celestial of the spiritual into the natural. This is clear from the meaning of 'being born' as being reborn, and so the birth of truth derived from good or faith derived from charity, dealt with in 4070, 4668, 5160 (for the generations described in the Word are spiritual ones, see 1145, 1255, 1330, 3263, 3279, 3860, 3866); and from the meaning of 'sons', who in this case are Manasseh and Ephraim, as good and truth, dealt with immediately below. For 'Manasseh' means the area of will belonging to the new natural, while 'Ephraim' means the area of understanding belonging to it. Or what amounts to the same, 'Manasseh' means the good present in the new natural, since good exists as an attribute of the will, while 'Ephraim' means the truth present there, since truth exists as an attribute of the understanding. One reads in other places about the birth of two sons. Good is meant by one, truth by the other, as for instance with Esau and Jacob. 'Esau' means good, see 3302, 3322, 3494, 3504, 3576, 3599, while 'Jacob' means truth, 3305, 3509, 3525, 3546, 3576. The like is meant by Judah's two sons by Tamar, Perez and Zerah, 4927–4929; and the same applies here in the case of Manasseh and Ephraim. The birth of these is dealt with here because the subject in what went immediately before this was the influx of the celestial of the spiritual into the natural and the consequent rebirth of it, which is effected solely by means of good and truth.

5349   'Before the year of the famine came' means which were born through the natural. This is clear from the meaning of 'before the year of the famine came' as while the state lasted when truth derived from good was multiplied. This state is meant by 'the years of abundance of corn', and so that which came before the state of desolation meant by 'the years of famine'. Because in the state that came first truth derived from good was multiplied in the natural, so that good and truth were born to the celestial of the spiritual through the natural, that which followed as a consequence is therefore meant by the words used here.

5350   'Whom Asenath, the daughter of Potiphera the priest of On, bore to him' means which were born from the marriage. This becomes clear from what has been stated above in 5332.

5351   'And Joseph called the name of the firstborn Manasseh' means a new area of will within the natural, and the essential nature of it. This is clear from the representation of 'Manasseh' in the Word as spiritual good within the natural, and so a new area of will there, dealt with below. This name also implies the essential nature of that good or new area of will. The fact that the name implies the essential nature of this may be recognized from the names given to other people. An explanation of the essential nature accompanies each name, like that given for Manasseh in the following words, For God has made me forget all my labour and all my father's house. These words describe the essential nature of what is meant by 'Manasseh'. What is more, when the phrase 'he called the name' is used, the meaning is that the actual name too contains that essential nature, since 'name' and 'calling the name' mean the essential nature, 144, 145, 1754, 1896, 2009, 2724, 3006, 3421.

2   The reason why the firstborn who was given the name Manasseh means spiritual good within the natural, or a new area of will there, is that good is in actual fact the firstborn in the Church. That is, with someone who is in the process of becoming a Church, truth is not the firstborn, though it appears to be so, see 352, 367, 2435, 3325, 3494, 4925, 4926, 4928, 4930. The same may also be recognized from the consideration that a person's will takes precedence over his understanding; for the desires in a person's will are the primary constituents of his life, while the ideas in his understanding are secondary to them; and he acts in accordance with the desires of his will. What goes forth from the will is called good in the case of those who through regeneration have received from the Lord a new will; but it is called evil in the case of those who have had no wish to receive such. What goes forth from the understanding however is called truth in the case of the regenerate but falsity in the case of the unregenerate. But because no knowledge of a person's will is possible except through his understanding – for the understanding is the outward form that the will possesses or the outward form taken by the will which enables it to be known – people therefore imagine that truth which goes forth from the understanding is the firstborn. But this is nothing else than the appearance, for the reason that has been stated.

3   This explains the controversy that existed in former times over whether the truth which is the essence of faith was the firstborn of the Church or whether good which is the essence of charity was such. Those who based their conclusions on the appearance said that truth was the firstborn, whereas those who did not base theirs on the appearance acknowledged that good was. This also explains why at the present day people make faith the primary and absolutely essential constituent of the Church, but charity the secondary and non-essential element. But by supposing that faith alone is what saves a person they have sunk into far deeper error than the ancients. (In the Church faith is used to mean all the truth of doctrine, while charity is used to mean all the good of life.) They do, it is true, call charity and the works of charity the fruits of faith. Yet does anyone believe that those fruits make any contribution to salvation when the belief exists that someone can be saved by faith in the final hour of his life, no matter what kind of life he led before then? More than this, does anyone believe that those fruits contribute in any way to salvation when people use doctrine to set faith apart from works that are the product of charity, saying that faith alone saves without good works, or that works which are matters of life contribute nothing to salvation? Dear, dear! What kind of faith is that, and what kind of Church is it when people cherish faith that is dead and reject faith that is living? For faith without charity is like a body

without a soul. But a body without a soul is removed from sight and put away because it stinks, as everyone knows; and in the next life faith without charity is just like this. All who possessed faith so-called which was devoid of charity are in hell; but all who had charity are in heaven. For everyone's life remains with him, whereas doctrine does so only insofar as it draws on that life.

It is less easy to show from other places in the Word that 'Manasseh' means a new area of will within the natural – or what amounts to the same, spiritual good there – than it is to show that 'Ephraim' means a new area of understanding within the natural, or spiritual truth there. Even so, inferences can be drawn regarding the meaning of 'Manasseh' from what is said about 'Ephraim', because in the Word when two are mentioned together in the way these are, one means good, the other truth. Therefore Manasseh's meaning – spiritual good within the natural, which is the essence of the new will there – will be seen in what follows shortly where Ephraim is the subject.

5352 'For God has made me forget all my labour' means a removal after temptations have finished. This is clear from the meaning of 'forgetting' as removal, 5170, 5278; and from the meaning of 'labour' as conflicts, and so temptations. From these meanings one may see that 'God has made me forget all my labour' means a removal after temptations – a removal of the evils that caused distress. The fact that these things are meant is also evident from what is recorded about Joseph in the land of Canaan when among his brothers, and after that in Egypt. In the land of Canaan he was thrown into the pit and sold; in Egypt he served as a slave and was kept in prison for several years. Temptations were meant by those experiences, as has been shown already; and the fact that those experiences are what is meant by 'labour' is self-evident.

5353 'And all my father's house' means the removal of hereditary evils. This is clear from the meaning of 'father's house' here as hereditary evils. In the internal sense 'house' means a person, more particularly his mind, either his rational mind or his natural mind. But specifically the will part there is meant, consequently good or evil since either of these can exist as an attribute of the will, see 710, 2233, 2234, 3128, 4973, 4982, 5023. This being so, 'father's house' here means hereditary evils. The essential nature meant by 'Manasseh' is contained in these words and in those immediately before them. In the original language Manasseh means forgetfulness, and so in the internal sense a removal is meant. That is to say, a removal of evils, both those of one's own doing and those which are hereditary; for once those evils have been removed a new area of will arises. This new will comes into being through an inflow of good from the Lord. Such an inflow of good from the Lord takes place constantly with a person, but evils exist there – both those of his own doing and those which he has inherited – which hinder and stand in the way of the reception of it. But once these have been removed a new area of will comes into being. Its coming into being at this time is clearly evident with those who suffer misfortunes, tribulations, or illnesses. During these experiences self-love and love of the world from which all evils spring are removed, and then a person entertains thoughts about God and about the neighbour that are good, and also desires his neighbour's welfare. It is similar with temptations, which are spiritual forms of distress and therefore inward experiences of tribulation and of despair. These experiences serve primarily to remove evils, and after these have been removed heavenly good from the Lord enters in, from which a new area of will is formed in the natural, which in the representative sense is 'Manasseh'.

5354 'And the name of the second he called Ephraim' means a new area of understanding within the natural, and the essential nature of it. This is clear from the meaning of 'the name' and 'calling the name' as the essential nature, dealt with in 144, 145, 1754, 1896, 2009, 2724, 3006, 3421; and from the representation of 'Ephraim' as the area of understanding within the natural, dealt with below. What the new area of understanding and what the new area of will are, meant by 'Ephraim and Manasseh', must be stated first. It is indeed well known in the Church that a person must be born again, that is, be regenerated, so that he may enter the kingdom of God. This is well known because the Lord has declared it quite explicitly in John 3:3,5; yet what being born again implies is still known to only a few. And the reason for this is that few know what good and evil are. The reason people do not know what good and evil are is that they do not know what charity towards the neighbour is. If they did know what this was they would also know what good was, and from good what evil was; for everything is good that springs out of genuine charity towards the neighbour.

2   But with no one can this good have its origin in the person himself, for it is something utterly heavenly flowing into him from the Lord. This heavenly good is flowing in constantly, but evils and falsities stand in the way and prevent the reception of it. So that it may be received therefore it is necessary for the person to remove the evils and, so far as he possibly can do so, the falsities too, and thereby bring himself into a condition to receive that good flowing in. When, after evils have been removed, he accepts the inflow of good he acquires a new will and a new understanding. The new will enables him to feel a sense of delight in doing good to his neighbour without any selfish end in view, and the new understanding enables him to take delight in learning what goodness and truth are for their own sakes and for the sake of the life he should lead. Because this new understanding and new will are brought into being by what flows in from the Lord, the person who has been regenerated therefore acknowledges and believes that the goodness and truth for which he feels an affection do not originate in himself but in

the Lord, and also that what does originate in himself or is properly his own is nothing but evil.

From all this one may see what is meant by being born again, and also what is meant by a new will and a new understanding. But regeneration, which brings the new will and the new understanding into being, does not take place in a single instant. Rather, it is taking place from earliest childhood through to the final phase of life, and after that for ever in the next life; and it is accomplished by Divine means that are countless and beyond description. In himself the human being is nothing but evil which is constantly radiating from him as if from a furnace and is constantly trying to smother good while it is still being born. The removal of that kind of evil and the firm implantation of good in its place cannot be effected except through the whole course of a person's life; nor can it be effected except by Divine means which are countless and beyond description. At the present time scarcely anything is known about these means, for the reason that people do not allow themselves to be regenerated. Nor do they believe that regeneration is anything, because they do not believe in a life after death. The process by which regeneration takes place, a process involving things beyond description, constitutes the major part of angelic wisdom; and that process is of such a nature that no angel can ever completely exhaust all there is to know about it. This is the reason why in the internal sense of the Word it is the chief matter that is dealt with.

It is evident from very many places in the Word that 'Ephraim' means a new understanding within the natural, above all in the prophet Hosea, who makes many references to Ephraim, the following among them,

> I know *Ephraim*, and Israel is not hidden from Me, that you have altogether committed whoredom, O *Ephraim*; Israel has been defiled. Israel and *Ephraim* will collapse through their iniquity; Judah also will collapse with them. *Ephraim* will become a lonely place on the day of reproach[1]. And I will be like a moth to *Ephraim*, and like a worm to the house of Joseph. And *Ephraim* saw his sickness, and Judah his wound; and *Ephraim* went *to Assyria* and sent to King Jareb, and he could not cure you.   Hosea 5:3,5,9,11–13.

After this in the same prophet,

> When I healed Israel the iniquity of *Ephraim* was revealed, and the evils of Samaria; for they practised a lie, and a thief came, a band spread itself outside. And *Ephraim* was like a silly dove with no heart; they called on *Egypt*, they went away to *Assyria*. When they go I will stretch My net over them.
> Hosea 7:1,11,12 and following verses.

And further on in the same prophet,

> Israel has been swallowed up, now they are going to be among the gentiles, like a vessel in which there is no desire. When they went up to *Assyria* [they were like] a wild ass alone by himself; *Ephraim* procures lovers[2] with a prostitute's hire.   Hosea 8:8,9.

---

[1] Reading *correptionis* (reproach), *which Sw. has in another place, for* *correctionis* (correction)
[2] lit. loves

Israel will not dwell in Jehovah's land, but *Ephraim* will return to Egypt, and in *Assyria* they will eat what is unclean.   Hosea 9:3.

Ephraim has encompassed Me with a lie, and the house of Israel with deceit; and Judah will have dominion still with God and with the saints of the Faithful One[1]. *Ephraim* feeds the wind, and pursues the east wind. All the day long he multiplies lies and devastation and makes a covenant with *Assyria*, and oil is carried down into *Egypt*.   Hosea 11:12; 12:1.

6   Ephraim is referred to by this prophet in many other places besides these, such as Hosea 4:16–18; 5:3,5,9,11–13; 7:8,9; 9:8,11,13,16; 10:6,11; 11:3,8,9; 12:8,14; 13:1,12; 14:8. In all these places 'Ephraim' is used to mean the area of understanding within the Church, 'Israel' the spiritual area within it, and 'Judah' the celestial area. Also, since the area of understanding within the Church is meant by 'Ephraim', frequent reference is therefore made to Ephraim going away into Egypt or into Assyria. This is because 'Egypt' means factual knowledge and 'Assyria' reasonings based on this; and factual knowledge and reasonings are things associated with the understanding. For the meaning of 'Egypt' as factual knowledge, see 1164, 1165, 1186, 1462, 2588, 3325, 4749, 4964, 4966; and for that of 'Asshur' or 'Assyria' as reason or reasoning, 119, 1186.

7   The understanding area of the Church is meant in a similar way by 'Ephraim' in the following places: In Zechariah,

Exult greatly, O daughter of Zion! Make a noise, O daughter of Jerusalem! Behold, your king comes to you. *I will cut off the chariot from Ephraim*, and the horse from Jerusalem, and I will cut off the battle bow; on the other hand he will speak peace to the nations. And his dominion will be from sea to sea, and from the river even to the ends of the earth. I will bend Judah for Me, *I will fill Ephraim with the bow*; and I will rouse your sons, O Zion, together with your sons, O Javan.   Zech.9:9,10,13.

This refers to the Lord's Coming, also to the Church among the gentiles. 'Cutting off the chariot from Ephraim, and the horse from Jerusalem' stands for the entire understanding which the Church possesses. 'Filling Ephraim with the bow' stands for imparting a new understanding. For 'the chariot' means doctrinal teaching, see 5321; 'the horse' means the power of understanding, 2760–2762, 3217, 5321; and 'the bow' too means doctrinal teaching, 2685, 2686, 2709. Doctrinal teaching is dependent on the power of understanding, for to the extent that a person understands it, he believes it; his understanding of doctrinal teaching determines what his faith is like.

8   For this reason the children of Ephraim are called 'archers' in David,

The children of *Ephraim* who were armed (they were *archers*) turned back on the day of battle.   Ps.78:9.

In Ezekiel,

---

[1] *The Latin means* Israel, *but the Hebrew means* the Faithful One.

Son of man, take a stick and write on it, For Judah and for the children of Israel, his companions. Then take another stick and write on it, Joseph's – *the stick of Ephraim* and of the whole house of Israel, his companions. After that join them together, one to the other into one stick for you, that both may be one in your[1] hand. Behold, I am about to take the stick of Joseph which is in the hands of *Ephraim* and of the tribes of Israel his companions, and I will add them who are on it to the stick of Judah, and will make them into one stick, that they may be one stick in My hand.   Ezek.37:16,17,19.

Here also 'Judah' is used to mean the celestial area within the Church, 'Israel' the spiritual area within it, and 'Ephraim' the understanding area. The idea that these will be made one through the good of charity is meant by the promise that one stick will be made out of two. For 'a stick' means good which is the good of charity and of works motivated by charity, see 1110, 2784, 2812, 3720, 4943.
In Jeremiah,

It is a day [when] the watchman will cry *from mount Ephraim*, Arise, let us go up to Zion, to Jehovah our God. I will be a father to Israel, and *Ephraim* will be My firstborn.   Jer.31:6,9.

In the same prophet,

I have surely heard *Ephraim* bewailing, You have chastised me and I was chastised, like an unruly calf. Direct me, that I may be directed. Is not *Ephraim* a precious son to Me? Is he not a delightful child? For after I have spoken against him I will surely remember him again.   Jer.31:18,20.

In the same prophet,

I will bring back Israel to his own habitation so that he may feed on Carmel and Bashan; and *on mount Ephraim* and in Gilead his soul will be satisfied.   Jer.50:19.

In Isaiah,

Woe to the crown of pride, to *the drunkards of Ephraim*, to the falling flower and the glory of its beauty, which is on the head of a valley of fat ones confused by wine.   Isa.28:1.

o In all these places too 'Ephraim' means the area of understanding within the Church. The area of understanding within the Church is that understanding which members of the Church have about truth and goodness, that is, about matters of doctrine regarding faith and charity. Thus it is the notions, conceptions, or ideas which they possess about these matters. Truth forms the spiritual area of the Church, and good the celestial area. But one member's understanding of truth and goodness is different from another's, and therefore the nature of each member's understanding of truth determines the kind of truth known to him. And the same is so with each person's understanding of goodness.

1 What the Church's area of will, meant by 'Manasseh', is exactly can be recognized from the area of understanding, which is 'Ephraim'. The

---

[1] *The Latin means* My, *but the Hebrew means* your.

nature of the Church's will is similar to that of its understanding in that it varies from one member to another. 'Manasseh' means that area of will in Isaiah,

Through the wrath of Jehovah Zebaoth the earth has been darkened, and the people have become as fuel for the fire; a man will not spare his brother. A man will eat the flesh of his own arm; *Manasseh* [will consume] *Ephraim*, and *Ephraim Manasseh*, and together they are against Judah.   Isa.9:19–21.

'A man will eat the flesh of his own arm, Manasseh [will consume] Ephraim, and Ephraim Manasseh' stands for the member of the Church when his will acts in opposition to the activity of his understanding, and his understanding acts in opposition to the activity of his will.

12 In David,

God has spoken by means of His holiness, I will exalt, I will divide up Shechem and portion out the valley of Succoth. Gilead is Mine, and *Manasseh* is Mine; and *Ephraim* is the strength of My head.   Ps.60:6,7.

In the same author,

Turn Your ear, O Shepherd of Israel, You who lead[1] Joseph like a flock; You who are seated upon the cherubim, shine forth. *Before Ephraim* and Benjamin and *Manasseh* stir up Your power.   Ps.80:1,2.

Here also 'Ephraim' stands for the area of understanding within the Church and 'Manasseh' for the area of will there. The same meaning is also evident from the blessing of Ephraim and Manasseh by Jacob before he died, and in addition from the fact that Jacob accepted Ephraim in place of Reuben, and Manasseh in place of Simeon, Gen.48:3,5. For Reuben had represented the Church's area of understanding, which is faith in the understanding, or doctrine, 3861, 3866. Also, Simeon had represented faith in action – or obedience and the will to put truth into practice – from which charity springs and through which charity expresses itself; thus he represented truth realized in action, which is good belonging to the new will, 3869–3872.

13 The reason why Jacob, who by then was Israel, blessed Ephraim more fully than Manasseh, by placing his right hand on the former and his left on the latter, Gen.48:13–20, was the same as the one involved in Jacob's procurement for himself of Esau's birthright. It was also the same as what was involved in the birth of Perez and Zerah, Judah's sons by Tamar; though he was the firstborn, Zerah nevertheless came out after Perez, Gen.38:28–30. The reason this happened was that the truth of faith, which belongs to the understanding, seems to occupy the first place while a person is being regenerated, and the good of charity, which belongs to the will, seems to occupy the second. But in actual fact good occupies the first place, as is plain to see once the person has been regenerated. On this subject, see 3324, 3539, 3548, 3556, 3563, 3570, 3576, 3603, 3701, 4243, 4244, 4247, 4337, 4925, 4926, 4928, 4930, 4977.

---

[1] *The Latin means* He who leads, *but the Hebrew means* You who lead.

5355   'For God has made me fruitful' means leading to a multiplication of truth from good. This is clear from the meaning of 'making fruitful' as a multiplication, that is to say, of truth from good, for fruitfulness is used in reference to good and multiplication to truth, 43, 55, 913, 983, 1940, 2846, 2847. In the original language the name Ephraim is derived from a word meaning fruitfulness, the essential nature of which is contained in the statement 'for God has made me fruitful in the land of my affliction'. That essential nature is one in which truth from good in the natural has been multiplied after the temptations undergone there have come to an end. But a brief description of what a multiplication of truth from good is must be given. When good, that is, love towards the neighbour, is present in a person, so also is the love of truth. Consequently, insofar as that good is present he feels an affection for truth, since good exists within truth like the soul within its body.

In the measure therefore that good multiplies truth it reproduces itself; and if it is the good of genuine charity it reproduces itself endlessly within truth and through truth. For there is no limit either to good or to truth; the Infinite is present within every single form of truth or good because each one has its origin in the Infinite. Yet that endless quality cannot ever match up to the Infinite itself, for what is limited or finite cannot be compared with the Infinite. In the Church at the present day scarcely any multiplication of truth takes place. The reason for this is that at the present day the good of genuine charity is non-existent. The Church believes that it is enough if a person knows simply the tenets of the Church within which he is born and in various ways firmly assents to these. But one with whom the good of genuine charity exists and who consequently feels an affection for truth is not content with that but wishes to clarify from the Word what the truth is and to see it before firmly assenting to it. Also, it is good that enables him to see it, for the discernment of truth originates in good, the Lord being within that good and imparting such discernment. When the person receives truth from Him he increases it to an unlimited extent. This may be likened to a tiny seed which grows into a tree and produces more tiny seeds, which then grow into a garden, and so on beyond that.

5356   'In the land of my affliction' means where the temptations were undergone. This is clear from the meaning of 'the land', in this case the land of Egypt, as the natural, dealt with in 5276, 5278, 5280, 5288, 5301; and from the meaning of 'affliction' as temptation, dealt with in 1846. From these meanings it is evident that 'in the land of my affliction' means in the natural where the temptations were undergone and therefore the place where truth from good was multiplied. Since that fruitfulness, or multiplication of truth from good, is brought about primarily by means of temptations, such words have therefore been used here. The reason why fruitfulness is brought about primarily by means of temptations is that temptations take away self-love and love of the world, and so evils too; and once these have been taken away, an affection for goodness and truth from the Lord flows in, see just above in 5354.

2   Another thing temptations do is to provide a person with the kind of discernment he has about what is good and true; they provide it through the opposites that evil spirits introduce at such times. From his discernment of those opposites a person can make comparisons which enable him to see what the whole is like. For no one can know what good is unless he also knows what is not good; and he does not know what truth is unless he knows what is not true. Also, temptations serve to strengthen goods and truths; for in temptations a person battles against evils and falsities, and through being victorious in such he goes on to hold on more firmly to those goods and truths. In addition to this temptations also serve to subdue evils and falsities so completely that they do not dare to rise up again. Thus temptations serve to cast evils and falsities away to the fringes, where they hang downwards, in a limp condition. But forms of good together with truths are in the centre, and in the measure that the zeal of genuine affection is present they are raised upwards – up to heaven, towards the Lord who does the raising up.

5357   Verses 53–57 **And the seven years of abundance of corn ended, which was in the land of Egypt. And the seven years of famine began to come, even as Joseph had said; and the famine was in all lands, and in all the land of Egypt there was bread. And all the land of Egypt suffered famine, and the people cried out to Pharaoh for bread. And Pharaoh said to all Egypt, Go to Joseph; do what he tells you. And the famine was over all the face of the earth; and Joseph opened all the places in which [there was grain] and sold to Egypt. And the famine was becoming great in the land of Egypt. And all the earth came to Egypt to buy [grain], to Joseph; for the famine became great in all the earth.**

'And the seven years of abundance of corn ended' means those states during which truth was multiplied. 'Which was in the land of Egypt' means within the natural. 'And the seven years of famine began to come' means the subsequent states of desolation. 'Even as Joseph had said' means as was foreseen by the celestial of the spiritual. 'And the famine was in all lands' means a desolation everywhere in the natural. 'And in all the land of Egypt there was bread' means the remnants of the truths from good that have been multiplied. 'And all the land of Egypt suffered famine' means desolation in both parts of the natural. 'And the people cried out to Pharaoh for bread' means the need of good which was felt by truth. 'And Pharaoh said to all Egypt' means a discernment. 'Go to Joseph' means that the celestial of the spiritual is the supplier of it. 'Do what he tells you' means provided that obedience exists. 'And the famine was over all the face of the earth' means when there was desolation even to the point of despair. 'And Joseph opened all the places in which [there was grain]' means a communication of remnants. 'And sold to Egypt' means a making over to. 'And the famine was becoming great in the land of Egypt' means an increasing severity. 'And all the earth came to Egypt' means that forms of truth and good were gathered into the facts known to the Church. 'To buy [grain]' means a making one's own. 'To Joseph' means where the celestial of the spiritual was. 'For the famine became great in all the earth' means that, apart from there, desolation existed everywhere in the natural.

5358   'And the seven years of abundance of corn ended' means after those states during which truth was multiplied. This is clear from the matters explained above in 5276, 5292, 5339, where similar words occur.

5359   'Which was in the land of Egypt' means within the natural. This is clear from the meaning of 'the land of Egypt' as the natural, dealt with in 5080, 5095, 5276, 5278, 5280, 5288.

5360   'And the seven years of famine began to come' means the subsequent states of desolation. This is clear from the meaning of 'years' as states, dealt with in 482, 487, 488, 493, 893; and from the meaning of 'famine' as an absence of cognitions of truth and good, dealt with in 1460, 3364, and consequently a desolation. The reason 'famine' means that absence of them, or a desolation, is that celestial and spiritual food consists in nothing else than goodness and truth. These are the food with which angels and spirits are fed and which they long for when they are hungry and thirst for when they are thirsty, and to which also material kinds of food therefore correspond. Bread corresponds to celestial love, wine to spiritual love, as does everything else which is a form of 'bread', meaning food, or of 'wine', meaning drink. When therefore these kinds of nourishment are lacking a famine exists, which in the Word is called desolation and vastation, desolation being when there is a lack of truths, vastation when there is a lack of forms of good.

Such desolation and vastation are spoken about in many places in the Word, where they are described as a desolation of the earth, kingdoms, cities, nations, or peoples. The same condition is also referred to as an emptying out, a cutting off, a bringing to a close, a wilderness, or a void, while the actual state is called the great day of Jehovah, the day of His wrath and vengeance, the day of darkness and thick darkness, of cloud and obscurity, the day of visitation, also the day when the earth will be destroyed, and so the last day or judgement day. But because people have not understood the internal sense of the Word they have imagined up to now that this is a day when the earth will be destroyed, at which point the resurrection and the judgement will begin to take place. Such people do not know that 'day' in this case means a state, and 'the earth' the Church, so that 'the day when the earth will be destroyed' means a state when the Church will pass away. In the Word therefore, when this passing away is referred to, a new earth is also mentioned, by which a new Church is meant, regarding which new earth together with a new heaven, see 1733, 1850, 2117, 2118(end), 3355(end), 4535. That final state of a Church which comes before the state of a new Church is meant and described in the Word, strictly speaking, by vastation and desolation. But desolation and vastation are also used to describe the state which comes before a person's regeneration; and that is the state meant here by 'the seven years of famine'.

5361 'Even as Joseph had said' means as was foreseen by the celestial of the spiritual. This is clear from the meaning of 'saying' in the historical narratives of the Word as perceiving, often dealt with in previous explanations, and therefore – when used in reference to the Lord, who is 'Joseph' here – perceiving from within Himself, and so foreseeing, is meant; and from the representation of 'Joseph' as the celestial of the spiritual, dealt with in 5249, 5307, 5331, 5332.

5362 'And the famine was in all lands' means a desolation everywhere in the natural. This is clear from the meaning of 'famine' as a desolation, dealt with above in 5360, and from the meaning of 'all lands' as everywhere in the natural. For 'land' or 'earth' is the natural mind, and so the natural itself, see 5276, 5278, 5280, 5288, 5301.

5363 'And in all the land of Egypt there was bread' means the remnants of the truths from good that have been multiplied. This is clear from the fact that 'bread in all the land of Egypt' is used to mean the grain which was gathered together in the seven years of abundance of corn and stored in the cities. This grain, as stated and shown in various places above, means the remnants stored away in the interior parts of the natural mind, and therefore 'bread in all the land of Egypt' means the remnants of the truths from good that have been multiplied. That remnants are meant here by 'bread in the land of Egypt' is in addition evident from the fact that the years of famine had already begun, years in which the land of Egypt suffered just as much as the rest of the earth did (except that it had grain laid aside, whereas the rest of the world did not), on account of which the statement 'And all the land of Egypt suffered famine' immediately follows.

5364 'And all the land of Egypt suffered famine' means a desolation in both parts of the natural. This is clear from the meaning of 'famine' as a desolation, dealt with above in 5360, 5362; and from the meaning of 'all the land of Egypt' as both parts of the natural, dealt with in 5276.

5365 'And the people cried out to Pharaoh for bread' means the need of good which was felt by truth. This is clear from the meaning of 'crying out' as the expression of someone enduring pain and grief, and so of someone in need; from the meaning of 'people' as truth, dealt with in 1259, 1260, 3295, 3581; from the representation of 'Pharaoh' as the natural, dealt with in 5079, 5080, 5095, 5160; and from the meaning of 'bread' as the celestial element of love, and so good, dealt with in 276,

680, 2165, 2177, 3464, 3478, 3735, 3813, 4211, 4217, 4735, 4976. From these meanings it follows that 'the people cried out to Pharaoh for bread' means the need of good that was felt by truth in the natural. This meaning seems, it is true, to be remote from the historical sense of the letter. Nevertheless, since people acquainted with the internal sense understand 'crying out', 'the people', 'Pharaoh', and 'bread' in no other way than mentioned above, such is the meaning that emerges from those words.

What is implied by the need of good which was felt by truth must be stated. Truth has a need of good, and good has a need of truth; also, when truth has a need of good, truth is joined to good, and when good has a need of truth, good is joined to truth. The reciprocal joining together of good and truth – that is to say, the joining of truth to good, and of good to truth – is the heavenly marriage. During the initial phases when a person is being regenerated truth is multiplied, but good less so. And because at these times truth has no good to which it is joined, truth is therefore drawn into and deposited within the interior parts of the natural, so that it may be called forth from there in the measure that good is increased. In this state truth stands in need of good, and in the measure that good enters the natural a joining of truth to good is effected. Even so, this joining together does not lead to any fruitfulness. But once the person has been regenerated good increases, and as it does so it stands in need of truth and also acquires truth to itself and becomes joined to it. This is a joining of good to truth, and when this takes place truth is made fruitful by good, and good by truth.

This process is one about which people in the world are totally ignorant, whereas those in heaven have a very good knowledge of it. If people in the world however knew, and not only knew but also had a perception of what celestial love or love to the Lord was, and what spiritual love or charity towards the neighbour was, they would also know what good was; for all good is the object of those loves. Above all they would know that good had a desire for truth, and truth had a desire for good, and that this desire and the essential nature of it determine the extent to which the two are joined together. Such would be evident to them from the fact that whenever they are thinking about truth, good presents itself linked together with that truth; and when good is stimulated, truth presents itself linked together with that good. And whenever both present themselves together they are accompanied by affection, desire, delight, or sacred yearning, from which they would then know what the joining together was essentially like. But because no knowledge is acquired by them as a result of an inner awareness or perception of what good is, such matters do not begin to be recognized by them. For what people know nothing about is unintelligible to them even if it happens to them.

Also, because people are ignorant of what spiritual good is – that it is charity towards the neighbour – controversy therefore exists in the world, especially among the learned, over what the highest good may be. Scarcely anyone says[1] it is the feeling of delight, bliss, blessedness, and happiness which flows from mutual love that does not have any selfish or worldly end in view attached to it and which constitutes heaven itself. From this it is also evident that the world at the present day knows nothing at all about what spiritual good is. Still less does it know that good and truth form themselves into a marriage, or that heaven consists in this marriage, or that those in whom the marriage exists possess wisdom and intelligence, or that they enjoy feelings of bliss and happiness in endless, indescribable variety. The world knows nothing about even a single one of those variations; consequently it neither acknowledges nor believes that any such thing exists, when in fact it is heaven itself or heavenly joy itself, about which the Church has so much to say.

5366   'And Pharaoh said to all Egypt' means a discernment. This is clear from the meaning of 'saying' in the historical narratives of the Word as perceiving, dealt with in 1791, 1815, 1819, 1822, 1898, 1919, 2061, 2080, 2862, 3395, 3509; from the representation of 'Pharaoh' as the natural in general, dealt with in 5160; and from the meaning of 'all Egypt' as both parts of the natural, dealt with in 5276, 5364. From these meanings it is evident that 'Pharaoh said to all Egypt' means a discernment in both parts of the natural in general and in particular.

5367   'Go to Joseph' means that the celestial of the spiritual is the supplier of it. This is clear from the representation of 'Joseph' as the celestial of the spiritual, often dealt with already. 'Going to him' means that this is the supplier of it, that is to say, of the good needed by truth, that need being meant by the people's cry to Pharaoh for bread, 5365.

5368   'Do what he tells you' means provided that obedience exists. This is clear from the meaning of 'doing what someone says' as being obedient. The meaning of this is that good becomes linked to truth in the natural provided that the natural conforms and is obedient. But something must also be said about such a conformity and obedience on the part of the natural. People absorbed solely in worldly interests, more so those absorbed in bodily interests, and more so still those absorbed in earthly ones cannot grasp what is meant by the need for the natural to conform and be obedient. They imagine that what is going on inside a person is the same throughout; thus they do not think of one part within him that commands and another part that obeys.

2   Yet within him there is an internal man that ought to command and an external man that ought to obey. The latter is obedient when it does not have the world but heaven, not self but the neighbour, as its end in view, consequently when bodily and worldly matters are thought of as means and not as an end. Such are thought of as means and not an end when that person loves his neighbour more than himself, and the

---

[1] *Reading* dicit (says), *which Sw. has in his rough draft, for* dixit (has said)

things of heaven more than those of the world. When this is so the natural is obedient, the natural being the same as the external man.

5369   'And the famine was over all the face of the earth' means when there was desolation even to the point of despair. This is clear from the meaning of 'famine' as desolation, dealt with above in 5360, 5362, 5364; and from the meaning of 'the earth' as the natural. When a famine is said to be 'over all the face of the earth' despair is meant, because in that case the desolation exists everywhere. For the fullest and uttermost degree of desolation is despair, 5279, 5280.

5370   'And Joseph opened all the places in which [there was grain]' means a communication of remnants. This is clear from the meaning here of 'opening' as communicating. 'All the places in which' are the storehouses where grain was kept and by which remnants are meant, as stated several times above. For remnants are forms of good and truth stored away by the Lord in interior parts, see 468, 530, 560, 561, 660, 661, 798, 1050, 1738, 1906, 2284, 5135, 5342, 5344.

5371   'And sold to Egypt' means a making over to. This is clear from the meaning of 'selling' as making over to another as his own, for that which is sold becomes the property of the one who buys it. That 'selling' and 'buying' mean a making over to or a making one's own will be seen below in 5374.

5372   'And the famine was becoming great in the land of Egypt' means an increasing severity, that is to say, of the desolation. This is clear from the meaning of 'the famine' and 'the land of Egypt' as a desolation within the natural, the increasing severity of which is meant by its 'becoming great'.

5373   'And all the earth came to Egypt' means that forms of good and truth were gathered into the facts known to the Church. This is clear from the meaning of 'the earth'. In the Word 'the earth' has various meanings, but in general it means the Church and also the things that constitute the Church, which are forms of good and truth. Also, because 'the earth' (or 'the land') means the Church it means the member of the Church as well since he is a Church on a particular level. And meaning a member of the Church, 'the earth' (or 'the land') means that which exists within him, namely his mind, which is why in various places above 'the land of Egypt' has meant the natural mind. Here however it is not the land of Egypt but the earth in general that is being referred to, and therefore those things that constitute the Church, which are forms of good and truth, are meant. For more about 'the earth' having various meanings, see 620, 636, 2571; but in general it means the Church, 566, 662, 1067, 1262, 1413, 1607, 1733, 1850, 2117, 2118(end), 2928, 3355, 3404, 4447, 4535.

2   As regards the phrase 'all the earth came to Egypt' meaning that forms of good and truth were gathered into the facts known to the Church,

this is clear from the meaning of 'Egypt' in its proper sense as knowledge, and then as known facts, see 1164, 1165, 1186, 1462; and the facts meant by 'Egypt' in the good sense are the facts that are known to the Church, 4749, 4964, 4966. It is indeed evident from the meaning of the expressions that are used – from the meaning of 'the earth' or 'the land' when this is used not for simply the land of Egypt, and also from the meaning of 'Egypt' in its proper sense – that such is the internal meaning of 'all the earth came to Egypt'. And it is also evident from the fact that the verb 'came' in this phrase is plural. But in addition to this it is evident from the actual sequence of ideas present in the internal sense. For there now follows in that sequence of ideas the thought that the forms of truth and good constituting the remnants are gathered into known facts.

3 For the situation is this: When a person's natural is being regenerated every single form of good and truth is gathered into the known facts there. Any that are not present within these facts are not in the natural. This is because that part of the natural mind which is subject to the understanding part is made up solely of factual knowledge; and this knowledge present in the natural is the last and lowest degree of order. To come forth and manifest themselves in that sphere things that are prior must exist within ones that are last and lowest. More than this, prior things all extend into their last and lowest forms which serve them as their boundaries or final limits. Prior things come into being simultaneously on that lowest level, in the same way as causes do within their effects, or as higher objects do within lower ones that serve as vessels to contain them. The known facts present in the natural are such last and lowest things. This being so, the final limit that holds the spiritual world within it is man's natural, in which things existing in the spiritual world reveal themselves in the form of representations. If spiritual things did not reveal themselves within the natural in the form of representations, thus with the help of such things as exist in the world, no one could have any awareness of them at all. From these considerations one may see that when the natural is being regenerated every form of interior truth and good which has its origin in the spiritual world is gathered into known facts to enable it to manifest itself.

5374 'To buy [grain]' means a making one's own. This is clear from the meaning of 'buying' as acquiring to oneself and so making one's own. Spiritually, acquiring and making one's own is effected by means of good and truth, to which the acquisition and ownership that are achieved in the world by the payment of silver and gold correspond; for in the spiritual sense 'silver' is truth, and 'gold' is good. Consequently 'buying' means a making one's own, as it also does in the following places in the Word: In Isaiah,

Everyone who thirsts, come to the waters, and he who has no money, come, *buy*, and eat! And come, *buy* wine and milk without money and without price. Isa.55:1.

Also in Jeremiah 13:1,2,11. In Matthew,

The kingdom of heaven is like treasure hidden in a field, which a man (*homo*) finds and hides, and in his joy he goes and sells whatever he has and *buys that field*. Again, the kingdom of heaven is like a trader seeking fine pearls, who, having found one pearl of great price, went and sold all that he had and *bought it*.   Matt.13:44-46.

And in the same gospel,

The wise virgins said to the foolish ones, Go *to those who sell* and *buy oil for yourselves*. While they were going *to buy*, the Bridegroom came.   Matt.25:9,10.

Because 'buying' meant a making one's own, a clear distinction is made in the Word between things bought with silver and those acquired in some other way. Slaves bought with silver were so to speak the buyer's own, and were like those born in the house, but in a lower degree. This also explains why the two are mentioned together in various places, as in the command in Gen.17:3, '*He who is born in your house* and *he who is bought with your silver* must be circumcised', or as in Lev.22:11, 'If a priest *buys* a person[1] – *a buying with silver* – [this person] and *one who is born in the house* shall eat of his bread'. From this one may see what is meant in the Word by 'the redeemed of Jehovah'[2], namely those who have acquired good and truth, thus those to whom things that are the Lord's have been made over as their own.

5375   'To Joseph' means where the celestial of the spiritual was. This is clear from the representation of 'Joseph' as the celestial of the spiritual, often dealt with already. The celestial of the spiritual is the good of truth from the Divine.

5376   'For the famine became great in all the earth' means that, apart from there, desolation existed everywhere in the natural. This is clear from the meaning of 'famine' as a desolation, dealt with previously; and from the meaning of 'the earth' as the natural, also dealt with previously. The idea that everywhere apart from there is meant, that is to say, apart from within the known facts where the celestial of the spiritual was, follows from what has gone immediately before. What the desolation of the natural, or the deprivation of truth there, is like has been stated already; yet as this is dealt with further still in what follows, let the nature of it be mentioned once again. From earliest childhood the person born within the Church learns from the Word and from the teachings of the Church what the truth of faith is and what the good of charity is. But when he grows up he begins either to confirm for himself or else to refuse to accept the truths of faith he has learned; for now he looks at them for himself and in so doing either makes those

[1] *lit.* soul
[2] *lit.* the bought back ones of Jehovah

truths his own or else casts them aside. For no truth can be made over to another person as his own unless he looks at it and accepts it for himself, that is, unless he knows for himself that it is true and does not rely simply on someone else. The truths therefore which he absorbed in childhood cannot enter any more deeply into his life than the outer gate, where they can either be let inside or else cast away outside.

2 With those who are being regenerated, that is, those who, as the Lord foresees, will allow themselves to be regenerated, those truths are multiplied exceedingly; for these people have an affection for knowing truths. But as they draw nearer to the point when their regeneration is actually carried out they are seemingly deprived of those truths. For those truths are withdrawn to a more interior position, and when this happens the person seems to experience desolation. Nevertheless those truths are returned in consecutive stages to the natural, where they are joined to good while the person is being regenerated. With those who are not being regenerated however, that is, those who, as the Lord foresees, will not allow themselves to be regenerated, truths are indeed usually multiplied, since these people possess an affection for knowing such truths for the sake of their own reputation, position, and gain. But as they advance in years and come to look at those truths for themselves, they either do not believe them, refuse to accept them, or else turn them into falsities. Thus in their case truths are not withdrawn to a more interior position but are cast away outside, though they remain in the memory to serve worldly ends, devoid of all life. In the Word this state is called desolation or vastation, though it differs from the state described first, in that the desolation belonging to that first state is only apparent, whereas the desolation belonging to the second state is total. For in the state described first the person is not deprived of truths, whereas in this latter state he is deprived of them altogether. The desolation belonging to the state described first is the subject in the internal sense of the present chapter and is again the subject in the next one; and that desolation is meant by a famine lasting for seven years.

3 This kind of desolation is referred to many times elsewhere in the Word, as in Isaiah,

Stir, stir, O Jerusalem, you who *have drunk from the hand of Jehovah the cup of His anger*. Two things have come upon you; who condoles with you? *Vastation* and *ruination, famine* and *sword*, who is there that I may comfort you? Your sons fainted, they lay at the head of every street. Therefore listen, do this, O afflicted one, and drunk though not from wine. Behold, I have taken out of your hand *the cup of trepidation, the dregs of the cup of* My *wrath*; you shall no longer drink it. But I will put it in the hand of those who oppress you. Isa.51:17–end.

This is a description of the state of desolation experienced by a member of the Church who is becoming a Church, that is, who is being regenerated. That desolation is called 'vastation, ruination, famine, and sword', also 'the cup of Jehovah's anger and wrath', and 'the cup of trepidation'. The truths that a person is deprived of at such times are 'the sons who faint and lie at the head of every street'. For 'sons' are truths, see 489, 491, 533, 1147, 2623, 2803, 2813, 3373, 'street' the place where the truths are, 2336; consequently 'lying at the head of every street' means that truths appear to exist in a dispersed condition. One can see that the desolation is only an apparent one and that regeneration is effected by means of it, as it also is by means of temptations; for it says that [Jerusalem] will no longer drink the cup but that [Jehovah] will put it in the hand of those who oppress her.

In Ezekiel,

Thus said the Lord Jehovih, Because they *devastated* you and *swallowed* you up from all around, so that you are an inheritance for the rest of the nations, therefore, O mountains of Israel, hear the word of the Lord Jehovih. Thus said the Lord Jehovih to the mountains and hills, the streams and valleys, and *the desolate wastes*, and *the deserted cities*, which became plunder and a derision to the rest of the nations all around: I have spoken in My zeal and in My wrath, because you have endured the shame of the nations. Surely the nations that are around you will bear their own shame. But you, O mountains of Israel, will shoot forth[1] your branches and yield your fruit to My people Israel. For behold, I am with you, and will turn to you, so that you are tilled and sown. Also I will multiply man (*homo*) upon you, the entire house of Israel; and *the cities will be inhabited*, and *the waste places will be built*. I will resettle you[2] to be as you were in former times and I will do more good than in your early days.   Ezek.36:3–12.

This too refers to the desolation that comes just before regeneration. That desolation is meant by 'the desolate wastes and the deserted cities, which became plunder and a derision', while such regeneration is meant by 'shooting forth a branch and yielding fruit', 'turning to them, so that they are tilled and sown', 'so that man is multiplied, cities inhabited, and waste places built', and 'resettling them to be as they were in former times, and doing more good to them than in their early days'.

What desolation is like is evident from those experiencing it in the next life. Those who experience desolation there are harried by evil spirits and genii; for these pour in evil desires and false ideas which are so strong that those people are almost submerged in them. As a consequence truths are not visible; but then as the time of desolation comes to an end those truths are lit up by light received from heaven, and the evil spirits and genii are driven away, each to his own hell, where they undergo punishments. Those punishments are what is meant by 'cities which became plunder and a derision to the rest of the nations all around' and by 'the nations that are around will bear their own shame'. Such punishments are also meant by 'the cup will be put in the hand of those who oppress you', in the passage quoted above from Isaiah, as well as in another place in the same prophet, where it says that 'the one who lays waste will be laid waste', Isa.33:1. And in Jeremiah,

I will visit those who lay waste, and I will consign them to everlasting desolations.   Jer.25:12.

---

[1] *lit.* give
[2] *lit.* I will cause you to inhabit

In Isaiah,

Your destroyers will hasten your sons, and *those who lay you waste* will go away from you. Lift up your eyes round about and see; they all gather together, they come to you. Because of *your waste places* and your desolate places, and *the land of your destruction*, you will be too restricted for the inhabitants; *those who swallow you up will have gone far away.* Isa.49:17–19.

6 These verses too, indeed that whole chapter in Isaiah, refer to the desolation suffered by those who are being regenerated, and to the regeneration and fruitfulness that follow desolation, verse 26 referring at length to the punishment of those who have been the oppressors. In the same prophet,

Woe to you who lay waste, though you have not been laid waste; when *you finish laying waste, you will be laid waste.* Isa.33:1.

This refers to the punishment of those who lay waste, as above. In the same prophet,

Let *My outcasts* dwell together in you; O Moab, be a refuge to them *in the presence of the one who lays waste.* For *the oppressor* has ceased, *vastation* has come to an end. Isa.16:4.

In the same prophet,

The day of Jehovah is near; like *vastation* from Shaddai it will come. Isa.13:6.

'Vastation from Shaddai' stands for vastation in temptations. For in ancient times God, when involved in temptations, was called Shaddai, see 1992, 3667, 4572.

7 In the same prophet,

At that time they will not thirst; *in the waste places* He will lead them; He will make water flow for them from the rock, and He will cleave the rock so that water flows out. Isa.48:21.

This has to do with the state that follows desolation. In the same prophet,

Jehovah will comfort Zion, He will comfort *all her waste places*, so much so that He will make *her wilderness* like Eden and *her desert* like the garden of Jehovah. Gladness and joy will be found in her, confession and the voice of song. Isa.51:3.

Here the meaning is similar, for as stated above, desolation occurs to the end that a person may be regenerated, that is, to the end that evils and falsities may first be separated from him and then truths may be joined to forms of good, and forms of good to truths. The regenerate person so far as good is concerned is the one who is being compared to Eden, and so far as truth is concerned to the garden of Jehovah. In David,

Jehovah caused me to come up *out of the pit of devastation*, out of the miry clay, and He set my feet upon a rock. Ps.40:2.

8 The vastation and desolation suffered by a member of the Church, or by the Church residing with him, was represented by the captivity of the

Jewish people in Babel, while the resurgence of the Church was represented by their return from that captivity, dealt with in various places in Jeremiah, especially in Chapter 32:37–end. Desolation is a captivity, for at that time a person is held so to speak in bonds, for which reason also 'the bound', 'those in prison', or 'those in the pit' mean those experiencing desolation, see 4728, 4744, 5037, 5038, 5085, 5096.

Reference to a state of desolation and vastation among those who are not being regenerated is also made in various places in the Word. It is a state passed through by those who utterly deny truths or else turn them into falsities; it is the state which the Church passes through around the time of its end, when there is no faith and no charity any longer. In Isaiah,

I will cause you to know what I am about to do to My vineyard, by taking away its hedge, so that it is destroyed[1], and by breaking down its wall, so that it is trodden down. *I will after that make it a desolation*; it will not be pruned or hoed, so that bramble and shrub will come up there; indeed I will command the clouds to rain no rain on it. Isa.5:5–7.

In the same prophet,

Say to this people, Hearing, hear – but do not understand; and seeing, see – but do not comprehend. Make the heart of this people fat and their ears heavy, and plaster over their eyes, lest they see with their eyes and hear with their ears, and their heart understands, and they turn again and be healed. Then I said, How long, O Lord? And He said, *Until cities will have been devastated*, so that they are without inhabitant, and houses, so that there is no one in them, *and the land is reduced to a lonely place*; He will remove man. And *the wilderness* will be multiplied in the midst of the land. Scarcely any longer will there be a tenth part in it; it will be however an uprooting. Isa.6:9–end.

In the same prophet,

A remnant will return, the remnant of Jacob, to the God of power. For *the close has been determined*, overflowing with righteouness; for the Lord Jehovih Zebaoth is bringing the whole earth to its *close* and to its *determined end*. Isa.10:21–23.

In the same prophet,

Jehovah is *emptying* the earth and *making* it *void*, and He will overturn the face of it. The earth will be *utterly emptied*. The inhabited earth will mourn, it will be turned upside down. The world will languish and will be turned upside down. *A curse* will devour the earth. The new wine will mourn, the vine will languish. What is left in the city will be *a waste*; the gate will be smashed *to devastation*. The earth has been utterly broken, the earth has been utterly split open, the earth has been made to quake violently; the earth staggers altogether like a drunken man. Isa.24:1–end.

In the same prophet,

The highways have been *devastated*, the wayfarer has ceased. The earth mourns, it languishes. Lebanon has become ashamed, it has withered away; Sharon has become like a wilderness. Isa.33:8,9.

---

[1] *lit*. depastured

In the same prophet,

I *will desolate* and at the same time swallow up; I *will lay waste* mountains and hills, and dry up every plant on them.   Isa.42:14,15.

11   In Jeremiah,

I will utterly destroy all the nations round about, and *make them into a desolation*, and a derision and *everlasting wastes*. And I will cast away from them the voice of joy and the voice of gladness, the voice of the bridegroom amd the voice of the bride, the sound of the mills, and the light of the lamp, so that the whole land will be *a desolation* and *devastation*. It will happen when seventy years have been fulfilled, that I will visit the king of Babel and this nation for their iniquity, and the land of the Chaldeans, and I will make it *everlasting desolations*. Jer.25:9–12 and following verses.

In the same prophet,

A desolation, a reproach, *a waste*, and *a curse* will Bozrah be; and all its cities will be *everlasting wastes*. Edom will be *a desolation*, all who pass by it will be astonished and will hiss at all its plagues.   Jer.49:13–18.

In Ezekiel,

Thus said the Lord to the inhabitants of Jerusalem upon the land of Israel, They will eat their bread with anxiety, and drink their waters with astonishment, *that her land may be devastated of the fullness that is in it*, on account of the violence of all who dwell in it. *The inhabited cities will be devastated*, and the land *desolated*.   Ezek.12:19,20.

12   In the same prophet,

When I make you *a desolate city*, like the cities that are not inhabited, when I shall cause the deep to come up against you, and many waters have covered you, I will cause you to go down with those going down to the pit, to the people of old, and I will cause you to dwell in the land of the lower ones, *in the desolations*[1] from eternity, with those going down to the pit.   Ezek.26:18–21.

This refers to Tyre. In Joel,

A day of darkness and thick darkness, a day of cloud and gloom. Fire devours before him, and behind him a flame burns; like the garden of Eden is the land before him, but behind him there is *a desert waste*.   Joel 2:2,3.

In Zephaniah,

The day of Jehovah is near. A day of wrath is that day, a day of anguish and repression, *a day of vastation* and *devastation*, a day of darkness and thick darkness, a day of cloud and clouding over. By the fire of Jehovah's zeal the whole land will be devoured, for He[2] will bring to *a close*, indeed to a hasty one, all the inhabitants of the earth.   Zeph.1:14–end.

In Matthew,

When you see *the abomination of desolation*, foretold by the prophet Daniel, standing in the holy place, then let those who are in Judea flee into the mountains.   Matt.24:15,16; Mark 13:14; Dan.9:27; 12:10–12.

---

[1] *Reading* in desolationibus *for* in desolationem
[2] *The Latin means* I, *but the Hebrew means* He, *which Sw. has in another place where he quotes this verse.*

From all these quotations it is clear that 'a desolation' means an apparent deprivation of truth in the case of those who are being regenerated, but a total deprivation in the case of those who are not being regenerated.

CORRESPONDENCE WITH
THE GRAND MAN – *continued*
IN THIS SECTION TOO THE CORRESPONDENCE
OF THE INTERNAL ORGANS WITH IT

5377   The subject at the end of the previous chapter was the correspondence of certain internal organs of the body with the Grand Man, that is to say, the correspondence of the liver, pancreas, stomach, and certain other organs with it. In this present section the same subject moves on to the correspondence of the peritoneum, kidneys, ureters, bladder, and also the intestines with it. Whatever exists in the human being, both in the external man and in the internal man, has a correspondence with the Grand Man. Without that correspondence with the Grand Man – that is, with heaven, or what amounts to the same, with the spiritual world – nothing can ever come into being and remain in being. This is because it does not have a connection with anything prior to itself or consequently with Him who is the First, that is, with the Lord. Nothing that lacks such a connection, thus that is independent, can remain in being for even a single instant. For everything that remains in being does so entirely by virtue of its connection with and dependence on what brings it into being; for remaining in being consists in a constant coming into being.
From this it follows that not only all the individual parts of the human being correspond to the Grand Man but also every single thing in the universe. The sun has a correspondence, and so does the moon; for in heaven the Lord is the Sun, and the Moon too. The fire and heat of the sun, as well as its light, have a correspondence, for it is the Lord's love towards the whole human race that its fire and heat correspond to, and His Divine truth that its light corresponds to. The stars too have a correspondence, the communities of heaven and their dwelling-places being what the stars correspond to. Not that the heavenly communities dwell in the stars, but that they have been set in order in the same kind of way as the stars. Everything under the sun has a correspondence – every single thing beneath it in the animal kingdom and every single thing beneath it in the vegetable kingdom. And unless the spiritual world were flowing into them all, every one, they would instantly break down and fall to pieces.

3 Considerable experience too has made me aware of all this, for I have been shown what very many things in the animal kingdom, and still more in the vegetable kingdom, correspond to in the spiritual world, as well as the fact that without the inflow of the spiritual world into them they cannot by any means at all remain in being. For once what is prior has been taken away what is posterior of necessity perishes, and likewise once what is prior has been severed from what is posterior. Since correspondence is primarily the correspondence of the human being with heaven, and through heaven with the Lord, the specific nature of each person's correspondence therefore determines what he looks like in the next life in the light of heaven. This explains why angels have an indescribably bright and beautiful appearance, whereas those in hell have an unspeakably dark and ugly one.

5378 Some spirits once came to me but remained silent. Then after a while they did speak, though not as a number of individuals but all of them together as a single person. I recognized from the way they spoke that they were the kind who wished to know everything and desired the explanation for everything, and who thereby became convinced that something was true. These spirits were modest, declaring that nothing done by them was their own idea but was inspired by others, even though it may have seemed to be their own idea. At this point they began to be troubled by some other spirits who, I was told, constituted the province of the kidneys, ureters, and bladder. They were modest in their response to these other spirits, who nevertheless continued to trouble and harass them; for that is what those connected with the kidneys are like. Consequently, since they were unable to prevail over them by their modest responses they resorted to behaviour in keeping with the disposition of the ones who troubled them. That is to say, they resorted to swelling themselves out and thereby striking terror. They therefore seemed to grow large, yet solely as a single person whose body swelled out just as Atlas seemed to tower up into the sky. A spear appeared in his hand; but for all the terror that he struck he had no desire at all to do harm. The spirits belonging to the kidneys fled from him, at which point a spirit was seen who pursued them as they fled, and then another was seen who set off from a forward position and flew between the feet of the enlarged one. The enlarged one also seemed to have wooden footwear which spread right out to those spirits belonging to the kidneys.

2 Angels told me that those modest spirits who so enlarged themselves are spirits who correlate with the *Peritoneum*. The peritoneum is a general membrane which envelops and holds within it all the internal organs of the abdomen, in the way that the pleura does all the internal organs in the chest. And because this membrane is so extensive and is a large one compared with other membranes, and is capable of swelling out as well, the spirits connected with the peritoneum are therefore allowed, when troubled by others, to display themselves visually as that

enlarged man and at the same time to strike terror, especially into those who constitute the province of the kidneys, ureters, and bladder. For these interior organs or vessels lie within the folds of the peritoneum and are held in place by it. The wooden footwear represented the lowest natural substances such as are absorbed and carried away by the kidneys, ureters, and bladder; for by 'shoes' are meant the lowest natural things, see 259, 4938–4952. The declaration made by those spirits that nothing done by them was their own idea but was inspired by others also correlated them with the peritoneum, for something similar is true of the peritoneum.

5379 I have also been shown by the use of representations what happens when those who constitute the colon trouble those in the province of the peritoneum. Those constituting the colon are puffed up, like the colon when it is distended by its own wind. When spirits in the colon wished to make an attack on the ones in the peritoneum, it seemed as though a wall was placed in their way; and whenever they tried to overturn the wall another one invariably rose up. This was how they were kept away from those in the peritoneum.

5380 It is well known that there are secretions and excretions and that there is a sequence of these extending from the kidneys through to the bladder. The kidneys come first in the sequence, then the ureters in the middle, and the bladder at the end of it. Those constituting these provinces in the Grand Man exist in a similar way in a sequence. But although they all belong to the same genus, they nevertheless differ from one another so far as species within that genus are concerned. When they speak their voices sound rough, as though split in two. They also have the desire to get into the body; but this remains as no more than their attempt to do so. Their position in relation to the rest of the human body is as follows: Those who correlate with the kidneys are very close to the body on the left hand side beneath the elbow; those who correlate with the ureters are further away from the body on the left hand side; and those who correlate with the bladder are still further away. All these together form, at the front on the left hand side, a virtual parabola; for they distend themselves into a shape like this at the front on the left hand side and in so doing occupy quite an elongated area. This path is the general one that leads to the hells, while another one passes through the intestines; for both these paths terminate in the hells. Those in the hells correspond to the kinds of waste products that are excreted through the intestines and bladder, the falsities and evils present with them being nothing else in the spiritual sense than urine and excrement.

5381 Those who constitute the province of the kidneys, ureters, and bladder in the Grand Man are by nature such that there is nothing they like more than to explore and examine closely other people's characters.

They are also ones who wish to correct and punish, provided that such an action is at all justly warranted. The functions of the kidneys, ureters, and bladder are also like this, for they explore the blood attracted into them to discover any useless or harmful fluid there. This they separate from what is useful and then purify it; for they send it down to lower parts, harrying it both on the way down and by various methods when it gets there. Such are the functions of those who constitute the province incorporating those parts. But the spirits and communities of spirits to which actual urine, especially stinking urine, corresponds are hellish ones. For as soon as the urine has been separated from the blood, even though still in the tubules of the kidneys or else held in the bladder, it is nevertheless outside the body, since what has been separated no longer circulates around the body and does not therefore contribute in any way to the continuing existence of its parts.

5382 I have learned from experience on many occasions that those who constitute the province of the kidneys and ureters are ready to explore and examine closely other people's characters to discover what their thoughts are and what their wishes are. They desire to find out the reasons why those people think and wish the way they do and to arouse a sense of guilt over any faults these may have, their primary purpose being to administer correction; and I have talked to such spirits about this desire and purpose of theirs. Many of their kind were judges when they lived in the world, at which time they felt glad at heart when they found the reason which, they believed, justly warranted the imposition of a fine, correction, or punishment. The work of such spirits is also felt in the region of one's back, where the kidneys, ureters, and bladder are situated. Those who belong to the bladder extend down towards Gehenna, where also some of them sit like a court of law.

5383 The methods used by them to explore and examine closely the minds of others are very many; but let simply the following be mentioned here. They induce the other spirits to speak, which is effected in the next life by means of an influx that defies any intelligible description. If the speech so induced flows readily, they judge from this the character of those other spirits. They also induce a state of affection. But those who explore the minds of others in this way are some of the rather obtuse ones. Others however are different, being spirits who discern in an instant, even while they are approaching someone, his thoughts, desires, and actions, including any grief felt by him over something he has done. Those spirits seize on such, and if they think the feeling is justified they also condemn him. One of the marvels in the next life which scarcely anyone in the world can believe is that as soon as any spirit approaches another spirit, more so when he approaches someone in the world, he knows in an instant his thoughts and affections and what he has been doing. Thus he knows the whole of the other's present state, altogether as though he has been constantly in his presence. This kind of communication exists there, though there are differences in such forms of discernment. Some spirits perceive another's interior thoughts and affections, others perceive solely his exterior ones. Yet if the latter wish to know others' interior thoughts and affections, they can employ various methods to explore them.

5384   The methods used by those who constitute the province of the kidneys, ureters, and bladder in the Grand Man when they do their work of correction are also various. For the most part they take away pleasant and cheerful feelings and introduce unpleasant and sad ones. Through their desire to do this those spirits communicate with the hells; but through the justice of the cause which they seek to establish before they administer any correction they communicate with heaven and are for that reason kept in that province.

5385   From all this one may see what is meant when it is stated in the Word that Jehovah tests and examines closely the kidneys and the heart, and also corrects the kidneys, as in Jeremiah,

Jehovah *testing the kidneys* and the heart.   Jer.9:20.

In the same prophet,

Jehovah testing the righteous, *seeing the kidneys* and the heart.   Jer.20:12.

In David,

You test the heart and *the kidneys*, a righteous God.   Ps.7:9.

In the same author,

O Jehovah, *explore my kidneys* and my heart.   Ps.26:2.

In the same author,

O Jehovah, You *possess my kidneys*.   Ps.139:13.

In John,

I am He who has *examined closely the kidneys* and the heart.   Rev.2:23.

Here 'the kidneys' means spiritual areas and 'the heart' celestial ones; that is, 'the kidneys' means areas of truth, while 'the heart' means areas of good. The reason for this is that the kidneys purify fluid whereas the heart purifies actual blood, and therefore 'testing, exploring, and examining closely the kidneys' means testing, exploring, and examining closely the amount and the essential nature of truth, that is, the amount and the essential nature of the faith present with a person. This meaning is also evident in Jeremiah,

O Jehovah, You are near in their mouth but far away *from their kidneys*.   Jer.12:2.

And in David,

O Jehovah, behold, You desire *truth in the kidneys*.   Ps.51:6.

The fact that in addition the ability to correct is attributed to the kidneys is also plain in David,

In the night seasons *my kidneys correct me.* Ps.16:7.

5386 Elsewhere in the body there are other secretory and excretory organs. In the brain there are ventricles amd mamillary processes which drain away viscid substances. In addition to this there are glands in all parts, such as those producing mucus and saliva in the head, and very many in the body. Also there are millions next to the skin through which sweat and more minute used matter are excreted. Those who in the spiritual world correspond to these are in general spirits who hold on tenaciously to their point of view and also spirits who take a conscientious stand on issues that are not vitally important. Some of these are seen midway overhead; their nature is such that they make meticulous enquiries into matters into which no such enquiries at all ought to be made. Consequently, because they burden the consciences of simple people they are called 'the conscientious ones'. Yet they have no knowledge of what true conscience is, because they make all issues into matters of conscience. For if a thing is subjected to minute questioning or to doubt and the mind is anxiously fixed on such, ideas supporting this attitude and weighing the mind down are never absent. When such spirits are present they also bring a feeling of anxiety that registers in the part of the abdomen located immediately beneath the diaphragm. They are also present with a person during temptations. I have talked to them and have noticed that their thoughts do not extend to any concern for matters that have greater purpose or that are vitally important. They were incapable of paying any attention to reasons offered to them because they persisted in holding on tenaciously to their own opinion.

5387 But the actual ones who correspond to urine are those in the hells, for urine, as stated above, is outside the body because it has already been separated from the blood and essentially is nothing else than unclean used fluid that has been cast away. Let the following details be given regarding such spirits. I once felt a certain spirit to be initially inside my body so to speak; but soon after he was outside it on my right where, once he had established himself, he could not be seen. For he had the ability to make himself unseen. When asked something he made no reply whatsoever. Others told me that during his lifetime he had engaged in piracy, for in the next life one can detect plainly from the sphere emanating from the life of a person's affections and thoughts who and what kind of person he has been. This is possible because everyone's life remains with him.

2 This spirit varied his position, appearing at one point on the right, at another on the left. I perceived that he did this because of a fear that people would know who he was and that he would be compelled to make some kind of confession. Other spirits told me that those like this

one are utterly afraid if there is the slightest danger; but when no danger at all exists they are full of courage. They also told me that such spirits are opposed to those to whom the function of expelling urine corresponds. They strive in whatever way they can to impair that function; and to remove any doubts I may have had, this was demonstrated to me by experience. When those who corresponded to the function of expelling urine departed only a little way off and that pirate was still present, the passing of urine was brought to a complete halt and was also filled with danger. But once they were called back the passing of urine was resumed, directed by their presence.

After this that spirit did confess that he had been a pirate. He said he had the ability to conceal himself skillfully, and by being cunning and painstaking to mislead his pursuers. Now, he added, he loved foul urinous places, much more than clean waters, and that the disgusting stench of urine gave him the greatest pleasure, so much so that he wanted a dwelling-place among pools, even among casks of stinking urine. I was also shown the kind of face he had. Really he had no face at all, but instead of a face something black and bearded.

After this some other pirates who were less painstaking than this one were summoned. These too hardly said a word, but – which was amazing – were gnashing their teeth. They likewise said they liked urine more than any other fluids, and foul waters more than any other kind. These however did not have for a face something bearded, like the first pirate, but a dreadful array of teeth, looking like a crate. For the beard and the teeth mean the lowest natural things. The absence of a face means that no rational life at all is present, for when no face is visible this is a sign that no correspondence exists of interior things with the Grand Man. In the next life correspondence determines what anyone looks like in the light of heaven, and therefore those in hell have horribly ugly appearances.

5388   There was once present with and talking to me a certain spirit who during his lifetime had had no faith at all and had not believed in any life after death. He had also been one of the quite hard-working. He had been able to captivate people's minds by speaking favourably to them and flattering them. For this reason it was not immediately evident from his conversation what he was really like. Also, he could speak fluently, like a running river, even as a good spirit can. Yet from this it was soon realized that he did not like to speak about matters of faith and charity, for being unable in his thinking to follow talk about these he was hesitant. Then I noticed from the particular things he said that he employed flattery that was intended to deceive; for the use of flattery is varied, depending on what its end in view may be. If the end in view, when someone resorts to flattery, is friendship, or the desire for social connections, or something similar, and also if material gain is allowable, then he is not behaving too badly. But if his end in view is to extract secrets from another person and in so doing to compel him to engage in wicked practices, in general if the end in view is to cause harm, he is behaving badly. And that was the kind of end that spirit had in view. He too was opposed to those in the province of the kidneys and ureters, and he too said he liked the stench of urine more than all other odours. He also inflicted a feeling of cramp or a painful tightness in the pit of my stomach.

5389   There are bands of spirits wandering about who return periodically to the same places. Evil spirits have a great dread of them because those bands torment them with a particular kind of torture. I have been told that they correspond to the fundus, or upper part of the bladder in general, and to the muscular ligaments leading from there which centre on the sphincter, where a twisting action is employed to release urine. These spirits attach themselves to that part of the back where the cauda equina is situated. Their method of working is effected by rapid movements to and fro which no one can resist. The method involves a tightening and relaxing action upwards, in the form of a cone pointing upwards. Evil spirits who are placed inside this cone, especially from above, are tortured pitiably by the twistings taking place in both directions.

5390   There are other spirits again who correspond to filthy excretions, these being the kind who in the world were firmly set on taking vengeance. I have seen these in front of me, over to the left. Also corresponding to those filthy excretions are people who have debased spiritual ideas into filthy earthly ones. Spirits such as these have also approached me, bringing their foul thoughts with them. Those thoughts also led them to say things that were foul; and worse than that, they turned pure ideas towards unclean ones and converted them into the same. A large number of spirits like these have sprung from the lowest level of society; but they also came from other levels of people who in the world were among the higher-ranking. During their lifetimes the latter did not, it is true, express foul ideas in company, even though they thought them; they refrained from speaking what they thought, to avoid ill repute or loss of the friendships, material advantages, and important positions they enjoyed. Otherwise, when among others like themselves and at liberty to do so, they uttered the same kinds of things as those belonging to the lowest level of society. Indeed what they spoke was even fouler because they had an intellectual ability which they misused to defile even those holy ideas contained in the Word and religious teaching.

5391   There are also kidneys which are called the *Subsidiary Kidneys* and also the *Renal Capsules*. The function of these is not so much to separate fluid as actual blood, sending the purer blood by a short route round to the heart, thus ensuring that neighbouring spermatic vessels do not take away all the purer blood. But their chief work is performed in embryos and also new-born babies. Chaste virgins are the ones who constitute that province in the Grand Man; easily given to anxious feelings and fearful of being disturbed, they lie quietly on the lower left side of the body. If I think about heaven or about a change in their state, they become anxious and sigh, as I have been allowed to detect plainly on several occasions. When my thoughts turned to young children those virgins felt a significant comfort and an inner joy, to which they openly bore witness. Also whenever my thought has dwelt on something unheavenly, they have again experienced anxious feelings. Those feelings stem primarily from the fact that those virgins have an innate disposition to keep their minds fixed on one particular concern and not get rid of those anxious feelings by turning to other matters. They belong to that province because by behaving in this way they can fix another's mind constantly on certain particular thoughts, as a consequence of which a succession of such matters as must be taken away from a person and from which he must be purified emerge and reveal themselves. In this way too interior things are made more evident to the angels, for once such things as cause obscurity and divert their attention are removed, clearer vision and influx result.

5392 Who exactly constitute the province of the *Intestines* in the Grand Man will become clear to some extent from those who correlate with the stomach. For the intestines are a continuation of the stomach, and the functions performed by the stomach increase in them and are intensified right through to the end of the intestines – to the colon and rectum. The spirits in the latter are therefore close to the hells which are called the excrementitious ones. In the region of the stomach and intestines are those on the lower earth. Because these have brought with them from the world forms of uncleanness clinging to their thoughts and affections, they are therefore detained for a while in that region until such forms of uncleanness have been wiped away, that is, cast away to the side. Once these have been cast away to the side those people can be raised up to heaven. People on the lower earth are not yet in the Grand Man, for they are like food which has been sent down into the stomach but which, until it has been purged, is not introduced into the bloodstream and so into the body. People contaminated with even worse earthly defilements are below those in the region of the intestines; but the actual excrement passed by the intestines corresponds to the hells called the excrementitious hells.

5393 It is well known that the colon[1] belonging to the intestines is extensive; and so also are those within that province. They extend, in a frontal direction on the left side, in a line that curves and leads to a hell. In that hell there are those who have been devoid of all pity, and having no conscience have been willing to destroy the human race. That is to say, they have been willing to kill and rob people, taking no account at all of whether or not their victims offer any resistance, or whether they

---

[1] *In this paragraph Sw. appears to mean the* colon descendens.

are men or women. A vicious disposition of mind such as this exists with a large section of soldiers and their officers; not during battles but after these are over they viciously terrorize the conquered and defenceless, and in their fury murder and rob them. I have talked to angels about spirits of this kind. Their essential nature is the same as that of human beings when left to themselves – when no law exists and they are permitted to act just as they like. In those circumstances they are far more savage than the most savage among animals, which are less inclined to plunge into killing members of their own species, except in self-defence. These also satisfy their hunger with those creatures assigned to them as their food; but once their hunger is satisfied they cease to behave in such vicious ways. But the human being, when motivated by cruel and savage feelings, is different.

2   Angels have been horrified that the human race is like this. For as soon as men see lines of troops strewn and streams of blood flowing over the whole field, their hearts are full of joy and their spirits are elated; yet they feel no joy that their country has been set free, only that they are hailed as mighty ones and heroes. Yet such men call themselves Christians and even believe that they will go to heaven, where however nothing but peace, pity, and charity dwell. Such are in the hell of the colon and rectum. Those however in whom some humanity is present are seen in a frontal direction on the left side, in the line that curves, yet on the inside of a kind of wall. But even within these people much self-love is present. Some do have a concern for what is good, which is sometimes represented by tiny stars that are almost fiery yet not bright. Once a wall appeared before me that seemed to be made of plaster and to have carved figures. This wall, which was near my left elbow, became more extensive and at the same time taller, the colour of the upper part verging on blue. I was told that this was representative of some of the better ones among this kind of spirits.

5394   People who have been both cruel and adulterous like nothing more in the next life than filth and excrement. To them the stink of these is most sweet and pleasant, and they prefer such odours to all other delights. The reason why lies in their correspondence. Those hells lie partly beneath the buttocks, partly beneath the right foot, and partly in a frontal direction, deep down. These are the hells to which the path through the rectum leads. Once a certain spirit was brought there, from where he spoke to me. He said there was nothing else in sight but latrines. Those there talked to him and led him to various other latrines, which were very numerous there. After that he was taken to another place situated a little to the left, and while he was in that place he said that an absolutely dreadful stench was emanating from caverns there and that he could not move a foot without almost falling into a cavern. The stink of dead bodies was also emanating from the caverns. The reason for this was that cruel and deceitful spirits were there, to whom the stink of dead bodies is most delightful. But these spirits are to be dealt with later on when the hells, especially the excrementitious and dead-body hells, will be the subject.

5395 There are some who live not for the sake of any useful service they may render to their country and its communities, only for themselves. They find no delight in the holding of offices, only in being honoured and respected, which is why they seek office. In addition they take delight in eating, drinking, games, and social intercourse, yet for no other reason than their own pleasure. In the next life these people cannot by any means remain in groups of good spirits, let alone among angels. For with good spirits and angels useful service is the source of their delight; and the services they perform determine the amount and the essential nature of the delight they receive. For the Lord's kingdom is nothing else than a kingdom of useful services. Since in an earthly kingdom the extent to which anyone is esteemed and honoured is determined by the useful purpose he serves, how much more must this be so in the case of the heavenly kingdom. Those who have lived solely for themselves and their own pleasure, without any useful purpose in view, are also beneath the buttocks; and in keeping with the types of pleasure they have sought and with their ends in view they spend their time in filth.

5396 By way of addition let the following be recounted. There was a large crowd of spirits around me, which sounded like a disorderly lot going by. They were all grumbling, declaring that everything was now being destroyed; for no unity at all was apparent among those who constituted that crowd of spirits, which made them fear destruction. They also imagined that they faced total destruction, such as takes place when the situation is as it was with them. But I detected in the midst of them a soft, sweet angelic sound, which was a wholly well-ordered one. Angelic choirs were present in the middle of them, while the actual crowd of spirits in all their disorder were on the outside. That angelic stream of sound lasted for a long time, and I was told that it served to represent the way in which the Lord regulates confused and disordered outward elements from a peaceful centre within them; He brings order into the disordered most outlying elements by withholding each one from the error peculiar to it.

42

1 And Jacob saw that there was corn in Egypt; and Jacob said to his sons, Why do you look at one another?

2 And he said, Behold, I have heard that there is corn in Egypt; go down there, and buy for us from there, and let us live and not die.

3 And Joseph's ten brothers went down to buy grain from Egypt.

4 And Benjamin, Joseph's brother, Jacob did not send with his brothers, for he said, Perhaps harm may come to him.

5 And the sons of Israel came to buy in the midst of others who came; for the famine was in the land of Canaan.

6 And Joseph, he was the governor over the land, he was selling to all the people of the land. And Joseph's brothers came and bowed down to him, faces to the earth.

7 And Joseph saw his brothers, and recognized them; and he acted as a stranger to them, and spoke hard words to them, and said to them, Where have you come from? And they said, From the land of Canaan, to buy food.

8 And Joseph recognized his brothers, and they did not recognize him.

9 And Joseph remembered the dreams which he had dreamed involving them; and he said to them, You are spies; you have come to see the nakedness of the land.

10 And they said to him, No, my lord; and your servants come to buy food.

11 All we, the sons of one man are we. We are upright men; your servants are not spies.

12 And he said to them, No, but the nakedness of the land you have come to see.

13 And they said, Twelve are your servants, brothers are we, the sons of one man in the land of Canaan; and behold, the youngest is with our father today, and one is not.

14 And Joseph said to them, It is as I spoke to you, saying, You are spies.

15 In this manner you will be tested: As sure as Pharaoh lives[1], you shall not go out of here unless your youngest brother comes here.

16 Send one of you and let him fetch your brother; and you will be in bonds, and your words will be tested, whether the truth is with you.

And if not, as sure as Pharaoh lives[1], you are spies.

17 And he shut them up in custody for three days.

18 And Joseph said to them on the third day, Do this and you will live, [for] I fear God:

19 If you are upright men, let one brother among you be in bonds in the house of your custody, and you, go, take corn for the famine of your houses.

20 And bring your youngest brother to me, and your words will be verified, and you will not die. And they did so.

21 And they said, a man to his brother, Assuredly we are guilty concerning our brother, whose anguish of soul we saw when he pleaded with us and we did not hear; therefore this anguish has come to us.

22 And Reuben answered them, saying, Did I not say to you, saying, Do not sin against the boy – and you did not listen? And also, his blood; behold, it is required.

23 And they did not know that Joseph was hearing, because the interpreter was between them.

24 And he turned away from them and wept; and he came back to them and spoke to them; and he took Simeon from them, and bound him before their eyes.

25 And Joseph gave the command to fill[2] their vessels with grain, and to restore their silver, each man's in his sack, and to give them provision for the way; and thus he did for them.

26 And they loaded their corn onto their asses, and went from there.

27 And one opened his sack to give fodder to his ass, in a lodging-place, and he saw his silver, and behold, it was in the mouth of his pouch.

28 And he said to his brothers, My silver has been restored, and also behold, it is in my pouch. And their heart went out of them, and they trembled [turning] a man to his brother, saying, What is this that God has done to us?

29 And they came to Jacob their father, to the land of Canaan; and they pointed out to him all that was happening to them, saying,

30 The man, the lord of the land, spoke hard words to us, and took us for men spying out the land.

31 And we said to him, We are upright men; we are not spies.

32 Twelve are we, brothers, the sons of our father; one is not, and the youngest is today with our father in the land of Canaan.

33 And the man, the lord of the land, said to us, By this I shall know that you are upright men: Cause one brother among you to remain with me, and take [food for] the famine of your houses, and go.

34 And bring your youngest brother to me, and I shall know that you are not spies, that you are upright men; I will give you your brother, and you will wander through the land, trading.

---

[1] *lit.* May Pharaoh live!
[2] *lit.* And Joseph commanded, and they [his servants?] filled

35 And so it was, as they were emptying their sacks, that behold, each man's bundle of silver was in his sack; and they saw their bundles of silver, they and their father, and they were afraid.

36 And Jacob their father said to them, You have bereaved me [of my children]; Joseph is not, and Simeon is not, and you take Benjamin. All these things will be upon me.

37 And Reuben said to his father – he said, Make my two sons die if I do not bring him back to you; give him into my hand, and I will bring him back to you.

38 And he said, My son shall not go down with you, for his brother is dead, and he, he alone, is left. And should harm happen to him on the road on which you go, you will cause my grey hair to go down in sorrow to the grave.

CONTENTS

5396[a]   The subject at the end of the previous chapter was the influx of the celestial of the spiritual into the known facts present in the natural and the joining of it to these. Now the subject is the influx of the celestial of the spiritual into the truths of faith there which are known to the Church and the joining of it to those truths.

5397   Dealt with first is the attempt to gain possession of these truths through the facts known to the Church, which are 'Egypt', and to do so without the intermediary, which is 'Benjamin', along with truth from the Divine, which is 'Joseph'. But this was a failure, and therefore they were returned to where they came from, together with a measure of the good of natural truth freely given.

THE INTERNAL SENSE

5398   This chapter and the ones that follow it concerning Jacob's sons and Joseph deal in the internal sense with the regeneration of the natural so far as the truths and goods of the Church are concerned – such regeneration being effected not by means of factual knowledge but by an influx from the Divine. Those who belong to the Church at the present day know so little about regeneration as to know virtually nothing at all about it. They do not even know that regeneration is a process that takes place throughout the whole course of the life of someone who is being regenerated and continues in the next life. Nor do they know that the arcana of regeneration are so countless that hardly the smallest fraction can be known even by angels, or that those which angels do know are what constitute the intelligence and wisdom they possess. Those belonging to the Church at the present day know so little about regeneration because they talk so much about the forgiveness of sins and justification, believing that sins can be forgiven instantaneously. Some believe that sins are washed away like dirt from the body by the use of water, and that a person is justified or made righteous by means of faith alone, that is, by means of trust of only a moment's duration. The reason people within the Church believe the way they do is that they do not know what sin or evil is. If they did possess such knowledge they would know that no one's sins can by any means at all be washed away, but that these are separated or cast away to the sides to prevent them from rising up, when the Lord maintains the presence of good within that person. They would also know that this cannot be accomplished unless evil is being cast out all the time, which is done by means that are numerically without limit and for the most part beyond description.

2   In the next life people who have brought with them the notion that a person is made righteous by faith in an instant and completely cleansed from sins are dumbfounded when they learn that regeneration is effected by means that are numerically without limit and beyond description. They laugh at their own ignorance, which they also call madness, that is, at the ideas they held to in the world regarding instantaneous forgiveness of sins and justification. Sometimes they are told that the Lord forgives the sins of everyone who in his heart desires forgiveness; but this does not mean that they are separated from the devil's crew, to whom they are bound through the evils which go along with the life which they bring with them in its entirety. After this they learn from experience that being separated from the hells is being separated from one's sins, and that this cannot possibly be accomplished except by thousands of ways known to the Lord alone, a process which, if you can believe it, continues for ever one stage after another. For the human being is so full of evil that he cannot ever be released from even one sin. But solely by the Lord's mercy, if he will accept that mercy, he is withheld from sin and maintained in good.

3   The way therefore in which a person receives new life and is regenerated is contained in the sanctuary of the Word, that is, in its internal sense. The primary reason why the internal sense contains that information is that when the Word is being read by man, it causes the angels to be aware of the bliss that wisdom brings them and at the same time to take delight in serving as means. The subject in the highest sense of this chapter and those that follow it, where the narrative concerns Joseph's brothers, is the glorification of the Lord's natural, and in the representative sense the regeneration by the Lord of man's natural, in this chapter so far as the truths of the Church are concerned.

5399   Verses 1-5 And Jacob saw that there was corn in Egypt; and Jacob said to his sons, Why do you look at one another? And he said, Behold, I have heard that there is corn in Egypt; go down there, and buy for us from there, and let us live and not die. And Joseph's ten brothers went down to buy grain from Egypt. And Benjamin, Joseph's brother, Jacob did not send with his brothers, for he said, Perhaps harm may come to him. And the sons of Israel came to buy in the midst of others who came; for the famine was in the land of Canaan.

'And [Jacob] saw' means the things that constitute faith. 'Jacob' means the natural so far as truth known to the Church is concerned. 'That there was corn in Egypt' means the intention to acquire truths to itself through factual knowledge, which is 'Egypt'. 'And Jacob said to his sons' means perception regarding truths as a general whole. 'Why do you look at one another?' means, Why did they fix their attention on these? 'And he said, Behold, I have heard that there is corn in Egypt' means that truths can be acquired through factual knowledge. 'Go down there, and buy for us from there' means making them its own through that knowledge. 'And let us live and not die' means spiritual life received from this. 'And [Joseph's ten brothers] went down' means an aim and endeavour. 'Joseph's ten brothers' means such truths known to the Church as were in agreement with one another. 'To buy grain from Egypt' means to make the good of truth its own through factual knowledge. 'And Benjamin, Joseph's brother' means the spiritual of the celestial, which is the intermediary. 'Jacob did not send with his brothers' means without that intermediary. 'For he said, Perhaps harm may come to him' means that without the celestial of the spiritual, which is 'Joseph', that intermediary will perish. 'And the sons of Israel came to buy in the midst of others who came' means the wish to acquire spiritual truths, like all other truths, through factual knowledge. 'For the famine was in the land of Canaan' means that desolation existed so far as things of the Church in the natural were concerned.

5400   'And [Jacob] saw' means the things that constitute faith. This is clear from the meaning of 'seeing' as those things that constitute faith, dealt with in 897, 2325, 2807, 3863, 3869, 4403-4421. When it has no link whatsoever with such things as exist in the world, sight – that is, spiritual sight – is nothing else than a perception of truth, that is, of such things as constitute faith. Therefore 'seeing' has no other meaning in the internal sense; for the internal sense emerges when everything of a worldly nature is set aside; for the internal sense concerns itself with the kinds of things that belong to heaven.

2   The light of heaven which enables one to see there is Divine Truth received from the Lord. This appears before angels' eyes as light a thousand times brighter than the light at midday in the world; and because it holds life within it, that light therefore brings sight to angels' understanding at the same time as it does so to their eyes, imparting a discernment of truth to them which is regulated by the amount and the

nature of good present within them. Because this chapter deals in the internal sense with those things that constitute faith, that is, with the truths known to the Church, the verb 'saw' is used at the very beginning of the chapter, 'saw' meaning the things that constitute faith.

5401 'Jacob' means the natural so far as truth known to the Church is concerned. This is clear from the representation of 'Jacob' as the doctrine of truth in the natural, and in the highest sense as the Lord's natural as regards truth, dealt with in 3305, 3509, 3525, 3546, 3599, 4009, 4538.

5402 'That there was corn in Egypt' means the intention to acquire truths to itself through factual knowledge, which is 'Egypt'. This is clear from the meaning of 'corn' as the truths known to the Church, or the truths of faith – 'an abundance of corn' being a multiplication of truth, see 5276, 5280, 5292; and from the meaning of 'Egypt' as factual knowledge, dealt with in 1164, 1165, 1186, 1462, and, in the genuine sense, facts known to the Church, see 4749, 4964, 4966. As is evident from the words that come immediately after them, the ones used here imply an intention to acquire these truths to itself. The expression 'facts known to the Church', which 'Egypt' stands for here, is used to mean all the cognitions of truth and good before they become linked to the interior man, that is, through the interior man to heaven, and thus through heaven to the Lord. The teachings of the Church and its religious observances, in addition to its cognitions about why and how these represent spiritual realities and the like, all exist as nothing more than known facts until a person sees from the Word whether they are truths, and having done so makes them his own.

2 There are two ways of acquiring the truths of faith, one way being through religious teaching, the other through the Word. When religious teaching alone is the way by which a person acquires them, he pins his faith on those who have deduced such truths from the Word, and assures himself that they are indeed truths because others have said that they are. Thus he does not believe those truths on account of any faith of his own but on account of that possessed by others. When however he gathers those truths for himself from the Word and assures himself for that reason that they are truths, he believes them on account of their Divine origin and so on account of a faith received from the Divine. Initially everyone within the Church acquires the truths that constitute faith from religious teaching; indeed this is how he ought to acquire them because he is not as yet equipped with judgement of his own that will enable him to see those truths from the Word. At this time those truths are for him no different from factual knowledge. But once he does possess the judgement to see them on his own, and if he does not consult the Word to the end that he may see from there whether they are indeed truths, they remain with him as factual knowledge. If however he does consult the Word with an affection for and an intention to know truths, and having found them there acquires them

from their own true source, he receives the truths of faith from the Divine and makes them his own. These and other matters like them are what the internal sense is dealing with here; for 'Egypt' is that factual knowledge, while 'Joseph' is truth received from the Divine and so truth obtained from the Word.

5403   'And Jacob said to his sons' means perception regarding truths as a general whole. This is clear from the meaning of 'saying' in the historical narratives of the Word as perception, dealt with in 1791, 1815, 1819, 1822, 1898, 1919, 2080, 2619, 2862, 3395, 3509; and from the meaning of 'sons' as the truths of faith, dealt with in 489, 491, 533, 1147, 2623, 3373, 4257. Also, because they were Jacob's sons, truths as a general whole are meant; for 'the twelve sons of Jacob', like the twelve tribes, meant all aspects of faith, and so truths as a general whole, see 2129, 2130, 3858, 3862, 3926, 3939, 4060.

5404   'Why do you look at one another?' means, Why did they fix their attention on these? This becomes clear without explanation.

5405   'And he said, Behold, I have heard that there is corn in Egypt' means that truths can be acquired through factual knowledge. This becomes clear from the explanation just above in 5402, where 'that there was corn in Egypt' means the intention to acquire truths to itself through factual knowledge, which is 'Egypt'. What is meant by factual knowledge, which is 'Egypt', may also be seen in the same place. 'Corn' here stands for a word in the original language which means *a breaking*, and also for a similar word meaning *to buy* or *to sell*, when it is said that Jacob's sons 'bought' corn in Egypt and that Joseph 'sold' it there. The reason for this is that in the Ancient Church bread was broken when it was given to another, by which action was meant the sharing of what was one's own and the passing of good from oneself to another to be his own. Thus it meant making love mutual. For when someone breaks bread and gives it to another he is sharing with him what is his own. Or when a loaf is broken and shared among many, the single loaf becomes one shared mutually by all, and all are consequently joined together through charity.

From this it is evident that the breaking of bread was a sign that meant mutual love. Because this had become an accepted and customary practice in the Ancient Church, the common availability of corn was therefore meant by such a breaking. 'Bread' means the good of love, see 276, 680, 1798, 2165, 2177, 3464, 3478, 3735, 3813, 4211, 4217, 4735, 4976; and this explains why, when the Lord gave bread, He broke it, as in Matthew,

Jesus taking the five loaves and the two fish, looking up to heaven, said a blessing, and *breaking* it gave *the bread* to the disciples. Matt.14:19; Mark 6:41; Luke 9:16.

In the same gospel,

Taking the seven loaves and the fish, giving thanks, Jesus *broke* and gave them to His disciples, and the disciples to the crowd. Matt.15:36; Mark 8:6.

In the same gospel,

Taking bread, saying a blessing, Jesus *broke* and gave to the disciples and said, Take, eat, this is My body. Matt.26:26; Mark 14:22; Luke 22:19.

In Luke,

It happened, when the Lord was at table with them, that taking *bread* He said a blessing, and *breaking* it gave it to them. And their eyes were opened and they recognized Him. The disciples told how the Lord was known to them in *the breaking of bread*. Luke 24:30,31,35.

In Isaiah,

This is the fast that I choose, *to break* your *bread* for the hungry. Isa.58:6,7.

5406 'Go down there, and buy for us from there' means making them its own through that knowledge. This is clear from the meaning of 'going down' as an expression used to describe movement towards things that are more external, dealt with below; and from the meaning of 'buying' as making one's own, dealt with in 4397, 5374. The accomplishment of this through that knowledge, factual knowledge, is meant by 'from there', that is to say, from Egypt; for 'Egypt' means factual knowledge, as shown above. Various places in the Word contain the expression to go up or to go down when a movement from one place to another is described. The reason for this usage is not that one place was higher than another but that going up describes a movement towards things that are more internal or superior, while going down describes a movement towards things that are more external or inferior. That is, 'going up' refers to movement towards things that are spiritual and heavenly since these are more internal and are believed to be superior, whereas 'going down' refers to a movement towards natural and earthly things as these are more external and also to outward appearance inferior. This explains why not only here but also everywhere else in the Word one is said to go down from the land of Canaan to Egypt and to come up from Egypt to the land of Canaan. 'The land of Canaan' means that which is heavenly, and 'Egypt' that which is natural; for in the representative sense the land of Canaan is the heavenly kingdom, and consequently celestial and spiritual forms of good and truth, which also reside more internally in a person who is the Lord's kingdom, whereas 'Egypt' in the representative sense is the natural kingdom, and consequently the forms of good and truth which belong to the external Church and exist for the most part as factual knowledge. For the use of 'going up' to describe a movement towards things that are more internal, see 4539.

5407 'And let us live and not die' means spiritual life. This is clear from the meaning of 'living and not dying' as spiritual life, for nothing else than this is meant in the internal sense by 'living and not dying'. In the next life 'life' generally means heaven, but specifically it means eternal happiness, while 'death' generally means hell, but specifically eternal unhappiness there, as is also evident from many places in the Word. The reason why heaven generally and eternal happiness specifically are called 'life' is that wisdom, which essentially is good, and intelligence, which essentially is truth, are present in heaven, and the life of such wisdom and intelligence is received from the Lord, the Source of the whole of life. But because the contrary of this exists in hell – that is to say, evil exists instead of good, and falsity instead of truth, so that spiritual life has been snuffed out there – what exists there, compared with that existing in heaven, is death. For spiritual death consists in evil and falsity, and it exists with man as the desire for what is evil and a consequent thinking what is false. Evil genii and spirits refuse to listen when it is said that they have no life or that they are dead. For they say that they do have life since they have the power of will and the power of thought. But they are told that since life resides in what is good and true it cannot possibly do so in what is evil and false, because the two are contraries.

5408   'And [Joseph's ten brothers] went down' means an aim and endeavour – an aim and endeavour to acquire truths to itself, and to make these its own, through factual knowledge. This is evident from the meaning of 'going down' – going down to Egypt – as an aim and endeavour.

5409   'Joseph's ten brothers' means such truths known to the Church as were in agreement with one another. This is clear from the meaning of 'brothers' as truths known to the Church. These truths are called 'Joseph's brothers' ('Joseph' representing truth received from the Divine) by virtue of their agreement with one another; for that agreement causes them to exist joined together like one brother to another. 'The sons of Jacob' means all the truths of faith or the truths as a general whole that are known by the Church, 5403; and the expression 'Joseph's brothers' has a similar meaning, though this is because of their agreement with one another. Jacob's ten sons by Leah mean the truths known to the external Church, but Jacob's two sons by Rachel mean the truths known to the internal Church, as is evident from what has been shown regarding Leah and Rachel. That is to say, it has been shown that 'Leah' is the affection for exterior truth and 'Rachel' the affection for interior truth, both dealt with in 3758, 3782, 3793, 3819. Also, the internal Church and the external Church are 'brothers', see 1222. The Lord Himself therefore uses the word 'brothers' to describe truths and resulting forms of good which exist in agreement with one another by virtue of charity and faith, that is, to describe people who know truths and from these desire what is good: In Matthew,

The king will say to them, Truly I say to you, Insofar as you did it to one *of the least of these My brothers* you did it to Me.   Matt.25:40.

And elsewhere,

Jesus answered them, saying, Who is My mother, or *My brothers*? And looking round about He said, Behold My mother and *My brothers*! For whoever does the will of God is *My brother*, and My sister, and My mother.
Mark 3:33–35; Matt.12:49; Luke 8:21.

5410 'To buy grain from Egypt' means to make the good of truth its own through factual knowledge. This is clear from the meaning of 'buying' as making one's own, dealt with in 4397, 5374, 5406; from the meaning of 'grain' as the good of truth, dealt with in 5295; and from the meaning of 'Egypt' as factual knowledge, dealt with above in 5402.

5411 'And Benjamin, Joseph's brother' means the spiritual of the celestial, which is the intermediary. This is clear from the representation of 'Benjamin' as the spiritual of the celestial, dealt with in 4592, where it may also be seen that the spiritual of the celestial is the intermediary. In general it should be recognized that what is internal cannot have any communication with what is external, or conversely what is external with what is internal, unless an intermediary exists. Consequently truth from the Divine, which is 'Joseph', cannot have any communication with the truths that exist as a general whole within the natural, which are 'the sons of Jacob', unless the intermediary that is represented by 'Benjamin' and is called the spiritual of the celestial is present. And to be the intermediary it must partake of both, of both the internal and the external. The reason an intermediary is needed is that the internal and the external are utterly distinct from each other, so distinct that they can be separated from each other, just as a person's external or lowest part, which is his body, can be separated when it dies from his internal part, which is his spirit. The external is dead when the intermediary is severed from it but living when the intermediary is in place; also, the amount and the nature of the life that the external possesses depends on the amount and nature of the life that the intermediary present within it possesses. Because Jacob's sons did not have Benjamin, who is the intermediary, with them, Joseph could not therefore reveal who he was to his brothers. He consequently spoke hard words to them, calling them spies and placing them in custody, as a consequence of which they did not recognize him as Joseph.

2 But the essential nature of this intermediary represented by 'Benjamin' and called the spiritual of the celestial defies any description that is intelligible. For not even any rough ideas exist about the celestial of the spiritual, which is 'Joseph', or about the truths of the Church existing merely as known facts, which are 'the sons of Jacob', and therefore no rough ideas exist either about the spiritual of the celestial, which is 'Benjamin'. But in the light of heaven the nature of this intermediary is seen as if in broad daylight. Its essential nature is revealed by the use of indescribable representatives seen in the light of heaven, which light at the same time holds perception within it. For the light of heaven is essentially intelligence flowing from the Divine which enables every

single thing represented in the light of heaven to be perceived. The same is not so with the light of the world, for that light does not hold any intelligence at all within it; yet the understanding is formed by means of it – by means of the inflowing light of heaven into it, and at the same time by means of the inflowing of the power of perception which the light of heaven contains within itself. This being so, a person dwells in the light of heaven insofar as intelligence exists with him, while intelligence exists with him insofar as the truths of faith do so, and the truths of faith exist with him insofar as the good of love does so. Consequently a person dwells in the light of heaven insofar as the good of love exists with him.

5412   'Jacob did not send with his brothers' means without that intermediary. This becomes clear from what has been stated immediately above.

5413   'For he said, Perhaps harm may come to him' means that without the celestial of the spiritual, which is 'Joseph', that intermediary will perish. This is clear from the meaning of 'coming to harm' here as perishing. These words were spoken by Benjamin's father because he loved him and was afraid that he would perish among his brothers, as Joseph had done. But they have been quoted and incorporated into the Word because of the internal sense, which is that if the intermediary is present with external things alone without the internal it will perish, the intermediary being 'Benjamin', the external things 'the sons of Jacob', and the internal 'Joseph'. Indeed the intermediary perishes whenever it exists with external things alone without the internal, for the situation with the intermediary is this: It derives its being from what is internal and is therefore also kept in being from there; for it is brought into being when the internal beholds the external, when the affection and intention exists there to link that external to itself. Accordingly what is intermediate exists joined to the internal; and extending from the internal it is joined to the external, but not to the external without the internal. From this it is evident that if the intermediary is present with the external alone it will perish. What is more, it is a law common both to things in the spiritual world and to those in the natural world that anything prior can remain in being with what is prior to that, but not with what is posterior without what is prior to it. If it exists solely with what is posterior it will perish. The reason for this is that everything unconnected to something prior to itself is unconnected to Him who is the First, the Source of all that comes into being and is kept in being.

5414   'And the sons of Israel came to buy in the midst of others who came' means the wish to acquire spiritual truths, like all other truths, through factual knowledge. This is clear from the meaning of 'the sons of Israel' as spiritual truths (for 'sons' are truths, see above in 5403, and 'Israel' is the celestial-spiritual man coming out of the natural, 4286,

4570, 4598, so that 'the sons of Israel' are spiritual truths within the natural); from the meaning of 'buying' as being acquired; and from the meaning of 'in the midst of others who came' as like all other truths, that is to say, ones acquired through factual knowledge.

5415 'For the famine was in the land of Canaan' means that a desolation existed so far as things of the Church in the natural were concerned. This is clear from the meaning of 'the famine' as an absence of cognitions and consequently as a desolation, dealt with in 3364, 5277, 5279, 5281, 5300, 5349, 5360, 5376; and from the meaning of 'the land of Canaan' as the Church, dealt with in 3686, 3705, 4447. And as the Church is meant, what belongs to the Church is meant also. So it is that 'the famine was in the land of Canaan' means a desolation so far as things of the Church are concerned. The reason the desolation exists in the natural is that the words used here have reference to the sons of Jacob, by whom aspects of the external Church are meant, 5409, and consequently such things as belong to the Church within the natural.

5416 Verses 6–8 **And Joseph, he was the governor over the land, he was selling to all the people of the land. And Joseph's brothers came and bowed down to him, faces to the earth. And Joseph saw his brothers, and recognized them; and he acted as a stranger to them, and spoke hard words to them, and said to them, Where have you come from? And they said, From the land of Canaan, to buy food. And Joseph recognized his brothers, and they did not recognize him.**
'And Joseph, he was the governor over the land' means that the celestial of the spiritual, or truth from the Divine, reigned in the natural where factual knowledge resided. 'He was selling to all the people of the land' means that this was what effected every making over. 'And Joseph's brothers came' means general truths known to the Church which were without any intermediary. 'And bowed down to him, faces to the earth' means an expression of humility. 'And Joseph saw his brothers, and recognized them' means perception and recognition by the celestial of the spiritual. 'And he acted as a stranger to them' means that in the absence of the intermediary no joining together took place. 'And spoke hard words to them' means no agreement therefore existed either. 'And said to them, Where have you come from?' means an investigation. 'And they said, From the land of Canaan' means from the Church. 'To buy food' means to make the truth of good their own. 'And Joseph recognized his brothers' means that the truths of the Church were visible to the celestial of the spiritual in the light that this possessed. 'And they did not recognize him' means that truth from the Divine was not seen in natural light that was not yet brightened with heavenly light.

5417 'And Joseph, he was the governor over the land' means that the celestial of the spiritual, or truth from the Divine, reigned in the natural where factual knowledge resided. This is clear from the representation of 'Joseph' as the celestial of the spiritual, dealt with in 4286,

4963, 5249, 5307, 5331, 5332 (as regards the celestial of the spiritual being truth from the Divine, this will be seen below); from the meaning of 'the governor' as the one who reigned; and from the meaning of 'the land', in this case the land of Egypt, as the natural mind, and so the natural, dealt with in 5276, 5278, 5280, 5288, 5301. Regarding the fact that the celestial of the spiritual reigned within the natural where factual knowledge resided, see 5313; and the fact that 'Egypt' in the internal sense means factual knowledge, see 1164, 1165, 1186, 1462, 4749, 4964, 4966. The reason why the celestial of the spiritual is truth from the Divine is that, until it had been fully glorified, the Lord's Internal Human – being the receptacle of His Divine – was the celestial of the spiritual. It has to be called this because no other terms or thought-forms exist to describe it. This receptacle or recipient of the Divine is the same as truth from the Divine; and 'Joseph' is that truth, see 4723, 4727.

5418   'He was selling to all the people of the land' means that this was what effected every making over. This is clear from the meaning of 'selling' as making over to another as his own, dealt with in 5371, 5374; and from the meaning of 'the people of the land' as truths known to the Church, dealt with in 2928, in this case truths in the natural, 5409.

5419   'And Joseph's brothers came' means the general truths known to the Church which were without any intermediary. This is clear from the meaning of 'Joseph's brothers' as general truths known to the Church, dealt with above in 5409. They lacked any intermediary because Benjamin who was the intermediary was not with them. As regards 'Benjamin' being that intermediary, see above in 5411, 5413.

5420   'And bowed down to him, faces to the earth' means an expression of humility. This is clear from the meaning of 'bowing down' as an expression of humility, dealt with in 2153, and of 'faces to the earth' as a reverent expression of humility, 1999. The phrase 'expression of humility' is not used here to mean that which arises out of acknowledgement or recognition and is therefore an inward humility. Rather, an outward humility is meant, because such a bowing down was the accepted way to behave in front of the governor of the land. No inward, only outward humility is meant because as yet no agreement existed, no agreement leading to a joining together. When such is the state of the natural it can indeed humble itself, doing so to the utmost; yet this is no more than an acquired habit. It is a posture devoid of genuine affection as the producer of it, and so is a bodily action lacking its own true soul. This kind of an expression of humility is meant here.

5421   'And Joseph saw his brothers, and recognized them' means perception and recognition by the celestial of the spiritual. This is clear from the meaning of 'seeing' as perception, dealt with in 2150, 3764, 4567, 4723; from the representation of 'Joseph' as the celestial of the spiritual, dealt with above in 5417; from the meaning of 'his brothers' as general truths known to the Church, also dealt with above, in 5419; and from the meaning of 'recognizing' as recognition resulting from perception. Regarding this recognition on Joseph's side and the non-recognition on his brother's side, see below in 5422, 5427, 5428.

5422   'And he acted as a stranger to them' means that in the absence of the intermediary no joining together took place. This is clear from the meaning of 'acting as a stranger' here as the fact that no joining together takes place because the intermediary is absent. For one who is not joined reciprocally to others because no intermediary is present seems to be a stranger, which is how internal truth, or truth coming directly from the Divine, is seen by people who are interested solely in external truths. This now explains why Joseph at this point acted as a stranger to his brothers. Not that he was really alienated from them; rather, he loved them, for verse 24 says that he turned away from them and wept. The alienation existed on their side, for the reason that they were not joined to him; and this was represented by his acting in the way he did. Let an exemplification of this be seen in those places in the Word which say that Jehovah or the Lord acts as a stranger towards people, sets Himself against them, casts them away, condemns them, sends them to hell, punishes them, and is delighted when such things are done. When these things are said of Him the meaning in the internal sense is that those people act as strangers towards Jehovah or the Lord, set themselves against Him, are subject to evils which cast these people away from His presence, condemn them, send them to hell, and punish them, and that Jehovah or the Lord is by no means at all the source from which such deeds spring. But the Word speaks as though He is since that is the appearance; for to the simple He does appear to do those very things.

2   Something similar is the case with internal truths. Looked at from the point of view of external truths that are not joined to them through an intermediary, those internal truths appear totally alien to them; indeed they are sometimes seen to be set in opposition to them. But there is no opposition on the part of the internal truths; rather it exists with the external ones. For when these have no intermediary to join them to internal truths they inevitably view the internal ones by the light of the world separated from the light of heaven, and consequently see them as strangers alienated from them. But more will be said about this further on.

5423   'And spoke hard words to them' means no agreement therefore existed either. This is clear from the same explanation offered above regarding his acting as a stranger, though 'acting as a stranger' has regard to affection, which is an activity of the will, whereas 'speaking hard words' has regard to thought, which is an activity of the understanding; for in the internal sense 'speaking' means engaging in thought, 2271, 2287, 2619. What is internal appears to what is external to be 'a stranger' when no affection is present, and it appears 'to speak hard words' when the two are not in agreement. Such agreement exists when the internal manifests itself within the external and produces a representation of itself within this, so that no agreement exists when the internal does not manifest itself within the external and does not therefore produce any representation of itself within it. And that leads to the hardness there.

5424   'And said to them, Where have you come from?' means an investigation. This is clear without explanation.

5425   'And they said, From the land of Canaan' means from the Church. This is clear from the meaning of 'the land of Canaan' as the Church, dealt with in 3705, 3686, 4447.

5426   'To buy food' means to make the truth of good their own. This is clear from the meaning of 'buying' as making one's own, dealt with in 4397, 5374, 5406, 5410; and from the meaning of 'food' as the truth of good, dealt with in 5293, 5340, 5342.

5427   'And Joseph recognized his brothers' means that the truths of the Church were visible to the celestial of the spiritual in the light that this possessed. This is clear from the meaning of 'recognizing' as perceiving, seeing, and so being visible; from the representation of 'Joseph' as the celestial of the spiritual, dealt with already; and from the meaning of 'his brothers' as the general truths known to the Church, dealt with above in 5409, 5419. And since 'Joseph recognized his brothers' means that those truths – the general truths known to the Church – were visible to the celestial of the spiritual, it follows that they were seen by the light in which the celestial of the spiritual dwells and so by the light which the celestial of the spiritual possesses. In this light, which is truth from the Divine, 5417, every single truth below – that is, within the natural – is visible. But the reverse is not possible if no intermediary is present, still less if no agreement between the two sides exists, no agreement enabling the two to be joined together. This becomes quite clear from the consideration that angels dwelling in the heavens, and so in the light of heaven, can see every single thing that happens in the world of spirits, which is immediately below the heavens, as well as every single thing that happens on the earth of the lower ones, and indeed that happens in the hells. But the reverse is not possible.

It is also the case that the angels of a higher heaven can see everything that is happening in the heaven beneath them, but the reverse is not so unless an intermediary exists. Intermediary spirits also serve as the means by which communication forward and back takes place. When therefore those who are in a lower position and have no intermediary, and more particularly those who are not in agreement with the ones above them, look at the light of heaven, they see absolutely nothing at all; everything there appears to them to dwell in total obscurity. But in fact those in the place where they look dwell in the brightest light. This may be illustrated by the following unique experience: A large city once appeared in front of me, where there were thousands of different, delightful and beautiful sights. I saw these because an intermediary had been provided; yet the spirits present with me could not see a single thing because they had no intermediary. I was told that even though they are present in that place those who are not in agreement with the ones above them discern nothing whatever of the things existing there.

3   The same is similarly true of a person's interior man or spirit, which is also called his soul. The interior man can see every single thing present and taking place in the exterior man; but the reverse is not possible unless the two are in agreement and an intermediary is present. To the exterior man therefore, when it is not in agreement with the interior man, the interior man does not appear to have any existence. It appears to be so completely non-existent that when anything is said about the interior man, it seems to the exterior man either to be so obscure that it is unwilling even to contemplate it or to be nothing it can believe in. But when agreement between the two does exist, the exterior man sees, with the help of the intermediary, what is going on in the interior man. For then the light which the interior man possesses enters into the light which the exterior or natural man possesses; that is, heavenly light passes into natural light and brightens it, and in this brighter light what is happening to the interior man is made visible. This is the origin of the intelligence and wisdom which the exterior man possesses. But if no intermediary is present, and especially if no agreement exists, the interior man sees and perceives what is going on in the exterior man and also to some extent guides it; the reverse however does not happen. More than that, if contrariety exists – that is to say, if the exterior man completely perverts or snuffs out what comes in by way of the interior man – the interior man is deprived of the light it receives from heaven, heaven is inaccessible to it, and a communication from hell with the exterior man is opened up. You may see more about these matters in what now follows below.

5428   'And they did not recognize him' means that truth from the Divine was not seen in natural light that was not yet brightened with heavenly light. This becomes clear from what has gone immediately before this, for since 'Joseph recognized his brothers' means that general truths known to the Church were seen by the celestial of the spiritual by the light this possessed, it follows that 'they did not recognize him' means that the celestial of the spiritual, which is truth from the Divine, was not seen by the general truths known to the Church while these were in natural light not yet brightened with heavenly light. This meaning may indeed be seen from what has been stated immediately above; but as it belongs among arcana let some examples be used to shed light on the matter. Take as an example the glory of heaven. Consider those who, when they think about the glory of heaven, see this in natural light that has not been brightened with heavenly light because no intermediary is present, especially if no agreement exists. Such people's idea of the glory of heaven cannot be anything different from the kind of idea they possess about the glory of the world when they read, for instance, about the revelations made to prophets, in particular those made to John and described in the Book of Revelation, in which everything is most magnificent. One may tell these people that the glory of heaven surpasses all worldly magnificence, so completely that one cannot begin to compare it with that glory. One may also tell them that even this is not really the glory of heaven, but that the glory of heaven consists in that which is of God shining out of every individual thing to be seen there, and in a perception of Divine realities and in the wisdom gained from that perception. One may tell these people too that this alone is the glory to those who are there, for they consider worldly magnificence, in comparison with such wisdom, to be nothing at all, and they attribute all wisdom to the Lord and none whatsoever to themselves. But if people behold the glory of heaven in natural light devoid of an intermediary, and especially if no agreement exists, that glory goes completely unrecognized.

Take angelic power as another example. Consider those who, when they think about angelic power, in particular that of the archangels who are mentioned in the Word, do so in natural light that has not been brightened with heavenly light because no intermediary is present, especially if because no agreement exists. Such people's idea of that power cannot be anything different from the idea they have of the power wielded by powerful rulers in the world. That is to say, they think that angels have thousands upon thousands of subordinates over whom they rule, and that high positions in heaven involve that kind of domination. One may tell these people that angelic power does indeed surpass all power wielded by powerful rulers in the world and is so great that just one of the subordinate angels can drive away millions of hellish spirits and send them down into their own hells, which is why in the Word angels are called 'powers' and 'dominions'. One may also tell those people that the least of the angels is the greatest; that is, the one who believes, wishes, and perceives that all power originates entirely within the Lord and never at all within himself is a very highly powerful ruler. And therefore those who are 'powers' in heaven utterly detest any power that derives from themselves. But neither is any of this recognized when beheld in natural light devoid of the intermediary, and more so if no agreement exists.

Take yet another example. Consider a person who looks at freedom from a natural idea devoid of an intermediary linking it to a spiritual one, and especially if no agreement exists between the two. He cannot see freedom as anything else than thinking and willing from what is within himself and being able to carry out without restriction whatever he so thinks and wills. More than that, to the end that he can have whatever he thinks and wills the natural man wishes to become very rich; and to the end that he can carry out whatever he thinks and wills he wishes to become very powerful. Once he has attained this he imagines that he is in perfect freedom and consequently possesses real happiness. If however one tells people like this that true freedom, called heavenly freedom, is not at all like that, but that it involves no willing from what is within oneself, only from the Lord, and does not involve any thinking from what is within oneself, only from heaven, and that feelings of pain and sorrow ensue if one is allowed to think from what is within oneself and to will from what is in oneself, nothing of this is recognized.

These examples may serve to some extent to show what is implied by truth from the Divine not being seen in natural light that has not yet been brightened with heavenly light, meant by Joseph's brothers not recognizing him.

5429 Verses 9–16 **And Joseph remembered the dreams which he had dreamed involving them; and he said to them, You are spies; you have come to see the nakedness of the land. And they said to him, No, my lord; and your servants come to buy food. All we, the sons of one man are we. We are upright men; your servants are not spies. And he said to them, No, but the nakedness of the land you have come to see. And they said, Twelve are your servants, brothers are we, the sons of one man in the land of Canaan; and behold, the youngest is with our father today, and one is not. And Joseph said to them, It is as I spoke to you, saying, You are spies. In this manner you will be tested: As sure as Pharaoh lives[1], you shall not go out of here unless your youngest brother comes here. Send one of you and let him fetch your brother; and you will be in bonds, and your words will be tested, whether the truth is with you. And if not, as sure as Pharaoh lives[1], you are spies.**

'And Joseph remembered the dreams which he had dreamed involving them' means that the celestial of the spiritual foresaw what was to happen to the general truths known to the Church in the natural. 'And he said to them' means the consequent perception. 'You are spies' means that they existed solely for the sake of gain. 'You have come to see the nakedness of the land' means that nothing would please them more than to know for themselves that they are not truths. 'And they said to him, No, sir, we are upright men[2]' means that truths are indeed present within them. 'And your servants come to buy food' means that they are present to enable the natural to make them its own by means of good. 'All we, the sons of one man are we' means that those truths all have the same origin. 'We are upright men' means that truths are accordingly present within them. 'Your servants are not spies' means that thus they are not there for the sake of gain. 'And he said to them,

---

[1] *lit.* May Pharaoh live!

[2] *Here and in* 5434 *Sw. has* Non domine, recti nos (No sir, we are upright men) *instead of* Non domine mi (No, my lord).

No, but the nakedness of the land you have come to see' means that they do not care whether they are truths. 'And they said, Twelve are your servants, brothers are we' means that all aspects of faith exist joined together in this manner. 'The sons of one man' means that they have the same origin. 'In the land of Canaan' means in the Church. 'And behold, the youngest is with our father today' means that they are also joined to spiritual good. 'And one is not' means that the Divine spiritual from which [the joining together begins] is not apparent. 'And Joseph said to them' means perception regarding that matter. 'It is as I spoke to you' means that the truth of the matter is as I thought. 'Saying, You are spies' means that they are interested in the truths known to the Church for the sake of gain. 'In this manner you will be tested' means it will be seen whether this is so. 'As sure as Pharaoh lives' means a certainty. 'You shall not go out of here unless your youngest brother comes here' means that truths with you cannot help being such unless these have been joined to spiritual good. 'Send one of you and let him fetch your brother' means provided that some kind of joining to that good exists. 'And you will be in bonds' means if all else is still separated. 'And your words will be tested, whether the truth is with you' means that in this way the fact of the matter will be established. 'And if not, as sure as Pharaoh lives, you are spies' means otherwise it is certain that truths exist with you solely for the sake of gain.

5430 'And Joseph remembered the dreams which he had dreamed involving them' means that the celestial of the spiritual foresaw what was to happen to the general truths known to the Church in the natural. This is clear from the meaning of 'remembering' as what exists at present, for whenever one calls something to remembrance it is brought into the present ('remembering' is used in references to foresight, see 3966); from the representation of 'Joseph' as the celestial of the spiritual, often dealt with already; and from the meaning of 'dreams' as foresight, foretelling, and outcome, dealt with in 3698, 5091, 5092, 5104, here therefore a foresight of what was to happen to the general truths known to the Church in the natural, these truths being meant by 'the sons of Jacob', 5409, 5419. This explains the addition of the phrase 'which he had dreamed'.

5431 'And he said to them' means the consequent perception. This is clear from the meaning of 'saying' as perception, dealt with in 1791, 1815, 1819, 1822, 1898, 1919, 2080, 2619, 2862, 3509.

5432 'You are spies' means that they existed solely for the sake of gain. This is clear from the meaning of 'spies' here as being bent on material gain; indeed it is clear from the train of thought that nothing else is meant in the internal sense by 'spies'. For the internal sense here deals with the truths known to the Church which are to be made over to the natural as its own. But such a making over is not possible unless an influx takes place from the celestial of the spiritual through the intermediary, those truths known to the Church being 'the sons of Jacob', who are 'Joseph's brothers', the celestial of the spiritual being 'Joseph', and the intermediary being 'Benjamin'. The implications of all this have been stated in 5402. There it is shown that when the truths of faith which are known to the Church and are called its teachings are learned at the earliest stage of life, they are taken in and consigned to the memory as facts in the same way as any other factual knowledge. And they remain there as factual knowledge until the person begins to use his own ability to look at those truths and see for himself whether they really are truths, and – having seen that they are such – to act in conformity with them. That ability to look at such truths and this willingness to act in conformity with them cause them to be factual knowledge no longer. Now they are commandments to be obeyed in life, till at length they are his life; for they then pass into the life he leads and are made his own.

2 People who have reached adult years, and especially those who have arrived at old age, but have not used their own ability to look at the truths known to the Church, called its doctrinal teachings, to see for themselves whether these really are truths, or to form any subsequent wish to live in conformity with them, inevitably retain them in exactly the same way as they do all other factual knowledge. Those truths remain solely in their natural memory, and from there in their mouth. When they speak truths they do so not from their interior man or heart, only from their exterior man or mouth. When this is a person's state he cannot possibly believe that the truths known to the Church are truths, no matter how much it might seem to him that he does believe that they are. The reason why it seems to him that he does believe they are truths is that he trusts other people and their ideas and firmly embraces them. To embrace firmly other people's ideas, no matter whether they are truths or falsities, is very easy, for it involves no more than the use of one's intellect.

3 These truths known to the Church – that is, those people with whom they exist in the way explained immediately above – are meant by spies coming to see the nakedness of the land. For their belief in the teachings of their Church does not spring from any affection for truth but from an affection for securing important positions and personal gain. For this reason they themselves have scarcely any belief, and there is denial for the most part in their hearts. They regard the Church's teachings in the way a merchant does his wares, in that they seem to themselves to be well-taught and wise when from within themselves they see those teachings as untrue and yet they are able to convince the common people that they are true. It is quite evident from those in the next life that very many leaders of Churches are like this. Wherever they go in the next life they take with them the sphere emanating from their affections and consequent thoughts, and that sphere is clearly percep- tible to others. From this sphere one can recognize quite plainly what kind of affection for truth and what kind of faith they have possessed.

The same is not made plain in the world because no spiritual perception of such things exists there. This being so, those leaders of Churches
do not reveal what they really think, for that would deprive them of
what they seek to gain.

The fact that these are 'spies' becomes perfectly clear from the consideration that they are the kind of people who do nothing else than
find fault with, so as to accuse and condemn, those who adhere to truths
grounded in good. Whether they belong to the Papists so-called, or to
the Reformed, or to the Quakers, or to the Socinians, or to the Jews, are
not such people, once they have firmly embraced the teachings of their
Church, nothing else than 'spies'? They deride and condemn absolute
truths, if these are known anywhere; for truths are not embraced by
them because they are truths, the reason for this being that they are not
moved by any affection for truth for its own sake, let alone for their
life's sake, only for the sake of personal gain. Also, when such people
read the Word they examine it closely with the sole intention of
confirming what is already known and taught, and for the sake of
material gain. Many of them examine the Word closely 'to see the
nakedness of the land', that is, to see there the truths known to the
Church not as truths but merely as means that will serve them to
convince others, for the sake of their own personal gain, that they are
truths.

People however who are moved by an affection for truth for its own
sake and for their life's sake, consequently for the sake of the Lord's
kingdom, do indeed have faith in the teachings of the Church. But even
so they examine the Word closely with no other end in view than to see
the truth itself, as a result of which they develop a faith and a
conscience that are their own. If anyone tells them that they ought to
keep to the teachings of the Church in which they were born, they then
think that they would have been told exactly the same if they had been
born within Judaism, within Socinianism, Quakerism, or Christian
Gentilism, or even outside the Church, and that everywhere they would
say, This is where the Church is, this is where the Church is; truths
exist here and nowhere else! This being what they think they decide to
examine the Word closely, praying sincerely to the Lord for enlightenment as they do so. People like these do not upset anyone else within
the Church, nor do they ever condemn others, for they recognize that
the life led by everyone who is a Church is founded on the faith that is
his own.

5433   'You have come to see the nakedness of the land' means that
nothing would please them more than to know for themselves that they
are not truths. This is clear from the meaning of 'coming to see' as
wishing to know that a thing is so, and therefore as nothing would give
greater pleasure than to know it; from the meaning of 'the nakedness'
as a lack of truths, thus that they are not truths, dealt with below; and
from the meaning of 'the land' as the Church (see 566, 662, 1067, 1262,

1733, 1850, 2117, 2118(end), 3355, 4447, 4535), so that 'the nakedness of the land' here means a lack of truths known to the Church. The reason 'the nakedness' means a deprivation or lack of truths is that 'clothes' in general means truths, while each specific type of garment means some particular kind of truth, see 2576, 3301, 4545, 4677, 4741, 4742, 4763, 5248, 5319, and therefore 'the nakedness' means a lack of truths, as will also be seen from the places below that are quoted from the Word.

2 The implications of this may be seen from what has been stated immediately above in 5432, where it is said that people who do not learn truths for truth's own sake and for their life's sake, but for the sake of material gain, inevitably think that the truths known to the Church are not truths. The reason for this is that the affection for gain is an earthly affection, whereas the affection for truth is a spiritual one. One or the other must have dominion, for no one can serve two masters. Consequently where one affection exists the other does not, so that where the affection for truth is present the affection for gain is absent, and where the affection for gain is present the affection for truth is absent. This being so, if the affection for material gain has dominion, then inevitably nothing pleases the person more than to know that truths are not truths. Yet nothing else pleases him more than when others believe that truths are truths. If the internal man looks downwards, that is to say, towards earthly things and makes these everything, he cannot possibly look upwards and have anything there since earthly things completely swallow up and smother everything. The reason for this is that the angels from heaven who are present with a person cannot dwell among earthly things; they therefore depart, in which case spirits from hell draw near who, while they are present with a person, cannot dwell among heavenly things. As a consequence he then thinks that heavenly things are of no importance, while earthly ones are everything. And when that person thinks that earthly things are everything, he believes himself to be more learned and wiser than everybody else, in that he himself does not accept the truths known to the Church, and at the same time says that they exist for those who are simple. The affection that moves a person is therefore either an earthly affection or else a heavenly one, for he cannot have his being simultaneously with angels from heaven and with spirits from hell; for if he did he would be left hanging between heaven and hell. But when he is moved by an affection for truth for truth's own sake, that is, for the sake of the Lord's kingdom (where Divine Truth is present) and so for the Lord's sake, he is among angels. He does not in this case despise material gain insofar as it enables him to lead his life in the world. But such gain is not his end in view, only the useful purposes it serves which are seen by him as intermediate ends leading on to an ultimate heavenly one. This being so, his heart is by no means at all set on material gain.

3 The fact that 'the nakedness' means a lack of truths may also be seen from other places in the Word, as in John,

To the angel of the Church of the Laodiceans write, Because you say, I am rich and have become wealthy, so that I have need of nothing – when you do not know that you are wretched and miserable, and needy, and blind, and *naked*.... Rev.3:17.

Here being 'naked' stands for suffering from a scarcity of truth. In the same place,

I counsel you to buy from Me gold purified in the fire, and white garments to clothe you, and do not let *the shame of your nakedness* be manifested. Rev.3:18.

'Buying gold' stands for acquiring good and making this one's own, 'that you may become wealthy' for acquiring it to the end that celestial and spiritual good may be present; 'white garments' stands for spiritual truths, 'the shame of nakedness' for the lack of any goodness or truth. For 'buying' means acquiring and making one's own, see 5374; 'gold' celestial and spiritual good, 1551, 1552; 'garments' truths, 1073, 2576, 4545, 4763, 5248, 5319; while 'white' is attributed to truth because this comes from the light of heaven, 3301, 3993, 4007, 5319.

In the same book,

Behold, I am coming like a thief. Blessed is he who is awake and keeps his garments, *so that he may not walk naked.* Rev.16:15.

'He who keeps his garments' stands for the person who hangs on to truths. 'So that he may not walk naked' stands for so that he is not without truths. In Matthew,

The King will say to those at His right hand, *I was naked* and *you clothed Me around*, and to those at His left, *I was naked and you did not clothe Me around.* Matt.25:36,43.

'Naked' stands for the good who acknowledge that within themselves no good or truth at all exists, 4958.

In Isaiah,

Is not this the fast, to break your bread for the hungry, and that you may bring afflicted outcasts to your house, *when you see the naked* and *cover him*? Isa.58:7.

Here the meaning is similar. In Jeremiah,

Jerusalem sinned grievously, therefore she became a menstruous woman; all who honoured her despised her, *for they saw her nakedness.* Lam.1:18.

Here 'nakedness' stands for a lack of truths. In Ezekiel,

You reached full beauty, your breasts were formed and your hair had grown; but you were *naked* and *bare.* I spread My wing over you and *covered your nakedness.* You did not remember the days of your youth, *when you were naked* and *bare.* Ezek.16:7,8,22.

This refers to Jerusalem, by which the Ancient Church is meant – what it was like when it was first established and what it came to be like after that. That is to say, initially it was lacking in truths, after which it was furnished with them, but finally it cast them aside. In the same prophet,

If a man is righteous, one who has executed judgement and righteousness, he gives his bread to the hungry and *covers the naked with clothing.* Ezek.18:5,7.

'Covering the naked with clothing' stands for furnishing with truths those who desire truths. In Hosea,

Lest *I strip her naked*, present her as she was on the day she was born, and make her like a wilderness, and set her like a land of dryness, and slay her with thirst. Hosea 2:3.

'Stripping her naked' stands for leaving her without truths. In Nahum,

I will show the nations *your nakedness*, and the kingdoms your shame. Nahum 3:5.

'Showing the nations its nakedness' stands for its ugliness. All ugliness is a result of the absence of truths, all beauty a result of the presence of them, 4985, 5199.

5434 'And they said to him, No, sir, we are upright men' means that truths are indeed present within them. This is clear from the meaning of 'saying to him, No, sir' as a denial that they existed for the sake of gain, meant by Joseph's words 'you are spies', 5432, and a denial that nothing would please them more than to know it for themselves that they are not truths, meant by Joseph's words 'you have come to see the nakedness of the land', 5433; and from the meaning of 'we are upright men' as that truths are indeed present within them, 'uprightness' meaning truth in the internal sense here, as also many times elsewhere in the Word. This meaning – that truths are indeed present within them – follows from the whole train of thought; for in the case of people who have acquired to themselves the truths known to the Church, doing so for the sake of their own material gain, those truths are not indeed truths to them, as shown above in 5433. But even so, truths can indeed be present within them, such truths known to the Church as a general whole being meant by 'the sons of Jacob'. The reason 'upright men' means truths quite apart from persons is that in the internal sense everything is withdrawn from ideas about persons; an idea in the literal sense describing a person becomes an idea describing some spiritual reality, see 5225, 5287. The reason for this is that otherwise the reader's thought and consequent speech are inevitably distracted and diverted from that spiritual reality and contemplation of it to details that have to do with the person. What is more, there is no other way in which the thought and consequent speech can become more universal, no other way in which just a number of ideas, let alone ideas that are countless and indescribable, can be taken in simultaneously, as is the case among angels. But although such spiritual images are withdrawn from ideas of persons they still have to do with persons; that is to say, they have to do with people in whom those spiritual realities are present. This is why 'upright men' means truths.

5435 'And your servants come to buy food' means that they are present to enable the natural to make them – these truths – its own by means of good. This is clear from the meaning of 'servants' as lower things and natural ones when considered in relation to others, dealt with in 2541, 3019, 3020, 5161, 5164, 5305, and consequently as truths too, 3409, since truths are subordinate to good and in the Word subordinates are called 'servants' (as is therefore the case here where, in relation to the celestial of the spiritual, truths in the natural are such); from the meaning of 'buying' as being made one's own, dealt with in 4397, 5374, 5406, 5410; and from the meaning of 'food' as celestial and spiritual good, dealt with in 5147, as well as truth linked to good, 5340, 5342, in this place truth that has to be linked to the natural by means of good and so made its own.

There is no other means than good by which truth can be made a person's own. But once it has been made his own by means of good, truth becomes good, for it now acts in unison with it. At the same time the two make so to speak one body, the soul of which is the good. The truths are present within that good like spiritual fibres forming the body. For this reason also the inmost forms going forth from good are meant by the fibres of the body, and truths by the sinews there, 4303, 5189(end).

5436   'All we, the sons of one man are we' means that those truths all have the same origin. This is clear from the meaning of 'the sons', who in this case are the sons of Jacob, as truths in general, often dealt with already. As regards 'of one man' meaning that they all have the same origin, this is evident without explanation.

5437   'We are upright men' means that truths are accordingly present within them. This is clear from the meaning of 'we are upright men' as the presence of truths within them, dealt with just above in 5434.

5438   'Your servants are not spies' means that they were not there for the sake of gain. This is clear from the meaning of 'spies' as the possession of truths known to the Church for the sake of gain, dealt with above in 5432, in this case a denial of this.

5439   'And he said to them, No, but the nakedness of the land you have come to see' means that they do not care whether they are truths. This is clear from the meaning of 'coming to see the nakedness of the land' as that nothing would please them more than to know for themselves that they are not truths, dealt with in 5433. Here something similar is meant – that they do not care whether they are truths.

5440   'And they said, Twelve are your servants, brothers are we' means that all aspects of faith existed joined together in this manner. This is clear from the meaning of 'twelve' as all, and when used as it is here in reference to the sons of Jacob, or to the tribes named after them, and also when used in reference to the apostles, all aspects of faith in their entirety are meant, dealt with in 577, 2089, 2129, 2130, 2553, 3272, 3488, 3858, 3862, 3913, 3926, 3939, 4060; and from the meaning of 'brothers' as their existing joined together through good, for when joined together through good truths assume a kind of brotherly relationship with one another. If in the absence of good they appear to be joined together, they are not in fact so joined; falsities resulting from evil always come in and set them apart. The reason this happens is that those truths do not then have the same origin from which they spring, nor do they have the same end to which they look. If they are to exist joined together they must do so from start to finish. Good from which they spring must be there right from the start, and good to which they look must be there through to the finish. Furthermore, that good must reign everywhere there if the truths are to exist joined together; for that which reigns everywhere effects the joining together. 'A brother' means the affection for good, and so good itself, see 2524, 2360, 3303, 3459, 3803, 3815, 4121.

5441 'The sons of one man' means that they have the same origin. This is clear from what has been stated just above in 5436, where similar words occur.

5442 'In the land of Canaan' means in the Church. This is clear from the meaning of 'the land of Canaan' as the Lord's kingdom and the Church, dealt with in 1413, 1437, 1607, 3038, 3481, 3686, 3705, 4447.

5443 'And behold, the youngest is with our father today' means that they are also joined to spiritual good. This is clear from the representation of Benjamin, to whom 'the youngest' refers here, as the intermediary effecting a joining together, dealt with below; and from the representation of Jacob, who by now was Israel, to whom 'father' refers here, as spiritual good, dealt with in 3654, 4598. 'Benjamin' is the spiritual of the celestial, which is the intermediary, see 4592, 5411, 5413, 5419. That is to say, it is the intermediary that links the natural, or what is present in the natural, to the celestial of the spiritual, which is 'Joseph'. And since 'Benjamin' is the intermediary, while 'Israel' is spiritual good, the words 'behold, the youngest is with our father today' therefore mean a joining to spiritual good.

5444. 'And one is not' means that the Divine spiritual from which [the joining together begins] is not apparent. This is clear from the representation of Joseph, to whom 'one' refers here, as the celestial of the spiritual, or what amounts to the same, the Divine spiritual, which is truth from the Divine, dealt with in 3969, 4286, 4592, 4723, 4727, 4963, 5249, 5307, 5331, 5332, 5417 (and since the whole joining together of truth in the natural begins from the Divine spiritual, the expression 'the Divine spiritual from which' is used); and from the meaning of 'is not' as the fact that it is not apparent. For Joseph was present there but did not make it apparent to them who he was because the intermediary, which is 'Benjamin', was not with them.

5445 'And Joseph said to them' means perception regarding that matter, that is to say, those things spoken by his brothers. This is clear from the meaning of 'saying' in the historical narratives of the Word as perceiving, dealt with in 1791, 1815, 1819, 1822, 1898, 1919, 2080, 2619, 3509.

5446   'It is as I spoke to you' means that the truth of the matter is as I thought. This is clear from the meaning of 'speaking' as thinking, dealt with in 2271, 2287, 2619. This meaning – that the truth of the matter is as he thought – is evident without explanation.

5447   'Saying, You are spies' means that they are interested in the truths known to the Church for the sake of gain. This is clear from the meaning of 'spies' as people who are interested in the truths known to the Church solely for the sake of gain, dealt with in 5432, 5438.

5448   'In this manner you will be tested' means it will be seen whether this is so. This is clear without explanation.

5449   'As sure as Pharaoh lives' means a certainty. This is clear from the fact that 'as sure as Pharaoh lives' is a phrase that is employed to say something emphatically, thus to state a certainty. Joseph, it is true, knew they were not spies and that they had not come to see the nakedness of the land; nevertheless he used that phrase because of the certainty described in the internal sense – the certainty that unless they are joined by means of good to the interior man, the truths known to the Church, with whomsoever they are present, possess no other end in view than material gain. But once they have become joined through good to the interior man they have what is really good and true, and so the Church, the Lord's kingdom, and the Lord Himself as their end in view. And when people have these as their end in view, material gain also comes their way, insofar as they have need of it, in keeping with the Lord's words in Matthew,

Seek first the kingdom of God and His righteousness, and all these things will be added to you.   Matt.6:33.

5450   'You shall not go out of here unless your youngest brother comes here' means that truths with you cannot help being such unless they have been joined to spiritual good. This cannot be explained very easily according to the meanings of the individual words that are used; it is however the meaning that springs from them, for here 'your youngest brother' means existing joined to spiritual good, see 5443.

5451   'Send one of you and let him fetch your brother' means provided that some kind of joining to that good exists. This is clear from the meaning of 'your brother' – the youngest one – as a joining to spiritual good, as immediately above in 5450; and from the meaning of 'send one and let him fetch him' as provided that some kind of joining to this exists. For a matter of doubt is being expressed.

5452   'And you will be in bonds' means if all else is separated. This is clear from the meaning of 'being in bonds' here as being separated.

For one who is held in bonds is separated, separated from spiritual good meant by their father Israel.

5453 'And your words will be tested, whether the truth is with you' means that in this way the truth of the matter will be established. This is clear from the meaning of 'words being tested' and of 'whether it is the truth' as its being a certainty that the truth will in that case come out, that is to say, it will be seen whether what they said was the truth. This certainty is concerned with what they stated and the things contained in the internal sense of their statements, dealt with above in 5434-5444.

5454 'And if not, as sure as Pharaoh lives, you are spies' means that otherwise it is a certainty that truths exist with you solely for the sake of gain. This is clear from the meaning of 'as sure as Pharaoh lives' as a certainty, dealt with in 5449, and from the meaning of 'spies' as ones who are interested in the truths known to the Church solely for the sake of material gain, dealt with in 5432, 5438, 5447. No fuller explanation of these words and those immediately before them is attempted here as a general explanation has appeared already in what went before, apart from which they are the kinds of matters that cannot possibly present themselves at all clearly to the understanding. For general ideas must exist first in the understanding, and only then can the particular details such as are contained in what went previously be added. If general ideas are not received first, particular details are by no means allowed in. Indeed they are a source of boredom since no affection for such details exists unless the general ideas have entered in with affection prior to that.

5455 Verses 17–20 **And he shut them up in custody for three days. And Joseph said to them on the third day, Do this and you will live, [for] I fear God: If you are upright men, let one brother among you be in bonds in the house of your custody, and you, go, take corn for the famine of your houses. And bring your youngest brother to me, and your words will be verified, and you will not die. And they did so.**
'And he shut them up in custody' means a separation of them from himself. 'For three days' means that which is complete. 'And Joseph said to them on the third day' means a perception of the celestial of the spiritual regarding those truths separated from itself, when completion is reached. 'Do this and you will live, [for] I fear God' means that so it will be if they have life from the Divine. 'If you are upright men' means if truths are indeed present within them. 'One brother among you is to be in bonds in the house of your custody' means that faith in the will must be separated. 'And you, go, take corn for the famine of your houses' means that in the meantime they will be left in freedom to consider their own interests. 'And bring your youngest brother to me' means until the intermediary is present. 'And your words will be verified' means that in this case those truths will be exactly as they have

been declared to be. 'And you will not die' means that the truths will thereby possess life. 'And they did so' means the end of this state.

5456   'And he shut them up in custody' means a separation of them from himself. This is clear from the meaning of 'putting (or shutting up) in custody' as a casting aside, and so a separation, dealt with in 5083, 5101.

5457   'For three days' means that which is complete. This is clear from the meaning of 'three days' as from beginning to end, and so that which is complete, dealt with in 2788, 4495. It is a new state that is now under description here. The entire state is meant by 'three days', its last phase, and so a new one, being meant by 'on the third day', dealt with in the next paragraph.

5458   'And Joseph said to them on the third day' means the perception of the celestial of the spiritual regarding those truths separated from itself, when completion is reached. This is clear from the meaning of 'saying' as perception, dealt with in 1791, 1815, 1819, 1822, 1898, 1919, 2619, 3509; from the representation of 'the sons of Jacob' as the truths known to the Church in general, dealt with already, here those truths when separated from the celestial of the spiritual, 5436; from the representation of 'Joseph' as the celestial of the spiritual, also dealt with already; and from the meaning of 'on the third day' as the last phase when another state begins, dealt with in 5159, 5457, and so when completion is reached. From all this it is evident that 'Joseph said to them on the third day' means the perception of the celestial of the spiritual regarding those truths separated from itself, when completion is reached.

5459   'Do this and you will live, [for] I fear God' means that so it will be if they have life from the Divine. This is clear from the meaning of 'do this' as so it will be; from the meaning of 'you will live' as that they – the truths meant here by 'the sons of Jacob' – will have life; and from the meaning of 'I fear God' as from the Divine. For 'Joseph' represents the Lord as regards truth from the Divine, which is the same as the celestial of the spiritual, and therefore 'I' here, in the highest sense, means truth from the Divine, while 'God' is the Divine itself that is present within the celestial of the spiritual or that is present within truth. In the highest sense, when it is used in reference to the Lord, 'fearing' does not mean fear but love. Also. 'the fear of God' mentioned in various places in the Word means a love that is felt for God, the exact nature of that love being determined by wherever it exists. Among those whose worship is external, devoid of anything internal, that love becomes fear; and among those whose worship is spiritual it becomes holy fear. But among those whose worship is celestial it becomes love that holds the feeling of sacred awe. Within the Lord however it was not fear at all but pure love. From this it may be seen that 'I fear God', when this has reference to the Lord, means Divine Love, and so the Divine.

5460   'If you are upright men' means if truths are indeed present within them. This is clear from the meaning of 'being upright men' as truths present within them, dealt with above in 5434, 5437.

5461   'One brother among you is to be in bonds in the house of your custody' means that faith in the will must be separated. This is clear from the representation of Simeon – who is the 'one brother who is to be in bonds', named in verse 24 – as faith in the will, dealt with in 3869–3872, 4497, 4502, 4503; and from the meaning of 'being in bonds in the house of custody' as being separated, dealt with in 5083, 5101, 5452, 5456. The implications of this are that when faith in the will – that is, when the will which desires to put the truth of faith into practice – is separated from people with whom the truths known to the Church are present, the link with the Divine is in that case so slender that it is little more than an awareness.

2   In the case of someone who has been regenerated the Divine flows from the Lord into good, and from this into truth; or what amounts to the same, it flows into his will, and from there into his understanding. To the extent therefore that someone with whom the truths of faith are present receives good from the Lord, the Lord forms for him a new will within the understanding part of his mind (why in the understanding part, see 927, 1023, 1043, 1044, 2256, 4328, 4493, 5113), and the Lord enters in there and creates an affection to do good, that is, to exercise charity towards the neighbour. From this one may see what is meant by the explanation that faith in the will must be separated, which faith is represented by 'Simeon', before the intermediary, which is 'Benjamin', comes to be present.

5462   'And you, go, take corn for the famine of your houses' means that in the meantime they will be left in freedom to consider their own interests. This is clear from the meaning of 'you, go', after they had been held in bonds and one was then kept back in place of them, as their being left in freedom in the meantime; from the meaning of 'corn' as truth, dealt with in 5276, 5280, 5292; from the meaning of 'the famine' as an absence of cognitions and a desolation, dealt with in 5360, 5376; and from the meaning of 'your houses' as the dwelling-places where specifically truths of every kind reside, namely the natural mind. For 'a house' is the natural mind, see 4973, 5023, and the truths represented by 'the sons of Jacob' here, are those known to the external Church, and so are truths in the natural, 5401, 5415, 5428. From all these meanings taken together one may see that 'take corn for the famine of your houses' means so as to consider their own interests amid the desolation of truth in which they find themselves.

5463   'And bring your youngest brother to me' means until the intermediary is present. This is clear from the representation of 'Benjamin' as the intermediary, that is to say, between the celestial of the spiritual and the natural, dealt with above in 5411, 5443.

5464   'And your words will be verified' means that in this case those truths will be exactly as they have been declared to be. This becomes clear without explanation. For what the brothers, and consequently what the truths known to the Church represented by those brothers, declared themselves to be, see above in 5434–5456. The implications of all this are as follows: People who are interested in the truths known to the Church solely for the sake of material gain can declare, just as well as others do, what the situation is with regard to truths. They can just as well declare, for example, that truths do not become a person's own unless they have been joined to the interior man, and indeed that they cannot be so joined except by means of good, and also that truths do not possess any life until this is done. At times they see these matters and others like them just as well as anyone else does, and sometimes their discernment of them seems even better. Yet this is so only when they talk to other people about such matters. When they talk to themselves about them, thus to their interior man – when, that is, they think about those matters – those who are interested in the truths known to the Church merely for the sake of their own gain contemplate ideas contrary to those truths. But even though they contemplate such contrary ideas and refuse in their hearts to accept those truths, they are still able to convince others that a thing is true, and indeed to do so in the same way as those who really are interested in truths.

The desire to earn material gain, position, and reputation for their own sakes adopts every means that can be employed to convince another; it adopts nothing more readily than such things as are essentially true since these have the power hidden within them to attract people's minds. Everyone – no matter who, provided that he is not mentally deficient – is endowed with such an ability, that is to say, the ability to understand whether things are true. He has been endowed with it to enable him to be reformed and regenerated through the understanding part of his mind. But although, once he has departed into wicked ways and has cast aside altogether what constitutes the faith of the Church, he still possesses the same ability to understand truths, he no longer has any wish to understand them and loathes them the moment he hears them.

5465   'And you will not die' means that the truths will thereby possess life, that is to say, when the truths will be as they have been declared to be. This is clear from the meaning of 'you will not die' as that you may live, thus that the truths represented by those men will possess life.

5466   'And they did so' means the end of this state. This is clear from the meaning of 'doing', or something that has been done, as the end of one state that comes first and by implication the beginning of another that follows, dealt with in 4979, 4987, 4999, 5074. A lengthier explanation of these matters is avoided here for the same reason as mentioned above in 5454. It should nevertheless be recognized that they contain arcana beyond description, which in heaven shine from every individual word, though not a trace of them is visible to man. The holiness which one can sometimes discern with a person reading the Word holds a large number of such arcana within it, for the holiness which fills a person possesses countless facets concealed within it which he does not see.

5467 Verses 21–24 **And they said, a man to his brother, Assuredly we are guilty concerning our brother, whose anguish of soul we saw when he pleaded with us and we did not hear; therefore this anguish has come upon us. And Reuben answered them, saying, Did I not say to you, saying, Do not sin against the boy – and you did not listen? And also, his blood; behold, it is required. And they did not know that Joseph was hearing, because the interpreter was between them. And he turned away from them and wept; and he came back to them and spoke to them; and he took Simeon from them, and bound him before their eyes.**

'And they said, a man to his brother' means a perception as to the reason why. 'Assuredly we are guilty concerning our brother' means that they were blameworthy because they had alienated the internal by their non-acceptance of good. 'Whose anguish of soul we saw' means the state of the internal in regard to good, once it was alienated. 'When he pleaded with us and we did not hear' means its constant entreaty without ever gaining acceptance. 'And Reuben answered them, saying' means that a perception nevertheless existed, springing from faith in doctrine and in the understanding. 'Did I not say to you, saying' means the degree of perception from there. 'Do not sin against the boy' means lest they become separated [the external from the internal]. 'And you did not listen' means non-acceptance. 'And also, his blood; behold, it is required' means the subsequent remorse of conscience. 'And they did not know that Joseph was hearing' means that the natural light in which those truths dwell does not engender any belief that spiritual light renders all things visible. 'Because the interpreter was between them' means that at this time spiritual things are understood in a completely different manner. 'And he turned away from them' means somewhat of a withdrawal. 'And wept' means mercy. 'And he came back to them and spoke to them' means an influx. 'And he took Simeon from them' means faith in the will. 'And bound him' means a separation. 'Before their eyes' means a discernment.

5468 'And they said, a man to his brother' means a perception as to the reason why. This is clear from the meaning of 'saying' in the historical narratives of the Word as perception, dealt with in 1791, 1815, 1819, 1822, 1898, 1919, 2080, 2619, 3509; and from the meaning of 'a man to his brother' as mutually, dealt with in 4725. The reason 'they said, a man to his brother' means a perception as to the reason why – why Joseph spoke hard words to them, calling them spies, and why he held them in custody for three days – is that what immediately follows contains their discussion with one another as to the reason why. Consequently a perception as to this is meant.

5469 'Assuredly we are guilty concerning our brother' means that they were blameworthy because they had alienated the internal by their non-acceptance of good. This is clear from the meaning of 'being guilty' as being blameworthy and subject to the imputation [of sin] because good and truth have been cast aside, dealt with in 3400; and from the representation of Joseph, 'their brother' concerning whom they were guilty, as the internal which they had cast aside or alienated. For Joseph and Benjamin represent the internal aspect of the Church, while the remaining ten sons of Jacob represent its external aspect – 'Rachel', from whom Joseph and Benjamin were born, being the affection for interior truth, and 'Leah' the affection for exterior truth, 3758, 3782, 3793, 3819.

In this chapter 'Joseph' represents the celestial of the spiritual or truth from the Divine, which is the internal; 'Benjamin' represents the spiritual of the celestial, which is the intermediary going forth from the internal; and the remaining 'ten sons of Jacob' represent the truths known to the external Church and so truths that are present in the natural, as stated many times above. This chapter also deals with the joining of the internal aspect of the Church to its external aspect, corporately and in every specific part; for each person individually must be a Church if he is to form part of the Church as a corporate whole. But in the highest sense the chapter deals with the way in which the Lord united the Internal to the External within His Human so as to make this Divine.

5470 'Whose anguish of soul we saw' means the state of the internal in regard to good[1], once it was alienated. This is clear from the meaning of 'anguish of soul' as the state which the soul passes through when it is alienated from the external. The nature of this state is as follows: The Lord comes to a person constantly, bringing good to him, and also truth within that good; but the person either accepts this or does not accept it. If he accepts it, all is well with him; but if he does not, all is ill. If, while not accepting it, he feels worried, described here as 'anguish of soul', the hope exists that he can be reformed; but if he has no such feeling, the hope disappears. For with every person two spirits from hell are present and two angels from heaven. These are present because a person is born in sins and cannot by any means live unless he is on one hand in communication with hell and on the other in communication with heaven. His entire life depends on having these on either hand. When a person is growing up he begins to be his own master, that is, it seems to him that his will and actions spring from his own power of judgement, and in matters of faith his thought and deductions

---

[1] *Reading* in bono (in regard to good) *for* interea (in the meantime); *cp above in* 5467, *where in his rough draft Sw. amends* interea *to* in bono.

are the result of his own power of understanding. If during this time he inclines to evils, the two spirits from hell draw closer to him and the two angels from heaven move a small distance away. But if he inclines to good the two angels from heaven draw nearer and the two spirits from hell are withdrawn.

2   If therefore a person when he inclines to evils – as most people do in adolescence – feels at all disturbed when he reflects on an evil deed he has committed, this is a sign that he will nevertheless accept what flows into him from heaven through the angels. It is also a sign that subsequently he will allow himself to be reformed. But if he does not feel in any way disturbed when he reflects on an evil deed he has committed, this is a sign that he no longer wishes to accept what flows into him from heaven through the angels; and it is a sign too that subsequently he will not allow himself to be reformed. Here therefore, where the subject is the truths known to the external Church, which are represented by 'the ten sons of Jacob', reference is made to 'the anguish of soul' which Joseph experienced once he was alienated from his brothers, and then to the fact that Reuben had warned them against doing what they did. By this is meant the consideration that once that state was under way reformation was to follow; that is, the internal came to be joined to the external, that joining together being the subject in what follows. For with people who feel disturbed during this state, an internal recognition of evil is present; and when the Lord calls that recognition to mind, it becomes confession and finally penitence.

5471   'When he pleaded with us and we did not hear him' means its constant entreaty without ever gaining acceptance. This is clear from the meaning of 'pleading' as an entreaty; for a plea not to be alienated, when the subject is the inflow of good from the Divine, is an entreaty to be accepted. Good which flows in from the Lord is constantly at hand and so to speak entreating; but it is up to the individual to accept it. This explains why a plea not to become alienated means a constant entreaty, from which it follows that 'not hearing' means non-acceptance. The sense of the letter refers to a number of persons – to the ten sons of Jacob and to Joseph; but the internal sense makes them all refer to the one same subject. The truths known to the external Church or truths present within the natural, which are represented by 'the ten sons of Jacob', are the truths present within a person's external man, while the celestial of the spiritual, which is represented by 'Joseph', is truth from the Divine present in his internal man. The situation is the same here as it is with historical descriptions in other places in the Word; different spiritual realities are meant by the persons in those descriptions, and those realities all have regard to the one same subject.

5472   'And Reuben answered them, saying' means that a perception nevertheless existed, springing from faith in doctrine and in the understanding. This is clear from the meaning of 'answering' or 'saying to his brothers' as perception, for 'saying' is perception, see above in

5468; and from the representation of 'Reuben' as faith in doctrine and in the understanding, which is the truth of doctrine by means of which one can arrive at the good of life, dealt with in 3861, 3866. Since the subject here is the entreaty made by good, or the Divine within good, to be accepted, reference is made to faith – to the kinds of things taught by this regarding the acceptance of good. For if a person departing from good feels at all disturbed, this is not due to an inner voice speaking to him but to the faith acquired by him since early childhood. This is what speaks to him at such times and gives rise to the disturbance felt by him. This explains why Reuben, who represents that faith, is the speaker here. The expression faith in doctrine and in the understanding is used to distinguish that faith from faith in life and in the will, which 'Simeon' represents.

5473   'Did I not say to you, saying' means the degree of perception from there. This is clear from the meaning of 'saying' in the historical narratives of the Word as perception, dealt with in 1791, 1815, 1819, 1822, 1898, 1919, 2080, 2619, 3509. And since the verb 'say' is used twice here, as well as immediately before this, it is the degree of perception that is meant.

5474   'Do not sin against the boy' means lest they become separated – the external from the internal. This is clear from the meaning of 'sinning' as a separation, dealt with in 5229, for all sin leads to separation; and from the representation of Joseph, to whom 'the boy' refers here, as the internal, as above in 5469.

5475   'And you did not listen' means non-acceptance. This is clear from the meaning of hearing or 'listening' as obeying, dealt with in 2542, 3869, 4652–4660, 5017. And since obeying is meant, so also is accepting, as above in 5471; for anyone who obeys what faith tells him is acceptive. Here non-acceptance is meant because the words used are 'you did not listen'.

5476   'And also, his blood; behold, it is required' means the subsequent remorse of conscience. This is clear from the meaning of 'blood' as violence done to good or charity, dealt with in 374, 1005. When this violence or blood 'is required' it gives rise to a disturbance within that is called the remorse of conscience. But this is the case only with those who have become disturbed once they have sinned, see 5470.

5477   'And they did not know that Joseph was hearing' means that the natural light in which those truths dwell does not engender any belief that spiritual light renders all things visible. This is clear from the representation of 'the sons of Jacob who did not know' as the truths which the external Church possesses, and so are present in the natural, often dealt with already – from which comes the meaning that the natural light in which those truths dwell does not engender any belief; and from the representation of 'Joseph' as the celestial of the spiritual, which dwells in spiritual light. But this spiritual light renders truths in the natural visible, and this is meant by 'Joseph was hearing'; for 'hearing' means both obeying and discerning, 5017. Thus spiritual light renders truths in the natural visible; but natural light cannot do the same for truths in the spiritual.

2 The situation with natural light and spiritual light is as follows. Natural light flows from the sun in the world, and spiritual light flows from the Sun in heaven, which is the Lord. All the truths of faith that a person has learned since early childhood come to be understood by him with the help of the kinds of objects, and the ideas formed from these, that originate in the light of the world. Thus every single thing is seen in a natural way; for as long as he lives in the world all the ideas constituting a person's thought are based on the kinds of things that exist in the world. If therefore these things are taken away from him his thought is totally destroyed. One who has not been regenerated has no knowledge at all of the existence of spiritual light, not even of the existence in heaven of a light that has nothing in common with the light of the world. Still less does that person know that spiritual light is what lights up ideas and objects that originate in the light of the world and is what enables a person to think, draw conclusions, and reflect on them. The reason such spiritual light enables him to do this is that that light is wisdom itself which goes forth from the Lord; and that wisdom manifests itself as the light which the angels in heaven see before them. That light renders visible every single thing beneath it, that is, every single thing present with a person which is a product of natural light. But the reverse does not happen unless the person has been regenerated, in which case the things that belong to heaven, that is, forms of goodness and truth, are lit up by spiritual light and become visible in the natural as if in a representative mirror.

3 From this it is evident that the Lord, who is Light itself, sees every single thing present in a person's thought and will, and present indeed in the whole natural creation; nothing at all escapes His notice.

From all this one may now recognize what is involved here – that natural light in which those truths dwell does not engender any belief that spiritual light renders all things visible, meant by the words 'they did not know that Joseph was hearing'. Much the same is implied by the statement above in verse 8, 'Joseph recognized his brothers and they did not recognize him'. For these words mean that the truths of the Church were seen by the celestial of the spiritual by the light it possessed, and that truth from the Divine was not seen in natural light that was not yet brightened with heavenly light; see 5427, 5428.

5478 'Because the interpreter was between them' means that at this time spiritual things are understood in a completely different manner. This is clear from the meaning of 'the interpreter was between them' as the fact that spiritual things are understood in a different manner. For an interpreter translates the language of one person into the language of another, and so enables the perceptions in the one person's mind to be understood by another person. This explains why 'the interpreter was between them' means that at that time spiritual things are understood in a completely different manner, that is, by those in possession of truths known to the Church which have not yet been joined through good to the internal man. The fact that the truths known to the Church are understood by those governed by good – that is among those with whom such truths have been joined to good – in a manner completely different from that in which those who are not governed by good understand them does indeed seem to be a paradox; but for all that, it is the truth. For truths are understood in a spiritual manner by those who are governed by good because such people dwell in spiritual light, whereas truths are understood in a natural manner by those who are not governed by good because they dwell in natural light. Consequently those who are governed by good are constantly linking truths to the truths they already have, whereas those who are not governed by good link very many illusions as well as falsities to the truths they have. The reason for this is that the truths present with people governed by good reach into heaven, whereas the truths present with those who are not governed by good do not reach into heaven. Consequently the truths present with those governed by good are filled out, whereas the ones present with those who are not governed by good are virtually empty. That fullness or emptiness is not seen by man as long as he lives in the world; but the angels see it. If man knew how much of heaven existed within truths that have been joined to good he would have a completely different conception of faith.

5479   'And he turned away from them' means somewhat of a withdrawal. This is clear from the meaning of 'turnng away from them', when it has reference to the inflow of good from the Divine or the Lord, as somewhat of a withdrawal. For the Lord never turns away from anyone, but He does regulate the inflow of good as a man's or angel's state requires. This regulating is what is meant by a withdrawal.

5480   'And wept' means mercy. This is clear from the meaning of 'weeping', when used in reference to the Lord, who is represented here by 'Joseph', as showing mercy. It is well known that weeping is an expression of grief and love; it is consequently an expression of mercy since mercy is love that is grieving. Divine love therefore is called mercy because left by itself the human race is in hell; and when a person recognizes within himself that this is the case he prays for mercy. Since in the internal sense 'weeping' also implies mercy, there are many occasions in the Word when Jehovah or the Lord is spoken of as weeping, as in Isaiah,

I shall weep with weeping over Jazer, the vine of Sibmah. *I will seek you with My tears*, O Heshbon and Elealeh.   Isa.16:9.

And in Jeremiah,

I know, says Jehovah, the indignation of Moab, that he is not right. Therefore *I will howl* over Moab and *will cry out* because of the whole of Moab. Above *the weeping* of Jazer *I will weep* because of you, O vine of Sibmah.   Jer.48:30–32.

'Moab' stands for those who are governed by natural good and allow themselves to be led astray; and once led astray they adulterate what is good, 2468. 'Howling, crying out, and weeping over Moab' stands for feelings of mercy and grief. Similarly in Luke,

As He drew near, Jesus saw the city and *wept over it*.   Luke 19:41.

The Jerusalem over which Jesus wept, that is, for which He had feelings of mercy and grief, was not only the actual city of Jerusalem but also the Church, whose last day, when there will no longer be any charity or consequently any faith, is meant in the internal sense. His feelings of mercy and grief led Him to weep. As regards 'Jerusalem' being the Church, see 2117, 3654.

5481 'And he came back to them and spoke to them' means an influx. This is clear from the meaning of 'coming back to them and speaking to them', after he had turned away from them, as an influx; for the celestial of the spiritual or truth from the Divine, which is represented by 'Joseph', flows into the truths present in the natural. This is expressed in the sense of the letter by 'his coming back to them and speaking to them'. 'Speaking' also means flowing in, see 2951.

5482 'And he took Simeon from them' means faith in the will. This is clear from the representation of 'Simeon' as faith in the will, dealt with in 3869–3872, 4497, 4502, 4503. The reason faith in the will was separated from them is that the intermediary, represented by 'Benjamin', was not yet present. For the inflow of truth from the Divine, represented by 'Joseph', goes through the intermediary into the good of faith, and then through this into the truth of faith; or what amounts to the same, it passes into the desire for truth, and then through this into the understanding of truth. Or what also amounts to the same, it passes into charity towards the neighbour, and then through this into faith. There is no other path along which it can flow in the case of one who has been regenerated; nor is there any other path along which it can do so in the case of angels.

2   This may be compared to the sun flowing into objects on earth. When it reproduces these from their seed and renews them, it flows in with heat, as it does in springtime and summertime, and also with light, and so reproduces them. Absolutely nothing at all is reproduced by light alone, as is evident from those objects in wintertime. Spiritual heat is the good of love, and spiritual light is the truth of faith. Also, spiritual heat present in objects in the animal kingdom gives them their vital heat, while spiritual light gives them life, which springs from that vital heat.

5483 'And bound him' means a separation. This is clear from the meaning of 'binding' as a separation, dealt with in 5083, 5101, 5452, 5456.

5484 'Before their eyes' means a discernment. This is clear from the meaning of 'the eyes' as understanding and discernment, dealt with in 2701, 4083, 4403–4421, 4523–4534.

5485 Verses 25–28 **And Joseph gave the command to fill[1] their vessels with grain, and to restore their silver, each man's in his sack, and to give them provision for the way; and thus he did for them. And they loaded their corn onto their asses, and went from there. And one opened his sack to give fodder to his ass, in a lodging-place, and he saw his silver, and behold, it was in the mouth of his pouch. And he said to his brothers, My silver has been restored, and also behold, it is in my pouch. And their heart went out of them, and they trembled [turning] a man to his brother, saying, What is this that God has done to us?**

'And Joseph gave the command' means an influx from the celestial of the spiritual. 'To fill their vessels with grain' means that factual knowledge was endowed with good produced from truth. 'And to restore their silver' means without the expending of any power of their own. 'Each man's in his own sack' means wherever a receptacle exists in the natural. 'And to give them provision for the way' means and that support should be supplied to the truths they had. 'And thus he did [for them]' means a putting into effect. 'And they loaded their corn onto their asses' means the truths gathered into factual knowledge. 'And went from there' means subsequent life. 'And one opened his sack' means a perusal. 'To give fodder to his ass, in a lodging-place' means when they stopped to reflect on the facts present in the exterior natural. 'And he saw his silver' means a discernment that no power of their own had been expended. 'And it was in the mouth of his pouch' means that this was returned as a gift and was put back in the opening of the exterior natural. 'And he said to his brothers' means a perception shared by all. 'My silver has been restored' means that nothing of their own resources was taken from them. 'And also behold, it is in my pouch' means its presence in the exterior natural. 'And their heart went out of them' means fear. 'And they trembled [turning] a man to his brother' means the dread shared by them all. 'Saying, What is this that God has done to us?' means owing to so great an act of providence.

5486 'And Joseph gave the command' means an influx from the celestial of the spiritual. This is clear from the meaning of 'giving the command', when used in reference to the celestial of the spiritual, or the internal, in relation to the external, as an influx, for the internal has no other way of 'giving the command' than by flowing into something and disposing it to serve some purpose; and from the representation of 'Joseph' as the celestial of the spiritual, often dealt with already.

---

[1] *lit.* And Joseph commanded, and they [his servants?] filled

5487 'To fill their vessels with grain' means that factual knowledge was endowed with good produced from truth. This is clear from the meaning of 'filling', because this was done freely, as being endowed with; from the meaning of 'vessels' as factual knowledge, dealt with in 3068, 3079; and from the meaning of 'grain' as good produced from truth, which is the good of truth, dealt with in 5295.

5488 'And to restore their silver' means without the expending of any power of their own. This is clear from the meaning of 'buying with silver' as acquiring to oneself by the use of what is one's own, so that here 'restoring their silver' means giving freely to them, or without their expending of any power of their own. The same is also meant in Isaiah,

Everyone who thirsts, come to the waters, and *he who has no silver*, come, *buy* and eat. And come, *buy* wine and milk *without silver* and without price. Isa.55:1.

5489 'Each man's in his own sack' means wherever a receptacle exists in the natural. This is clear from the meaning of 'a sack' as a receptacle, dealt with below; and this exists in the natural because truths and factual knowledge in the natural are the subject. The reason 'a sack' has the specific meaning here of factual knowledge is that just as a sack is a receptacle for grain, so is factual knowledge a receptacle for good, in this case for good that is the product of truth, as above in 5487. Few people know that factual knowledge is a receptacle for good because few stop to reflect on such matters. Yet they can know it from the following considerations: When facts enter the memory some affection is always instrumental in their introduction there. Facts that are not introduced by means of some affection do not remain but slip away. The reason for this is that life is present within an affection but not within factual knowledge except through an affection. From this it is evident that linked to factual knowledge there are always those kinds of impulses that belong to an affection, or what amounts to the same, that are the expressions of some love or other. Consequently it has some form of good linked to it, for every expression of love is called a form of good, whether it is real good or what is mistakenly thought to be such. Factual knowledge together with such forms of good therefore constitute a kind of marriage. This being so, when that good is stimulated, so instantly is the factual knowledge to which it is linked; and conversely, when facts are called to mind, the good to which they are linked comes forth. Anyone can learn of this, if he so pleases, from what goes on within himself.

2 From this one may now conclude that, among unregenerate persons who have cast aside the good of charity, facts existing as truths known to the Church have the kinds of impulses expressing self-love and love of the world attached to them. Thus attached to those facts there are forms of evil which, because of the delight these hold within them, are called forms of good by those unregenerate persons, who also employ

wrong interpretations to present them as such. Those facts take on an attractive appearance, when self-love and love of the world reign throughout, assuming it in the degree in which these are reigning. But among regenerate persons facts existing as truths known to the Church have the kinds of impulses that belong to love towards the neighbour and love to God, thus forms of genuine good, attached to them. These forms of good are placed by the Lord within the truths known to the Church that are present with all undergoing regeneration. Therefore when the Lord inspires these people with a zeal for what is good, those truths come forth at the same time in their own proper order; and when He inspires a zeal for truth, that good is present and sets it ablaze. From all this one may see the situation so far as factual knowledge and truths are concerned – that they are the receptacles for good.

5490   'And to give them provision for the way' means and that support should be supplied to the truths they had. This is clear from the meaning of 'giving provision' as support, and from the meaning of 'the way' as truth, dealt with in 627, 2333. In this case however 'on the way' means as long as they were passing through that state, for 'being on the way' means a state when truth exists joined to good, 3123. The support received from truth and good is also meant by 'provision' in David,

He caused manna to rain down onto them for food, and gave them the grain of heaven. Man ate the bread of the mighty; He sent them *provision* to satiety. Ps.78:24,25.

5491   'And thus he did [for them]' means a putting into effect. This is clear without explanation.

5492   'And they loaded their corn onto their asses' means the truths gathered into factual knowledge. This is clear from the meaning of 'corn' as truth, dealt with in 5276, 5280, 5292, 5402; and from the meaning of 'ass' as factual knowledge, dealt with in 2781. From these meanings it follows that 'they loaded their corn onto their asses' means that truths were gathered into factual knowledge. Such a meaning of these words will seem strange to someone who fixes his mind on the historical sense of the letter. It will seem even stranger to him if he does not believe in the existence of any internal sense other than the one which lies in close proximity to and shines out of the letter. For that person will say to himself, How can 'loading corn onto their asses' mean truths gathered into factual knowledge? But let him know that in the Word the sense of the letter passes into a sense of a spiritual kind when it passes from man to the angels, that is, into heaven. Indeed it passes into a sense stranger still when it passes into the third heaven, where every single detail in the Word passes into affections belonging to love and charity, which the internal sense serves as the foundation for it to rest upon.

2   The fact that the historical descriptions in the Word move away into another sense when they are raised into heaven may become clear to anyone who uses his reason to draw conclusions and who knows

something about the natural and the spiritual. He can see that 'loading corn onto their asses' is a purely natural action and has absolutely nothing spiritual about it. He can also see that angels in heaven, that is, in a spiritual world, cannot grasp those words in any but a spiritual manner and that they do grasp them in a spiritual manner when corresponding entities are understood in place of them, that is to say, when they understand truth known to the Church in place of 'corn' and facts present in the natural in place of 'asses'. It has been shown previously that in the Word 'asses' means objects of service and so known facts, for in relation to spiritual ideas and also to rational concepts such facts are objects of service, see 2781. From all this one may also see what the thought and speech of angels are like compared with men's thought and speech. That is to say, one may see that angels' thought and speech are spiritual whereas men's are natural, and that when angels' thought and speech move downwards they pass into men's, and that men's are converted into angels' when they move upwards. If this were not so there would not be any communication at all between mankind and the angels, that is, between the world and heaven.

5493 'And went from there' means subsequent life. This is clear from the meaning of 'going' as living, dealt with in 3335, 3690, 4882. The way in which 'going' in the spiritual sense means living is similar to that involved in the matters discussed immediately above in 5492.

5494 'And one opened his sack' means a perusal. This is clear from the meaning of 'sack' as a receptacle within the natural, dealt with above in 5489; this was endowed with good that was a product of truth, 5487. 'Opening it', it is evident from the train of thought, means perusing it, for the words that follow 'to give fodder to his ass, in a lodging-place' mean when they stopped to reflect on the facts present in the exterior natural.

5495 'To give fodder to his ass, in a lodging-place' means when they stopped to reflect on the facts present in the exterior natural. This is clear from the meaning of 'giving fodder to his ass' as stopping to reflect on facts (for fodder is the food, made up of straw and chaff, that asses are fed with, and therefore all reflection on facts is meant by it since reflection primarily is what nourishes these; as regards 'an ass' meaning factual knowledge, see just above in 5492); and from the meaning of 'a lodging-place' as the exterior natural. The meaning of 'a lodging-place' here as the exterior natural cannot, it is true, be substantiated from other places in the Word; even so it is evident from the consideration that facts are in their proper lodging-place so to speak when they are present in the exterior natural. For the natural has two parts, the exterior natural and the interior natural, see 5118. When facts exist in the exterior natural they have a direct communication with the external senses of the body, where they install themselves and so to speak rest. Therefore the exterior natural provides a lodging-place for facts, that is, a place for them to rest or spend the night.

5496   'And he saw his silver' means a discernment that no power of their own had been expended. This is clear from the meaning of 'seeing' as understanding and discerning, dealt with in 2150, 2325, 2807, 3764, 3863, 4403–4421, 4567, 4723, 5400; and from the meaning of 'silver that was restored' as without the expending of any power of their own, dealt with in 5488.

5497   'And it was in the mouth of his pouch' means that it was returned as a gift and was put back in the opening of the exterior natural. This is clear from the meaning of 'the mouth of the pouch' as the opening of the exterior natural. Its having been put back there is implied from its very presence there, while its return as a gift follows from what was stated immediately before this, that no power of their own had been expended. Because 'the pouch' was in the preliminary part where the sack opened, nothing else is meant by 'the pouch' than the preliminary part of the receptacle, which is the exterior natural since this too is a preliminary part – 'a sack' being a receptacle, see 5489, 5494. So that anyone may know what the exterior natural and the interior natural are, let a further brief statement be made about them.

One who is still a child cannot begin to think from anything higher than the exterior natural, for he composes his ideas out of sensory impressions. But as he grows up, employing sensory impressions to work out the reasons for things, he begins to think from the interior natural. For he begins to employ his sensory impressions to formulate ideas about truths which essentially are higher than sensory impressions; yet such ideas are still on a level with things in the natural world. But as he grows into a young adult, if he develops his power of reason, he employs what is in his interior natural to work out the reasons for things, which are truths of a yet higher nature. These are extracted so to speak from what is present in the interior natural. (The learned world calls the ideas composing thought which originate in this way intellectual and immaterial ideas, whereas ideas formed from factual knowledge present in both parts of the natural, insofar as these originate in the world and come through the senses, they call material ideas.) This is the manner in which a person rises with his understanding from the world up to heaven. Yet he does not go on into heaven with that understanding unless he accepts good from the Lord which is constantly present and flowing into him. If he does accept that good he is also endowed with truths, for in good all truths are welcome guests. And as he is endowed with truths, so he is endowed with understanding enabling him to have his being in heaven.

5498   'And he said to his brothers' means a perception shared by all. This is clear from the meaning of 'saying' in the historical narratives of the Word as perception, often dealt with already, and from the meaning of 'to his brothers' as shared by all, for what is said to all becomes something shared by all.

5499 'My silver has been restored' means that nothing of their own resources was taken from them. This is clear from the meaning of 'restoring silver' as without the expending of any power of their own, or what amounts to the same, nothing of their own resources was taken from them, dealt with above in 5488, 5496.

5500 'And also behold, it is in my pouch' means its presence in the exterior natural. This is clear from the meaning of 'the pouch' as the exterior natural, dealt with just above in 5497.

5501 'And their heart went out of them' means fear. This is clear from the meaning of 'the heart going out' as fear. The reason 'the heart going out' means fear is that in fear one's heart begins to throb.

5502 'And they trembled [turning] a man to his brother' means the dread shared by them all. This is clear from the meaning of 'trembling' as dread, and from the meaning of 'a man to his brother' as shared by all, as just above in 5498. The reason why fear is expressed by these two phrases, by 'their heart went out' and 'they trembled', is that one has reference to the will and the other to the understanding. For it is quite usual in the Word, especially in the prophetical part, for the same matter to be described twice, though with a change of words. Anyone unacquainted with the hidden reason for this may imagine that it is pointless repetition; but that is not the case. One expression has reference to good, the other to truth; and because good belongs in the will and truth in the understanding, one has reference at the same time to the will and the other to the understanding. The reason for this is that in the Word everything is holy, and this holiness comes from the heavenly marriage, which is the marriage of goodness and truth. This being so, heaven is present within the Word, and so too is the Lord, the All in all of heaven – present so fully that He is the Word. The Lord's two names Jesus Christ entail the same, the name Jesus entailing Divine Good and the name Christ Divine Truth, see 3004, 3005, 3008, 3009. From this it is also evident that the Lord is present in every part of the Word, present so fully that He is the Word itself. Regarding the marriage of goodness and truth, which is the heavenly marriage, in every detail of the Word, see 683, 793, 801, 2516, 2712, 5138. From this a further conclusion may be reached, that to live in expectation of heaven a person must have within him not only truth that is the truth of faith but also good that is the good of charity. Otherwise no heaven is present within him.

5503 'Saying, What is this that God has done to us?' means owing to so great an act of providence. This is clear from the meaning of 'God doing' as providence, for no other expression than providence can be used to describe everything done by God. The reason for this is that everything done by God or the Lord has an eternal quality and an infinite one; and the word 'providence' has the same implication. The amazement of the brothers is the reason for the meaning here – owing to so great an act of providence.

5504   Verses 29–34 **And they came to Jacob their father, to the land of Canaan; and they pointed out to him all that was happening to them, saying, The man, the lord of the land, spoke hard words to us, and took us for men spying out the land. And we said to him, We are upright men; we are not spies. Twelve are we, brothers, the sons of our father; one is not, and the youngest is today with our father in the land of Canaan. And the man, the lord of the land, said to us, By this I shall know that you are upright men: Cause one brother among you to remain with me, and take [food for] the famine of your houses, and go. And bring your youngest brother to me, and I shall know that you are not spies, that you are upright men; I will give you your brother, and you will wander through the land, trading.**

'And they came' means a subsequent state of reformation. 'To Jacob their father' means the good of natural truth. 'To the land of Canaan' means which is that of the Church. 'And they pointed out to him all that was happening to them' means reflection made by the good of that truth on what was provided up to then. 'Saying' means perception. 'The man, the lord of the land, spoke' means the celestial of the spiritual ruling in the natural. 'Hard words to us' means that no joining together with this took place because no agreement existed. 'And took us for men spying out the land' means that it saw the truths known to the Church as ones existing for the sake of gain. 'And we said to him, We are upright men; we are not spies' means a denial that they were interested in the truths known to the Church for the sake of gain. 'Twelve are we, brothers' means all truths in their entirety. 'The sons of our father' means having the same origin. 'One is not' means that the Divine spiritual from which their joining together begins is not apparent. 'And the youngest is today with our father in the land of Canaan' means that from itself [the celestial of the spiritual] had a link with spiritual good. 'And the man, the lord of the land, said to us' means a discernment regarding the celestial of the spiritual ruling in the natural. 'By this I shall know that you are upright men' means its willingness, provided that they were not interested in truths for the sake of gain. 'Cause one brother among you to remain with me' means that faith in the will was to be separated from them. 'And take [food for] the famine of your houses' means that in the meantime they should provide for their own needs in that desolation. 'And go' means so that they may thereby live. 'And bring your youngest brother to me' means that if the intermediary were there the joining together would take place. 'And I shall know that you are not spies' means that they are no longer truths existing for the sake of gain. 'That you are upright men' means that agreement accordingly exists. 'I will give you your brother' means that truths will thereby be made forms of good. 'And you will wander through the land, trading' means that truths from good will thereby be made fruitful and will all afford some useful purpose and lead to some form of gain.

5505 'And they came' means a subsequent state of reformation. This is clear from the meaning here of 'coming', coming to Jacob their father, as a subsequent state of reformation. 'Jacob their father' represents the good of truth in the natural, and 'coming' to this good means being reformed thus far. For the subject in the internal sense is how the truths known to the Church, which are represented by 'the sons of Jacob', were implanted in the natural and after that became joined to the celestial of the spiritual, or what amounts to the same, how truths in the external man became joined to truths from the Divine in the internal man. From all this it is evident that here 'they came' means a subsequent state of reformation.

5506 'To Jacob their father' means the good of natural truth. This is clear from the representation of 'Jacob' as the good of natural truth, dealt with in 3659, 3669, 3677, 3775, 4234, 4273, 4538, and also from the meaning of 'father' as good, 3703. 'Coming' to this good is being reformed thus far. Afterwards, as the intermediary represented by 'Benjamin' appeared on the scene, that good enabled the joining to the internal represented by 'Joseph' to be effected.

5507 'To the land of Canaan' means which is that of the Church. This is clear from the meaning of 'the land of Canaan' as the Church, dealt with in 3705, 4447. This good of truth represented by 'Jacob' is the good of the external Church, whereas in relation to this what is represented by 'Israel' is the good of the internal Church.

5508 'And they pointed out to him all that was happening to them' means reflection by the good of that truth on what was provided up to then. This is clear from the meaning of 'pointing out' as thought and reflection, dealt with in 2862, for what is pointed out to someone is thought based on reflection; and from the meaning of 'all that was happening to them' as what was providential or provided, dealt with below. The reason why it is the good of truth that reflects is that the one to whom 'they pointed out' was Jacob their father, who represents the good of truth, 5506. The reflection did not originate in the truths represented by 'the sons of Jacob', as the sense of the letter implies, for the reason that all reflection and thought based on it which take place in what is lower or more external begin in what is higher or more internal, though they appear to begin in what is lower or more external. And because the good of truth, which 'Jacob' represents, is more internal, reflection by the good of truth is therefore meant.

2   The reason 'what is happening' means what is providential or has been provided is that every happening or contingency which is otherwise described as fortuitous and attributed to chance or luck is something

providential. Divine Providence does its work out of sight and in ways beyond comprehension, for the reason that a person may be able in freedom to attribute that work either to providence or else to chance. For if providence performed its acts in seen and comprehensible ways the dangerous condition would then exist in which a person would first believe, because of what he has seen and comprehended, that those acts were providential, but after that would move away into a contrary belief. In that case truth and falsity would then be joined together in his interior man and the truth would be rendered profane – a condition that holds eternal damnation within it. The retention therefore of a person such as this in a state of disbelief is preferable to his having faith at one point and then departing from it.

This condition is meant in Isaiah,

Say to this people, Hearing, hear – but do not understand; and seeing, see – but do not comprehend. Make the heart of this people fat and their ears heavy, and plaster over their eyes, lest they see with their eyes and hear with their ears, and their heart understands, and *they turn again* and *are healed.*
Isa.6:9,10; John 12:40.

This also explains why miracles do not take place at the present day. For as with everything else that is seen and comprehensible, miracles would compel a person to believe; and anything that compels takes freedom away. But the whole of a person's reformation and regeneration takes place while he is in freedom; nothing implanted in him if he is not in freedom remains fixed in him. Things are implanted in freedom if an affection for goodness and truth are present in the person, 1937, 1947, 2744, 2870–2893, 3145, 3146, 3158, 4031.

The reason why great miracles occurred among the descendants of Jacob was that they were compelled by those miracles to fulfill in their outward form the religious laws they were given; for no more than this was required of those limited to representatives of the Church. With those people things of an external nature were separated from internal ones, which was why they could not undergo any interior reformation. They completely rejected things of an internal nature and were therefore unable to render truths profane, 3398, 3399, 3479, 4680. Such people could be subjected to compulsion without any danger of their profaning what was holy.

People of today ought to believe what they do not see, as is also clear from the Lord's words to Thomas, in John,

Because you have seen Me, Thomas, you have believed; blessed are those who do not see and yet believe.   John 20:29.

The truth that contingencies which are otherwise attributed to chance or luck are due to Divine Providence is indeed accepted by the Church; yet there is no real belief in it. Who does not say that God has saved him, who does not give thanks to God when, seemingly by good fortune, he gets out of some great danger? Also, when he is promoted to important positions or comes into wealth, does he not also call this a blessing received from God? Thus the member of the Church accepts that all contingencies are attributable to providence, even though he does not really believe this. But more on these matters will in the Lord's Divine mercy be presented elsewhere.

5509 'Saying' means perception. This is clear from the meaning of 'saying' in the historical narratives of the Word as perceiving, often dealt with already.

5510 'The man, the lord of the land, spoke' means the celestial of the spiritual ruling in the natural. This is clear from the representation of Joseph, to whom 'the man, the lord of the land' refers here, as the celestial of the spiritual ('the man' is used to refer to the spiritual, and 'the lord' to the celestial; for in the internal sense 'the man' is truth and 'the lord' good, truth from the Divine being what is called spiritual, and good from the Divine being what is called celestial); and from the meaning of 'the land', in this case the land of Egypt, as the natural mind, dealt with in 5276, 5278, 5280, 5288, 5301. The idea that the celestial of the spiritual, represented by 'Joseph', ruled in both parts of the natural is contained in the internal sense of the previous chapter; and to represent its rule Joseph was set in authority over the land of Egypt.

2 There are within the natural these two: known facts and the truths known to the Church. The placing of facts into their proper order by the celestial of the spiritual, which is truth from the Divine, has been dealt with already. Now the truths known to the Church, which are represented by 'the ten sons of Jacob', are the subject. Facts must be placed in order within the natural before the truths known to the Church are placed in order there, for the reason that those facts are needed for the grasping of these truths. For nothing can enter a person's understanding without ideas formed from such factual knowledge as has been acquired by him since early childhood. For man is totally ignorant of this, that every truth known to the Church that is called a truth of faith is founded on the facts he knows, or that he comes to grasp that truth, retain it in his memory, and recall it from there with the help of ideas formulated from the facts he knows.

3 It is quite normal in the next life to demonstrate in a visual way to those who desire it what those ideas are like; for things like this can be presented clearly in visual ways in the light of heaven. At the same time that visual presentation demonstrates in what darkness or else in what kind of beaming light they have kept the truth taught by the Church. With some people that truth is shown to be lying among falsities, with some among absurd, even scandalous ideas, with others among illusions of the senses, with others again among apparent truths, and so on. If a person has been governed by good, that is, if he has led a charitable life, truths are lit up by good, as if by fire sent down from heaven, and the illusions of the senses holding those truths within them are made beautifully radiant. And when they have innocence introduced into them by the Lord they actually look like truths.

5511   'Hard words to us' means that no joining together with this took place because no agreement existed. This is clear from the meaning of 'speaking hard words', when used to refer to the internal in relation to the external separated from it, as no joining together because no agreement existed, dealt with above in 5422, 5423. For if no agreement of the external with the internal exists, everything in the internal and coming from the internal seems 'hard' to the external, because the two are not joined together. Take for example a situation in which the internal, that is, someone living in his internal, declares that nothing at all of a person's thought begins in himself, but that his thought comes to him either from heaven (that is, from the Lord by way of heaven) or else from hell: he declares that any thought he has of good comes from the Lord by way of heaven, while any thought of evil comes from hell. Such an idea seems to be a thoroughly 'hard' one to anyone who wants what he thinks to come from himself and who believes that if that 'hard' idea is true, he is nothing. Yet that idea is absolutely true, and all in heaven perceive it to be so.

It is similarly the case when the internal, or those living in their internal, declare that the joy experienced by the angels originates in love to the Lord and charity towards the neighbour, that is to say, when they are actually engaged in performing deeds of love and charity, and that those deeds hold within them so much joy and happiness that these are beyond description. This will come as a 'hard' idea to those whose joy springs solely from self-love and love of the world and who take no interest in their neighbour other than for their own selfish reasons. Yet heaven and heavenly joy start to exist in a person when self-regard vanishes from the useful deeds he performs.

Take as yet another example the situation in which the internal declares that a person's soul is nothing else than the internal man and that after death the internal man appears to be exactly the same person as lived in the world, having a similar face, similar body, similar sensory powers, and a similar power of thought. People who have entertained the idea that the soul exists only on the level where thought does and is for that reason something ethereal lacking any outward form, and that the soul is to be reclothed with its body, imagine that what is declared by the internal about the soul is very far from the truth. Indeed those who believe that there is nothing more than the body to a human being will find the idea 'hard' when they hear that the soul is the real person and that the body which is buried serves no use at all in the next life. I know this is true because I have in the Lord's Divine mercy gone among such people, not among just some but among many, not just once but often, and I have talked to them on this matter. The same may also be said about countless other matters.

5512   'And took us for men spying out the land' means that it saw the truths known to the Church as ones existing there for the sake of gain. This is clear from the representation of the sons of Jacob, to whom 'us' refers here, as the truths known to the Church that were present in the natural, dealt with in 5403, 5419, 5427, 5458; and from the meaning of 'spies' or 'men spying out the land' as people interested in the truths known to the Church solely for the sake of gain, dealt with in 5432.

5513 'And we said to him, We are upright men; we are not spies' means a denial that they were interested in truths for the sake of gain. This is clear from the meaning of 'saying to him' as a reply, in this case a denial; from the meaning of 'we are upright men' as having an interest in truths which are indeed truths, dealt with in 5434, 5437, 5460; and from the meaning of 'spies' as those interested in the truths known to the Church for the sake of gain. Here it is denied that gain was the reason for their interest in them.

5514 'Twelve are we, brothers' means all truths in their entirety. This is clear from the meaning of 'twelve' as all, and – when used, as it is here, in reference to the sons of Jacob, or else to the tribes named after them, as well as to the twelve apostles – as all aspects of faith in their entirety, dealt with in 577, 2089, 2129, 2130, 2553, 3272, 3488, 3858, 3862, 3913, 3926, 3939, 4060.

5515 'The sons of our father' means having the same origin. This is clear from the meaning of 'the sons' as truths, dealt with in 489, 491, 533, 1147, 2623, 3373, and from the meaning of 'father' as good, dealt with in 2803, 3703, 3704. Consequently 'the sons of our father' means truths springing from good, thus truths having the same origin; they are all truths originating in one and the same good.

5516 'One is not' means that the Divine spiritual from which their joining together begins is not apparent. This is clear from what has been stated above in 5444, where the same words occur.

5517 'And the youngest is today with our father' means that from itself [the celestial of the spiritual] had a link with spiritual good. This too is clear from the explanation above in 5443, where the same words occur. The expression from itself is used because the intermediary represented by 'Benjamin' goes forth from the celestial of the spiritual, which is 'Joseph'.

5518 'And the man, the lord of the land, said to us' means a discernment regarding the celestial of the spiritual ruling in the natural. This is clear from the meaning of 'saying' in the historical narratives of the Word as discerning, often dealt with already; and from the meaning of 'the man, the lord of the land' as the celestial of the spiritual ruling in the natural, dealt with above in 5510.

5519 'By this I shall know that you are upright men' means its willingness, provided that they were not interested in truths for the sake of gain. This is clear from the meaning of 'knowing' here as being willing, for the train of thought leads on to this; and from the meaning of 'that you are upright men', and so not spies, as people whose interest in truths was not for the sake of gain, dealt with in 5432, 5512.

5520   'Cause one brother among you to remain with me' means that faith in the will was to be separated. This is clear from the representation of Simeon, to whom 'one brother' refers here, as faith in the will, dealt with in 5482; and from the meaning of 'causing to remain' as being separated. The implications of all this have been stated already.

5521   'And take [food for] the famine of your houses' means that in the meantime they should provide for their own needs in that desolation. This is clear from what has been stated above in 5462, where similar words occur. In that desolation is meant because 'a famine' means a desolation.

5522   'And go' means so that they may thereby live. This is clear from the meaning of 'going' as living, dealt with in 3335, 3690, 4882, 5493.

5523   'And bring your youngest brother to me' means that if the intermediary were there the joining together would take place. This is clear from the representation of Benjamin, to whom 'youngest brother' refers here, as the intermediary, dealt with in 5411, 5413, 5443; and from the meaning of 'bringing him to me' as a consequent joining together. For the intermediary effects the joining of the internal represented by 'Joseph' to the externals represented by 'the sons of Jacob', as shown above in 5411, 5413, 5427, 5428.

5524   'And I shall know that you are not spies' means that they are no longer truths existing for the sake of gain. This is clear from the meaning of 'spies' as those interested in the truths known to the Church for the sake of gain, in this case those who no longer have such an interest, that is to say, if the joining together is effected through the intermediary.

5525   'That you are upright men' means that agreement accordingly exists. This is clear from the meaning of 'you are upright men' as the fact that truths are present within them, for 'uprightness' consists in the truth, 5434, 5437. And because, once agreement exists, gain ceases to be the reason for their interest in truths, that agreement is meant as well by 'you are upright men'.

5526   'I will give you your brother' means that truths will thereby be made forms of good. This becomes clear from the representation of Simeon, who is 'the brother' here whom he would give them, as faith in the will, dealt with in 5482; and from the representation of the ten sons of Jacob, who are the ones here to whom he would be given, as the truths known to the Church present within the natural, dealt with in 5403, 5419, 5427, 5428, 5512. The reason 'I will give you your brother' means that truths will thereby be made forms of good is that when faith in the will is 'given', truths are made forms of good.

2 For as soon as the truth of faith, which is a matter of doctrine, enters the will it is made the truth of life and truth put into practice, in which case it is called good and also becomes spiritual good; and the Lord uses this good to form a new will in the person. The will causes truth to exist as a form of good for the reason that essentially the will is nothing else than love (for whatever a person loves he wills, and whatever he does not love he does not will), and also for the reason that everything which is a product of love or flows from love is perceived by a person as a form of good since he takes delight in it. From this it follows that everything which is a product of the will or flows from the will is a form of good.

5527 'And you will wander through the land, trading' means that truths from good will thereby be made fruitful and will all afford some useful purpose and lead to some form of gain. This is clear from the meaning of 'trading' as acquiring for oneself cognitions of good and truth, and so truths known to the Church, and communicating the same, dealt with in 4453; and those who possess such truths are called 'traders', 2967. Consequently 'going through the land, trading' is gathering such truths, wherever they are. From this it follows that 'going through the land, trading' also means the fruitfulness of truths from good. For once the joining together through the intermediary, which is 'Benjamin', has been accomplished, that is to say, once the external man, which is 'the ten sons of Jacob', has been joined to the internal, which is 'Joseph' – which joining together is dealt with here – or what amounts to the same, once a person has been regenerated, good is constantly making truths fruitful.

2 For someone who is governed by good possesses the ability to see particular truths that derive from general ones, and to see them in a continuing sequence. This is more especially the case at a later stage in the next life when worldly and bodily matters cease to cast a shadow over them. I have been allowed to know from considerable experience that good brings this ability with it. Such experience has included spirits who had possessed not so much of that ability when they lived as people in the world but who had nevertheless led charitable lives. I have seen those spirits raised up into heavenly communities, where they have then possessed intelligence and wisdom akin to that of the angels there; indeed these knew no other than that such intelligence and wisdom existed within those spirits. For the good which had governed the lives they had led gave them the ability to receive everything that flowed into them from the angelic communites in which they were present. This kind of ability exists within good and so therefore does that kind of fruitfulness. But the truths which with them are made fruitful by good do not remain as truths; these people make them matters of life, in which case they come to be assigned to some useful purpose. Therefore 'wandering through the land, trading' also means that all truths will afford some useful purpose and lead to some form of gain.

5528   Verses 35–38 And so it was, as they were emptying their sacks, that behold, each man's bundle of silver was in his sack; and they saw their bundles of silver, they and their father, and they were afraid. And Jacob their father said to them, You have bereaved me [of my children]; Joseph is not, and Simeon is not, and you take Benjamin. All these things will be upon me. And Reuben said to his father – he said, Make my two sons die if I do not bring him back to you; give him into my hand, and I will bring him back to you. And he said, My son shall not go down with you, for his brother is dead, and he, he alone, is left. And should harm happen to him on the road on which you go, you will cause my grey hair to go down in sorrow to the grave.

'And so it was, as they were emptying their sacks' means the use performed by truths in the natural. 'That behold, each man's bundle of silver' means truths in ordered groups freely given. 'Was in his sack' means in each one's receptacle. 'And they saw their bundles of silver' means a discernment that this was so. 'They and their father' means by the truths and the good of truth in the natural. 'And they were afraid' means a holy influence. 'And Jacob their father said to them' means a perception that came to them from the good of truth. 'You have bereaved me [of my children]' means that thus no Church existed any longer. 'Joseph is not' means that the internal does not exist. 'And Simeon is not' means that faith in the will does not exist either. 'And you take Benjamin' means if the intermediary also is taken away. 'All these things will be upon me' means that, when this is so, that which constitutes the Church will have been destroyed. 'And Reuben said to his father' means matters of faith present in the understanding were discerned by the good of truth. 'He said, Make my two sons die' means that neither of the two kinds of faith will survive. 'If I do not bring him back to you' means if no joining of the intermediary takes place. 'Give him into my hand' means insofar as it was in its power. 'And I will bring him to you' means that it will be restored. 'And he said, My son shall not go down with you' means that it will not move down towards inferior things. 'For his brother is dead' means because the internal is not present. 'And he, he alone, is left' means that this one now exists in place of the internal. 'And should harm happen to him on the road on which you go' means that, when in the company of truths alone in the natural that have been separated from the internal, it will perish. 'You will cause my grey hair to go down' means that this will accordingly be the final phase of the Church. 'In sorrow to the grave' means without hope of a restoration to life.

5529   'And so it was, as they were emptying their sacks' means the use performed by truths in the natural. This is clear from the meaning of 'emptying' – emptying out the corn they had brought back from Egypt – as the use performed by truths (for 'corn' means truth, 5276, 5280, 5292, 5402); and from the meaning of 'sacks' as receptacles within the natural, dealt with in 5489, 5494, and so the natural itself. Regarding the receptacles in the natural, see below in 5531.

5530 'That behold, each man's bundle of silver' means truths in ordered groups freely given. This is clear from the meaning of 'bundle' as an ordered group, dealt with below; and from the meaning of 'silver' as truth, dealt with in 1551, 2954 – 'each man's in his sack' meaning that the ordered groups were freely given. The reason why 'bundle' means an ordered group is that the truths present with a person are arranged and ordered into sequences. The truths most in harmony with his loves lie in the middle; ones less in harmony with his loves lie immediately around those in the middle, while truths that are not at all in harmony with his loves lie pushed back to the peripheries. And lying outside that whole sequence are those which are contrary to his loves. The truths in the middle are therefore called kindred ones since love is the creator of kinship; those that are more remote are called associated ones, extending to and ending with associates that are on the fringes. All the truths present with a person are arranged into sequences like this and are meant by 'bundles'.

2 From this one may see quite clearly what the situation is with those governed by self-love and love of the world and what it is with those governed by love to God and towards their neighbour. With people governed by self-love and love of the world the kinds of truths that lend support to these loves are in the middle, while those giving them little support are on the peripheries, and those contrary to them, such as truths to do with loving God and loving their neighbour, are cast to the outside. Such is the state of those in hell. This also explains why sometimes a band of light is seen around them; but inside this band where they themselves are, there exists a dark, gruesome, and horrible centre. With angels however there is a radiance at the centre, fuelled by the good of celestial and spiritual love, with a band of light or shining whiteness clothing it round about. Those who appear like this are likenesses of the Lord, for when He Himself revealed His Divinity to Peter, James, and John, He shone with His face like the sun, and His garments became like the light, Matt.17:2. The fact that angels, who are likenesses of Him, are seen in a radiance with a surrounding whiteness is evident from the angel who came down from heaven and rolled the stone away from the door of the tomb,

His appearance was like lightning, and his clothing white as snow.   Matt.28:3.

5531 'Was in his sack' means in each one's receptacle. This is clear from the meaning of 'a sack' as a receptacle, dealt with in 5489, 5494, 5529. What is meant by a receptacle here must also be stated briefly. A person's natural is divided into receptacles. Each receptacle comprises a general whole within which there are, in ordered groups, less general or relatively particular parts, and specific parts within these. Each general whole, together with its particular and its specific parts, includes within itself its own receptacle which can activate itself, that is, can achieve variations in form and effect changes of state within itself. The receptacles present with a person who has been regenerated are as many in number as the general truths present with him, and each receptacle corresponds to some community in heaven. This ordered condition exists with the person in whom the good of love and consequently the truth of faith are present. From all this one may gain some idea of what is meant by each one's receptacle when this phrase is used to refer to general truths in the natural which are represented by 'the ten sons of Jacob'.

5532 'And they saw their bundles of silver' means a discernment that this was so – that ordered groups of truths had been freely given. This is clear from the explanation just above in 5530.

5533 'They and their father' means by the truths and the good of truth in the natural. This is clear from the representation of the sons of Jacob, to whom 'they' refers here, as the truths in the natural, dealt with in 5403, 5419, 5427, 5458, 5512; and from the representation of Jacob, to whom 'their father' refers here, as the good of truth which is also in the natural, dealt with in 3659, 3669, 3677, 3775, 4234, 4273, 4538. An explanation of what a discernment by truths and the good of truth in the natural is can indeed be given; but when that explanation passes into the understanding the matter will seem to be extremely obscure. Yet it will be seen in so to speak the clear light of day by spirits when it passes into their understanding. Such matters are for them some of the less hard to understand. This also makes clear to some extent the nature of the difference between a person's intelligence while he is in the world and the inferior light shining here and when he is in heaven and the superior light shining there.

5534 'And they were afraid' means a holy influence. This is clear from the meaning of 'being afraid', when happenings such as those that are attributable to Divine Providence take place, like the one here involving the free gift of truths, meant by 'each man's bundle of silver was in his sack'. The holy influence at work at this time leads to a certain kind of fear that is coupled to a feeling for what is holy and to be reverenced.

5535 'And Jacob their father said to them' means a perception that came to them from the good of truth. This is clear from the meaning of 'saying' in the historical narratives of the Word as perception, often dealt with already; and from the representation of 'Jacob' as the good of truth, dealt with just above in 5533.

5536 'You have bereaved me [of my children]' means that thus no Church existed any longer. This is clear from the representation of Jacob, the one who says this about himself, as the good of truth, dealt with in 3659, 3669, 3677, 3775, 4234, 4273, 4538 (and as the good of truth is represented, so also is the Church because good is the essential element of the Church. It therefore amounts to the same whether you say the good of truth or the Church, for the person who has the good of truth present with him has the Church present with him. 'Jacob' represents the Church, see 4286, 4520, and that being so his sons represent the truths known to the Church, 5403, 5419, 5427, 5458, 5512); and from the meaning of 'bereaving' as depriving the Church of its truths and forms of good, such as those here which are represented by Joseph, Benjamin, and Simeon, to whom reference is made directly after the words 'you have bereaved me'.

2 'Bereaving' is depriving the Church of its truths for the reason that the Church is likened to a marriage. Good is likened to the husband and truth to the wife, while the truths born from that marriage are likened to 'the sons' and the forms of good to 'the daughters', and so on. When therefore a state of bereavement or an action causing this is mentioned, the meaning is that the Church has been deprived of its truths and as a consequence ceases to be a Church. The expressions 'bereft' and 'bereavement' are also used in various other places in the Word, as in Ezekiel,

I will send famine and evil wild animals upon you, and *I will make you bereft.* Ezek.5:17.

In the same prophet,

When I cause evil wild animals to pass through the land and *they leave it bereft* so that it becomes a desolation, with the result that no one passes through on account of the wild animals. Ezek.14:15.

In Leviticus,

I will send into you the wild animals of the field, which *will leave you bereft* and will cut off your beasts[1], and make you few in number, so that your roads are laid waste. Lev.26:22.

3 In these quotations 'famine' stands for an absence of cognitions of good and truth and the consequent desolation, 'evil wild animals' for falsities derived from evils, and 'the land' for the Church. 'Sending famine and evil wild animals, and leaving the land bereft' stands for destroying the Church by means of falsities derived from evils and so depriving it completely of truths. In Jeremiah,

I will winnow them with a winnowing-fork in the gates of the land; *I will bereave,* I will destroy My people. Jer.15:7.

Here also 'bereaving' stands for depriving of truths. In the same prophet,

Give their children over to the famine, and cause them to be wiped out by the power of the sword[2], *so that their wives become bereaved* [of children] *and widows.* Jer.18:21.

---

[1] *i.e.* cattle
[2] *lit.* cause them to flow down by means of the hand of the sword

'So that their wives become bereaved and widows' stands for their being left without truths or good.

In Hosea,

As for the Ephraimites, their glory will fly away like a bird, away from birth, and from the belly, and from conception. Even if they bring up their sons, *I will make them bereft* of human beings.   Hosea 9:11,12.

Here the meaning is similar. In Ezekiel,

I will cause human beings to walk upon you, even My people; and those human beings will by inheritance take possession of you and you will be an inheritance to them; *no more will you bereave them* [of their children]. Thus said the Lord Jehovih, Because they say to you, You have been one devouring human beings *and one bereaving your peoples* [of children].   Ezek.36:12,13.

Here also 'bereaving' stands for depriving of truths.

In Isaiah,

Now hear this, you lover of pleasures, sitting securely, saying in her[1] heart, I am, and there is no one else like me; a widow I shall not sit, *nor shall I know bereavement* [of children]. But these two things will come to you in a moment in one day – *bereavement* and widowhood.   Isa.47:8,9.

This refers to the daughter of Babel and to Chaldea, that is, to those who are outwardly holy but inwardly unholy and who call themselves the Church by virtue of that outward holiness. 'Bereavement and widowhood' stands for a deprivation of truth and good. In the same prophet,

Lift up your eyes round about, and see; they all gather together, they come to you. *The children of your bereavements* will say again in your ears, The place is too narrow for me; yield me a place to dwell in. But you will say in your heart, Who has begotten these for me, when yet I am *bereft* [of children] and alone, an exile and one who has been displaced? Who therefore has brought these up? I was left, alone. These, where were they?   Isa.49:18,20,21.

This refers to Zion, which is the celestial Church, and to its fruitfulness after it had been laid waste. 'The sons of bereavements' stands for the truths of which it was deprived when laid waste, but which were restored and underwent enormous increase.

5537   'Joseph is not' means that the internal does not exist. This is clear from the representation of 'Joseph'; since he represents the celestial of the spiritual, his representation is the internal aspect of the Church, dealt with in 5469.

5538   'And Simeon is not' means that faith in the will does not exist either. This is clear from the representation of 'Simeon' as faith in the will, dealt with in 3869–3872, 4497, 4502, 4503, 5482.

5539   'And you take Benjamin' means if the intermediary also is taken away. This is clear from the representation of 'Benjamin' as the intermediary, dealt with in 5411, 5413, 5443.

----

[1] *The Latin means* your *but the Hebrew means* her, *which Sw. has in another place where he quotes this verse.*

5540 'All these things will be upon me' means that, when this is so, that which constitutes the Church will have been destroyed. This is clear from the representation of Jacob, who says this about himself, as the Church, dealt with in 5536. When neither the internal represented by 'Joseph' nor faith in the will represented by 'Simeon' exist within the Church, and if the intermediary, represented by 'Benjamin', that effects the joining together is taken away, that which constitutes the Church has been destroyed. These are the factors meant by 'all these things will be upon me'.

5541 'And Reuben said to his father' means matters of faith in the understanding were discerned by the good of truth. This is clear from the meaning of 'saying' in the historical narratives of the Word as discerning, often dealt with already; from the representation of 'Reuben' as faith in doctrine and in the understanding, dealt with in 3861, 3866, 5472, and therefore matters belonging to that faith; and from the representation of Jacob, 'his father' whom Reuben addresses here, as the good of truth, dealt with in 3659, 3669, 3677, 3775, 4234, 4273, 4538, 5533. From all this it is evident that 'Reuben said to his father' means matters of faith present in the understanding were discerned by the good of truth. The reason Reuben is the speaker here is that the subject is the Church in which faith present in doctrine and in the understanding seemingly takes the lead and teaches. Here it teaches what must be done if the destruction of what constitutes the Church is to be averted.

5542 'He said, Make my two sons die' means that neither of the two kinds of faith will survive. This is clear from the meaning of Reuben's 'two sons' as both kinds of faith. For 'Reuben' represents faith in doctrine and in the understanding, while his 'sons' are the two kinds of teaching existing within the Church – teaching about what is true and teaching about what is good, that is, teaching about faith and teaching about charity. The thought that neither of these two kinds of faith or the Church will survive unless a joining of the intermediary represented by 'Benjamin' takes place is meant by 'make my two sons die if I do not bring back Benjamin to you'. In saying this Reuben certifies that the Church would be at an end unless the intermediary were present. But for the internal sense contained in those words Reuben would never have told his father to make his two sons die if he did not bring back Benjamin; for in telling him this Reuben would have been suggesting that he should subsequently wipe out an entire family. Such a course of action, being contrary to all that is right, would have been utterly wicked. But what the internal sense teaches explains why he spoke in the way he did.

5543 'If I do not bring him back to you' means if no joining of the intermediary takes place. This is clear from the representation of Benjamin, to whom the one he would bring back refers here, as the intermediary, dealt with in 5411, 5413, 5443, 5539; and from the meaning of 'bringing back' as being joined.

5544   'Give him into my hand' means insofar as it was in its power. This is clear from the meaning of 'hand' as power, dealt with in 878, 3387, 4931–4937, 5327, 5328. Correctly understood 'giving him into his hand' means entrusting him [Benjamin] to himself [Reuben]. But since faith in the understanding, represented by 'Reuben', possesses little power in which trust can be placed – for the truth of faith receives its power from the good of charity, 3563 – 'give him into my hand' therefore means insofar as it was in its power.

5545   'And I will bring him back to you' means that it will be restored. This is clear without explanation.

5546   'And he said, My son shall not go down with you' means that it will not move down towards inferior things. This is clear from the meaning of 'going down' as an expression used of movement towards inferior things, dealt with in 5406, in this case towards truths existing as factual knowledge in the exterior natural, 5492, 5495, 5497, 5500, which are represented by 'the sons of Jacob'.

5547   'For his brother is dead' means because the internal is not present. This is clear from the representation of Joseph, to whom 'brother' refers here, as the celestial of the spiritual, or truth from the Divine, and therefore the internal aspect of the Church, dealt with in 5469; and from the meaning of 'being dead' here as not being present. For though not present there he was still among the living.

5548   'And he, he alone, is left' means that this one now exists in place of the internal. This becomes clear from the consideration that because the internal, represented by 'Joseph', was not present and he alone [Benjamin] was born from the same mother, he was now one and the same as Joseph. For 'Joseph' and 'Benjamin' both represent the internal, while 'the remaining ten sons of Jacob' represent the external, 5469.

5549   'And should harm happen to him on the road on which you go' means that, when in the company of truths alone in the natural that have been separated from the internal, it will perish. This is clear from the explanation above in 5413, where similar words occur.

5550   'You will cause my grey hair to go down' means that this will accordingly be the final phase of the Church. This is clear from the meaning of 'grey hair', when the Church is the subject, as its final phase. A final phase is also meant by 'grey hair' in Isaiah,

Hearken to Me, O house of Jacob, and all the remnant of the house of Israel who have been carried from the womb, borne from the belly. *Even to* [your] *old age* I am the same, and *even to grey hair* I will carry [you].   Isa.46:3,4.

'The house of Jacob' stands for the external Church, 'the house of Israel' for the internal Church. 'From the womb and the belly' stands for since it began. 'To old age and to grey hair" stands for the final phase of it. And in David,

Planted in the house of Jehovah, they will flourish in the courts of our God. They will still have produce when *in grey hair*. Ps.92:13,14.

'When in grey hair' stands for when in the final phase.

5551 'In sorrow to the grave' means without hope of a restoration to life. This is clear from the meaning of 'sorrow' here as without hope, for sorrow comes when no hope exists any longer; and from the meaning of 'the grave' as resurrection and regeneration, dealt with in 2916, 2917, 3256, 4621, and so a restoration – a restoration of the Church – to life. For if neither the internal represented by 'Joseph' is present within the Church, nor the intermediary represented by 'Benjamin', nor faith in the will, which is charity, represented by 'Simeon', no hope of its restoration to life exists any longer.

2 It does indeed seem strange that 'the grave' means a restoration to life; but that strangeness is due to man's idea about the grave. He makes no distinction between the grave and death, nor even between the grave and the corpse lying in it. But angels in heaven cannot have any such idea about the grave; theirs is an entirely different one from man's, namely the idea of resurrection and restoration to life. For when a person's corpse is committed to the grave he himself is raised into the next life. When thinking about the grave therefore the angels have no idea of death, only of life and consequently of a restoration to life.

CORRESPONDENCE WITH
THE GRAND MAN – *continued*
IN THIS SECTION THE CORRESPONDENCE OF
THE SKIN, HAIR, AND BONES WITH IT

5552 Correspondence is by nature such that the parts in the human being which possess the greatest amount of life correspond to those communities in heaven which possess the greatest amount of life and consequently the greatest amount of happiness there, such as those communities to which a person's external and internal sensory powers correspond, and which have a link with his understanding and his will. But parts in the human being which possess less life correspond to the the kinds of communities where less life is present, such as the layers of the skin which cover the whole body, also the cartilages and the bones which hold together and support everything within the body, as well as the hairs that grow out of the skin. The identity and nature of those communities to which all these parts of the body correspond must also be stated.

5553 The communities to which the layers of the skin correspond are at the entrance to heaven. They are able to perceive what spirits are like who arrive at the outer threshold of heaven, who are then either turned away or taken inside. So those communities may be called the entrances to or places on the threshold of heaven.

5554 Very many communities exist which constitute the outer coverings of the body, all differing from one another from the face down to the soles of the feet; for differences exist wherever you choose to look. I have had many conversations with these communities. So far as their spiritual life was concerned they were the kind of people who had allowed themselves to be convinced by others that this or that was the truth; and once they had heard proofs drawn from the sense of the letter of the Word they fully believed it and stuck firmly to the opinion they had received. They also based the life they led, though this was not an evil one, on the same convictions. But other spirits who do not possess a similar frame of mind to theirs find it difficult to have any dealings with them because of their rigid adherence to the ideas they have accepted and because of their refusal to be led away from these by reasonable thinking. Very many spirits like that come from this'planet, for our own globe is taken up with things of an external nature and responds to internal ones in the way that the skin usually does.

5555 There are spirits who during their lifetime knew no more than the general outlines of faith, such as the requirement to love their neighbour, and in obedience to this general basic command did good no less to the wicked than to the upright, without discriminating between those two kinds of people; for they said that everyone was their neighbour. When spirits like these lived in the world they allowed themselves to be led astray greatly by deceitful, hypocritical, and fraudulent persons. Much the same happens to them in the next life, where they do not bother to listen to what anyone else tells them because they are ruled by their senses and do not go in for rational ideas. These spirits constitute the skin – the outer part where there is not so much feeling. I have talked to those who constitute the skin which covers the skull. These differ considerably, as does the skin on various parts of the body, such as that on different areas of the skull to the back of it, to the front of it, and on the temples, or that on the face, and over the chest, abdomen, loins, feet, arms, hands, and fingers.

5556 I have also been allowed to know who those spirits are that constitute the scaly area of the skin. This area of the skin, more than any other casings of the body, possesses the least amount of feeling, since it is thickly covered with scales which are rather like soft gristle. The communities constituting that scale-like skin are ones who engage in reasoning about everything, about whether such-and-such a thing is true or not, yet go no further than just reasoning. When I spoke to them I was allowed to perceive that they had no understanding at all of what was true or untrue; and the more they go on reasoning the less they understand. Even so, they seem to themselves to be wiser than others, for they identify wisdom with an ability to reason. They are totally unaware of the fact that the chief characteristic of wisdom is perceiving, without the use of reasoning, that a thing is true or untrue. Many of these spirits belong to those who in the world became like this because of the confusion into which goodness and truth had been thrown by philosophical arguments, as a result of which they possess less common sense than anybody else.

5557 There are also spirits who serve as mouthpieces for others, while they themselves understand scarcely anything of what they utter. They have confessed that this is so, yet they go on acting as those mouthpieces. This is what those people come to be like who during their lifetime simply babbled on without giving any thought to what they were saying and who loved to speak on every subject. I have been told that they exist in groups and that some of them correlate with the membranes that cover the internal organs of the body, others with those layers of skin where little feeling exists. For they are wholly passive forces which do not act of themselves but are moved by others.

5558 There are spirits who, when they wish to know something, declare an idea to be true; and they declare this one after another in their community. As they do so they watch to see whether that declaration flows freely, unimpeded by any spiritual resistance to it. For when the idea is not true they usually notice some resistance coming from within. If no resistance to it is detected by them they suppose that the idea is true, and they have no other way of knowing it. Spirits like this are the ones who constitute the glands associated with the skin; yet there are two kinds of these spirits. The first kind affirm that the idea is true because the declaration they make appears, as stated, to flow freely, from which they assume, because there is no resistance to it, that it accords with the heavenly form and consequently with the truth. So it is affirmed by them. The second kind of those spirits boldly affirm, without knowing it to be so, that an idea is true.

5559 I have been shown in a representative manner the pattern produced by the interweavings present in different parts of the skin. With those spirits among whom those outermost coverings of skin corresponded to inner realities – that is, material things acted in agreement with spiritual ones – a beautiful pattern existed that was formed from coils wonderfully linked together like lacework that defies description. They were azure-coloured. After that forms still more continuous, neat and attractive were represented, which is how the skin of a person who has been regenerated is seen. But among those who have been deceitful persons those outermost coverings look like clumps consisting solely of snakes, while magicians look like foul entrails.

5560   The communities of spirits to which the cartilages and bones correspond are very many. But they are the kind that have very little spiritual life within them, even as very little life is present in the bones when compared with the softer parts which they encompass, such as the skull and bones belonging to the head when compared with both parts of the brain, the medulla oblongata, and the substances within these that belong to the senses, or, for instance, the vertebrae and ribs when compared with the heart and lungs; and so on.

5561   I have been shown how small is the amount of spiritual life present in those spirits who correlate with the bones. Used as mouth-pieces by other spirits, they know little about the things they declare. Even so they do declare things, taking delight solely in the act of so declaring them. Reduced to a state like this are those people who led an evil life and yet had certain remnants of goodness stored away within them. These remnants, after vastations lasting for ages and ages, are what produce that small amount of spiritual life. For what remnants are, see 468, 530, 560, 561, 660, 1050, 1738, 1906, 2284, 5135, 5342, 5344. As has been stated, these spirits possess only a small amount of spiritual life, by which life is meant the life that angels in heaven possess. While in the world a person is introduced to it by means of matters of faith and charity. An actual affection for the good of charity, an affection also for the truth of faith, is what constitutes spiritual life. Without that affection a person's life is a natural, worldly, bodily, and earthly one, which is not spiritual life if it does not hold such an affection within itself but a life such as animals in general possess.

5562   Those who are released from vastations and correlate with the purposes served by the bones do not have any clear and precise ideas, only general and most imprecise ones. They are like those who are called the distracted, not fully in their bodies so to speak. They are sluggish, dim-witted, and stupid; they are slow at grasping anything at all. What is more, they frequently lack any feelings of uneasiness because anxious cares do not get through to them but become lost in their overall dull-wittedness.

5563   Occasionally pains are felt in the skull, sometimes in one part, at other times in another, when what seem like nodules which are separate from all other bones and so are the source of the pains are detected there. Experience has taught me that things of this nature are caused by falsities originating in evil desires. And what is a marvel, the genera and species of falsities have their own particular locations in the skull, as considerable experience has also enabled me to know. In the case of people undergoing reformation such nodules, which are pieces of hardness, are broken down and made soft; and this is done in a variety of ways. In general it is done by means of instruction in what is good and true, by means of incisive inroads made by truths, an activity accompanied by pain inwardly, and also by means of actual tearings apart, an activity accompanied by pain outwardly. For falsities originating in evil desires are of such a nature as to cause hardness; they are the opposite of truths. In the case of truths, because they take shape in accord with the shape heaven takes, they flow so to speak spontaneously, freely, gently, and softly. But the shape taken by falsities is the opposite because they incline in the opposite direction from heaven. As a consequence that flow associated with the form taken by heaven is blocked and hardnesses develop. For this reason those in whom deadly hatred and desires for revenge accompanying such hatred have existed, and in whom falsities originating in such desires have been present, possess skulls that are completely hardened. Some have skulls like ivory, which no rays of light, which are truths, can penetrate but are altogether turned back.

5564   There are spirits, low in stature, who boom when they speak; sometimes they do this all together, like a column of troops. They are born with this method of speaking. They do not come from this planet but from some other one which in the Lord's Divine mercy will be described when the inhabitants of various planets are the subject. I have been told that these spirits correlate with the shield-shaped cartilage which is situated in front of the cavity of the chest and which serves as a support for the front of the ribs and also for various voice muscles.

5565   There are spirits too who correlate with the bones that are much harder, such as the teeth; but I have not been allowed to know very much about these. All I have been allowed to know is that when these spirits, with whom scarcely any spiritual life at all remains, are brought into view in the light of heaven, they do not appear to possess a face, only teeth instead of a face. This is because the face represents a person's interiors, thus his spiritual and celestial endowments, which are matters of faith and charity. Spirits therefore who during their lifetime did not acquire any such spiritual life have the kind of appearance that has just been described.

5566   As a certain spirit came towards me I saw what looked like a black cloud that had stars around it which were wavering. Falsities are meant when stars that are wavering appear in the next life, but truths when those that are firmly fixed appear there. I noticed that this was a spirit who wanted to get near me; and when he did so he struck fear into me, an ability that certain spirits, especially robbers, possess. It was that fear which led me to deduce that he was a robber. While he was near me he sought to do all he could with the aid of magical devices to disturb me, but without success. He stretched out his hand to exercise the power he imagined himself to possess, but that action achieved absolutely nothing. After that I was shown what his face was like. He had no face but instead something very black, where a mouth appeared, opened wide in a dreadful and fierce manner to produce gaping jaws in which a row of teeth stood out. In short it was like a mad dog with its jaws opened wide, so wide that it had jaws but no face.

5567 A certain spirit once positioned himself by my left side, at which point I did not know where he came from or what kind of spirit he was; he also acted in an obscure manner. In addition he wished to get right inside me; but he was thrust away. He emitted a general sphere of ideas constituting thought, a sphere such as cannot be described; I do not remember ever detecting any sphere like it before then. He had not given his allegiance to any basic convictions but was in general opposed to everyone, whom he had been able to refute and disparage by the use of adroit and clever arguments without even knowing what the truth might be. I was astonished that he was gifted with such cleverness, that is to say, with the ability to refute others by the use of clever arguments while having no actual knowledge of the truth. After this he went away, but he soon returned with an earthenware flask in his hand, from which he wanted to give me something to drink. The flask contained some brew produced from false notions that would take away the understanding from those who drank it. This representation took place because he had deprived those who had been his adherents in the world of their understanding of truth and good; yet they remained his adherents. This spirit too, when seen in the light of heaven, did not seem to have a face, only teeth, for the reason that he had been able to deride other people's ideas even though he himself had no knowledge at all of the truth. I was told who he was. During his lifetime he existed among the famous and was recognized by some as such.

5568 Sometimes spirits have been present with me who ground their teeth. They came from hells in which the inhabitants had not only led an evil life but also firmly rejected the Divine and traced everything back to natural forces. Those spirits grind their teeth when they speak, which is hideous to listen to.

5569 Just as there is a correspondence of the bones and skin, so there is also a correspondence of the hairs on the body; for hairs come up out of roots in the skin. Whatever is part of the correspondence with the Grand Man exists with spirits and angels; for each one is related to the Grand Man as an image of the same. Angels therefore have hair, neatly and tidily arranged; their hair represents their natural life and the correspondence of this with their spiritual life. For 'the hair' or 'hairs' means the strands of one's natural life, see 3301, while 'cutting one's hair' means attending to natural things so as to make them tidy and so attractive, 5247.

5570 Many spirits exist, especially female ones, who have imagined that having an attractive appearance was all that mattered and who have thought about nothing deeper than this. They have given scarcely any thought to eternal life. This is excusable in females up to the time of young womanhood, when the burning desire which usually comes before marriage has died down. But if, when they become more mature adults and are able to understand something better, they continue in those ways, they acquire a character that remains with them after death. Such women are seen in the next life, possessing long hair which falls over their faces and which, in their imagination that such makes them elegant, they are also combing. (For 'combing one's hair' means making natural things look attractive, 5247.) From this other spirits recognize what those women are like; for spirits can know from their hair – from its colour, length, arrangement – what those women have been like so far as their natural life in the world is concerned.

5571   There are spirits who have believed that natural forces accounted for everything and who were thoroughly convinced of this. They have also led a carefree life on the basis of this belief, without recognizing any life after death or thus the existence of hell and of heaven. Being wholly naturally-minded, when such spirits are seen in the light of heaven they do not seem to have a face at all but instead something bearded, very hairy, and uncut. For, as stated above, the face represents the spiritual and celestial endowments existing with a person interiorly, whereas the hair on the head represents natural ones.

5572   At the present day there are very many people in the Christian world who attribute everything to natural forces and scarcely anything to the Divine. But more of these people exist in one nation than in another. Let me therefore record a conversation I had with certain members of that nation in which there are very many who think like that.

5573   A certain spirit was once present, but was invisible over my head. I was led to perceive his presence from a stench of burnt horn or bone and from stinking teeth. After that a large crowd looking like a cloud appeared on the scene, coming up from below towards a higher position behind my back. These too were invisible; and they came to a halt above my head. I assumed that their invisibility was due to their own cleverness. I was told however that where the spiritual sphere obtained they were not visible, but where the natural sphere did so they were visible. They were therefore called 'the invisible natural ones'. Regarding those spirits let me record first the disclosure that they endeavoured in a most zealous, cunning, and skillful manner to prevent any exposure at all of themselves. Having this end in view they also knew how to take away from other people the ideas they possessed and to replace these with different ones with which they prevented their own disclosure. Their endeavour to do this lasted for quite a long time. From all this I was led to see that during their lifetime those spirits had been the kind of people who did not want any of their actions or thought to be exposed, which they achieved by assuming a different countenance and a different manner of speaking. Nevertheless they had not employed any kind of pretence so as to lie and deceive.

2 I perceived that the spirits present with me had been traders during their lifetime; yet they were the kind whose delight in life lay in trading itself and not so much in riches, so that trading itself was so to speak the driving force (*anima*) within them. I therefore spoke to them about this, and was led to say that trading in no way prevented them from entering heaven and that in heaven there were rich people no less than poor ones. But they objected to this, saying it had been their opinion that if they were going to be saved, they would need to give up trading, donate all their possessions to the poor, and reduce themselves to a pitiable condition. I was led to answer that what they said was not true and that those among them who were in heaven because they had been good Christians and yet had been wealthy, some extremely wealthy, thought otherwise. These people had had as their end in view the common good and love towards their neighbour; and they had engaged in commerce solely for the sake of service in the world and had not, what is more, set their heart on wealth. But the reason why those to whom I was speaking were on a lower level was that they were wholly naturally-minded and therefore had no belief in a life after death, or in hell, or in heaven; indeed they had no belief in the spirit. I also told them that by the use of all kinds of ingenuity they had heartlessly robbed others of their goods and without feeling any pity could for their own gain watch entire households perish, and that they consequently derided everyone who talked to them about the spiritual life.

3 I have also been shown the kind of belief those spirits had had regarding life after death, and regarding heaven and hell. A certain person appeared who was carried up to heaven, going up from the left over to the right. I was told that this was someone who had recently died and was being taken off immediately by angels into heaven. There followed a discussion concerning that person, but although those spirits too saw this take place, they possessed a sphere of disbelief which was an extremely powerful one and which they diffused around themselves. It was so powerful that they were willing to convince themselves and others not to believe what they had seen. Because their disbelief was so strong I was led to tell them that if in the world they had by chance witnessed the restoration to life of someone lying dead on a catafalque they would first of all have said that they refused to believe it unless they had seen many dead persons restored to life, and that if they had seen this they would have attributed such to natural causes. After this, when those spirits had been left to think for a while, they said that at first they would have believed that what they had seen was some trick. But once, they added, it proved to be no trick they would have believed that the soul of the dead person had some secret communication with the one restoring him to life, and at length that this was some secret which they could not comprehend; for the natural

world contains very many incomprehensible secrets. So they could not have been led to believe that such a happening was attributable to some force outside the natural order. This revealed the kind of faith that had been theirs, that is to say, a faith which could not possbly lead them to believe in a life after death, or in hell, or in heaven. Thus it revealed that they were naturally-minded. When spirits like these are seen in the light of heaven they too seem to have no face, only a thick growth of hair in place of it.

43

1 And the famine grew more serious in the land.

2 And it happened, when they had finished eating the corn which they had brought from Egypt, that their father said to them, Turn back, buy a little food for us.

3 And Judah said to him – he said, The man issued a solemn warning to us, saying, You will not see my face unless your brother is with you.

4 If you are willing to send our brother with us, we will go down and buy food for you.

5 And if you are not willing to send him, we will not go down; for the man said to us, You will not see my face unless your brother is with you.

6 And Israel said, Why did you treat me so badly as to tell the man that you had still [another] brother?

7 And they said, The man questioned us closely about ourselves and our generation, saying, Is your father still alive? Have you a brother? And we told him according to the tenor[1] of these words. Could we possibly have known that he would say, Cause your brother to come down?

8 And Judah said to Israel his father, Send the boy with me, and we will rise up and go, and we will live and not die – even we, even you, even our young children.

9 I myself will be surety for him; from my hand you will require him. If I do not bring him to you and set him before you, then I shall be sinning against you every day.

10 For if perhaps we had not delayed we would by now have returned these two times[2].

11 And Israel their father said to them, If this therefore has to be, do it. Take some of the much-sung-about produce[3] of the land in your vessels, and cause a gift to go down to the man – a little resin and a little honey, wax and stacte, pistachio nuts and almonds.

---

[1] *lit.* mouth

[2] *i.e.* they would by now have returned home a second time

[3] much-sung-about produce *translates the single Latin word* decantatio, *which Sw. uses to represent the Hebrew* zimrath, *a word meaning* products celebrated and praised in song.

12 And take a double amount of silver in your hands. And the silver that was put back in the mouth of your pouches you are to take back in your hand; perhaps it was a mistake.

13 And take your brother; and rise up, return to the man.

14 And may God Shaddai grant you mercy before the man, and may he release[1] to you your other brother and Benjamin; and I, even as I have been bereaved, I shall be bereaved.

15 And the men took this gift, and took the double amount of silver in their hand, and Benjamin; and they rose up, and went down to Egypt, and stood before Joseph.

16 And Joseph saw Benjamin with them, and he said to the one who was over his house, Bring the men to the house, and slaughter and prepare [an animal]; for the men will eat with me at midday.

17 And the man did as Joseph said, and the man brought the men to Joseph's house.

18 And the men were afraid because they were brought to Joseph's house; and they said, Over the matter of the silver put back in our pouches at the beginning are we brought to [this place], so that he may come down on us and fall on us[2], and take us as slaves, and our asses.

19 And they came near the man who was over Joseph's house, and they spoke to him [at][3] the door (*ostium*) of the house.

20 And they said, On my honour[4], my lord, we certainly came down at the beginning to buy food.

21 And it happened, when we came to the lodging-place and opened our pouches, that behold, each man's silver was in the mouth of his pouch, our silver in its full weight; and we are bringing it back in our hand.

22 And we are causing other silver to come down in our hand to buy food; we do not know who put our silver in our pouches.

23 And he said, Peace to you, do not be afraid; your God and the God of your father has given you the concealed gift in your pouches; your silver came to me. And he brought Simeon out to them.

24 And the man brought the men to Joseph's house and gave them water, and they washed their feet; and he gave fodder to their asses.

25 And they made ready the gift, until Joseph's coming at midday, for they heard that they would eat bread there.

26 And Joseph came to the house, and they brought him the gift that was in their hand, to the house, and bowed down to him to the earth.

27 And he questioned them about their peace[5], and said, Does your father, the old man of whom you spoke, have peace? Is he still alive?

---

[1] *lit.* send
[2] *lit.* roll down onto us and throw himself onto us
[3] *See* 5653.
[4] *The Latin* In me *here represents the Hebrew* Bi, *which is usually regarded as an expression of entreaty rather than validity, cp* Chapter 44:18.
[5] *i.e.* their welfare

28 And they said, Your servant our father has peace; he is still alive. And they bowed, and bowed down.

29 And he lifted up his eyes and saw Benjamin his brother, his mother's son, and said, Is this your youngest brother, whom you said [something about] to me? And he said, God be gracious to you, my son.

30 And Joseph hastened, because feelings of compassion were being roused in him towards his brother, and he sought [somewhere] to weep; and he went to his bedchamber and wept there.

31 And he washed his face and went out; and he contained himself and said, Set on bread.

32 And they set for him by himself, and for them by themselves, and for the Egyptians eating with him by themselves; for the Egyptians cannot eat bread with the Hebrews, since that is an abomination to the Egyptians.

33 And they sat in front of him, the firstborn according to his birthright, and the youngest according to his youth; and the men were astonished [and looked] each at his companion.

34 And he took portions from before his face to them, and he multiplied Benjamin's portion above the portions of all theirs – five measures more. And they drank, and drank plentifully with him.

CONTENTS

5574   The description of the joining of the truths known to the Church and present in the natural, which are 'the ten sons of Jacob', to the celestial of the spiritual or truth from the Divine, which is 'Joseph', through the intermediary, which is 'Benjamin', is continued. But this chapter confines itself in the internal sense to the general influx which comes before the joining together.

THE INTERNAL SENSE

5575   Verses 1–5 **And the famine grew more serious in the land. And it happened, when they had finished eating the corn which they had brought from Egypt, that their father said to them, Turn back, buy a little food for us. And Judah said to him – he said, The man issued a solemn warning to us, saying, You will not see my face unless your brother is with you. If you are willing to send our brother with us, we will go down and buy food for you. And if you are not willing to send**

him, we will not go down; for the man said to us, You will not see my face unless your brother is with you.

'And the famine grew more serious' means the desolation resulting from the dearth of spiritual things. 'In the land' means in the case of the integral parts of the Church. 'And it happened' means a new situation. 'When they had finished eating the corn' means when there was a deficiency of truths. 'Which they had brought from Egypt' means which had been obtained from factual knowledge. 'That their father said to them' means a perception received from the things that constituted the Church. 'Turn back, buy a little food for us' means that, so as to have life, they should acquire the good of spiritual truth. 'And Judah said to him' means the good which existed in the Church. 'He said, The man issued a solemn warning to us' means the turning away from them of the spiritual from the internal. 'Saying, You will not see my face' means that no compassion will show itself. 'Unless your brother is with you' means unless the intermediary is with you. 'If you are willing to send our brother with us' means if the Church desires a linking to take place, the intermediary must be there. 'We will go down and buy food for you' means that in this case the good of truth will be acquired. 'And if you are not willing to send him' means if that is not so. 'We will not go down' means that it cannot be acquired. 'For the man said to us' means a perception regarding the spiritual. 'You will not see my face' means that no compassion will show itself. 'Unless your brother is with you' means unless the intermediary is with you.

5576 'And the famine grew more serious' means the desolation resulting from the dearth of spiritual things. This is clear from the meaning of 'the famine' as an absence of cognitions of goodness and truth, dealt with in 3364, 5277, 5279, 5281, 5300, and the consequent desolation, 5360, 5376, 5415. And because desolation can arise from a shortage and consequent dearth of spiritual realities, 'the famine' has this meaning too. A famine in the spiritual world or heaven is not a hunger for [bodily] food, for angels do not feed on material food, which is the food for that body which a person carries around in the world. Rather it is a hunger for the kind of food that nourishes their minds, and this, which is called spiritual food, consists in understanding what is true and in having a wise discernment of what is good. And what is amazing, angels are nourished with this food.

2 This has been made clear to me by the fact that after young children, who have died as young children, have been furnished in heaven with truths that are the constituents of intelligence and with forms of good that are the essence of wisdom, they no longer look like young children but adults, increasingly so as goodness and truth increase with them. The nourishment of angels by spiritual food has also been made clear to me by the fact that they have a constant desire for those things that are the constituents of intelligence and wisdom. At their eveningtime, that is, when they pass through a state in which they lack what they desire,

that state compared with other states holds no happiness for them. In that state there is nothing that they hunger and long for more than a new dawning of morning light upon them and their return to the life filled with happiness that comes with intelligence and wisdom.

It may also be seen by anyone who stops to reflect on the matter that understanding what is true and desiring what is good constitute spiritual food. If someone who is enjoying material food that serves to nourish the body is at the same time in a cheerful state of mind and is engaged in conversation about the kinds of things that accord with that state of mind, the material food for the body becomes all the more nourishing. This is an indication of the existence of a correspondence between spiritual food, which feeds the soul, and material food, which feeds the body. The same is clear in addition from the experience of someone who has the desire to furnish his mind with ideas that constitute knowledge, intelligence, and wisdom. If he is denied these he begins to feel sad and distressed, and like somebody in time of famine he has the desire to return to his spiritual food and so to the nourishment of his soul.

It may also be seen from the Word that spiritual food is what nourishes the soul in the way material food nourishes the body, as in Moses,

Man does not live by bread only, but *man lives by every utterance of the mouth of Jehovah.* Deut.8:3; Matt.4:4.

In general 'utterance of the mouth of Jehovah' is the Divine Truth which goes forth from the Lord, and so is every truth contained in wisdom; specifically it is the Word, the foundation and source of ideas constituting wisdom. And in John,

Do not labour for *the food* which perishes, *but for the food which endures to eternal life,* which the Son of Man will give you. John 6:27.

This 'food' is clearly the truth that is contained in wisdom and that goes forth from the Lord.

From this one may also recognize what is meant by these words of the Lord recorded in the same chapter,

My flesh is truly *food,* and My blood truly is drink. John 6:55.

That is to say, 'the Lord's flesh' is Divine Good, 3813, and 'His blood' Divine Truth, 4735. For now that the Lord has made His Human completely Divine, His 'flesh' is nothing else than Divine Good, and His 'blood' nothing else than Divine Truth. One has to understand that in the Divine there is nothing material; therefore in the highest sense, that is, where it has reference to the Lord, 'food' is the Good of Divine Love directed towards the salvation of the human race. This food is also the kind that is meant by the Lord's words in John,

Jesus said to the disciples, *I have food to eat* of which you do not know. *My food* is to do the will of Him who sent Me, and to finish His work. John 4:32,34.

'Doing the will of Him who sent Me, and finishing His work' is saving the human race; and the Divine attribute which motivates this is Divine Love.

From all this one may now see what is meant in the spiritual sense by 'the famine'.

5577 'In the land' means in the case of the integral parts of the Church. This is clear from the meaning of 'the land' in the Word as the Church, and therefore here the integral parts of the Church; for whatever serves to mean the Church also means its integral parts since it is made up of these. The reason why in the Word 'the land' means the Church is that the land of Canaan was the one in which the Church had existed since most ancient times. Consequently when the expression 'the land' appears in the Word it is used to mean the land of Canaan; and when this particular land is meant one understands the Church. For when the expression 'the land' appears there, people in the spiritual world do not concern themselves with the idea of a land, only with the idea of the nation inhabiting it; yet not with an idea of that nation but with an idea of the essential nature of it. Consequently they concern themselves with an idea of the Church when 'the land', used to mean the land of Canaan, appears there.

2 From this one may see how deluded those people are who believe – on the basis of prophetical utterances in the Old Testament, and in John in the New – that on the day when the last judgement takes place a new earth or land and a new heaven or sky are going to be created, when in fact nothing else than a new external Church is meant by 'a new earth' and a new internal Church by 'a new heaven'. These deluded people also believe that something other than the Church is meant when the expression 'the whole earth' is used in the Word. This shows how little understanding of the Word exists with those who imagine that the Word does not contain any meaning more holy than that shining out of the letter alone.

Regarding the existence of the Church in the land of Canaan since most ancient times, 3686, 4447, 4454, 4516, 4517, 5136.
Regarding 'the land' in the Word meaning the Church, 662, 1066, 1067, 1262, 1413, 1607, 2928, 4447.
Regarding 'a new heaven and a new earth' meaning a new Church, internal and external, 1733, 1850. 2117, 2118(end), 3355(end), 4535.

5578 'And it happened' means a new situation. This is clear from the meaning of 'so it was' or 'it happened' as that which implies a new state, dealt with in 4979, 4987, 4999, 5074, 5466. In the original language used in ancient times the meaning was not indicated with the aid of punctuation marks; rather the text continued without any breaks in the same way as speech does in heaven. Instead of punctuation marks the conjunction 'and' was used, also the verb 'so it was' or 'it happened'. This explains why these expressions occur so many times and why 'so it was' or 'it happened' means a new situation.

5579   'When they had finished eating the corn' means when there was a deficiency of truths. This is clear from the meaning of 'the corn' as truth, dealt with in 5276, 5280, 5292, 5402 – the fact that there was a deficiency of such truth being meant by 'they had finished eating it'. The situation in the spiritual world is that those there satisfy their hunger with truths and forms of good; for they constitute the food for those there, 5576. But once that food has served its purpose those people enter a further state of dearth. It is like the nourishing of a person with material food, in that once this food has served its purpose that person feels hungry again. This kind of hunger, which is a dearth of spiritual things, is eveningtime for those in the spiritual world, or the darkest part of their day; but this is followed by twilight and morning. Those there pass through alternating phases like these. They enter that eveningtime or state of spiritual hunger to the end that they may long for and have a desire for truths and forms of good, which are more nutritious when they are hungry for them, even as material food is for someone who is famished. From this one may see what is meant by a dearth of spiritual things when there was a deficiency of truths.

5580   'Which they had brought from Egypt' means which had been obtained from factual knowledge. This is clear from the meaning of 'Egypt' as factual knowledge, dealt with in 1164, 1165, 1186, 1462, *from this knowledge* being meant by 'they had brought from there'. In the good sense 'Egypt' means the facts which the Church possesses, that is to say, which serve the Church in the outward form it takes, 4749, 4964, 4966. Facts of this kind, like the porch leading into a house, serve to introduce a person into the truths which the Church possesses.

[2] For the impression of those facts on a person's senses takes place first, and this opens the way into the more internal parts of the mind. Indeed it is well known that the area of external sensory perception is opened up first in a person, then that of the more internal sensory perceptions, and finally that where intellectual concepts reside; and that once the area where those concepts reside has been opened up, such concepts there are represented, to enable them to be understood, within those sensory impressions. The reason for this is that intellectual concepts spring up out of sensory impressions by a process of extraction from them; for intellectual concepts are deductions which, once they have been made, are separated from and rise far above sensory impressions. The presence of spiritual influences coming from the Lord by way of heaven is what accomplishes all this. From these things one may see what is implied by truths obtained from factual knowledge.

5581   'That their father said to them' means a perception received from the things that constituted the Church. This is clear from the meaning of 'saying' in the historical narratives of the Word as perception, often dealt with already, and from the representation of Israel, to whom 'father' refers here, as the Church. For 'Israel' is the internal spiritual Church, and 'Jacob' the external Church, see 4286, 4292, 4570.

The word 'father' is used because in the Word 'father' as well as 'mother' means the Church; but 'mother' means the Church so far as truth is concerned, and 'father' the Church so far as good is concerned. The reason for this is that the Church is a spiritual marriage formed from good as the father and truth as the mother.

5582 'Turn back, buy a little food for us' means that, so as to have life, they should acquire the good of spiritual truth. This is clear from the meaning of 'buying' as acquiring and making one's own, dealt with in 4397, 5374, 5397, 5406, 5410, 5426; and from the meaning of 'food' as the good of truth, dealt with in 5340, 5342. Here the good of spiritual truth is meant, because this kind of good is the subject in what follows. That the purpose was for them to have life follows from this.

5583 'And Judah said to him' means the good which existed in the Church. This is clear from the representation of 'Judah' as the good existing in the Church, dealt with in 3654. The fact that now Judah speaks about Benjamin, whereas previously, in verses 36 and 37 of the previous chapter, Reuben was the one to do so, is an arcanum which only the internal sense can bring to light. The same applies to the fact that when Reuben spoke about Benjamin, Jacob is referred to in verse 36 of the previous chapter as Jacob, whereas now, when Judah is speaking about Benjamin, Jacob is referred to in verses 6,8,11 as Israel. No one can deny that some such arcanum lies within this, but what that arcanum is cannot possibly be known simply from the story told in the sense of the letter, as is also the case in other places where Jacob is sometimes referred to as Jacob, and at other times as Israel, 4286. The actual arcanum embodied in all this will in the Lord's Divine mercy be stated in what follows. The reason Judah is the speaker now is that the subject is the good of spiritual truth which needs to be acquired, 5582. Therefore here Judah, who represents the good existing with the Church, is the one to speak to Israel, who represents the good of spiritual truth. He also offers himself as a surety for Benjamin, who represents the intermediary; for the intermediary must be joined by means of good to what has to be acquired.

5584 'He said, The man issued a solemn warning to us' means the turning away from them of the spiritual from the internal. This is clear from the meaning of 'issuing a solemn warning' as the turning away of [the spiritual from the natural], for Joseph had warned them that they would not see his face unless their brother was with them (this warning is the threat of a turning away, for 'not seeing his face' means that no compassion will show itself, dealt with in the next paragraph); and from the representation of 'Joseph' as the Divine Spiritual, or what amounts to the same, truth from the Divine, dealt with in 3969, which at this point is the spiritual or truth flowing in from the internal since the expression 'the man' is used.

366

5585 'Saying, You will not see my face' means that no compassion will show itself. This is clear from the meaning of 'face', when used in reference to a person, as his interiors, that is to say, his affections and consequent thoughts, dealt with in 358, 1999, 2434, 3527, 3573, 4066, 4796, 4797, 5102. But when used in reference to the Lord, for the Lord is represented in the highest sense by 'Joseph', 'face' means mercy and compassion, and therefore 'not seeing his face' means a lack of mercy or absence of compassion. Not that the Lord lacks any compassion, for He is pure mercy; but when the intermediary that effects the joining to Him is not present it does seem to a person as though there is no compassion in the Lord. The reason for this is that if no intermediary effecting the joining together is present, no acceptance of good takes place. And if there is no acceptance of good, evil is present instead. If at this time the person calls out to the Lord because evil prompts him to do so, thus for selfish reasons in defiance of anyone else's needs, he is not heard, in which case it seems as though no compassion shows itself.

2 As regards 'Jehovah's (or the Lord's) face' meaning mercy, this is evident from the Word; for understood properly 'Jehovah's (or the Lord's) face' is Divine love itself, and being Divine love it is the face of mercy since mercy is the expression of love towards the human race set in such miseries. The truth that 'Jehovah's (or the Lord's) face' is Divine Love may be seen from the Lord's face when He was transfigured in the presence of Peter, James, and John; that is, when He displayed His Divinity to them,

His face shone like the sun. Matt.17:2.

It has been shown already that 'the sun' is Divine Love, see 30-38, 1521, 1529-1531, 2441, 2495, 3636, 3643, 4060, 4321(end), 4696. The Lord's actual Divinity had never previously appeared in any face; but His Divine Human had so appeared, through which, seemingly within which, Divine Love – which in relation to the human race is Divine Mercy – showed itself. This Divine Mercy within the Divine Human is called 'the angel of His face' in Isaiah,

I will cause *the mercies of Jehovah* to be remembered. He has rewarded[1] them according to His mercies, and according to the abundance of *His mercies*; and He became their Saviour. And *the angel of His face* saved them; *in His love* and in His pity He redeemed them. Isa.63:7-9.

The expression 'the angel' is used because 'angels' in the Word means in the internal sense some attribute of the Lord, 1925, 2821, 4085, in this case His mercy, which is why the phrase 'the angel of His face' is used.
3 'Jehovah's (or the Lord's) face' is not only mercy but also peace and goodness since these are attributes of mercy, as may also be seen from the following places: In the Blessing,

---

[1] *Reading* retribuit (has rewarded), *which Sw. has in his rough draft and also in 222, for* retribuet (will reward)

Jehovah make His face shine upon you and *be merciful to you. Jehovah lift up His face upon you* and give you *peace.* Num.6:25,26.

Here it is quite evident that 'making His face shine' means showing mercy, and 'lifting up His face' means granting His peace. In David,

God *be merciful to us* and bless us, and *make His face shine upon us.* Ps.67:1.

Here also 'face' stands for mercy. In the same author,

Turn us back, O God, and *make Your face shine*, that we may be saved. Ps.80:3,7,19.

Here the meaning is similar. In the same author,

Deliver me from the hand of my enemies and my pursuers. *Make Your face shine upon Your servant.* Ps.31:15,16.

Likewise in Ps.119:134,135. In Daniel,

Hear, our God, the prayer of Your servant, and his supplications, *and make Your face shine upon Your sanctuary* that has been made desolate. Dan.9:17.

Here also 'making His face shine' stands for showing mercy.

4 In David,

Many are saying, Who will cause us to see *good? Lift up the light of Your face upon us.* Ps.4:6,7.

'Lifting up the light of His face' stands for His imparting good because of His mercy. In Hosea,

Let them seek My face; when they are in distress, in the morning let them seek Me. Hosea 5:15.

In David,

Seek My face! Your face, O Jehovah, will I seek. Ps.27:8,9.

In the same author,

Seek Jehovah and His strength; *seek His face* continually. Ps.105:4.

'Seeking Jehovah's face' stands for seeking His mercy. In the same author,

I, in righteousness, *shall see Your face.* Ps.17:15.

And in Matthew,

See that you do not despise any of these tiny ones; for I say to you that their angels in heaven *always see the face of My Father* who is in heaven. Matt.18:10.

'Seeing God's face' stands for the enjoyment of peace and good because of His mercy.

5 But the contrary of this is the hiding or concealment and also the turning away of the face, by which showing no compassion is meant, as in Isaiah,

In an overflowing of My anger *I hid My face* from you for a moment; but with eternal *mercy I will have mercy* on you. Isa.54:8.

'An overflowing of anger' stands for temptation in which, because the Lord does not seem to show mercy, the words 'I hid My face from you for a moment' are used. In Ezekiel,

I will turn My face away from them. Ezek.7:22.

In David,

How long, O Jehovah, will You forget me [as if] for ever? *How long will You hide Your face from me?* Ps.13:1.

In the same author,

Do not hide Your face from me; do not cast aside Your servant in anger. Ps.27:8,9.

In the same author,

Why, O Jehovah, do You abandon my soul? *Why do You hide Your face from me?* Ps.88:14.

In the same author,

Make haste, answer me, O Jehovah. My spirit is consumed. *Do not hide Your face from me,* lest I become like those going down into the pit. Cause me to hear *Your mercy* in the morning. Ps.143:7,8.

And in Moses,

My anger will flare up against this people on that day, so that I forsake them, and *I will hide My face from them,* and they will be devoured. *I will certainly hide My face* on that day, because of all the evil which they have done. Deut.31:17,18.

'Anger flaring up' stands for turning oneself away, 5034, and 'hiding one's face' for not showing any compassion.

These actions are attributed to Jehovah or the Lord, for the reason that although He is never angry and never turns away or hides His face He is said to do so because that is how it seems to someone under the influence of evil. For the person under the influence of evil turns himself away and hides the Lord's face from himself; that is, he removes His mercy from himself. The fact that it is the evils present with a person that do this is also clear from the Word, as in Micah,

Jehovah will hide His face from them at that time, *inasmuch as they have rendered their deeds evil.* Micah 3:4.

In Ezekiel,

Because they transgressed against Me, therefore *I hid My face from them.* According to their uncleanness and according to their transgressions I have dealt with them and *have hidden My face from them.* Ezek.39:23,24.

In particular in Isaiah,

Your iniquities are what separate you from your God, and *your sins what cause His face to hide from you.* Isa.59:2.

From these and many other places one may see the internal sense, which shows itself in various places and is discovered by one who is looking for it.

5586 'Unless your brother is with you' means unless the intermediary is with you. This is clear from the representation of 'Benjamin' as the intermediary, dealt with in 5411, 5413, 5443. The intermediary represented by 'Benjamin' serves as the link between the internal and the external, that is, between the spiritual man and the natural man; also, it is the truth of good that goes forth from truth from the Divine, represented by 'Joseph'. This truth of good is called the spiritual of the celestial – 'Benjamin' being the spiritual of the celestial, see 3969, 4592. A person's internal and external are completely distinct and separate from each other; for his internal dwells in the light of heaven, his external in the light of the world. And being completely distinct and separate they cannot be joined together except through the intermediary which derives its existence from both of them.

5587 'If you are willing to send our brother with us' means if the Church desires a linking together to take place, the intermediary must be there. This is clear from the representation of 'Israel', who was to be the sender, as the Church, dealt with in 4286 – 'if you are willing to send' consequently meaning if the Church so desires; and from the representation of Benjamin, to whom 'brother' refers here, as the intermediary, dealt with immediately above in 5586. From this it is evident that 'if you are willing to send our brother with us' means if the Church desires a linking together to take place between its external and its internal, the intermediary must be there.

5588 'We will go down and buy food for you' means that in this case the good of truth will be acquired. This is clear from the meaning of 'buying' as acquiring and making one's own; and from the meaning of 'food' as the good of truth, both of which meanings are dealt with above in 5582.

5589 'If you are not willing to send him' means if it does not act in that way, that is to say, if the Church does not desire the linking together. This is evident from what has been stated just above in 5587.

5590 'We will not go down' means that it cannot be acquired. This is clear from what has been stated just above in 5588.

5591 'For the man said to us' means a perception regarding the spiritual. This is clear from the meaning of 'the man' as the spiritual from the internal, dealt with above in 5584; and from the meaning of 'saying' in the historical narratives of the Word as perception, often dealt with already.

5592 'You will not see my face' means that no compassion will show itself. This is clear from the explanation above in 5585, where the same words occur.

5593 'Unless your brother is with you' means unless the intermediary is with you. This is clear from what has been stated above in 5586,

5587, about Benjamin, to whom 'brother' refers here, being the intermediary.

5594   Verses 6–10 **And Israel said, Why did you treat me so badly as
to tell the man that you had still [another] brother? And they said, The
man questioned us closely about ourselves and our generation, saying,
Is your father still alive? Have you a brother? And we told him
according to the tenor[1] of these words. Could we possibly have known
that he would say, Cause your brother to come down? And Judah said
to Israel his father, Send the boy with me, and we will rise up and go,
and we will live and not die – even we, even you, even our young
children. I myself will be surety for him; from my hand you will
require him. If I do not bring him to you and set him before you, then I
shall be sinning against you every day. For if perhaps we had not
delayed we would by now have returned these two times[2].**

'And Israel said' means a perception received from spiritual good. 'Why
did you treat me so badly as to tell the man that you had still [another]
brother?' means that they separated the truth of good from spiritual
good, so as to join it to the spiritual from the internal. 'And they said,
The man questioned us closely about ourselves' means the clear
perception this had regarding what existed within the natural. 'And our
generation' means regarding the truths of faith there. 'Saying, Is your
father still alive?' means and regarding spiritual good from which those
truths sprang. 'Have you a brother?' means regarding interior truth.
'And we told him according to the tenor of these words' means its
accordant discernment of these matters. 'Could we possibly have
known that he would say, Cause your brother to come down?' means
that we did not believe that he would want the truth of good to be
joined to him. 'And Judah said to Israel his father' means a perception
received from the good of the Church regarding these matters. 'Send
the boy with me' means so that he would be attached to him. 'And we
will rise up and go, and we will live and not die' means spiritual life
entered into by degrees. 'Even we' means the external aspect of the
Church. 'Even you' means the internal aspect of it. 'Even our young
children' means aspects even more internal. 'And I will be surety for
him' means that in the meantime [the truth of good] will be attached to
it [the good of the Church]. 'From my hand you will require him' means
that [the truth of good] will not be snatched away, insofar as it lies
within its power to prevent it. 'If I do not bring him to you and set him
before you' means the complete restoration of it to the Church. 'Then I
shall be sinning against you every day' means that the good of the
Church will not exist any longer. 'For if perhaps we had not delayed'
means lingering in a state of indecision. 'We would by now have
returned these two times' means that spiritual life, exterior and interior,
[would have been restored].

---

[1] *lit.* mouth
[2] *i.e.* they would by now have returned home a second time

5595 'And Israel said' means a perception received from spiritual good. This is clear from the meaning of 'saying' as perceiving, dealt with already; and from the representation of 'Israel' as spiritual good, dealt with in 3654, 4598. And as 'Israel' represents spiritual good, he also represents the internal Church, 3305, 4286; for that Church is a Church by virtue of its spiritual good. Spiritual good is truth made into good; for truth is made into good when a person leads a life in keeping with that truth. When he does this, truth passes into his will and from there into action and becomes part of his life; and when truth becomes part of his life it is no longer called truth but good. But the will which transforms truth into good is the new will formed in the understanding part of his mind; and that good is called spiritual good. Spiritual good differs from celestial good in that celestial good is implanted in the will part of a person's mind. But this matter has been dealt with quite a number of times before.

2 The reason why Jacob is not called Jacob now, as he is in verse 36 of the previous chapter, but Israel is that good is the subject here, whereas truth was the subject in the previous chapter. In the previous chapter the speaker was therefore Reuben, who represents the truth of doctrine taught by the Church, 3861, 3866, 4731, 4734, 4761, 5542; but in the present chapter the speaker is Judah, by whom the good of the Church is represented, 3654, 5583. Good becomes the subject now because this time the joining together is effected of the internal , which is 'Joseph', and the external, which is 'the ten sons of Jacob', through the intermediary, which is 'Benjamin'. That joining of the internal to the external is effected through good.

5596 'Why did you treat me so badly as to tell the man that you had still [another] brother?' means that they separated the truth of good from spiritual good, so as to join it to the spiritual from the internal. This is clear from the meaning of 'treating badly' as separating, for it is their separation of Benjamin from him that Israel calls 'treating badly'; and from the meaning of 'telling' or 'pointing out' as imparting knowledge about what another thinks and reflects on, 2862, 5508, consequently communicating, 4856, and therefore joining together too (for when what is imparted passes into another's will, that communication leads to a joining together, as when Joseph heard that Benjamin was still alive and present with his father, he wanted Benjamin to come to him, and then, when alone with him, wanted to be joined to him, as is evident from the historical details that come after this); from the representation of Joseph as the Divine Spiritual, who, when he is called 'the man', means the spiritual from the internal, dealt with in 5584; and from the representation of Benjamin – to whom their brother, whose existence they had told him about, refers here – as the truth of good, dealt with in 5586. From all this it is evident that 'why did you treat me so badly as to tell the man that you had still [another] brother?' means that they separated the truth of good from spiritual good, so as to join it to the spiritual from the internal.

5597   'And they said, The man questioned us closely about our-selves' means the clear perception this had regarding what existed within the natural. This is clear from the meaning of 'questioning' as perceiving another's thought, dealt with below; and from the representation of the ten sons of Jacob, to whom 'us' refers here, as the truths known to the Church which were present in the natural, dealt with in 5403, 5419, 5427, 5458, 5512. The reason 'questioning' means perceiving another's thought is that in heaven all thoughts are communicated, so clearly that no one needs to ask another what he thinks. This is why 'questioning' means perceiving another's thought; for things as they exist on earth become in the internal sense things as they exist in heaven.

5598   'And our generation' means regarding the truths of faith there. This is clear from the meaning of 'generation' as the birth of truth from good or faith from charity, dealt with in 1145, 1255, 4070, 4668. The reason 'generation' has this meaning in the internal sense is that in heaven no other kind of birth is meant than what is called regeneration, which is effected by means of the truth of faith and the good of charity. By this kind of generation or birth the children of men become the children of the Lord; these are they who are called 'the born of God' in John 1:13. The variations that exist in the offspring of good from truth and truth from good within that kind of generation are what determine the brotherly or blood relationships and the relationships by marriage that exist in heaven.

In heaven unending variations exist; but those variations are effected by the Lord in such a way that they resemble families in which there are brothers, sisters, sons-in-law, daughters-in-law, grandsons, grand-daughters, and so on. In general however all are organized into the kind of form that makes one united whole. They are like the variations within the human body, in which no one member is exactly the same as any other; indeed no one part within any member is the same as any other part. Even so, all those varying parts are organized into the kind of form in which they act as a single whole, and each fits in directly or remotely with the activity of another. Seeing a form such as this in the human being, one may deduce what the form must be like in heaven, with which there is a correspondence – a most perfect one – of everything in the human being.

5599   'Saying, Is your father still alive?' means and regarding spiritual good from which these sprang. This is clear from the representation of Israel, to whom 'father' refers here, as spiritual good, dealt with in 3654, 4598, 5595. Since the truths of faith descend from that good as their father, 5598, the expression from which they sprang is used here.

5600   'Have you a brother?' means regarding interior truth. This is clear from the representation of 'Benjamin' as the spiritual of the celestial, or what amounts to the same, the truth of good, which is interior truth. For 'Benjamin' is truth that has good within it, or the spiritual of the celestial, see 3969, 4592. This interior truth is what acts as the intermediary between truth from the Divine and truth within the natural.

5601 'And we told him according to the tenor of his words' means its accordant discernment of these matters. This is clear from the meaning of 'telling' or 'pointing out' as discerning, dealt with in 3608, for in the spiritual world or heaven those there have no need to tell what they are thinking since all thoughts are communicated, 5597, which is why 'telling' in the spiritual sense means discerning; and from the meaning of 'according to the tenor of his words' as in an accordant manner, for they are matters that he wished to discern.

5602 'Could we possibly have known that he would say, Cause your brother to come down?' means that we did not believe that he would want the truth of good to be joined to him. This is clear from the meaning of 'could it possibly be known that he would say?' as not believing; and from the representation of Benjamin, to whom 'brother' refers here, as the truth of good, dealt with just above in 5600. The joining of this truth of good to the spiritual from the internal is meant by the command that they should cause him to come down, as is evident from what has been stated above in 5596.

5603 'And Judah said to Israel his father' means a perception received from the good of the Church regarding these matters. This is clear from the meaning of 'saying' in the historical narratives of the Word as perceiving, often dealt with already; from the representation of 'Judah' as the good of the Church, dealt with above in 5583; and from the representation of 'Israel' as the internal spiritual Church, dealt with in 3305, 4286. From this it is evident that 'Judah said to Israel his father' means a perception the Church had which it received from its own good.

5604 'Send the boy with me' means that he would be attached to him, that is to say, to the good of the Church represented by 'Judah'. This is clear from the meaning of 'sending with him' as being attached to him and not to the rest, for in what follows it is stated, 'I will be surety for him; from my hand you will require him'; and from the representation of Benjamin, to whom 'the boy' refers here, as interior truth, dealt with just above in 5600. The expression 'the boy' is used because in the Word that which is more internal, when compared with what is external, is called a boy or child, for the reason that more innocence is present in what is more internal than in what is more external, innocence being meant in the Word by 'a young child' and also by 'a boy (or child)', 5236.

5605 'And we will rise up and go, and we will live and not die' means spiritual life entered into by degrees. This is clear from the meaning of 'rising up' as a raising up to higher or more internal things, and therefore to those that constitute spiritual life, dealt with in 2401, 2785, 2912, 2927, 3171, 4103, 4881; from the meaning of 'going' as living, dealt with in 3335, 3690, 4882, 5493 (and since 'and we will live' follows, 'going' means the earliest stage of spiritual life); from the meaning of 'living' as spiritual life, for no other kind of life is meant in the internal sense of the Word; and from the meaning of 'not dying' as standing condemned no longer, that is, standing outside a state of condemnation, for no other kind of death is meant in the internal sense of the Word than spiritual death, which is condemnation. From all this it is evident that 'we will rise up and go, and we will live and not die' means life entered into by degrees. That is to say, an introductory phase leading into life is meant by 'rising up', the earliest stage of that life by 'going', that life fully under way by 'living', and guidance away from everything alien to that life by 'not dying'.

The idea that living is meant in the internal sense by 'going' will seem strange to one who does not know anything about spiritual life. But much the same is involved here as with the expression 'travelling on', namely an ordered life and a further stage of life, 1293, 4375, 4554, 4585; and the expression 'sojourning' involves much the same, namely receiving instruction and leading a life in keeping with it, 1463, 2025, 3672. The reason why 'going', 'travelling on', and 'sojourning' have these meanings can, it is true, be stated; yet it is the kind of reason that makes little sense to those who have no knowledge of the exact nature of people's movements in the next life. Moving about and advancements made by people there are nothing else, since they have no other origin, than changes in their states of life. Such changes present themselves in outward actions as nothing other than advances from one place to another. The truth of this has been proved to me from many an experience I have had in the next life. In my spirit I have walked with and among those there, and have moved through their many dwelling-places; and I have done so even though my body remained all the time in the same place. I have talked to them about how this could be so and have learned that changes in their states of life are what constitute the advances people make in the spiritual world.

The same has also been proved to me by the fact that spirits are able, through changes of state that are effected, to be somewhere high up and then in an instant somewhere deep down, or to be far away in the west and then in an instant in the east, and so on. But, as stated, this is bound to seem strange to someone who does not know anything about life in the spiritual world. For in that world no intervals of space or of time exist, but states of life instead of these. Such states produce externally a visible scene with all the appearance of life involving advances and movement. The scene that appears is so vivid and real that it is an appearance of life itself; that is to say, the appearance is that life exists inherently within us, and so is essentially our own, when in actual fact life flows into us from the Lord, the source from which all life springs, see 2021, 2658, 2706, 2886–2888, 3001, 3318, 3337, 3338, 3484, 3619, 3741–3743, 4151, 4249, 4318–4320, 4417, 4523, 4524, 4882. Because 'going' and 'moving' mean living, the ancients had the saying, *In God we move*, and live, and have our being. By 'moving' they meant the external degree of life, by 'living' the internal degree, and by 'having one's being' the inmost degree.

5606 'Even we' means the external aspect of the Church. This is clear from the representation of the ten sons of Jacob, to whom 'we' refers here, as the external aspect of the Church, dealt with in 5469.

5607 'Even you' means the internal aspect of the Church. This is clear from the representation of Israel, to whom 'you' refers here, as the internal aspect of the Church, dealt with in 4286, 4292, 4570.

5608 'Even our young children' means aspects even more internal. This is clear from the meaning of 'young children' as things that are more internal, 5604. The reason more internal things are meant by 'young children' and also by 'boys (or older children)' is that innocence is meant by both these, and innocence is something inmost. The situation in heaven is that the inmost or third heaven consists of those in whom innocence dwells because they are moved by love to the Lord. For the Lord is Innocence itself, so that those who are there because they are moved by love to Him have innocence dwelling within them. And although they are the wisest ones of all in heaven, they look to others there like young children. For this reason, as well as for the reason that innocence dwells in young children, innocence is meant in the Word by 'young children'.

2 Since innocence is the inmost virtue of heaven, innocence must exist inwardly with all who are in heaven. It is like entities of a consecutive nature in relation to those that come into being simultaneously, that is, entities existing separated from one another in distinct degrees in relation to ones that come into being from these. For everything that comes into being simultaneously has its origin in entities of a consecutive nature. When simultaneous things take rise from consecutive ones they position themselves in the same order as that in which they existed initially, separated into distinct degrees. Take, by way of illustration, end, cause, and effect. These exist consecutively, distinct and separate from one another. When they come into being simultaneouly they position themselves in the same order; that is to say, the end takes up the inmost position, the cause the position after this, and the effect the one that comes last. The effect comes into being simultaneously with the others; for unless the cause is present within the effect, and the end within the cause, no effect exists. If you remove the cause from the effect you destroy the effect, and all the more so if you remove the end from the cause. The end enables the cause to be a cause, and the cause enables the effect to be an effect.

3 The same is so in the spiritual world; just as end, cause, and effect are

distinct and separate from one another, so in the spiritual world are love to the Lord, charity towards the neighbour, and the deeds of charity. When these three are made one, that is, when they come forth simultaneously, the first has to be within the second, and the second within the third. Likewise within the deeds of charity: unless charity flowing from affection or the heart is present inwardly in those deeds, they are not the deeds of charity; and unless love to the Lord is present inwardly in charity it is not charity. If therefore you take away the inward substance, the outward form perishes; for the outward form is brought into being and kept in being by the loves existing in order within it. The same is so with innocence. It makes one with love to the Lord. Unless innocence is present inwardly in charity it is not charity. Consequently unless charity that has innocence within it is present inwardly in the deeds of charity, they are not the deeds of charity. This being so, innocence must be present inwardly with all who are in heaven.

The truth of this, as well as the fact that innocence is meant by 'young children', is clear in Mark,

Jesus said to the disciples, Let *the young children* come to Me and do not hinder them; for of such is the kingdom of God. Truly I say to you, Whoever has not received the kingdom of God like *a young child* will not enter into it. Taking them up therefore in His arms, He laid His hand upon them, and blessed them. Mark 10:14–16; Luke 18:15–17; Matt.18:3.

Here 'the young children' clearly means innocence, for the reason that innocence resides with young children, and for the reason that in heaven forms of innocence are seen as young children. No one can enter heaven unless he possesses some measure of innocence, see 4797.

What is more, young children allow themselves to be governed by angels who are filled with innocence; children do not act independently, the way adults govern personal behaviour by the exercise of their own judgement and will. The fact that young children allow themselves to be governed by angels is clear from the Lord's words in Matthew,

See that you do not despise any one *of these little ones*, for I say to you *that their angels in heaven* always see the face of My Father.　Matt.18:10.

No one can see God's face except by virtue of having innocence.

Innocence is meant by 'young children' in the following places as well: In Matthew,

Out of the mouth of *young children* and *sucklings* You have perfected praise. Matt.21:16; Ps.8:2.

In the same gospel,

You have hidden these things from the wise and intelligent and have revealed them to *young children*.　Matt.11:25; Luke 10:21.

The innocence meant by 'young children' is true wisdom; for genuine innocence dwells within wisdom, 2305, 2306, 4797. This explains why it is said that 'out of the mouth of young children and sucklings You have perfected praise', and also that such matters 'have been revealed to young children'.

7 In Isaiah,

The young cow and the bear will feed; their young will lie down together. And *a suckling will play over the viper's hole.* Isa.11:7,8.

This refers to the Lord's kingdom, specifically to the state of peace and innocence there. 'Suckling' stands for innocence. The impossibility that any evil can befall those in whom innocence is present is meant by 'the suckling will play over the viper's hole' – 'vipers' being utterly deceitful persons. This chapter in Isaiah refers quite explicitly to the Lord. In Joel,

Blow the trumpet in Zion; gather the people, sanctify the congregation, assemble the elders, gather *the young children* and *those sucking at the breast.* Joel 2:15,16.

'The elders' stands for the wise ones, 'the young children and those sucking at the breast' for the innocent ones.

8 In the following places too 'young children' is used to mean innocence, but here innocence that has been destroyed: In Jeremiah,

Why are you committing great evil against your own souls, to cut off from you man and woman, *young child* and *suckling* from the midst of Judah, so that I leave you no remnant? Jer.44:7.

In the same prophet,

Lift up to Him your hands for the soul of *your young children* who faint through famine at the head of every street. Lam.2:19.

In Ezekiel,

Go through Jerusalem and strike; do not let your eye spare, and show no pity. [Utterly slay] old man, young man, virgin, and *young child.* Ezek.9:5,6.

In Micah,

The women of My people you cast out from each one's pleasant house; *from her young children* you take away My honour for ever. Micah 2:9.

9 As regards the innocence present in young children, this is solely external, not internal; and because it is not internal it cannot be linked to any wisdom and exist together with it. But the innocence in angels, especially in those of the third heaven, is internal, and so exists joined to wisdom, 2305, 2306, 3494, 4563, 4797. Furthermore the human being has been created in such a way that when he grows old and becomes like a young child, the innocence of wisdom links itself to the innocence of ignorance that had been his when he was a young child, and in this condition, as a true young child, he passes over into the next life.

5609 'And I will be surety for him' means that in the meantime [the truth of good] will be attached to it [the good of the Church]. This is clear from the meaning of 'being surety for someone' as being responsible for him, as is also evident from what immediately follows, especially from what Judah told Joseph regarding his being surety, Gen.44:32,33. And because 'being surety' is being responsible for that person, even while on the way the truth of good exists attached to it [the good of the Church].

5610   'From my hand you will require him' means that [the truth of good] will not be snatched away, insofar as it is within its power to prevent it. This is clear from the meaning of 'hand' as power, dealt with in 878, 3387, 4931–4937, 5327, 5328, 5544 (insofar as it is within its power is meant because the surety or pledge does not extend beyond [the good of the Church]; the explanation of the truth and the nature of this matter is contained in the internal sense); and from the meaning of 'requiring from him' as not being snatched away, for the one 'required' from another must be attached to that other and remain inseparable from him.

5611   'If I do not bring him to you and set him before you' means the complete restoration of it to the Church. This is clear from the meaning of 'bringing him and setting him before him' as completely restoring; and from the representation of 'Israel', to whom Benjamin would be restored, as the Church, dealt with in 3305, 4286, 5595.

5612   'Then I shall be sinning against you every day' means the good of the Church will not exist any longer. This is clear from the representation of Judah, who says this about himself, as the good of the Church, dealt with in 5583, 5603; from the meaning of 'sinning' as a separation, dealt with in 5229, 5474, thus the fact that it will not exist since that which is separated from someone does not exist with him any more; and from the meaning of 'every day' as for ever, thus not any longer. These words were spoken by Judah because the good of the Church has no existence without the intermediary, which is represented by 'Benjamin', between the internal and the external. For when either the good or the truth of the Church flows from the internal into the external it does so through the intermediary; consequently the existence of the intermediary is just as vital as the existence of the good of the Church, which is why Judah goes as surety for Benjamin. The non-existence of the good of the Church unless the intermediary is present is meant by these words spoken by Judah, while the non-existence of the truth of the Church is meant by those uttered by Reuben, 5542.

5613   'For if perhaps we had not delayed' means lingering in a state of indecision. This is clear from the meaning of 'delaying' as a state of indecision. For just as 'going', 'advancing', 'travelling', and 'sojourning' mean a state of life, 5605, so 'delaying' means a state of indecision; for when a state of life passes into a state of indecision, the external enters a state involving delay. Visual evidence of this presents itself in the person concerned; when his mind is at all undecided he stops in his tracks and ponders what to do. The reason for this is that indecision brings about a state of life in which a person is hesitant and vacillates between two different courses of action, and as a consequence produces a faltering step as the outward effect of that hesitancy. From this it is evident that 'if perhaps we had not delayed' means lingering in a state of indecision.

5614 'We would by now have returned these two times' means that spiritual life, exterior and interior, [would have been restored]. This is clear from the meaning of 'going' as living, dealt with above in 5605, and therefore 'going back' is a subsequent phase of living (for they went to Egypt to acquire grain for themselves, and 'grain' means the good of truth that is the product of spiritual life); and from the meaning of 'these two times', since this has reference to life, as exterior life and interior life. The corn which they received the first time meant exterior life, which is life in the natural, for the reason, dealt with in the previous chapter, that they did not have the intermediary with them. But the grain which they receive this time means interior life, for now they did have Benjamin, who is the intermediary, with them, this being the subject in the present chapter and the next one. All this explains why 'we would by now have returned these two times' means spiritual life, exterior and interior.

2   It is bound to seem strange that these things are meant, especially to someone who has no knowledge of what is spiritual; for it seems as though 'returning these two times' does not have the vaguest connection with what is actually meant, namely spiritual life. But this really is the inner meaning of these words. Indeed – if you are willing to believe it – that spiritual meaning is what the interior thought of a person moved by good comprehends, for that interior thought exists on the same level as the internal sense, though the person himself is totally ignorant of this while he lives in the body. For the internal or spiritual sense, which exists on the level of his interior thought, comes down without him knowing it into material ideas formed by his senses. These ideas rely for their formation on time and space and on the kinds of things that exist in the world, so that it is not evident to him that his interior thought is of such a nature. His interior thought is by nature the same as that of the angels, for his spirit dwells in communion with them.

3   The fact that the thought of a person moved by good accords with the internal sense may be recognized from the consideration that when he enters heaven after death he knows that internal sense without ever at all having to learn about it, which would by no means be possible if in the world his interior thought had not existed on the same level as that sense. It exists on the same level because of the correspondence between spiritual things and natural ones, the nature of which is such that not even the smallest thing is without correspondence. Therefore since the interior or rational mind of a person moved by good is in the spiritual world and his exterior or natural mind is in the natural world, both of these parts of his mind inevitably engage in thought. But his

interior mind thinks on a spiritual level, his exterior mind on a natural level; also what is spiritual comes down into what is natural, and then through correspondence the two act as one.

A person's interior mind, in which the ideas constituting the thought there are called intellectual concepts and are referred to as immaterial ideas, does not rely, when it is engaged in thought, on verbal expressions belonging to any language. Consequently it does not rely on any natural forms. This may be recognized by anyone who is able to stop and reflect on these matters; for he can in an instant see in his mind what he can hardly express verbally in an hour, by the use of general observations which include very many details. The ideas constituting his thought are spiritual ones and are no different in nature, when the Word is read, from the spiritual sense. Even so, that person is quite unaware of this, for the reason already stated that those spiritual ideas flow into the natural and present themselves within natural ideas. Thus those spiritual ideas are inapparent, so completely that unless a person has received instruction in the matter he imagines that the spiritual does not exist unless it is like the natural, indeed that he does not think within his spirit in any different way from that in which he speaks in the body. Such is the way that the natural conceals the spiritual.

5615   Verses 11–14 **And Israel their father said to them, If this therefore has to be, do it. Take some of the much-sung-about produce[1] of the land in your vessels, and cause a gift to go down to the man – a little resin and a little honey, wax and stacte, pistachio nuts and almonds. And take a double amount of silver in your hands. And the silver that was put back in the mouth of your pouches you are to take back in your hand; perhaps it was a mistake. And take your brother; and rise up, return to the man. And may God Shaddai grant you mercy before the man, and may he release[2] to you your other brother and Benjamin; and I, even as I have been bereaved, I shall be bereaved.**

'And Israel their father said to them' means a perception received from spiritual good. 'If this therefore has to be, do it' means if it cannot be done in any other way, let it be done in that way. 'Take some of the much-sung-about produce of the land in your vessels' means the choicer things of the Church among the truths of faith. 'And cause a gift to go down to the man' means to obtain favour. 'A little resin and a little honey' means the truths of exterior natural good, and the delight that goes with these. 'Wax and stacte' means the truths of interior natural good. 'Pistachio nuts and almonds' means forms of the good of life that agree with those truths. 'And take a double amount of silver in your hands' means truth received by the powers. 'And the silver that was put back in the mouth of your pouches you are to take back in your hand'

---

[1] much-sung-about produce *translates the single Latin word* decantatio, *which Sw. uses to represent the Hebrew* zimrath, *a word meaning* products celebrated and praised in song.
[2] *lit.* send

means that through the truth freely given and present in the exterior natural they were to make themselves submissive as far as was possible. 'Perhaps it was a mistake' means lest he becomes unfriendly. 'And take your brother' means that by that self-submission they would receive the good of faith. 'And rise up, return to the man' means the life received from spiritual truth. 'And may God Shaddai' means the comfort that follows hardships. 'Grant you mercy before the man' means so that spiritual truth may accept you favourably. 'And may he release to you your other brother' means so that it may grant the good of faith. 'And Benjamin' means so that interior truth may be granted also. 'And I, even as I have been bereaved, I shall be bereaved' means that before these things take place the Church must be so to speak deprived of its own truths.

5616 'Israel their father said to them' means a perception received from spiritual good. This is clear from the meaning of 'saying' in the historical narratives of the Word as perception; and from the representation of 'Israel' as spiritual good, both of which matters are dealt with above in 5595. The word 'father' is used because the truths that his sons represent spring from that good as their father.

5617 'If this therefore has to be, do it' means if it cannot be done in any other way, let it be done in that way. This becomes clear without explanation.

5618 'Take some of the much-sung-about produce of the land in your vessels' means the choicer things of the Church among the truths of faith. This is clear from the meaning of 'the much-sung-about produce' as choice things, dealt with below; from the meaning of 'the land' as the Church, dealt with above in 5577; and from the meaning of 'vessels' as the truths of faith, dealt with in 3068, 3079, 3316, 3318. The expression 'the much-sung-about' (*decantatio*) is used because in the original language it is derived from a word meaning 'singing' (*cantatio*), and therefore 'the much-sung-about produce of the land' means products that are highly commended and praised; and that is why choicer things are meant in the internal sense.

5619 'And cause a gift to go down to the man' means to obtain favour. This is clear from the meaning of 'taking a gift to the man' – 'the man' being Joseph, who is called the lord of the land – as to obtain favour. It was customary in the representative Ancient Church, and so in the Jewish Church, when people went to the judges, and at a later time to the kings or priests, to present them with a gift; indeed the people were commanded to do this. The reason for the custom was that the gifts people presented to those men represented the kinds of things mankind possessed that ought to be offered to the Lord when any approach is made to Him. Such gifts are ones that a person offers in freedom and therefore ones that come truly from himself. For his freedom resides in what comes from his heart; and what comes from his heart comes from his will. Also what comes from his will comes from a desire arising out of his love; and a desire arising out of his love constitutes his freedom, thus what is truly his own, 1947, 2870–2893, 3158. Such should be the origin of any gift made by man to the Lord when making any approach to Him. This kind of gift was represented by the gifts mentioned above, for 'kings' represented the Lord as regards Divine Truth, 1672, 2015, 2069, 3009, 3670, 4581, 4966, 5044, while 'priests' represented Him as regards Divine Good, 1728, 201-5(end), 3670. Those gifts also served as introductions, see 4262, which were made to obtain favour.

5620   'A little resin and a little honey' means the truths of exterior natural good, and the delight that goes with these. This is clear from the meaning of 'resin' as the truth of good, which is truth derived from good, dealt with in 4748. The reason 'resin' has this meaning is that it belongs among unguent-like substances and also among aromatic ones. Aromatic substances mean those kinds of entities that belong to truth derived from good, the more so when those substances also resemble unguents and consequently have oil among their ingredients; for 'oil' means good, 886, 3728, 4582. Since this resin was aromatic, see Gen.37:25, the same word in the original language also means balm; it was also, it is clear, unguent-like or thick with oil. From this one may now see that 'resin' means the truth of good present in the natural, in this case in the exterior natural since 'resin' is mentioned first, then 'honey', meaning the delight there, is added. 'Honey' means delight because it is sweet and everything sweet in the natural world corresponds to some delight or pleasure in the spiritual world. The reason for the use of the expression 'the delight that goes with this' – that is to say, with truth derived from good present in the exterior natural – is that every truth, and more so every truth of good, possesses its own delight. But that delight springs from an affection for such truths and consequently for the use they serve.

[2] The fact that 'honey' means delight may be seen also from other places in the Word, as in Isaiah,

A virgin will conceive and bear a son, and will call His name Immanuel (God with us). Butter and *honey* will He eat that He may know to refuse the evil and choose the good. Isa.7:14,15.

This refers to the Lord. 'Butter' stands for what is celestial, 'honey' for what is derived from the celestial.

[3] In the same prophet,

It will be, because of the abundance of the milk which they give, that he will eat butter; both butter and *honey* will everyone eat that is left in the midst of the land. Isa.7:22.

This refers to the Lord's kingdom. 'Milk' stands for spiritual good, 'butter' for celestial good, and 'honey' for what is derived from these, namely happiness, pleasure, and delight.

4 In Ezekiel,

Thus were you adorned with gold and silver, and your robes were fine linen, and silk, and embroidered cloth. You ate fine flour, and *honey*, and oil; therefore you became extremely beautiful, and attained to a kingdom. With fine flour, oil, and *honey* I fed you; but you set this before them as a pacifying odour. Ezek.16:13,19.

This refers to Jerusalem, by which the spiritual Church is meant; it describes what that Church was like among the Ancients, and what it came to be like after that. Its adornment with gold and silver is the furnishment of it with celestial and spiritual good and truth. Its robes of fine linen, silk, and embroidered cloth stand for truths present in the rational and in both parts of the natural. 'Fine flour' stands for what is spiritual, 'honey' for the pleasure accompanying this, and 'oil' for the good that goes with it. The fact that all these, each one, mean things of a heavenly nature may be recognized by anyone.

5 In the same prophet,

Judah and the land of Israel were your traders in wheat of minnith and pannag, and *honey*, and oil, and balm.   Ezek.27:17.

This refers to Tyre, by which is meant the spiritual Church, what it was like initially and what it came to be like subsequently so far as cognitions of good and truth were concerned, 1201. Also, 'honey' in this quotation stands for the pleasure and delight gained from affections for knowing and learning about celestial and spiritual forms of goodness and truth.

6 In Moses,

He causes[1] him to ride over the heights of the land and he eats from the produce of the fields; he causes him to suck *honey out of the crag*, and oil out of the stony rock.   Deut.32:13.

This too refers to the spiritual Ancient Church. 'Sucking honey from the crag' stands for the delight taken in factual knowledge that holds truths within it.

7 In David,

I feed them with the fat of wheat, and with *honey out of the rock* I satisfy them. Ps.81:16.

'Satisfying with honey out of the rock' stands for the delight gained from the truths of faith.

8 In Deuteronomy,

Jehovah is bringing you to a good land, a land of rivers of water, springs, and depths gushing out of valleys and mountains; a land of wheat and barley, and vines, and fig trees, and pomegranates; a land of olive oil and *honey*. Deut.8:7,8.

---

[1] *The Latin means* You cause, *but the Hebrew means* He causes, *which Sw. has in other places where he quotes this verse.*

This refers to the land of Canaan, in the internal sense to the Lord's kingdom in heaven. 'A land of olive oil and honey' stands for spiritual good and the pleasure that goes with it.

For the same reason the land of Canaan is called 'a land flowing with *milk* and *honey*', Num.13:27; 14:7,8; Deut.26:9,15; 27:3; Jer.11:5; 32:22; Ezek.20:6. In these places 'the land of Canaan' is used, as has been stated, to mean in the internal sense the Lord's kingdom. 'Flowing with milk' stands for an abundance of celestial-spiritual things, while 'honey' stands for an abundance of forms of happiness and delight received from these.

) In David,

The judgements of Jehovah are truth; they are righteous altogether – more desirable than gold, and much fine gold; and *sweeter than honey* and *what drops from honeycombs*.   Ps.19:9,10.

'The judgements of Jehovah' stands for Divine truth, 'sweeter than honey and what drops from honeycombs' for the delights received from good and the pleasures received from truth. In the same author,

Sweet are Your words to my taste[1], *more than honey* to my mouth.   Ps.119:103.

Here the meaning is similar.

1 The manna which the descendants of Jacob received in the wilderness as their bread is described in Moses as follows,

The manna was like coriander seed, white, and its taste was like *wafers made with honey*.   Exod.16:31.

Because 'the manna' meant the Divine truth which came down from the Lord by way of heaven, it is the Lord's own Divine Human, as He Himself teaches in John 6:51,58. For the Lord's Divine Human is the source from which every truth that is Divine springs; indeed it is what every truth that is Divine has reference to. This being so, the manna, the taste of which gave delight and pleasure, is described as being 'like wafers made with honey' – 'taste' being the delight which good provides and the pleasure that truth affords, see 3502.

2 Because John the Baptist represented the Lord as to the Word, which is Divine Truth on the earth – in the same way as Elijah had represented Him, 2762, 5247(end), making him the Elijah who was to come ahead of the Lord, Mal.4:5; Matt.17:10–12; Mark 9:11–13; Luke 1:17 – his clothing and food were therefore meaningful signs. They are described in Matthew as follows,

John had a garment of camel hair and a skin girdle around his waist; his food was locusts and *wild honey*.   Matt.3:4; Mark 1:6.

'A garment of camel hair' was a sign of what the literal sense of the Word is like so far as truth there is concerned. That sense – the natural sense – serves as a garment for the internal sense; for 'hair' and also

[1] *lit.* palate

'camels' mean what is natural. Food consisting of 'locusts and wild honey' was a sign of what the literal sense is like so far as good there is concerned, the delight belonging to that good being meant by 'wild honey'.

13 In addition the delight afforded by Divine truth as this exists in the external sense is described by 'honey', in Ezekiel,

He said to me, Son of man, feed your stomach and fill your inward parts with this scroll that I am giving you. And when I ate it, *it was in my mouth like honey as regards sweetness.* Ezek.3:3.

And in John,

The angel said to me, Take the little book and eat it up; it will indeed make your stomach bitter, *but in your mouth it will be sweet as honey.* I therefore took the little book out of the angel's hand and ate it up, and it was *in my mouth like sweet honey.* But when I had eaten it, my stomach was made bitter. Then he said to me, You must prophesy again over many peoples, and nations, and tongues, and many kings. Rev.10:9–11.

'The scroll' in Ezekiel, and 'the little book' in John, stand for Divine truth. The delight this appears to possess in the outward form it takes is meant by the taste being sweet as honey; for Divine truth, like the Word, is full of delight in the outward form it takes, which is the literal sense, because this allows everyone to interpret and explain it in whatever way it suits him. But the internal sense does not allow him to do so, and this is meant by its bitter taste; for the internal sense discloses what man is like inwardly. The external sense is full of delight for the reason just stated, that a person can explain things there in whatever way it suits him. The truths contained in the external sense are all general ones and remain such until particular truths are added to qualify them, and specific ones to qualify these. The external sense is also full of delight because it is natural, concealing what is spiritual within itself. It needs to be full of delight too if a person is to accept it, that is, to be taken into it and not left standing on the threshold.

14 The honeycomb and the broiled fish which after His resurrection the Lord ate in the presence of the disciples was also a sign of the external sense of the Word, 'the fish' meaning the truth associated with that sense and 'the honeycomb' the pleasure attached to it, described in Luke as follows,

Jesus said, Do you have any food at all here? They gave Him part of *a broiled fish* and some *honeycomb*, which He took and ate in their presence. Luke 24:41–43.

And because the fish and the honeycomb had that meaning the Lord therefore tells them,

These are the words which I spoke to you while I was still with you, that all things must be fulfilled which were written in the law of Moses, and the Prophets, and the Psalms concerning Me. Luke 24:44.

The appearance is that nothing of the sort is meant, for it seems to have been purely by chance that they had part of a broiled fish and a honeycomb. But in fact their possession of these was providential – as is not only this but every other smallest fact mentioned in the Word. Because matters such as have been described were indeed meant, the Lord therefore referred to the Word, declaring that the things written in it had reference to Himself. But the things which have been written in the Old Testament Word regarding the Lord are but few in the sense of the letter, whereas everything contained in the internal sense has to do with Him; and it is from this that the Word gets its holiness. Everything contained in the internal sense is what is meant in the statement that 'all things must be fulfilled which were written in the law of Moses, and the Prophets, and the Psalms concerning Him'.

5 From all this one may now see that 'honey' means the delight that is received from goodness and truth, that is, from the affection for these, and that specifically external delight and so that belonging to the exterior natural is meant. Because this delight is the kind that is gained from the world through the senses, and so contains within it much that springs from love of the world, people were forbidden to use honey in their minchahs. This is expressed in Leviticus as follows,

Every minchah which you bring to Jehovah shall be made without yeast; for no yeast *nor any honey* shall be used along with the fire-offering you burn to Jehovah. Lev.2:11.

'Honey' stands for the kind of external delight which, containing something of love of the world within it, was similar to yeast and therefore forbidden. What yeast or made with yeast implies, see 2342.

5621 'Wax and stacte' means the truths of interior natural good. This is clear from the meaning of 'wax', in this case aromatic wax, as the truth of good, dealt with below; and from the meaning of 'stacte' too as truth derived from good, dealt with in 4748. The truths of interior natural good are meant because these spices are purer substances than resin or honey, and for that reason the mention of them comes second. For in the Word order determines the way in which such substances are listed. 'Wax' is not used here to mean ordinary wax but an aromatic kind, such as storax. This kind of wax is what the word in the original language is used to describe; and the same word is used for spice. From this one may see why this aromatic wax means the truth of good; for all spices, because they are sweet smelling, mean in the internal sense truths that are derived from good.

2 This may be recognized from the consideration that in heaven truths derived from good are perceived with the same pleasure as sweet scents in the world. Also, when angels' perceptions are converted into odours, which in the Lord's good pleasure happens frequently, they are therefore detected as fragrances coming from spices and from flowers. This is why frankincense and incense were prepared from odiferous substances and put to a sacred use, and also why aromatic substances were mixed with oil for anointing. Anyone who does not know that the cause behind those practices lay among the perceptions enjoyed by those in heaven may suppose that they were practices enjoined solely to

make external worship pleasant and that they held nothing of heaven and nothing holy at all within them, consequently that such religious practices held nothing Divine within them. See what has been shown already on these matters:

Frankincense and incense, as well as the fragrant substances in oil for anointing, were representative of spiritual and celestial things, 4748.
Spheres of faith and love are converted into pleasant odours; and therefore pleasant and sweet-smelling odours, also aromatic ones, mean the truths of faith which are derived from the good of love, 1514, 1517–1519, 4628.

5622 'Pistachio nuts and almonds' means forms of the good of life that agree with those truths. This is clear from the meaning of 'pistachio nuts' as forms of the good of life that agree with the truths of exterior natural good, meant by 'resin', dealt with below; and from the meaning of 'almonds' as forms of the good of life that agree with the truths of interior natural good, meant by 'aromatic wax and stacte'. Those nuts have that meaning because they are fruits, and 'fruits' in the Word means deeds – fruits produced by useful trees meaning good deeds, or what amounts to the same, forms of the good of life, since these, so far as the use they serve is concerned, are good deeds. The reason 'pistachio nuts' means forms of the good of life that agree with the truths of exterior natural good is that they are the fruit borne by an inferior kind of tree, and things of an exterior nature are meant by objects of an inferior kind, for the reason that essentially exterior things are not so specific as interior ones since they are the general appearances produced by large numbers of inner components.

2 The reason 'almonds' means forms of the good of life that agree with the truths of interior natural good is that the almond is a superior kind of tree. In the spiritual sense the tree itself means a perception of interior truth derived from good, its blossom means interior truth derived from good, while its fruit means the good of life resulting from that truth. The word 'almond' is used with this meaning in Jeremiah,

The word of Jehovah came [to me], saying, What do you see, Jeremiah? And I said, A rod of almond do I see. Then Jehovah said to me, You have seen well[1], for I am watching over My word to perform it. Jer.1:11,12.

'A rod' stands for power, 'almond' for a perception of interior truth; and because this rod is said to be Jehovah's it stands for a watching over that truth – 'word' standing for truth.

3 The almonds which blossomed on Aaron's rod for the tribe of Levi also mean the good deeds of charity or forms of the good of life. They are described in Moses as follows,

It happened the next day, when Moses went into the tent of meeting, that

[1] *lit.* Well have you done in seeing

behold, Aaron's rod for the house[1] of Levi had blossomed, and had produced buds[2], so that it flowered and produced *almonds*.   Num.17:8.

This was the sign that that tribe had been chosen for the priesthood; for charity was meant by that tribe, 3875, 3877, 4497, 4502, 4503, and charity is the essential characteristic of the spiritual Church.

5623   'And take a double amount of silver in your hands' means truth received by the powers. This is clear from the meaning of 'silver' as truth, dealt with in 1551, 2954; from the meaning of 'a double amount' as in succession, a second time, dealt with in 1335, that is to say, it was truth which had been given to them freely, and was to be given once again; and from the meaning of 'hands' as powers, dealt with in 878, 3387, 4931–4937, 5327, 5328. Truth present in the powers is truth within, thus subject to, people's abilities to accept it. But people's abilities or powers to accept truth are utterly dependent on good. They are linked by the Lord to good. For when the Lord enters with good He also enters with that kind of ability. Consequently the reception of truth by a person's powers is dependent on what forms of good are present. The fact that people's abilities to accept truth are determined by the good that is present becomes clear from much experience in the next life.

2   Those there who are moved by good have not only the ability to perceive truth but also the ability to accept it; yet this is conditioned by the amount and the kind of good that moves them. Those on the other hand who are moved by evil do not have any ability to accept truth. That ability of the former and this inability of the latter to accept truth are the outcome of each one's pleasure and consequent desire. The pleasure of those moved by good consists in the accomplishing of what is good by means of truth; for the specific nature of their good is derived from truths, and therefore they also have a desire for those truths. But the pleasure of those moved by evil consists in evil and the justification of it by the use of falsities, which they also consequently have a desire for; and in their desire for falsities they turn away from truths. Consequently, having no ability to accept truths, those moved by evil therefore cast these aside, or smother them, or pervert them as soon as they reach their ears or enter their heads. Furthermore every individual person of sound mind has the ability to accept truths; but those who turn to evil annihilate that ability, whereas those who turn to good enhance it.

5624   'And the silver that was put back in the mouth of your pouches you are to take back in your hand' means that through the truth freely given and present in the exterior natural they were to make themselves submissive as far as was possible. This is clear from the meaning of 'the

---

[1] *The Latin means* tribe *but the Hebrew means* house.
[2] *lit.* flower

silver that was put back' as truth freely given, dealt with in 5530; from the meaning of 'in the mouth of a sack' as in the opening of the exterior natural, dealt with in 5497; and from the meaning of 'in the hand' as within one's power, dealt with immediately above in 5623, thus as far as possible. Making themselves submissive through that truth is meant by the instruction that 'they were to put back' the silver; for when people in the spiritual world 'take back' truth to the Lord from whom they have received it freely they are making themselves submissive through it. But in what way they made themselves submissive through such truth is evident from the conversation, included in verses 18–24, which they had with the man who was over Joseph's house.

5625 'Perhaps it was a mistake' means lest he becomes unfriendly. This is clear from the meaning of 'a mistake' as an unfriendly act, for an error of that kind is meant here. The mistake could have been that they had forgotten to hand over their silver and so had brought it back, each man's in his own sack; it could have been this that had caused the unfriendliness towards them. Indeed they themselves believed this to be so, for when in their fear they were brought to Joseph's house they said,

Over the matter of the silver put back in our pouches at the beginning are we brought to this place, so that he may come down on us and fall on us, and take us as slaves, and our asses. Verse 18.

Furthermore 'sin' means separation and an unfriendly turning away, 5229, 5474; so too does 'a mistake' if this entails some sin, though a minor one. This is why the expression 'lest he becomes unfriendly' is used.

5626 'And take your brother' means that by that self-submission they would receive the good of faith. This is clear from the representation of Simeon[1], to whom 'brother' whom they were to take refers here, as faith in the will, dealt with in 3869–3872, 4497, 4502, 4503, 5482, and so the good of faith since the truth of faith becomes the good of faith when it passes over into the will. For when this happens that truth passes over into the person's life, and when it is there it is not seen as something to be known but as something to be done. That truth then changes its essential nature and becomes truth realized in action, as a consequence of which it is no longer called truth but good.

5627 'And rise up, return to the man' means the life received from spiritual truth. This is clear from the meaning of 'rising up' as a raising up to interior and therefore to spiritual things, dealt with in 2401, 2785, 2912, 2927, 3171, 4103, 4881; from the meaning of 'returning' as the life received from, dealt with above in 5614; and from the representation of Joseph, who is called 'the man', as spiritual truth, dealt with in 5584.

[1] *The brother referred to at this point was in fact* Benjamin, *whose spiritual representation is indicated in* 5600.

5628   'And may God Shaddai' means the comfort that follows hardships. This is clear from the meaning of 'Shaddai' as temptation, also the comfort that follows temptation, dealt with in 1992, 4572, here therefore the comfort which followed all the hardships they experienced in Egypt. The meaning here – the comfort that follows severe sufferings – is also evident from the words 'grant you mercy before the man' which immediately follow. The reason why 'Shaddai' means temptation, also the comfort that follows temptation, is that the ancients gave the one and only God various illustrious names which were descriptive of the various things that came from Him; and because they believed that even temptations came from Him they called Him 'God Shaddai'. They did not understand some other God by this name but the one and only God so far as temptations were concerned. When however the Ancient Church went downhill they began to worship as many gods as there were names of the one and only God; indeed they increased the number of them with many more which they themselves invented. This trend continued until at length each family had its own god whom that family kept quite distinct and separate from all other gods worshipped by other families.

[2]   The family of Terah, which Abraham came from, worshipped Shaddai as its particular god, see 1356, 1992, 2559, 3667. Consequently not only Abraham but Jacob too recognized Shaddai as their god; and they did so in the land of Canaan. But to avoid any compulsion of them to forsake the form of religion they had – for no one is compelled to forsake what for him is holy – they were allowed to keep to it. However, because the ancients had meant Jehovah Himself or the Lord by the name Shaddai, which they used when they underwent temptations, Jehovah or the Lord took this name in His dealings with Abraham, as is evident from Gen.17:1, and also in His dealings with Jacob, Gen.35:11.

[3]   The reason why not only temptation but also comfort is meant by 'Shaddai' is that comfort follows all spiritual temptations, as I have been allowed to know from experience in the next life. When anyone there is subjected to hardships at the hands of evil spirits, who attack him, incite him to evil practices, and persuade him to accept falsities, he is subsequently received by angels, once the evil spirits have been turned away, and he is brought into a state of consolation by means of some delight in keeping with his character.

5629   'Grant you mercy before the man' means so that spiritual truth may accept you favourably. This is clear from the meaning of 'granting mercy' as accepting favourably, and from the representation of Joseph, when he is called 'the man', as spiritual truth, as above in 5627.

5630   'And may he release to you your other brother' means so that it may grant the good of faith. This is clear from the representation of Simeon, to whom 'other brother' refers here, as the good of faith, as above in 5626. The reason 'releasing' or 'sending' means granting is that the expression 'sending' applies to the person but 'granting' to the spiritual reality meant by that person.

5631 'And Benjamin' means so that interior truth may be granted also. This is clear from the representation of 'Benjamin' as interior truth, dealt with above in 5600.

5632 'And I, even as I have been bereaved, I shall be bereaved' means that before these things take place the Church must be deprived of its own truths. This is clear from the representation of Israel, who says this regarding himself, as the Church, dealt with in 3305, 4286; and from the meaning of 'being bereaved' as being deprived of the truths which belong to the Church, dealt with in 5536. The fact that such a deprivation must occur before these things take place is a self-evident one. For if the good of faith represented by 'Simeon', 5630, does not exist, and if interior truth, which is the intermediary, represented by 'Benjamin' does not exist, no truth belonging to the Church exists other than the kind of truth which is solely on the lips and not in the heart.

5633 Verses 15–17 **And the men took this gift, and took the double amount of silver in their hand, and Benjamin; and they rose up, and went down to Egypt, and stood before Joseph. And Joseph saw Benjamin with them, and he said to the one who was over his house, Bring the men to the house, and slaughter and prepare [an animal]; for the men will eat with me at midday. And the man did as Joseph said, and the man brought the men to Joseph's house.**
'And the men took [this] gift' means that the truths had with them the means to obtain favour. 'And took the double amount of silver in their hand' means also truth received by the power. 'And Benjamin' means the intermediary also. 'And they rose up, and went down to Egypt' means a raising up so as to acquire life from the interior areas of factual knowledge. 'And stood before Joseph' means the presence there of the celestial of the spiritual. 'And Joseph saw Benjamin with them' means the discernment by the celestial of the spiritual that the spiritual intermediary was present with the truths. 'And he said to the one who was over his house' means that which belongs to the external Church. 'Bring the men to the house' means that the truths in the natural were to be introduced into it. 'And slaughter and prepare [an animal]' means through the forms of good belonging to the exterior natural. 'For the men will eat with me at midday' means that they will be joined together when accompanied by the intermediary. 'And the man did as Joseph said' means a putting into effect. 'And the man brought the men to Joseph's house' means the first introduction into good coming from the celestial of the spiritual.

5634 'And the men took this gift' means that the truths had with them the means to obtain favour. This is clear from the meaning of 'the men' as the truths, dealt with in 3134; and from the meaning of 'the gift' presented by people when they went to kings and priests, as to obtain favour, dealt with in 5619.

5635   'And took the double amount of silver in their hand' means also truth received by the power. This is clear from what has been stated above in 5623, where the same words occur, and where one may also see what is meant by truth received by the power.

5636   'And Benjamin' means the intermediary also. This is clear from the representation of 'Benjamin' as the intermediary, dealt with in 5411, 5413, 5443.

5637   'And they rose up, and went down to Egypt' means a raising up so as to acquire life from the interior areas of factual knowledge. This is clear from the meaning of 'rising up' as a raising up to the things that belong to spiritual life, dealt with in 2401, 2785, 2912, 2927, 3171, 4103, 4881; from the meaning of 'going down' as to acquire life, for 'going down' here implies much the same as the words used previously in verse 8 – 'Send the boy with me, and we will rise up and go, and we will live and not die' – which mean spiritual life entered into by degrees, dealt with in 5605; and from the meaning of 'Egypt' as factual knowledge, dealt with in 1164, 1165, 1186, 1462, 4749, 4964, 4966, in this case the interior areas of such knowledge since the celestial of the spiritual represented by 'Joseph' is there, which is why the statement 'and stood before Joseph' follows directly after.

2   The interior areas of factual knowledge are facts existing in the natural which are spiritual ones; and they are spiritual ones there when such facts in the natural have been illuminated by the light of heaven. They have been so illuminated by the light of heaven when a person has a real belief in teachings that are based on the Word; and he has a real belief in these when the good of charity is present in him. For then the good of charity, like a flame, sheds light on the truths and so on the facts he knows. This is how they get the spiritual light they possess. From this one may see what is meant by the interior areas of factual knowledge.

5638   'And stood before Joseph' means the presence there of the celestial of the spiritual. This is clear from the meaning of 'standing before someone' as the presence; and from the representation of 'Joseph' as the celestial of the spiritual, often dealt with already. The presence of the celestial of the spiritual in both parts of the natural was represented by Joseph's being made the lord over the whole of Egypt. That is, his lordship over it meant the presence of the celestial of the spiritual within the interior areas of factual knowledge; and this knowledge exists within the natural. Regarding the lordship of the celestial over both parts of the natural, see 5316, 5324, 5326–5328, 5333, 5337, 5373, the truths represented by 'the ten sons of Jacob' being truths within the natural.

5639 'And Joseph saw Benjamin with them' means the discernment by the celestial of the spiritual that the spiritual intermediary was present with the truths. This is clear from the meaning of 'seeing' as understanding and discerning, dealt with in 2150, 2807, 3764, 4567, 4723, 5400; from the representation of the ten sons of Jacob – to whom 'with them', that is, the ones whom Joseph saw Benjamin with, refers – as the truths within the natural, dealt with in 5403, 5419, 5427, 5458, 5512; and from the representation of 'Benjamin' as the intermediary, dealt with in 5411, 5413, 5443. The reason the expression 'spiritual intermediary' is used here is that the truths which are represented by 'the ten sons of Jacob' had now to be joined to truth from the Divine, which was 'Joseph'; but that joining together does not take place except through an intermediary that is a spiritual one. Therefore immediately after that intermediary had been recognized, Joseph told the man over his house, 'Bring the men to the house, and slaughter and prepare [an animal]; for the men will eat with me at midday', meaning that they would be brought in and joined to him because they were accompanied by the intermediary.

2 A further brief statement needs to be made about what the spiritual compared with the natural is since the majority living in the Christian world do not know what the spiritual is. They are so ignorant of what it is that when they hear the term they are at a loss, saying to themselves, What the spiritual is, no one knows. Essentially the spiritual existing with a person is his actual affection for what is good and true, loved for its own sake and not for any selfish reason, as well as an affection for what is right and fair, likewise loved for its own sake and not for any selfish reason. When a person has inward feelings of delight and pleasure, and more so if feelings of blessedness and bliss flow from them, they constitute the spiritual present with him, which does not come to him from the natural world but from the spiritual world or heaven, that is, from the Lord by way of heaven. This then is the spiritual which, when it reigns in a person, influences and so to speak gives colour to everything he thinks, wills, or does, and which causes his thoughts and acts of will to partake of what is spiritual, till at length these too become spiritual qualities present with him when he passes from the natural world into the spiritual world. In short, the spiritual consists in an affection stirred by charity and faith, that is, an affection for what is good and true, and in the delight and pleasure, and even more so in the blessedness and bliss that flow from them, which are feelings residing with a person inwardly and making him someone truly Christian.

3 The majority in the Christian world are ignorant of what the spiritual is for the reason that they make faith, not charity, the essential virtue in the Church. Consequently, since the few who do bother about faith give little if any thought at all to charity or know what charity is, and since therefore they have no knowledge or any perception of the affection characteristic of charity, an affection that is not present in

them, they cannot possibly know what the spiritual is. This is especially so at the present day when scarcely any charity exists with anyone, for now is the final period of the Church. But it should be recognized that in a general sense the spiritual means an affection both for what is good and for what is true, which is why heaven is called the spiritual world and the internal sense of the Word is called the spiritual sense. But more specifically what is essentially an affection for good is called the celestial, while that which is essentially an affection for truth is called the spiritual.

5640   'And he said to the one who was over his house' means that which belongs to the external Church. This is clear from the representation of 'the one who was over the house' as the external Church, when 'the one who is in the house' is the internal Church, dealt with in 1795. And since no attention is paid in the internal sense to the person, only to the spiritual reality, 5225, 5287, 5434, 'the one who was over the house' means that which belongs to the external Church.

5641   'Bring the men to the house' means that the truths in the natural were to be introduced into it. This is clear from the meaning of 'the sons of Jacob' as the truths known to the Church that were present in the natural, dealt with in 5403, 5419, 5427, 5428, 5512 – their introduction into the external Church being meant by 'bring them to the house'.

5642   'And slaughter and prepare [an animal]' means through the forms of good belonging to the exterior natural. This is clear from the meaning of 'slaughtering' – implying that which was slaughtered, namely an ox, young bull, he-goat or other member of the flock – as forms of good belonging to the natural. 'An ox' and 'a young bull' mean forms of good belonging to the natural, see 2180, 2566, 2781, 2830, in this case forms of good belonging to the exterior natural because they are the means by which the truths are first introduced to effect a joining together. For 'he brought the men to Joseph's house' means the first introduction into good coming from the celestial of the spiritual, see below in 5645. Because 'a young bull and an ox' meant forms of good in the natural, every activity involving these meant that good too; for the one entailed the other.

5643   'For the men will eat with me at midday' means that they will be joined together when accompanied by the intermediary. This is clear from the meaning of 'eating' as being communicated, being joined together, and being made one's own, dealt with in 2187, 2343, 3168, 3513(end), 3596, 3832. And because they were accompanied by the spiritual intermediary represented by 'Benjamin', 5639, the expression 'at midday' is used; for 'midday' means a state of light, and so a spiritual state which the intermediary is instrumental in bringing about, 1458, 3708.

5644 'And the man did as Joseph said' means a putting into effect. This is clear without explanation.

5645 'And the man brought the men to Joseph's house' means the first introduction into good coming from the celestial of the spiritual. This is clear from the meaning of 'bringing to' as an introduction, as above in 5641; from the meaning of 'the sons of Jacob' as truths known to the Church that are present within the natural, dealt with in 5403, 5419, 5427, 5428, 5512; from the meaning of 'the house' as good, dealt with in 3652, 3720, 4982, on account of which 'the house' is also the Church, 3720, for the Church is the Church by virtue of good; and from the representation of 'Joseph' as the celestial of the spiritual, often dealt with already. From all this it is evident that 'the man brought the men to Joseph's house' means that truths in the natural were introduced into good coming from the celestial of the spiritual. The reason why a first introduction is meant is that at this point they merely ate with Joseph but did not recognize who he was. By this is meant a general joining together, which is a first introduction; for at this point there is a general inflow of truth from the Divine, but it is not recognized. When however a discernment of that inflowing truth does exist a second joining together is effected, and this is meant by Joseph revealing who he was to his brothers, dealt with further on in Chapter 45.

5646 Verses 18–23 **And the men were afraid because they were brought to Joseph's house; and they said, Over the matter of the silver put back in our pouches at the beginning are we brought to [this place], so that he may come down on us and fall on us[1], and take us as slaves, and our asses. And they came near the man who was over Joseph's house, and they spoke to him [at][2] the door (*ostium*) of the house. And they said, On my honour[3], my lord, we certainly came down at the beginning to buy food. And it happened, when we came to the lodging-place and opened our pouches, that behold, each man's silver was in the mouth of his pouch, our silver in its full weight; and we are bringing it back in our hand. And we are causing other silver to come down in our hand to buy food; we do not know who put our silver in our pouches. And he said, Peace to you, do not be afraid; your God and the God of your father has given you the concealed gift in your pouches; your silver came to me. And he brought Simeon out to them.**
'And the men were afraid' means a drawing back. 'Because they were brought to Joseph's house' means that the truths belonging to the natural were to be linked and made subservient to the internal. 'And they said, Over the matter of the silver put back in our pouches at the beginning are we brought to [this place]' means that because truth in the exterior natural appears to be something freely given, they were

---

[1] *lit.* roll down onto us and throw himself onto us
[2] *See 5653.*
[3] *The Latin* In me *here represents the Hebrew* Bi, *which is usually regarded as an expression of entreaty rather than validity, cp* Chapter 44:18.

being made subservient. 'So that he may come down on us and fall on us' means that for this reason they were subjected to its absolute power and control. 'And take us as slaves, and our asses' means even to the point where whatever exists in either part of the natural is of no worth. 'And they came near the man who was over Joseph's house' means the teachings of the Church. 'And they spoke to him [at] the door of the house' means a consultation of these regarding the introduction. 'And they said, On my honour, my lord' means an attestation. 'We certainly came down at the beginning to buy food' means a mind set on acquiring good for truths. 'And it happened, when we came to the lodging-place and opened our pouches' means an inspection of the exterior natural. 'That behold, each man's silver was in the mouth of his pouch' means that it was observed that the truths had been so to speak freely given. 'Our silver in its full weight' means truths commensurate with each one's state. 'And we are bringing it back in our hand' means the submission as far as possible of what had been freely given. 'And we are causing other silver to come down in our hand to buy food' means that the mind is set on acquiring good through truth from some other source. 'We do not know who put our silver in our pouches' means an absence of faith owing to ignorance of where the truth present in the exterior natural came from. 'And he said, Peace to you, do not be afraid' means that all is well, they should not despair. 'Your God and the God of your father' means the Lord's Divine Human. 'Has given you the concealed gift in your pouches' means that it came from Him without the exercise of any prudence by them. 'Your silver came to me' means that it will seem as though truth has been acquired by them. 'And he brought Simeon out to them' means that he linked to those truths the will to practise them.

5647 'And the men were afraid' means a drawing back. This is clear from the meaning here of 'being afraid' as a drawing back, a drawing back from being joined to the internal. Fear arises from various causes, such as those dangerous situations when people can lose their lives, the gains they have made, and also both their positions and reputations, as well as the fear that they may be led into some kind of slavery, resulting in the loss of freedom together with the delight life holds within itself. This matter is dealt with below, for the men's fear was that they would become linked to the internal, which would cause them to lose their own identity, and with their own identity their freedom, and with their freedom the delight life holds within itself since that delight depends on the existence of freedom. This is the reason why 'the men were afraid' means a drawing back, a drawing back lest they should become linked [to the internal].

2   Let a brief preliminary statement be made here about the nature of that joining together, that is to say, of the external or natural man to the internal or spiritual man. The external or natural man reigns from the earliest period in life, unaware of the existence of the internal or

spiritual man. That being so, when a person undergoes reformation and from being a natural or external man starts to become a spiritual or internal one, the natural rebels initially. For that person receives teaching to the effect that the natural man must be made subservient; that is, all his strong evil desires and the accompanying ideas that lend support to these must be rooted out. Consequently when left to himself the natural man thinks that in that case he may be completely destroyed, since he knows nothing other than that the natural is all there is, being totally ignorant of the fact that things beyond measure or description reside within the spiritual. When the natural man thinks like this he draws back, having no wish to be made subservient to the spiritual. This then is what is meant here by 'fear'.

5648 'Because they were brought to Joseph's house' means that the truths belonging to the natural were to be linked and made subservient to the internal. This is clear from the meaning of 'being brought to Joseph's house' as being joined and made subservient to the internal. For 'Joseph' represents the internal since he represents truth from the Divine, which is the celestial of the spiritual, dealt with in 5307, 5331, 5332, 5417, 5469; 'the house' means both a person's internal and his external, 3128, 3538, 4973, 5023, in this case the internal because the expression 'Joseph's house' is used; and 'being brought to' – to the internal – means becoming linked to it. And as becoming linked to it is meant, being made subservient to it is meant as well, the reason being that when the natural becomes linked to the internal it is made subservient to it. For the dominion which has belonged previously to the natural man comes to belong subsequently to the spiritual. This dominion will in the Lord's Divine mercy be discussed later on.

2 Let a brief statement be made about what the situation is with the internal sense. The internal sense of the Word exists primarily for the benefit of those in the next life. When present with someone [on earth] who is reading the Word those in the next life perceive it according to its internal sense, not its external sense. For they do not understand any expressions used by man, only the sense lying behind those expressions; nor to understand that sense do they employ the natural thoughts that are men's, only their own thoughts, which are spiritual ones. The transformation of the natural sense residing with man into that spiritual sense takes place instantaneously, like a person's immediate conversion of someone else's language into his own which is a different one. It is in that kind of way that the natural sense proper to man's thought is converted into the spiritual sense; for spiritual language or speech belongs properly to angels, but natural language properly to man. The reason for the immediate transformation of the one sort of language into the other is that a correspondence exists between every single thing in the natural world and every single thing in the spiritual world.

3 Now because the internal sense of the Word exists primarily for the

benefit of those in the spiritual world, the kinds of details contained here in the internal sense that have been mentioned are ones that exist for their benefit and give them pleasure and delight. But the more internal those details are the further removed they are from the range of understanding present in men, for whom none but matters of a worldly and bodily nature bring pleasure and delight. When this is the situation they consider the spiritual matters contained in the internal sense as of little value; indeed they loathe them. Let anyone examine himself to see whether or not the ideas contained in the internal sense of the narrative that follows below are to him worthless and loathsome. Yet such ideas are what give angelic communities utmost delight. From this anyone who stops to reflect may also see the kind of difference there is between men's delights and angels' delights, as well as what it is that angels consider wisdom to consist in and what it is that men consider it to consist in. That is to say, angels consider wisdom to consist in the kinds of things that man regards as being worthless and that he is averse to, while man considers wisdom to consist in the kinds of things in which angels have no interest at all; indeed many people consider it to consist in the kinds of things which angels cast aside and have nothing to do with.

5649 'And they said, Over the matter of the silver put back in our pouches [at the beginning] are we brought to [this place]' means that because truth in the exterior natural appears to be something freely given, they were being made subservient. This is clear from the meaning of 'the silver put back' as truth freely given, dealt with in 5530, 5624; from the meaning of 'the pouch' as the opening to the exterior natural, dealt with in 5497; and from the meaning of 'brought to' as being linked and made subservient to, dealt with immediately above in 5648.

2 The implications of all this are as follows: Because it had been perceived that the facts present in the exterior man which held truths within them had been freely given and were therefore being led on to become joined to the internal, which would make them subservient to it, it was consequently perceived that, as stated just above, they would be deprived of their freedom and so of all the delight that life holds within itself. But man has no conception of such a thing, that is to say, of its being perceived that facts holding truths within them can be given freely and that this happens in the natural, in either the exterior part or the interior part of it. The reason he has no conception of this is that he does not enjoy any kind of perception like that, for he does not have the vaguest idea about what is given to him freely, let alone about what is stored away in the exterior natural and what in the interior natural. The common reason why he does not have any perception of this is that his heart is set on worldly and earthly things, not on celestial and spiritual ones, and therefore he has no belief in any influence coming from the Lord by way of heaven and so no belief whatever in the gift of any such

things to him. Yet in actual fact all the truth which he arrives at by the use of reason based on factual knowledge and which he imagines he arrives at by his own power of understanding is something that is given to him. And man has even less ability to perceive whether that truth is stored away in the exterior natural or in the interior natural, because he is ignorant of the fact that the natural has two parts, namely an exterior part which leans towards the external senses and an interior part which leans away from these and turns towards the rational.

3   Since man has no knowledge of any of these matters he cannot have any perception at all regarding such ideas; for acquaintance with a reality must come first if there is to be any perception about it. But angelic communities are properly acquainted with and have a right perception of those matters. They are acquainted with and perceive not only what is given them freely but also in what place this exists, as the following experience makes clear: When any spirit who is moved by good, and therefore has the ability to do so, enters some angelic community, he enters at the same time into all the knowledge and intelligence belonging to this community, which he had not possessed before. At such a time he is not aware of anything different from this – that he was already in possession of such knowledge and understanding, and through his own deliberation. But when he stops to reflect he realizes that it is something freely given him by the Lord through that angelic community. He also knows, from the angelic community where he is, whether that truth exists in the exterior natural or in the interior natural; for there are angelic communities situated in the exterior natural, and there are those situated in the interior natural. But their natural is not like man's natural; rather it is a natural that is spiritual – one that has been made spiritual by having become joined and made subservient to the spiritual.

4   From all this one may see that the matters mentioned here in the internal sense describe what actually happens in the next life. That is to say, those there are quite aware of what is freely given them and also of where it is stored away, even though man at the present day knows nothing at all about such matters. In ancient times however those who belonged to the Church did know about them; their factual knowledge told them about such matters, and so did their religious teachings. They were people of a more internal frame of mind; but since those times people have become progressively more externally minded, so much so that at the present day they live in the body, thus in what is the most external. A sign of this is seen in the fact that people do not even know what the spiritual is or what the internal is; and they do not believe even in the existence of such realities. Indeed people have moved so far away from things on a more internal level to what is most external within the body that they do not even believe in the reality of a life after death, or in the existence of heaven or hell. Indeed because of their departure from things on a more internal level into what is most external they have become so stupid, so far as spiritual realities are

concerned, as to believe that man's life is similar to that of beasts, so that in death man is no different from them. And what is so surprising, the learned believe these kinds of things more than the simple; and anyone whose belief is different from theirs is thought by them to be a simpleton.

5650   'So that he may come down on us and fall on us' means that for this reason they were subjected to its absolute power and control. This is clear from the meaning of 'coming down on someone' as considering him blameworthy; and from the meaning of 'falling on someone' as making him subject to one's own power and control, which in this case is absolute since the statement 'take us as slaves, and our asses' follows after this. The implications of all this are as follows: Before the natural man is joined to the spiritual, or the external man to the internal, he is left to consider whether he wants the strong desires that spring from self-love and love of the world, also such ideas as he has used to defend those desires, to be done away with, and whether he wants to surrender dominion to the spiritual or internal man. He is left to consider this so that he may choose in freedom what he pleases. When the natural man without the spiritual contemplates this possibility he rejects it; for he loves his strong evil desires for the reason that he loves himself and the world. Such a contemplation fills him with anxiety and he imagines that if those desires are done away with his life would be finished; for he locates everything in the natural or external man. Alternatively he imagines that after they have been done away with he will be left with no power of his own and that all his thought, will, and action will come to him through heaven, so that he will no longer have any responsibility for these. Once the natural man has been left to himself in this condition, he draws back and becomes resistant. But when some light flows from the Lord through heaven into his natural he starts to think differently. That is to say, he now prefers the spiritual man to have dominion, for then he is able to think what is true and to will what is good and so is able to enter heaven, which is not possible if the natural man has dominion. And when he considers that all the angels in the whole of heaven are like this and as a consequence experience joy defying description, he goes to war with the natural man and at length wishes to make the same subject to the spiritual. This is the condition into which someone who is to be regenerated is brought, so that he can in freedom turn where he wills; and insofar as he does in freedom turn in that direction he is being regenerated. All these matters are the things under consideration here in the internal sense.

5651   'And take us as slaves, and our asses' means even to the point where whatever exists in either part of the natural is of no worth. This is clear from the representation of the ten sons of Jacob – who say this about themselves – as the truths in the natural, dealt with in 5403, 5419, 5427, 5458, 5512; from the meaning of 'slaves' or 'servants' as things which are of little value, 2541, in this case those that are of no worth, dealt with below; and from the meaning of 'asses' as what was present in the natural, namely factual knowledge, dealt with in 5492, in this case facts present in the exterior natural since the truths meant by 'the sons of Jacob' reside in the interior natural.

2 The implications of this, that whatever exists in either part of the natural is of no worth, are as follows: If a person is to become spiritual his natural must come to be of no worth, that is, it must cease to have any power that is essentially its own; for to the extent that the natural has any power of its own the spiritual lacks it. Since earliest childhood the natural has been acquiring no other ambitions than those that spring from selfish and worldly desires, thus ones that are the opposite of charity. These evil ambitions make it impossible for good to flow in from the Lord by way of the internal man; for whatever flows in is turned within the natural into what is evil, the natural being the final level into which what is inflowing goes. Consequently unless the natural, that is, the evil and falsity that have been giving shape to the natural, comes to be of no worth, no good can possibly flow in from the Lord by way of heaven. It finds no dwelling-place there and is dissipated, for it cannot stay in what is evil and false. For this reason the internal remains closed to the extent that the natural fails to become of no worth. This is something known within the Church from the teaching that one should put off the old man in order that one may put on the new[1].

3 Regeneration consists in nothing else than the natural being made subservient and the spiritual becoming its lord; and the natural is made subservient when it is made to correspond to the spiritual. Once the natural is made to correspond it is no longer reactionary but acts as it is commanded, answering the beck and call of the spiritual, almost as the actions of the body are answers to the beck and call of the will, or as speech and facial expressions conform to the thought flowing into them. From this it is evident that for a person to become spiritual, his natural must come to be, so far as his power of will is concerned, of no worth whatsoever.

4 But it should be realized that it is the old natural that must come to be of no worth, since it is shaped by evils and falsities. Once it has been made of no worth the person is endowed with a new natural, called the spiritual natural. This is called spiritual because the spiritual is what acts by means of it and also makes itself known through it, in the way a cause does through its effect – the cause, as is well known, being the entire reason for the effect. Consequently the new natural, so far as the activities of thought, will, and putting into effect are concerned, is nothing else than the representative of the spiritual. When this new natural comes into being a person receives good from the Lord; when

---

[1] *A Pauline teaching; see for example Eph.4:22–24; Col.3:9,10.*

he receives that good truths are conferred on him; when those truths are conferred on him his intelligence and wisdom are made more perfect; and when his intelligence and wisdom are made more perfect he is blessed with happiness that lasts for ever.

5652   'And they came near the man who was over Joseph's house' means the teachings of the Church. This is clear from the meaning of 'the man over Joseph's house' as that which belongs to the external Church, dealt with above in 5640, thus religious teaching since this belongs to the Church. In addition 'the man' means truth, and so religious teaching, 3134, while 'the house' means the Church, 1795; and since 'Joseph' is the internal, 5469, 'Joseph's house' is the internal Church. Teaching drawn from the Word is what is set over that house, serving and ministering to it.

5653   'And they spoke to him [at] the door of the house' means a consultation of these regarding the introduction. This is clear from the meaning of 'speaking to him', to the man over Joseph's house, as a consultation of these – of these teachings of the Church; and from the meaning of 'the door of the house' as the introduction, dealt with in 2356, 2385, in this case the introduction of the natural or external man to the spiritual or internal man, which is the subject here. This being the meaning the original language does not say 'at the door of the house', only 'the door of the house'.

5654   'And they said, On my honour, my lord' means an attestation. This is clear from the stock phrase itself that is used here as the making of an attestation, which was that what they said about the silver found in each man's sack was the truth.

5655   'We certainly came down at the beginning to buy food' means a mind set on acquiring good for truths. This is clear from the meaning of 'coming down' as a mind set on something, that is, an intention; for a person who goes down or betakes himself to any place does so from a set purpose, the purpose being in this case to acquire good for truths, meant by 'buying food'. For 'buying' means acquiring and making one's own, 5374, 5397, 5406, 5414, 5426, while 'food' means the good of truth, 5340, 5342, in this case good for truths which are represented by 'the sons of Jacob' who spoke these words regarding themselves.

5656   'And it happened, when we came to the lodging-place and opened our pouches' means an inspection of the exterior natural. This is clear from the meaning of 'the lodging-place' as the exterior natural in general, dealt with in 5495; from the meaning of 'opening' as an inspection, for when someone opens something he does so to inspect it; and from the meaning of 'a pouch' as the exterior natural more specifically, dealt with in 5497.

5657 'That behold, each man's silver was in the mouth of his pouch' means that it was observed that the truths had been so to speak freely given. This is clear from the meaning of 'each man's silver in his sack' as truths freely given, dealt with in 5530, 5624, 'each man's silver in the mouth of his pouch' meaning much the same. The difference is that the latter statement means that the truths which were freely given were placed in the opening of the exterior natural; for 'the mouth of the pouch' means the opening of the exterior natural, 5497. The reason why *so to speak* freely is meant at this point is that they dwell in a state of uncertainty, unsure whether they want to be joined to the internal, for fear that they will cease to be of any worth. And when anyone dwells in a state of uncertainty he feels unsure about the truths that serve to corroborate.

5658 'Our silver in its full weight' means truths commensurate with each one's state. This is clear from the meaning of 'silver' as truth, dealt with in 1551, 2954; and from the meaning of 'weight' as the state of something as regards good, dealt with in 3104, so that truths commensurate with each one's state means commensurate with the good they are able to receive. Many places in the Word make reference to weights or to measures, but no weight nor any measure is meant in the internal sense. Rather states so far as the good involved in some reality is concerned are meant by 'weights', while states so far as the truth involved in it is concerned are meant by 'measures'. The same applies to the properties of gravity and spatial magnitude; gravity in the natural world corresponds to good in the spiritual world, and spatial magnitude to truth. The reason for this is that in heaven, where correspondences originate, neither the property of gravity nor that of spatial magnitude exists because space has no existence there. Objects possessing these properties do, it is true, seem to exist among spirits, but those objects are appearances that have their origins in the states of goodness and truth in the heaven above those spirits.

2 It was very well known in ancient times that 'silver' meant truth; therefore the ancients divided up periods of time ranging from the earliest to the latest world epochs into the golden ages, the silver ones, the copper ones, and the iron ones, to which they also added the clay ones. They applied the expression 'golden ages' to those periods when innocence and perfection existed, when everyone was moved by good to do what was good and by righteousness to do what was right. They used 'silver ages' however to describe those times when innocence did not exist any longer, though there was still some sort of perfection, which did not consist in being moved by good to do what was good but in being moved by truth to do what was true. 'Copper ages' and 'iron ages' were the names they gave to the times that were even more inferior than the silver ones.

3 What led those people to give periods of time these names was not comparison but correspondence. For the ancients knew that 'silver'

corresponded to truth and 'gold' to good; they knew this from being in communication with spirits and angels. For when a discussion takes place in a higher heaven about what is good, this reveals itself among those underneath them in the first or lowest heaven as what is golden; and when a discussion takes place about what is true this reveals itself there as what is silvery. Sometimes not only the walls of the rooms where they live are gleaming with gold and silver but also the very air within them. Also, in the homes of those angels belonging to the first or lowest heaven who are moved by good to live among what is good, tables made of gold, lampstands made of gold, and many other objects are seen; but in the homes of those who are moved by truth to live among what is true, similar objects made of silver are seen. But who at the present day knows that correspondence was what led the ancients to call ages golden ones and silver ones? Indeed who at the present day knows anything at all about correspondence? Anyone who does not know this about the ancients, and more so anyone who thinks pleasure and wisdom lie in contesting whether such an idea is true or untrue, cannot begin to know the countless facets there are to correspondence.

5659   'And we are bringing it back in our hand' means the submission as far as possible of what had been freely given. This is clear from the meaning of 'bringing back' here as submitting, and from the meaning of 'in our hand' as as far as possible, dealt with above in 5624. The fact that it had been given freely is meant by 'the silver in the mouth of each man's pouch' which they were returning, 5657.

5660   'And we are causing other silver to come down in our hand to buy food' means that the mind is set on acquiring good through truth from some other source. This is clear from the meaning of 'silver' as truth, dealt with just above in 5657, and as 'silver' means truth, some other truth and therefore truth from some other source is meant by 'other silver' (for no other truth that is genuine truth exists apart from that received from the Lord, who gives it freely, so that there is no other source than He from which real truth is derived); and from the meaning of 'causing to come down' as a mind set on acquiring – on acquiring the good of truth, which is meant by the grain they bought. The story told in the sense of the letter implies that the other silver came to Joseph, for the purchase of food from him and so from no other source. But the internal sense is not subject to any limitation set by the story told in the sense of the letter; indeed it is not concerned with that sense, only with the real matter under discussion here, which is this: If they were to make themselves subservient like slaves owing to the fact that some truths were freely given within the exterior natural, they would from some other source acquire good through truth. This idea also forms the train of thought in the internal sense, for immediately after this the words 'we do not know who put the silver in our pouches' are used, meaning their lack of belief because they did not know where truth present in the exterior natural came from.

2   Something like this happens in the next life in the case of spirits who are being introduced by means of truths into good, especially into this – that everything good and true flows in from the Lord. When they learn that everything they think or will flows into them, so that they themselves cannot be the source of their thinking and willing, they fight all they can against the idea. For they believe that, if this idea is true, they cannot have any life within themselves that is entirely their own and that all delight is therefore destroyed, for they make the existence of separate selfhood vital to delight. Furthermore those spirits think that if they do not have any power entirely their own to do what is good and to believe what is true, they must let their hands hang down, not do or think anything on their own initiative, and wait for influx. They are allowed to go on thinking in this kind of way until they reach the point when they almost decide that they do not want to receive what is good and true from such influx but from some other source which does not involve their being deprived in this manner of their selfhood. Sometimes they are even allowed to make enquiries about where they may find that kind of goodness and truth. But when after this they do not find such goodness and truth anywhere, those who are being regenerated come back and freely choose to let the Lord lead their will and thought. They are also told at the same time that they are going to receive a heavenly selfhood such as the angels possess, and along with this the gift of everlasting bliss and happiness.

3   As regards this heavenly selfhood, it is a product of the new will conferred by the Lord. It is different from the selfhood properly man's own, in that those who have received that heavenly selfhood no longer see only themselves in every single thing they do or in every single thing they learn about and convey to others. Instead they see their neighbour, the general public, the Church, the Lord's kingdom, and so the Lord Himself. The ends they have in life are what undergo change; for ends which have lower things – namely self and the world – in view are removed and higher ones introduced to replace them. Ends in life are nothing else than the actual life in a person, for a person's ends in view are the things that his will desires. They are also the actual loves present in him, for what a person loves is what his will desires and what constitute his end in view. The person who is given a heavenly selfhood enjoys too a state of serenity and peace, for he trusts in the Lord and believes that no evil at all can come to touch him, knowing too that no strong evil desires can molest him. More than that, those who have received a heavenly selfhood enjoy true freedom; for being led by the Lord constitutes freedom since one is then led within the sphere of good, from good, and to good. From this it becomes clear that they enjoy bliss and happiness, for nothing exists to disturb them – no self-love at all, consequently no enmity, hatred, or vengeance at all; nor any love of the world at all, consequently no deceitfulness, fear, or unease at all.

5661 'We do not know who put the silver in our pouches' means an absence of faith owing to ignorance of where truth present in the exterior natural came from. This is clear from the meaning of 'not knowing' in the spiritual sense as not believing, or an absence of faith; from the meaning of 'who put' as ignorance of where it came from; from the meaning of 'silver' as truth, dealt with in 5658; and from the meaning of 'a pouch' as the exterior natural, dealt with in 5497.

5662 'And he said, Peace to you, do not be afraid' means that all is well, they should not despair. This is clear from the meaning of 'peace' as what is well, dealt with below; and from the meaning of 'do not be afraid' as they should not despair. The subject in the internal sense is a change of state. No longer were they by their own power acquiring truths; now they were acquiring good by means of truths, which however were truths given them by the Lord. But because they imagined that they would then be losing their selfhood, and so would be losing their freedom and consequently their entire delight in life, they were plunged into despair, as is evident from what has gone before. So it is that here 'do not be afraid' means that they should not despair; for fear arises from various different causes, 5647, and therefore has various different meanings.

The reason 'peace' means all is well is that peace is what is central and consequently what reigns universally within every single thing in heaven. For the peace that reigns in heaven is like spring on earth, or like the dawn. What moves a person's feelings when spring or dawn arrives is not the discernible changes that take place then but the loveliness reigning universally, which pervades every individual thing he perceives and fills not only that perception but also each individual object with loveliness. Scarcely anyone at the present day knows what peace is when it is mentioned in the Word, as, besides other places, in the Blessing,

Jehovah lift up His face upon you and *give you peace.* Num.6:26.

Almost everyone believes that peace consists in being kept safe from enemies and in serenity reigning at home and among companions. That kind of peace is not however what is meant here but another kind that is immensely superior, namely heavenly peace, described immediately above. No one can be granted this peace unless he is led by the Lord and abides in the Lord, that is, unless he is in heaven where the Lord is the All in all. For heavenly peace enters in when the desires that spring from self-love and love of the world are removed; for those desires take peace away, molesting a person inwardly and causing him at length to consider rest to consist in unrest and peace in molestations, because he considers delight to consist in evil desires. All the time a person is subject to these desires he cannot by any means know what peace is; indeed during all that time he believes that such peace is of no worth. And should anyone say that one experiences this peace when the delights that spring from self-love and love of the world are removed he laughs at the idea, for the reason that he considers peace to consist in the delight taken in evil, which is the opposite of peace.

3   Such being the nature of peace, that is to say, it is what is central to every form of happiness and bliss and is therefore what reigns universally within every individual thing, the ancients therefore used the common saying 'Peace to you', meaning May all be well; or else they would ask people 'Did they have peace?' meaning Was all well with them? See what has been stated and shown already regarding peace,

Peace in heaven is like spring and the dawn on earth, 1726, 2780.
In the highest sense 'peace' is the Lord; in the representative sense it is His kingdom, also the Lord's Divine affecting inmostly what is good, 3780, 4681.
All unrest is due to evil and falsity, whereas peace is due to goodness and truth, 3170.

5663   'Your God and the God of your father' means the Lord's Divine Human. This becomes clear from the fact that where the name God or the name Jehovah is used in the Word, the Lord and no one else is meant, 1343, 1736, 2921, 3035. And when the words 'your God and the God of your father' are used – that is, the God of Israel and Jacob and of his sons – the Lord's Divine Human is meant, in particular His Divine Natural, 3305, 4286, 4570; for 'Israel' represented the Lord's interior Natural, 'Jacob' His exterior Natural, and 'his sons' the truths present in that Natural.

2   The truth that the Lord was meant by God and Jehovah in the Word was unknown to the Jewish Church; and the Christian Church at the present day does not know it, the reason for its ignorance of this truth being that it has distinguished the Divine into three separate persons. But the Ancient Church which existed after the Flood, and especially the Most Ancient Church which existed before the Flood, did not understand by Jehovah and God anyone else than the Lord, in particular His Divine Human. They did know about the Divine Himself who dwells within the Lord, and whom the Lord calls His Father; but they could not engage in any thought about the Divine Himself who dwells within the Lord, only about His Divine Human, and consequently could not be joined to any other that is Divine. For that linking together is effected through thought which is the activity of the understanding and through affection which is the activity of the will, thus through faith and love. When anyone thinks about the Divine Himself his thought becomes lost so to speak in boundless space and so is dissipated. As a consequence no joining together can result. But it is different when anyone thinks about the Divine Himself as the Divine Human. Those people living in former times also knew that unless they were joined to the Divine they could not be saved.

3   It was therefore a Divine Human that the Ancient Churches worshipped, and it was Jehovah in this Divine Human that revealed Himself among them. That Divine Human was also the Divine Himself

in heaven, for heaven consists of a single human being called the Grand Man, dealt with at the ends of chapters up to this point. The Divine in heaven is essentially the Divine Himself; but He exists in heaven as a Divine Man. This Man is the one the Lord took upon Himself, made Divine within Himself, and made one with the Divine Himself, even as He had from eternity been made one with Him; for He has from eternity been one. He acted in that way because the human race could not otherwise be saved. The channel formed by heaven, and so by the Divine Human there, by means of which the Divine Himself came into people's minds was no longer adequate; therefore the Divine Himself was willing to make the Divine Human one with Himself through the Human He actually took upon Himself in the world. This Divine Human and that Divine Himself are the Lord.

5664   'Has given you the concealed gift in your pouches' means that it came from Him without the exercise of any prudence by them. This is clear from the meaning of 'the concealed gift' as truth and good conferred by the Lord without man's knowledge; and from the meaning of 'the silver put back in their sacks (or in their pouches)' as without expending any power of their own, dealt with in 5488, 5496, 5499. From this it is evident that 'has given you the concealed gift in your pouches' means that from Him – that is to say, from the Lord's Divine Human – came truth and good in the natural, without the expenditure of any power of their own. And because the gift comes without the expenditure of any power of their own, it comes without the exercise of any prudence by them. The expression prudence is used for the reason that prudence is the virtue [in man] that answers to providence [in God]; and what is attributable to Divine Providence is not attributable to human prudence.

5664[a]   'Your silver came to me' means that it will seem as though truth has been acquired by them. This is clear from the meaning of 'silver' as truth, dealt with in 1551, 2954. The coming of their silver to him implies that payment had been made by them, thus that they had made an acquisition for themselves; for 'buying' means acquiring, 5655. This explains why 'your silver has come to me' means that truth has been acquired by them. Yet because the truth which constitutes faith is never an acquisition that a person makes but is a gift instilled and conferred by the Lord, though it seems to be an acquisition made by that person, the expression it *will seem* as though truth has been acquired by them is used.

2   The fact that truth is instilled and conferred by the Lord is also well known in the Church, for the Church teaches that faith does not originate in man but comes from God, so that not only confidence but also the truths that constitute faith come from Him. Yet the appearance is that truths of faith are acquired by the person himself. The fact that they flow into him is something he is totally unaware of because he has no perception of their doing so. The reason he has no such perception is

that his interiors are closed, so that he is unable to have any communication with spirits and angels that is perceptible by him. When a person's interiors are closed he cannot know anything whatever about what is flowing into him.

3 But it should be recognized that it is one thing to know the truths of faith, another thing to believe them. Those who merely know the truths of faith consign them to their memory in the way they do anything else that is an item of knowledge. A person can acquire those truths without any such inflow into himself; but they do not possess any life, as is evident from the fact that a wicked person, even a very wicked one, can know the truths of faith just as well as an upright and God-fearing person. But in the case of the wicked, as stated, truths possess no life; for when a wicked person brings them forth he sees in each one either his own glory or personal gain. Consequently it is self-love and love of the world that fill those truths and give what seems like life. But this life is akin to that in hell, which life is called spiritual death. Consequently, when such a person brings forth those truths he does so from his memory, not from his heart. But someone who has a belief in the truths of faith is bringing them forth from his heart when they pass through his lips; for in his case the truths of faith have so taken root in him that they strike root in the external memory and then, like fruitful trees, grow up into interior or higher levels of the mind, where tree-like they adorn themselves with leaves and at length blossom, to the end that they may bear fruit.

4 This is what someone with belief is like. He too has nothing else in mind, when employing the truths of faith, than the performance of useful services or the exercise of charity, which is his 'fruit'. These are not the kind that anyone can acquire by himself. Not even the smallest can be so acquired by him; rather, the Lord gives such to him freely, doing so every single moment of his life. Indeed, if he will but believe it, countless gifts are imparted every single moment. But man's nature is such that he has no perception of the things that flow into him; for if he did have that kind of perception he would fight against the idea, as stated above, for he would then think that if the idea was true he would lose his selfhood, and with this his freedom, and with his freedom his delight, and so would be left with nothing. And without that perception a person knows no other than that such things originate in himself. This then is the meaning of the explanation '*it will seem* as though truth has been acquired by them'. What is more, if a person is to have a heavenly selfhood and heavenly freedom conferred on him, he must do what is good as though he himself were the source of it and think what is true as though he were the source of that. But when he stops to reflect he must ackowledge that such goodness and truth have their origin in the Lord, see 2882, 2883, 2891.

5665 'And he brought Simeon out to them' means that he linked to those truths the will to practise them. This is clear from the representation of 'Simeon' as faith in the will, or a will that desires to put the truth of faith into practice, dealt with in 3869–3872, 4497, 4502, 4503, 5482; and from the representation of the sons of Jacob, the ones here to whom he brought out Simeon, as truths known to the Church which were present in the natural, dealt with in 5403, 5419, 5427, 5458, 5512. From this it is evident that 'he brought Simeon out to them' means that he linked to those truths the will to practise them.

5666   Verses 24–28 **And the man brought the men to Joseph's house and gave them water, and they washed their feet; and he gave fodder to their asses. And they made ready the gift, until Joseph's coming at midday, for they heard that they would eat bread there. And Joseph came to the house, and they brought him the gift that was in their hand, to the house, and bowed down to him to the earth. And he questioned them about their peace[1], and said, Does your father, the old man of whom you spoke, have peace? Is he still alive? And they said, Your servant our father has peace; he is still alive. And they bowed, and bowed down.**

'And the man brought the men to Joseph's house' means an introductory stage to the joining to the internal. 'And gave them water' means a general influx of truth from the internal. 'And they washed their feet' means a consequent purification of the natural. 'And he gave fodder to their asses' means instruction regarding good. 'And they made ready the gift' means an instillation. 'Until Joseph's coming at midday' means up to when the internal would be present with light. 'For they heard that they would eat bread there' means a discernment that good was to be linked to the truths. 'And Joseph came to the house' means the presence of the internal. 'And they brought him the gift that was in their hand, to the house' means an instillation as far as this was possible. 'And bowed down to the earth' means an expression of humility. 'And he questioned them about their peace' means a perception that all is well. 'And he said, Does your father, the old man of whom you spoke, have peace?' means with spiritual good too. 'Is he still alive?' means that this has life. 'And they said, Your servant our father has peace' means a perception gained from there by the natural that all is well with the good from which it springs. 'He is still alive' means and that it has life. 'And they bowed, and bowed down' means an expression of humility, exterior and interior.

5667   'And the man brought the men to Joseph's house' means an introductory stage to the joining to the internal. This is clear from the meaning of 'bringing the men to Joseph's house' as the linking of the truths belonging to the natural to the internal, dealt with above in 5648. It is quite clear from the details that follow that an introductory stage to that joining together is meant – from their eating there, and from Joseph's not revealing to them who he really was, which details mean

---

[1] *i.e.* their welfare

the general influx which is dealt with in what now follows and which is the introductory stage.

5668   'And gave them water' means a general influx of truth from the internal. This is clear from the meaning of 'water' as truth, 2702, 3058, 3424, 4976, in this case truth in general. This is why 'giving water' means a general influx of truth; and the reason it comes from the internal is that this took place in Joseph's house, 5667. A general influx of truth is enlightenment that makes it possible for truth to be discerned and understood. This enlightenment is provided by the light of heaven which flows from the Lord, a light which is nothing else than Divine Truth, 2776, 3138, 3167, 3195, 3222, 3339, 3485, 3636, 3643, 3993, 4302, 4413, 4415, 5400.

5669   'And they washed their feet' means a consequent purification of the natural. This is clear from the meaning of 'washing one's feet' as the purification of the natural, dealt with in 3147.

5670   'And he gave fodder to their asses' means instruction regarding good. This is clear from the meaning of 'giving fodder' as providing instruction in good; for 'fodder' means the good that goes with known facts that are factual truths, 3114; and 'giving fodder', which is feeding, means providing instruction in that good, for the reason that 'feeding' means providing instruction, see 5201, while 'asses' means factual knowledge, 5492. From this it is evident that 'giving fodder to asses' means instruction regarding the good that goes with known facts. The good that goes with known facts is the delight gained from factual truths. Factual truths are very general truths which are seen in natural light received from the light of the world. But if they are to be seen as truths, a general influx from the internal must take place, 5668; and this is an enlightenment received from the light of heaven.

5671   'And they made ready the gift' means an instillation. This is clear from the meaning of 'the gift' as the obtaining of favour, dealt with in 5619, so that 'making ready the gift' is an instilling.

5672   'Until Joseph's coming at midday' means up to when the internal would be present with light. This is clear from the meaning of 'until his coming' as up to when it was present; from the representation of 'Joseph' as the internal, dealt with in 5648; and from the meaning of 'midday' as a state of light, 1458, 3195, 3708[1]. The reason 'midday' means a state of light is that the times of day, such as morning, midday, and evening, correspond to states of light in the next life; and states of light there are states of intelligence and wisdom, for the reason that the light of heaven holds intelligence and wisdom within it. The changing states of light there are like those times of day on earth – morning, midday, and evening. The states of shade akin to evening do not

---

[1] *The Latin word used here may mean* midday, *or it may mean* the south.

however have anything to do with the sun there, which is the Lord who is constantly shedding His light, but with the selfhood that is essentially the angels' own. For insofar as this selfhood takes over in their lives they pass into a state of shade or evening; but insofar as this selfhood gives way to the heavenly selfhood they move into a state of light. From this one may see where the correspondence of midday to a state of light has its origin.

5673 'For they heard that they would eat bread there' means a discernment that good was to be linked to the truths. This is clear from the meaning of 'hearing' as discerning, dealt with in 5017; from the meaning of 'eating' as being made one's own and being joined together, dealt with in 2187, 3168, 3513(end), 3596, 3832, 5643; and from the meaning of 'bread' as the good of love, dealt with in 2165, 2177, 2187, 3464, 3478, 3735, 3813, 4211, 4217, 4735, 4976.

5674 'And Joseph came to the house' means the presence of the internal. This is clear from the meaning of 'coming to the house' as being present or the presence of, as above in 5672; and from the representation of 'Joseph' as the internal, dealt with in 5648.

5675 'And they brought him the gift that was in their hand, to the house' means an instillation as far as this was possible. This is clear from the meaning of 'the gift' that was given to kings and priests as the obtaining of favour, and so also an instillation, dealt with just above in 5671; and from the meaning of 'that was in their hand' as as far as possible, also dealt with above, in 5624, 5659.

5676 'And bowed down to the earth' means an expression of humility. This is clear from the meaning of 'bowing down to the earth' as expressing humility, dealt with in 2153. See also below, in 5682.

5677 'And he questioned them about their peace' means a perception that all is well. This is clear from the meaning of 'questioning' as perceiving another's thought, dealt with in 5597; and from the meaning of 'peace' as all being well, dealt with in 5662.

5678 'And he said, Does your father, the old man of whom you spoke, have peace?' means with spiritual good too. This is clear from the meaning of 'peace' as all being well, as above in 5677; and from the representation of Israel, to whom 'father' refers here, as spiritual good, dealt with in 3654, 4286, 4598.

5679 'Is he still alive?' means that this has life. This is clear from the meaning of 'being alive' as spiritual life, dealt with in 5407.

5680 'And they said, Your servant our father has peace' means a perception gained from there by the natural that all is well with the good from which it springs. This is clear from the meaning of 'saying' as perceiving, dealt with in 1898, 1919, 2080, 2619, 2862, 3395, 3509; from the meaning of 'peace' as all being well, dealt with in 5662, 5677; and from the representation of 'Israel' as spiritual good, dealt with just above in 5678. This good is called their 'father' because the truths and forms of good present in the natural, which are represented by Israel's ten sons, spring from it as their father. And as the truths and forms of good in the natural are represented by those sons, the natural is also meant by them; for the natural is the container, while the truths and forms of good there are its contents which make one with it. From all this it is evident that 'they said, Your servant our father has peace' means a perception gained from there by the natural that all is well with the good from which it springs.

2 The perception is said to be gained *from there* – from the internal represented by 'Joseph', 5648 – because every perception gained by the natural comes from the spiritual; and because it comes from the spiritual it comes from the internal, that is, from the Lord through the internal. The natural cannot possibly have any perception, nor even any life present within thought and affection, other than that which comes from the spiritual. For all things within the natural that are essentially its own are dead; but they receive life through what flows in from the spiritual world, that is, from the Lord by way of the spiritual world. In the spiritual world everything receives life from the light flowing from the Lord, for that light holds wisdom and intelligence within. The meaning here – that the perception is gained *from there*, from the internal, in the natural – also follows from what has gone before in 5677.

5681 'He is still alive' means and that it has life. This is clear from what was suggested just above in 5679 – that one should compare what is mentioned in 5407.

5682 'And they bowed, and bowed down' means an expression of humility, exterior and interior. This is clear from the meaning of 'bowing' as an expression of exterior humility, and from the meaning of 'bowing down' as an expression of interior humility. For bowing is something less than bowing down and is therefore an expression of exterior humility, whereas bowing down is something more and is therefore an expression of interior humility. In addition to this, 'bowing' is the humility expressed by truth, that is, by those motivated by truth, and so is the humility of those who are spiritual; but 'bowing down' is the humility expressed by good, that is, by those motivated by good, and so is the humility of those who are celestial. Thus 'bowing' also means the expression of exterior humility, and 'bowing down' the expression of interior humility; for those motivated by good are people who are more interior than those motivated by truth. The explanation of the major part of the contents of the internal sense in this section has been confined simply to the meanings of the words that are used, for the reason that they are matters such as have appeared in explanations prior to this.

5683   Verses 29–34 **And he lifted up his eyes and saw Benjamin his brother, his mother's son, and said, Is this your youngest brother, whom you said [something about] to me? And he said, God be gracious to you, my son. And Joseph hastened, because feelings of compassion were being roused in him towards his brother, and he sought [somewhere] to weep; and he went to his bedchamber and wept there. And he washed his face and went out; and he contained himself and said, Set on bread. And they set for him by himself, and for them by themselves and for the Egyptians eating with him by themselves; for the Egyptians cannot eat bread with the Hebrews, since that is an abomination to the Egyptians. And they sat in front of him, the firstborn according to his birthright, and the youngest according to his youth; and the men were astonished [and looked] each at his companion. And he took portions from before his face to them, and he multiplied Benjamin's portion above the portions of all theirs – five measures more. And they drank, and drank plentifully with him.**

'And he lifted up his eyes' means reflection. 'And saw Benjamin' means a discernment of the intermediary. 'His brother, his mother's son' means the internal born from the natural as its mother. 'And said' means perception. 'Is this your youngest brother, whom you said [something about] to me?' means born after all of them, as they well knew. 'And he said, God be gracious to you, my son' means that the Divine was also present with the spiritual of the celestial, which is the intermediary, because it goes forth from the celestial of the spiritual, which is truth from the Divine. 'And Joseph hastened' means from what is inmost. 'Because feelings of compassion were being roused in him' means mercy springing out of love. 'Towards his brother' means towards the internal going forth from himself. 'And he sought [somewhere] to weep' means an expression of mercy springing out of love. 'And he went to his bedchamber and wept there' means within itself, in an unseen manner. 'And he washed his face' means that it took steps to ensure this. 'And went out' means by means of a removal. 'And he contained himself' means a concealment. 'And said, Set on bread' means a perception of a joining, through the intermediary, to the truths in the natural. 'And they set for him by himself, and for them by themselves' means the outward appearance that the internal was seemingly separated from them. 'And for the Egyptians eating with him by themselves' means the separation of factual knowledge existing in an inverted state of order. 'For the Egyptians cannot eat bread with the Hebrews' means that these could not by any means be joined to the truth and good of the Church. 'Since that is an abomination to the Egyptians' means that they are in a contrary position. 'And they took their seats in front of him' means that they were ranged in order, as determined by his presence. 'The firstborn according to his birthright, and the youngest according to his youth' means in conformity with the order truths take beneath good. 'And the men were astonished [and looked] each at his companion' means a change of state that took place in each one among them. 'And he took portions from before his face to them' means forms of good applied with mercy to each one. 'And he multiplied Benjamin's portion above the portions of all theirs' means the good imparted to the intermediary exceeded the forms of good imparted to the truths in the natural. 'Five measures more' means that it was much increased. 'And they drank' means the application of the truths beneath good. 'And drank plentifully' means in abundance.

5684 'And he lifted up his eyes' means reflection. This is clear from the meaning of 'lifting up the eyes' as thought and attention, dealt with in 2789, 2829, 4339, and also observation, 4086, and so reflection; for reflecting is turning one's attention, which is the sight of one's understanding, to observe whether something is true, and having done this to observe that it is indeed so.

5685 'And saw Benjamin' means a discernment of the intermediary. This is clear from the meaning of 'seeing' as understanding and discerning, dealt with in 2150, 2325, 3764, 3863, 4403–4421, 4567, 4723, 5400; and from the representation of 'Benjamin' as the intermediary, dealt with in 5411, 5413, 5443, 5639.

5686 'His brother, his mother's son' means the internal born from the natural as its mother. This is clear from the representation of Benjamin, to whom 'brother' and 'mother's son' refer here, as the internal, dealt with in 5469. And since this is the intermediary it comes into being from the celestial of the spiritual, represented by 'Joseph', as its father, and from the natural as its mother; for it must have its beginning in both these if it is to serve as an intermediary. So this is what is meant by the internal born from the natural as its mother. Also because the celestial of the spiritual, which is 'Joseph', had come into being in a similar way from the natural as its mother, but from the Divine as its father, 'Benjamin' is therefore called, as he was in actual fact by birth, 'his brother, his mother's son'; and in what immediately follows he is also addressed as 'son'. The name 'brother' is used by the Lord, who is meant here in the highest sense by 'Joseph', to refer to everyone who has any good of charity which he has received from the Lord. He is also referred to as 'his mother's son', but in this case 'mother' is used to mean the Church.

5687 'And said' means perception. This is clear from the meaning of 'saying' in the historical narratives of the Word as perception, often dealt with already. The reason 'saying' means perceiving is that in heaven, quite differently from what happens in the world, the actual thoughts that give rise to an utterance are perceived. And this is the reason why perceiving in the spiritual sense is 'speaking' or 'saying' in the literal sense, or what amounts to the same, the natural sense.

5688 'Is this your youngest brother, whom you said [something about] to me?' means born after all of them, as they well knew. This is clear from the meaning of 'youngest brother' as the one born after all of them, dealt with in what follows; and from the meaning of 'whom you said to me' as that which was perceived by them. For 'saying' means that which has been perceived, see immediately above in 5687, and so means what is well known. The reason Benjamin is called here, as he in fact was, their 'youngest brother' – that is, the one born after all of them, or the youngest by birth – is that in the spiritual sense the intermediary, which 'Benjamin' represents, is likewise the one that comes last. The intermediary in a person is born last of all; for when a person is undergoing spiritual birth – that is, when he is being born again – his rational, which is his inner man, is regenerated first by the Lord, then the natural after that, the rational being the means by which the Lord regenerates the natural, 3286, 3288, 3321, 3493, 4612. Now since the intermediary must be derived from both these – both from the spiritual rational or rational that has been made new, and from the natural – and since the intermediary cannot be derived from the natural unless this too has been made new, the intermediary is inevitably born at a later stage, and then only insofar as the natural is regenerated.

Everything recorded in the Word regarding the sons of Jacob happened for a providential reason, which was that the Word might be written dealing with them and their descendants. This Word was to contain heavenly realities, and in the highest sense Divine ones, which those sons in actual fact represented. This was no less so in the case of Benjamin who, being the one born last of all, represented the intermediary between the internal and the external, that is, between the celestial of the spiritual which was the Lord's when He was in the world and the natural which was also the Lord's and which He was to make Divine.

Everything recorded about Joseph and his brothers represents in the highest sense the glorification of the Lord's Human, that is, the way in which the Lord made the Human within Himself Divine. The reason this is what is represented in the inmost sense is so that in its inmost sense the Word may be completely holy. A further reason is that every detail recorded may contain within itself what can pass into angelic wisdom; for it is well known that angelic wisdom so surpasses man's wisdom that man can hardly begin to comprehend any of it. The actual happiness of the angels resides in the fact that every detail has to do with the Lord; for they abide in Him. Furthermore the glorification of the Lord's Human is the pattern for a person's regeneration, which is why a person's regeneration is also presented in the internal sense at the same time as the subject of the Lord's glorification is dealt with. A person's regeneration and the countless arcana associated with it also passes into angelic wisdom and brings the angels happiness insofar as they apply those arcana to useful services, which look to a person's reformation.

5689 'And he said, God be gracious to you, my son' means that the Divine was also present with the spiritual of the celestial, which is the intermediary, because it goes forth from the celestial of the spiritual, which is truth from the Divine. This is clear from the meaning of 'God be gracious' – when this is said by the celestial of the spiritual, which is 'Joseph', to the spiritual of the celestial, which is 'Benjamin', and when the latter is also addressed by the former as 'son' – as the Divine presence also with the spiritual of the celestial, which is the intermediary, because this goes forth from the celestial of the spiritual, which is truth from the Divine. For 'Benjamin' is the spiritual of the celestial, see 3969, 4592; he is the intermediary too, 5411, 5413, 5443, 5639.

2 Since, as stated above, the Lord's inner man was the celestial of the spiritual, and this was truth from the Divine or the clothing next to the Divine Himself within the Lord, and since the spiritual of the celestial, which is the intermediary, went forth from that, it follows that the Divine was also present with this intermediary. What goes forth from something acquires its essential being from that from which it goes forth; but it is clothed with coverings such as serve to enable communication to take place and thereby enable a useful purpose to be realized in a lower sphere. The coverings that clothe it are derived in part from such things as exist in that lower sphere, to the end that the internal from which it goes forth can operate in the lower sphere through the kinds of things present there.

3 What provides its essential being is so to speak its father, since that essential being is its soul; and what provides its clothing is its mother, for that clothing is the body belonging to this soul. This is why, as stated above, the intermediary must be derived from both if it is to be an intermediary – from the internal as its father and from the external as its mother.

5690 'And Joseph hastened' means from what is inmost. This is clear from the meaning of 'hastening' here as that which bursts forth from what is inmost, for the statement follows 'because feelings of compassion were being roused in him', by which mercy springing out of love is meant. When mercy bursts forth it does so from what is inmost; and it does so as fast as the blink of an eye or flash of an idea. This is why 'hastening' here means nothing else than from what is inmost.

5691 'Because feelings of compassion were being roused in him' means mercy springing out of love. This is clear from the meaning of 'feelings of compassion being roused' as mercy springing out of love. The word 'mercy' is used because Benjamin had not yet recognized who Joseph really was, and the expression 'out of love' because as the intermediary Benjamin went forth from him. In the original language 'feelings of compassion' is expressed by a word which describes inmost or tenderest love.

5692   'Towards his brother' means towards the internal going forth from himself. This is clear from the representation of Benjamin, to whom 'brother' refers here, as the intermediary, and so also the internal, dealt with in 5469; and because he goes forth, as the intermediary and the internal, from the celestial of the spiritual, which is 'Joseph', the words of explanation are 'towards the internal going forth *from himself*'. Anyone who receives anything of a Divine nature from the Lord, whom 'Joseph' represents here in the highest sense – for example, someone who receives any good of charity from Him – is called 'brother' by the Lord as well as 'son'.

5693   'And he sought [somewhere] to weep' means an expression of mercy springing out of love. This is clear from the meaning of 'weeping' as an expression of mercy springing out of love, dealt with in 3801, 5480.

5694   'And he went to his bedchamber and wept there' means within itself, in an unseen manner. This is clear from the meaning of 'going to one's bedchamber' as within oneself, in an unseen manner. To say someone was 'entering his bedchamber' and also 'shutting the door' was a commonplace expression which the ancients used when they meant an action that should remain unseen. The expression had its origin in the meaningful signs which existed in the Ancient Church. For they would speak of 'the house', which they used in a spiritual sense to mean a person, 3128, and of its 'chambers' and 'bedchambers' to mean the person's interiors. This is the reason why 'going to (or entering) one's bedchamber' meant within oneself, consequently so that one could not be seen. And since 'entering one's bedchamber' had this particular meaning, the expression is used in various places in the Word; as in Isaiah,

Go away, my people, *enter your bedchambers*, and *shut your door behind you.* Hide yourself, so to speak, for a little moment, until the anger passes over.   Isa.26:20.

Quite clearly 'entering bedchambers' does not in this case mean entering bedchambers but keeping out of sight and within oneself. In Ezekiel,

He said to me, Have you not seen, son of man, what the elders of the house of Israel are doing in the dark, each in *the chambers of his own idol?* For they say, Jehovah does not see us.   Ezek.8:12.

'Doing in the dark, each in the chambers of his own idol' stands for within themselves inwardly, in their thoughts. The interior aspects of their thought and affection were being represented to the prophet by means of 'chambers', and they were called 'the chambers of an idol'. In Moses,

Outside the sword will bereave – and *out of the chambers* terror – both young man and virgin, suckling together with a man in old age.   Deut.32:25.

'The sword' stands for the vastation of truth and the punishment of falsity, 2799. 'Out of the chambers terror' stands for a person's interiors;

for here too it is self-evident that one should not take 'the chambers' to mean chambers.

4   In David,

He waters the mountains *from His chambers*. Ps.104:13.

In the spiritual sense 'watering the mountains' is blessing those in whom love to the Lord and love towards the neighbour are present. For 'a mountain' means the celestial element of love, see 795, 1430, 4210, and therefore 'from His chambers' means from the interior parts of heaven. In Luke,

Whatever you have said in the dark will be heard in the light; and what you have spoken in the ear *in bedchambers* will be proclaimed on the housetops. Luke 12:3.

Here also 'bedchambers' stands for a person's interiors – what he has thought, what he has intended, and what he has mulled over. In Matthew,

When you pray, *enter your bedchamber*, and *shut your door*, and pray in secret. Matt.6:6.

'Entering one's bedchamber and praying' stands for acting in an unseen manner; for these words had their origin in things of a representative nature.

5695   'And he washed his face' means that it took steps to ensure this. This is clear from the meaning of 'washing his face' here as taking steps to ensure that it remained unseen; for Joseph's face was washed, and so steps were taken by him to ensure that his tears remained unseen. The full implications of this will in the Lord's Divine mercy be stated further on; but let something be said at this point about the correspondence of a person's face with his interiors. His face is what is external serving to represent his interiors. For the face has been designed in such a way that a person's interiors may be seen there as if in a mirror that reflects things in a representative fashion; it has been so designed that another may know its owner's attitude of mind towards himself, so that the owner reveals his sentiments when he speaks not only through his speech but also through his face. This was the kind of face possessed by the most ancient people who belonged to the celestial Church, and it is the kind that all angels have. Angels have no wish to conceal from others anything they think, for they think solely of their neighbour's well-being. Nor do they have any thought hidden away which desires their neighbour's well-being for some selfish reason of their own.

2   But those in hell, as long as they are not seen in the light of heaven, have a face other than the one that corresponds to their interiors. The reason for this is that during their lifetime they bore witness by means of their face to charity towards the neighbour solely for the sake of their own position and gain; they did not desire their neighbour's well-

being except insofar as it was identical with their own. Consequently the expression on their face is at variance with their interiors. Sometimes that variance is so great that feelings of enmity, hatred, and revenge, and the desire to murder are inwardly present, yet their face is set in such a way that love towards their neighbour is beaming from it. From this one may see how far people's interiors disagree at the present day with their exteriors, and why they resort to those kinds of practices to serve their own interests.

5696   'And went out' means by means of a removal. This is clear from the meaning here of 'going out' as a removal; for one who removes himself goes out or departs from another. The matter contained in the internal sense is as follows: 'Joseph' in the highest sense represents the Lord; 'the ten sons of Israel' represents the truths and the forms of good present in the natural in the case of those who are being regenerated; while 'Benjamin' is the intermediary. Mercy springing out of love is shown towards the intermediary because this is the means by which what is below, that is, in the natural, is regenerated. But the Lord's love and mercy remain unseen until the joining together has been effected by means of the intermediary. Steps are also taken to prevent their being seen; for if they did come to be seen no regeneration would be possible. Those steps involve removal and concealment. Not that the Lord ever removes or conceals His mercy; but when the evils present in one who is being regenerated are brought to the fore it appears to that person as though the Lord has been removed and is concealed from him; for those evils stand in the way and are responsible for that appearance. One may compare what they do to dark clouds which stand between him and the sun, causing this to be absent and concealed from him. It is that kind of concealment and removal that is meant here.

5697   'And he contained himself' means a concealment. This is clear from the meaning of 'containing himself' as concealing; for a person who contains himself conceals his inward desires. For what concealment is used to mean here, see immediately above in 5696.

5698   'And said, Set on bread' means a perception of a joining, through the intermediary, to the truths in the natural. This is clear from the meaning of 'saying' as perceiving, often dealt with already; and from the meaning of 'setting on bread' as a joining, through the intermediary, to the truths in the natural. 'Setting on bread' is used to mean an actual meal; and meals and feasts mean a joining together, in particular the introductory stage to a joining together, 3596, 3832, 5161. A joining, through the intermediary, to the truths in the natural follows from the train of thought – 'Benjamin' being the intermediary, and 'the ten sons of Jacob' the truths in the natural, as shown already. And since the intermediary is the one through whom the joining together is effected, Joseph gave the command, on seeing Benjamin, that they should eat with him,

And Joseph saw Benjamin with them, and he said to the one who was over his house, Bring the men to the house, and slaughter and prepare [an animal]; for the men will eat with me at midday.   Verse 16.

5699   'And they set for him by himself, and for them by themselves' means the outward appearance that the internal was seemingly separated from them. This is clear from the meaning of 'setting for him by himself, and for them by themselves' as a separation; and since 'Joseph' represents the internal, and 'the ten sons of Israel' the external, 5469, the words used here mean a separation of the internal from the external, which was only an apparent separation, for he gave them food from his own table, sending portions to each of them.

5700   'And for the Egyptians eating with him by themselves' means the separation of factual knowledge existing in an inverted state of order. This is clear from the representation of 'the Egyptians' as factual knowledge present in an inverted state of order, dealt with below; and from the meaning of 'eating with him by themselves' as a separation, dealt with immediately above in 5699. 'The Egyptians eating with him' means Egyptians who were eating at Joseph's house; yet it is evident that they did not do so with Joseph since it says that they ate 'by themselves'. In the good sense facts known to the Church are meant by 'Egypt' or 'the Egyptians', see 1462, 4749, 4964, 4966; but in the contrary sense facts existing in an inverted state of order, and so ideas contrary to the truths known to the Church are meant by them, 1164, 1165, 1186. And many places in the Word contain some reference to Egypt in this contrary sense. The reason why 'Egypt' means those facts existing in an inverted state of order is that the facts known to the Ancient Church which were the representatives and meaningful signs of celestial and spiritual realities, and which were fostered among those people more than others, were converted by them into magic. Consequently the facts known to the representative Church were brought by them into a completely inverted state of order.

2   Facts are said to exist in an inverted state of order when people intent on doing what is evil violate heavenly order; for heavenly order intends that good should be done to everyone. The result of this therefore is that once people cause heavenly order to become inverted in this way they ultimately reject what is of God, what is of heaven, and consequently what constitutes charity and faith. People who have come to be like this know how to use factual knowledge to engage in keen and skillful reasoning; for their use of reason relies on sensory evidence, and reasoning reliant on sensory evidence relies on considerations of an external nature – on bodily and worldly matters which instantly absorb a person's thoughts and feelings. Unless such factual knowledge has had the light of heaven shed upon it and has thereby been brought into a completely different state of order, it sets the person in obscurity. This obscurity is so pronounced, so far as heavenly matters are concerned, that he not only fails to understand them but also utterly refuses to

accept them, and at length casts them aside and, so far as he is allowed to do so, says blasphemous things about them. When factual knowledge exists in a proper state of order it has been arranged by the Lord into the same form as heaven takes. But when it exists in an inverted state of order it has been arranged into the form hell takes, a form in which the worst falsities are in the centre, supporting ideas come next, and truths on the outside. And as those truths are on the outside they cannot have any communication with heaven where truths are predominant. For this reason the interiors are closed, since it is through those interiors that the way to heaven lies open.

5701   'For the Egyptians cannot eat bread with the Hebrews' means that these could not by any means be joined to the truth and good of the Church. This is clear from the representation of 'the Egyptians' as those with whom an inverted state of order, and so evil and falsity, exists, dealt with immediately above in 5700; from the meaning of 'eating bread' as being joined together, also dealt with above, in 5698; and from the representation of 'the Hebrews' as those with whom genuine order, and so the truth and good of the Church, exists – 'the land of the Hebrews' meaning the Church, see 5136, 5236, for the reason that the Hebrew Church was the second Ancient Church, 1238, 1241, 1343. The expression 'eating bread' is used, and the command 'set on bread' mentioned just above, because 'bread' means all food in general, 2165, and so means a meal. The reason 'bread' means all food and an actual meal is that in the spiritual sense 'bread' is heavenly love; and heavenly love includes every aspect of good and truth, and so everything constituting spiritual food. For the meaning of 'bread' as heavenly food, see 276, 680, 2165, 2177, 2187, 3464, 3478, 3735, 4211, 4217, 4735, 4976.

5702   'Since that is an abomination to the Egyptians' means that they are in a contrary position. This is clear from the representation of 'the Egyptians' as those with whom order has been inverted, 5700; and from the representation of 'the Hebrews', to eat with whom was an abomination to the Egyptians, as those with whom genuine order exists, 5701. Thus the two are set in contrary positions, and this gives rise to strong dislike and at length to what is an abomination. Regarding this abomination, it should be recognized that people with whom an inverted state of order, that is, evil and consequent falsity, exists, thereby come at length to acquire a strong dislike for the goodness and truth of the Church the moment they hear it referred to. This is even more true when they hear reference made to the interior aspects of that goodness and truth; they find these so abominable that so to speak they feel nauseated and wish to vomit. This is what I have been told and shown to be so when I have wondered why the Christian world does not accept the interior teachings of the Word. Spirits from the Christian world have appeared on the scene and have been compelled to hear about the interior teachings of the Word; they were then so nauseated by these that they said they felt within themselves the great need to vomit. I have also been told that this is what the Christian world is like virtually everywhere at the present day. The reason it is like this is that it has no affection for truth for its own sake, still less any affection for good motivated by good. Anything they think or say that is based on the Word or their religious teachings is due to habit followed since early childhood and to religious custom, and so is something external devoid of anything internal.

2 The fact that all aspects of the Hebrew Church, the one established at a later time among the descendants of Jacob, were an abomination to the Egyptians is evident not only from their refusal even to eat with them but also from the fact that sacrifices, in which the Hebrew Church made its main worship consist, were an abomination to them, as is evident in Moses,

Pharaoh said, Go away, sacrifice within the land. But Moses said, It is incorrect to do so, for *we shall be sacrificing* to Jehovah our God *what is an abomination to the Egyptians*; behold, if *we sacrifice what is an abomination* to the Egyptians in their eyes, will they not stone us?   Exod.8:25,26.

Also, feeding cattle and being a shepherd was an abomination to them, as is evident again in Moses,

Every shepherd is an abomination to the Egyptians.   Gen.46:34.

Thus every aspect of that Church was an abomination to the Egyptians. The reason was that initially even the Egyptians had been among those who constituted the representative Ancient Church, 1238, 2385. But after that they rejected the God of the Ancient Church, who was Jehovah or the Lord, and served idols, in particular calves. Also the actual representatives and meaningful signs of the celestial and spiritual realities of the Ancient Church, which they came to know while part of that Church, were turned by them into magical practices. This being so, order with them became inverted, as a consequence of which everything constituting the Church was an abomination.

5703 'And they took their seats in front of him' means that they were ranged in order, as determined by his presence. This is clear from the meaning of 'taking one's seat' here as being ranged in order, for they were placed in order by Joseph, as is evident from what immediately follows – they were astonished that the firstborn took his seat according to his birthright, while the youngest took his according to his youth; and from the meaning of 'in front of him' as determined by his presence.

2 The truth of the matter is that in the highest sense 'Joseph' represents the Lord, 'the sons of Israel' the forms of good and the truths in the natural. When the Lord is present His very presence arranges everything into order. The Lord is order itself, and therefore wherever He is present order exists, and wherever order exists He is present. That order is described in what follows next, the aim of that order being to see that truths are properly arranged beneath good.

5704   'The firstborn according to his birthright, and the youngest according to his youth' means in conformity with the order truths take beneath good. This is clear from the meaning of 'taking seats according to birthright, and according to youth' as in conformity with the order truths take beneath good. The sons of Israel represent the truths known to the Church existing in their proper order, see the explanation at Chapters 29 and 30 of Genesis, and therefore taking their seats according to their order of birth means in conformity with the order truths take. But the truths known to the Church, which 'the sons of Israel' represent, do not come to be arranged into any kind of proper order except through Christian good, that is, through the good of charity towards the neighbour and of love to the Lord. For good has the Lord within it, and therefore has heaven within it. Good consequently has life within it, making it a force that is active and filled with life. But truth devoid of good cannot possibly have any life within it. Good arranges truths into order in keeping with itself, as is quite evident from every kind of love, including self-love and love of the world, and so such love as gives rise to vengeance, hatred, and other evils like these. People governed by those loves call evil good because they take delight in evil. This so-called good of theirs imposes a certain kind of order on those falsities which to them are truths – a kind of order that enables these falsities to lend support to it, till at length all those falsities, which they call truths, are arranged into an order that becomes a sequence of false beliefs. But this order is the kind of order that exists in hell, whereas the order in which truths are ranged beneath the good of heavenly love is the kind that exists in heaven. This also explains why a person with whom the latter kind of order resides, that is, a person who has been regenerated, is called a miniature heaven and also is heaven in the smallest form of all that it can take; for his interiors correspond to the heavens.

2   The fact that good is what brings order to truths is evident from order as it exists in the heavens. All the communities there are ranged in conformity with the order in which truths that are received from the Lord exist beneath good. For [in His own Being] the Lord is nothing else than Divine Good, while Divine Truth, which does not exist within Him, goes forth from Him. And it is in conformity with this Divine Truth ranged beneath Divine Good that all the communities of heaven have been arranged into order. As regards the Lord's being nothing else than Divine Love whereas Divine Truth does not exist within Him but goes forth from Him, this can be illustrated by a comparison made with the sun of this world. The sun is nothing else than fire, while its light does not exist within it but goes forth from it. What is more, objects in the world dependent on light, such as plants, are subject to the order imparted to them by the heat that goes forth from the fire of the sun and exists within the light of the sun, as is evident in springtime and summertime. For since the whole natural order is a theatre representative of the Lord's kingdom, so is this whole situation involving the sun

representative. The sun represents the Lord; its fire represents His Divine Love; the heat from it represents the good that flows from this Love, and its light the truths that constitute faith. And since they have these representations, 'the sun' is also used in the spiritual sense of the Word to mean the Lord, 1053, 1521, 1529–1531, 3636, 3643, 4321(end), 5097, 5377, 'fire' to mean love, 934, 4906, 5071, 5215, so that the sun's fire in a representative sense is Divine Love, while the heat from that fire is good flowing from Divine love. As regards 'light' meaning truth, see 2776, 3138, 3190, 3195, 3222, 3339, 3636, 3643, 3862, 3993, 4302, 4409, 4413, 4415, 4526, 5219, 5400.

5705 'And the men were astonished [and looked] each at his companion' means a change of state that took place in each one among them. This is clear from the meaning of 'being astonished' as an unexpected and sudden change in the state of their thoughts (and since this change causes astonishment, the same is meant in the internal sense); and from the meaning of 'each at his companion' as in each one among them. For the subject is the order of the truths beneath good, determined by the presence of the internal, 5703, 5704, which order, being a new one, leads to a change of state in each one among them, meant by 'the men were astonished [and looked] each at his companion'.

5706 'And he took portions from before his face to them' means forms of good applied with mercy to each one. This is clear from the meaning of 'portions' – portions of food – as forms of good (for forms of good are meant by all 'foods', while 'drink' means truths of every kind) – to be exact, an application of those forms of good to each one, as is evident from what follows and is meant by 'he took to them'; and from the meaning of 'face', when used in reference to the Lord, who is represented by 'Joseph', as mercy, dealt with in 222, 223, 5585.

5707 'And he multiplied Benjamin's portion above the portions of all theirs' means that the good imparted to the intermediary exceeded the forms of good imparted to the truths in the natural. This is clear from the meaning of 'portions' as forms of good, dealt with immediately above in 5706; from the representation of 'Benjamin' as the intermediary, dealt with in 5411, 5413, 5427, 5428, 5443, 5586, 5612; and from the representation of the ten sons of Jacob, above whose portions he multiplied Benjamin's portion, as the truths present in the natural, dealt with in 5403, 5419, 5427, 5458, 5512. From all this it is evident that 'he multiplied Benjamin's portion above the portions of all theirs' means the good imparted to the intermediary exceeded the forms of good imparted to the truths in the natural.

2 The reason why the good imparted to the intermediary exceeded the forms of good imparted to the truths in the natural is that the intermediary is interior, and what is interior possesses forms of good in greater abundance than what is exterior. Few know what is implied by

this – by what is interior possessing forms of good and truth in greater abundance than parts that are more external do. The reason for this is that up to now few, if any, have known that what is interior is distinct and separate from what is exterior, so distinct that the two can be separated from each other; and that once they have been separated the interior goes on living but the exterior dies. But as long as they exist joined together what is exterior receives life from what is interior. If people knew this first they could then know what the interior is like compared with the exterior – that what is interior possesses thousands of things which are seen in the exterior only as a simple whole. For what is interior exists in a purer sphere, what is exterior in a grosser one; and what exists in a purer sphere is capable of receiving individually thousands of things more than that which exists in a grosser sphere can. This is the reason why, when a person who has led a good life enters heaven after death, he is able to receive thousands and thousands more of those things that constitute intelligence and wisdom, and also happiness, than when he had been living in the world. For in heaven he lives in a purer sphere and in the interior parts of his being, having cast off the grosser parts belonging to the body. From all this one may now see what is implied by the statement that the good imparted to the intermediary exceeded the forms of good imparted to the truths in the natural, meant by 'he multiplied Benjamin's portion above the portions of all theirs'.

5708   'Five measures more' means that it was much increased. This is clear from the meaning of 'five' as much, dealt with below; and from the meaning of 'measures' as states of truth received from good, dealt with in 3104. As regards 'five', this is a number which can mean little, or else something, or even much. Whatever its specific meaning, this stems from its relationship with the number of which it is a factor, 5291. When it is a factor of ten, much the same as ten, but in a smaller degree, is implied, five being half the number ten. For just as compound numbers have a similar meaning to the simple ones of which they are the product, 5291, 5335, so do divisors have a similar meaning to the compound numbers they divide, as with the relationship of five to ten, also to twenty, as well as to a hundred, a thousand, and so on. 'Ten' means what is full and complete, see 3107, 4638. 'Five measures more' were given to Benjamin than to the rest of his brothers on account of what was meant by this in the spiritual sense. Ten measures could not be given because that amount would have been far too much. The ancients knew from what had been handed down to them from the Most Ancient Church the meanings that certain numbers carried; they therefore used those numbers whenever something cropped up, the meaning of which could be conveyed by those numbers, as is the case with five here. At other times they employed many other numbers, such as three to mean what was complete from start to finish, seven to mean what was holy, or twelve to mean all things in their entirety.

5709 'And they drank' means the application of the truths beneath good. This is clear from the meaning of 'drinking' as the communication of truth and making it one's own, dealt with in 3168, 3772, 4017, 4018, and therefore an application of it also. The reason beneath good is meant is that whenever there is any application of truth, this takes place beneath good, see above in 5704.

5710 'And drank plentifully' means in abundance. This is clear from the meaning of 'drinking' as applying truths beneath good, dealt with immediately above in 5709; therefore 'drinking plentifully' means an application of truths in abundance.

From the explanations given in this chapter it is evident that the subject has been an introductory stage to the joining of the natural to the celestial of the spiritual. But the subject in the next chapter is the first stage when they are actually joined together, that first stage being represented by Joseph's revelation of himself to his brothers, and the second stage by his going to meet his father and his brothers and bringing them down into Egypt.

CORRESPONDENCE – *continued*
IN THIS SECTION THE CORRESPONDENCE OF
SICKNESSES WITH THE SPIRITUAL WORLD

5711 Since the subject is to be the correspondence of sicknesses, it should be recognized that all human sicknesses too have a correspondence with the spiritual world. For nothing at all comes into being in the natural creation that does not have a correspondence with the spiritual world; it has no cause from which it may be brought into being and from which it may be kept in being. Things existing in the natural world are nothing else than effects; their causes exist in the spiritual world, while the causes behind those causes, which are the ends, exist more internally in heaven. No effect can remain in being unless its cause is present within it constantly; for the instant a cause ceases to exist, so does its effect. Essentially an effect is nothing else than its cause; but a cause so clothes itself outwardly with an effect that it is enabled to act as a cause in a lower sphere than its own. And similar to the relationship between an effect and its cause is the relationship between a cause and its end. Unless a cause likewise comes into being from its own cause, which is the end, it is not a cause; for without an end a cause is devoid of order, and where there is no order nothing is brought into being. From this it is now evident that the essence of an effect is its cause, while the essence of a cause is its end, and that an end which has good in view exists in heaven and comes forth from the Lord. Consequently an effect is not an effect unless there is a cause within it, constantly there, and a cause is not a cause unless there is an end within it, constantly so. Nor is an end an end that has good in view unless the Divine which goes forth from the Lord is present within it. From this it is also evident that even as every single thing in the world has been brought into being from the Divine, so it is kept in being from the Divine.

5712 All this has been stated so that people may know that even sicknesses have a correspondence with the spiritual world. They do not have a correspondence with heaven, which is the Grand Man, but with those in a contrary place, thus with those in hell. The expression spiritual world is used in an all-embracing sense to mean both heaven and hell; for when a person dies he passes from the natural world into the spiritual world. The reason sicknesses have a correspondence with those in hell is that sicknesses correspond to the evil desires and cravings of the lower mind (*animus*), and these desires and cravings are the origins of those sicknesses, the origins of sicknesses in general being various kinds of intemperance and self-gratification, wholly physical pleasures, as well as feelings of envy, hatred, revenge, lust, and the like, which destroy a person's interiors. Once these are destroyed his exteriors suffer and subject him to sickness and so to death. The fact that human death is the result of evils or due to sin is well known in the Church; so too are sicknesses, for these are bringers of death. From all this it may be seen that sicknesses too have a correspondence with the spiritual world, with the forms of uncleanness there; for essentially sicknesses are forms of uncleanness. As stated above, they have their origin in uncleanness.

5713 All who are in hell are the causers of sicknesses, though varying ones, for the reason that all the hells are steeped in desires and cravings for what is evil. That being so, they are antagonistic to the things of heaven, and for this reason they exert an opposite influence on man. Heaven, which is the Grand Man, preserves the interconnection of all things and keeps them safe from harm; hell, having opposite intentions, is destructive of all things and sets them at variance with one another. This being so, if those in hell are brought into contact with man they bring sicknesses and at length death. But they are not allowed to enter the actual solid parts of a person's body, nor the parts making up his internal organs or his other organs and limbs; they do not enter anything else than his evil desires and false ideas. Only when he falls sick do they enter any further, into the kinds of uncleanness that are the essence of sicknesses. For as has been stated, nothing ever comes into being with man unless a cause also exists in the spiritual world. If the natural part of a person's being were separated from the spiritual part it would be separated from the entire cause from which it has its being and so from all that brings it life. Even so, this does not make it impossible for a person to be healed by natural remedies, for the Lord's providence works in co-operation with means such as these. I have been enabled through much experience to know the truth of this, on so many occasions and during such lengthy periods that I have not been left in any doubt at all. For evil spirits from such places have been brought in contact with me often and for lengthy periods; and according to their presence they introduced feelings of pain and also sicknesses. I was shown where those spirits were and what they were like, and I was also told where they came from.

5714   There was a spirit who during his lifetime had been very much an adulterer. His greatest delight had lain in committing adultery with many women, whom he instantly cast aside and detested after committing it; and he had continued in such ways even in old age. In addition he had been given to sensual pleasures and was unwilling to treat anyone well or render any service other than for his own sake, especially for his adultery. This spirit was with me for several days; I saw him beneath my feet. And since the sphere emanating from his life was communicated to me, he caused wherever he went a painful feeling in my periostea and nerves, that is, in those in the toes of my left foot. Then, when he was allowed to leave those parts where he was, he caused painful feelings in particular in the periostea of my hips, also in the periostea in my chest below my diaphragm, as well as in my teeth, right inside them. While his sphere was at work it also caused severe stomach-ache.

5715   A large four-sided opening appeared, falling away at an angle down to a considerable depth. At the bottom I saw a round opening which then lay open but was soon closed. A vexatious heat rose up from there, being a collection emanating from various hells. It arose out of various kinds of evil desires, such as pride, lack of sexual restraint, adultery, hatred, revenge, quarreling and fighting. These desires present in those hells were the origin of the heat that was rising up. When it acted on my body it instantly caused a sickness like that of a burning fever; but once that heat ceased to come into me, this form of sickness instantly departed. When a person falls sick in this way he has contracted his sickness from the life that is his; in his case an unclean sphere corresponding to the sickness attaches itself and is present as the cause from which the sickness springs. To enable me to know for certain that this is the case spirits from many hells have been present with me. Through them the sphere created out of emanations from them has been communicated to me; and as that sphere has been allowed to act on the solid parts of my body, I have been seized by an ache, pain, and indeed the corresponding sickness. But these feelings departed the instant those spirits were driven away. And to leave me in no doubt the experience has been repeated a thousand times.

5716   There are also spirits, not far away from those just described, who can bring on filthy chills such as are accompanied by feverish shivering, as again I have been allowed to know about through experiences I have had. The same spirits are also responsible for influences that lead to disturbance of the mind; and they can cause fainting-fits too. The spirits from that place are very wicked ones.

5717   There are spirits who not only correlate with the very sticky substances in the brain, which are its waste products, but who also know how to infect those substances with what are like poisons. On arrival spirits of this kind charge inside the skull and continue without stopping right on into the spinal cord. This is not something that people whose interiors have not been opened are able to feel; but I have been allowed to feel them entering in, and to feel their endeavour to destroy, which however was to no avail because the Lord was protecting me. Their intention was to remove my entire power of understanding from me; I felt their activity clearly as well as the resulting pain, which however soon ceased. When I spoke to those spirits subsequently they were compelled to confess where they were from. They said they lived in dark forests where they do not dare to do anything at all to their companions, for if they do do anything their companions are allowed to treat them cruelly. Thus they are kept in bonds; and they are ugly, having faces that look like wild beasts, and they are covered with hair.

2   I have been told that those in former times who slew entire armies, such as one reads about in the Word, were like them. They charged into the cells of each man's brain and introduced terror there, together with a kind of madness that caused one man to slay another. At the present day such spirits are kept locked up in their own hell and are not let out. They also correlate with malignant swellings of the head inside the skull. I have described those spirits as ones that charge inside the skull and continue without stopping right on into the spinal cord; but it should be realized that this charging in by them is an appearance. They are actually conveyed along a route outside the body which corresponds to those areas inside it; but it feels as though the force of them were inside. Correspondence is the explanation for this, for it enables the operation they are carrying out to be concentrated on the person at whom it is directed.

5718   A certain type of spirits exists who wish to dominate and have sole control over all others; and to achieve this end they stir up all kinds of enmity, hatred, and conflict among those other spirits. I have seen the conflicts stirred up by them and have been astonished. I have asked who these spirits were and have been told that they are a particular kind who stir such troubles up because their intention is to have sole dominion, acting according to the principle Divide and Rule. I was also allowed to talk to them, when immediately they said they were going to govern everyone. I was led to reply that they were madmen if they sought to gain dominion for themselves by creating those kinds of disturbances. These spirits spoke to me from a position above, a fair way up at the centre above my forehead. Their words flowed from them like a stream, for during their lifetime they had been clever speakers. I was informed that these spirits are ones that correlate with the crude mucus secreted in the brain, from which by their very presence they remove vitality and into which they introduce a sluggishness that leads to obstructions – which are the major causes of many forms of sickness – and to slowness of thought also.

2   I noticed that these spirits were devoid of any conscience and that they thought that human prudence and wisdom lay in stirring up all kinds of enmity, hatred, and internal conflicts for the purpose of gaining dominion over others. I was led to ask them whether they knew that they were now in the next life where they were going to live for ever and where spiritual laws existed that completely forbade such actions. I also told them that while in the world they may have been considered and thought to be wise ones among the stupid, but in fact they had been the insane among the wise – which they did not like to be told. I went on to say that they ought to know that heaven consists in mutual love, or the love of one person towards another, which love gives rise to order in heaven and which love governs so many millions as a single whole. But the contrary of this, I said, existed with them since they filled others with nothing else than feelings of hatred, revenge, and cruelty towards their companions. They replied that they could not be anything other than what they were, to which I responded that from this they could know that each person's life remained with him.

5719   There are spirits who despise and ridicule what appears in the letter of the Word, and more so what is contained in the higher sense there, and also consequently the religious teachings that are drawn from the Word. When at the same time such spirits do not have any love towards their neighbour, only self-love, they correlate with corruptions of the blood which pass into all the veins and arteries and contaminate the whole of the blood. To prevent by their presence the introduction of anything like this into a person, those spirits are kept apart from others, in their own hell, where they communicate with none but others like themselves; for such spirits cast themselves into the whole sphere emanating from that hell.

5720   There have been times when hypocrites were present with me. That is to say, spirits have been present who spoke with reverence about Divine matters, and with affection and love about society and their neighbour, declaring a belief in what was right and fair. Yet in their heart they rejected all this and scorned it. When they were allowed to flow into those parts of my body to which they corresponded in a contrary sense, they introduced pain into my teeth; and when they were very close they introduced pain so severe that I could not bear it.

But in the measure that they were moved away the pain left off. This has been demonstrated to me repeatedly, to remove all shadow of doubt. Those spirits included someone whom I had known during his lifetime, and therefore I spoke to him. Again, as was his presence, so was the pain I felt in my teeth and gums. When he was being raised up towards the left the pain moved into my left jawbone and the bone forming my left temple, and from these into my cheekbones.

5721   The most ungovernable spirits of all are those who in their life in the world appeared to be more just than others, and who were at the same time appointed to high offices, for both of which reasons they had authority and great influence. Yet they did not have any real belief and led a wholly selfish life, being fired by the utter hatred of, and desire for revenge on all who failed to show them any favour or pay them any respect, and even more so on those who opposed them in any way. If they discovered in the latter any imperfection they made a great evil of it and denigrated those persons, even though they may have been some of the finest citizens.

2   In the next life spirits like these speak as they did in the world, that is to say, with authority and great influence, and seemingly from an awareness of what is just, as a consequence of which many think that people should trust what they say more than what others say. But they are very wicked spirits. When they come into contact with a person they introduce intense pain through a feeling of fatigue which they instill and increase all the time to a point when it is totally unbearable, a fatigue which renders the mind and consequently the body so weak that the person can hardly get out of bed. This has been demonstrated to me by the experience that when those spirits were present weakness like that overcame me; yet the weakness left me to the extent they were moved away from me.

3   They employ many a device to infuse that feeling of fatigue and consequent weakness; in particular they introduce the general sphere that is a product of insults and slanders they hurl at one another and at family and friends. When they engage within their own chambers in reasoning about Divine worship, faith, and eternal life, they sweep these completely aside, doing so, it seems, with a wisdom that is greater than anyone else's. In the next life they are quite prepared to be called devils provided that they are allowed to reign over hells, and by reigning over these, so they believe, to act in opposition to the Divine. Inwardly they are foul, for they surpass all others in self-love, consequently in hatred and revenge, and in cruelty to all who do not pay them any respect.

4   They undergo severe punishment, which I have also heard taking place, until they leave off misleading others by their outward pretence of being just. When that pretence is removed from them they speak in a different tone of voice. After this they are cast away from the world of spirits, to the left hand side, where they are sent to a hell very deep down. That hell is positioned on the left, a fair distance away.

5722 There are others who during their lifetime were utterly foul; that foulness was such that it must be passed over in silence here. By their presence and influx into the solid parts of the body they introduce a fatigued feeling of weariness with life and such sluggishness in one's members and limbs that one cannot get out of bed. They are most ungovernable; they are not deterred by punishments the way other devils are. They appear next to one's head, where they seem to be lying down. When they are driven away this is not achieved all of a sudden but slowly; they are rolled away gradually into the nether regions. When they reach a position deep down they suffer such great torment there that they are compelled to desist from plaguing others. So great is their delight in doing evil that nothing gives them greater delight.

5723 Spirits have been present with me who brought on a stomach-ache so bad that I felt I could scarcely live; it was such as would have caused other people to faint. But those spirits were removed and the ache immediately ceased. I was told that they were the kind of spirits who during their lifetime had had no interest in anything at all, not even in their own home, only in sensual pleasure. They had led disgracefully lazy and inactive lives, showing no concern whatsoever for others. They had also cast all belief aside with contempt. In short, they were simply animals, not human beings. Among people who are sick the sphere emanating from those spirits introduces sluggishness into their members and limbs.

5724 In the brain there are viscous substances that have something spirituous or life-giving mixed into them. Once those substances have been expelled from the blood in the brain, they first of all move in among the meninges, then among the fibres; some of them move into the large ventricles in the brain, and so on. The spirits who are related by correspondence to those viscous substances that have something spirituous or life-giving in them are seen almost directly above the middle of the head, a fair distance away. They are the kind who, from habit acquired during their lifetime, raise conscientious objections, introducing them where conscience has no part to play, and thereby over-burdening the consciences of simple persons. They are unaware of what ought to be a matter of conscience; for they bring conscience into everything that happens to them. These spirits also introduce a feeling of anxiety that is located in the abdomen underneath the diaphragm. They are present too in temptations, introducing feelings of anxiety that are sometimes unbearable. Those among them who correspond to phlegm that is not so life-giving keep a person's thought fixed on such anxious feelings. I have also been with them in their discussions so that I might know what those spirits were like. They try by various methods to over-burden a person's conscience. To do this had been the delight of their lives, and I was led to observe that they could not pay attention to reasons presented to them, and that they were unable to take the overall view of things from which they might then look at specific details.

5725   Experience has enabled me to learn what is implied in the spiritual sense by a deluge or flood. Understood in this spiritual sense a deluge is two-sided, being on the one hand a deluge of evil desires, on the other a deluge of falsities. The deluge of evil desires affects the will part of the mind and the right side of the brain, whereas that of falsities affects the understanding part, with which the left side of the brain is connected. When a person who has led a good life is taken back into his own selfhood, and so into the sphere that emanates from the life properly his own, it seems like a deluge. Caught in this deluge he is annoyed and angry, has unpeaceful thoughts and wildly evil desires. It is one thing when the left side of the brain, where falsities exist, is under deluge, another when the right, where evils reside, is under it.

2   But when a person is kept within the sphere emanating from the life he has received through regeneration from the Lord he is completely outside such a deluge. He is so to speak in a calm and sunny, cheerful and happy place, and so is far removed from annoyance, anger, unpeacefulness, evil desires, and the like. The latter state is for spirits morning or spring, the former state their evening or autumn. I was led to perceive myself outside such a deluge; this lasted quite a long time, during which I saw other spirits caught in it. But after that I too become submerged in it, when I experienced what felt like a deluge. This is the kind in which people undergoing temptations are caught. From this I learned what is meant in the Word by the Flood, namely that the final descendants of the most ancient people who belonged to the Lord's celestial Church were completely submerged in evils and falsities, so that they perished.

5726   Since death is due entirely to sin, and sin consists in everything contrary to Divine order, evil therefore closes the tiniest and completely invisible blood vessels out of which the immediately larger, yet also invisible, vessels are constructed. For the tiniest and completely invisible vessels extend into a person's interiors. This is where the first and innermost obstruction develops and where the first and innermost impairment enters the blood. As this impairment grows it causes sickness, and at length death. But if it were the case that the person was leading a good life his interiors would lie open into heaven, and through heaven towards the Lord, and so too would his tiniest invisible *vascula* (the mere traces of first threads may by virtue of correspondence be called *vascula*). If this were so man would not know any sickness and would grow weak only as he approached extreme old age, until he became a young child again, but now a young child with wisdom. And when his body was no longer able to serve his internal man, which is his spirit, he would pass, without knowing any sickness, from his earthly body into a body such as angels possess, and so would pass from the world directly into heaven.

5727   This brings the subject of correspondence to an end. At the ends of chapters after this the subjects discussed will in the Lord's Divine mercy be Spirits and Angels present with Man; then Influx, and the Interaction of the Soul and the Body; and after that the Inhabitants of other Planets.

WORD LIST

Celestial. Apart from the rare occasions in *Arcana Caelestia* when it obviously refers to the visible heavens or sky, the Latin adjective *caelestis*, formed from the noun *caelum* meaning 'heaven', is translated either as 'heavenly' or as 'celestial'. The former is usually adopted when Swedenborg is referring to something that belongs to heaven in general as against that which is of hell, or of the world, or of the flesh, e.g. 'the heavenly marriage' or 'heavenly joy'. But 'celestial' is used when Swedenborg is describing that which belongs to the highest heaven or degree as against the spiritual beneath it, e.g. 'the celestial heaven', 'celestial angels', or 'celestial good or truth'.

Chaste and **chastity** are used in reference to the married as well as to the single state and therefore describe the pure and undefiled rather that the virginal and celibate.

Cognitions is used throughout this work as a translation of the Latin *cognitiones*, a word to which Swedenborg often gave the special sense, when contrasted with *scientifica* 'known facts', of 'items of knowledge relating to interior things'.

Conjugial. Swedenborg regularly uses the Latin adjective *conjugialis* 'of marriage', instead of the usual *conjugalis* 'conjugal, marital'. Since this was clearly a deliberate choice, the word 'conjugial' was coined by early translators into English.

Minchah, generally rendered 'offering' in English versions of the Scriptures, is a Hebrew word. The 'ch' in it has a hard or guttural pronunciation, as in German *buch* or Scottish *loch*.

Proprium is a Latin word meaning 'one's own (thing)'. Swedenborg uses it in the specialized sense of 'what is of the self'.

Real things translates Latin *res*, a word which ordinarily means 'things, matters, affairs, cases, conditions, etc.', but which is also used to mean the spiritual realities behind material things.

Further Erratum in Volume One

Page	Line				
121	28	*For*	bread, the produce	*read*	bread of the produce

Further Errata in Volume Two

Page	Line				
31	1	*For*	let evil hunt	*read*	evil hunts
39	40	*For*	the border	*read*	their border

Further Erratum in Volume Five

Page	Line				
183	3	*For*	hands	*read*	hand

Errata in Volume Six

Page	Line				
137	16	*For*	means as an area	*read*	means an area
318	19	*For*	Divine	*read*	Divine Human
331	2	*For*	fire,	*read*	fire
371	38	*For*	to to	*read*	so to